"*Rise* is informative, thoughtful, beautiful, and full of love. It has literally expanded my idea of American culture and American history. A must-read for anybody and everybody."
—**IJEOMA OLUO,** author of *So You Want to Talk About Race* and *Mediocre*

"*Rise* is smart, funny, and entertaining.... Get two copies because the first is definitely gonna get swiped off your coffee table."
—**SHEA SERRANO,** author of *Hip-Hop (And Other Things)* and *Movies (And Other Things)*

"If you think you already know, [*Rise*] will teach you tons you didn't. If you don't know anything, get reading: It's a perfect introduction to the wildly diverse and ever-evolving Asian American community."
—**CELESTE NG, author of** *Everything I Never Told You* and *Little Fires Everywhere*

"Finally, the book on Asian American pop culture that needed to be made. Don't be fooled by the fun presentation because this book has serious substance. Also, I'm in it."
—**RONNY CHIENG,** senior correspondent on *The Daily Show*

"An accessible, informative, and fun compendium.... A vivid and readable tour of Asian American representation."
—**CATHY PARK HONG,** author of *Minor Feelings*

JEFF YANG    PHIL YU    PHILIP WANG
ILLUSTRATED BY JULIA KUO

RI

Mariner Books
An Imprint of HarperCollinsPublishers
Boston   New York

**A Pop History of Asian America
from the Nineties to Now**

marinerbooks.com

Designed by Allison Chi
Unless otherwise noted, all other art credited on page 484.

Library of Congress Cataloging-in-Publication Data has been applied for.

ISBN 978-0-358-50809-0

Printed in Italy

RTL   10 9 8 7 6 5 4 3 2 1

This book is dedicated to
the ones who come next

# CONTENTS

# Introduction

STORY: JEFF YANG, PHIL YU, & PHILIP WANG    ART: KRISTAN LAI

VISIBILITY DOESN'T HAPPEN OVERNIGHT.

1. JOY LUCK CLUB
2. [SOMETHING HAPPENS]
3. CRAZY RICH ASIANS

WE DIDN'T JUMP FROM **VINCENT CHIN** TO HAVING AN **ASIAN AMERICAN WOMAN** AS VICE PRESIDENT.

WE DIDN'T GO FROM ALL-AMERICAN GIRL TO FRESH OFF THE BOAT, OR JOY LUCK CLUB TO CRAZY RICH ASIANS, WITHOUT SWEAT, TEARS, SACRIFICE, AND DISAPPOINTMENT -- AND A LOT OF FORGOTTEN **HEROES** IN BETWEEN.

THIS BOOK IS ABOUT THE OFTEN **OVERLOOKED** WORK OF THE LAST 30 YEARS THAT MADE OUR BREAKTHROUGHS POSSIBLE,

BOTH STUFF THAT MADE **HEADLINES** AND THINGS THAT STAYED IN THE INTIMATE CONVERSATIONS WE WERE HAVING AMONG **OURSELVES** -- IN PART BECAUSE NO ONE ELSE WOULD LISTEN.

IT'S ABOUT THE EXPERIENCES THAT **SHAPED** US, THE WORKS THAT **INFLUENCED** US, THE PEOPLE THAT **LED** US AND THE EVENTS THAT INSPIRED AND **GALVANIZED** US TO DO MORE AND DO BETTER --

-- OVER THREE DECADES IN WHICH OUR COMMUNITIES FIGURED OUT **WHO WE ARE**, AND HOW WE COULD **EXPRESS** THAT TO THE WORLD.

# BEFORE

# Before

BY JEFF YANG

**WHERE DO WE** begin? Or rather, *when* did we begin?

If you go by the history books, Asians have been in America since the 19th century, when Chinese immigrants toiled to build the infrastructure of America's manifest destiny and fed the hungry bellies of goldstruck prospectors (and, after hours, took a turn at panning the glittering streams of California themselves).

If you go by the records that never seem to make it into textbooks, Asians have been in America since Filipino slaves jumped ship from Spanish galleons in Louisiana in the 1760s, where they built secret villages in the swamplands, hid from their kidnappers, fished to survive, and eventually, were recruited to defend a young America from a new British invasion in 1812.

If you crawl through the weird fringes of antiquarianism, you'll find people who claim that a Chinese admiral landed his fleet of ships on the East Coast of the United States in 1421; that Japanese fishermen "discovered" America in the 13th century; that wandering Buddhist monks floated to a place called "Fusang"— *California, maybe!*—in AD 499. And if you dive down into evolutionary anthropology, you'll probably read about the Bering land bridge, crossed by ancient Asian migrants who trekked over from Siberia some 16,000 years ago and spread out all across what's now America.

But none of these moments, real or fake, really answer the question of when Asian America began . . . because none of the protagonists in these journeys ever thought of themselves as "Asian." After all, Asia is a huge land mass, made up of wildly disparate states, most of whom have spent centuries trying hard to kill each other, or alternatively, trying hard to resist killing each other. It's difficult to imagine that these remarkably different peoples might choose to identify as a collective group—which makes the term "Asian" meaningless. In *Asia,* anyway.

## Inventing Asian America

But this is *America*. And in America, not only does "Asian" mean something, we can pinpoint when that meaning came into being, and where: in May 1968, in the apartment of two grad students, Yuji Ichioka and Emma Gee, at 2005 Hearst Avenue in Berkeley, California.

During the late Sixties, UC Berkeley and other San Francisco Bay Area universities bubbled with activist activity, carbon-charged by the fight for civil rights, the rise of the Black Power Movement, and growing outrage over

AAPA's Victor Ichioka, Phil Nakamura and Yuji Ichioka march in support of Black Panther Huey Newton (courtesy: AAPA Archive Project)

the war in Vietnam. Ichioka and Gee recognized that the absence of a common banner under which to rally made activists of Asian descent invisible. They decided it was time to found an organization to unify, amplify, and uplift these voices—to allow them to stand side by side and shoulder to shoulder with Black, Chicano, and Native liberation movements. But what would this group be called?

The answer emerged from the first organizing meeting that took place in the living room of Ichioka and Gee's apartment, after they'd made cold calls to every activist they could find who had a Chinese, Japanese, or other "Oriental"-sounding surname. The half-dozen students who gathered to plan the nascent group's June 2 kickoff—Ichioka, Gee, Ichioka's brother Victor, Vicci Wong, Floyd Huen, and Richard Aoki—dubbed themselves the "Asian-American Political Alliance," coining "Asian-American" in emulation of their Afro-American fellows in the fight, a point that Ichioka made abundantly clear in a statement that stands as something of a manifesto: Asian-Americans have been, and still are,

Under the freshly painted AAPA banner, a membership that included Chinese, Japanese, Korean, and Filipino Americans organized and marched for Third World Liberation, for civil rights, for worker unionization, and for the release of Black Panther leader Huey P. Newton—rallies that marked the first recorded usage of the term "Asian-American" in a public context.

This wasn't the first time Asians of different ethnicities had been classified as a single group: at various times before this moment, we'd been lumped together as "Mongoloids," "Orientals," "Asiatics," and a variety of interchangeable slurs related to the color of our skin, the shape of our eyes, and the things we eat (or are alleged to eat).

But it did represent the first time Asians had embraced a sense of common identity for *ourselves,* by *choice,* and the discovery of a budding power in that choice. As charter member Huen later wrote, this invention of Asian America "represented the learnings of a racially common group of American youth who were tired of being labeled 'meek and passive,' and wanted to self-define like other groups." Vicci Wong, another founding member, put it even more simply: "I went into AAPA 'Oriental,' and left as an Asian American."

Though **AAPA** was only around for a few short years, in that time it was a visible and powerful presence as part of the Third World Liberation Front, a coalition with African American, Mexican American, and Native American groups.

used politically to the detriment of oppressed minorities. AAPA will break the silence [of the Asian-American community] on the issues now confronting America . . . a nation which shows every evidence of liquidating Black people, and is waging the politically and morally insane war in Vietnam. We must redefine our relationship to the Black, Mexican-American and Indian liberation movements [because] all existing organizations in our community are too committed to the status quo.

It wasn't a coincidence that the impetus for taking this first step together was politics. In majority-rules America, size matters, and grouping together into larger coalitions is a necessity to be seen, to be heard, and to get anything done. As Ichioka told Yến Lê Espiritu in an interview for her book *Asian American Panethnicity,* "There were so many Asians out there [but] everyone was lost in the larger rally. We figured that if we rallied behind our own banner, behind an Asian American banner, we would have an effect on the larger public."

They certainly did. Though AAPA was only around for a few short years, in that time it was a visible and powerful presence as part of the Third World Liberation Front, a coalition with African American, Mexican American, and Native American groups. The Front rocked Bay Area campuses with four months of demonstrations, student strikes, and acts of resistance that ultimately led then-governor Ronald Reagan to send in the National Guard. AAPA chapters sprang up at other colleges across California and then beyond, from New York to Hawaii—fighting, like their Berkeley flagship, for social justice, progressive change, and inclusion and representation for Asian Americans and other underrepresented groups.

But the biggest and most important legacy of the Alliance was, of course, the concept of "Asian America" itself. After taking root on college campuses, use of the term "Asian American" spread with shocking speed across academia, media, and business. By 1971, it had already reached government, with then-congressman Glenn Anderson, a Democrat from California, proposing the creation of a "Cabinet Committee for Asian-American Affairs" in a bill called the "Asian-American Affairs Act" (HR 12208) that would have the power to "advise and direct Federal agencies for assuring that Federal programs are providing appropriate assistance for Asian-Americans. Additionally, the bill provides for the investigation of possible discriminatory practices against Asian-Americans."

The bill didn't pass. (Thank you anyway, former congressman Anderson.) Nevertheless, for all intents and purposes, we—Asian Americans—had arrived. It would be up to the next wave of Asian Americans to begin the process of figuring out who we were meant to become.

## Filling in the Blank

The Asian American political movement had staked a claim to relevance in society, to a voice in the civic debate, to solidarity in struggle. But newly minted Asian Americans found themselves with the awkward task of giving meaning to the label that they'd defiantly willed into existence, since in its first few years, the definition of "Asian American" was still a shaky, thinly traced boundary that was better described by what it didn't represent (e.g., not "Oriental," and certainly not white) than what it did.

Coloring in that outline, bringing texture and depth and nuance to our family self-portrait, would require the creation of an *Asian American culture*: collective experiences and memories; shared heroes, symbols, traditions, and lore. Politics made Asian America go viral, but only culture could ensure it would sustain and grow.

The leaders of AAPA recognized this; it's why they made the establishment of Asian American Studies a central pillar of the Alliance's mission, in an effort to reclaim the centuries of our presence that were missing from America's textbooks and canon. The leaders of AAPA Berkeley created and taught a guerrilla Asian American Studies curriculum, and soon had hundreds of fellow students attending their classes. During the Third World Liberation Front strikes of 1968, the San Francisco State University chapter of AAPA was part of the coalition that successfully demanded that SFSU establish the nation's first College of Ethnic Studies. And in 1969, Yuji Ishioka and Emma Gee moved to Los Angeles to help found the first Asian

CLOCKWISE FROM TOP LEFT: **1.** The UCLA Asian American Studies Center was the initial home of Visual Communications, the nation's first organization for Asian American film and video creators—founded in 1970 with the mission of "promoting intercultural understanding through the creation, presentation, preservation and support of media works by and about Asian Americans." **2.** By 1972, L.A.'s East West Players, the nation's first Asian American theater company—which actually dates back to 1965, before the term "Asian American" existed, and began with the original goal of encouraging "cultural understanding between the East and West" via productions of classic Asian and European plays—had decided to refocus their repertory on the production of original works from Asian American playwrights instead. **3.** 1970 saw the opening of Manhattan Chinatown's Basement Workshop, an early incubator for Asian American artists and activists, whose members would go on to establish most of New York's major Asian American arts organizations, including Asian CineVision, the Museum of Chinese in America, the Asian American Arts Centre, Asian American Dance Theater, and many more. **4.** Founded in San Francisco in 1972, the Kearny Street Workshop was a multidisciplinary collective that quickly became the epicenter of the Bay Area's nascent Asian American arts and literary community.

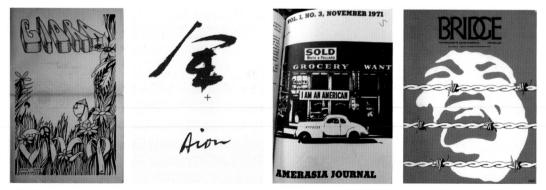

L-R: *Gidra,* "the Monthly of the Asian American Experience," was a radical, raw, and unabashedly unfiltered monthly newspaper that challenged racism, imperialism, colonialism, and anti-Asian stereotypes with activist coverage, interviews, essays, poetry, and cartoons. In the Bay Area, poets Janice Mirikitani and Francis Oka formed the literary magazine *Aion* in 1970, which during its brief two-issue existence published early work by seminal Asian American authors like Lawson Inada, Al Robles, Toshio Mori, Jeffrey Paul Chan, and Mirikitani herself. In 1971 at Yale University, members of the AAPA chapter founded *Amerasia Journal,* the first academic review of Asian American Studies, which migrated to the UCLA Asian American Studies Center and continues to publish today. Later that same year, members of the Basement Workshop led by Frank Ching launched *Bridge,* whose purpose, as Ching wrote, was to "foster a sense of solidarity and promote understanding among Asians, whether Chinese, Japanese, Koreans, et cetera."

American Studies Center at the University of California, Los Angeles, with Ishioka as its first instructor.

By instilling a mutual awareness of history, Asian American Studies laid a critical foundation for the construction of new Asian American stories and creative expressions; as a result, in the late Sixties and early Seventies, Asian American arts organizations began springing up like bamboo shoots after the rain, bringing together novice culture creators and wide-eyed audiences, who in many cases had never seen themselves on-screen, onstage, or on paper.

## Pushing Back the Torrent

Even as Asian Americans began the slow process of creating a cultural infrastructure, we faced the reality that we were a tiny minority, just a half percentage point of the population, in a country that had spent much of its past centuries colonizing, exploiting, competing with, or waging war against people who looked like us and in some cases *were* us, our relatives, or our ancestors.

As a result, we were swimming against a flood of social preconceptions, wartime propaganda, and government policies that targeted Asians in historically unique ways: Chinese were the first and only group to ever be federally prohibited from coming to the United States based on nationality. Japanese Americans were the first and only group to ever be mass incarcerated by the federal government without trial or evidence, solely on the basis of ethnicity. Indian Americans were the only group to be acknowledged as being "Caucasian" but nevertheless "not white," and thus ineligible for citizenship. Filipino Americans made up the only group of veterans to fight under the U.S. flag without receiving the benefits promised them by the federal government.

All of this took place against a backdrop of laws designed to make sure we stayed a minority in a predominantly white, largely Christian, mostly Protestant America. In 1882, the Chinese Exclusion Act had been signed, barring most Chinese entry to the United States. The act was later expanded to include most other Asian countries, what was known as the "Asiatic Barred Zone," making up most of East, Southeast, and South Asia, other than Japan, which had brokered a "Gentleman's Agreement" for exemption, and the Philippines, which was an American protectorate. But in 1924, even the Gentleman's Agreement was broken, as President Calvin Coolidge signed a new act that effectively banned all immigration from Asia, including from Japan, declaring that "America must remain American."

That restriction would stay in place for the next three decades, during which the Asian population would barely grow at all.

But in the mid-Fifties, the first hairline crack appeared in the dam barring Asian immigration. The Immigration and Nationality Act of 1952, also known as the McCarran-Walter Act, finally abolished race-based restrictions against naturalization as a U.S. citizen, which had, since 1790, been limited to "free white persons of good character." This allowed Asians to begin coming to America again, albeit in minute numbers: just 100 immigrants per year were allowed in from each Asian country, with an overall cap of 2,000 per year from the "Asiatic Barred Zone." And then, 13 years later, in 1965, the Hart-Celler Act finally took a sledgehammer to the dam, eliminating racist nationality quotas and creating a set of preferences that prioritized family reunification—giving precedence to close relatives of existing U.S. citizens and legal residents—and professional skills and education. As a result, a stream of immigration began that quickly transformed Asian America from the smallest, slowest-growing minority in the United States into the fastest-rising population in the nation.

Hart-Celler didn't just change the pace of immigration from Asia; it also altered the makeup. The Chinese Communist Party's effective ban on emigration from the mainland after it took power in 1949 meant that the primary sources of Chinese immigration to the United States shifted to Hong Kong and, especially, Taiwan. While immigration from Japan and the Philippines continued at a steady pace, for the first time new regions of Asia began sending people to America in sizable numbers. Hundreds of thousands of South Koreans left a nation still struggling from the aftereffects of the Korean War. Indians and other South Asians headed for America to escape regional food shortages, spiraling inflation, and ongoing social unrest. By the mid-Seventies, the Vietnam War led large numbers of displaced Southeast Asians to seek asylum and resettlement in America as well.

In 1960 there were fewer than a million Asians in America, less than half of whom were foreign-born. By 1970, five years after Hart-Celler, the Asian American population had grown to 1.5 million, 55 percent foreign-born—and by 1980, it had more than doubled to 3.5 million, 71 percent of whom were foreign-born.

## Martyrdom and Media

The vast new tide of migration unleashed by Hart-Celler meant that by the end of the Seventies, most Asians in America were recent immigrants, who naturally weren't inclined to see themselves through the lens of being "Asian." They thought of themselves first as members of their own specific ethnic communities, and second as aspirational Americans; the pan-ethnic organizing work of the Asian American pioneers of the Sixties made as little sense to them as it might to the relatives they'd left behind in Asia.

And the extraordinary new diversity of ethnicities, tongues, and traditions they brought with them made defining a common Asian American identity even more of a baffling challenge—complicated further by the "plane versus boat" divide. The Hart-Celler Act's prioritization of skilled immigrants meant that from the late Sixties onward, a sizable percentage of Asian arrivals would land with diplomas in hand, ready to step into the suits, scrubs, and lab coats of the professional elite, while others came as refugees, escaping war and disaster with little but their lives.

As the Eighties progressed, however, an event occurred that would fundamentally reshape the way that the next chapter of Asian America would evolve.

On June 19, 1982, in Detroit, Michigan, 27-year-old Vincent Chin[*] got into an altercation with a pair of white unemployed autoworkers while celebrating his last days of bachelorhood with friends. Mistaking him for Japanese, the two men, Ronald Ebens and Michael Nitz, made statements blaming him for the collapse of the American car industry, then chased him into a nearby parking lot and

---

[*] See page 34, "Why Vincent Chin Still Matters"

used a baseball bat to batter him into a coma. Chin never returned to consciousness, dying in the hospital a few days later.

The killing galvanized Detroit's Asian population, across ethnic lines. It was bad enough that white rage against the economic rise of Japan, fueled by poisonous political rhetoric, had exploded into murderous violence. But the fact that the crime happened to a U.S.-born Chinese American, a college graduate, a white-collar worker, awakened the local community to the fact that bigotry ignores national origin, supersedes socioeconomic status, and can't be deflected with a diploma.

It wasn't a new lesson, but it was a vital refresher course. Anti-Chinese caricatures and slurs dating back to the 1800s had been reused in turn against Japanese, Koreans, and Vietnamese; inability to tell Asians apart was a cliché in popular culture, to the point where in 1941, the iconic periodical *Life* published an article called "How to Tell Japs from the Chinese" to prevent vigilantes from accidentally attacking Chinese "allies" as they went out to hunt "enemy" Japs, pointing out the "parchment yellow complexion" and "scant beard" of Chinese versus the "earthy yellow complexion" and "heavy beard" one would expect to see among Japanese. It didn't matter then that any people of Chinese or Japanese ancestry that readers were likely to encounter would be innocent fellow Americans, and it clearly didn't matter in 1982, in the case of Vincent Chin, something made clear by the outcome of the criminal trial against Chin's killers.

While Wayne County Circuit Judge Charles Kaufman found Ebens and Nitz guilty, it was of the lighter charge of manslaughter, not murder, and the punishment he sentenced them to was probation and a $3,000 fine, declaring that they were "not the kind of men you send to jail." Kin Yee, president of the Detroit Chinese Welfare Council, which had been supporting the Chin family during the case, dubbed the results a "license to kill [Asians] for $3,000."

The shocking outcome of the trial reinforced to Chin's supporters that Ebens and Nitz weren't the only ones responsible for his death. The killers had been primed for anti-Asian violence by an ongoing campaign to frame "the Japanese" as an existential threat to America.

In 1980 John Connally, a former Democratic governor of Texas turned Republican presidential candidate, made it a habit to point out on the campaign trail that Japan seemed to have forgotten that the United States was the victor in World War II, and delivered one memorable stump speech in which he warned Japanese in their little cars to "be prepared," because Americans, he thundered, had taken "all we're going to take." Representative John Dingell complained to fellow congressmen about the problems his Detroit constituents were having with the "little yellow people." California governor Jerry Brown, running for the Senate, suggested that America was in danger of becoming a Japanese colony. In 1982, legendary Speaker of the House Tip O'Neill promised to "fix the Japanese like they've never been fixed before," while eventual Democratic presidential candidate Walter Mondale exhorted the United States to "stop showing the white flag [and] start running up the American flag—to turn around, fight and make America number one again," lest American children end up in a future where their jobs consisted of "sweeping up around Japanese computers."

The mass media aided and abetted this culture war, putting the rants of nativist politicians in headlines, airing interviews with conspiracy theorists, and running editorial cartoons showing Japanese factory workers dropping Toyotas on Detroit, the "new Pearl Harbor."

It became clear that if the media was being wielded as a weapon against Asians, the only recourse Asians had was to wield it right back. During a gathering of supporters at the Golden Star restaurant, where Vincent Chin had worked as a waiter to help put himself through school, a former autoworker turned journalist named Helen Zia urged the assembled group to bring the case to the national press: "We must let the world know that we think this is wrong," she told them. With the assent of Chin's mother, Lily, Zia wrote and issued the first national press release aimed at drawing attention to Chin's killing, the disturbingly minimal punishment its perpetrators received, and what this said about the value of Asian lives in America.

As word of the case spread in print and on the airwaves, Zia and others, including lawyers Liza Chan, James Shimoura, and Roland Hwang and educator Parker Woo, founded American Citizens for Justice, the first national advocacy organization with an explicitly pan–Asian American membership, to organize the fight for a new trial. With support from Asians across the country, as well as the NAACP, the Anti-Defamation League, and prominent Black leaders like Representative John Conyers and the Reverend Jesse Jackson, ACJ successfully convinced the Justice Department to file a federal civil rights case that led to Ebens being convicted and sentenced to 25 years in prison. Though the conviction was overturned on a legal technicality, ACJ lawyers subsequently filed a civil lawsuit on Lily Chin's behalf that

Ebens and Nitz settled for over $1.5 million—a small and hard-won victory for Chin, and a milestone for Asian America.

## A Truer Reflection

The term "Asian American" originated as a way to make sure that we'd be seen and heard in a crowd, and that we'd have a seat at the tables where coalitions were built, decisions were made, and resources were apportioned. But it also set us on the path toward controlling our own narrative—becoming the protagonists of our own stories, rather than blank screens upon which others could project their fantasies and nightmares.

If the early Asian American movement was focused on creating a culture of our own, after Vincent Chin a new emphasis would be placed on changing the one around us as well, because of how it demonstrated that cultural visibility, representation, and authorship weren't just important for our self-esteem. They were necessary for our survival.

And the rest of the Eighties showed how much work we had ahead of us to even be seen at all, much less to be seen as human—as something other than cartoons or playthings, hapless victims or insidious villains.

In 1984, teens across America would roar at the spectacle of Long Duk Dong, the comical exchange student played by Gedde Watanabe in John Hughes's iconic adolescent sex comedy *Sixteen Candles*. "The Donger," as the character refers to himself, is bizarre, horny, incomprehensibly foreign, his every appearance announced with a soundtrack gong. He's despised or condescended to by everyone other than his "sexy American girlfriend," a wallflower athlete who towers over him. When he goes missing and turns up unconscious on a lawn, the elder patriarch of his host family points him out by saying "There's your Chinaman!" His wife, upon learning Dong has trashed the car he borrowed, kicks him in the balls. All of this was enough to make growing up in the decades that followed miserable for Asians, especially Asian men.

But Long Duk Dong wasn't just an offensive racial caricature. He was a probably-Chinese character with a Vietnamese-sounding name played by a Japanese American actor (born and raised in Utah!), with an accent inspired by actor Watanabe's Korean friend. Arriving just two years after the killing of Vincent Chin, the Donger was a reminder that Asians, as imagined by white America, were still a cultural blur, fungible and interchangeable.

That same year saw the heralded sequel to Steven Spielberg's blockbuster homage to the 1940s adventure serial, *Raiders of the Lost Ark. Indiana Jones and the Temple of Doom* took the action to Asia, where the eponymous Jones shot Shanghainese gangsters and picked up a love interest and an 11-year-old Chinese sidekick named "Short Round," before facing off against murderous brown death cultists in Darkest India (whose creepy acts of ritual sacrifice were synthesized from the practices of Aztecs, Native Hawaiians, and European devil worshippers, because the actual practices of Kali worshippers weren't creepy at all).

For Indian Americans, however, the most traumatic scene in the movie was actually one in which the local maharajah presents an extravagant feast featuring such "traditional" Indian fare as roasted giant beetles, eyeball soup, and for dessert, chilled monkey brains served in the severed heads of monkeys. *Temple of Doom* sub-jected Desi kids to a generation of lunchroom mockery. It also reinforced the association of South Asians with bad hygiene, weird religious practices, and a lack of concern for human life.

In 1985, the year after *Temple of Doom* was released, a series of anti-Indian assaults were carried out in New York and New Jersey by an anonymous group calling itself the "Dotbusters." While no direct connection has been alleged between the movie and the subsequent violent outbreak of anti–South Asian violence, a letter purporting to have been written by a representative of the Dotbusters to the *Jersey Journal* expresses the same tenor of disgust toward Indians that's expressed in the movie. The hate campaign culminated in 1987 with the fatal beating of 30-year-old Navroze Mody in Hoboken, New Jersey, and, three nights later, in the brutal ambush of Dr. Kaushal Sharan by a gang of white men in nearby Jersey City. All charges against the perpetrators were dismissed, because the permanent brain damage Sharan suffered made it impossible for him to identify his attackers. The weapons they used to put Sharan into a coma were the same as the ones used against Vincent Chin: the good old American baseball bat.

Growing up in the Eighties taught a rising generation of young Asian Americans, the first to be referred to by that label from birth to adulthood, that images have consequences.

Upon emerging into adulthood in the Nineties, a surprising number of them—especially surprising, perhaps, to their immigrant parents—would decide to see for themselves whether the pen, the podium, the screen, and the stage could be mightier than the Louisville Slugger.

# Who's Asian American?

BY FRANCES KAI-HWA WANG

**IF YOU'RE LOOKING** for evidence that race is a social construct, there's no better place to start than the constantly evolving definition of "Asian American," as determined by the federal government. To be clear, it wasn't an easy task from the very beginning: "Asian" could refer to people with origins from a huge continent stretching as far north as Russia and as far west as Iran, home to over 50 countries whose people speak in excess of 2,000 different languages.

Currently, the U.S. Census Bureau—the government entity tasked with counting heads and classifying them into different groups—uses the following definition, based on 1997 standards on race and ethnicity created by the Office of Management and Budget: "Asian" refers to "A person having origins in any of the original peoples of the Far East, Southeast Asia, or the Indian subcontinent, including, for example, Cambodia, China, India, Japan, Korea, Malaysia, Pakistan, the Philippine Islands, Thailand and Vietnam."

It's a definition that excludes people from Central Asia, even if they have features that may resemble those of East Asians, as do many ethnic groups from Kazakhstan, Kyrgyzstan, Tajikistan, Turkmenistan, Uzbekistan, and parts of eastern Russia, or have deep cultural ties with neighboring countries that are considered Asian, like Afghanistan, which until 2019 had a mostly porous border with Pakistan.

The Middle East is also a complicated issue for racial taxonomists: Though it was historically referred to as part of the "Orient," through the early 1900s courts went back and forth in determining the racial status of Arabs, Turks, and Persians, until the federal government finally ruled in 1943 that Arabs, North Africans, and other Middle Eastern and Southwest Asian peoples would all be classified as white. In most cases, this was due to hard-fought campaigns by those communities, seeking to avoid the penalties associated with being Asian (e.g., inability to own land or to naturalize as U.S. citizens).

So yes: race is a social construct. But it's one with real and significant implications. Here's a rundown of the many configurations of Asian America, and how they've evolved over the years.

# Major Milestones in the Categorization of Asians in the United States

**1852**

Chinese are enumerated for the first time, as a subset of "white" residents of California, in a special supplementary census of the state.

**1854**

In the California Supreme Court case of *People v. Hall*, the court determined that Chinese should not have been allowed to testify against George Hall at his trial for murdering Ling Sing, a Chinese man, due to a state law barring "Blacks, Mulattos and Indians" from serving as witnesses against whites. The court's rationale: because Native Americans had originally trekked across the land bridge into the United States from Asia, Asiatic peoples like the Chinese should legally be counted as equivalent to "Native Americans" for the purposes of court testimony.

**1870 Census**

Chinese are counted for the first time as a separate group, alongside whites, Blacks, "mulattoes," and Indians (meaning Native Americans). Japanese are included in the tally of "Chinese." In a subsequent Congressional report challenging the Census results, Chinese were referred to as "Celestials," and framed as a racial problem that raised "grave questions" (questions that were presumably answered by the Chinese Exclusion Act of 1882).

**1860 Census**

Chinese are the only Asian ethnicity enumerated, and bizarrely, are counted as white everywhere except in California, where they are counted as "Asiatic."

**1877**

Testimony is delivered to a California Senate committee that "it is generally supposed that they [Chinese and Japanese] are the same race; but this is not so. They are of absolutely different origin, and there is no sympathy, no similarity between them," suggesting that "Japanese are of Turkish blood; of the same race as the Turks or Arabians." Other witnesses claim that "some similarities of race exist between . . . [Koreans] and Japanese, while the Chinese are quite singular and unlike."

**1878**

Ah Yup sues in the Ninth Circuit Court in California to be declared white, on the basis of having light-colored skin. He loses his case and is denied the right to naturalize.

## 1880 Census

A brief reference is made of "Asiatic" as a racial umbrella category for Chinese and Japanese, and the first mention occurs of the existence of "Hindus"/"Hindoos," although they are not enumerated.

## 1883

Following the lead of Congress, courts hold that, despite being British subjects, people of Chinese ancestry from Hong Kong were still "Chinese" under exclusion laws, and barred from naturalization.

## 1900 Census

Chinese and Japanese are counted as separate groups.

## 1906

The Census publishes a Supplementary Analysis on Race that finds "little scientific ground" for separating Chinese and Japanese as different races, calling them "closely related branches of the great Mongolian, or yellow, race."

## 1910 Census

Chinese and Japanese are counted as separate groups; non-Chinese or Japanese Asian groups are tabulated as part of "Other." A supplementary table identifies Hindus, Koreans, and Filipinos in the population schedule, but does not enumerate them. However, the supplement outlines the rationale for including Hindus as "non-white Asiatics," which acknowledges that they are "Caucasian" but explains that their civilization is "distinctly different from that of Europe," making it improper to classify them as "white."

## 1920 Census

Racial categories include Chinese, Japanese, Filipino, Hindu, Korean, and Other, with supplementary publications adding categories such as Asian Hawaiian, Part Hawaiian, "Mixed (rather than Chamorro or Polynesian)," and "Mixed (rather than Filipino)."

## 1930 Census

Racial categories include Chinese, Japanese, Filipino, Hindu, Korean, and Other.

## 1922

Takao Ozawa petitions the Supreme Court for naturalization, on the basis of having pale skin and being "American in his heart." The court rules that Ozawa is not white within the meaning of the law and denies his petition.

## 1925

Bhagat Singh Thind*—a Sikh Indian American veteran of the U.S. Army—petitions the Supreme Court for naturalization, citing that "Hindoos" (the term used for Indians and other South Asians, regardless of their actual religious belief) have a common "Aryan" ancestry with Europeans. Though common ancestry is acknowledged, Thind's petition is denied, and Indians in the United States who had been allowed to naturalize find themselves stripped of their citizenship.

---

* See page 28: "Twelve Court Cases That Shaped Asian America: A Dozen Decisions That Changed Our World—and Yours"

## 1968

First public use of the term "Asian American," on the banners of the Asian American Political Alliance, founded by students in Berkeley, California.

## 1960 Census

For the first time, self-response ("I am . . .") replaces enumeration by a census taker. Only Chinese, Japanese, and Filipinos are tallied nationally; Native Hawaiians (and "Part Hawaiians") are counted in the state of Hawaii only. Multiracial people are categorized as their predominant nonwhite race if part white, and by father's race if multiracial nonwhite.

## 1970 Census

Koreans are added back into racial categories; Native Hawaiians are officially counted on a national basis for the first time.

## 1977

The Office of Management and Budget issues Directive 15, formally defining the basic racial and ethnic categories to be used across the federal government.

## 1950 Census

Hindus and Koreans are inexplicably removed from racial categories; only Chinese, Japanese, and Filipinos are enumerated.

## 1980 Census

The first census to use Directive 15 categories, adding "Asian Indian," "Vietnamese," "Guamanian," and "Samoan" to the list of possible self-designations. Multiracial persons are designated as a single race (generally, the race of their mother).

## 1940 Census

Racial categories include Chinese, Japanese, Filipino, Hindu, Korean, and Other.

## 1990 Census

In addition to the Directive 15 categories, Asians are given the option of volunteering their identity, with examples that include Hmong, Fijian, Laotian, Thai, Tongan, Pakistani, Cambodian, "and so on." Multiracial persons are still categorized by maternal race. For the first time, Asians are placed in a common racialized category, "Asian and Pacific Islanders" (APIs).

## 2000 Census

"Guamanian" is expanded into "Guamanian or Chamorro." Asian Americans and Pacific Islanders are separated into two different racial categories, which include the options of "Other Asian" and "Other Pacific Islander," though no examples are listed. For the first time, respondents are told they can mark multiple racial and ethnic categories.

## 2010 Census

Largely the same as 2000, except that examples are added to the "Other Asian" and "Other Pacific Islander" designations.

# The Ascent of AAPI

## Oriental

The word "oriental" has been used as a collective term to refer to things and people from the "East" since the Roman empire, though at the time it referred to territories that ended in what is now Syria. As Europeans traveled farther east, the boundaries of the "Orient" were pushed outward as well, shifting from the Middle East to the countries of East, South, and Southeast Asia. The murky boundaries of the term and its roots in a long history of conquest, colonialism, exploitation, and abuse led to its falling out of use as a classification for people (though it's still used for objects, such as rugs and perfumes). In 2016, New York representative Grace Meng successfully led the passage of HR 4238, a bill that finally struck the terms "Oriental" and "Negro" from federal law books, replacing them with Asian American and African American.

## Asian American

When first coined in 1968, Asian American was hyphenated, both as a noun and as an adjective. The hyphen eventually became seen as a symbol of subordinated identity, as nativists began using the term "hyphenated American" as an anti-immigrant insult. As a result, Black and Asian groups began pressuring to end the use of hyphens, noting that removing it turned "African American" and "Asian American" into phrases where both words stand alone. But it wasn't until 2019 that the Associated Press, a major arbiter of journalistic style, finally stopped hyphenating.

## Asian Pacific American

In the 1980s, the term "Asian Pacific American" (APA) began to be used as an inclusive term for Asian Americans, Native Hawaiians, and other Pacific Islander Americans. However, the term has been criticized for obscuring the very different histories and challenges faced by the two groups, and for concerns that Pacific Islanders were frequently included in name (and acronym) only.

## Asian/Pacific Islander American (A/PIA)

In the 1990s, "Asian/Pacific Islander American (A/PIA)" grew in usage. The slash, significantly, was intended to preserve Asian Americans and Pacific Islanders as distinct groups (as opposed to APA, where the P was just wedged in).

## Asian Americans and Pacific Islanders (AAPI)

By the 2000s, Asian Americans and Pacific Islanders (AAPI) became the most commonly used term, reflecting how, in the 2000 U.S. Census, "Asian" and "Pacific Islander" were once again divided into two separate racial categories. The "and" was intended to make the distinct and equal statuses of both Asian Americans and Pacific Islanders in this grouping clearer than the use of the slash, which was often dropped.

**WHO ARE WE GENERALLY TALKING ABOUT WHEN WE TALK ABOUT ASIAN AMERICANS TODAY?** The U.S. Census Bureau officially tracks and reports on the following 21 Asian American ethnic groups:

| | | | |
|---|---|---|---|
| Bangladeshi | Hmong | Malaysian | Taiwanese |
| Bhutanese | Indian | Mongolian | Thai |
| Burmese | Indonesian | Nepali | Vietnamese |
| Cambodian | Japanese | Okinawan | |
| Chinese | Korean | Pakistani | |
| Filipino | Lao | Sri Lankan | |

# THE PACIFIC ISLANDER STORY ISN'T THE ASIAN AMERICAN STORY

BY JES VU AND JEFF YANG

**IT'S ALMOST A** reflexive thing these days for people to use the term "Asian American and Pacific Islander"—or AAPI, for short—to refer to an expansive definition of our community, which includes not just those of Asian descent, but people hailing from the island nations of Polynesia, Micronesia, and Melanesia. It's done with good intentions, as an attempt to create coalitions and build bridges between cultures that have undoubtedly intersected, cross-pollinated, and influenced one another over centuries. But for many Pacific Islanders, the notion of a hybrid "Asian/Pacific Islander" community overlooks the very different histories of the two groups, which include in many cases colonization, exploitation, and displacement of Pacific Islanders by Asians, and their equally different present statuses. We brought together a group of diverse Pacific Islander voices—**DIONNE FONOTI** of the National University of Samoa, filmmaker **CONRAD LILIHI**, Oregon State University's **PATRICIA FIFITA**, and **KEITH CAMACHO** of the UCLA Asian American Studies Department—to discuss the complicated and even problematic issues that emerge from the reflexive inclusion of Pacific Islanders into the "AAPI" coalition.

## Don't Worry, Be AAPI?

**PATRICIA:** The Asian American ethnic category really evolved out of organizing in the 1960s seeking appropriate representations of unique histories, experiences, and identities in culture, politics, and academic curricula. But after that, for reasons of "inclusion," government entities like the U.S. Census decided to put Pacific Islanders under that umbrella.

**DIONNE:** The government lumps people together and has been doing it forever. You can draw links to how the government lumped together all Native Americans, and how even in tenuous ways this links to issues Native American tribes face today in getting recognition. These were the sorts of games the govern-

ment has played in how it categorizes people.

**KEITH:** But those government categories lead to institutional, organizational, faith-based, sports, and cultural classifications which conflate Asians and Pacific Islanders.

**CONRAD:** By the time you get the Internet, "AAPI" is just flying around in the atmosphere as an acronym, despite it being coined without discussion by those of us impacted by it.

## Indigenous Versus Immigrant

**PATRICIA:** When I see announcements of, for example, Asian Pacific American Heritage Month—I feel like I have to prepare myself, because I know there isn't going to be an appropriate inclusion of "PI" in these "AAPI" month celebrations. We're just going to be further marginalized. There are so many different instances where this plays out. It's political. And it's economic. When there's money involved, a need for resources, apportionment, whatever, these classifications matter.

**CONRAD:** If you go to an "Asian American and Pacific Islander" event, you're not going to see Samoans, you're not going to see Tongans, you're not going to see Māori. We're half of the acronym, but not even close to half the representation. The Indigenous story is always washed away by the immigrant story. Americans are proud to say that "we're a nation of immigrants," but that's also saying "f*ck the Indigenous people."

We're proud to be mixed in Hawaii, but we need to acknowledge that that comes at the price of Indigenous people. We can support each other, but there's a difference between inclusion and erasure.

## We Are Not the Same

**PATRICIA:** It's also the case that there are stark differences between different Asian ethnic groups and different Pacific Islander groups. We don't all have the same identities, we don't all have the same language or forms of expression. When you push all of us together, you create layers and layers of confusion. And that has real consequences for how people look at health outcomes, educational attainment, and income. On that level alone, there needs to be a disaggregation, so the differences in groups can be tracked.

**CONRAD:** The fact is if you look at things sta-

tistically, where we as Pacific Islanders are falls more in line with other Indigenous communities. If we were to be grouped with anyone, it would make sense to be grouped with them.

## Occupied Territories

**CONRAD:** I think what's often missing is the role of colonialism in Pacific Islander histories. While Asians are fighting for representation, you have to realize that part of the Indigenous struggle is fighting for our land. So that's why I don't identify as "Asian Pacific American" or feel connected to the idea of "AAPI." That language seems to apply only toward "positive" things like Jason Momoa and his accomplishments, or Disney's *Moana*. But there's no "AAPI" support when you're talking about the occupation of Mauna Kea or other Indigenous-specific issues or even how AAPI resources are distributed, because the fact is they'll likely go toward East Asians.

**KEITH:** It's not just about America, either. You have to think about the old and ongoing colonial cartography of the Asia-Pacific region. For example, West Papuans reside in Indonesia and are technically Indonesian nationals, but culturally and linguistically, West Papuans are closer to Indigenous Papuans and Pacific Island peoples. But the map just says they're "Indonesian."

## Pop Culture

**DIONNE:** If you're looking at popular media, say, something like cinema, there's no connection between Pacific Islanders and Asians. Our trajectories have been very independent of each other. You might see some weird mixes, like in the musical *South Pacific,* where Bloody Mary is portrayed as a blend of Asian and Pacific Islander.

**KEITH:** She's supposed to be "Tonkinese" from Vietnam. I mean, the Pacific is one big seascape and landscape. But in this film Bloody Mary represents a Southeast Asian reference and a Pacific Islander French colonial reference.

**DIONNE:** When you look at Pacific Islander representation in media, it all stems from very broad connections that non–Pacific Islanders made up about Tiki culture beginning in the 1940s and 1950s, with Pacific Islanders being portrayed as savage island people.

## So Should AA and PI Be Separated?

**CONRAD:** For what reason are we even together? Even among Asian Americans, there's South Asia, Southeast Asian, East Asian, and now you want to add Pacific Islanders? The term is very Asian American. It's not coming from the Pacific Islander community. It's not coming from anybody else.

**KEITH:** I don't think we should be limited by the term "AAPI." What's more helpful is to focus our energies on topics and themes that are important to the communities around us. If you're trying to include everything in this "multicultural apple pie," it's a sky-high ambition to have every group represented. For example, if you are a program in Long Beach, California, it behooves you to work with the Chumash, Tongva, Black, Cambodian, Latinx, Samoan, and Chamorro people who are in that area. I think a lot of times we get overstretched with coalition building at the regional and global

levels. Instead, we should be fiercely local. Who is around you? What do these communities want? What are their needs and aspirations? How can we support each other? That's a good place to start.

**PATRICIA:** At no point do I ever use AAPI to represent myself or to identify myself. It doesn't make sense to me. In my efforts to situate myself, I say I'm Tongan. I think it's important for you to exercise your own right to articulate who you are. I think that does more justice than to fool ourselves into thinking that these umbrella terms will fully represent everybody. What's most important is to represent what you're rooted and grounded in and what you can speak from. I think that clarity is super important. I don't take offense at all if I'm not included in spaces where I'm not being asked to speak about myself or for my people.

**DIONNE:** Especially because I don't live on the mainland, "AAPI" doesn't really bother me. But when I come across it, it's just sort of one of those "other things." Because it's clear to me that it doesn't mean much to me, nor would I ever identify that way. I'm just Samoan. Let the next generation of people coming up figure out if this is who they are for whatever reason. They can define it for themselves.

"AAPI" is a term specific to the United States. It doesn't mean anything anywhere else. When I got to Samoa, as somebody who grew up in a Pacific Islander enclave in Hawaii, it was a shock to me to see how the classification of the Pacific by Samoans was so different from even Pacific Islanders in Hawaii, who may not see Hawaii as part of the Pacific. Even in the Pacific, the people who are actually there define everybody differently than how you, in the United States, do.

JEFF YANG     PHIL YU     PHILIP WANG

# THE ASIAN AMERICAN SYLLABUS

**1980S AND BEFORE**

**WHAT ARE THE** essential texts that best tell the story of "how we got to here"? What are the movies, television shows, and literature that have informed our collective understanding of Asian America? That's the challenge we posed to ourselves as we started this exercise of curating what we're calling the Asian American Syllabus. It's not meant to be a library of great, or even consequential, art, literature, or entertainment. It's also not exhaustive; this is just a survey of our world, an introductory course to the works that shaped us, reflected us, or otherwise impacted how we lived through our own history. As we examined what works we felt we needed to include, we were once again reminded that, especially early on, the times we got to tell our own story were far too often overwhelmed by others telling it for us. For better or for worse, we found ourselves assembling this library of primary sources as a collage of both narratives told by us, and told about us.

**NOTE:** We've focused on works that were either critical touchpoints for those of us growing up in each era, or provide a nostalgic porthole into the era's aesthetics and sensibilities. That means an important novel written in the 1990s that focuses on events of the 1940s might not make it into our picks . . . unless it was also a novel that everyone we knew felt like they had to read, in the 1990s.

**ANOTHER NOTE:** We're not creating a "canon." We're pulling threads to weave a larger tapestry of who we are and how we're seen. That means not all of our picks are Asian American—or even American—and some of them are racist garbage, because that's what we had to deal with then, so you'll have to deal with it too.

**FINAL NOTE, JUST FOR THIS SECTION:** This installment covers everything up through the 1980s, which is a lot. Think of it as a stretch for your cultural muscles before the real exercise begins in the next chapter.

### The Cheat (1915)

**PHIL:** This was the film that made Sessue Hayakawa the first Asian American screen idol . . . in 1915! It's hard to imagine that there was an Asian heartthrob back in the silent era. How did that even happen?

**PHILIP:** I think it was so early that people were like, anything goes. Hollywood hadn't had time to develop their filters yet about what should be on-screen.

> "[*Daughter of the Dragon*] actually radicalized Anna May Wong. It was so racist that being in it made her start calling out how racist Hollywood was!"

### Daughter of the Dragon (1931)

**JEFF:** In this almost unwatchable film, icon Anna May Wong plays the daughter of Fu Manchu! Who's played by Warner Oland in yellowface! And her romantic lead, Chinese detective Ah Kee, is none other than Sessue Hayakawa! They never kiss, of course, and spoiler, he ends up killing her, then dying himself. Also Oland was paid more for being a fake Asian than either of the real Asians. This movie encapsulates the Asian American experience in Hollywood for the next half century.

**PHIL:** It actually radicalized Anna May Wong. It was so racist that being in it made her start calling out how racist Hollywood was!

### *Mrs. Spring Fragrance* (1912) by Sui Sin Far; *East Goes West* (1931) by Younghill Kang; *Father and Glorious Descendant* (1937) by Pardee Lowe; *America Is in the Heart* (1943) by Carlos Bulosan; *Fifth Chinese Daughter* (1943) by Jade Snow Wong

**JEFF:** This is your "early Asian America" bundle—five books that everyone should read to get a sense of what it was like being a pioneer in a country that really didn't want us here. Bulosan's book in particular is a searing, bitter, hopeful piece of activist art that should be required reading for everyone. This line: "All of us, from the first Adams to the last Filipino, native born or alien, educated or illiterate—We are America!" Chills.

### *Nisei Daughter* (1953) by Monica Sone; *No No Boy* (1957) by John Okada; *Farewell to Manzanar* (1972) by Jeanne Wakatsuki Houston

**PHIL:** You can't understand Asian Americans, or America for that matter, without knowing about the incarceration of Japanese Americans. Since you probably didn't learn about it in school, read these books.

### Sayonara (1957)

**PHILIP:** This film stars Marlon Brando as an American air force pilot in postwar Japan, but you really only need to watch it because of Miyoshi Umeki, whose performance won her an Oscar. It also has Ricardo Montalban in it as a Japanese man. *Khaaaaaannnnn!*

### The Crimson Kimono (1959)

**JEFF:** A Sam Fuller noir starring the great James Shigeta as the cop hero . . . who actually gets the girl. They even share the first onscreen kiss between an Asian man and a white woman! Remember, interracial marriage wasn't even legal everywhere in the U.S. until 1967.

### Flower Drum Song (1961)

**PHIL:** A Rodgers and Hammerstein musical. An almost all-Asian cast. With Chinese American characters, set in San Francisco's Chinatown. Great songs, great dancing, flimsy plot, but you can't not love it.

**PHILIP:** Nancy Kwan at the top of her game. Jack Soo is hilarious in it.

**JEFF:** The wild thing is that Madame Liang, who sings the big dance number "Chop Suey," is played by Black actress Juanita Hall and no one even notices.

### Star Trek: The Original Series (1966)

**PHILIP:** Diversity in space.

**PHIL:** And it blessed us with George Takei as Sulu.

**JEFF:** It proved Asians can drive!

### Kung Fu (1972)

**PHIL:** A hit TV show, starring a not-Asian man, from an idea that was probably stolen from Bruce Lee. That is all.

### Zoom (1972)

**JEFF:** The *Zoom* I grew up with, not the Zoom that COVID built. I don't know any Asian guy my age who didn't have a crush on Bernadette.

**PHIL:** Why, because of that thing she did with her hands?

**JEFF:** Don't make it sound weird.

> "I've never seen [Sixteen Candles]. People have always told me to watch it and I'm like, nah, I heard that one's racist."

> "Here's a little secret: All of John Hughes's movies are racist."

### Enter the Dragon (1973)

**PHILIP:** We all hate this. Just kidding.

**PHIL:** Bruce's best film, and the one that propelled him to global stardom.

**JEFF:** And he didn't live to see it released.

### Aiiieeeee! (1974) by Frank Chin, Jeffery Paul Chan, Lawson Fusao Inada, and Shawn Wong; The Woman Warrior (1976) and China Men (1980) by Maxine Hong Kingston

**JEFF:** More for your essential Asian American library—*Aiiieeeee!*, the first Asian American literature anthology, edited with a very particular angry Asian male POV.

**PHIL:** Not gonna take that personally. Also, two works by Maxine Hong Kingston that you can't not read.

### The Year of the Dragon (1974) by Frank Chin; And the Soul Shall Dance (1977) by Wakako Yamauchi; The Wash (1985) by Michael Toshiyuki Uno; M. Butterfly (1988) by David Henry Hwang

**PHIL:** Groundbreaking plays. If you can't see them, read them.

**PHILIP:** *M. Butterfly* won the Tony for Best Play and Best Actor. It put David Henry Hwang and B. D. Wong on the map.

### Mr. T & Tina (1976)

**PHIL:** This was the *Welcome Back, Kotter* spinoff!

**JEFF:** The first Asian American family sitcom starring Pat Morita and Pat Suzuki as his sister-in-law, and June Angela, who was Julie on the *Electric Company*, another of my childhood crushes. It lasted five episodes.

**PHILIP:** The credits were in chopstick font.

### Chan Is Missing (1982)

**PHIL:** Wayne Wang's first film and one of the first Asian American indies to really receive recognition. It still holds up!

### They Call Me Bruce? (1982)

**PHIL:** It's a terrible movie but it starred pioneering Korean American comic Johnny Yune as a guy who gets mistaken for Bruce Lee because he's Asian.

**JEFF:** So relatable. It was a surprise hit and even had a sequel, *They Still Call Me Bruce!*

**PHIL:** We named our podcast after it.

### Gandhi (1983)

**PHILIP:** A blockbuster hit, which won Oscars for Best Picture and Best Director, and Best Actor for Ben Kingsley, making him still the only Asian to ever win a Best Actor Oscar.

**JEFF:** Did you know Alec Guinness almost played Gandhi?

### Indiana Jones and the Temple of Doom (1984)

**PHIL:** If you ask any South Asian who grew up in this era, this movie fucked up their lives, with every kid asking you if you ate monkey brains at home.

**PHILIP:** Not gonna lie, though—when I was a kid I used to pretend to be Short Round. "Doctor Jones! Doctor Jones!"

### Sixteen Candles (1984)

**PHIL:** If *Temple of Doom* fucked up lives for South Asians, *Sixteen Candles* did it for East Asians. Long Duk Dong!

**PHILIP:** I've never seen it. People have always told me to watch it and I'm like, nah, I heard that one's racist.

**JEFF:** Here's a little secret: all of John Hughes's movies are racist.

### The Karate Kid (1984) and The Karate Kid Part II (1986)

**JEFF:** Not gonna lie, I have a love-hate relationship with these movies. Yeah, nostalgia! Pat Morita! But it's still the series that copied everything good about martial arts films and made it all about white people.

**PHIL:** But *The Karate Kid Part II* gave us Kumiko, Tamlyn Tomita's first feature role.

### The Killing Fields (1984)

**PHIL:** Nobody really knew about the horrors of the Khmer Rouge before this film, and it made Haing S. Ngor one of three Asian actors to win an Oscar.

### The Goonies (1985)

**PHILIP:** Data was our hero.

### Year of the Dragon (1985)

**JEFF:** Just wall-to-wall racism. Mickey Rourke as a white cop trying to clean up Chinatown. His character is literally named Captain White.

### Big Trouble in Little China (1986)

**JEFF:** Crazy stuff happens underneath Chinatown.

**PHILIP:** I think it's subversive that the white hero is actually a dummy and the guy you're rooting for is Dennis Dun's character.

**PHIL:** Half the Asians who ever played bad guys are in this movie.

### Sidekicks (1986)

**PHIL:** This did not last long, but it starred Ernie Reyes Jr. as a kid martial artist whose foster dad is Gil Gerard, and it only worked because of Ernie Reyes Jr.

### The Baby-Sitters Club series (1986–2000) by Ann M. Martin

**PHIL:** For a certain generation of Asian American women, Claudia Kishi is arguably the most important literary character ever.

### 21 Jump Street (1987)

**JEFF:** This was the TV version of that "How do you do, fellow kids" meme, but it did give us Dustin Nguyen.

### Who Killed Vincent Chin? (1987)

**PHILIP:** An essential documentary about the murder that galvanized the Asian American movement. Nominated for an Academy Award for Best Documentary.

### Forbidden City USA (1989)

**JEFF:** If you loved *Flower Drum Song*, you need to watch this doc. There really was a "chop suey circuit" of Asian singers, dancers, and showgirls in the 1930s and 1940s!

### The Joy Luck Club (1989) by Amy Tan

**PHILIP:** Love it or hate it, this book was a gateway to Asian American literature for nearly everyone, and it was hugely empowering for a generation of Asian American women who could not find a way to voice the kinds of struggles they faced growing up..

# UNDERCOVER ASIANS

**1980S AND BEFORE**

BY PHIL YU, ILLUSTRATED BY EC YI

**WHEN YOU RARELY** see yourself in mass media, you'll sometimes seek out representation clumsily, in fractions, grasping at rumors of the possible Asian parentage of public figures in an effort to find some kind of connection to celebrity. This dimension of multiracial identity and belonging was hilariously explored in the now-classic "Racial Draft" sketch from *Chappelle's Show,* in which representatives from different racial groups officially selected celebrities as one of their own, once and for all, in a pro-sports-styled public selection ceremony. The Black delegation got to claim 100 percent of Tiger Woods; in response, the Asian delegation chose Wu-Tang Clan.

For years, Team Asian's number-one draft pick was Keanu Reeves, whose multiracial identity was always the stuff of speculation among Asian Americans (before simple facts were simply Google-able). Was he "one of us"? Could we "claim" him? For the record, Keanu is English on his mother's side and Native Hawaiian, Chinese, English, Irish, and Portuguese on his father's side—in total, three-quarters European, 7/32 Native Hawaiian, and 1/32 Chinese. (Also, for the record? He's Canadian.)

Still, for many of us, that was more than enough rationale to include him in our roster. And when he started making films like *47 Ronin,* in which he played a biracial Japanese hero, our stakehold in him felt validated.

But does Keanu, or any multiracial public figure, want to be claimed? Would they claim us back? What even gave us the authority to do the claiming in the first place? These are all valid—and essential—questions to ask against the backdrop of our changing and expanding understanding of who makes up Asian America. At the end of the day, identity can't and shouldn't be measured in percentages. But the need to find needles of representation in the pop-culture haystack continues.

For fellow Asianspotters, here are some noteworthy figures from the Eighties or before who you might be surprised to learn have a connection to the clan (and one who absolutely doesn't).

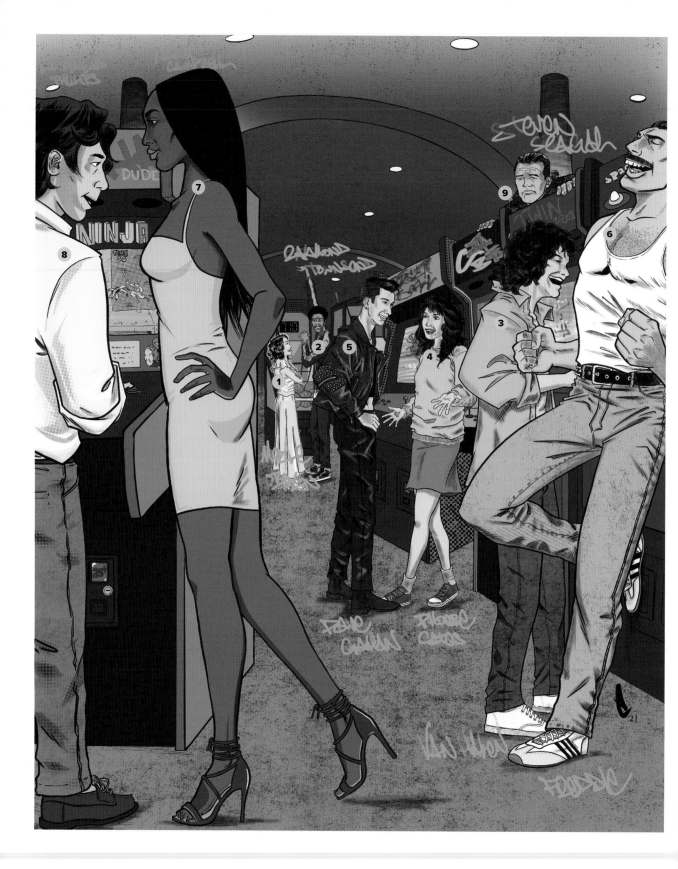

### 1. MERLE OBERON
Fearing the repercussions of racism, actress Merle Oberon, who was nominated for an Academy Award for her performance in *The Dark Angel* (1935), hid her South Asian and Maori heritage for most of her life.

### 2. RAYMOND TOWNSEND
Point guard Raymond Townsend, who played for the Golden State Warriors and the Indiana Pacers, was the first Filipino American to play in the NBA.

### 3. EDDIE VAN HALEN
Van Halen's celebrated lead guitarist was born Edward Lodewijk van Halen to a Dutch father and a Eurasian mother from Indonesia.

### 4. PHOEBE CATES
Eighties icon Phoebe Cates, star of *Fast Times at Ridgemont High* and maybe your adolescent dreams, is of Chinese Filipino descent on her maternal grandmother's side.

### 5. DAVE GAHAN
Dave Gahan, frontman for the essential new wave band Depeche Mode, has an Irish surname, but his birth father was Malaysian.

### 6. FREDDIE MERCURY
The legendary rock icon was born Farrokh Bulsara in Zanzibar to Parsi Indian parents, but legally changed his name upon embracing his genre-bending persona as lead singer of Queen.

### 7. NAOMI CAMPBELL
British supermodel Naomi Campbell is of Afro Jamaican and Chinese Jamaican heritage (on her paternal grandmother's side).

### 8. LOU DIAMOND PHILLIPS
Despite his breakthrough roles playing Mexican American characters in *La Bamba* (1987) and *Stand and Deliver* (1988), actor Lou Diamond Phillips is actually Filipino American.

### 9. STEVEN SEAGAL
Has actually claimed to be a reincarnated Tibetan buddha. He is not Asian at all, not even a little, no matter how hard he tries.

# ORIGINAL SYNTH:
## The Anthems of
## Young Asian America

BY TODD INOUE, ILLUSTRATED BY JEF CASTRO

**IF YOU FLIPPED** through the record collections (remember records?) of many Asian Americans who came of age in the early Nineties, you'd probably have seen an endless lineup of dour, pale faces—members of bands on the danceable fringes of new wave and punk, like Depeche Mode, Erasure, New Order, Pet Shop Boys, OMD, and The Cure. For Asians living in the mostly white suburbs, eager to express adolescent angst without triggering parental crackdown, their affectless vocals and synthesized melodies were a low-risk, profanity-free alternative to hip-hop. Blame cable TV and Kurt Loder: access to 100 channels was an affordable symbol of upward mobility for aspirational middle-class Asian families. For parents, cable was about access to CNN, ESPN, and shows from the motherland. For kids, it meant endless streams of synthpop and modern rock videos—back when MTV played videos; to not-so-reckless suburban youth, having *120 Minutes* and *Alternative Nation* on in the background made cramming for midterms actually bearable. When we were in high school, the music invoked our yearning for individuality and independence, speaking directly to our passive aggression and repressed passion. Upon reaching the relative freedom of college, it became eternally linked to moments of camaraderie and shared milestones, dorm-room drinking games and torrid make-out/break-up sessions. And after we graduated to the so-called real world, it entered into permanent rotation in our car ride mixes, wedding reception playlists, photo-slideshow soundtracks, and weekend noraebang sessions.

Here are the alt-anthems that have staked out a permanent slot on Asian America's nostalgic Nineties playlist:

**"Bizarre Love Triangle,"
New Order (1986)**

When you're in a group of Asians of a certain age and this song comes on, a circle—the Asian version of the *Soul Train* line—will inevitably form, and you'll find yourself pushed into the middle and be expected to throw down. Melodramatic and propulsive, with lyrics speaking to alienation and urgent, unrequited love, "BLT" was the GOAT, the Alpha, the definitive Asian American Nineties anthem, period.

**"A Little Respect," Erasure (1988)**

Andy Bell sings with a rarefied fearlessness and vulnerability, to which Asians are hardwired to respond, and this song's themes of experiencing disrespect and (ahem) erasure were particularly evocative to Asian Americans in the Nineties era of near-invisibility. Warning: If you dare to sing this at karaoke, it will change you forever. Wield its power wisely.

**"People Are People," Depeche Mode (1984)**

Depeche Mode had many songs worthy of this honor, but "People Are People" remains undefeated, given the instantly memorable chorus, the industrial-strength production values, the easy-to-dance-to BPM. And it's an anti-racism plea sung by lead singer Dave Gahan, who's British Malaysian!

**"The Promise," When in Rome (1988)**

Manchester's When in Rome probably weren't aiming for the quintessential "sing at the top of your lungs until you ugly cry" last-dance song, but they made it anyway. A solemn keyboard riff blossoms with lush romanticism atop winding bass roots. The lyrics document a pledge of trust, an acknowledgment of wrongdoing, and a firm commitment to do better—a better background track to a climactic K-drama scene has yet to be written.

**VERY HONORABLE MENTIONS:**

"Only You," Yazoo (1982); "Forever Young," Alphaville (1984); "What's on Your Mind (Pure Energy)," Information Society (1985); "Just Like Heaven," The Cure (1987); "I Beg Your Pardon," Kon Kan (1988); "What Have I Done to Deserve This?," Pet Shop Boys (1988)

## TWELVE COURT CASES
## THAT SHAPED ASIAN AMERICA:

# A DOZEN DECISIONS THAT CHANGED OUR WORLD— AND YOURS

### BY JENN FANG

**THE MEEK, PASSIVE** Asian stereotype has persisted to this day—but history shows that it's a false one. Asians have played a critical role in resisting injustice and winning rights since the beginning of our arrival in this country, writing op-eds, organizing boycotts and protests, pressuring political leaders, and yes, challenging systemic bigotry, persecution, and exploitation in the courts. Here are a dozen court battles waged by Asian plaintiffs— some successfully, some not—whose outcomes continue to shape our lives today.

### Ho Ah Kow v. Nunan, 12 Fed. Cas. 252 (1879)

Throughout the latter half of the 19th century, numerous anti-Chinese laws were passed at the federal, state, and local levels aimed at discouraging Chinese American migration to the United States. One such law was San Francisco's 1876 Pigtail Ordinance, under which Chinese men were, if arrested, required to have their traditional long hair queues forcibly cut short (ostensibly for sanitary reasons). Ho Ah Kow challenged the law's constitutionality, arguing that it was disproportionately enforced against Chinese men, and that it caused him "irreparable harm"—because in China, should he ever visit, not having a queue was punishable by death. In 1879, the California State Supreme Court agreed, striking down the law and awarding him $10,000 in damages.

**IMPACT:** Asserted that the Fourteenth Amendment's guarantee of equal protection to all persons under the law included Chinese, who were not eligible to become citizens.

### Tape v. Hurley, 66 Cal. 473 (1885)

During the late 19th century, Chinese children throughout California were barred by both law and social custom from enrolling in public schools. When Joe and Mary Tape sued to allow their eight-year-old American-born daughter Mamie to attend her local San Francisco primary school, the California State Supreme Court ruled that all Chinese children "are entitled to admission into the public school of the district in which they reside." Unfortunately, the victory was short-lived: because the *Tape v. Hurley* decision did not challenge the prevailing separate-but-equal doctrine used to broadly justify racial segregation, the San Francisco School Board quickly established new, segregated schools for Chinese and other Asian American children.

**IMPACT:** One of the earliest attempts to break down school segregation, which continued for several more decades—especially after the U.S. Supreme Court formally established the constitutionality of separate-but-equal in *Plessy v. Ferguson* in 1896. It wasn't until 1954, in the landmark Supreme Court *Brown v. Board of Education* decision, that segregated schools were finally ruled unconstitutional.

### *Yick Wo v. Hopkins,* 118 U.S. 356 (1886)

In 1880, San Francisco passed a city ordinance barring the operation of a laundry business in a wooden building without a permit. At the time, two-thirds of the city's laundries were Chinese-owned, most were run out of wooden buildings, and almost all Chinese laundry owners had their permit applications denied. Yick Wo sued after being imprisoned for continuing to operate his laundry without a permit. The Supreme Court ruled in Yick Wo's favor, reinforcing the Fourteenth Amendment's guarantee of equal protection under the law.

**IMPACT:** A bedrock decision establishing that even if a law was written with race-neutral language, it could still be seen as a violation of equal protection if it is enforced in a racially biased fashion.

### *United States v. Wong Kim Ark,* 169 U.S. 649 (1898)

Throughout the 19th and early 20th centuries, most Asian and other nonwhite immigrants were denied the right to naturalize as United States citizens. Wong Kim Ark was born in San Francisco in 1873 to parents who were Chinese nationals. After traveling as an adult to China to visit family in 1894,

Wong was denied re-entry to the United States on the grounds that by virtue of his parents' foreign nationality, he was not "subject to the jurisdiction of the United States" and therefore not a natural-born U.S. citizen. Wong challenged that reasoning in the courts and won.

**IMPACT:** The landmark *Wong Kim Ark* decision has been used as legal precedent for the citizenship rights of marginalized U.S.-born persons ever since.

### *Dorr v. United States,* 195 U.S. 138 (1904)

In 1898, the Philippines were ceded by Spain to American colonial control. Shortly thereafter, newspaper editor and Filipino citizen Fred Dorr was arrested and charged with libel. He petitioned for—and was denied—a trial by jury, a right that Dorr argued was granted to him under American law and by the Philippines' status as a U.S. territory. The U.S. Supreme Court ruled against Dorr on the basis that Congress determines the laws that govern unincorporated U.S. territories and therefore, Dorr was not guaranteed that right under the U.S. Constitution.

**IMPACT:** The outcome of *Dorr* and related cases involving U.S. territories established precedent for the denial of full constitutional rights to U.S. citizens residing in unincorporated U.S. territories—a framework that continues to frustrate access to legal rights for many Asian Americans and Pacific Islanders today, not to mention Black and Latinx residents of American territories and protectorates.

### *United States v. Ju Toy,* 198 U.S. 253 (1905)

In the years following the 1882 Chinese Exclusion Act, federal law further sought to limit the Chinese population in the United States by facilitating their deportation and by barring their re-entry following overseas travel. Ju Toy, an American-born citizen who was denied re-entry to the nation of his birth, sued on the grounds that he was a U.S. citizen, and won in federal court. However, the government appealed to the U.S. Supreme Court, arguing that the judicial system should not be used to overrule immigration officials' decisions, except when there is evidence of mistaken application of the law. The Supreme Court ruled in favor of the government.

**IMPACT:** The much-criticized *United States v. Ju Toy* decision effectively ceded control over most immigration matters to the Bureau of Immigration, closing an important avenue for Chinese American citizens and prospective immigrants to appeal immigration decisions that excluded them from the country through the courts, while helping to birth the modern immigration judicial system that continues to adjudicate all immigration claims today.

### *United States v. Bhagat Singh Thind,* 261 U.S. 204 (1923)

Until the mid-20th century, America explicitly forbade the naturalization of any immigrant who was not a "person of African descent" or a "person of what is popularly known as the Caucasian race." In 1919, writer Bhagat Singh Thind—a Sikh Indian—petitioned for the right to naturalize on the grounds that he was descended from people of the Caucasus mountains, and as such was a "Caucasian" with the right to apply for U.S. citizenship. The Supreme Court ruled against Thind. Instead, the courts held that the interpretation of "free white persons" should be drawn upon popular understanding of the racial distinctions between white and nonwhite people.

**IMPACT:** This decision reinforced the white supremacist assumptions at the heart of America's citizenship laws, regardless of common lineage with people of European descent.

### *Korematsu v. United States,* 323 U.S. 214 (1944)

In 1942, President Franklin D. Roosevelt signed Executive Order 9066, directing the forcible relocation and incarceration of hundreds of thousands of Japanese Americans for several years during World War II. Fred Korematsu was arrested for refusing to comply with the order, and became one of a handful of Japanese Americans to challenge the constitutionality of the Japanese American incarceration in the courts. In the landmark *Korematsu v. United States* decision—now considered one of the worst Supreme Court decisions in U.S. history—the Court ruled that the military interest of national defense outweighed the rights of Japanese American citizens, while representing the first use of the "strict scrutiny" standard to evaluate whether a restriction of a particular racial group's civil rights may be justified by public necessity.

In the decades following their eventual release, Japanese American activists succeeded in having the convictions of Korematsu and fellow resisters Minori Yasui and Gordon Hirabayashi overturned, following the emergence of new evidence in the 1980s that the government had used debunked intelligence to allege the disloyalty of Japanese American citizens.

**IMPACT:** Japanese Americans eventually also successfully won a formal apology and reparations payments to surviving incarcerees. Unfortunately, the *Korematsu v. United States* decision has since been used to politically defend such abhorrent policies as the proposed creation of a national registry of Muslim immigrants and citizens.

### *Oyama v. California,* 332 U.S. 633 (1948)

In the early 20th century, California and several other states passed a series of Alien

Land Laws barring "aliens ineligible for citizenship"—a phrasing that at the time included all Asian migrants—from owning land. Instead, they could only lease land in increments of up to three years, a measure aimed at reducing competition for white farmers. In the 1930s, Kajiro Oyama purchased eight acres in Chula Vista, California, in the name of his six-year-old American-born son, Fred Oyama. After the Oyamas' forced incarceration in 1942, the government filed to seize their land on the grounds that the original purchases violated the Alien Land Laws. In 1948, the U.S. Supreme Court ruled that this violated Fred Oyama's equal protection rights.

**IMPACT:** The Court's ruling provided an early challenge to the constitutionality of Alien Land Laws, which California's Supreme Court eventually struck down as unconstitutional. Other states eventually repealed their own Alien Land Laws—although in Florida, this didn't occur until a ballot measure passed . . . in 2018!

### *Mangaoang v. Boyd,* 205 F.2d 553 (1953)

Born in the Philippines in 1902 when it was under American colonial control, Ernesto Mangaoang was a prominent American labor activist who was arrested under the 1917 anti-communist McCarran Act and threatened with deportation on the grounds that the Philippines' 1946 declaration of independence from the U.S. made Filipinos alien immigrants. Mangaoang sued, arguing that because he was a U.S. citizen at the time of his entry, he could not be deported as an alien. The 9th Circuit Court of Appeals agreed, ruling that Filipino Americans were not aliens and that to deport Mangaoang would be unnecessarily punitive.

**IMPACT:** After the U.S. Supreme Court declined to hear the government's appeal of the decision, attempts to quell Filipino American political and labor organizing in the mid-20th century using the threat of forcible deportation effectively ended.

### *Lau v. Nichols,* 414 U.S. 563 (1974)

During the 1970s, at the height of school desegregation efforts in California and around the country, thousands of limited-English-proficiency Chinese students in San Francisco were integrated into public schools without adequate supplemental English language support. The parents of Kinney Kinmon Lau sued, and in 1974, the U.S. Supreme Court ruled in Lau's favor, saying that the 1964 Civil Rights Act required public schools to provide equal educational opportunities and access to all students.

**IMPACT:** By stating that lack of adequate supplemental English support deprived English-language-limited students from meaningful access to a public education, the ruling established that this was a form of discrimination, paving the way for more extensive bilingual education access in public education today.

### *Department of Homeland Security v. Thuraissigiam,* 140 S. Ct. 1959 (2020)

In the face of mounting deportation efforts against refugees and asylum seekers in the United States, Vijayakumar Thuraissigiam—a member of the Tamil ethnic minority from Sri Lanka—sued, arguing that expedited removal proceedings that denied him the right to judicial review were a violation of his constitutional rights to habeas corpus and due process. In March 2020, the U.S. Supreme Court ruled against Thuraissigiam, upholding the constitutionality of expedited removal procedures.

**IMPACT:** This decision is one of several by the courts that continue to limit access to federal judicial review of immigration and deportation proceedings and other rights for refugees and asylum seekers.

# The Propaganda Family Tree

BY JEFF YANG

**WHETHER OUT OF** fear of competition or hatred of a wartime enemy, America has spent much of its history creating grotesque images of Asians in propaganda posters, political cartoons, and editorial illustrations. These images have been recycled again and again: stereotypes first created to stir rage against Chinese workers in the early 19th century were later adapted for use in anti-Japanese propaganda during World War II, and then again for conflicts in Korea and Vietnam, before surfacing in the Eighties as weapons against an economically resurgent Japan. Most recently, we've seen them deployed against a rising China in an era of global pandemic. If some of these images are familiar to you, it's not a coincidence: over the decades they've also seeped their way into pop culture, becoming a permanent part of how Asians are depicted in media and entertainment even during times of "peace."

Ad, "Rough on Rats" (1886)

U.S. Marine Corps (1945)

R. McKee (2020)

U.S. Information Service (1942)

Ashtray (1944)

**LOATHSOME VERMIN**

(2020)

(1887)

Tribune Review, 2003

BAD CHINESE TAKE-OUT

(19th C.)

New York Post, 2003

**PLAGUE CARRIERS**

JAP BLOOD CULT
(1899)

MAN'S ACTION
THOSE NUDE TEEN HEATHEN JOYGIRLS
Man's Action (1967)

12 CHINAMEN and a WOMAN
12 Chinamen and a Woman (1950)

(1899)

**VIOLATORS OF MAIDENHOOD**

JAP BEAST
AND HIS PLOT TO RAPE THE WORLD
(1942)

The Green Mask (1941)

THIS IS THE ENEMY
(1942)

Dr. Seuss (1942)

JAPAN CAKES PEARL HARBOR / MAN SUES PEARL HARBOR
Mike Luckovich (1987)

TIME
Time (1971)

(1870s)

**SNEAKY INVADERS**

Newsweek
Japan Invades Hollywood
Newsweek (1989)

32

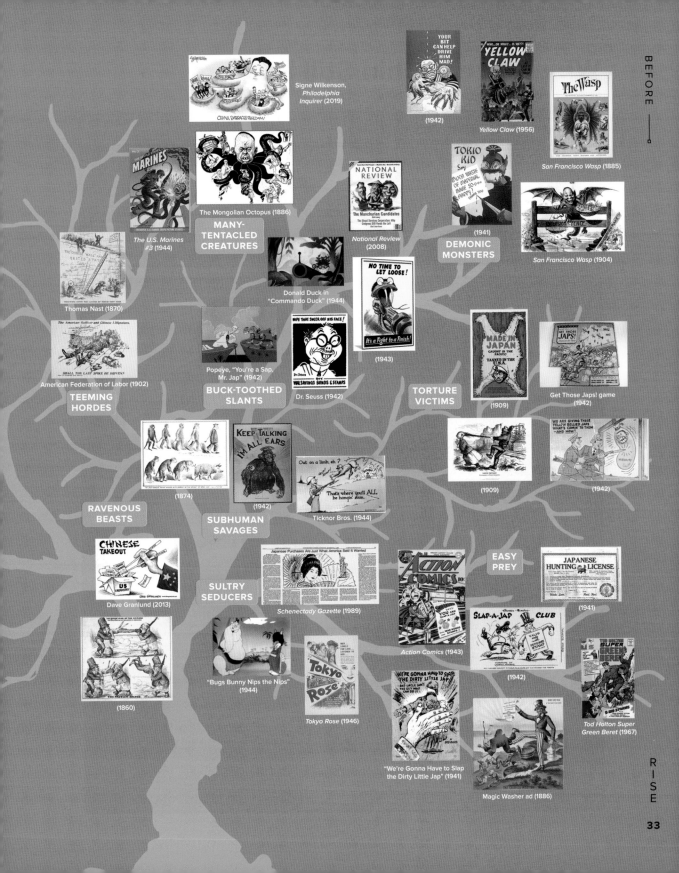

Signe Wilkenson, *Philadelphia Inquirer* (2019)

(1942)

*Yellow Claw* (1956)

*San Francisco Wasp* (1885)

The Mongolian Octopus (1886)

*The U.S. Marines #3* (1944)

**MANY-TENTACLED CREATURES**

*National Review* (2008)

(1941)

*San Francisco Wasp* (1904)

**DEMONIC MONSTERS**

Thomas Nast (1870)

Donald Duck in "Commando Duck" (1944)

(1943)

American Federation of Labor (1902)

Popeye, "You're a Sap, Mr. Jap" (1942)

**BUCK-TOOTHED SLANTS**

Dr. Seuss (1942)

**TEEMING HORDES**

(1909)

Get Those Japs! game (1942)

**TORTURE VICTIMS**

(1909)

(1942)

(1874)

(1942)

**RAVENOUS BEASTS**

Ticknor Bros. (1944)

**SUBHUMAN SAVAGES**

**EASY PREY**

JAPANESE HUNTING LICENSE

(1941)

Dave Granlund (2013)

*Schenectady Gazette* (1989)

**SULTRY SEDUCERS**

*Action Comics* (1943)

SLAP-A-JAP CLUB

(1942)

(1860)

"Bugs Bunny Nips the Nips" (1944)

*Tokyo Rose* (1946)

"We're Gonna Have to Slap the Dirty Little Jap" (1941)

*Tod Holton Super Green Beret* (1967)

Magic Washer ad (1886)

# Why Vincent Chin Still Matters

BY PAULA YOO, ILLUSTRATED BY LOUIE CHIN

AS A 24-YEAR-OLD IN THE SUMMER OF **1993**, FRESHLY GRADUATED FROM COLUMBIA JOURNALISM SCHOOL, I GOT AN OFFER FOR MY FIRST FULL-TIME REPORTING JOB, FROM THE **DETROIT NEWS**.

I WAS EXCITED TO MOVE TO DETROIT, NOT REALIZING HOW **ALONE** I'D FEEL IN A CITY THAT, AT THE TIME, WAS LESS THAN ONE PERCENT ASIAN.

YOUR ENGLISH IS SO GOOD!

WHAT IS SHE?

SHE'S AN **ORIENTAL**. DON'T POINT.

AS YOU MIGHT GUESS, I WAS ALSO ONE OF THE VERY FEW ASIAN AMERICANS AT MY **PAPER**, WHICH MEANT THAT I FELT PRESSURE TO WORK HARDER TO PROVE I WASN'T A "**TOKEN**."

I USED MY LUNCH HOURS TO RESEARCH OUR **ARCHIVES** FOR STORIES ABOUT PEOPLE WHO LOOKED LIKE ME, MOSTLY COMING UP **EMPTY**...

...UNTIL I GOT TO **VINCENT CHIN**.

CHIN WAS A 27-YEAR-OLD CHINESE AMERICAN MAN WHO'D BEEN BRUTALLY KILLED BY **TWO WHITE MEN** IN 1982.

THE WEEK BEFORE HIS WEDDING, HE WAS OUT FOR A **BACHELOR CELEBRATION** WITH HIS FRIENDS, WHEN HE GOT INTO AN ALTERCATION WITH **RONALD EBENS** AND HIS STEPSON **MICHAEL NITZ** AT A CLUB. ALTHOUGH EBENS AND NITZ DENIED IT, WITNESSES TESTIFIED THEY HEARD **RACIST SLURS** FROM THEIR DIRECTION, INCLUDING EBENS ALLEGEDLY SHOUTING, "IT'S BECAUSE OF YOU LITTLE M*****F*****S THAT WE'RE OUT OF **WORK**."

THE MEN CHASED CHIN DOWN THE STREET, AND EBENS BEAT HIM WITH A **BASEBALL BAT**. ACCORDING TO ONE WITNESS, CHIN'S LAST WORDS AS HE SANK INTO UNCONSCIOUSNESS, NEVER TO AWAKEN, WERE "**IT'S NOT FAIR**."

CHIN'S KILLING HAPPENED AT THE HEIGHT OF **ANTI-JAPANESE** SENTIMENT IN THE AMERICAN AUTO INDUSTRY, WHEN MANY FORD, GM, AND CHRYSLER AUTOWORKERS TOOK THEIR ANGER OVER **MASS LAYOFFS** OUT ON THE ASIAN COMPETITION.

MEANWHILE, CHIN LAY IN A **COMA** FOR FOUR DAYS. HE DIED **JUNE 23, 1982**. ON JUNE 29, THE DAY AFTER HIS WEDDING SHOULD HAVE TAKEN PLACE, HIS FIANCÉE AND FAMILY ATTENDED HIS **FUNERAL** INSTEAD.

ONE GROUP OF DETROITERS GOT ON THE NEWS FOR HOLDING A FUNDRAISER WHERE PEOPLE COULD TAKE A **SLEDGEHAMMER** TO A TOYOTA FOR A DOLLAR A SWING.

BOTH MEN PLEADED GUILTY TO MANSLAUGHTER. AT THEIR HEARING IN MARCH 1983, **JUDGE CHARLES KAUFMAN** ANNOUNCED THAT HE BELIEVED BOTH MEN WERE NOT "THE KIND OF PEOPLE YOU SEND TO PRISON." IN LIEU OF JAIL, HE GAVE THEM A FINE OF **$3,000** EACH AND **THREE YEARS PROBATION.**

YOU DON'T MAKE THE PUNISHMENT FIT THE CRIME, YOU MAKE THE PUNISHMENT FIT THE **CRIMINAL.**

THIS SHOCKINGLY **LENIENT** SENTENCE DEVASTATED CHIN'S **MOTHER,** LILY.

IT'S NOT FAIR!

IT **ENRAGED** DETROIT'S ASIAN AMERICAN COMMUNITY.

A GROUP OF ACTIVISTS LED BY HELEN ZIA, ROLAND HWANG, JAMES SHIMOURA, AND KIN YEE FORMED **AMERICAN CITIZENS FOR JUSTICE** TO BRING ATTENTION TO THE CRIME, GARNERING SUPPORT FROM ASIAN AMERICANS ACROSS THE COUNTRY, AND EVEN FROM LEADERS OF **OTHER** DIVERSE COMMUNITIES...

...SUCH AS **REVEREND JESSE JACKSON,** A CANDIDATE AT THE TIME FOR THE DEMOCRATIC PRESIDENTIAL NOMINATION.

IN 1984, THEIR ORGANIZING LED TO THE FIRST-EVER FEDERAL TRIAL OVER THE CIVIL RIGHTS OF AN ASIAN AMERICAN **HATE-CRIME VICTIM.** EBENS WAS FOUND **GUILTY** AND SENTENCED TO 25 YEARS.

BUT EBENS DIDN'T SPEND A DAY IN JAIL; HIS CONVICTION WAS **OVERTURNED** IN 1986 DUE TO A LEGAL TECHNICALITY. CHIN WOULD **NEVER** RECEIVE THE JUSTICE HE DESERVED.

IN 2020, CHIN'S NAME RESURFACED IN THE NEWS, AS PRESIDENT **DONALD TRUMP** USED RACIST LANGUAGE TO DESCRIBE **COVID-19.**

BETWEEN MARCH AND AUGUST 2020, MORE THAN **2,500** ASIAN AMERICANS REPORTED BEING ATTACKED BY PEOPLE **BLAMING** THEM FOR THE PANDEMIC. MOST WEREN'T OF CHINESE ORIGIN.

AND AS FOR ME, MY YEARS OF LUNCHTIME RESEARCH FINALLY LED ME TO WRITE A NONFICTION BOOK FOR **TEENS** ABOUT CHIN AND HIS ROLE IN ASIAN AMERICAN HISTORY. AS DIFFICULT A STORY AS IT IS TO HEAR, IT'S ONE THAT WE NEED TO LEARN EARLY.

AZNS 4 BLM

BLM!

ASIANS FOR BLACK LIVES

CHIN'S DEATH WAS A TRAGEDY. BUT IT **GALVANIZED** THE ASIAN AMERICAN MOVEMENT, AND SERVES AS A CONSTANT REMINDER THAT WE CAN'T BE COMPLACENT IN THE FACE OF INJUSTICE, WHETHER IT OCCURS TO US OR TO **OTHERS.**

BECAUSE FOR SOME OF US, LIKE **VINCENT CHIN,** THEIR TWENTIES ARE TOO LATE.

Adapted from *A WHISPER TO A RALLYING CRY: The Killing of Vincent Chin and the Trial That Galvanized the Asian American Movement,* published by Norton Young Readers (W. W. Norton & Co.) in April 2021.

# How to Yellowface

BY NANCY WANG YUEN

1. Darken hair or wear a black wig, ideally slicked back or in a blunt bowl cut; shorter 'dos can feature hair ornaments, such as food utensils. Longer hair should extend at a minimum to the top of the buttocks.

2. For East/Southeast Asians, use tape, eyepieces, or rubber bands to "slant" eyes; exaggerate eye corners with eyeliner for maximum feline/Asian effect. Squinting and wearing glasses may help sell the look.

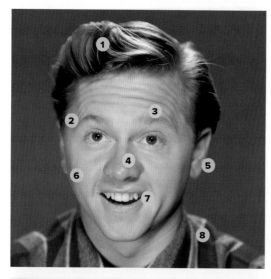

3. For East/Southeast Asians, make eyebrows high, narrow, and boomerang-shaped. For South Asians, the darker and bushier the brow, the better; think two caterpillars about to engage in mortal combat.

4. For East/Southeast Asians, diminish the bridge of the nose; flatten and flare nostrils or turn them up in piglike fashion. If male, consider wispy lip strands or a goatee. For South Asians, build up the nose to comically large proportions. If male, consider adding giant mustache or, for older men, a luxurious beard.

5. Extra credit for making ears demonically pointed (villains) or spread out like mighty wings (buffoons).

6. Darken skin with foundation, preferably yellow or brown pigments not found in nature; remove all pink or other organic undertones.

7. Prosthetics should be used to make face round, flat, and moon-shaped, or to architecturally enhance cheekbones. For men, oversized incisors are a must.

8. Where feasible, native or traditional garments are preferred; mix and match among kimonos, qipaos, saris, tunics, embroidered robes, or ninja gear. No one will know the difference.

9. And, of course, garnish with an impenetrable accent, or flowery pidgin English and plenty of bowing.

**Welcome to Asian!**

# YELLOWFACE: IN THE BEGINNING

## BY NANCY WANG YUEN

**"Cho Cho San" in *Madame Butterfly* (1915), Mary Pickford**
*Madame Butterfly* was the first Hollywood feature film to feature a white person playing an Asian character. Pickford played the stereotypical tragic Japanese girl who marries a white American soldier, has his child, and then sacrifices herself. The director thought Pickford was "too Americanized to play a Japanese," and wanted her to play Cho Cho San in a "more reserved 'Oriental' manner."
**CONVINCING OR NOT? NOT CONVINCING.** Basic white girl playing dress-up in a geisha wig and kimono.

**"Fu Manchu" as portrayed by a series of white actors, including Warner Oland, Boris Karloff, Peter Sellers, Christopher Lee, and Nicolas Cage (1920s to 2000s)**
Since his screen debut in 1923's *The Mystery of Fu Manchu,* the "Devil Doctor" created by British pulp author Sax Rohmer established himself as one of pop culture's most infamous yellowface creations. An Asian parent's dream—with an M.D. from Harvard, J.D. from Christ's College, and Ph.D. from Edinburgh!—he used his brilliant mind to become every white person's nightmare, embodying the idea of the "yellow peril" seeking to take over the West. The Chinese embassy in Washington, D.C., actually issued a formal complaint against *The Mask of Fu Manchu* (1932), which featured Dr. Fu inflaming the peoples of Asia and the Middle East to launch a war to wipe out the "white race."
**CONVINCING OR NOT? NOT CONVINCING.** Fu Manchu put the Orientalist supervillain on the pop culture map, instilling fear, fascination, and loathing in the West. But the performances just looked like white dudes in bad Halloween costumes.

**"Charlie Chan" as portrayed by a series of white actors including Warner Oland, Sidney Toler, Roland Winters, and J. Carrol Naish (1920s to 1980s)**
Charlie Chan, a fictional Chinese detective from Hawaii, was initially created as a "positive" alternative to the sinister criminal mastermind Fu Manchu, by American author and Sax Rohmer contemporary Earl Derr Biggers. The very first Charlie Chan was actually played by Japanese American actor George Kuwa, in a supporting role in the 1926 film serial *The House Without a Key.* But once Chan became the lead, studios cast white actors in yellowface to play him. Swedish American actor Warner Oland—who also robed up as Fu Manchu—played Chan in a staggering sixteen films. (He claimed the key to his successful Asian performances was a trace of "Mongolian ancestry," a claim without evidence.) The yellowface portrayals of Charlie Chan solidified

certain Asian stereotypes in popular culture, including the "so solly" accent, mock Confucian proverbs, and constant deferential bowing.

**CONVINCING OR NOT? NOT CONVINCING.** Every version was a cringey racist caricature.

### "O-Lan" in *The Good Earth* (1937), as portrayed by Luise Rainer

The movie was based on Pearl S. Buck's book of the same name, and she wanted Chinese actors to star in the film but said an MGM executive told her that would be "impossible." Anna May Wong, the biggest Chinese American actor at the time, auditioned for O-Lan—one of the extremely rare Chinese female leads; MGM denied her the role and offered her the concubine role instead. Wong refused, saying: "I won't play the part. If you let me play O-Lan, I'll be very glad. But you're asking me—with Chinese blood—to do the only unsympathetic role in the picture."

**CONVINCING OR NOT? THE OSCARS WERE CONVINCED.** The Academy thought Luise Rainer was convincing enough to award her a Best Actress Oscar, something no Asian woman has ever won as of this writing.

### "Genghis Khan" in *The Conqueror* (1956), as portrayed by John Wayne

Wayne said he wanted to play Genghis Khan as a cowboy, and that's exactly what he did. Even with taped eyes and a Fu Manchu mustache, John Wayne sounded and acted exactly like . . . John Wayne. The movie was filmed in Utah, 130 miles downwind from a major U.S. nuclear testing site—over 40 percent of the cast and crew, including the director and John Wayne, either developed or died of cancer.

**CONVINCING OR NOT? HORRIFYING.** The film was such a travesty that its producer, Howard Hughes, purchased every print of the film for $12 million to keep it out of circulation.

### "King Mongkut" in *The King and I* on Broadway and the film adaptation (1956), as portrayed by Yul Brynner

While some biographies cite Brynner as having Mongolian forebears on his father's side, the Russian American still chose to darken his skin and wear eye makeup to play his signature role. Brynner gave a total of 4,625 performances of the Siamese king on stage, taking his last curtain call in 1985. For his performances, he won two Tony Awards (1952, 1985) and a Best Actor Oscar (1956). Though considered a classic, the Rodgers and Hammerstein musical nevertheless exoticized Thai culture—even as it was one of the first major musicals to depict an interracial romance between an Asian man and a white woman.

**CONVINCING OR NOT? CONVINCING.** Brynner was so effective in the role that he became synonymous with the King of Siam on stage and screen for over thirty years. That doesn't excuse his decision to cosmetically alter his appearance to boost his Asianness.

### "Mr. Yunioshi" in *Breakfast at Tiffany's* (1961), as portrayed by Mickey Rooney

Rooney's bumbling Yunioshi, with his bug eyes, exaggerated buck teeth, and cringe-inducing accented screeching, may take the prize as the most humiliating yellowface buffoon in Hollywood history, especially as contrasted with the glamorous Holly Golightly (Audrey Hepburn) and suave Paul Varjak (George Peppard).

**CONVINCING OR NOT? NO, JUST NO.** Mr. Yunioshi goes down in history as one of the most racist yellowface performances in Hollywood. After defending the role for decades, Rooney himself finally admitted in 2008 that if he'd known people would be so offended, he "wouldn't have done it."

**"Indian Physician" in *The Road to Hong Kong* (1962); "Dr. Ahmed el Kabir" in *The Million-airess* (1960); "Hrundi V. Bakshi" in *The Party* (1968), all portrayed by Peter Sellers**
British comic chameleon Peter Sellers, best known as *The Pink Panther*'s Inspector Clouseau, donned brownface for Indian roles no fewer than three times in widely distributed movies—playing an unnamed "Indian Physician" in the Bob Hope/Bing Crosby movie *The Road to Hong Kong*; the British Indian romantic lead (!) of *The Millionairess,* opposite Sophia Loren; and finally, as a blundering Indian actor who gets mistakenly invited to a big Hollywood gala in *The Party*. (He'd also be the last white actor to don yellowface to play Fu Manchu in that franchise, though Nicholas Cage did a brief yellowed-up Fu cameo in the 2007 horror anthology *Grindhouse*.)
**CONVINCING OR NOT? FRUSTRATING.** Sellers not only took roles away from actual Indian actors, his performance served as an inspiration for later brownface interpretations: Hank Azaria admitted he drew inspiration from Sellers's performance in *The Party* to voice Apu's character on *The Simpsons*.

**"Kwai Chang Caine" in *Kung Fu* (1972–1975, ABC), as portrayed by David Carradine**
Yellowface enables racist caricature—but it also denies Asian actors the opportunity to play Asian roles. In the case of *Kung Fu,* not only did Warner Brothers pass on casting Bruce Lee as its lead, it's alleged that they took the basic concept for the series from an idea he pitched. Carradine would reprise the role in its 1990s sequel *Kung Fu: The Legend Continues* (1993–1997, ABC), which paired him with also-white Chris Potter playing his son, Peter Caine, a Chinatown-based detective.
**CONVINCING OR NOT? IT SHOULD HAVE BEEN BRUCE.** Racist concerns about Lee's accent, and the belief that "you can't make a star out of a 5'6" Chinese actor," per one executive, meant that audiences would have to wait until 2019—nearly half a century after Lee's death—to see Lee's original TV concept come to fruition as the Cinemax series *Warrior,* developed by his daughter, Shannon Lee.

**"Billy Kwan" in *The Year of Living Danger-ously* (1982), portrayed by Linda Hunt**
Amazingly, Linda Hunt won a Best Supporting Actress Oscar for a yellowface performance as a Chinese Australian *man*. Yes, you read that right: for the role, white American actor Linda Hunt shaved her eyebrows, dyed her hair black, and wore body and face makeup to "give her skin an Oriental cast," according to the *Washington Post*'s Joyce Wadler, in an admiring profile.
**CONVINCING OR NOT? WELL, IT FOOLED THE ACADEMY—AGAIN.** It's truly incredible that as many white actresses have won Oscars for yellowface performances as Asian actresses have won Oscars for anything. (Just two Asian actresses have ever won an Oscar—Miyoshi Umeki, for *Sayonara* in 1957—and Yuh-Jung Yoon for her performance in *Minari* in 2021.)

**"Ben Jahveri" in *Short Circuit 2* (1988), portrayed by Fisher Stevens**

When Indian American actor Aziz Ansari saw sci-fi comedy *Short Circuit 2,* with its Indian lead character and white love interest, he says he thought it was a "bold foray into diversity, far ahead of its time"—until he found out that the Indian character was played by a white actor in brownface. To his credit, Stevens has since said he never should have taken the role.

**CONVINCING OR NOT? CONVINCING—BUT STILL PROBLEMATIC.** If it's any consolation (it isn't), Stevens says he went full method to avoid playing the role as a caricature: he studied with a dialect coach, read R. K. Narayan's *The Guide* and Hesse's *Siddhartha,* and even lived in India for a month before shooting. How much easier would it have been to just hire an Indian actor?

# POSTCARD FROM ASIAN AMERICA

BY CHELSEA ST. CLAIR

Dear RISE,

Growing up in Iowa, my identity was an aspiration, not a steady foundation. My mom was adopted at birth into a Japanese family. Her birth parents chose a closed adoption, sealing her records. She found out she was Chinese when she took a DNA test connecting her to a woman who, genetically, had to be her mother.

But for most of my life, being Black and Japanese was the uncertain foundation I rested on as people asked me prying questions about who I was, where I was from, and why I had such pretty hair. When my mother wasn't present, my Asian American identity always seemed like an inconvenient truth. When we're together it's unmistakable—the way that genetics copy-and-pasted her face onto mine. We share the same crinkle in our eyes and megawatt smiles. When we're apart, people tend to see only what they want, and Asian American isn't it.

In high school, I would always be called on to speak for the minority because "we don't know what she's mixed with, but we know she's not white." In college, as I moved even further from home, most stopped listening after "Black and . . ."

Now as an adult, I am working to reclaim being Asian while reconciling what it means to be Black in America. How do I honor both identities as I grow and build my own traditions, tendencies, and talismans? But that's the story of being Asian in America; we defy definition, breaking free of the shackles of convention and model-minority myth. We can be Black and Asian, with a Chinese mother raised in a Japanese family. We still persist, even under the monstrous pressure to assimilate into what's expected.

Love,
Chelsea

RISE
HERE AND NOW,
ASIAN AMERICA

DIEP TRAN

VIVIEN NGÔ

# *Miss Saigon,* but Not Forgotten

## BY JES VU

**CLAUDE-MICHEL SCHÖNBERG** and Alain Boublil's musical *Miss Saigon* is a global success, with 10-year runs in London and on Broadway (a 2017 revival added on another 340 performances) and multiple touring companies whose performances have been seen by over 16 million people across North America. But for Asian and particularly Vietnamese Americans, its legacy is more tangled. As one of a handful of musical theater productions with a predominantly Asian cast, it's launched the careers of hundreds of talented Asian performers. And yet, by resetting Giacomo Puccini's *Madama Butterfly*—the opera that stamped the stereotype of the self-sacrificing "lotus blossom" onto the Western cultural landscape—in a Vietnam War brothel, it presents cliché, racist images of Asian women and men, while reinforcing the tradition of projecting the war through a strictly American lens.

We invited theater critic **DIEP TRAN** (*American Theatre* magazine, NBC *Asian America*) and actor **VIVIEN NGÔ** (*Queen Sugar*) to comment on their personal relationships with *Miss Saigon,* and as we guessed . . . it's complicated.

## Meeting *Miss Saigon*

**VIVIEN:** My introduction to *Miss Saigon* came when I was 15—it was the year I was introduced to theater. My high school did a production of it, and the idea that there was a musical, of all things, centered on a Vietnamese girl around my age meant the world. I auditioned and got cast as a bar girl. It was . . . a strange experience. You had teenage girls cage-dancing on stage . . . and the girl who got cast to play Kim wasn't even Asian; I remember her being of white and Mexican descent.

Looking back, I recognize how problematic it all was, but I do credit it with giving me something to dream of as a young performer. Like, "well, I can't play all these other things, but if I train for it, someday I can be in *Miss Saigon*!" I held on to a complicated love for the show for a long time before finally realizing I didn't have to accept something that participated in such harmful narratives about my people's trauma.

**DIEP:** When I first heard about it, I went online and read the summary. "Oh, it's based on *Madama Butterfly*; it's a tragic story about this Vietnamese woman who suffers and dies!" And even then I was like, "That doesn't sound fun, or familiar, or accurate to what actually happened in Vietnam."

Eventually, I finally went to see it. I knew it was going to be bad, but I thought, maybe I can just go and be entertained? And then the bar girls came on; the audience was having a good time and they were openly ogling them. They were all white and old, and I was sitting in there going, "Why am I here? Why did I do this to myself?"

## Who Are We, Really?

**DIEP:** Growing up in Orange County next to Little Saigon, my whole family used to watch Vietnamese variety shows like *Paris by Night*. We saw how talented Vietnamese Americans can be—dancing, doing comedy, singing with insane vocal runs—but we also knew that the show was for Vietnamese people. We were not visible in American entertainment. Even then I was aware of that disconnect—that we were a really strong, really overlooked people but Americans didn't want to see us, so we had to create our own space.

> "In pop culture about the Vietnam War, the narrative is all about what Americans went through, using Vietnamese people and the setting of Vietnam as props and backdrop. There's no concern over the interiority of the people who live there."

What a lot of white people don't understand about *Miss Saigon* is that for Vietnamese people, the Vietnam War was a civil war. Where Vivien and I grew up, if you put a photo of Ho Chi Minh up in your store, people would protest outside. It's triggering for a lot of us in the West. So putting Ho Chi Minh on a shirt, as the 2017 revival of *Miss Saigon* did, and selling it as musical merchandise is inappropriate. It shows it's not for us, because they didn't care how I or my community might take it.

**VIVIEN:** Agreed. It is obvious the show is not for us, really. *Miss Saigon* depicts Vietnamese women like the exact opposite of who we are. It frames us as helpless with a constant need to be saved. But in the North, women fought in the tunnels. In the South, they held their families together when all their husbands were imprisoned. And today, it's not like we're these perfect, prim and proper innocent beings. Nothing about me is proper. My grandma liked smoking cigarettes, she'd organize gambling parties for her girlfriends to come over and play cards.

## Through Western Eyes

**DIEP:** American culture tends to see Asians as weak and in need of white people to come save us. That's especially true in pop culture about the Vietnam War. The narrative is all about what Americans went through, using Vietnamese people and the setting of Vietnam as props and backdrop. There's no concern over the interiority of the people who live there. *Miss Saigon* is the largest manifestation of this. It says, "You're never going to be the hero. We cannot relate to you. You're always going to just be the sidekick in our stories or a trigger for our feelings."

Maybe they never allow us to be the lead in our stories because they think that without them, our stories are not worth telling.

**VIVIEN:** Also, let's remember that *Miss Saigon* was originally written by a French team. The irony—our colonizers rewriting our history to tell a story for Western sensibilities. It's not surprising that they built it around this clichéd archetype of a virginal sex worker who's yearning for love. It's clearly written from a white male gaze that doesn't understand the experience of a woman during this time, much less a sex worker. And yet, it may now be the preeminent depiction of Vietnamese women.

**DIEP:** I hate that *Miss Saigon* was adapted from *Madama Butterfly,* because the Japanese have a tradition of honorable suicide. That's not a part of Vietnamese culture. To transpose that story into a Vietnamese setting makes it seem like all Asians are the same, that all we care about is honor and self-sacrifice. And of course, they make that sacrifice all about motherhood, and letting your child go to have a better life in a better place. It's a gratuitous romanticization of Third World tragedy that frames Americans as heroes and America as paradise.

## The Legacy

**VIVIEN:** I want to create stuff for my community. I want to support the work of other Vietnamese and other Asian American play-wrights. *Miss Saigon* and the Western narratives of the American War (as it's called in Vietnam) take up all this space. I think there're other ways to remember the war, but also I don't want us to forever be stuck in that trauma when it comes to telling stories about who we

> "[*Miss Saigon*] is clearly written from a white male gaze that doesn't understand the experience of a woman during this time, much less a sex worker. And yet, it may now be the preeminent depiction of Vietnamese women."

are. I used to feel compelled to defend *Miss Saigon* because I felt that if I didn't embrace it, what else would I have? But I've realized we can have so much more than these inauthentic characters and stories that just make me feel dirty, other, and less than.

**DIEP:** We all recognize that it opened doors for a lot of Asian American performers. But I was so upset when Qui Nguyen's *Vietgone* came to New York Off-Broadway and it didn't get love from the mostly white drama critic establishment, because they didn't understand it. It went against the narratives that white people expect from us. And it didn't transfer to Broadway, and it should have.

It's not like there's a lack of Vietnamese and other Asian American people writing musical theater—it's that they never get funding to put their shows on Broadway because white people think the only people white people want to watch are other white people. But in my perfect Broadway world, instead of *Miss Saigon* revivals, you'd have Lauren Yee's *Cambodian Rock Band* and David Henry Hwang's *Soft Power* and *Vietgone.*

# The *Miss Saigon* Family Tree

BY ERIN QUILL, ILLUSTRATED BY LEI DE LOS REYES

One of the biggest controversies to erupt out of *Miss Saigon*'s original 1991 run was the producers' decision to cast white British actor Jonathan Pryce—wearing bronzer and eye prosthetics—in the showpiece role of the Engineer, who is supposed to be half French and half Vietnamese. In the wake of the uproar over that casting, the decision was made to only cast Asian actors in the role, underscoring the fact that this show remains the largest musical theater employer of Asian actors, singers, and dancers, and the training ground for some of Asian America's brightest stars.

COSTARS IN *YELLOW ROSE*

**LEA SALONGA** leapt into the spotlight as Broadway's first Kim—a performance for which she became the first Asian to win a Tony Award for Best Actress. She was the first Asian to play the roles of Fantine and Eponine in *Les Misérables,* and was the lead in David Henry Hwang's Broadway reimagining of *Flower Drum Song* and in the Japanese American incarceration saga *Allegiance.* She has been the singing voice of not one, but two Disney Princesses, Mulan and Jasmine.

MEMBERS OF POP COVER GROUP "MAMA BARES"

**JOAN ALMEDILLA** appeared as Kim on Broadway in 1995. She went on to play Fantine in the third national tour of *Les Misérables.* In 2007 she starred as Imelda Marcos in the concert version of David Byrne's *Here Lies Love.*

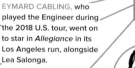

**JENNIFER PAZ** played Kim on the first national tour, and went on to play both Eponine and Cosette in *Les Misérables* on Broadway, and to originate the role of Mei-Li in the pre-Broadway. She voices Lapis Lazuli in the Cartoon Network hit *Steven Universe.*

COSTARS IN *STEVEN UNIVERSE*

MEMBERS OF POP COVER GROUP "MAMA BARES"

**DEEDEE MAGNO HALL** played Kim on Broadway and in one of the national tours, then went on to voice the role of Pearl on the hit Cartoon Network show *Steven Universe.*

**AI GOEKU CHEUNG** played Yvette in the original Broadway production and eventually took over the role of Ellen.

**PLAYED ELLEN**

**MARGARET ANN GATES** was in the ensemble of the original production, then went on to be the first Asian American to perform the role of Ellen, Chris's American wife, opposite Lea Salonga as Kim.

**EYMARD CABLING, who** played the Engineer during the 2018 U.S. tour, went on to star in *Allegiance* in its Los Angeles run, alongside Lea Salonga.

**PLAYED THE ENGINEER**

MET ON NATIONAL TOUR AND GOT MARRIED

**THOM SESMA** starred as the Engineer in the second national tour, and is a veteran of many Broadway productions, including *The Times They Are A-Changin',* *Man of La Mancha, Search and Destroy, Nick & Nora, Chu Chem,* and *Titanic: The Musical.*

**FRANCIS JUE** has played the Engineer in multiple regional productions. He is best known for creating the role of Bun Foo in the original Broadway production of *Thoroughly Modern Millie,* as well as lead turns in a number of David Henry Hwang productions—*M. Butterfly,Yellow Face,* and *Soft Power.*

**JON JON BRIONES** was part of the original West End production in 1989, then joined the show's European tour as the Engineer; he met his wife, Megan Johnson, in Germany, where she played the role of Ellen. He returned to the role in 2014 for the West End revival, receiving a Laurence Olivier Award nomination, then followed the show to Broadway, to play the Engineer in its 2017 revival there. Briones and his family now reside in L.A., where he has been cast in major roles on TV, including *American Crime Story: The Assassination of Gianni Versace* and *Ratched.*

**FRANCIS RUIVIVAR** was the first Asian American to play the role of the Engineer. He sadly passed away from leukemia in 2001 at the age of 40.

**CLIFTON HALL** was in the ensemble for the original production, and then starred as Chris on its first national tour.

EVA NOBLEZADA was nominated for a Tony Award for her portrayal of Kim in the 2017 Broadway revival, and again in 2019 as the lead in *Hadestown*. In 2019, she played the country-singing lead in the movie *Yellow Rose*.

CALUD IS NOBLEZADA'S AUNT

ANNETTE CALUD played Kim during the original Broadway run and went on to play dance teacher Celina on *Sesame Street* for half a decade.

SHARON LEAL broke into Broadway as head bar girl Gigi, and went on to play Mimi in the Broadway production of *Rent* before launching an illustrious TV and film career, appearing alongside Beyoncé and Jennifer Hudson in the movie version of *Dreamgirls*.

RONA FIGUEROA played Kim on Broadway and, later, Eponine in the Broadway production of *Les Misérables,* and was a lead in the 2003 revival of *Nine*.

**PLAYED KIM**

HAZEL ANN RAYMUNDO played Kim in the Chicago company while still attending Northwestern University. Since then she's appeared on Broadway in *Pacific Overtures* and *Avenue Q*.

**PLAYED GIGI**

EMILY HSU was in the Pittsburgh Civic Light Opera production and later joined the Broadway cast as Gigi.

# MISS SAIGON

BARRY K. BERNAL, who originated the role of Thuy on Broadway, also starred in the national tour of *Cats* as Mr. Mephistopheles. He passed away of complications from AIDS in 1993, at the age of 31.

STARRED IN *ALLEGIANCE* AND *FLOWER DRUM SONG* TOGETHER

**PLAYED THUY**

DEVIN ILAW played Thuy in Toronto in 2010 and went on to star as Marius in the 2014 revival of *Les Misérables* and its national tour, before returning to the role of Thuy for the 2017 Broadway revival.

MARC DELACRUZ played Thuy in a regional production in North Carolina; in 2018, he became the first Asian American to play Alexander Hamilton in the production of *Hamilton* on Broadway.

KRISTI TOMOOKA played Mimi in the second national tour, where she met her future husband, Christopher Russo, who understudied Chris on the tour. The two toured the country for ten years in *Wicked,* and have a daughter, Isabella Russo, who went on to star in the Broadway production of *School of Rock*.

STARRED IN *ALLEGIANCE* TOGETHER

TELLY LEUNG played Thuy in the 2003 Pittsburgh Civic Light Opera production, and has since become a mainstay on Broadway, starring in the reboot of *Flower Drum Song* and *Allegiance*.

KELVIN MOON LOH played Thuy in the Pioneer Theater Company's regional production and has since gone on to five Broadway productions.

MANU NARAYAN was on the second national tour as Thuy. Since then, he's gone on to star in a Broadway musical built around him, *Bombay Dreams*.

**PLAYED OTHER ROLES**

MICHAEL K. LEE played Thuy in the second national tour and went on to take over the role in the original Broadway run.

LEON LE, one of the few Vietnamese performers who has appeared in the show, toured the Midwest with the show, and made it to Broadway as part of *Spider-Man: Turn off the Dark.*

RACHEL ANN GO made her Broadway debut as Gigi in the 2017 revival, but she'd already become a singing sensation in the Philippines, after winning one of the nation's most popular TV talent competitions, *Search for a Star*. She went on to play Fantine in the 30th-anniversary production of *Les Misérables* and Eliza Hamilton in the West End production of *Hamilton.*

NINA ZOIE LAM is a member of the ensemble in the original Broadway company, she became a cofounder of the National Asian Arts Project.

REGGIE LEE was in the ensemble for the second national tour, and has gone on to become a regular on TV series like *Prison Break, Grimm,* and *All Rise.*

# THE ASIAN AMERICAN PLAYLIST:

BY RICHIE "TRAKTIVIST" MENCHAVEZ

# 1980s and Before

**IT'S SURPRISING HOW** many Asian American artists broke through to mainstream success in the decades before the Nineties; it's outright shocking how invisible these pioneers are to present-day Asian Americans. In this first installment of our Asian American Playlist, Filipino American DJ and music archivist Richie Menchavez, better known as "Traktivist," takes a look back at the groundbreaking artists who make up our hidden pop music history.

A Rise 1980s + BEFOR

### "Jump Children" (1946), the International Sweethearts of Rhythm

An all-woman jazz orchestra featuring 16 teen-aged girls of various heritages—Asian, Black, Latin, white, and Indigenous—the International Sweethearts of Rhythm pushed the boundaries of race and gender in a sexist and segregated America. One of its original members was Willie Mae Wong, a baritone saxophonist of mixed Chinese and Indigenous heritage. This track is one of a handful of surviving sound recordings from this popular, boundary-breaking big band.

### "I Enjoy Being a Girl" (1959), Pat Suzuki

Chiyoko "Pat" Suzuki was a legendary Japanese American actor best known for originating the role of Linda Low in the Broadway musical *Flower Drum Song* in 1958. Suzuki, who as a child was incarcerated during WWII, was discovered at a local Seattle nightclub by Bing Crosby, and ended up winning a recording contract with major label RCA Victor after her Broadway success. Suzuki's third RCA album, *Broadway '59*, featuring this rendition of "I Enjoy Being a Girl," scored her a Grammy Award nomination.

### "Charlie Brown" (1962), the Kim Sisters

The Kim Sisters were the original K-pop crossover stars. In the early days of the Korean War, Lee Nan-young, one of Korea's most famous singers, found herself widowed after her husband was kidnapped and killed by the North Korean army. To survive, she trained her daughters Sue and Aija and their cousin Mia as a singing group under the name the Kim Sisters. They were discovered and brought to the U.S. in 1959, where they became resident artists in Las Vegas. An invitation to appear on *The Ed Sullivan Show* would catapult them to national success. "Charlie Brown," a cover of the Coasters classic, was their biggest hit, reaching number 7 on the *Billboard* pop charts.

### "Killer Joe" (1963), the Rocky Fellers

The Rocky Fellers were a Filipino American pop band composed of four Filipino brothers—Tony, Junior, Eddie, and Albert Maligmat—and their father, "Moro" Maligmat. A brief appearance on *The Ed Sullivan Show* led producer Stanley Kahn to sign them to Florence Greenberg's legendary Scepter Records, home of the Isley Brothers, Dionne Warwick, and other R&B greats. This hit single reached number 16 on the *Billboard* charts in April 1963.

### "Tiny Bubbles" (1966), Don Ho

Born Donald Tai Loy Ho to a family of mixed Chinese, Hawaiian, and Portuguese descent, Don Ho's music would serve as the soundtrack to the rise of Polynesian chic and Hawaii tourism. "Tiny Bubbles" is his signature song; it was so popular that his album of the same name would stay on the Billboard Top 200 for almost a year.

### "Walkin' My Cat Named Dog" (1977), Norma Tanega

Don't search for any mysterious meaning behind the lyrics; this song by folk pop artist Tanega, of Filipino and Panamanian descent, is literally about walking her cat named "Dog." She was discovered by a producer who was visiting a summer camp where she worked as a counselor. Released as Tanega's first single in 1966, it became an international hit, peaking at number 22 on the *Billboard* charts.

### "Windy" (1967), The Association

Filipino American Larry Ramos became the first Asian American to win a Grammy Award in 1962, as a backup vocalist and banjo player for the New Christy Minstrels. In 1967, he would go on to join the sunshine-pop band The Association, as colead vocalist and guitarist. He sang colead on their hit single "Windy," which would top the *Billboard* charts in July and eventually rank as the number 4 song of the year.

### "Ain't That Peculiar" (1972), Fanny

The first all-women rock band to release an album on a major label, Fanny was founded and led by Filipina American sisters June and Jean Millington. These ass-kicking godmothers of rock were signed to Reprise Records, the label founded by Frank Sinatra, and released four albums, the third and most critically acclaimed of which was named *Fanny Hill,* after the erotica classic. This hard-driving cover of the Marvin Gaye classic was the biggest single from that album, hitting number 85 on the *Billboard* charts. They remain today one of the most important and influential bands of their era, for their groundbreaking music and their rejection of the expectations of women in rock music.

### "We Are the Children" (1973), *A Grain of Sand*

Written and performed by activists and musicians Chris Kando Iijima, Joanne Nobuko Miyamoto, and William "Charlie" Chin, *A Grain of Sand: Music for the Struggle by Asians in America* has been called "the first album of Asian American music"—a powerful collection of protest songs proclaiming solidarity with the antiwar, Black, and Latin American social movements of the early 1970s. This track was the first English language track in history to discuss the incarceration of Japanese Americans during World War II.

### "If I Can't Have You" (1977), Yvonne Elliman

Born and raised in Hawaii to a Japanese mother and Irish father, Elliman spent four years in the cast of the Broadway musical *Jesus Christ, Superstar,* but her biggest claim to fame is this legendary disco track, written by the Bee Gees and included on the soundtrack for the film *Saturday Night Fever.* The song became a number-one hit on the *Billboard* charts, and the soundtrack would win a Grammy in 1978 for Album of the Year.

### "Rap-O Clap-O" (1979), Joe Bataan
Black and Filipino musician Bataan may be best known for coining the phrase "Salsoul" and playing a leading role in the movement that mixed Latin boogaloo and Black doo-wop. However, he also released this hit single—one of the first rap music recordings, and an early and influential hip-hop hit.

### "Roomful of Mirrors" (1979), Hiroshima
"Asians don't sing and Asians don't dance." The members of Hiroshima remember hearing these mocking words from Arista Records staff members as the band recorded their debut album. Over four million records, two Grammy nominations, and a career spanning over 40 years later, Hiroshima has proven their doubters wrong, galvanizing the music world with its unique mixture of R&B, jazz, and pop. This track is a classic R&B hit from their debut album in 1979.

### "Jump" (1984), Van Halen
Even most of their superfans don't know that the Van Halen brothers, Alex and Eddie, were born in the Netherlands to a Dutch father and Indonesian mother. The family moved to Pasadena, California, in 1962; the brothers formed Van Halen in 1974 with Eddie as lead guitarist, Alex as drummer, Michael Anthony on bass, and David Lee Roth as vocalist. Ten years later, already rock legends, they'd release their biggest-selling album featuring this monster number-one track.

### "If You Leave Me Now" (1989), Jaya
This cover of the freestyle classic, which hit number 44 on the *Billboard* charts, features María Luisa Ramsey, the Jamaican Filipino singer better known as Jaya. Jaya wasn't even supposed to be visible—she'd originally been hired as an anonymous backup singer for legendary producer Stevie B, the "King of Freestyle"—but her talent convinced management to reposition her as the song's main artist. She returned to the Philippines in 1995, and continues to be a star there today, both as a singer and a television personality.

### "Walking on Thin Ice" (1981 re-edit), Yoko Ono
To many, Ono is an artist, singer-songwriter, and peace activist. To others, she's the Japanese woman who broke up the Beatles. But both groups would acknowledge that from the late Sixties to the Eighties, Ono was one of the most visible Asian figures in the world. This was her first *Billboard* charting record. It was also John Lennon's final creative project; he'd recorded lead guitar work for it and was holding a tape of the final mix when he was shot and murdered four days later.

### "Baroque in Rhythm" (1983), Yo-Yo Ma (with Claude Bolling)
Ma was born in 1955 to Chinese parents in Paris, France, then moved with his family to New York in 1957, already a child prodigy cellist. He would go on to become one of the most acclaimed classical musicians in history, while also constantly pushing the boundaries of the genre; in this outing, he partnered with piano great Claude Bolling for a jazz-meets-classical fusion.

SCAN THE QR CODE TO DOWNLOAD THE PLAYLIST

# Asian Ethnic Enclaves

BY JEFF YANG

**CHINATOWN. KOREATOWN.** Little Saigon. Little Tokyo. The largest and best-known Asian ethnic enclaves in America tend to be framed as mini theme parks—pocket-sized versions of their counterparts across the Pacific that exist to provide a fun and inexpensive day-trip experience for non-Asian culture tourists. But to Asian Americans, they represent much more: For those who live beyond their borders, they're a spiritual tether to the motherland, a gathering point for families and friends, and a refueling station for supplies and ingredients that just can't be found anywhere else. For those who live within them, they're a place of safety from the assimilationist pressure and casual racism of a society where Asians are still a minority in all but a handful of cities in all but a handful of states. Here's a look at some of the most important Asian enclaves in the United States—some thriving, some faded and forgotten.

## Lost Towns

Before we look at the enclaves of the present, we wanted to pay respect to some of the most important, and now largely vanished, communities of the earliest days of Asian immigration to America.

### SAINT MALO, LA

The oldest Asian American settlement in U.S. history, Saint Malo was a fishing village founded in the 1760s by Filipino slaves escaping the brutality of the Spanish galleon trade, which brought goods from China, through Manila in the Philippines, and eventually to Western ports like New Orleans. The village's residents were generally called the "Manilamen" or "Tagalas" by their neighbors; as an all-male community, many intermarried with Native Americans and Isleñas (migrants from the Canary Islands, brought to America by the Spanish as colonials). Manilamen who were recruited to fight by the pirate Jean Lafitte helped to successfully defend New Orleans from British attack during the War of 1812. The village was completely destroyed by a massive hurricane in 1915, and survivors decamped to New Orleans, where some of their descendants still live to this day.

### MARYSVILLE, CA

Founded in 1843, the Marysville Chinatown was at one point the second largest in America after San Francisco, home to thousands of Chinese drawn to the area along with many others by the nearby Yuba Goldfields, the largest and richest site for gold panning in California. While few Chinese live there now, it's still the sole surviving community out of dozens built in "gold country" during the Rush, with one of the oldest operating Taoist temples in California, and a century-and-a-half-old annual celebration called the Bok Kai Festival, a uniquely Chinese American event that takes place on or near the second day of the second month of the lunar calendar. The festival features

California's oldest continuously held parade, with a 175-foot-long golden dragon and the exploding of giant firecrackers that shoot bamboo rings wrapped with fortunes into the air, to be caught by the crowd—a practice that has given the Bok Kai Festival the common name of "Bomb Day."

### TERMINAL ISLAND, CA

Beginning in the 1890s, Japanese immigrants began flocking to San Pedro Bay to catch fish and shellfish. By the early 1900s, a small but thriving Japanese American community of around 600 had sprung up around the area, which spoke its own unique pidgin dialect that blended Japanese and English and developed an innovative and wildly successful tuna fishing technique, which led to canning factories being constructed on the island. By 1942, Terminal Island had around 3,500 residents. After the attack on Pearl Harbor, the FBI arrested all of the island's adult males and then sent the remaining population to internment camps—the first mass "evacuation" of Japanese Americans under Executive Order 9066—before the entire town was razed to the ground. The second season of AMC's horror anthology series, *The Terror: "Infamy,"* is set on Terminal Island.

### LOCKE, CA

Locke was the first town in the United States to be entirely built and settled by its Chinese residents. In 1915, displaced by a fire that had burned them out of their homes in the nearby town of Walnut Grove, a group of Chinese businessmen struck a deal with local landowner George Locke to build a new town on his property. What started out as a small group of stores and homes eventually expanded to a full 14 acres of one- and two-story wooden buildings, which became a hotbed of economic activity during the Prohibition era due to Locke's thriving, not-so-secret speakeasies. At its peak, Locke had a population of some 1,500 residents, all Chinese. Its population rapidly dwindled in the 1980s and 1990s, and now the town is home to just 80 people, 10 of them Chinese. It was registered as a National Historic Landmark in 1970.

## Towns of Today

The Asian ethnic enclaves of the present are divided into three categories: a handful of major historical commercial and population centers with a national profile, what we'll call the Homelands; smaller ethnic clusters that are regional cultural hubs or emerging communities, which we'll call the Homesteads; and a few large and rising representatives of a different kind of enclave, the modern ethnoburb, which we'll call the New Territories.

## The Homelands

These are the enclaves you've heard of, and maybe visited, even if you're an international tourist. They tend to have "town" or "little" in their names, reinforcing a sense of quaintness and diminutive stature. But in the spirit of the nicknames of New York City and Atlanta, Georgia—the "Big Apple" and "Big Peach" respectively—we'd like to propose new nicknames that reflect how large they loom in our history and present:

### CHINATOWN, SAN FRANCISCO, CA

Founded in the early 1850s, San Francisco's Chinatown is the oldest continuous Asian ethnic enclave in the nation. It consists of about 24 square blocks, centered on the legendary Grant Avenue (as immortalized in the musical *Flower Drum Song*\*), and even today is the most densely populated urban area west of Manhattan: some 15,000 residents live within its boundaries, along with hundreds of stores, restaurants, and other businesses. It has survived earthquakes, fires, the bubonic plague, and full-blown anti-Chinese race riots, including one in 1877 that killed four Chinese and caused massive damage to Chinese-owned businesses. Though it has been eclipsed as a residential center by newer enclaves in SF's Richmond and Sunset districts and in the South Bay, it continues to be the cultural mothership for Bay Area Chinese Americans today.

### CHINATOWN, NEW YORK, NY

Manhattan's Chinatown is home to the densest concentration of Chinese people in the Western Hemisphere, and the oldest and largest of at least nine Chinatowns in the New York City metropolitan area, with an estimated population of over 90,000 people. Unlike most other ethnic enclaves, the name and identity of Chinatown's original resident is actually known—Ah Ken, who was the first Chinese person to permanently settle in the area. In 1858, Ah Ken arrived in Manhattan from Guangdong and used the money he brought with him to buy a building on lower Mott Street, which he turned into a bunkhouse for fellow Chinese immigrants. He used his profits of about $100 per month to open a cigar store on Park Row, which was successful enough that it encouraged other businesses

\* See page 19, "The Asian American Syllabus"

to open around it—the nucleus of what would become the largest and most prominent Asian enclave on the Eastern Seaboard.

### LITTLE TOKYO, LOS ANGELES, CA

The cultural heart of the largest Japanese American population in North America, Little Tokyo was founded in 1905, and continued to grow rapidly until the 1924 Exclusion Act halted further immigration from Japan. Still, by 1941, Little Tokyo was home to around 30,000 Japanese Americans. World War II incarceration emptied the neighborhood; Black and Mexican American migrants moved into the vacant properties, leading to its being renamed as "Bronzeville." As a result, after the war, returning Japanese Americans found themselves unable to return to their homes. It wasn't until the late Seventies that Little Tokyo began to actively be redeveloped as a Japanese American community. Japanese corporations began setting up their U.S. headquarters in the area and Los Angeles–based Japanese Americans focused their efforts on historical reclamation, making it the site of the Japanese American National Museum.

### JAPANTOWN, SAN FRANCISCO, CA

One of the oldest and largest ethnic enclaves in the United States, Japantown was settled by immigrants who began moving into the area after San Francisco's 1906 earthquake. World War II incarceration emptied Japantown as it did L.A.'s Little Tokyo. After the war, many residents returned, and the area was rejuvenated in the 1960s by Japanese retailer Kintetsu's decision to build the shopping mall Japan Center to serve as the neighborhood's commercial hub.

### INTERNATIONAL DISTRICT IN SEATTLE, WA

THE BIG COMBO PLATTER

After being relocated several times by disaster or racist mobs, the center of Seattle's historical Chinese American community finally anchored itself in the King Street area in the early 1900s. Japanese and Filipino Americans (including the iconic activist and author Carlos Bulosan) also migrated to the vicinity, and in the 1970s, Vietnamese Americans began to move into the neighborhood as well. In 1999, the area was formally dubbed the Chinatown/International District, reflecting its pan-Asian cultural context.

### KOREATOWN, LOS ANGELES, CA

THE BIG KALBI

America's biggest Koreatown was formed as a satellite to the tiny original L.A. Korean community that was centered about a dozen blocks south, adjacent to the University of Southern California. "Old Koreatown," as it was known, grew to about 650 residents by the 1930s, but because of the growing use of racist "exclusionary covenants" to prevent the sale or rental of properties to nonwhite persons beyond a several-block radius in that area, the commercial and cultural center of K-Town, as it's affectionately known today, shifted north in the mid-Sixties, to the area it occupies today.

### KOREATOWN, NEW YORK, NY

THE BIG BULGOGI

Centered around West 32nd Street in lower midtown Manhattan, New York's Koreatown is a dense cluster of around 150 businesses, which range from restaurants and bars to the U.S. branches of major Korean conglomerates. Unlike its sprawling Los Angeles counterpart, K-Town New York is mostly vertical: Multistory elevator buildings have different businesses on every floor, which draw in traffic with window displays or signage at street level. As a result, the single block of 32nd between 5th and 6th Avenues, commonly referred to as "Korea Way," boasts more than 100 bars, salons, restaurants, groceries, bakeries, karaoke lounges, and other small businesses, arranged in stacks. Because of the heated competition they face, these establishments stay open into the wee hours of the morning, making New York's K-Town as much of a nightlife destination as its West Coast alter ego.

### FLUSHING, QUEENS, NY

THE BIG HOT POT

In the late Sixties, the first major wave of immigrants from Taiwan and Korea arrived in New York after the passage of Hart-Celler,[*] and large numbers of them gravitated to Flushing, Queens, an area whose early Dutch settlers had issued a public declaration of tolerance (the "Flushing Remonstrance"), making it the "birthplace of religious freedom in the New World," which may be why it has emerged as one of the most ethnically diverse areas in the United States. Though it would be wrong to call it a "melting pot"—different communities,

---

\* See page 1, the introduction to "Before"

many of them Asian, live side by side and generally interact in harmony, but retain their cultural distinctions—the result is delicious nevertheless.

## LITTLE SAIGON, ORANGE COUNTY, CA

Established when Vietnamese refugees began moving to and reviving the city of Westminster in the 1970s, Little Saigon soon expanded to include the neighboring city of Garden Grove, and beyond. With nearly 200,000 residents, Orange County's Little Saigon is the largest community of Vietnamese outside of Vietnam itself. Westminster has emerged as the cultural center of the national Vietnamese American community. It is the home of many of the in-language media companies that provide news and entertainment to Vietnamese throughout the U.S. and to expatriates abroad—most notably Thuy Nga Productions, creators of the beloved and wildly influential *Paris by Night* musical variety series, which has been watched by millions of Vietnamese around the world since it first began in the early 1980s.

## The Homesteads

A selection of smaller Asian ethnic enclaves—many of them in areas you might find surprising.

## BANGLADESHI
**LITTLE BANGLADESH, LOS ANGELES, CA:** Mostly a commercial nexus but with around a hundred permanent residents.

## BURMESE
**FORT WAYNE, IN:** Home to over 6,000 Burmese, the largest such community in the U.S.

## CAMBODIAN
**CAMBODIA TOWN, LONG BEACH, CA:** A mile-long stretch of businesses and restaurants on Anaheim Street was officially designated as "Cambodia Town" in 2007; the area is home to over 2,000 Cambodians.
**LOWELL, MA:** The city with the highest concentration of Cambodians in the U.S., around 25,000 residents.

## CHINESE
**RICHMOND AND SUNSET DISTRICTS, SAN FRANCISCO, CA:** Beginning in the late 1960s, these two neighborhoods of San Francisco began to emerge as satellite "new Chinatowns"; both now have greater Chinese populations than the original, and thriving ethnic commercial strips.
**SUNSET PARK AND BENSONHURST, BROOKLYN, NY:** To understand why the Sunset Park and Bensonhurst areas of Brooklyn have emerged as magnets for Chinese immigrants, turning them into the "third" and "fourth" New York Chinatowns, all you need to know is that the epicenter of the Sunset Park Chinese neighborhood is 8th Avenue, and for Bensonhurst, it's 18th Avenue. Yes: these areas have surged in part due to the Chinese belief that eight is a lucky number. Both are now the favored destinations of more recent Chinese immigrants, from Fuzhou and Guangdong respectively.

## FILIPINO
**DALY CITY, CA:** Just south of San Francisco, Daly City has the highest concentration of Filipino Americans in the U.S., who make up 27 percent of the city's population. The area's status as a Filipino magnet soared as San Francisco's historic Manilatown was erased by gentrification in the Sixties and Seventies.

**HISTORIC FILIPINOTOWN, LOS ANGELES, CA:** In 2002, Filipinotown became the first officially designated geographic area in the U.S. to honor Filipinos, commemorating one of the first large-scale Filipino communities in Southern California, which still is home to over 10,000 Filipino American residents and hundreds of businesses today.

## HMONG

**FROGTOWN, ST. PAUL, MN:** Also known as "Little Mekong," the Frogtown area of St. Paul is the largest urban community of Hmong Americans in the U.S.

## INDIAN

**LITTLE INDIA, ARTESIA, CA:** Though Indians only make up 8 percent of the town's resident population, over the past 20 years, Artesia has become home to hundreds of Indian businesses and restaurants, making it the largest Indian commercial enclave in Southern California, and a cultural hub for Indians throughout Greater Los Angeles.

**LITTLE INDIA, EDISON, NJ:** Oak Tree Road, stretching from Edison out to Iselin, is known as the first Little India in the U.S., with over 400 South Asian businesses and a local population that's nearly 50 percent Indian American.

**JACKSON HEIGHTS, QUEENS, NY:** Centered on 74th Street and Roosevelt Avenue, Jackson Heights is the center of New York's South Asian community, with hundreds of businesses and a population in the tens of thousands, though a rival "Little India" has emerged in suburban Hicksville, Long Island.

## JAPANESE

**NIHONMACHI, SAN JOSE, CA:** San Jose's Japantown developed alongside the city's historical Chinatown, and more than a century later, it remains one of the last three historical Japantowns in the United States.

**SAWTELLE, LOS ANGELES, CA:** If Little Tokyo is the historic center of Japanese American culture in L.A., "Little Osaka" is its smaller cousin on the west side, with perhaps an even greater allure for the hungry.

## KOREAN

**ANNANDALE, VA:** With a population that's a quarter Korean and approximately 350 Korean-owned businesses and restaurants, this town is a hub for Korean Americans from throughout the D.C. metropolitan area.

## LAOTIAN

**CHOLLAS VIEW, SAN DIEGO, CA:** Chollas View is the focal point of San Diego's 8,000-strong Laotian community.

## SRI LANKAN

**LITTLE SRI LANKA, STATEN ISLAND, NY:** The borough of Staten Island is home to an enclave of over 5,000 Sri Lankans, surprisingly making it the largest Sri Lankan community outside of Sri Lanka itself.

## THAI

**NORTH SIDE, CHICAGO, IL:** Chicago was an early magnet for Thai professional immigrants, many of them doctors and nurses, who clustered on Chicago's North Side and in adjacent suburbs. While the population numbers about 10,000, the Thai presence is amplified by the huge number of restaurants the enterprising community has opened—about one for every 33 Thai residents.

**THAI TOWN, LOS ANGELES, CA:** A six-block area in the East Hollywood neighborhood of

Los Angeles, this is the only officially recognized Thai Town in the United States, and the home to the bulk of Southern California's 80,000-strong Thai American community.

## VIETNAMESE

**LITTLE SAIGON, HOUSTON, TX:** The community centered around Bellaire Boulevard in Houston may be the largest Vietnamese enclave in the United States, though a second major Vietnamese cluster is centered around the north Texas city of Arlington.

## The New Territories

Traditionally, ethnic enclaves were seen as temporary refuges for new immigrants. Cramped, expensive, with old housing stock and restrictive professional opportunities, these urban population clusters were used as a way station for those seeking to eventually move themselves—or their children—out into America beyond. That started to change in the 1970s, with the emergence of a new type of Asian ethnic enclave on the suburban outskirts of major metropolitan centers. Arizona State University professor Wei Li dubbed these enclaves "ethnoburbs," home to affluent immigrants as well as second-generation Asians for whom living in cultural proximity is a matter of lifestyle choice, not necessity. Rising ethnoburbs include communities along Atlanta's DeKalb Corridor; towns like Bayside and Little Neck in Queens, NY; Fort Lee, NJ; Cupertino, CA; and Bellevue, WA, among many others—but the phenomenon arguably started in one place: Monterey Park, CA, thanks to an enterprising real estate developer named Frederic Hsieh.

In the 1970s, Hsieh recognized that educated professionals from Taiwan and Hong Kong were migrating to the U.S. in rising numbers, and that they had little interest in living in traditional urban Chinese enclaves. He hit upon the idea of purchasing tracts of land for development in the San Gabriel Valley gateway town of Monterey Park, advertising it as "the Chinese Beverly Hills," while pointing to the city's "lucky" area code—818—as a marketing device. It worked. By the mid-1990s, Monterey Park was 65 percent Asian American, predominantly Chinese and Taiwanese.

From there, the ethnoburb phenomenon spread ever deeper along Valley Boulevard's 25 miles—transforming along the way towns like Alhambra, Arcadia, Rosemead, San Marino,

> "Ethnoburbs" [are] home to affluent immigrants as well as second-generation Asians for whom living in cultural proximity is a matter of lifestyle choice, not necessity.

San Gabriel, South Pasadena, Temple City, Diamond Bar, Hacienda Heights, Rowland Heights, West Covina, and Walnut into communities with sizable or even majority Asian populations. The SGV's unique string of middle-class Asian American communities has forged its own culture—one that's defiantly global, firmly local, and unafraid to represent itself. If the ethnic enclaves explored above represent the rich past of the Asian American community, the SGV may well be a look at our future.

# Asian American Atlas
BY PHIL YU

Asian America is a community, a shared history of people, ideas, celebration, and struggle. It's also a place. It occupies meaningful physical space, from the shores where the first migrants stepped foot before it was called "America," to the Detroit street where an act of hate ignited a cry for justice, to the Manhattan sports arena that gave birth to basketball's greatest underdog story. This map highlights sites of significance—some that you can actually still visit—that declare we're here, we've been here, and this is where we're "really" from.

33

JUSTICE FOR VINCENT CHIN

KUM☺N

36

26

3
4
24
5
35

NEW YORK

17

FORT CHAFFEE

25

2

28

**1 Morro Bay, California**
The first Filipinos—or "Luzon Indios," as they were known back then—on a Spanish galleon set foot on what is now the United States near Morro Bay, California, on October 18, 1587. That's 33 years before Pilgrims from England arrived at Plymouth Rock.

**2 St. Malo, Louisiana**
Sometime in the 1760s, Filipino sailors—then called "Manilamen"—disembarked from Spanish trade ships to establish a small fishing village, believed to be the first recorded Asian settlement in America. The site is commemorated with a historical marker in Saint Bernard.

### 3 Salem, Massachusetts

The earliest recorded arrival of an Indian immigrant in the U.S. was a young man from Madras, who traveled to Massachusetts in 1790.

### 4 Fairhaven, Massachusetts

The first Japanese immigrant, Nakanohama Manjiro, arrived on American soil on May 7, 1843, and settled in Fairhaven, Massachusetts.

### 5 New Haven, Connecticut

In 1854, a Chinese student named Yung Wing graduated from Yale University, becoming the first Asian American to graduate from a U.S. college.

### 6 Promontory, Utah

The first transcontinental railroad was completed on May 10, 1869, connecting the East and West Coasts of the United States. Almost two-thirds of the workforce were Chinese laborers—though none were included in the iconic photograph of the "Golden Spike" ceremony.

### 7 Calle de los Negros, Los Angeles, California

On October 24, 1871, a mob entered Old Chinatown and attacked, robbed, and murdered Chinese residents in one of the worst mass lynchings in U.S. history.

### 8 Oklahoma City, Oklahoma

After the Chinese Exclusion Act passed, Chinese Americans unable to return to China were pushed out of California toward other states with greater leniency and more opportunities—including Oklahoma, where a small Chinese population began to grow between 1900 and the 1920s, 250 of whom were living in a network of underground tunnels beneath the city.

### 9 Honolulu Harbor, Hawaii

On January 13, 1903, the first wave of Korean immigrants in America stepped off the S.S. *Gaelic* to work on the islands' sugar and pineapple plantations.

### 10 Bellingham, Washington

On September 4, 1907, a mob of white men in Bellingham, Washington, violently attacked a community of South Asian workers, driving them out of the city.

### 11 Butte, Montana

Built in 1909, the Pekin Noodle Parlor is the oldest known continuously operating Chinese restaurant in the United States. Still open for business, the restaurant is now one of the last surviving properties from Butte's once-thriving original Chinatown neighborhood.

### 12 Angel Island, San Francisco Bay, California

From 1910 to 1940, immigrants entering the U.S., primarily from Asia, were detained, examined, and interrogated at the Angel Island Immigration Station.

### 13 Stockton, California

Founded in 1912, the Stockton Gurdwara Sahib was the first Sikh house of worship in the United States, and became a major religious, social, and political hub for South Asian pioneers.

### 14 Astoria, Oregon

On July 15, 1913, a meeting of expatriate Punjabi Indians in Astoria, Oregon, officially founded the Ghadar Party, an international political movement to overthrow British rule in India.

### 15 Harada House, Riverside, California

A four-bedroom, two-story house in Riverside, purchased by the Harada family in 1915, became the focal point of a landmark court case testing the constitutionality of laws preventing immigrants from owning property in California.

### 16 Watsonville, California

On January 19, 1930, violence erupted in the farming town of Watsonville, California, where white marauders targeted and attacked Filipinos in a brutal racist riot that lasted five days.

### 17 Manzanar, California

The Manzanar War Relocation Center was one of ten concentration camps where more than 120,000 Japanese Americans were detained during World War II.

### 18 Sacramento, California

The first Indian American hotelier in the U.S. was a Gujarati immigrant named Kanji Manchhu Desai, who took over a 32-room hotel in Sacramento in 1942.

### 19 Imperial Valley, California

In 1956, Dalip Singh Saund was elected to the U.S. House of Representatives from California's 29th District, becoming the first Asian American and first Indian American elected to Congress.

### 20 Seattle, Washington

Bruce Lee, a philosophy student at the University of Washington, opened his first martial arts school, the Jun Fan Gung Fu Institute, in 1960. The first lessons were held in a parking garage in Seattle's First Hill neighborhood.

**21 Delano, California**

In 1965, Filipino American grape pickers, led by Larry Itliong, Philip Vera Cruz, and others, organized a strike to fight against the exploitation of farmworkers. Joined by Mexican American laborers, their efforts ultimately led to the creation of the nation's first farmworkers' union, and revolutionized the farm labor movement in America.

**22 Berkeley, California***

In 1968, Yuji Ichioka and Emma Gee cofounded the Asian American Political Alliance at UC Berkeley, effectively coining the term "Asian American" to frame a new inter-ethnic Pan-Asian political consciousness.

**23 Pasadena, California**

The Cherng family opened the Panda Inn restaurant in 1973, serving up Mandarin and Szechuan-style cuisine. A decade later, they opened the first fast-food version of their restaurant at the Glendale Galleria. They named it Panda Express.

**24 Larchmont, New York**

The first overseas Kumon Math Center opened in Larchmont, New York, in 1974.

**25 Fort Chaffee, Arkansas**

Fort Chaffee was the largest of four military bases to take in Southeast Asian refugees for resettlement at the end of the United States' official involvement in the Vietnam War.

**26 Detroit, Michigan**

Vincent Chin, a 27-year-old Chinese American drafts-man, was killed by two white autoworkers. His death and the ensuing fight for justice galvanized an Asian American civil rights movement and became a rallying cry for hate crimes legislation.**

**27 Westminster, California**

99 Ranch Market opened its first location in Little Saigon in 1984. It grew to become the largest Asian supermarket chain in the United States.

**28 Kennedy Space Center, Florida**

On January 24, 1985, Ellison Onizuka was on board the launch of space shuttle *Discovery*, becoming the first Asian American to reach space.

**29 Monterey Park, California**

The first city with an Asian-majority population in the continental United States, dubbed "the first suburban Chinatown."

**30 Koreatown, Los Angeles, California***

Korean American businesses were looted and burned in the 1992 uprising triggered by the acquittal of four police officers in the beating of Rodney King.

**31 Arcadia, California**

In the late 1990s, the first dedicated boba shop in the U.S. opened in a food court in Arcadia, California.

**32 Long Beach, California**

Long Beach is home to the nation's first officially des-ignated Cambodia Town and the largest population of Cambodians outside of Cambodia.

**33 Minneapolis–St. Paul, Minnesota**

Home to the largest population of Hmong Americans in the United States.

**34 Mesa, Arizona**

Balbir Singh Sodhi, a Sikh American gas station own-er, was murdered in the first known hate crime in the aftermath of the September 11 terrorist attacks.****

**35 Madison Square Garden, New York City, New York**

Jeremy Lin came off the bench to score a then-career-high 25 points and lead the New York Knicks in a come-from-behind victory against the New Jersey Nets, kicking off the phenomenon known as "Linsanity."*****

**36 Oak Creek, Wisconsin**

On August 5, 2012, a white supremacist gunman en-tered the Sikh Temple of Wisconsin and opened fire, fatally shooting six people and wounding four others.

**37 Main Library, San Francisco, California**

The 1906 earthquake destroyed all records at San Francisco City Hall, enabling thousands of Chinese to enter America as "paper sons" of U.S.-born Chinese American citizens. This site is also where the riot of 1877 started, igniting two days of ethnic violence against the city's Chinese immigrant population.

***   See page 352, "A Night in Koreatown"

****   See page 209, "9/11: Remembering a Tragedy and the Dark Days That Followed"

*****   See page 322, "Remembering Linsanity"

_____

*   See page 1, the introduction to "Before"

**   See page 34, "Why Vincent Chin Still Matters"

# FOUNDING FATHERS AND MOTHERS

**1980S AND BEFORE**

BY JEFF YANG, ILLUSTRATED BY SOJUNG KIM-McCARTHY

**IT'S IMPOSSIBLE TO** celebrate all of the individuals whose political and activist leadership laid the foundations of Asian America, but here's a selection of the builders and barrier-breakers whose achievements defined our communities in the 1980s and before.

**CHIN FOO WONG:** Anti-exclusion activist, journalist, and founder of the Chinese Equal Rights League

**REP. DALIP SINGH SAUND:** First Asian American in Congress

**BENITO LEGARDA** and **PABLO OCAMPO:** First Philippine resident commissioners in U.S. Congress

**SEN. HIRAM FONG:** First Asian American senator

**SEN. SAMUEL ICHIYE HAYAKAWA:** First Asian American senator from the mainland

**PHILIP JAISOHN:** Activist, physician, publisher, and first Korean naturalized citizen of the U.S.

**AHN CHANGHO:** Activist and Korean American leader

**PHILIP VERA CRUZ** and **LARRY ITLIONG:** Co-heads of the Agricultural Workers Organizing Committee

**YOUNG-OAK KIM:** Decorated Army colonel who was one of the few non-Japanese in the 442nd/100th; cofounder of Koreatown Youth and Community Center

**442ND REGIMENT/100TH BATTALION:** All-Asian WWII army unit—the most decorated in American combat history

**SAKHARAM GANESH PANDIT:** Advocate who fought against the denaturalization of Indian Americans

**THOMAS YATABE:** Cofounder and first national president of the Japanese American Citizens League

**SEN. DANIEL INOUYE:** U.S. representative and senator; Medal of Honor decorated war hero

**SPARK MATSUNAGA:** U.S. representative who fought for redress for Japanese Americans

**FRED KOREMATSU, MINORU YASUI, GORDON HIRABAYASHI:** Civil rights activists and WWII resisters

**YURI KOCHIYAMA:** Activist and founder of the Day of Remembrance Committee

**GRACE LEE BOGGS:** Activist, scholar, and founder of Detroit Summer

**SIRDAR JAGJIT SINGH:** President of India League of America

**MARII HASEGAWA:** Pioneering peace activist

**TSUYAKO "SOX" KITASHIMA:** Primary spokesperson for the campaign to win redress

**MITSUYE ENDO:** Activist and plaintiff in *Ex parte Endo*

**AIKO HERZIG-YOSHINAGA:** Primary researcher behind campaign for redress

**KIYOSHI KUROMIYA:** AIDS activist, cofounder of the Gay Liberation Front, editor of ACT UP's *Standard of Care*

**K. W. LEE:** Journalist covering civil rights issues; editor of the *Korea Times English Edition*

**THELMA BUCHHOLDT:** First Filipino American woman elected to a state legislature

**YUJI ICHIOKA** and **EMMA GEE:** Founders of the Asian American Political Alliance

**K. L. WANG:** Cofounder and first national president of the Organization of Chinese Americans

# STUFF ASIANS LIKE

*Jeff Yang and Shing Yin Khor*

If you tried to define what it means to be Asian American, you'd probably begin with the things that make us different from those around us: the way we look, the food we eat, the cultural legacies we have from our ancestors. But spread out as they are across a vast spectrum of heritages and traditions, these are often things that also make Asians different from one another. When we think about the things we share in common, the reality is that many of them come from our mutual experience of exposure to Western culture, rooted in colonialism and the experiences of growing up in communities shaped by immigration. So here's a list of things shared with us when we asked our friends and networks for examples of non-Asian stuff that Asians like:

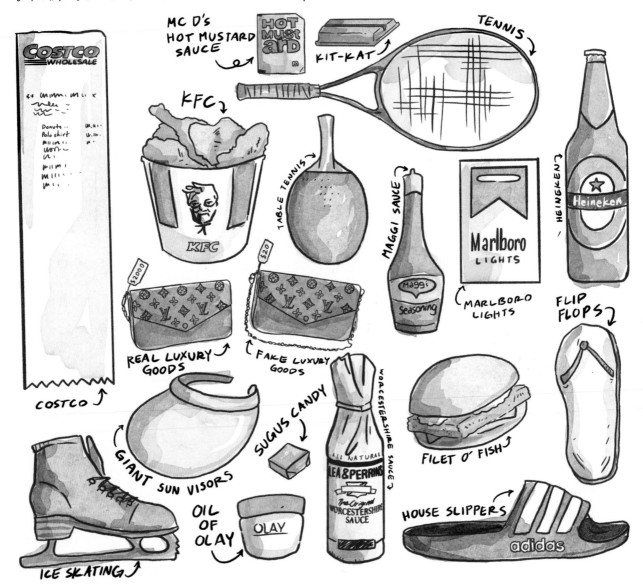

COSTCO

MC D's HOT MUSTARD SAUCE

KIT-KAT

TENNIS

KFC

TABLE TENNIS

MAGGI SAUCE

MARLBORO LIGHTS

HEINEKEN

REAL LUXURY GOODS

FAKE LUXURY GOODS

SUGUS CANDY

WORCESTERSHIRE SAUCE

FILET O' FISH

FLIP FLOPS

GIANT SUN VISORS

OIL OF OLAY

HOUSE SLIPPERS

ICE SKATING

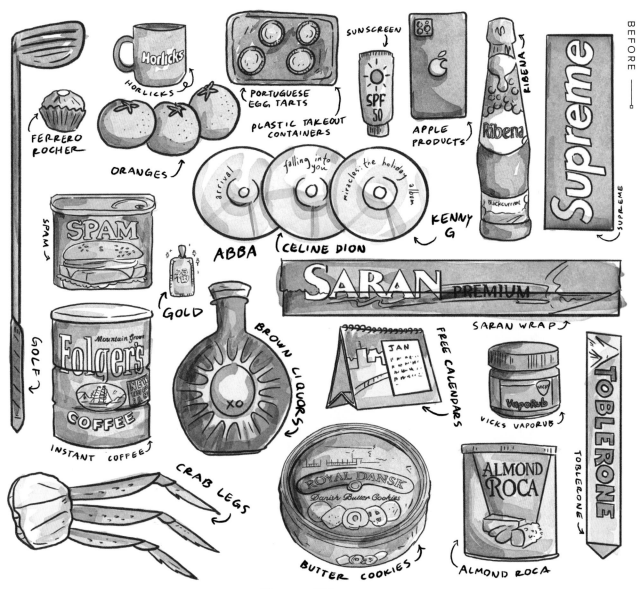

FERRERO ROCHER

HORLICKS

ORANGES

PORTUGUESE EGG TARTS

PLASTIC TAKEOUT CONTAINERS

SUNSCREEN
SPF 50

APPLE PRODUCTS

RIBENA
Ribena
Blackcurrant

SUPREME

SPAM

arrival
ABBA

falling into you
CELINE DION

miracles: the holiday album
KENNY G

GOLF

GOLD

Mountain Grown
Folgers
NEW
COFFEE
INSTANT COFFEE

BROWN LIQUORS
XO

SARAN PREMIUM
SARAN WRAP

JAN
FREE CALENDARS

VapoRub
VICKS VAPORUB

TOBLERONE

CRAB LEGS

ROYAL DANSK
Danish Butter Cookies
BUTTER COOKIES

ALMOND ROCA
ALMOND ROCA

# NOT PICTURED:

Apple picking
Bargains
Bleached, brown, or ombre hair
British last names as first names
Buffets and salad bars
Cartoon mascots
Classical music
Condensed milk
Cruises
Enormous suitcases

Exclusive public schools
Extra credit
Fighting for the check
German cars
Hawaii
Hip-hop
Ivy League schools
Las Vegas, especially on holidays
Logos
Made in America anything

Matchmaking
Multilevel Marketing
New-agey women's names
Photo booths
Preppy style
Ronald Reagan
Small white dogs
Synth pop and techno
Taco Bell
Taking pictures of food

Thanksgiving
The UCs in general
Throwing up peace signs
Vancouver

1990S

# The 1990s

BY JEFF YANG

**I WAS BORN** in 1968. I'm starting with that because since I first became aware of it, I've always been a little bit haunted by the fact that I was born in the same year as Asian America itself. Because of the timing of my birth, I ended up as one of the first wave of kids asked to reckon with what the term "Asian American" meant from as soon as we could hear and speak, when the idea of Asian America was still just a faint, smoke-ring outline in the culture.

Growing up in the Seventies in a paper-white part of Staten Island, the whitest borough of New York City, I was used to being called Chinese, and occasionally to being referred to as "oriental." When I ran into the latter, it almost always came from older white people, almost always in a tone of benign condescension: "Oriental kids are just the cutest little things!" "My housekeeper is oriental too, they're *so* hardworking." I wasn't offended, because it meant nothing to me. It wasn't an identity. It was a flavor of Maruchan Ramen.

But "Asian": "Asian" was the term that I was supposed to understand and embrace and celebrate. It was the box I was told to check off, without explanation and without question. And yet I did have questions, many of them, and so did people around me, often delivered in a passive-aggressive barrage. Sometimes aggressive-aggressive.

The first time I faced the "Asian interrogation," it was Halloween. I was maybe 10 or 11 years old, and I'd managed to convince my parents to let my sister and me go trick or treating on our very safe suburban block for the first time. My parents had no interest in spending money on fake clothes that we'd only wear one day of the year. As a result, we both went out dressed in the closest thing we had to masquerade: our Chinese-school activity clothes. Almost as soon as we left our house—me in my kung fu outfit of black drawstring pants, rubber-soled shoes, and a T-shirt with a tiger on it, my sister in the silk pajamas and parasol she wore for the school's Chinese dance troupe—we ran into a scrum of teens from the neighborhood, armed with the traditional weapons of Halloween mischief: shaving cream, cartons of eggs, rolls of toilet paper. Seeing us in our outfits, they began hooting and hollering. *"It's those Asian kids!" "What are you? Chinese? Japanese? Where are you from, anyway?" "They aren't even in costume. That's just what they wear at home, haaaaa."*

It didn't take an experienced Halloweener to predict what would happen next. As we bolted down the block, pelted with eggs the whole way, my sister flipped open her parasol, which protected her from the worst. I had nothing, and was quickly drenched, the cartoon

---

1990

🏛 Committee of 100, group of prominent Chinese Americans, founded by I. M. Pei, Yo-Yo Ma, and others

💼 Apu's first appearance on *The Simpsons*. The Indian convenience store owner became an iconic stereotype, much to the chagrin of many South Asian Americans.

💡 *A. Magazine* founded; becomes biggest Asian American periodical over the next decade, part of a wave of AAPI indie publishing

💡 Vera Wang opens her first design salon in NYC, at the Carlyle Hotel. Wang becomes a primary force in shaping the look of formal wear and wedding gowns.

tiger on my shirt turning a realistic shade of orange-yellow.

Once we made it home, sent to the shower, never to trick or treat again, the shouted questions echoed in my head as driblets of yolk swirled down the drain: "What are you? Where are you from?" I knew it wasn't the last time I'd hear those questions. And they weren't ones I could easily answer. At least not then, and not there.

## Becoming Asian American

The answers would begin to come in college. I'd gotten through the rest of my adolescence mostly intact, but still puzzled enough about what it meant to be an apparently "Asian" kid growing up in white America that I wrote my college personal essay on my "divided self"— *"What am I? Where am I from?"*—like probably 500,000 other Asian Americans applying to colleges in the 1980s.

It was on campus that I met for the first time people who helped me to answer those questions in ways that began to make sense, but it took a tragedy to connect me with them. My rooming group lost one of its members midway through my freshman year—a white football player who'd subjected me to a first semester full of weird pranks and racial microaggressions. The guilt and horror I felt after his passing sent me into a spiral: I stopped going to classes. I con-sidered withdrawing from school. I distanced myself from friends, until one of them, an officer in our school's Asian American Association, reached out to me out of concern and recruited me to work on a project: relaunching the organization's magazine, *East Wind*. She knew I was an aspiring journalist, a truth I'd still not yet had the guts to share with my parents, and thought it might offer a way for me to stretch my editorial ambitions while working out some of the issues I was struggling with about what it meant to check off the Asian box.

I told her I would, if I could pivot it from being a typical literary journal, full of essays like the cliché "my Asian side/my American side" personal statement that almost got me not accepted to Harvard, into something that tore off the scab of politeness that prevented us from talking about what it meant to be Asian and what it meant to not be white. I didn't know what that looked like—I'd never seen an Asian American magazine before—and so my friend suggested I check out the Asian American Resource Workshop, one of Boston's original Asian American social justice organizations, which at the time was nestled in a third-floor Chinatown space near a seedy red-light area nicknamed the "Combat Zone." It was there, in their library, that I found what I was looking for: copies of *Gidra*, the first Asian American newspaper, dating back to 1969. And *Bridge*, launched in New York City in 1971, arguably the first Asian

1990

1991

*Miss Saigon* debuts on Broadway. Becomes lightning rod for discussion about stereotypes and yellowface, but also offers rare opportunity for Asian American stage performers

Jessica Hagedorn's *Dogeaters* is published. Seminal Filipino American work wins American Book Award and is nominated for National Book Award

*Hook* features Dante Basco as Rufio, one of the most iconic Asian American characters in modern pop culture

Peter Chung's strange dystopian animated series *Aeon Flux* debuts on MTV

American magazine, and the most influential. And in a decaying yellow box with cellophane-taped corners, a copy of *Yellow Pearl*, an unbound art book, consisting of printed sheets of art, essays, poetry, and comics. I sat reading for hours, until the volunteers at the workshop kindly told me they were closing up, and also that I should keep my eyes sharp walking back to the subway, because, hello, *Combat Zone*.

I and a group of volunteers published the rebooted *East Wind* for three years, trying to bring the spirit of those early Asian American periodicals into the present—while aspiring to make what we created professional enough to sit next to "real" magazines at the Out of Town News that dominated Harvard Square. (We'd sometimes sneak copies of our mag and surreptitiously stock them there, just to see if anyone would notice. It was ironic that the wild rebellion of our angry Asian youth consisted not of stealing or breaking things, but secretly trying to give stuff away for free.)

And then I was graduating. And then it was over. There was no room for an Asian American magazine in the "real world." Or was there?

## Start Up

While planting copies of *East Wind* at Out of Town News, I'd come across copies of a few magazines that called themselves Asian American magazines. One was called *Rice*,

*A. Magazine*'s annual Bridge Builder Awards

because even then Asians couldn't resist naming our things that are not food after food—it was glossy, businesslike, and blandly safe, with articles, in the words of its editor, on "issues that have an impact on both Asian American groups and Asians in the Pacific Rim," like how to get SBA loans and Asian vacation destinations. The other was *AsiAm*, and it was obsessed with presenting a middle-aged man's wannabe-baller image of being Asian, with James Bond–inspired pictorials of Asian men in tuxes leaning against midprice luxury vehicles and a racy feature called "Little Black Dress," which featured Asian women in little black dresses, or less.

On the one hand, the two titles proved that pretty much anyone could launch a magazine; *Rice* was started by a dentist and a restaurant owner; and *AsiAm*'s head honcho was a lawyer. On the other, it felt like Asian Americans deserved more. Both magazines focused on how Asians had "made it" in America, steering

---

Super Nintendo changes the face of leisure; console becomes a prime gateway for Japanese popular culture

Designer Anna Sui has breakthrough runway show in NYC; Sui becomes one of the key drivers of the rise of Asian Americans in haute fashion

Hundreds protest the casting of Jonathan Pryce, a white actor, as a biracial Vietnamese character in the Broadway musical *Miss Saigon*

Lea Salonga becomes first Asian woman to win a Tony, for playing Kim in *Miss Saigon*

away from the controversial realities of who we were, where we came from, and where we fit in a society that wasn't always as welcoming as their glossy pages suggested.

And then, in 1989, right as I was graduating, both *Rice* and *AsiAm* disappeared as if they'd never existed. There was no announcement that they were shutting down; mainstream media was barely aware of them, so of course they didn't cover their demise, and the Internet had literally just been invented.

It felt like a sign. Or at least enough of one to convince three of my friends, Amy Chu, Bill Yao, and Sandra Kim, that we might somehow be able to succeed at publishing an Asian American magazine where those before us had failed. My friends agreed to come along for the ride—for a postcollegiate summer, at least.

The four of us moved into an apartment in Brooklyn, gathered a volunteer staff, put together a promo piece describing our ambitions, and got a local printer to print copies of it for us at a discount, because the affable salesman we worked with, Corky Lee, was also a photographer who'd documented much of the history of post-1968 Asian America (our little promo was full of his photos). With the summer fading and our saved red-envelope and graduation money almost gone, it looked like our chance at filling the gap left by the demise of *AsiAm* and *Rice* was over.

It was then that Leon Wynter, a Black journalist who had carved out a column for himself at the *Wall Street Journal* titled "Business and Race," chanced on our promo piece and dropped in on one of our volunteer meetings. The resulting story he wrote led to our phone ringing off the hook for days—mostly from friends of ours shocked to see our names in print. But there were also calls from ad agencies who'd tracked us down through our printers, a few prominent Asian American journalists, who asked if we were taking submissions for our promised first issue, and even outreach from tentative investors.

And then, at the end of that heady week, we got a Federal Express package (this was before they were known by the jaunty contraction FedEx). It was from Knapp, then a major publishing company. Its arrival filled us with wild hope. Was this influential media concern, owners of the aspirational *Bon Appétit* (we were on a 100 percent ramen and pizza diet), perhaps reaching out with a bolt-from-the-blue offer to back our idea?

No. Because, you see, we'd dubbed our still-just-a-dream publication "*A.D.*, the Magazine for Americans of Asian Descent." And in addition to food porn, Knapp also published house porn, which is why lawyers for Knapp's *Architectural Digest* had preemptively chosen to make it clear that if our mag

1991

1992

ever landed in Out of Town News bearing their trademarked initials, a hammer would fall on us, our families, and probably, Asians everywhere.

The legal nastygram took the wind out of our sails. My three co-conspirators shared plans to get jobs, go back to grad school, and otherwise not get sued. As editor-in-chief, I didn't want to let go, but we didn't seem to have much choice, and it was my responsibility to share this news with our squad of volunteers.

It turned out those volunteers didn't want to let go either. Our shut-down meeting instead turned into a brainstorming session for alternative names. After eliminating all the suggestions that had anything to do with food, we were left with one: the letter A. Half of our original name, but also the first letter of the alphabet—and the first letter of both *Asian* and *American*. And all three of these things made sense: the magazine was going to be about the intersection of being Asian and American, and it was going to trace the evolution of that identity and culture from our vantage point as members of that first generation to grow up wholly within that intersection, trying to figure out what it meant.

In effect, *A. Magazine: Inside Asian America* would try to answer the handful of questions each of us had faced repeatedly since we first heard the word "Asian": *When you say you're Asian, what are you?*

I'm one of millions of different people, from thousands of different backgrounds, who nevertheless share common experiences and a joint political purpose. *Where are you from?* I'm from the same place you're from, pal: America.

*But where are you* really *fr—* Don't say it.

## Notes from Underground

We began publishing *A. Magazine* furtively, out of our common rooms and day-job workplaces, liberating reams of paper and standing nervously next to fax machines, waiting for responses to surreptitiously sent queries, and meeting at night to edit and design our quarterly issues in sleepy clusters. We were assistants, junior staff, admins with supportive or lax white bosses. At work, we typed notes, filed paper, and made endless photocopies. At our work after work, we assigned stories, conducted interviews, planned photo shoots, commissioned illustrations, and on weekends, threw nightclub parties for Asian banker bros to raise money to print each issue.

There were moments of despair and desperation and occasional dissent. But we kept on going, fueled by will and grit and passion—and the company of a rising generation of fellow twentysomethings who shared our convictions. It seemed like we were surrounded by a startling array of offbeat, outspoken,

*Wayne's World*, the *SNL* sketch turned movie, introduces the world to Tia Carrere as Cassandra

During the L.A. Riots, the Korean community in Los Angeles suffers devastating losses: 2,000 to 2,500 Korean businesses are damaged or destroyed. More than two-thirds are not insured.

The Asian Pacific American Labor Alliance founded in Washington, D.C.; 500 unionists form the first national Asian Pacific American labor group as a subgroup of the AFL-CIO

Disney's *Aladdin* premieres; the film, with its South Asian–ish themes, becomes the first animated feature to reach half a billion dollars at the box office

and idealistic Asian American artists, activists, entrepreneurs, and organizers. Most of them, like us, were children of immigrants and students of the first wave of Asian American Studies, steeped in the striver ethics of our hardworking parents, but rebelling against the burden of expectations they'd placed on our shoulders.

We'd learned from and paid homage to the rich creativity and bright ideals of our cultural godparents as well, the original Asian American movement members, listening to their stories, volunteering for their organizations—but secretly (and sometimes not-so-secretly) thinking we could go farther, climb higher, do more, building on the foundations they'd laid. And together, overeducated and underemployed, working feverishly and quietly in the shadows of primordial Asian American institutions, we built nonprofits and coalitions, movements and a new wave of media: *Yolk Magazine*, *Giant Robot*, *KoreAm Journal*, *Filipinas*, and *Little India* all launched in this decade.

One of the first major events that drew together New York's emergent next-generation Asian American community was the 1991 protests against *Miss Saigon*. The announcement drew an unprecedented backlash from Asian Americans in the city, but what was less evident was that the reaction was bifurcated: There was a group of pioneering Asian American creatives, like playwright David

Henry Hwang, who were horrified at the musical's yellowface casting, demanding opportunity for Asian actors to play a role that had won Pryce enormous acclaim in the U.K. And then there was a group of younger Asian Americans who were appalled that a musical based on the racist Puccini opera *Madame Butterfly* had been made even more racist by resetting it in a Saigon brothel—especially since Hwang himself had eviscerated *Madame Butterfly* with his brilliant disruption of the opera's tropes, the play *M. Butterfly*, and scored multiple Tony Awards for its Broadway staging just three years before.

Even with their divergent viewpoints and ultimate failure (far from being Miss Sai-gone, the musical became a long-running hit and Pryce was honored with a Tony of his own for his performance), the Miss Saigon protests sparked among Asian Americans the recognition that challenging gross distortions of our image could rally our very diverse community together, and garner coverage in the media itself.

## Breaking the Ice

The following February, Asian Americans encountered another, slightly different kind of media distortion, but one stemming from a similar source. The Winter Olympics were taking place in Albertville, France, and I had the

1992

1993

🏛 George Bush signs a proclamation declaring May to be Asian Pacific American Heritage Month

🏛 16-year-old Japanese exchange student Yoshihiro Hattori is shot and killed in Louisiana by Rodney Peairs after Hattori, wearing an Elvis costume, knocked on Peairs's door, mistakenly thinking it was the site of a Halloween party. Peairs is acquitted of all charges.

🏛 Bobby Scott is elected to Congress from Virginia's 3rd congressional district, becoming the first member of the U.S. Congress of Filipino ancestry

🎬 *The Joy Luck Club*, directed by Wayne Wang from Amy Tan's bestselling 1989 book, jerks tears to the tune of $33 million at the box office

unexpected opportunity to be present for them in person, in part due to the fact that my friend and *A. Magazine* cofounder Bill Yao was working in Europe at the time, and in part because I was then writing for the New York–based alternative weekly the *Village Voice*, which offset some of my expenses on the chance I'd run into something interesting to cover.

And as it turned out, I did. Kristi Yamaguchi, the Japanese American figure skating champion whose grandparents had been incarcerated by the U.S. government in World War II, won the gold medal in a hotly contested women's singles competition—beating her rival Midori Ito of Japan and two beloved U.S. skaters who would later be part of an infamous incident just two years later at the Winter Olympics in Lillehammer, Nancy Kerrigan and Tonya Harding. But Yamaguchi's victory wasn't the story—or at least, it was only part of the story. The story was about how the media depicted Yamaguchi, in the runup to and aftermath of her victory: as an outsider, as a foreigner, as an Asian upstart in a spotlight that belonged to lily-white "golden girls" of the ice.

The most egregious, and frankly racist, example of how news media treated Yamaguchi was *Newsweek*, which had run a lengthy editorial noting that "She comes at precisely that moment when so many Americans are blaming the Japanese, rounding on them, making devils of them. . . . What's a good ole boy to

do if there's not only a Toyota in the driveway and a Sony in the bedroom and a Mitsubishi in the family room—but on the screen there, as the band plays the 'Star-Spangled Banner,' is the All-American girl of 1992, and her name is Yamaguchi?"

Well, the right answer to that question is, he should damn well cheer. But the article was just the first to frame Yamaguchi as less-than-American, in an age when Americans were loudly blaming Japan for the U.S.'s economic woes.

I wrote about that incident then, and would later return to the subject in 1998, when MSNBC ran the headline "American Beats Out Kwan" in announcing Tara Lipinski's victory over her fellow very much American Michelle Kwan, and again in 2014, when the latest golden girl, Ashley Wagner, was picked over Japanese American Mirai Nagasu to represent the U.S. at the Olympics—despite Nagasu winning a bronze medal at the U.S. Nationals, traditionally the event used to select Olympians, while Wagner, having fallen multiple times, placed a distant fourth. Figure skating wasn't my beat— the lane that I was finding for myself was being an Asian American commentator writing about Asian American issues—a rare one at the time, when there were few of us at all in journalism, with those that were part of the industry largely avoiding topics that were too close to home, for fear of being boxed in.

---

📽 *Dragon: The Bruce Lee Story* debuts, reintroducing Lee's story to a new generation

📽 Brandon Lee, son of Bruce, is killed in a tragic accident on the set of *The Crow*—the movie that would have made him a star

📽 *Mighty Morphin Power Rangers* features Thuy Trang as Yellow Ranger Trini Kwan

📽 Connie Chung is named co-anchor of the CBS *Evening News* with Dan Rather, becoming the first Asian American to be a main anchor of a national network news program

## L.A. Burning

But events a few months later would show the real need for journalists occupying that box. In April, an all-white jury of seven men and five women failed to convict four white officers who'd been caught on tape brutally beating Black motorist Rodney King. Black neighborhoods like South Central erupted in rage, unleashing long-simmering anger at mistreatment by law enforcement, at white supremacy—and at Asian Americans, who were widely seen as a "middleman minority" that had adopted many of the racist attitudes and fears of the white mainstream, exemplified in the killing earlier that year of a young Black girl named Latasha Harlins, shot by a Korean American grocer, Soon Ja Du.*

By the end of the first night of six straight days of rioting, much of Koreatown was in rubble or in flames. The Los Angeles Police Department had fallen back to positions protecting affluent white communities like Beverly Hills and West Hollywood, treating the Asian immigrant enclave as a buffer to absorb the rage, looting, and destruction of its neighbors without restriction. And some Korean Americans, with nowhere to turn, decided to protect their own businesses, crouching on rooftops with rifles in silhouettes that some decried as looking like "North Korean snipers."

These images ran incessantly on newscasts for a week, dehumanizing both the Black and the Korean American communities, turning them into armies at war with one another, a crazed mob versus robotic assassins, in an egregious distraction from the reality that the chaos had been unleashed by the racist actions of white cops, a white judge, and a white jury—that storyline wasn't as effective or as popcorn-ready as the "Black and Asian Race War."

For Korean Americans, the Riots were a call to action, birthing a new wave of activists and political leaders intent on building a civic infrastructure for a community that until then had kept their head down and their profile low. For Asian Americans more broadly, they were a reminder that the perils of not controlling our own narrative extended beyond entertainment and into the newsroom.

## Shadow of *The Crow*

By 1993, *A. Magazine* had grown to the point where we had a handful of full-time staffers, though I was still pulling double duty, researching and editing for the *Village Voice* while editorial-directing *A.* In March of that year, the *Voice*'s film editor gave me a rare opportunity to write a feature profile: Brandon Lee, son of Bruce, was shooting a movie that was

---

* See page 87, "Sai-I-Gu 1992"

**1993**

**1994**

♫ Smashing Pumpkins breaks into pop superstardom with *Siamese Dream*, turning Japanese American guitarist James Iha into an alt-rock It Boy

🎬 *The Wedding Banquet* debuts; the gay romantic drama jumpstarts the career of filmmaker Ang Lee

⚾ Pitcher Chan Ho Park makes his debut as a Los Angeles Dodger, thrilling Korean Americans. He goes on to win the most victories of any Asian-born player in major league history.

🏛 Ben Cayetano is elected governor of the state of Hawaii, becoming the first Filipino American to serve as a U.S. state governor

being buzzed about as a breakout role for the young actor, who had struggled to free himself from the shadow of his father, and his father's untimely death. My conversation with Lee while he was in the throes of completing production was extended and rich. He was open about his love and respect for his father, as well as his desire to carve out his own identity, which he hoped this role as Eric Draven might do. He discussed his extended conversations about mortality and hope and loss with James O'Barr, author of the original comic book that was the film's source, and how challenging it was to compare his own vision of the character with that of its creator: "It's a difficult thing to meet your maker," he joked.

That line took on a new and darker meaning just a few days later, when I heard from the production's PR person that Brandon, in a tragic accident, had died. A gun that was supposed to contain blanks had somehow been misloaded. The scene was supposed to show the death of Brandon's character; it ended up causing his actual demise instead.

The reason the publicist was calling ahead of news reports of Brandon's death was because I was the last journalist to speak to him before the tragedy, and people were already trying to reach me. Different media entities soon came calling, asking for me to write the story for them, offering different kinds of promises—freelance fees I hadn't ever seen before as a journalist, and even a staff writer position at a major entertainment publication.

I turned them down, partly because the angle those periodicals wanted was one I was determined not to pursue—a ghoulish dive into the weird "curse" of the Lee family, a betrayal of both the kindness that Brandon had shown to me and his last ambitions to be defined as his own person. Instead, I completed the assignment I'd been given for the *Village Voice*, writing my profile, titled "Nevermore," as an obituary and epitaph for a young man who got his wings too soon.

## A Page of Our Own

The *Voice* didn't have the money that other publications had, but they did respond with gratitude. On the heels of that assignment and the strength of that piece, they made me a full-fledged member of the masthead, promising me the autonomy to keep doing *A. Magazine*, which is where my secret heart lay, while also giving me the agency to write a monthly full-page column about race and culture from an Asian American perspective, as well as a regular gig as one of the weekly's small team of TV critics.

It was the best of a number of worlds for me: I could spend as much time as I wanted at *A. Magazine*'s office, just a few blocks away from the *Voice*, while writing about both the

---

*Vanishing Son* gives *Joy Luck Club*'s Russell Wong a rare lead role in a TV series

*All-American Girl*, a family sitcom based on the comedy of Margaret Cho, hits primetime on ABC. It lasts 19 episodes before being canceled.

*Real World: San Francisco* introduces Pam Ling, the first Asian American to be cast in MTV's seminal reality franchise

*Speed* is released to theaters, turning Keanu Reeves into an action icon

Openly queer Japanese American Jenny Shimizu becomes a model for CK1

issues that concerned me and about one of the parts of the pop culture world that was facing unprecedented change and disruption: television. I was able to ask for my longtime friend and mentor Andrew Hsiao as editor. Andy and I chose our friend Florian Bachleda, one of the *Voice*'s designers, as the "house artist" for my monthly column. Bachleda being Filipino American meant that every month, one page in the paper was an oasis written, edited, and illustrated by Asian Americans.

From that vantage point we covered incidents like the wreck of the *Golden Venture*, a ship carrying undocumented Chinese immigrants that crashed into the far rocks of Far Rockaway, causing hundreds in its human cargo to swim to shore and immediately be placed into detention, and about the rising shadow of nativist hysteria that led to the passage of initiatives like Proposition 187 in liberal California, which would have barred undocumented immigrants from public schools and from any health or welfare service other than emergency medical treatment, while requiring doctors and teachers to serve as spies for immigration enforcement. (The law was instantly blocked by the courts, bounced around on appeal for years, and was eventually repealed without ever taking effect.)

I also wrote about technology, and how it was transforming Asian America, tying the scattered members of our community closer together, while creating a generation of Asian American tech moguls — the most visible of whom was Jerry Yang, cofounder of Yahoo, whose name was close enough to mine that on the day of Yahoo's IPO, leading Chinese newspaper *World Journal* accidentally ran a file photo of me to accompany their front-page story, causing my parents to get a flood of confusing calls from friends and extended family congratulating them on their son's success. ("We do not have a successful son by that name here," I can still imagine my father saying.) A year later, when Yahoo celebrated the launch of its Finance platform with a ceremonial "pushing the opening button" at NASDAQ, Jerry actually reached out to me to have lunch, and began the conversation by joking, "Nice to meet you, Jeff. I believe I've been getting some of your mail."

## Cho Stopper

But the biggest turning point for my career as a journalist didn't come because of my column, but because of my other gig, as television critic. In early 1994, news broke that ABC was working with comedian Margaret Cho to develop her stand-up* material into a series that

---

* See page 152, "It All Began with Margaret Cho"

**1994**

**1995**

💡 **Jerry Yang** cofounds Yahoo, one of the early dot-com "unicorns"

🏛 California voters pass Proposition 187, which seeks to cut off health, education, and other social services to undocumented immigrants. It is later deemed unconstitutional.

🎴 Nomomania is unleashed as Japan's Hideo Nomo becomes Rookie of the Year and All Star for the L.A. Dodgers

📺 *Star Trek: Voyager* premieres as the fledgling UPN network's flagship show, introducing to the world Garrett Wang as Ensign Harry Kim

would focus on her immigrant Korean family; the announcement meant that for the first time since 1976, a show with a predominantly Asian American cast might land on primetime network television. I knew Margaret; I'd interviewed her for *A. Magazine*, we'd occasionally connect when I was in L.A. or she was in New York—I considered her to be a friend. She'd even announced that her show *All-American Girl* was getting picked up to series from the stage at an Asian American stand-up comedy event that I and Corky Lee, whom I'd stayed close to from the days when he was our printer's rep, had organized as an Asian Pacific American Heritage Month charity fundraiser.

But it never quite hit me that that friendship would be tested this way. I was still just five years out of college, and, while I couldn't claim to be naive, it was the first time my personal and professional worlds had collided quite so directly. While uncomfortable, my editor was firm: this would be a key opportunity for me—and it made little sense to put the piece into the hands of one of the more senior (white) critics. I took the tapes of the show and watched them that night. It was not like anything I expected.

Not because it featured Asian Americans, although that was truly amazing, almost unbelievable in an era where we still excitedly called roommates or family members into the room if we happened to see an Asian person on an advertisement. But because it was objectively not good TV, despite having so much talent on screen. And the humor barely resembled Margaret's bawdy, anarchic comedy at all, eschewing bitter, edgy insights on sex, queerness, racism, and misogyny for door-slamming sitcom antics and all-too-typical couch jokes.

I wrote what I saw, lacing my review with what I thought at the time were bitter, edgy insights of my own, but which ultimately read like an unnecessary pile-on. (For example, bemoaning Margaret's flattening into sitcom two-dimensionality, I compared her portrayal on the show to a hostage proof-of-life video.) It wasn't meaningful—it was *mean*. And I regretted it even as I turned it in to publish.

I'd regret it more when Margaret called me the day after the review ran, angrily informing me that the piece would be used as an excuse to kill the show, with my rare status as an Asian American TV reviewer cited as ultimate proof that the show was deemed unsalvageable by both critics and the A community. She was right. ABC yanked the show after 19 episodes, ostensibly to "reboot"— word was they were going to try to surround Margaret with a group of white friends, like the existing hit show about white friends, *Friends*. But it never came back from hiatus.

The incident underscored to me how vulnerable our community still was to critique at the time—not because our creators were weak or untalented, but because the mostly white

---

## 1996

Chang-Rae Lee's *Native Speaker* is published and wins the American Book Award and the PEN/Hemingway Award for Best First Novel

Pokemon is released and becomes a global multimedia phenomenon

Influential rock band Linkin Park forms, originally under the name Xero, with Mike Shinoda and Joe Hahn among its members

*The Mystery Files of Shelby Woo* becomes first Nickelodeon show to feature Asian American leads (Irene Ng and Pat Morita)

executives backing them offered only conditional access to the gold mountain of production, distribution, and promotion. Any excuse to pull out the rug would be taken, and the slot of opportunity transferred to a "safer" white performer or storyteller instead. It didn't matter if the safer option had shat the bed a dozen times before, against a handful of successes: The successes were proof of the artist's potential, failures were evidence of their ability to "rebound."

By contrast, Asians—as individuals, and as a community—only got one shot, and if missed, back to square one. Primetime network TV wouldn't see another sitcom focused on an Asian American family for 20 more years . . . when *Fresh Off the Boat* hit the airwaves, starring my son Hudson Yang.* (The irony was palpable, and I've written about it many times over the years. Coincidence or karma? Who can tell.)

## The City Wide Web

But while all this was happening, *A. Magazine* continued to grow. We wrote our first book—*Eastern Standard Time*, a mini-encyclopedia of Asian influences on American culture, "from Astro Boy to Zen Buddhism." The whole Margaret Cho debacle felt like a great excuse

to do what I'd wanted to do for a while: start working on *A.* full-time. I threw myself into the magazine, perhaps trying to wash my feelings of guilt away in ink.

As part of going all-in on *A.*, I reimmersed myself in Asian New York, which had evolved into a wildly dynamic and eclectic subculture with a perspective and purpose wholly distinct from that of California's big and densely populated Asian communities. There were fewer footholds for those who wanted to get involved; most of the establishment institutions of Asian New York were run by their charismatic original founders, all first-wave activists from the Sixties, Seventies, and early Eighties; they were tough and battle-scarred and proud and not going anywhere, which left very little opportunity for young guns looking to shoot their shot.

But ours was a generation—we'd finally been given the moniker "Gen X"—whose mindset and identity had been intrinsically shaped by the first-order technological ground shift happening all around us: the cheaply available personal computer, the mobile phone, desktop publishing, the Internet. Suddenly, anyone could start an organization, launch a campaign, or yes, found a magazine, but thousands did. We were all auteurs of our own pet endeavors and actors in many others—an iridescent, undulating constellation composed of cosmic

---

* See page 368, "*Fresh Off the Boat:* A Retrospective"

1996

| | | | | |
|---|---|---|---|---|
| 🎬 *Rumble in the Bronx* released in the U.S., becomes Jackie Chan breakthrough movie in the U.S. | 💡 Dr. David Ho named *Time* Man of the Year for his work on an effective treatment for AIDS | 🏛 Campaign finance controversy hits Clintons, Democrats; allegations of funds funneled from China to Democratic Party spark congressional investigations | 🏛 Gary Locke is elected governor of Washington, making him the first Asian American governor on the U.S. mainland | 🏛 California passes Proposition 209, which strikes down gender and racial preferences in the state, ending most forms of affirmative action |

bodies who were at once both sun and satellite.

By the end of the decade, a spectacular array of organizations, coalitions, and ad hoc collusions had emerged from our entanglements: *A. Magazine* and the Writers Workshop and Kaya Press and the Second Generation Theater Company and the Asian Pacific Islander Coalition on HIV and AIDS (APICHA) and Asian Professional Extension (APEX) and Arkipelago and Godzilla and Peeling the Banana and Gay Asian Pacific Islander Men of New York and Ma-Yi Theater and the National Asian American Theater Company and so many others.

Everything seemed possible, on a local level and on a global one. Hatred of Japan, which had fueled much of the 1980s, had swung over to fascination with its pop culture: video games, toys, anime, manga. Hong Kong, too, was getting its time in the limelight,** as the island's stars and cinematic treasures made a bid for American audiences, aware of the impending arrival of 1997 and the uncertain implications of the transfer of the island to mainland Chinese control.

The rise of Hong Kong had a direct impact on me: Based on my writing about martial arts cinema—including that last profile I wrote of Brandon Lee—I was picked by Jackie Chan and his publishers to ghostwrite his auto-

biography, *I Am Jackie Chan: My Life in Action*. It gave me a unique front-row seat for Jackie's big American breakthrough with the movie *Rush Hour*, which made $140 million in the U.S. and $244 million worldwide and spawned two sequels and a short-lived TV series remake; it taught me a lesson about the huge opportunities that lay in connecting Asia to the Asian diaspora, but it also made me sharply aware of how poorly global fame and success translated into respect in Hollywood. Jackie was at the time the biggest star in Asia, and quite possibly the world, recognized and beloved everywhere—in the Netherlands, in South Africa, in Eastern Europe—but when I saw him meet with American entertainment execs, their eyes flickered around the room as if they couldn't rest for too long on his Asian features, they betrayed impatience with his English, sometimes correcting him or leaping in with words to fill the gaps in his sentences, they talked about their own tedious tourist experiences in China (or other Asian countries, all same same) or asked him if he might be related to random Chinese people in places where Jackie had never been, like Chicago and Long Beach. Maybe! It's possible! We do get around! (But did they ever ask Hugh Grant if he was related to Cary and Ulysses S.?)

---

** See page 133, "How the Golden Age of Hong Kong Cinema Gave Us Hope"

See page 133

## 1997

🎬 *Tomorrow Never Dies* is released, with Michelle Yeoh as a "Bond Girl" who's the equal of Bond

⛳ Golfer Tiger Woods, son of a Thai American mother and an African American father, wins the Masters

💡 Asian Avenue launches as one of the first—and most influential—early Asian American social networking sites

## 1998

⛳ "American Beats Out Kwan" headline appears on MSNBC, announcing U.S. skater Tara Lipinski's win of the gold over her teammate Michelle Kwan; headline reinforces notion that Asian Americans are foreigners

## End of an Era

Meanwhile, two big shifts occurred toward the end of the 1990s, both of which would help to shape the immediate years after the millennium, and which continue to influence our community decades later.

The first was a passing of the baton of populist fear and hatred from Japan to China, now seen as the "next great superpower," made more scary by its ostensibly Communist ideology. In 1996, the *Washington Post* broke news about a Department of Justice investigation into alleged attempts by the People's Republic of China to funnel money into the Clinton reelection campaign, using Asian Americans as cutouts. The investigation identified some campaign finance violations tied to a number of colorful characters, but no evidence of a concerted effort by China to undermine American democracy. Meanwhile, Asian Americans of all backgrounds were getting called to the table and interrogated—not just Chinese Americans, but Indonesian, Taiwanese, Korean, and Filipino donors were being put under suspicion, with the media grabbing onto new persons of interest with "exotic" surnames and recklessly flipping them into the headlines. When nothing came of the investigations, intelligence officials and right-wing activists, looking for any kind of dirt that would stick

to China, seized on evidence that Dr. Wen Ho Lee,* a nuclear physicist for the Los Alamos National Laboratory, had downloaded classified research files to his personal computer as signs of a vast Chinese conspiracy.

The second was the frothy arrival of the finale to the so-called "dot-com" era—where venture capitalists started getting wild and throwing money at anything with a domain name. A friend of a friend, a Wall Street banker looking for the chance to break into the startup space, approached *A. Magazine* with the proposal to build a "targeted community portal" around the brand. The magazine business was already looking unsteady. As an independent publication surviving on sweat and hope, the offer of a digital zipline off the precipice seemed too good to be true. Is it a spoiler to say "it was"?

The year 1999 marked the start of an unbelievable final chapter for *A.*, as we successfully raised $5 million to launch a digital version of the magazine—trading stock and a few thousand bucks to an Alaskan domain squatter for the rights to the name "AOnline.com," and then going on a wild spending spree, egged on by the former banker, now the president, CFO, COO, head of business development, and primary strategist for the company. I remained nominal CEO, with ownership diluted down to a fraction, but, he said to me, this was necessary

---

* See page 224, "The Trials of Dr. Wen Ho Lee"

1998

🏛 **80-20 Initiative** is founded by S. B. Woo and others; while initially a "non-partisan" group focused on electoral politics, it eventually becomes a point of organizing for Asians against affirmative action

🎬 Disney's *Mulan*, based on a Chinese folk tale, becomes its first film to feature a largely Asian American voice cast

🎬 **Lucy Liu** first appears on *Ally McBeal* as the memorable Ling Woo; though controversial for reinforcing the "dragon lady" stereotype, the role serves as a launchpad for Liu's career

🎬 *Rush Hour* is released; blockbuster hit finally establishes martial arts icon Jackie Chan as a Hollywood star

given the New Rules our Old Media was now operating by. After all, just a few months after we raised our round, upstart digital titan AOL would take over legendary "bricks and paper" giant Time Warner!

"You can't raise more until you spend what you've got," our new president told us. So we acquired companies—a web development operation and an Asian American record label in San Francisco, a sales consultancy in Los Angeles—and we rented and built out offices in three different cities, and we committed money toward long-term software licenses for content management systems, intelligent search tools, embedded video, streaming audio. Our payroll alone was creating a biweekly bonfire of cash, as our head count went from seven to over a hundred in a few months. But the whole "spend money so you can raise money" mantra only made sense if you could raise money, and that seemed less likely every day.

For one, the only thing bringing in income was the magazine, which was doing better than ever. But it certainly wasn't generating the revenue needed to prop up over a hundred people across three cities. Our president/CFO/COO/head of biz dev/primary strategist declared that we had two choices: shut down, or merge with someone bigger. Of course, we chose the latter, accepting a "merger" with a nominally more established Asian American Internet player on terms that erased most of our value, with the promise that at least jobs would be saved and assets like the magazine would be preserved.

Then that company announced it was out of money too—after spending the money that remained in our coffers. Everything would have to shut down, I was told by the new owners. (Our P/C/C/HBD/PS was long since gone, having resigned after the merger and headed off to greener pastures in Europe.) The decade was over, the bubble was over, the magazine was over. The millennium was here, out with the old, in with the new, and we woke up to the painful realization that "the old" meant us.

I'm not great at sports analogies—or sports—but if I had to describe what the Nineties were to Asian America, I'd say they were like a baseball pitcher's windup. Standing on the mound of the original movement activists of the Sixties and Seventies, following the signals thrown by the organization builders of the Eighties, the work we did in this decade identified targets, coiled muscles, and shifted our collective center of balance for a pitch we'd be making for relevance, visibility, and influence in the decades to come. It was hard enough work in this era to even be acknowledged as part of a growing "trend" of diversity. It would pass to those who emerged in the 2000s to stake a claim to a cultural lane within our multicultural America, and the 2010s to affirm that our culture deserved and needed to be included, to be respected, and yes, to be seen.

**1999**

🎬 Cartoon Network's *Toonami* launches, with series like *Sailor Moon*, *Dragon Ball Z*, and *Naruto*, bringing anime out of the cult underground and into the mainstream

🎬 *Lethal Weapon 4* becomes wushu legend Jet Li's American debut

📖 Kenneth Li writes "Racer X" for *Vibe*, an article about street racing in New York. The article is optioned for film and becomes the source for Rob Cohen's reboot of *The Fast and the Furious*—now a multibillion-dollar franchise.

🏛 General Eric Shinseki becomes the chief of staff of the U.S. Army, making him the first Asian American to head a military service branch

# Asian Americans on Campus

BY JEFF YANG

**IN 1987,** *TIME* published a cover story, titled "Those Asian-American Whiz Kids," that stands as one of the earliest pop-culture eruptions of a new Asian stereotype: the Asian American (specifically, the East/South Asian American) as academic overachiever.

The feature marveled at the way that the children of Asian immigrants were crushing grade point averages, "setting the educational pace for the rest of America and cutting a dazzling figure at the country's finest schools." What could explain their success? Was it due to the fact that they worked harder? ("They have almost a maniacal attitude that if they just work hard enough, they can do it.") Could it be because of Confucius? ("The Confucian ethic drives people to work, excel and repay the debt they owe their parents.") Or were they just genetically primed for intellectual success? ("One claim is that Asians are simply smarter than other groups.")

Like most trend pieces, "Whiz Kids" was focused on generalizations that were misleading at best and dangerous at worst, something that the article itself acknowledged, noting non-Asian "resentment" at this "updated 'yellow peril,'" and speaking to the stress many Asians faced over being dismissed as "grade grinds" and the trauma experienced by Asians who didn't conform to the stereotype.

What the article didn't acknowledge was that many East and South Asian Americans going through high school and college in the 1980s were children of the first wave of Asians to come to the U.S. after 1965, a disproportionate number of whom were hyper-educated superachievers themselves, because of the Hart-Celler Act's preferences for immigrants capable of contributing to the scientific, medical, and engineering professions. (And meanwhile, the experiences of children of Asian immigrants who arrived through other channels, for example as refugees of war, did not match the stereotype.)

As a result, the post-'65ers were pre-filtered to be educated, and to value education for their offspring. So it hardly takes pathological work ethics, Confucian values, or natural evolutionary superiority to explain why Asian American presence at elite colleges boomed beginning in the Nineties. Our parents survived war, occupation, economic collapse, and natural disaster and in many cases earned advanced degrees anyway, then dragged themselves to a whole new country to build a life and family in an alien culture where they were exploited and underappreciated. Out of that came a rock-hard determination to see their kids do better, and have a life less bitter, than themselves. The statistics here are the result.

## 1990:*

% of Asian Americans with an 8th-grade education or less: **10.8**
% of white Americans with an 8th-grade education or less: **3.1**

% of Asian Americans with a bachelor's degree or more: **34.7**
% of white Americans with a bachelor's degree or more: **28.1**

## 2020:

% of Asian Americans with an 8th-grade education or less: **4.8**
% of white Americans with an 8th-grade education or less: **3.9**

% of Asian Americans with a bachelor's degree or more: **58.1**
% of white Americans with a bachelor's degree or more: **36.3**

Average amount of time spent studying by Asian youth:** **13 HOURS A WEEK**
Average amount of time spent studying by white youth: **5.6 HOURS A WEEK**

Average amount of time spent on sports by Asian youth: **3.4 HOURS A WEEK**
Average amount of time spent on sports by white youth: **5.1 HOURS A WEEK**

Average amount of time spent on socializing by Asian youth: **5.2 HOURS A WEEK**
Average amount of time spent on socializing by white youth: **8.5 HOURS A WEEK**

Average amount of time spent on computer games by Asian youth: **8.5 HOURS A WEEK**
Average amount of time spent on computer games by white youth: **5.6 HOURS A WEEK**

## % ASIAN AMERICAN ENROLLMENT AT SELECTED ELITE COLLEGES***

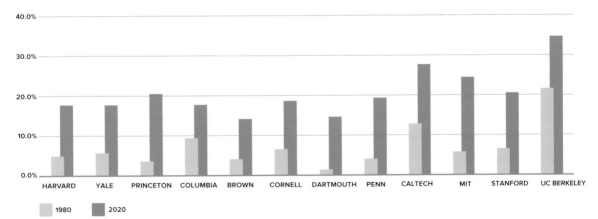

1980   2020

\*   https://www.census.gov/content/census/en/data/tables/2019/demo/educational-attainment/cps-detailed-tables.html
\*\*  https://ucsdnews.ucsd.edu/archive/newsrel/soc/5-4-11tiger_mother.asp
\*\*\* https://www.theamericanconservative.com/articles/meritocracy-appendices/#tophttps://www.collegefactual.com/

**88%*** of Asian Americans agree that "People who did not receive education beyond high school are limited in how much they can grow in their careers."

**73%** of white Americans agree that "People who did not receive education beyond high school are limited in how much they can grow in their careers."

**41%** of Asian Americans agree that "There are lots of well-paying, stable jobs that people can find with only a high school diploma or GED."

**55%** of white Americans agree that "There are lots of well-paying, stable jobs that people can find with only a high school diploma or GED."

**33%** of Asian Americans agree that "Race and ethnicity should positively factor into college or university admission standards if academic and extracurricular qualifications are equal."

**25%** of white Americans agree that "Race and ethnicity should positively factor into college or university admission standards if academic and extracurricular qualifications are equal."

**65%** of Asian Americans agree that they "would be more likely to support a candidate who favored free college tuition."

**46%** of white Americans agree that they "would be more likely to support a candidate who favored free college tuition."

## Aggregate Numbers Suggest Asian Americans Excel in Educational Attainment:**

Asian Americans: **58%** have bachelor's degree
White Americans: **40%** have bachelor's degree

## Disaggregated Numbers Show a Vast Spectrum:

Chinese, Taiwanese Origin: **75%** have bachelor's degree
Asian Indian: **73%**
Korean: **54%**
Pakistani: **52%**
Chinese, not of Taiwanese Origin: **51%**
Japanese: **50%**
Filipino: **47%**
Vietnamese: **29%**

### ASIAN AMERICANS LIVE IN AREAS WITH BETTER SCHOOLS***

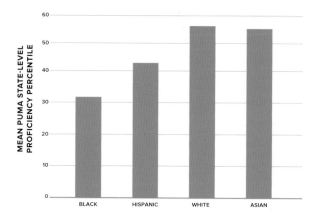

\* https://www.newamerica.org/education-policy/reports/varying-degrees-2020/explore-the-data

\*\* https://equitablegrowth.org/how-data-disaggregation-matters-for-asian-americans-and-pacific-islanders/

\*\*\* https://www.brookings.edu/research/asian-american-success-and-the-pitfalls-of-generalization/

# SO EXTRA

**BY PHILIP WANG**

School was just our day job. Outside of class and on weekends, many of us made friends and developed passions (or traumas) in courses and clubs that kept our schedules packed. How many extracurricular activities on this bulletin board were you signed up for?

| | | | |
|---|---|---|---|
| **1.** Piano | **9.** Coding school | **16.** Basketball | **23.** Calligraphy |
| **2.** Violin | **10.** Saturday language school | **17.** Tennis/badminton | **24.** Choir |
| **3.** Marching band | **11.** Model UN | **18.** Martial arts (karate, taekwondo, judo, etc.) | **25.** Key Club/Circle K |
| **4.** Guitar/ukulele | **12.** Speech/debate | | **26.** National Honor Society |
| **5.** Drums: drumline or cultural (*taiko*, Korean drums) | **13.** Academic Decathlon/Mathlete | **19.** Golf | **27.** Hospital |
| **6.** Kumon | **14.** Odyssey of the Mind | **20.** Figure skating | **28.** Youth group |
| **7.** A Kumon knockoff | **15.** Robot Wars | **21.** Painting | **29.** Alpha Phi Omega |
| **8.** SAT prep | | **22.** Dance: ballet, ethnic dance | **30.** A job |

JEFF YANG    PHIL YU    PHILLIP WANG

# THE ASIAN AMERICAN SYLLABUS 1990s

**HERE'S OUR LIST** of must-consume media to understand being Asian American in the 1990s, the decade in which we made our first real forays into mainstream visibility, exposing to the world the talent that had been overlooked—or been forcibly rendered invisible—within our creative communities.

*Dogeaters* by Jessica Hagedorn (1990); *Pangs of Love* by David Wong Louie (1991); *China Boy* by Gus Lee (1991); *American Knees* by Shawn Wong (1995); *Native Speaker* by Chang-Rae Lee (1995); *Typical American* by Gish Jen (1998); *Interpreter of Maladies* by Jhumpa Lahiri (1999)

**JEFF:** Here's your mini-library of Asian American literature from the 1990s. Gonna call out *Native Speaker* here, the first book that spoke to the sense that when you're an Asian American, especially if you're an immigrant, you kind of feel like a double agent. That insider-outsiderness.

**PHIL:** I'll do the same for *Interpreter of Maladies,* Jhumpa Lahiri's debut book, a collection of short stories about Indians and Indian Americans that won the Pulitzer Prize.

### *The Simpsons* (1990)

**PHIL:** Apu. But really, every Asian on this show is a stereotype.

**PHILIP:** And it's conscious, because the characters basically say, "I am aware I am a stereotype."

**JEFF:** The first time I watched it, I thought it was interesting that the white people are yellow, and the Asians are a lighter shade of yellow. I can't remember if I thought that was empowering or if I felt cheated.

**PHILIP:** How did you feel about Legos?

**JEFF:** Philip, this literally is the first time I've ever thought about Lego guys being yellow.

### *Hook* (1991)

**PHILIP:** Okay, everyone together: RU-FI-OOOOOOOO!

**PHIL:** Dante Basco still gets called Rufio because of this movie. It is that iconic of a performance.

### The Joy Luck Club (1993)

**PHILIP:** Take this off. It had no impact. I'm kidding.

**PHIL:** There is no more consequential Asian American film than this one in the Nineties. It's like our mile marker—the standard by which other Asian American movies have been measured ever since.

**JEFF:** And it basically brought us the next generation of Asian American woman actors: Ming-Na, Tamlyn, Lauren, Rosalind . . . and the best of the older generation too. Tsai Chin is a legend.

**PHILIP:** Plus, Russell Wong eating watermelon.

### Dragon: The Bruce Lee Story (1993)

**PHIL:** Not directed by an Asian American, and it had a lot of issues, but it was the film that introduced Bruce Lee to a new generation.

**JEFF:** The scene in which Bruce and Linda Lee watch *Breakfast at Tiffany's* together, even though it's probably fictional, is enough to make the movie worth watching.

### The Wedding Banquet (1993)

**JEFF:** *The Wedding Banquet* deserves more retroactive honor than it gets. It brought Ang Lee to the attention of Hollywood as a star director in the waiting.

**PHIL:** And at the same time, it was also intersectional. I don't know that prior to this, LGBTQ issues within the Asian American community, especially immigrant communities, were put on screen at all, and certainly not in a narrative fashion.

### Mighty Morphin Power Rangers (1993)

**PHILIP:** For a lot of us, Trini Kwan was our first superhero. But I'll always wonder if the Yellow Ranger was intentionally Yellow Ranger because she was Asian.

**PHIL:** Oh, a hundred percent. The Asian ranger is yellow, the Black ranger is black. And then of course the white guys are red, white, and blue,

and the white girl is pink. Not a coincidence.

**JEFF:** Weird how no one notices that in all the action sequences, which are clipped in from the original Japanese series, the Yellow Ranger is a guy.

### All-American Girl (1994)

**PHIL:** Short-lived, but groundbreaking. And if you watch it now, it's not nearly as bad as it was made out to be back when. It's not worse than a lot of stuff that ended up surviving.

**JEFF:** It was just a disappointment that it was so far away from Margaret's actual comedy and personality. But as a TV critic back then who reviewed it harshly, I still stay up nights wondering what might have happened if it was given the chance to evolve.

### Vanishing Son (1994)

**PHIL:** Chances are you've never heard of it. But it was a cross between *The Fugitive* and *Kung Fu*.

**JEFF:** It starred Russell Wong as a classical music prodigy who knows kung fu, like he had all the Asian superpowers.

### The Crow (1994)

**PHIL:** This was the movie that would've made Brandon Lee a star, had he lived to see it.

**PHILIP:** I was a kid when I heard about his death on the set, but I still remember everyone talking about it: "Did you hear about Bruce Lee's son?"

**JEFF:** I was the last journalist to interview him before he died. I found out right after I got back home. It was horrific. My profile became an obituary.

### Street Fighter (1994) and Mortal Kombat (1995)

**PHILIP:** Objectively bad movies, but because they were based on games with incredibly popular Asian characters in them, Hollywood was forced to cast Asian actors.

**PHIL:** *Street Fighter* had Ming-Na Wen as Chun Li, Byron Mann as Ryu, Roshan Seth as Dhalsim, but of course the poster was Jean-Claude Van Damme's giant head.

**PHILIP:** At least in *Mortal Kombat,* the main protagonist and the main villain are both Asian: Robin Shou played Liu Kang and Cary-Hiroyuki Tagawa was Shang Tsung. And it made $121 million and the soundtrack went platinum.

### Rumble in the Bronx (1995)

**JEFF:** The movie that finally broke Jackie Chan through as an American action star, *Rumble in Vancouver.*

**PHIL:** It's got some awful racial stereotypes in it and the most ridiculous portrayal of gangsters since Michael Jackson's "Bad" video, but it's a fun movie that made you wonder how America took so long to realize what they were missing.

### The Mystery Files of Shelby Woo (1996)

**JEFF:** Nickelodeon's first live-action kids' show featuring an Asian American cast—Irene Ng as Shelby Woo, and Pat Morita as her grandfather, solving crimes. Ripe for a reboot, I'd say.

**PHILIP:** Pat Morita just kept on breaking ground.

### Ally McBeal (1997)

**PHIL:** So this is the show that introduced the world to Lucy Liu. It was problematic in a lot of ways, but she was excellent in it.

**PHILIP:** This was on when I was in middle school, and my parents wouldn't let me watch it because they thought it was about sex stuff.

**PHIL:** You were not its primary target audience.

### Shopping for Fangs (1997); Yellow (1997); Sunsets (1997); Strawberry Fields (1997)

**PHIL:** Four films that all came out the same year and made everyone believe for a minute that it was Asian America's time in the indie movie spotlight. All worth finding and watching.

### Fakin' Da Funk (1997)

**PHIL:** This movie is a trip. Read the synopsis and you're like, how did they even make this movie? Dante Basco stars as an Asian American kid who was accidentally adopted by Black parents, and who learns to be Asian from a Chinese exchange student . . . played by Margaret Cho!

**JEFF:** The cast blows my mind. Pam Grier? Tone Lōc? Bo Jackson? Rudy Ray Moore?

**PHILIP:** Dante Basco makes out with Tatyana Ali!

### Face/Off (1997)

**JEFF:** This movie was such a crazy idea—a cop surgically swaps faces with a terrorist!—that the only person who could've made it was John Woo. To his credit, he made it 100 percent a John Woo movie.

**PHILIP:** Of course it has a sequence with flying doves in a church. Margaret Cho has a cameo!

**PHIL:** This was the biggest hit to come out of that moment when all these Hong Kong stars were trying to figure out if they could make it in Hollywood, because they didn't know what would happen when China took over.

### Cinderella (1997)

**PHIL:** This Disney made-for-TV movie taught a generation of kids that their Prince Charming looked like Paolo Montalban.

### Rush Hour (1998)

**JEFF:** The Hollywood blockbuster Jackie Chan was always looking for, and deserved.

**PHILIP:** It set the template for pairing up Black and Asian leads in buddy action movies.

**PHIL:** It also set the template for Tzi Ma playing Asian dads who lose track of their daughters. Gotta keep a closer eye out, Tzi.

### Martial Law (1998)

**PHIL:** It's kind of wild in general that the decision was made to try to turn Sammo Hung into an American action star . . . and then to pair him up with Arsenio Hall.

**JEFF:** It was like a blurry photocopy of *Rush Hour?*

### Mulan (1998)

**PHIL:** This was our Disney movie.

**PHILIP:** It's a movie about a cross-dressing Chinese heroine who saves the kingdom. The very fact that it got made is kind of miraculous.

**JEFF:** It has issues but it's still beloved, and for good reason.

# Sa-I-Gu 1992: Remembering the Los Angeles Riots

BY JEFF YANG, ILLUSTRATED BY JESSICA HJ LEE

**FOR KOREAN AMERICANS,** 4/29 is a date that has been seared into cultural memory, so much so that it's known by just the digits themselves—"Sa-I-Gu," "four-two-nine"—in much the same way as 9/11 has been for Americans in general. April 29 was the date in 1992 when L.A. exploded with unrest in reaction to the acquittal of the police officers who'd brutally beaten Rodney King on camera. The news beamed stereotypical images of African Americans, Latinos, and Koreans as both victims and perpetrators of violence across the nation, with little context as to the triggers or roots of the events as they happened. For Korean Americans, Sa-I-Gu was a community-wide trauma, and a rude awakening: Over 2,200 Korean-owned businesses in L.A.'s Koreatown were damaged or destroyed, resulting in an estimated $400 million in damages—while municipal services like firefighting, law enforcement, and emergency medical teams largely pulled back from the majority Black, Latino, and Asian neighborhoods in the vicinity of the unrest, to ensure the safety and security of wealthier and whiter neighborhoods like West Hollywood and Beverly Hills. As a result, violence and destruction continued for days, and those in the Koreatown and South Central communities were left to fend for themselves. In a landmark video project, KTown92.com, documentarians **GRACE LEE** and **EURIE CHUNG** assembled a vast archive of news footage and original interviews with a multiracial array of observers and survivors, to tell a set of stories about the events leading up to, during, and following the Riots that's more nuanced, complex, and comprehensive than any other to date. "Every five years or so, on the anniversary of the Riots, you'll see the same footage recycled over and over again—the Rodney King video, Latasha Harlins, hordes of people looting shops, and then, the Korean shopkeepers with the guns," says Lee. "If that's your first image of Korean Americans on television, it really shapes your perception in a shocking way. We wanted to challenge that representation, and bring out a full spectrum of voices to talk about what happened."

## The Long, Slow Burn

*Seeking justice for decades, Black Angelenos finally hoped that the videotaped beating of Rodney King would lead to a crackdown on abusive police—only to see the perpetrators acquitted*

**EURIE CHUNG:** As one of our interviewees, Abraham Torres, said, it was on tape. Everyone saw it happen, and it seemed like finally there was going to be justice for victims of law enforcement brutality. There was no doubt in most of our minds that the officers were guilty. And in that context, when they were acquitted, it became almost impossible to not respond— much like in the George Floyd case. The tape was a representation of what was going on already in the United States for centuries.

**GRACE LEE:** Right. And when people are saying this over and over again for years and decades, that these abuses are happening, and

1990s

RISE

87

then we finally have evidence, it's even more devastating when justice still doesn't happen. But I would say that many Korean Americans' response to this was "What does this have to do with us? Like, why would you target us?"

## Koreatown Abandoned

*Korean Americans realized too late that they were being used as human shields*

**LEE:** Long before the Riots, organizers in different communities—Black, Latinx, Korean American—knew that the living and working conditions in and around Koreatown were untenable. That there was a simmering situation and unresolved racial tensions that could erupt at any time. But still, when the King verdict came out, everyone was caught flat-footed—no one expected a complete acquittal.

So the explosion that they were all anticipating actually happened.

**CHUNG:** One of our interviewees told us that to him, the Riots reaffirmed the status of Korean immigrants in American society, that Koreans were meant to be scapegoats to distract the Black community from their tensions with the white community. A buffer zone between the folks in Beverly Hills and Hollywood, and the folks in South Central.

## Save What You Can

*With no time to prepare, they salvaged what they could from their businesses*

**CHUNG:** When the Riots began, the community network activated, and people just began passing warnings to one another by word of mouth, that it was time to pack things up and

leave. We had interviewees talking about being brought by their parents to their stores and restaurants to grab everything that could be salvaged, because it was clear that the fire was headed their way.

**LEE:** Koreans are good at being resilient. Our parents grew up in war. They're used to getting ready to run.

## An Eruption of Rage

*Anger at the verdict turned into displaced violence against those seen as the face of oppression*

**LEE:** One of the most striking interviews we did was with Annetta Wells, who was a schoolgirl on a bus at the time, watching the Reginald Denny incident occur right in front of her. He was the white trucker who was pulled from his vehicle and beaten with bats. She said that

it felt like a knee-jerk response to decades of affliction, like they were screaming "you need to feel what it feels like to be one of us." How do you forget seeing something like that, as a child?

## Fire in the Night

*Fury was directed at Korean Americans in memory of the deadly shooting of a young Black girl, Latasha Harlins, by Korean grocer Soon Ja Du, just two weeks after the video-taped beating of Rodney King. Du, who submitted a self-defense plea, had been sentenced only to five years probation and a fine.*

**CHUNG:** We spoke to Brenda Stevenson, who's a historian and author, who told us that the Denny incident wasn't actually the first eruption in the Riots. There was a Korean liquor shop that had been targeted earlier, about a block and a half away. So the Korean community was where it started, and that's also where it ended. As people left South Central Los Angeles, they headed to Koreatown. She told us that people were chanting, "Let's go to Koreatown!" and shouting Latasha [Harlins]'s name. When we talked to people who were part of it, they said, "They take our money, but they don't respect us as people." So even if it was misdirected anger, it was anger that had been simmering a long time—it wasn't a coincidence.

## Taking Flight

*Korean Americans caught up in the chaos didn't just lose their businesses; many feared for their lives*

**LEE:** Korean American business owners were running all-night businesses in high-crime neighborhoods—Angela Oh, who became a spokesperson for Koreatown during and after the Riots, says she has a huge file of shop owners who'd been killed in the years before 1992. So that generated a constant feeling of fear and suspicion that contributed to the tensions they were having with the Black community. And a lot of that came to a head during Sa-I-Gu. One older woman we interviewed talked about trying to flee her shop incognito, knowing that mobs were targeting the cars they knew were owned by Koreans. That interviewee later learned more about the history of racism in this country, and she ended up becoming an organizer among fellow senior citizens to try to open up discussions about the conditions that have led to hostility between Black and Korean communities.

## Who Else Will Help Us?

*With L.A. police and fire departments refusing to respond to calls from Koreatown, the community had no choice but to save itself*

**CHUNG:** Koreatown felt completely abandoned. A lot of the interviewees told us that in that moment, the only thing they could trust in, the only way they had to communicate and ask for help was Radio Korea, the local Koreatown radio station. People would call in live to Radio Korea and say, my building is on fire, I need help, someone please come. And five minutes later, other Koreatown residents would drive over to help fight the fire with buckets of water from nearby stores. As Richard Choi, who was vice president of Radio Korea at the time, told us, "At the time, if 100,000 Koreans were living in L.A., 100,000 were listening to Radio Korea."

But there's a darker side to this too. The one Korean American who was killed during the Riots, the word is that he was part of a young group of vigilantes wearing white headbands, roving through Koreatown with walkie-talkies and guns, trying to "defend" the neighborhood. There was definitely a siege mentality in place, and it's something that you see the residue of today. Before 1992, there were no walls around all the parking lots—those were put up immediately afterwards.

## Unseen and Unheard

*The narrative politicians and the media put forth around Korean Americans erased their struggles—and the sacrifice and generosity of the community as it came together*

**LEE:** When we talk about Koreatown rebuilding, it's not just about physical property. It's about civic infrastructure. There was a generation of young Korean Americans who came to this understanding that we have to become more politically involved. I know a lot of people in my generation who went into law and media and activism as a result, because they felt they had to speak up for our community. We have to be seen. We have to be heard. That's the only way we can be safe.

## Koreatown Rebuilds

*It would take months for Koreatown to recover, with the help of thousands of volunteers and unprecedented support from within and beyond the community*

**CHUNG:** As Korean, Black, and Latinx communities began the process of rebuilding after the Riots, there was an understanding that we needed to learn each other's histories, understand commonalities, acknowledge our tension points. One outcome that we thought was really important was that a major labor organization in the area, the Korean Immigrant Workers Association, changed its name to the *Koreatown* Immigrant Workers Association. It was a recognition that there are enough similarities between the immigrant populations of low-wage workers who live in Koreatown, that they can find solidarity, regardless of whether they speak Spanish or Korean or English.

## Hiding the Memory

*After the Riots, many Korean Americans chose to hide their scars and forget*

**LEE:** One of the catalysts for our project was a woman named Leslie Shim, who came up to me after a screening of one of my documentaries and said, I want to tell you an odd story. And it was about how she went to the basement of UCLA's Powell Library to do research on Korean Americans who had been affected by the Riots. She was going through documents, and saw one that was a government list of all the businesses that had been burned or looted—and her family's dry cleaners was on the list. She was shocked. She called her mother and her mother matter-of-factly told her that yes, the store had been burned, and that's why they had sent her to live in Korea for a while until they could rebuild. Their family had never talked about it, because as Leslie put it, "We only talk about good things."

## Telling the Story

*The tragedy is painful to remember, but keeping memories alive is key to preventing something like this from happening again*

**LEE:** At the core of what we were trying to do with KTown92 was to question who gets to tell the story. Once you hear all the different voices, you begin to realize there is no one master narrative. It was important to us that we didn't privilege one perspective over another, because that's something that happened back then and has been recycled for years since.

**CHUNG:** Journalists we spoke to said they were told to specifically find certain people to interview—a Latino looter. A traumatized Korean store owner. We need to ask, what are the consequences of those editorial choices? We still live with them. We don't know where some of these narratives come from, but we do know this: they have long-standing consequences.

# The Long Dark Shadow of
## "Me Love You Long Time"

BY THUC NGUYEN

**FOR SOME PEOPLE,** the phrase "me love you long time" might be most familiar as the chorus of the infamous 1989 hit "Me So Horny," by the Miami rappers 2 Live Crew. For Asian women, however, it's something we've heard time and again, as a "harmless" joke, as a vicious taunt, and even as a questionable catcall. (A great on-screen example of what we have to deal with can be seen in season one of Hulu's Emmy-nominated *PEN15,* when the phrase is used by a white boy to bully the series' half-Japanese lead, Maya Erskine, in a scene Erskine says was inspired by personal middle-school experiences.)

But "me love you long time," along with its partner phrase "me so horny," first appeared as dialogue in Stanley Kubrick's 1987 Vietnam War film *Full Metal Jacket,* in a cameo appearance by British actress Papillon Soo Soo as a Vietnamese prostitute soliciting American GIs. Though brief and largely unimportant to the film, that two-minute scene established the phrase in popular culture, and as the bane of English-speaking Asian women everywhere.

Since its sampling by 2 Live Crew, the phrase has popped up in cartoons like *South Park, Family Guy,* and *American Dad!*; on primetime TV shows like *The Office* and *Parks and Recreation*; and in the movies *The 40-Year-Old Virgin, Disturbia* (where, as a prank, it's turned into a ringtone for the male protagonist's Asian best friend), *Bruce Almighty, Be Cool, How to Lose Friends and Alienate People, American Pie: Reunion,* and *The To Do List.* And 2 Live Crew aren't the only musicians who've embraced the phrase—*female* singers like Fergie of the Black Eyed Peas, Nelly Furtado, and Mariah Carey have also put it into their music.

When challenged, their argument is that by using "me love you long time" in a way that doesn't reference Asian women, they're actually reclaiming and liberating it. But the phrase's use of accented broken English, its association with prostitution and deceitfulness—no one who uses the phrase is ever actually horny, or interested in loving you a long time—and its general dehumanizing misogyny all feed into the stereotypes of Asian women that have been rampant throughout entertainment history, as seen on stage everywhere from the opera *Madama Butterfly* (1904) to the musical *Miss Saigon* (1989), on TV shows from *Shogun* to *Ally McBeal,* in movies from *The World of Suzie Wong* to *The Last Samurai.* In each, Asian women have been framed as exotic objects to be lusted after by or sacrificed for white male consumption, sexual and otherwise.

Those who suggest the phrase should just be taken in fun ignore the fact that, by denying Asian women's lived reality in favor of sexualized stereotypes, it puts them at direct risk of assault—or worse. "At its core, it reduces [Asian] women to an accent and sex work," says TV writer Lauren Bradley. "I think it's the duty of people in control of culture—entertainment, fashion, et cetera—to not use it as a joke." And ultimately, to not use it at all.

# Asian American Food Glow Up

BY AGNES CHUNG TALDE, ILLUSTRATED BY ROBIN HA

# ASIAN AMERICANS
## DOT COM
### The Wild Rise and Hard Fall of the Nineties Startup Kings

BY JEFF YANG, ILLUSTRATED BY CHI-YUN LAU

IN THE 1980S and early 1990s, two things were clear: Asian Americans—both immigrants and fresh-out-of-university children of immigrants—were becoming a growing force in the fast-growing world of technology. The problem was that the world of technology didn't have room for them where they belonged—at the top. Asians were seen as gifted engineers, but not leaders or managers, a perception that would lead to what author Jane Hyun would later dub the "Bamboo Ceiling": a cap on opportunity for Asian Americans in corporate America that prevented them from joining the executive suites. But a series of disruptive technology shifts in the mid-1990s—most notably, the explosive commercialization of the shiny new global network known as "the Internet"—opened up a new way for young Asian Americans to become top management: Armed with a bright idea and some venture capital dollars, they could launch their *own* companies. Some of these startups thrived; some survived; others hit a wall called financial reality and shattered into a billion pieces, as part of the broad collapse of the "dot com" bubble. Here are some of the notable Asian American entrepreneurs of the era, and the companies they founded.

## JERRY YANG

While still a student at Stanford in 1994, Yang and his friend David Filo built a directory of web pages they initially called "Jerry and David's Guide to the World Wide Web." As it became increasingly popular, they changed its name to the shorter and catchier Yahoo!—later claiming that the name stood for the longer and much less catchy "Yet Another Hierarchical Officious Oracle." Venture money quickly came calling, and Yang and Filo turned their weird hobby into a startup, which went public in 1996.

**VALUE AT PEAK:** Around $50 billion

**VALUE NOW:** It was quietly sold to wireless giant Verizon in 2017 for about $4.5 billion.

**WHAT'S HE UP TO TODAY:** Investing in companies through his fund, AME Cloud Ventures, sitting on the board of Chinese commerce giant Alibaba, and making charitable donations. (He gave $25 million to the Asian Art Museum, the largest donation in its history.)

## TONY HSIEH

In 1996, Hsieh and his friend Alfred Lin founded LinkExchange, an early ad network for the web. By 1998, the site was serving over 5 million ads to 400,000 participating web pages; Microsoft bought it that year for $265 million. Hsieh and Lin then launched an investment firm called "Venture Frogs" (a joke name suggested by a friend that they adopted on a bet), which in 1999 helped to incubate an online shoe company called Zappos. A few months later, Hsieh took over as Zappos's CEO. Within a decade, Zappos was doing $1 billion in annual revenues, based on a mantra that customer happiness should be everything. Hsieh sold the company to Amazon in 2009, and then shifted his attention to other lofty goals—including rejuvenating the decaying downtown area of Las Vegas, his adopted home.

**VALUE AT PEAK:** Zappos sold to Amazon for $1.2 billion.

**VALUE NOW:** Hard to say, but Amazon is the most valuable retailer in the world.

**WHAT'S HE UP TO TODAY:** Hsieh passed away in November 2020 due to injuries from a fire; the circumstances under which he died are unclear, though friends—including singer Jewel—had expressed concern over his health and drug use in the months before his death.

## SABEER BHATIA

In 1996, on the Fourth of July, Bhatia and his colleague Jack Smith launched Hotmail, one of the first web-based email systems (they chose the date because they believed their startup symbolized "freedom from ISP-based email," surely what the founding fathers had in mind). Bhatia continued to lead the company as CEO until it was acquired by Microsoft.

**VALUE AT PEAK:** Microsoft bought it for $400 million.

**VALUE NOW:** Nothing. Microsoft shut Hotmail down in 2011, and launched Outlook.com the following year.

**WHAT'S HE UP TO TODAY:** Bhatia has launched a number of other startups, but none have garnered the same heat as Hotmail.

## JOSEPH PARK

Investment banker Park and his friend Yong Kang had an idea for a service that would deliver a bunch of things—DVDs (remember those?), books, food, and gadgets—to residents of major cities in the U.S. within one hour. They convinced investors to give them close to $280 million, including $60 million from Amazon. The company, Kozmo.com, crashed in April 2001, laying off 1,100 employees.

Within a decade, Zappos was doing $1 billion in annual revenues, based on a mantra that customer happiness should be everything. Hsieh sold the company to Amazon in 2009, and then shifted his attention to other lofty goals—including rejuvenating the decaying downtown area of Las Vegas, his adopted home.

**VALUE AT PEAK:** They filed to go public in May 2000 with an expected valuation of over $1 billion.

**VALUE NOW:** It's a smoking crater.

**WHAT'S HE UP TO TODAY:** Park went on to work at Amazon, where he founded a Q&A site called "Askville" (now shuttered), then joined Zondervan to help them develop their online site BibleGateway.com. After a stint at Forever 21 as global VP of e-commerce, he joined Mattel as the toy company's global chief e-commerce officer.

## RAM SHRIRAM

Shriram was an early member of the executive team at Netscape, then was recruited to become president of an online shopping comparison startup called Junglee, which Amazon bought in 1998. Shriram joined Amazon and worked with the company until 2000, when he left to launch his own venture fund, Sherpalo Ventures.

**VALUE AT PEAK:** Amazon bought it for $280 million.

**VALUE NOW:** A donut hole. Amazon shut it down in 2012 after a brief attempt to use it to crack the India market.

**WHAT'S HE UP TO TODAY:** Shriram was smart enough to invest in a company called Google, and was a member of its founding board. Between that and his investments via Sherpalo (which include Paperless Post and Yubico), he's worth an estimated $2.3 billion.

## NAVEEN JAIN

After graduating from college in 1983, Jain worked for Unisys in New Jersey, and then moved to Silicon Valley for better weather, bouncing around different companies before landing at Microsoft in 1989, where he rose to the position of manager of the fledgling Microsoft Network. But after seeing Netscape raise $2.2 billion in an IPO in 1995, a restless Jain quit Microsoft to launch InfoSpace with six employees. The business was essentially copying phone books and other databases onto the Internet and then providing the content to websites and mobile companies. Somehow the business managed to get to a size where it was able to go public, in December 1998, raising $75 million and making Jain a billionaire.

**VALUE AT PEAK:** As of early 2000, over $20 billion

**VALUE NOW:** The directory and mobile content businesses, the heart of InfoSpace, were sold for $360 million in 2007; the sodden rags of the original company's assets were sold off for $45 million in 2016. In the interim, the company, renamed Blucora for some reason, had acquired a tax-prep company called TaxACT, which became its new focus. Today, that business is worth about $850 million.

**WHAT'S HE UP TO TODAY:** Jain allegedly engaged in various shady practices that led him to get forced out as CEO in 2002. He and his wife were then forced to make a $105 million settlement with his former company for insider trading. Since then, he's founded other companies, like Intelius, TalentWise, and BlueDot, as well as Moon Express, which is building robot spacecraft to mine the moon. He also collects meteorites.

## GUNJAN SINHA

Sinha began his career as an engineer at Olivetti, before launching his first startup in 1994, Parsec Technology. The following year, he created one of the first search engines, called WhoWhere? In 1998, he sold it to Lycos.

**VALUE AT PEAK:** Lycos bought it for $133 million.

**VALUE NOW:** Nada. Lycos went public, and then in 2000 was acquired by Terra Networks, the Internet arm of Spanish telecom Telefonica, for $12.5 billion. Just four years later, Terra sold Lycos to Korean software giant Kakao for $95.4 million. Kakao tried to sell Lycos to Ybrant Digital for $36 million in 2010, but Ybrant was unable to come up

with the funds, so the assets reverted to Kakao. It somehow . . . still exists? But WhoWhere? long ago turned to vapor.

**WHAT'S HE UP TO TODAY:** Sinha went on to found eGain, a software company that went public in 1998. He's the chairman of an incubator and holding company called OpenGrowth, as well as its nonprofit arm, OpenGrowth.org.

## JAMES HONG AND JIM YOUNG

In 2000, Hong and Young created a voting site, "Am I Hot Or Not," to settle an argument between them over whether a passing woman was attractive. Within a week, the site was getting two million page views a day. The duo added features allowing people to upload their own photos for evaluation, as well as to vote on the hotness (or notness) of others, renaming

After seeing Netscape raise $2.2 billion in an IPO in 1995, a restless Jain quit Microsoft to launch InfoSpace with six employees. The business was essentially copying phone books and other databases onto the Internet and then providing the content to websites and mobile companies.

it simply HotOrNot.com. Within a few months, the site was among the top 25 most visited content sites on the Internet, and the duo added a matchmaking/dating element to the service, which became extremely popular. In 2008, they sold the site to Avid Life Media, parent company of Ashley Madison, a dating site for partnered people who want to have affairs.

**VALUE AT PEAK:** Avid Life Media was rumored to have bought HotOrNot.com for about $20 million.

**VALUE NOW:** Hard to say. HotOrNot.com now redirects to "ChatDate.app," a dating site of mysterious provenance and ownership.

**WHAT THEY'RE UP TO TODAY:** Both founders are living lives as investors, world travelers, and parents of multiple children.

# How to "AZN"

**BY PHILIP WANG**

**IN THE MID-1990S,** a new generation of Asian Americans took control of their youth culture, finding a deep sense of pride—or rather "PrYdE"—in their identity. Thanks to the early Internet, Asians across the country could connect with each other and their motherlands through dial-up modems, overcoming the social and geographical isolation experienced by many in our community. We could complain about school and parents, talk about anime and cars, find friends and flirt, in different chatrooms and forums. These were a digital third place relatively free of adult supervision, where new interests, styles, and trends could evolve, creating a brand-new, uniquely Asian American subculture that burst free of its online origins and into RL: AZN Culture. Young Asians gravitated to the three-letter shorthand because it distanced them from nerdy, submissive stereotypes, giving them a persona that was defiant enough to be cool, but not so

rebellious as to get into trouble. AZN Pryde had slang, syntax, a soundtrack, and a sense of style—much of it heavily borrowed from Black culture—plus a uniquely dawn-of-the-digital-era visual aesthetic, defined by rotating dragon GIFs, yin-yang symbols, and the alternately rebellious and romantic cartoon art of Jonny Ngo, a.k.a. "Jonny Angel," whose doodles celebrated teen love and AZN self-esteem. "I've always been a hopeless romantic," says Ngo. "I grew up in a time when you'd express how you felt about someone with 'Precious Moments' cartoons. But I wanted those cartoons to represent who I was and what my heritage meant to me. So I expressed that through these drawings. And something that started off very personal to me grew to become a reflection of how the Asian community was starting to see itself." Here's a guide to the things that made up the AZN lyfe for bOiZ and GuRlz of the Nineties and early 2000s.

# The Words

AZN-speak was a bizarre fusion of the hacker/gamer dialect known as 1337 (e.g., "leet," short for "elite"), borrowed hip-hop diction, and text-messaging shorthand that existed only on and for the Internet. Here were the rules of AZN-speak:

- Type words with rAndOMLy AltTerNAtIng upper and lowercase letters, and occasional stray numbers
- Use obscure acronyms (the randoms hitting you up in chat with "ASL?"—Age, Sex, Location)
- Drop hip-hop slang (wassup, yo, aite, dawg, gangstas, killa, etc.) where possible*
- Reclaim slurs: Chink, Jap, slant, yella, gook, FOB are okay if you say it, not okay if they do
- Replace hard S with Z ("boyz"), Y for I and vice versa ("lyfe," "boi"), use texting shortcuts (U for "you," UR for "your" and "you're," R for "are," N for "and"), truncate Ts (like you jus don care)
- Punctuation is unnecessary, but *asterisks*, ~ tildes ~, and xxxtra xxxxs are your friends. So are emoticons, the all-text emoji that existed before emoji :-), especially the extreme Japanese versions (ō_ō)

**EXAMPLE:**

*("Hey, baby, what are you doing? Would you like to spend time with me this evening? I miss you.")*
*("Okay.")*

# The Platforms

**AIM:** Short for AOL Instant Messenger. AZNs lived by the buddy list and the digital sounds of doors opening and closing that told them their crush had signed on and off without responding to that late-night "sup."

**ICQ:** All the normies were on AOL; people on ICQ were special.

**ASIAN AVENUE:** Imagine, an entire social media platform just for Asians.

**ANGELFIRE:** The go-to place to build your own aZn PrYdE website from scratch, or check out the soft-focus low-res pics on your bestie's. Don't forget to sign the guestbook!

**XANGA:** Launched in 1999, and immediately became the blogging platform of choice for AZNs graduating from Angelfire, but wanting somewhere to be emo in public.

**LIVEJOURNAL:** Also launched in 1999, but catering to a crowd that had aged out of Xanga. Xanga was so high school! LiveJournal was where you could, like, talk about life and philosophy and stuff and also post your Cloud and Tifa fanfic.

> Young Asians gravitated to the three-letter shorthand because it distanced them from nerdy, submissive stereotypes, giving them a persona that was defiant enough to be cool, but not so rebellious as to get into trouble.

---

\* See page 425, "Black and Asian: A Conversation"

## The Visuals

**JONNY NGO GRAPHICS:** Somehow these crude, bite-sized cartoon images created by "Jonny Angel," a.k.a. Jonny Ngo, ended up being the preferred decor for everyone's Angelfire website. If you didn't email one of these to your BB, were you *even* in love?

**BAD BADTZ-MARU, POCHACCO, KEROPPI:** Your favorite Sanrio character was like a K-pop bias. Once you picked yours, you were loyal (guys too).

**MORNING GLORY:** There were Sanrio girls, and there were Morning Glory girls. Either way, these were an improvement over Lisa Frank rainbow dolphins.

**PHOTO STUDIOS AND KIOSKS:** Selfies before selfies existed. Grab your boo, or your crew (because you had to have a crew), and head to the mall's photo studio. Girls in matching outfits, boys doing their best to mean mug, all trying to look as cute and cool as possible in front of generic color gradient backdrops and fake Doric columns. The next evolution: those Japanese "purikura" photo booths that started popping up in Asian shopping centers across North America, which drew AZN kids in like moths with soft-focus lighting, digital stickers, and of course the ability to adjust eye and nose size.

**DRAGONS & BRUSH STROKES:** Cliché? Stereotypical? Sure. But AZN boiz owned these tropes, Photoshopping them with drop shadows and 3-D edges into all of their web art and mix CD covers.

## The MP3s

**"GOT RICE?":** Half-tacky homage to a milk slogan, half-racist/problematic lyrical content, this song, created in 1998 by a young Chinese American rapper from Texas named "Joey Lo Flow," became the anthem for "AZN PrYde," blasted from the windows of lowered Honda Civics across the country.

**R&B:** For the wannabe love thugs: wall-to-wall slow jams and ballads by Black soul artists and a few Asian American ones (Kai, Drop n Harmony, Innerlude, One Vo1ce, Pinay, Premiere), interspersed with Canto/Mando/K/J-pop faves.

**TRANCE:** For the ravers, high-tempo techno tracks to get the glowsticks swinging and the LED "photons" spinning.

My first screenname was actually JonnyAzn. The term AZN Pride wasn't really a big thing when I started my drawings but feeling like an outcast most of my life, finding a great group of friends that had similar interests really made me proud to be who I was and for sure had major influence at the height of my art.

# Asian Avenue, Annotated

## BY ESTHER TSENG

**IN THE MID-NINETIES,** even the earliest social network pioneers, like Friendster and MySpace, didn't exist. In fact, social networks as a concept didn't exist. But across America, there were millions of young Asian Americans thirsting to connect with one another, and many of them were doing it on the nascent platform of the World Wide Web.

Seeing this surge of activity online firsthand, in July 1997, a group of entrepreneurial twenty-somethings—Benjamin Sun, Peter Chen, Grace Chang, Michael Montero, and Calvin Wong—were inspired to launch a website that sought to bring online Asian Americans together: a little cul-de-sac off the digital superhighway they dubbed Asian Avenue.

Asian Avenue was one of those classic startup success stories: It was cobbled together in the apartment the founders shared, pooling their savings from jobs in finance (cofounder Sun had left a job with Merrill Lynch to lead the startup as CEO) and seed money from friends and family. Targeting Asian Americans on campus, it grew to thousands of members almost entirely by word of mouth, enough for them to raise $1.3 million in venture capital—a relief to the team, who had gone unpaid for much of their first year and, as they prominently noted on their corporate site, largely subsisted on Kentucky Fried Chicken. As they continued to grow Asian Avenue, driving membership growth by giving away free promo CDs featuring tracks from popular Asian American musicians, they also launched sites targeted at other culturally cohesive groups, under the banner of their parent company, Community Connect:

BlackPlanet for African Americans, MiGente for Hispanics, and eventually, GLEE for "gays, lesbians, and everyone else" and FaithBase. com for Christians.

Of these, only BlackPlanet approached, and eventually exceeded, the membership and activity volume of Asian Avenue, which at its peak had 2 million users with 5,000 online at any given time. Ultimately, with the advent of other, broader-reaching social networking sites, Asian Avenue met its end; Community Connect, which had raised around $22 million in funding over its lifetime, was sold to Black media titan UrbanOne for $38 million. Though UrbanOne still operates a version of BlackPlanet, it shut the other sites down almost immediately, including Asian Avenue. Regardless, the site will always hold a special place for Asian Americans who, at that time, were just beginning to unlock the potential of connecting with others of a shared identity across the wide expanse of the Internet.

It might be easy to dismiss Asian Avenue as a site for idle socializing, and yes, it absolutely was that. But at the same time, it also served as one of the few online hubs for young Asian Americans to share their opinions on social issues. One such example was when, during the 1998 Winter Olympics, the MSNBC headline "American Beats Out Kwan" caused an uproar. Tuned-in Asian Avenue members flooded the newsroom with angry emails. MSNBC subsequently apologized. A year later, members also united to protest a SKYY Vodka ad campaign in which a white woman was depicted being served by an Asian woman dressed in a

1. **MEMBER COUNTER:** Asian Avenue encouraged FOMO (fear of missing out) in two ways: first, by letting you know how many members were already on the site, kind of like McDonald's tracking the number of cheeseburgers it's sold (billions and billions, at this point) . . .

2. **"WHO'S ONLINE" COUNTER:** . . . and by telling you how many members were logged in *at this very moment,* what are you waiting for? The "who's online" counter always seemed to be in the thousands; who knows if it was just a ploy.

3. **FREE MEMBERSHIP:** It cost nothing to join, as Asian Avenue repeatedly said, except if you wanted to see your "secret admirers" and identify your "crushes" it did in fact cost $19.99 per month. But getting that free account as "AZNcy00tipYe" cost nothing, and gave you access to a bunch of features available elsewhere (but not as Asian): Chats, Personal Pages, IMs, Articles, Forums, Events, and Free Internet Email (assuming you wanted to actually get email at AZNcy00tipYe@mail.asianavenue.com).

4. **MAIN PAGE:** Once you'd logged in, you faced a bunch of options. The green area let you access your mail (called "Notes") to see who was sending you random "add me" requests, your friends list to see what randos you'd already added, and your

personal page, where you could share photos to encourage more people to send you random add requests.

5. **THE PINK SECTION:** Let you check your flirting activity in a more direct way.

6. **JOBS:** Did anyone really get a job through Asian Avenue?

7. **NEWS:** News of interest to Asians . . . but also, FLIRT with other members!

8. **GIANT AD:** Asian Avenue had to make money somehow, and advertising was the main way it did it. By 2000, they'd scored 20 sponsorship deals generating around $100,000 apiece.

9. **MEMBER OF THE WEEK:** Who knows how Asian Avenue picked its MotW, but if you got selected, you'd get a ton of profile views.

10. **FIND A DATE:** If you're getting the feeling that the reason people were on Asian Avenue was to hook up, you're not wrong.

11. **EDIT YOUR PAGE:** Asian Avenue began as a site that let people create their own web pages. Its founders decided to emphasize the "social" aspect of the community when a tool that let you see which people had stalked—er, visited—your site emerged as the site's most actively used feature.

12. **MAIN PHOTO:** If you were a girl, it really didn't matter what you put here, you'd still get 15 Notes a day from random guys.

13. **PERSONAL MESSAGES:** "Sup, ur cute."

14. **MEMBER DOCK:** Yet another way to scour through Asian Avenue to find that special someone. Or you could use the "surprise me!" feature, if you dared.

15. **ASIANAVE.COM:** In 2007, Asian Avenue relaunched as "AsianAve," with a new logo and look, and an even heavier emphasis on meeting people. Register now! It's free and easy.

qipao and chopsticks in her hair. The liquor company pulled the campaign. Asian Avenue also brought its membership together for positive causes, such as the Asian bone marrow registry, created to make it easier to find matching donors for cancer patients in need of transplants. The website was a primary advocate on behalf of Cindy Moy, a 28-year-old Chinese American New Yorker with leukemia. Over 7,000 Asians around the world underwent tests to see if they were marrow matches, and ultimately a match was found in Singapore. Though Moy ultimately passed away despite the surgery, the match gave her a few more months to spend with her friends and family—and provided proof that the Internet offered Asians scattered across a nation and even around the globe a new and powerful way of connecting, collaborating, and creating community.

# POSTCARD FROM ASIAN AMERICA

BY JAMIE FORD

Dear RISE,

I'm stealth Asian. Not like a ninja, though that would be cool, too. I'm half-Chinese with the last name Ford, so I confuse people. Growing up in Seattle, Washington, in the 1980s, strangers would assume I was Amerasian and that my father had been a GI in Vietnam. Or they'd think I was Native. Or—and this was always a favorite—they'd think I was Russian. The Cold War was still smoldering in the American psyche, so that was as good a guess as any, comrade. I looked so different from my classmates in high school that one Halloween, when I worked in our class haunted house as the Devil—complete with red cape, pitchfork, and a devil mask—my pimple-faced peers said "Wow, you really do look like Satan!" That was without my mask.

Now I live in Montana, where I'm devilishly handsome, and once again, ethnically ambiguous. I fly beneath the radar in a town founded by a man who, in the 1800s, famously ran off all of the Chinese. There's even a statue of him in a park. Whenever I walk by, I take a selfie and say, "Look who's back, bitch."

Yours,

Jamie

P.S. In case you're wondering, around 1890, my great-grandfather changed his name from "Min Chung" to "William Ford." When people ask if he was a pioneer I say, "Yeah, he pioneered identity theft."

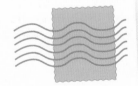

RISE
HERE AND NOW,
ASIAN AMERICA

# THE STYLE LIST

## BY FAWNIA SOO HOO

**THE EARLIEST WAVES** of Asian immigration may have been involved with fashion primarily through garment factories or storefront tailor shops—but by the 1990s, Asian Americans, many of whom had grown up as the children or grandchildren of textile workers, had started to step into the couture-world spotlight. Here are five Asian Americans who played an outsized role in defining the decade's lines and looks.

## ANNA SUI

**BEST KNOWN FOR:** Her 1991 debut at New York Fashion Week, with supermodel friends Naomi Campbell, Linda Evangelista, and Christy Turlington walking for free

**SIGNATURE LOOK:** Pop culture fever dream

**ASIAN INSPIRATION:** Shades of lucky red; her Fall 2014 collection, featuring '20s silhouettes that paid homage to the first Chinese American Hollywood starlet, Anna May Wong

Originally from Dearborn, Michigan, the Chinese American designer was a stalwart fixture of the New York club scene, who launched her self-titled label in 1981 and steadily grew it into a global powerhouse brand that has expanded into beauty, home, and accessories. Her career skyrocketed after Madonna wore her dress to Jean Paul Gaultier's Paris Fashion Week show in 1991; Sui continues to be a favorite of the supermodel set decades later.

## VERA WANG

**BEST KNOWN FOR:** Designing wedding gowns for A-list brides, including Mariah Carey, Victoria Beckham, Alicia Keys, and Chrissy Teigen

**SIGNATURE LOOK:** Uptown romantic meets downtown edge

**ASIAN INSPIRATION:** The floral prints, kimono and origami silhouettes, and obi belts in her Spring 2011 ready-to-wear collection

After 15 years as an editor at *Vogue,* Chinese American Wang launched her own bridal specialty line in 1990, quickly becoming the most sought-after wedding-dress designer in America. It was only natural that Wang's expansion into evening wear would become a red carpet staple—and a White House favorite: she designed Michelle Williams's iconic marigold dress for the 2006 Oscars and First Lady Michelle Obama's glamorous off-the-shoulder gown for the 2015 China State Dinner.

## VIVIENNE TAM

**BEST KNOWN FOR:** The short-sleeve dress from her "Mao" collection featured in the 2015 exhibit "China: Through the Looking Glass" at the Metropolitan Museum of Art's Costume Institute

**SIGNATURE LOOK:** Sinocentric glamour meets New York City chic

**ASIAN INSPIRATION:** Floral and nature embroideries, qipao silhouettes, Buddha and watercolor prints

Born in Guangzhou and raised in Hong Kong, Tam established her fashion line in New York in 1982, debuting with her brand East Wind Code, and then, in 1993, launching her own self-named line at New York Fashion Week. She scored her first *Vogue* spot with her spring 1995 "Mao" collection, featuring colorful T-shirts, mesh dresses, and suits emblazoned with cheeky pop art of Mao Zedong by Chinese American artist Zhang Hongtu. Fran Drescher wore one of her black and white Mao miniskirts on an episode of her '90s hit sitcom, *The Nanny,* while Jennifer Aniston wore another signature Tam piece, a floral-embroidered mesh dress, in season four of *Friends.*

## TYSON BECKFORD

**BEST KNOWN FOR:** Starring in that 1993 campaign, shot by Bruce Weber, for usually WASP-y Ralph Lauren Polo Sport

**SIGNATURE LOOK:** That "Blue Steel" gaze (Beckford had a cameo in 2001's *Zoolander*)

**ASIAN INSPIRATION:** His paternal grandmother is Jamaican Chinese.

As a child, Beckford, who is of Afro-Jamaican, Panamanian, and Chinese heritage, faced racist taunts from classmates calling him "Mr. Chin" for his multiracial features (and maybe his chiseled chin?). The Bronx native was discovered in 1992 by a scout looking to cast for a photo spread in hip-hop magazine *The Source.* Beckford went on to become the first Black male supermodel, lending his devastating cheekbones to numerous brands, including Ralph Lauren, Gucci, Karl Kani, and Calvin Klein.

## JENNY SHIMIZU

**BEST KNOWN FOR:** Starring alongside in 1994's iconic Steven Meisel–shot Calvin Klein CK1 fragrance campaign

**SIGNATURE LOOK:** Choppy pixie cut and badass tattoos

**ASIAN INSPIRATION:** She's third-generation Japanese American.

Shimizu was discovered while working as an auto mechanic in Los Angeles, and quickly booked gigs with top designers, including Calvin Klein, Anna Sui, Jean Paul Gaultier, Yohji Yamamoto, and Donna Karan. She became the first Asian model to walk the Prada runway at Milan Fashion Week in October 1993. She also fronted Banana Republic's "American Beauty" campaign in the '90s. An out lesbian and longtime LGBTQ+ activist, Shimizu is now married, but once upon a time was in and out of tabloids for relationships with Ione Skye, Madonna, and Angelina Jolie (her costar in the 1996 indie film *Foxfire*).

# GENERASIAN GAP

BY TESS PARAS, FEATURING PHILIP WANG, SONAL SHAH, TESS PARAS, AND NATHAN RAMOS PARK

PHOTOGRAPHED BY MOLLY PAN

## AZN BOiz:

Nike warmup over white T-shirt or tank top (or Nautica/Polo Sport/Tommy Hilfiger if you're trying to impress). JNCO jeans, you know the ones, made with five yards of denim, pockets that go down to your knees, and hems so wide they scream "I also DJ on the side!" Immaculate white K-Swiss kicks. Hair buzzed tight around the back and sides, long on top with spikes, a middle split, or "antenna bangs," probably with blond tips. Liberal splash of Cool Water or Curve cologne. Typical accessories: a visor or ski goggles (for some reason). A Honda Civic with spoiler, or Acura Integra, RSX, or S2000 for the players. Make sure to top it off with as hard a "mean mug" as you can manage.

## AZN BaBy GuRLs:

Marshmallow jackets or Adidas warmup over skin-tight baby tee (because nothing says women's fashion like literally infantilizing yourself to appeal to guys!). Make sure that shirt is small enough to show your pierced belly button. If you don't want the commitment of a piercing (and who needs commitment?), why not a belly chain? Bottom this with JNCO flares or tight jeans and three-inch platform shoes. As far as hair goes, start with highlights or full-on contrasting streaks; pull most of it up in that bun and make sure to leave out two tendrils to frame your face. If you have a little edge, go for that blunt bob that stops at your—you guessed it—choker necklace. Makeup? Brown lipstick (something with the word "toast" in the name usually did the trick) or brown lip liner with some of that sticky, icky lip gloss. Make friends with your tweezer for those super-thin, high-arched eyebrows. Make friends with your optometrist and snag some colored contacts because, sure, we think you were born with those violet-gray eyes. Top with a spritz of Tommy Girl perfume. Accessorize with a baby backpack—so small that the only thing that fits is your pager, with a saved message from boyfriend: 143-637-823-247 = "I love you always and forever, thinking about you 24 hours and 7 days a week."

# SPEED RACERS

BY PHILIP WANG

**NOWHERE IN THE** world is car culture more deeply ingrained than in America—the nation with the biggest road and highway network in the world, the nation that invented the hot rod and the muscle car, the nation that's written over 70,000 songs about cars and driving. In America, automobiles are a symbol of belonging, status, and freedom. So it's not surprising that as immigrant cultures integrated into American society, their kids embraced American car culture as well . . . while making it uniquely their own. Latinx teens invented the lowrider: vintage cars whose lowered blocks allowed them to hover inches above the tarmac. For Asian youth of the 1990s and beyond, car culture expressed itself via the import tuning scene, whose enthusiasts took Japanese vehicles often handed down by their parents and turned them into eye-catching cultural statements with upgraded engines and custom body kits wringing performance and swagger out of unassuming econoboxes.

Import tuning was as much about resistance and identity as it was about cars. When the founding fathers of import culture, Frank Choi and Ken Miyoshi, first showed up at the drag races held regularly at the Los Angeles County Raceway in Palmdale, California, in the late Eighties, they weren't allowed to race because the event was for "domestics only"—a phrase that probably wasn't meant to apply solely to the vehicles.

In response, the pair regrouped and took over the entire track themselves. In the summer of 1990, Choi and Miyoshi hosted the first "import-only" race, Battle of the Imports. The event jumpstarted an import car culture that would accelerate through the Nineties and 2000s, and eventually go mainstream via the billion-dollar *Fast & Furious* franchise, albeit with Asians pushed into the background. Here's a look at the import scene from four different perspectives, each representing a unique and critical element of the subculture: **MICHAEL CHANG**, CEO of aftermarket performance parts supplier Evasive Motorsports; **CARTER JUNG**, former editor in chief of the scene's bible, *Import Tuner*; **MIKE MUNAR**, CEO of the biggest import car show, Hot Import Nights; and actress/singer **KAILA YU**, one of the most popular models on the import scene.

## Wheels Make the Man

**MICHAEL CHANG:** Cars are part of American culture, but Asian Americans have our own take on what's cool, and being able to personalize our cars meant everything to us. A customized car was a way to show who was driving it, a form of identity expression. In some ways it was a rebel culture; back in the Nineties, everyone had a car crew, and everyone wanted to know the guy who had the coolest car. When I was 19, I got my first car—an Integra—and I started messing with it right away. My hobby quickly turned into a business. I started selling parts out of my garage in 2000. I'd meet people at car shows, figure out how to get parts at a discount, and then I'd sell them to people around the country who had no idea how to get them. Remember, this was before e-commerce was big. These days, most of our customers are

Photo courtesy of Carter Jung

still Asian, but we get people from all walks of life. We've expanded beyond just imports, but haven't lost that Japanese tuning style. We put pieces together to create a look, and essentially show people, "This is how your car should be built." Because even though people can have the same parts, it's about technique, assembly, and presentation. It's like cooking. You can have the same ingredients and come out with totally different dishes.

> Growing up as an Asian guy in the Nineties, before social media, your car was part of your identity. So I wasn't Carter, I was "Carter with the Integra."

Tuning culture allowed Asians to feel like rock stars. The entry point was a Honda Civic, but if you could build it up, you could get respect and publicity. Anyone could become the coolest guy ever.

## Social Before Social Media

**CARTER JUNG:** Asians were shunned by white guys who were into muscle cars, but imports were uniquely ours. Growing up as an Asian guy in the Nineties, before social media, your car was part of your identity. So I wasn't Carter, I was "Carter with the Integra."

As the tuning/show scene was emerging, major publishing companies realized they had to start covering it. *Motor Trend* was the first to create an offshoot dedicated to Japanese imports, called *Super Street. Import Tuner* was an offshoot of *Turbo* magazine, which at the time also only focused on domestics. At one time there were around 12 magazines dedicated to the culture! But *Import Tuner* became part of the lexicon. I remember Asian kids would carry around issues with them. It was a platform for an audience that didn't have a voice in the media.

Above: Kaila Yu, photo courtesy of Chris Carlo

When magazines started covering what we were doing, it was like our real lives were being reflected for the first time—we had never seen our interests portrayed in media like this. Even if you weren't into cars yourself, you had a friend who was, and it was our first taste of authentic representation. When I became editor of *Import Tuner,* I felt that responsibility. I'm proud that we provided an outlet and a tangible space to congregate.

On another front, cars have always been associated with showgirls and race queens, but *Import Tuner* magazine really made "import modeling" a term. We brought in stylists and real production value. And we put Asian women on the cover.

## Make and Model

**KAILA YU:** Growing up, my idol was Sung Hi Lee, the first Asian *Playboy* cover model. She was the only one I had to look up to. I feel like the previous generations of Asian girls maybe didn't think they were attractive, but my generation thought Asian women were beauti-

ful because of Sung Hi. So there was an intersection of girls trying to be like her—with the import scene rising at the same time, they just kind of merged together, which led to this burst of Asian models all at once.

Still, in terms of the modeling industry, the import scene definitely elevated models far more quickly than anywhere else. Getting covers was such a big deal to us. No other magazine would put Asian girls on a cover. And we'd be right there on the supermarket newsstand! So it became aspirational.

It was empowering, but I do sometimes question, if there were different representations in media, whether that would've been the path I'd choose. Looking back I have mixed feelings about my modeling days. We were celebrated and vilified at the same time. We had lots of fans, but many outside the industry called us slutty, or thought it was an easy job. I'm excited to see that now, for example on Instagram, there are Asian female influencers showing that "sexy" isn't the only road that they can choose to go down—women whom this generation can look up to so they can have a choice.

Photo courtesy of Carter Jung

## Hot Summer Nights

**MIKE MUNAR:** It started for me in the mid-Nineties at UCLA, as a Filipino with friends in the Chinese, Vietnamese, and Korean student unions and in the Asian Greek system. I started throwing massive parties bringing together all these organizations, and doing car meetups at my car shop. Using early social media platforms, we were uniting Asian Americans across the country, and our social events were getting too big for even the biggest nightclubs in L.A.—we spilled into the parking lots. In 1998, we decided to combine the parties *with* the cars *with* the early social media connection, and "Hot Import Nights" was born. Out of our desire to be connected, we were able to get multiple Asian communities to come together and take pride as a larger group.

Assimilation is such a big part of being first-generation Asians. Car shows allowed us to take things that were specifically Asian, put them on a pedestal, and attract mainstream attention and support. And once it went mainstream, it became acceptable. That's when we saw Latinos, Caucasians, everybody saying, "I want to be part of that culture." Nowadays, Hot Import Nights is like a festival, with DJs, dance competitions, e-sports—even drone racing. But it always still has to come back to showcasing the best vehicles: whether it's exotics, Japanese classics, drift cars, we find the best. And no matter what we expand into and what content we make, we hope it still has the DNA of Asian American culture.

## Furious over *Fast & Furious*

**MICHAEL CHANG:** I was actually an extra on the first film. I was there when they filmed it. Although I'm not particularly fond of how they portrayed everything, it transformed what import culture was. Before that movie, import culture was underground, but now businesses are thriving from selling performance parts because of the film alone.

**CARTER JUNG:** When that movie first came out, I hated it. A lot of us in the industry did. The cars were ugly, the graphics were over the top. Plus, where were the Asians? This was *our* culture, and we were erased. There was a casting call for cars to be featured, and I didn't want to be in it. Nowadays, though, I can see how it brought the culture to the masses, and I can appreciate it for that at the very least.

# The 1990s

BY RICHIE "TRAKTIVIST" MENCHAVEZ

**WHAT SONGS BY** Asian American artists dominated our mixtapes and playlists in the Nineties? Filipino American DJ and music archivist Richie Menchavez, better known as "Traktivist," gives his authoritative take.

## "Say You'll Stay," KAI

If you're older, you probably requested this song on late-night slow-jam radio. If you're younger, chances are some of you were conceived to it. KAI, a close-harmony boy group featuring the vocal talents of Leo Chan, Andrew Gapuz, AC Lorenzo, and later, Andrey Silva, Errol Viray, and Johnny Misa, made history as the first all–Asian American group to sign a major record contract, with Geffen Records/Universal Music Group. Their biggest hit, "Say You'll Stay," reached #59 on the Billboard Hot 100 in 1998, which led to a world tour alongside the likes of NSYNC, Usher, and Aaliyah. KAI pioneered the brief Asian American R&B/pop wave of the late 1990s, influencing a generation of artists who'd later conquer YouTube in the 2000s.

## "Galaxies (The Next Level)," Mountain Brothers

As someone who grew up during the Golden Age of Hip-Hop, nothing was more mind-blowing and empowering than watching the music video for "Galaxies" play on MTV's *Total Request Live*. A hip-hop trio consisting of Taiwanese and Chinese American MCs CHOPS (Scott Jung), Peril-L (Christopher Wang), and Styles Infinite (Steve Wei), Mountain Brothers are rightfully revered as Asian American cultural pioneers. With "Galaxies," whose playful original lyrics lace around a head-nodding, sample-free beat, Mountain Brothers took Asian Americans out of the hip-hop periphery and into national underground success—which, startlingly, came after they began releasing their music independently.

## "Do You Miss Me?," Jocelyn Enriquez

If you were a West Coast Asian, you probably heard the remix of this song blasting from the speakers of a souped-up Honda Civic at Hot Import Nights. Jocelyn Enriquez was the first Filipina American solo act to be signed to major label Tommy Boy Records. "Do You Miss Me?" was a Top 40 dance hit, co-released by Tommy Boy and Enriquez's original record label, Classified Records, an indie Asian American–owned label that helped fuel the Bay Area American R&B/soul scene in the late 1990s.

## "1979," Smashing Pumpkins

One can argue that no other musician of this decade shifted the public perception of Asian American men in music more than alt-rock poster boy James Iha, the Japanese American cofounder and contributing songwriter of Smashing Pumpkins. Iha's smoldering good looks made girls swoon (and not just Asian ones), while his fuzzy, growling guitar helped establish the Pumpkins' signature sound. Wistful and dreamy, "1979" was the Pumpkins' biggest mainstream hit, a brilliant and defining electro-pop departure from the grunge decade's predominant rock sound.

## "Is It Real?," Pinay Divas

Whether at your Filipina friend's 18th birthday cotillion, a Club Platinum event in San Francisco, or Legend Entertainment parties in Los Angeles, this high-energy dance track always got the crowd bumping. "Is It Real?," released by Classified Records in 1997, reached #41 on the Billboard Hot Dance chart, the same year when former Pinay Divas member Jocelyn Enriquez broke out as a solo artist. (The group continued on as simply "Pinay" after she left.) Their soulful, versatile voices and captivating beauty led to frequent references to the group as the "Asian En Vogue"; Asian parents loved them because while performing they were also attending grad school and went on to careers in medicine and law.

## "When U Think About Me," One Vo1ce

At the tail end of the decade, the all–Filipina American group One Vo1ce, consisting of Monica Castillo, Marie Ceralvo, Mae Ceralvo, and former members Melissa Ruiz Moreno and Aimee Castillo, stood out among a surge of Asian American R&B groups. Their sultry single "When U Think About Me" was their biggest hit, breaking into the Billboard Top 100 and catching the attention of major record label MCA.

## "Reflection" (Mulan soundtrack version), Lea Salonga

Yes, it's a Disney Princess song, but this theme from the animated feature resonated with many Asian Americans with its lyrics about searching for self-identity. The fact that it was also an emotionally dramatic ballad with a belt-out-loud power chorus made it a carpool karaoke staple and a frequent winning performance at school talent shows. Though

Christina Aguilera sang the pop radio track, the version styled by iconic Filipina diva and actress Lea Salonga (who also served as the singing voice of Princess Jasmine in Disney's earlier Aladdin) was naturally preferred.

## "Before I Fall in Love," Coco Lee

Born in Hong Kong and raised in San Francisco, Lee moved back to Hong Kong as an adult and became one of the region's biggest stars, dubbed the "Asian Mariah Carey" for her vocal range and her platinum sales success. Her record of hits convinced her label, Sony Music, to try to launch her as the first Asian pop star to cross over into the mainstream American pop market. A wedding-reception-friendly mid-tempo romantic ballad, "Before I Fall in Love" landed on the soundtrack of the Julia Roberts hit Runaway Bride. Though it didn't crack the U.S. Hot 100, it topped Asian charts and paved the way for Sony to release her first English-language album, Just No Other Way.

### "Don't Sit Next to Me Just Because I'm Asian," Bruce Lee Band

Smart kids—or "presumed smart" kids—intimately related to this Asian American acoustipunk classic. Comedic yet straight-forward, it hilariously captured the angst and rage of those victimized by test cheaters: *"So I fill out my scantron and then I erase / And the poor guy fails his exams to graduate."* The song was by Mike Park, Korean American founding member of the seminal ska-punk band Skankin' Pickle and creator of DIY punk record label Asian Man Records.

### "Can You Hear It?," Key-Kool & DJ Rhettmatic

This West Coast underground classic by rapper Key-Kool (Japanese American Kikuo Nishi) and Beat Junkies deejay Rhettmatic (Filipino American Nazareth Nirza) embodies the signature Golden Age sound: crafty lyrics, sample-laden melodies and basslines, and the use of a notoriously popular drum loop from Skull Snaps' "It's a New Day." This track, along with their entire critically acclaimed album *Kozmonautz,* was the first hip-hop album released by an Asian American emcee/deejay duo. Key-Kool and Rhettmatic were instrumental in opening up both the possibilities and the opportunities for young Asian Americans who couldn't imagine acceptance and participation in this genre.

### "Berlitz," Seam

One of the most influential groups in the post-punk/emo scene of the Nineties was Seam, the Chicago-based band fronted by Korean American guitarist and vocalist Sooyoung Park. "Berlitz" was released in 1995 with a lineup that included fellow Korean American bassist William Shin. Park and Shin, along with journalist Ben Kim, would go on to curate and release the Asian American indie-rock compilation *Ear of the Dragon.*

SCAN THE
QR CODE TO
DOWNLOAD
THE PLAYLIST

# Asian Home

BY JEFF YANG

Some of us live in apartments, and others in multistory houses. Some of us are more traditional in our decor and design, and others more contemporary. Despite the diversity in our heritages and the distinct stamp they put on our domestic lives, one thing remains consistent: home is where the heart is, where generations—sometimes four or more—and extended family gather, and where old and new worlds intersect.

## Entryway

1. Shoes removed by the door, because we're not barbarians
2. House slippers, because the floors are cold
3. Urn full of umbrellas, walking sticks, and backscratchers

## Living Room

4. Fish tanks, for aesthetic purposes and maybe good fortune
5. Photo albums full of pictures of "uncles" and "aunties" you don't recognize
6. Piano; tearstains have been wiped away
7. Pop sheet music hidden behind classical sheet music
8. Huge TV (not pictured)
9. Remotes, wrapped in plastic
10. Satellite box to pipe in news and variety shows from the "old country" (not pictured)
11. Industrial-strength karaoke machine with multiple microphones
12. Small white dog, not allowed on furniture (on furniture)
13. Ethnic art that's not very attractive but someone famous painted it
14. Ethnic art that's downright ugly but a close family friend gave it as a gift

15. Immersive massage chair
16. Low coffee table
17. Tea set
18. Lucky plants
19. Shrine

## Kitchen

20. Tupperware
21. Takeout containers used as Tupperware
22. Neatly flattened aluminum foil for reusing
23. Plastic bag full of other plastic bags
24. Kitchen scissors (not pictured)
25. Lazy Susan
26. Water dispenser
27. Steamer
28. Daily rice cooker
29. Big rice cooker (special events) (not pictured)
30. Jars, for reusing
31. Ancient wok with the terroir of a thousand meals
32. Grocery bag used as trash bag
33. Dishwasher used as drying rack
34. Grandma asking if you've eaten yet
35. Multiple shelves of spices
36. A section of the pantry just for dried meat and fish (not pictured)
37. 50-pound bag of rice
38. Cubic meter of instant ramen
39. Scallion butts being regrown in little cups of water

# Setting Sail on the Love Boat

## BY VALERIE SOE

**ASK ANY CHINESE** American of a certain age and they'll probably know exactly what you're talking about when you mention the "Love Boat," better known as the Overseas Compatriot Youth Taiwan Study Tour.

It's not the only government-subsidized summer exchange program that sends Asian Americans overseas for cultural immersion, light political indoctrination, and the tantalizing chance to party in a parentally approved-but-not-supervised fashion—there's also the Yonsei International Summer School program, which offers a similar experience for Korean teens—but it's the biggest, the oldest, and maybe the most infamous, allowing hundreds of college-aged Chinese and Taiwanese Americans to run rampant in Taiwan for six weeks every summer at the rock-bottom government-subsidized price of $400 plus airfare.

The Study Tour officially had its start in 1967 with fewer than 50 participants, but by the Eighties, the number of students had already multiplied by a factor of ten. In 1989, attendance was increased to 1,200 per summer, where it stayed through much of the 1990s, turning it into an iconic coming-of-age experience for thousands of college-aged Chinese and Taiwanese Americans.

Yes, the program's high-minded cultural aspirations included Mandarin-language classes, martial arts, and brush painting. But it

wasn't called the Love Boat for nothing. It was notoriously known for fostering summer hookups and romances among its students, an outcome that Chinese parents winked at so long as no one came home pregnant (something that's happened more than once). After all, it was a way to increase the probability of their offspring finding a Nice Chinese Boy/Girl to marry and eventually, not right now, produce Nice Chinese Grandchildren.

For Taiwan, the Love Boat was a handy political tool, an engine of soft-power diplomacy that helped generations of overseas-born Chinese and Taiwanese to immerse themselves in Taiwanese culture and perhaps sympathize with the island's plight, after the United Nations and most of the world's nations severed diplomatic relations with Taiwan in 1971 in favor of recognizing the People's Republic of China instead. (China defines Taiwan as a "rogue province," and is adamant about preventing any of its diplomatic partners from acknowledging otherwise.)

And for many attendees, it worked. "While I was there, I remember I felt a very deep connection to Taiwan," says Love Boat alumnus Justin Tan. "I was like, 'What's happening to me right now? Am I falling in love with this country?' And I absolutely was."

And for participants coming from parts of the world with relatively few fellow Chinese—

**Clockwise from top left:** Image from promotional recruitment video for the Love Boat, circa 1994; friends on the Love Boat, 1982; Love Boat attendees prowling the night market in Taipei, Taiwan, 2016

All images from the documentary *Love Boat: Taiwan* (2019), director: Valerie Soe

like Sweden or the American Midwest—the Love Boat gave them a chance to fall in love with undiscovered aspects of themselves as well. "On the Love Boat, I was amazed to meet Asian Americans my age who were as enthusiastic about scallion pancakes and dragon's beard candy as my Ohio friends were about pizza and donuts," says Abigail Hing Wen, who turned her experiences on the tour into the inspiration for the *New York Times* bestselling YA novel *Loveboat, Taipei.*

The Love Boat as it was in its Nineties heyday no longer exists, though a much reduced, three-week form of the program with around a hundred participants per summer still continues to this day. But the Study Tour's thousands of alumni are out there, most of them still with fond memories of those six summer weeks.

Some of the more notable alums include:

**ELAINE CHAO**, U.S. secretary of transportation and wife of Mitch McConnell

**REP. JUDY CHU**, congresswoman from California

**ROGER FAN**, actor, *Better Luck Tomorrow*

**EDDIE HUANG**, celebrity chef and author of the memoir turned sitcom *Fresh Off the Boat*

**COCO LEE**, Hong Kong pop superstar

**WANG LEEHOM**, Taiwanese American pop superstar

**GARRETT WANG**, actor, *Star Trek: Voyager*

**KRISTINA WONG**, comedian and performance artist

## Bedroom

**40.** Foot massage device

**41.** Back massage device

**42.** Shoulder massage device (not pictured)

**43.** Massage device for part of body that's not quite clear (it was a gift)

**44.** USB sockets everywhere

**45.** An Asian-origin piece of furniture, inherited and somewhat out of place

**46.** Air conditioner, rarely used

**47.** Fan, even more rarely used, because fan exposure can be deadly

## Bathroom

**48.** Rubber bath sandals

**49.** Plastic stool to sit on while washing in the tub

**50.** Second shower head on hose for close-up washing

**51.** Sheet masks in a wide variety of shapes and flavors (not pictured)

**52.** Scrubbies that resemble kitchen scouring pads, but used for turbo exfoliation (not pictured)

**53.** Magic Japanese-made toilet seat that heats, jets, plays music, and maybe massages

**54.** Well-used electric gadgets for dental hygiene and complexion maintenance

**55.** Infrequently used electric razor (not pictured)

## Garage (not pictured)

**56.** Second fridge for spare meat and pungent food

**57.** Tesla or German "show" car plus Honda or Toyota "go" car

**58.** Doilies on car headrests

**59.** Bicycles

**60.** Bags of outgrown clothes, waiting for next child to grow into them

## Outdoors

**61.** Garden, producing surprising quantity of produce

**62.** Replanted scallion butts

**63.** Badminton/volleyball net

## Basement (not pictured)

**64.** Ping-pong table that parents use to demonstrate there's one thing the kids will never be better at

**65.** Play area with baby toys; will be here long after kids have gone off to college

**66.** Pullout couch for kids to sleep on when relatives visit from the old country

**67.** Random unfinished storage space full of dry goods, vintage hoardings, holiday decorations

# Boba Triumphant

BY CLARISSA WEI, ILLUSTRATED BY STEPHANIE LIN

THAT VERSION OF BOBA WAS BROUGHT TO THE STATES BY ENTERPRISING TAIWANESE IMMIGRANTS IN THE 1990S.

BOBA to GOGA

By the way, the reason it's called "boba" is because it looks like boo--

Don't say it.

YES, IN TAIWAN, "BOBA" IS SLANG FOR BOOBS.

DEDICATED *BOBA CAFES* SOON POPPED UP IN EAST AND SOUTHEAST ASIAN ENCLAVES ACROSS THE NATION.

Chatime

Quickly

CoCo

Tapioca Express

Tea Station

TenRen's Tea

We don't even have to try...

.....'Cause we're livin' boba life

BY THE 2000S, IT WAS THE DRINK OF A GENERATION OF *YOUNG ASIANS* -- THE *BOBA GENERATION.*

BUT THINGS DIDN'T STOP *THERE.* BOBA SHOPS POPPED UP IN *SHOPPING MALLS* AND ON BUSY *STREET CORNERS,* OPERATED BY HIP CHAINS LIKE BOBA GUYS AND KUNG FU TEA, AND 7 LEAVES IN 2017, THE *NEW YORK TIMES* EVEN WROTE UP BOBA AS A *HOT NEW TREND.*

"BLOBS" IN YOUR TEA?

TODAY, THE BOBA CAFE IS A *GATHERING GROUND* FOR YOUNG AND OLD—*FAMILIES* AND GROUPS OF *FRIENDS, ASIANS* AND *NON-ASIANS.*

BOPOMOFO

*THAT* DIDN'T GO SO WELL, BUT NOTHING COULD SLOW THE *BOBAMENTUM.* BY 2019, THERE WERE AT LEAST 3,000 BOBA CAFES IN AMERICA, AND THE GLOBAL BOBA MARKET WAS WORTH OVER *$2 BILLION.*

BOBA IS SOMETHING THAT'S ASIAN AMERICAN WITHOUT NEED FOR *TRANSLATION* OR *EXPLANATION.* WHICH IS WHY FOR MANY OF US, IT ISN'T JUST A DELICIOUS DRINK: IT'S A DEFIANT PART OF OUR *IDENTITY* AND *CULTURE.*

ROSALIND CHAO

LAUREN TOM

# *The Joy Luck Club* Remembered

BY PHIL YU

**WHEN *CRAZY RICH ASIANS*** was released to widespread fanfare in 2018, it seemed as though journalists were all legally obligated to note that it was the first major Hollywood studio film with an all-Asian cast in a full quarter-century—that is, since 1993's *The Joy Luck Club*. The oft-cited fact not only serves to highlight the infrequency of representation for Asian Americans in feature films, it also speaks to *The Joy Luck Club*'s enduring status as arguably the most influential Asian American film of the past three decades.

TAMLYN TOMITA

MING-NA WEN

Adapted from the bestselling novel by Amy Tan, directed by Wayne Wang and starring an octet of Hollywood's most talented Asian American actresses, *The Joy Luck Club* interweaves the stories of four Chinese American women and their immigrant mothers, exploring their complex relationships, painful personal histories, and tangled bicultural identities. Ultimately, the film was just a modest critical and commercial success, but it served as perhaps the first real demonstration of what Asian American cinema with a meaningful budget and star-studded cast could look like. Unfortunately, even that didn't trigger the deluge of cinematic opportunity that some predicted and many hoped for. It would take decades, with many false starts along the way, before Hollywood gave it another go. But its impact on Asian American culture persists—and it still sparks spirited debate and unleashes tears at revival screenings today.

Nearly 30 years later, much like their movie moms gathering around a mah-jongg table, the *Joy Luck* daughters—**ROSALIND CHAO** ("Rose"), **LAUREN TOM** ("Lena"), **TAMLYN TOMITA** ("Waverly"), and **MING-NA WEN** ("June")—joined us to take a nostalgic look back at their career-defining roles, the unique sisterhood the movie inspired, the unfair burdens of being "the one," and this special film's lasting legacy.

## Joining the Club

*When the movie's producers sent out the call for eight—eight!—Asian female leads, it shook the firmament of Asian American Hollywood. Actresses auditioned from all across the nation, recognizing that this was a unique, perhaps once-in-a-lifetime opportunity. For some,*

*getting cast meant meeting their fellow "sisters" for the first time; for others, it represented a rare chance to work alongside friends, rather than competing with them for roles.*

**MING-NA:** At the time, I was doing theater and soap operas. I thought of myself as a theater girl at the time—my dream was to be on Broadway, I'd never really considered Hollywood. But they were auditioning a bunch of girls in New York, so I decided to give it a shot. I'd known of everyone's careers, but getting *Joy Luck Club* was when I actually met the other girls for the first time. I was very much the new kid in town.

**TAMLYN:** It was the late Eighties when I first heard of this actress named "Ming-Na"—she was playing Lien Hughes in the soap opera *As the World Turns*. And the soap *Santa Barbara* brought me in to audition for the role of Ming Li, who was apparently *inspired* by Ming-Na, so her name stuck in my head. When I met her, all the pieces came together. I was like, so this is Ming! This is the gal from New York.

**ROSALIND:** Meanwhile, I happened to be a soap opera freak, so I knew Ming and her work too. And Tamlyn and I knew each other from the *Miss Saigon* protests. I still remember holding her hand and crying in the Equity office. You could say it was a bonding experience.

**LAUREN:** I'd been in New York for a decade, and finally came out to L.A. in 1990. I started as a dancer, but was pushed to study acting because I was told dancing is like being an athlete—you're usually done by 35. That was *really* good advice, and I gave up dancing.

**ROSALIND:** I did this movie *Thousand Pieces of Gold,* and Wayne Wang was working in San Francisco with the movie's costume designer,

Lydia Tanji, which is how I first heard that they were making the film. I'd read the book, of course. *Joy Luck Club*'s casting director happened to have lunch with a friend of mine and asked her for recommendations of Asian actresses. She said, "Wayne wants someone like Rosalind Chao, but he heard she's pregnant." And my friend said, "She's not going to be pregnant *forever*." And that's how I ended up getting the audition. That's how this business is: once you're pregnant, you're put out to pasture, so I'm very grateful to my friend. If she hadn't said that, I probably wouldn't have even been considered.

**LAUREN:** When we went in, Wayne asked us which character we resonated with the most after having read the book. That's what he wanted to go with. So I actually read for Lena.

**MING-NA:** I auditioned for Waverly and June.

**TAMLYN:** Same!

**MING-NA:** But there was never any competitiveness between us! We somehow knew in our hearts that what was important was this journey that all four of us were going on together, with our "moms" in tow.

## Buzz and Backlash

*Though the film was anticipated and warmly welcomed, it was also criticized—often by people who hadn't even seen it. Some naysayers had issues with the way that the film seemed to exploit immigrant trauma for melodrama; others, with its portrayal of Asian men. Over time, those critiques have faded. But did they prevent the film from getting the audience it deserved in its original release?*

**ROSALIND:** The community then was not as supportive as it is now. It's a bit of a shame because it's wonderful how Wayne brought this diverse Asian cast—Japanese American, Vietnamese American, Chinese American— together as one group. I thought that would work in our favor, but unfortunately at the time we were a little more fractured as a community. Every Q&A, we had somebody who stood up to complain about the way men were portrayed.

**LAUREN:** I remember we were all on a panel, with Wayne and Amy, and an audience member asked, "Why are the Asian men in the film portrayed as such jerks?" And Wayne, without missing a beat, said, "Because Asian men *are* jerks." That unleashed chaos. Amy tried to calm people down and explain, "Look, these characters are a conglomeration of different people I've known in my life, and this is just my personal story. If you don't like it, the antidote is for many more writers and people to come out with their stories, so that we have a balance." It put a lot of pressure on her.

It makes me wish our movie had come out during a time when social media existed. We were making something special. And there was a buzz, but not as much as one might expect, given that the book was so popular.

**MING-NA:** But with social media, it could have been even worse, you know? It's frightening how people can tear things down into little pieces, and it makes them feel good. It's very different from *Crazy Rich Asians* in the sense that that movie had such a glamorous spin. Of course everybody's going to be mesmerized by these wealthy fabulous Asians. Our film had a universality to it. It wasn't glamorous, it's more poignant, and it's also not as linear—it's eight stories of people intertwined together, and it takes a little bit more focus to understand how all these stories relate to one another. So it's a different conversation.

But the fact is, we were received with a lot of excitement and we've had a lasting effect. The movie is being taught in schools! There's a timelessness to *Joy Luck Club*.

## Mothers Know Best

*The younger actresses would go on to become the most beloved and visible Asian American actresses of their generation. But what made the film so powerful wasn't just their performances—it was the dynamic they had with the grande dames who played their mothers.*

**ROSALIND:** Lisa Lu and I had a similar relationship offscreen as we had on camera. But then again, I've known Auntie Lisa since I was a little girl. She came over on the boat from China with my mom and was like a big sister to her; Auntie Lisa is the one who recruited me into acting when I was tiny because they needed to cast a kid in a project she knew about, and she kind of pushed me in that direction. So, unbeknownst to Wayne, Auntie Lisa had already been a big part of my life. And of course France Nuyen was the goddess that we all knew, right? Remember her as Liat in the movie version of *South Pacific*? Oh my God!

**MING-NA:** Don't forget Kieu Chinh—she was such a prolific icon even prior to *Joy Luck Club*.

**TAMLYN:** The film was actually the second time I got to work with Kieu. She was such a powerhouse. I knew France and Lisa, but Tsai Chin was the new one to me—holy shit! Tsai is a force

of nature. Whatever comes out of her mouth is just uncensored honesty, and it's hilarious.

**MING-NA:** Tsai wanted to come out to Hollywood. She was like, "Ming! Go find me a place to live! It has to have a pool." So I literally took my big-ass camcorder and went to various residence hotels and took video of the facilities for her because I was scared of her—but in a loving way. We all did whatever Tsai needed and wanted from us. I don't even know if I would do that for my mom. [laughs]

**ROSALIND:** When we did the publicity junket, we were at the Four Seasons in New York eating fancy food—oysters, Dom Pérignon, we went to town. Tsai and the other moms were sitting at the next table, but they pulled up their chairs afterwards and sat down. I remember France saying, "I want to tell you, it's never going to be like this again. Enjoy this! I wish someone had told me that when *I* was young."

**MING-NA:** And I'm just trying to think . . . we're kind of their age now?

**LAUREN:** No! Really?

**ROSALIND:** Weren't they older? I could have sworn they were in their late sixties.

**MING-NA:** Sorry to bring it up, girls. We just have better creams!

## Not Quite *Crazy Rich Asians**

*The reality, perhaps, is that* Joy Luck Club *might have been a little ahead of its time. Hollywood didn't know how to effectively market the film; there wasn't the viral platform of the Internet to spread the word about it; and of course, the Asian American community*

---

* See page 388, "The Road to *Crazy Rich Asians*"

*was smaller, less cohesive, and less equipped to mobilize behind a project like this. And of course, it took 25 years for Asian Americans to realize that it would be another 25 years before an opportunity like this one came along again.*

**LAUREN:** Hollywood runs where the money is. If they'd made more money on *The Joy Luck Club,* producers would have felt encouraged to make other Asian movies. *Crazy Rich Asians* really took off—people saw it four times in theaters. And then, all of a sudden, I saw so many other Asian projects happening, because studios realized there was money to be made.

**TAMLYN:** We have to remember *The Joy Luck Club* was not the only touchstone for telling the Asian American story. That's the problem with the politicization of the Asian American "umbrella." It's like every story has to be *the* Asian American story. The effect was that America, through this movie, thought it finally "understood" what it meant to be Asian American or specifically Chinese American.

But *The Joy Luck Club* was not only an Asian American film. It was a chick flick. It was a love story of mothers and their daughters. The husbands and boyfriends were secondary—this was about these women finding who they were at a particular, critical moment in their lives, and the lessons they passed down to their daughters, and then their daughters finding their own voices in America.

**LAUREN:** I remember hearing Amy say something as a guide to young writers: "The more personal it is, the more universal it becomes. So write from your heart and what you know." And that turned out to be true.

**MING-NA:** Yes! This was a true immigrant story of hope and the cultural differences between the younger and older generation. And that made it very impactful, not just for Asian Americans, but people of all ethnicities—that was a big surprise to me, that there was such a universality to the response: "I didn't have a Chinese mom, but I certainly had an immigrant mom."

## The *Joy Luck* Group Text

*For the four actresses, making the film wasn't just a career opportunity, it also gave them a permanent extended family: three new sisters who would stay connected for life.*

**MING-NA:** For me, the film was like my green card into Hollywood. I didn't know anybody—casting people, producers, directors, nobody knew me. But afterwards, when I went into a casting room and told them I was June in *The Joy Luck Club,* it definitely opened up a lot of doors. I still had to earn the part, but at least I had a way in. So I will forever be grateful to Amy, Wayne, and Janet [Yang, the film's producer] for this opportunity, on a professional and personal level and on a friendship level too.

**LAUREN:** It's one of the projects I'm the proudest of. It came from such beautiful material and it was done with so much integrity. And I felt like it legitimized my place as an actress, and balanced out some of the other goofy roles that I've chosen to take on.

**ROSALIND:** I don't know if it really "transformed" my career. I feel like I've always been more of a journeyman actor. But the film has made such a big difference in a lot of people's lives. It's so comforting to me when somebody says how much it meant for them to see themselves reflected on screen. One way *The Joy Luck Club* was definitely life-changing, though, was that we have this sisterhood now. We're all on a group text—Tamlyn and I are really bad late-night texters.

**TAMLYN:** I echo every single one of these sisters. I treasure our sisterhood here. And I'm just glad that the four of us had a fucking blast shooting the movie.

## More Joy, Better Luck Tomorrow

*While the movie didn't "change everything" then, it set Hollywood and Asian America on a course for transformation—led by a multiracial movement of diverse storytellers who are actively engaging with and uplifting one another, across cultural lines.*

**ROSALIND:** I'm optimistic for the future. Asians are not as invisible as we were 10 years ago, and we're learning a lot from our Black and brown brothers and sisters. But we do have to speak up for ourselves. The anti-Asian racism that we're seeing now—it's been happening for a long time. And that's only been possible because they don't see us. We've been invisible for so long. I did not feel seen for a long time, and sometimes I still don't.

**MING-NA:** I think that's cultural too: We're often told, put your head down, do the work, don't complain. Don't make waves. Be humble, be grateful. I think you can be, but at the same time, you don't have to be a pushover. You shouldn't let yourself be walked all over.

**ROSALIND:** Ming, you've always had a really good sense of yourself. I remember you always had a voice that I definitely felt I didn't have. And I remember you would fight for us. If something happened that was inappropriate, you're the one who spoke up. I learned a lot from watching you, to be honest.

**MING-NA:** Yeah, I have a big mouth.

**ROSALIND:** But you spoke up, while I was like, "Oh, don't make waves. Just pretend it didn't happen." You know, which really sucks.

**LAUREN:** I'm optimistic, too. There are more projects out there that let younger generations actually see themselves on screen. My parents were really traditional and wanted me to be in academics or education, science, math, and I just sucked at all of that. In a way, I had no choice but to do this! But we need to encourage parents to see that the arts are something noble. I want to give back and invest time in the younger generation, so I've been teaching acting and voiceover skills at my son's high school, and directing their school plays. I feel like if I can be any inspiration at all, that's going to keep things moving. To any parents who happen to be reading this book: Encourage your kids. If they're into the arts, let them be into the arts. Because we need that.

**TAMLYN:** All it takes is a platform. And I think our stories will continue to gain momentum, because they're showing to everyone, not just fellow Asians, what takes place in every single generation, across all cultures. They explain what it means to be American.

# How the Golden Age of
# Hong Kong Cinema Gave Us Hope

BY JEFF YANG
ILLUSTRATED BY LINDA CHUNG

**I GREW UP** with an uncle who babysat me by taking me along to matinee double features at the Music Palace in New York's Chinatown, where we'd sit in the back row and watch the incredible antics of Hong Kong's finest unfurl onscreen, amid sunglass-sporting gangsters (who'd regularly pop out to check their beepers) and grandmas gnawing on dried squid. I didn't know then that the films I'd come to love would also shape the tastes and sensibilities of many of Hollywood's most influential creators, who watched them on scratchy bootleg videotapes and memorized their action choreography and visual conceits—or that in the Nineties and early 2000s, many of the stars who lit up our immigrant screens would leap over into mainstream American multiplexes. But I also didn't know then that this sudden eruption of talent would be the last hurrah for the Hong Kong film industry as we knew it: the reason why the likes of Jackie Chan, Chow Yun-Fat, Jet Li, and others were looking for footholds in America was due to the uncertainty fostered by the island's reunification with the mainland. The years since then haven't been kind to Hong Kong cinema, which has seen its industry become a commercial afterthought and creative backwater, as the island's most prominent performers and directors either "crossed the border" to make movies in the mainland or simply retired.

But even if the industry's best years are past, its fingerprints can still be seen all over our pop culture, in every half-decent stunt sequence and action framing you'll see on American screens today. And of course, for Asian Americans coming of age in the Eighties and Nineties, Hong Kong cinema offered us an aspirational set of reflections to counter the buffoonish depictions of Asians we saw all around us. We were Maggie Cheung charming the camera with her catlike smile, we were Jackie Chan taking flight off of a seven-story skyscraper, we were Chow Yun-Fat giving a cocky thumbs-up in aviator shades before smashing through a doorway into a deadly hail of gunfire.

Here are some of the most influential icons of Hong Kong's golden age, and the ways they indelibly changed and inspired us.

> For Asian Americans coming of age in the Eighties and Nineties, Hong Kong cinema offered us an aspirational set of reflections to counter the buffoonish depictions of Asians we saw all around us.

## The Cool Cat

As action auteur John Woo's avatar in movies like *A Better Tomorrow* (1986) and *The Killer* (1989), **CHOW YUN-FAT** exuded an effortless, bulletproof chill that every Asian guy wished we could achieve simply by donning his signature trench coat and striking a rakish grin. He landed on American screens in a couple of forgettable films (remember 1990's *The Corruptor*? No, you don't) before smashing into the marquee mainstream in the most unlikely of ways, as swordsman Li Mu-Bai in

Ang Lee's wuxia blockbuster *Crouching Tiger, Hidden Dragon*. Did anyone imagine a subtitled all-Chinese-language period epic would make $100 million in America? If you'd seen the work of Chow and its other stars Michelle Yeoh and Zhang Ziyi before, you would have believed.

## The Survivor

**JACKIE CHAN** has put himself at death's door more times than any of us can count, all in the service of entertaining the world in classics like *Project A* (1983) and *Supercop* (1992), and every single time he's shaken it off and done another take. Even when he scored monster U.S. box-office success in the *Rush Hour* films (1998, 2001, 2007) and *Shanghai Noon* (2000) and its sequel *Shanghai Knights* (2003), Hollywood never quite understood just how big a star he was everywhere else in the world—or the price he paid for that stardom. For those of us who really knew his career, and who saw his early brilliance, he'll always be the epitome of the guy who gets back up one more time than you do.

## The Genius

Jackie Chan was all about showing the effort behind his spectacular screen achievements. **JET LI**, meanwhile, exemplified the kind of magical grace and precision that you only see in natural-born prodigies—not least because many of his roles in films like the *Once Upon a Time in China* movies (1991, 1992, 1993, 1997) and *Hero* (2002) showcased gravity-defying wirework, making hand-to-hand combat look like bone-crunching ballet. Li blew minds as the villain in 1998's *Lethal Weapon 4,* and followed that up with an incredible leading performance in *Romeo Must Die* (2000), marred only by the film's refusal to give his romantic subplot with Aaliyah closure (in the final scene of the movie, they hug and walk off instead of kiss). But Jet Li was still an inspiration to every one of us who ever struggled to learn a crappy piano concerto for a church recital our parents were forcing us to play—the guy who would've rolled in, taken a look at the keys, and performed it at first glance, making it look easy.

## The Enigma

She bent boundaries as genderqueer sorcerer Asia the Invincible in *The Swordsman* films (1992 and 1993), and broke hearts as the blond-wigged femme fatale in Wong Kar-Wai's 1994 masterpiece *Chungking Express*. If Chow Yun-Fat epitomized debonair cool, **BRIGITTE LIN** was the unfathomable ice queen who said more with the quirk of an eyebrow than most actors could manage in a ten-minute monologue. Though she never made a film in Hollywood, anyone who's seen what she accomplished in her two-decade career knows why she's been called the last and brightest star of her era. Her

Jackie Chan has put himself at death's door more times than any of us can count, all in the service of entertaining the world. . . . Hollywood never quite understood just how big a star he was everywhere else in the world—or the price he paid for that stardom.

perfect poker face is what we all wanted when we had to walk through embarrassment with our backs ramrod straight.

> Brigitte Lin was the unfathomable ice queen who said more with the quirk of an eyebrow than most actors could manage in a ten-minute mono-logue. Though she never made a film in Hollywood, anyone who's seen what she accomplished in her two-decade career knows why she's been called the last and brightest star of her era.

## The Queen

Brigitte Lin's brilliance was in some ways impossibly remote—in her most notable roles, she was an unworldly, unknowable presence. But **MAGGIE CHEUNG** was the warm, fiery glow at the center of every movie in which she starred—raw, passionate, and emotionally available, whether submerged in tragedy or suffused with comic hysteria. She had us roaring in her slapstick turns alongside Jackie Chan, and melted us in dramas like 1996's romance-through-the-decades epic *Comrades: Almost a Love Story*; no one will ever wear a qipao as well as she did in Wong Kar-Wai's *In the Mood for Love* (2000). When we wish we could shake off passive-aggressiveness and express ourselves fully and openly, she's our inspiration.

## The Smooth Operator

There's something about **TONY LEUNG CHIU WAI**—short in stature, slender in build, with striking but ordinary looks—that's a testament to being unafraid to be who you are, and owning yourself with such complete confidence that everyone around you is swept up into your wake. One of two Tony Leungs in the constellation of Hong Kong stars of the Eighties and Nineties, he was sometimes referred to as "Little" Tony Leung while Tony Leung Kar Fai, taller and more conventionally handsome, was called "Big"—but when Leung Chiu Wai was onscreen, in Wong Kar-Wai's *Chungking Express* and *In the Mood for Love,* in 2002's *Infernal Affairs* and *Hero,* there was no one bigger. He's finally making his Hollywood crossover in 2021, in Marvel's *Shang-Chi and the Legend of the Ten Rings,* and for those of us who know him from his Hong Kong canon, all we can say is, better late than never.

## The Wild One

**STEPHEN CHOW** is perhaps the most talented comic artist that Hong Kong has ever produced. As both actor and director, his innovations transformed the comedy genre, literally creating an entire new form of onscreen humor, referred to as "mo lei tau" in Cantonese—literally, "nonsense," a rapid-fire collage of incongruous words, surreal images, and bizarre ideas that cascade across the screen in films like *Fight Back to School* (1991) and *From Beijing with Love* (1994). But it was his unpredictable, indelible later outings, *Shaolin Soccer* (2001) and *Kung Fu Hustle* (2004), that brought him to global attention. For those of us who wish we had the (soccer) balls to defy oppressive expectations and unleash the anarchy we secretly hid inside, Chow was our patron saint.

# Bollywood Saved Us

## How Indian Cinema Blurred Boundaries,
## Bridged Generations, and Brought Together a Diaspora

**BY JEFF YANG, ILLUSTRATED BY LINDA CHUNG**

**BACK IN THE** Nineties and 2000s, movie industry pundits noticed an odd pattern. Every couple of weeks, a movie might pop into the top ranks of weekend box-office earners and then disappear—and the films would have non-English titles, unfamiliar directors, and stars with last names like Khan, Singh, Kumar, and Kapoor. This phenomenon had a simple explanation: There was a circuit of small theater venues in cities with large South Asian populations that would host single-weekend showings of recent Bollywood releases, to completely packed houses—drawing audiences from dozens of miles around. Hotly

anticipated films might earn as much as $5 or $6 million from these screenings—Indian Americans spend 50 percent more on movie tickets per capita than other moviegoers, and they disproportionately spend it watching Indian movies. On any given weekend, there might be as many as 1,000 movie screens in the United States showing Indian movies, an amazing statistic given that two-thirds of all Hollywood movies get theatrically released on under 100 screens.

What makes this all possible is the deep cultural connection that Indian Americans and many other South Asians have to Bollywood—and how these movies and the stars that light them up serve to tie together populations that have been scattered and dispersed, and bridge the cultural and linguistic gaps between generations. We asked comedians **SAAGAR SHAIKH**, who can be seen in Disney's hotly anticipated *Ms. Marvel,* and **SHAAN BAIG**, who performs with L.A.'s Upright Citizens Brigade, to share their thoughts and reminiscences about growing up Bollywood.

## Together in the Dark

**SHAAN:** When my family first immigrated to the United States, theaters showing Bollywood films were the only place where they could meet other South Asians. These were little theaters that were rented out every other week for Bollywood movie screenings. On those weekends, my family and pretty much everyone else in the greater Detroit Indian American community would come together to watch them. Going to a Bollywood theater is an experience unlike anything else. It's not just about sitting quietly in your seat—you interact with the screen, people are hollering and cheering at

certain moments, booing when there's a villain. And during intermission, something that happens in every Bollywood movie, there'll be like a 15-minute break, and outside, somebody will be selling samosas, chaat, things like that. It's a party. So for a lot of us, Bollywood has a big nostalgia factor to it. You hear the songs, and it feels like you're with family.

**SAAGAR:** It was the same for me. Growing up in Houston, there was this place called FunPlex that had an arcade, a bowling alley, a roller skating rink, a bumper car area, and the only movie theater in the area that showed Bollywood films. I'd go there with my mom to watch films all the time. Bollywood was the medium I used to connect with my parents, aunts, and uncles. Weddings wouldn't be the same without Bollywood music. And it connected us brown kids together—when I saw other South Asian kids at my school, it was our little thing to talk about that no one else knew.

## The Secret Recipe

**SAAGAR:** Bollywood movies are their own mini universes, and you have to just accept anything that the film gives you. When Bollywood suspends reality, it *really* suspends reality. A movie could belong to three or more different genres at once—it's a rom-com, it's an action comedy, it's a serious drama, and whoa, now it's a murder mystery.

**SHAAN:** There's a reason for that: In India, going to the movies is like a whole-day family event—everyone goes together, the grandparents, the parents, and the little kids. So movies had to have something for literally every single demographic in the family. So you're going to have comedy. You're going to have romance. And then of course there's the music. Every Bollywood movie has its own original soundtrack; the music and film industries are totally intertwined in India. A Bollywood film is like an all-in-one entertainment package.

## Khan Khan Khan

**SAAGAR:** During the early Nineties, the three biggest actors were the three Khans: Shah Rukh Khan, Aamir Khan, and Salman Khan. Everybody had their favorite Khan, and they were all badass in different ways. But it didn't matter what roles they played, because in every movie, their characters were the same—just in a different scenario with a different name.

**SHAAN:** These were our heroes growing up, literally—in Bollywood culture, they don't even use terms like "lead actor" or "lead actress." They say "hero" and "heroine." They were always flexing their muscles, and if they weren't bare-chested, they were wearing mesh shirts, so you could see their bare chests. If you were a guy, you aspired to be them. If you were a girl, you aspired to be their girl. It really meant something for us to be able to see heroes that looked like us on screen.

## From India with Love

**SHAAN:** Bollywood isn't just a thing in India, or among South Asians. Brown countries all over the world have embraced the industry with a fervent fandom. Because seeing other brown people is like the first inroad to seeing yourself on screen. It's like the next closest thing, you know? So even if you're from Africa or other parts of Asia, I definitely think you'd see yourself more in these films than you would in a Hollywood movie.

**SAAGAR:** Across the Arab world, they love Bollywood films. You'll find people that don't speak Hindi or even English, living in Arab and African countries, who can quote Bollywood films and sing along with Bollywood songs.

## Finding Your Way Back Home

**SAAGAR:** As you get older, like in high school, you start to spend more time with your friends outside of school. You realize you want to fit in, and you resent being different. So there's this period in my life when I refused to watch Bollywood films.

**SHAAN:** Coming of age, especially post-9/11, we experienced terrorist jokes and Muslim jokes. We ended up having an adverse reaction to anything that made us stand out. Bollywood felt like something that was a taboo to talk about with anyone outside of our families.

**SAAGAR:** I rejected Bollywood for so long and eventually went crawling back, to experience that familiar roller coaster of emotions. There's just no substitute. These movies have a kind of passion that you don't find anywhere else, even though they also have some unique blind spots. Like, they didn't allow kissing on screen until pretty recently. The camera would just move to the side, the couple would neck-nuzzle, and the kissing would be sort of implied.

**SHAAN:** It was specifically kissing that was taboo, though. They might be half naked and rolling around together in a field, but kissing was a line they did not cross. Also, Bollywood has had problems with representation. You'll see in some films the token "Muslim friend"—

which are sometimes portrayed as not-so-bright characters.

**SAAGAR:** My dad would fast-forward through the Hindu prayer scenes in Bollywood films. We're Muslim and they didn't want me to get confused, seeing people who look like us onscreen, praying in a different way.

**SHAAN:** But you're starting to see things change. There's more nuanced inclusion of minority groups. There's LGBTQ+ stories being told now. It takes time. Like America, India is both a very red and very blue country.

## Bollywood Brought Us Together

**SAAGAR:** When you're in a country where everyone looks like you, you're tempted to ask, well, who acts like me? Who worships or talks like I do? Who speaks the same language as me? You always want to find a group that's more specific. You're never happy just all being together, man.

**SHAAN:** That's why in India, it's more taboo for Muslims and Hindus or Indians and Pakistanis to be close friends. But over here? We don't care about that at all. I'm Indian and Saagar is Pakistani, and we got to be close friends because of our mutual love of Bollywood.

## POSTCARD FROM ASIAN AMERICA

BY DR. THAO HA

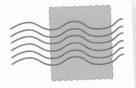

Yo RISE,

Wassup from Houston!

I was born in Vietnam, but the Dirty South is where I stake my roots. Viet refugees came here in droves, making the third coast the third largest target for the Viet diaspora.

The air is sweltering and bugs bite, but housing and gas are hella cheap. Shrimpers trawl the Gulf. Nail techs brush the tips of women with big hair and big trucks. Guns, poverty, racism, and Bibles are abundant.

As a petulant teen, I defied the wrath of God and embraced a Vietnamese gang. I ditched Sunday school and the university library for Rainbow Karaoke and Club Bayou Mama. I was a model-minority failure, but damn, it felt good to be a gangster.

But thug life leads to rude reckonings. We clung to a dangerous lifestyle because we were looking for somewhere to belong and someone to feel like family, and the gang felt like home. One by one, my crew met misery, learning how life turns out when you're lost. Our karmic debts came due, and we paid for our stupid choices. I lost the love of my life to his life sentence in prison. I nearly lost my own life to a hollow-point bullet during a pool hall brawl. They shot me, but the punks didn't finish.

After the violence, instead of turning to vengeance, I steered my rice rocket toward calm, eventually earning a doctorate at The University of Texas at Austin and a gig as a college professor. My passion for lifting the up the less fortunate is grounded in my own rise from the bottom. Now I'm here.

Peace,

Dr. Ha

RISE
HERE AND NOW,
ASIAN AMERICA

# Awesome Asian Bad Guys

BY PHIL YU

**THE HISTORY OF** Asians in Hollywood has largely been scrawled in invisible ink. For decades, an Asian American actor's fleeting moment of screen time has been mostly relegated to playing yellow-peril villains and nameless, soulless henchmen populating a cop show's biannual "Chinatown" episode or falling to the spray of Rambo's machine gun.

After a while, you start noticing the same Asian faces popping up (and getting killed) over and over again—a phenomenon celebrated in the 2014 indie action comedy *Awesome Asian Bad Guys* from directors Patrick Epino and Stephen Dypiangco—because Asian bad guys deserve their moment in the limelight too.

For veteran actors like Keone Young, the bit roles were about finding the humanity within the scarcity. "You go in and see this stereotypical shit and you're like, *not this again*. But in those days, what were we going to do—beat [leading man] Jimmy Shigeta?" Young says. "There was none of that for us. So we had to go in, attack, and take what was there. And try and turn it into something special."

This is a tribute to ten unsung, hey-it's-that-guy! Asian American character actors of a certain generation who came up during a time when substantial roles for Asians were laughably scarce but who somehow made it work, blazing trails in their own way and building careers on playing Tong Boss, Master Chan, and Yakuza Enforcer Numbers 1, 2, and 3.

## Al Leong

Having tussled with the toughest guys in Hollywood, the immortal Al Leong has been killed onscreen possibly more times than anyone on this list.
**BADDEST ROLE:**
Genghis Khan, *Bill & Ted's Excellent Adventure*

## James Hong

A legend. With over 600 acting credits to his name, the instantly recognizable James Hong has probably been in more movies and TV shows than anyone in Hollywood history.
**BADDEST ROLE:**
David Lo Pan, *Big Trouble in Little China*

### Ric Young

His roles have ranged from Confucius to Bruce Lee's dad to Mao Tse-Tung, but this British-born veteran actor is never more deliciously watchable than when he's playing a baddie.
**BADDEST ROLE:** Dr. Zhang Lee, *Alias*

### Simon Rhee

Hundreds of stunt credits, from *The Dark Knight Rises* to *Rush Hour*. But he'll always be the badass with an eye patch who killed your brother.
**BADDEST ROLE:** Dae Han Park, *Best of the Best*

### Gerald Okamura

Once dubbed "The Scariest Man in Martial Arts," the stone-faced 5th-degree black belt is, naturally, a veteran of films with titles like *Ninja Busters, Samurai Cop,* and *Karate Wars.*
**BADDEST ROLE:** Hagata, the Torturer, *Showdown in Little Tokyo*

### Cary-Hiroyuki Tagawa

He's played cops, robbers, ambassadors, and assassins. But one thing is certain: you do not want to be on the receiving end of Cary-Hiroyuki Tagawa's death stare.
**BADDEST ROLE:** Shang Tsung, *Mortal Kombat*

### George Cheung

The roles of "Vietcong Leader," "Korean Elvis," and many more have been blessed with the charm of George Cheung and his signature thin mustache.
**BADDEST ROLE:** Lt. Tay, *Rambo: First Blood Part II*

### Keone Young

The Honolulu-born actor's prolific oeuvre includes an astronaut, an Elvis impersonator, and yes, many gangsters.
**BADDEST ROLE:** Voice of Storm Shadow, *G.I. Joe: A Real American Hero*

### Tzi Ma

After a 40-year career playing criminals, detectives, doctors, and generals, Tzi Ma seems to have settled comfortably into the role of Asian American cinema's favorite father.
**BADDEST ROLE:** Lee Hei, *Martial Law*

### Yuji Okumoto

In the sequel to *The Karate Kid,* Daniel-san went to Okinawa and got a serious villain upgrade. If you are the man who will fight for someone's honor, this is the guy you have to fight.
**BADDEST ROLE:** Chozen, *The Karate Kid Part II*

# Reflections on Mulan

FEATURING PEILIN CHOU AND RITA HSIAO
BY PHIL YU, ILLUSTRATED BY LINDA CHUNG

We're a community that has become accustomed to scant inclusion—or flat-out invisibility—over decades of Hollywood films and television. But during the summer of 1998, representation unexpectedly showed up in the most mainstream package possible: a Disney animated feature. And for a generation of Asian Americans that grew up watching Disney movies, *Mulan* was a moment. *Mulan* was *our* Disney movie.

The film is based on the legendary Chinese folk tale of Fa Mulan, a girl who disguises herself as a man and takes her ailing father's place when he is conscripted by the military to defend against the invading Huns. Though that tale is thoroughly Disney-fied, complete with catchy musical numbers, a wisecracking dragon sidekick, and some truly cringeworthy Nineties-era gender jokes, *Mulan* offered Asians something recognizably rare and resonant: a hero who looked like many of us, fighting her family and the world's expectations of her, in an effort to be seen for *who* she is, *as* she is. And despite its ancient Chinese inspiration, with Ming-Na Wen as the voice of the titular heroine—and Lea Salonga singing her soaring musical numbers—leading a multiethnic, mostly Asian voice cast, *Mulan* was a pop culture artifact that felt decidedly familiar, contemporary, and Asian American.

In retrospect, it feels like a minor miracle that this film got made at all. **PEILIN CHOU**, development exec at Walt Disney Feature Animation, and **RITA HSIAO**, screenwriter on the film, look back at the triumphs and challenges of bringing Disney's first Asian heroine to the screen, and the meaningful lasting legacy of *Mulan* over two decades later.

## "A Girl Worth Fighting For"

**PEILIN:** The project was already in development before I joined the division. I was at Touchstone Pictures in live action, and I had heard that they were doing *Mulan,* it was picking up heat, and they were interested in moving it beyond development. That was actually the reason why I went over to Disney Feature Animation. I was like, if they're going to make *Mulan,* I have to be a part of it, because this isn't going to happen again for 20 more years. And in fact, the next time there was a Chinese family in a global animated film, it was *Abominable,* 21 years later. [Note: Chou was the executive behind *Abominable,* as creative head of its production company, Pearl Studios.]

Rita and I were two of the only Asian people involved with the production, and we became instant kindred spirits and best friends. Officially, I was one of the development execs on the movie, but unofficially, Rita and I were the cultural safeguards of the film. We were the ones who'd go into an office behind a closed door and say, "Oh my God, can you believe they said that? That's so wrong! What are we going to do?"

**RITA:** At the time, I was a writer on *All-American Girl*. There were already three writers on *Mulan* and they wanted to add me, but I was on the show. So what happened was they would send me scenes, and I'd read them and give my thoughts on the script. But then when *All-American Girl* went into hiatus, which would end up being permanent, I said, "Okay, I'll jump in." I was just going to be on it for two months, but ended up staying on in some capacity for two years. There was already a script in place, but in animation, everything constantly gets changed. You actually want to be the last writer on the project, because then your stuff makes it into the movie.

## So That's Why the Dragon's Called "Mushu"

**PEILIN:** At Disney Feature Animation, there's a slate of, I don't know, 20 to 30 projects in development at any given time. In the time I was there, I worked on *Frozen*. I worked on *Tangled*. I worked on all these movies that were released like a decade or more after I left. It's pretty typical that projects can just kick around for years and years until one day the powers that be decide, *that's* the one we're going to make.

In the genre of animation in particular, there's a desire to explore different worlds and different cultures. There's an openness in animation that's very different from live action. But at the time, it was really about [Disney CEO] Jeffrey Katzenberg and [Chairman] Michael Eisner, and what films they deemed worthy of being made. And Jeffrey had made *The Joy Luck Club* at Hollywood Pictures, the only place that would make that movie; later, he went on to do a joint venture with China

in the form of Oriental Dreamworks [which would eventually become Pearl Studios]. So I like to think that his affinity for China—and his personal love of Chinese food—actually had some impact.

## "The Greatest Honor . . ."

**RITA:** For me, it was about finding Mulan's emotional throughline. I think she was very relatable in the sense that every kid wants to please their parents, but at the same time, it's like, what if you don't look like what everybody expects? How you look on the outside doesn't reflect how you feel on the inside, which is something I think I always felt. Also, in terms of my parents' friends growing up, their kids knew they were going to be doctors or engineers or whatever. I didn't know what I wanted to do. And certainly, there weren't a lot of creative Asian people [to look up to] at the time.

When I wrote the line "The greatest honor is having you for a daughter" at the end, it meant a lot to me, because that's kind of what I always wanted to feel. And then in a weird fluky thing, my parents actually gave me a greeting card with that on it, like, years later. Somebody had put it on a card, and I was like, oh my God, it's come full circle.

**PEILIN:** Your parents put that on a greeting card? You clearly don't have Asian parents.

**RITA:** No, they bought it from a store.

**PEILIN:** Did they buy it for you because they knew you had written it, or did they buy it for you because they believe in that sentiment?

**RITA:** Oh no, they bought it because they knew I wrote it.

## "Punch Him. It's How Men Say Hello"

**RITA:** We really pushed for the movie not to be a romance, like all Disney movies were.

**PEILIN:** They originally kissed at the end when Shang comes to her home—in front of her parents! Mortifying in every way. Rita and I, from a very visceral place, were like, "Oh my God, no. You can't do that." But there was a lot of pushback. There was a creative involved with the film who wrote a 10-page essay about why the kiss needed to remain in *Mulan*. Rita and I chose to respond verbally, not in the form of an essay. Of course, we didn't have the final call on it at all, but thankfully the powers that be ultimately decided to take it out. And I actually heard recently that there was also a kiss filmed for the live-action *Mulan* that they ended up taking out. I was like, what is it with that moment?

**RITA:** To this day, there's one thing that still kills me. After she gets to the emperor, everyone's like, "You have saved China!" and then Shang is supposed to come up and say how he feels about her. But he just stutters and says, "You fight good." And she's like, "Oh. Thank you." She's disappointed. It's really weird, because *this girl just saved China.* Don't be depressed and ride off on your horse; you should be like, "Fuck it and fuck you! I'm out!" My point is we were trying to keep it about her story and journey, not about romance. What she was doing was showing up for herself; that's where the accomplishment was coming from. And not, you know, that she got a guy.

## "Brave and True"

**RITA:** I like writing strong female characters. But when I see movies and they write women just like men . . . I liked that Mulan used her brains to solve problems in a way that was true to herself. You didn't feel like she suddenly became this totally different person.

Mulan's problem is something that everybody feels: *I don't feel comfortable where I am because of society's expectations and rules for me.* "Mulan, you're a girl, you're going to get married. You've got to please the matchmaker. That is what you do, and that's it." We were like, no, there's more to you than somebody else's label. *You* get to figure out who you are. So we made sure that tracked throughout the whole film, and that as she grew as a person, others came to respect her. I love that when the guys are singing "A Girl Worth Fighting For," and they're imagining women who are going to cook for them or whatever, the person they thought was their buddy is eventually revealed to be a woman so outside of their stereotypes that it broadens everybody's minds. A lot of LGBTQ people later told me how *Mulan* resonated with them, and you can see why.

**PEILIN:** There were a lot of conversations about what Mulan should look like. She had one of the most authentically proportionate real-girl figures that there had been in the Disney canon. That was due to conversations with a lot of people—mostly women—pushing for it. And then culturally, it was like, if you had a big-breasted Asian girl, that would be a little ridiculous, right? I'm really happy about where we landed with it, but it didn't happen without a lot of conversation for sure.

## "Here I Stand, Proof That There Is a Place for People Like Us"

**PEILIN:** I think casting Asian American voices was more about authenticity of the storytelling than, like, *let's do this for Asian America.* They didn't care about Asian America. And it definitely wasn't catering to China. But there was a history there. Inside Disney, there was a consciousness about cultural authenticity. Not that they went that way 100 percent of the time, but at least it was in consideration, and the desire to do that when they could.

This is a conversation we're still having in current-day projects. One of the creative reasons is that it simply makes the movie better. Because if you have actors who have an actual, real, emotional connection they bring to the role, it makes a huge difference. In [the Netflix animated feature I produced] *Over the Moon,* we have Phillipa Soo playing Chang'e, the Lady in the Moon. Being half-Chinese, she grew up with the legend, hearing it from her father and her grandmother, and it was a really deep, meaningful thing for her. She definitely brought something that a white actress, even a fantastic one, couldn't have brought in the same way. The other thing is: Why not? Why wouldn't you do it that way? Because in the past we've heard like, "Oh, the talent's not there, we just can't limit ourselves in that way." That's just absolutely not true.

And then we have Eddie Murphy as Mushu. I have to say, at the time I thought he was hilarious. With a story like that, you wanted a big comedic presence; it was Eddie Murphy in his prime and it was a huge get. Obviously he wasn't Chinese, but I guess on some level I thought, well, he's a *dragon,* he's not a Chinese person. So, I never personally struggled with that. But I know a lot of people did.

## "You Brought Honor to Us All"

**RITA:** We all liked it, but we had no idea if it was going to work. Because when you break it down, it's Asian and it's war, and there's cross-dressing and all this stuff. Like, how is that going to do out in the world? You just don't know.

And then to see how everybody else reacted . . . to me, it was like, okay, you know you've made it when your parents are like, "It's in the Chinese papers!" They're reading about it and it's getting good reviews. So then they were super proud and they had all of their friends calling them. Of course part of it was that you hadn't seen anything with Asian people of any sort, real or not, on screen. That was exciting. You know, how your parents are always calling you, "There's a Chinese person on TV!" And it's an ice skater, so you'd have to run and see.

**PEILIN:** I think for me, the moment where I thought, "Oh, maybe this is really going to be a thing that's received well," was actually this small, tiny moment during the opening weekend. I had friends that were living in Utah—a very blond-haired, blue-eyed family, by the way—who took their son and daughter to see it opening weekend. I think their kids were six and eight or something at the time. She called me and said, "We came home and my daughter went into the kitchen, got a butter knife, and tried to cut her hair off." I was like, okay. She wants to be Mulan. I think this is going to work.

# SuChin Pak on How Connie Chung Opened the Door for Asian American Women in Broadcast News

**ILLUSTRATED BY TAYEN KIM**

**FOR ASIAN AMERICANS** growing up in the 2000s, MTV News correspondent SuChin Pak was the face and voice of millennial pop culture—sharp, funny, and totally unafraid to go toe to toe with A-list talent like diva Mariah Carey, *Star Wars* creator George Lucas, and the boys from NSYNC in her celebrity interviews. She was also unabashedly willing to get both political and personal, in her "Choose or Lose" coverage of national elections and in her series *My Life, Translated*—one of the first mainstream documentary shows to delve into issues of race, identity, and representa-tion from a first-person Asian American perspective. But Pak has made it clear that she wouldn't have been able to break into the business of news at all had it not been for the pioneers who came before her . . . most notably, Connie Chung, the broadcast trailblazer who in 1993 became the first woman of color (and just the second woman ever, after Barbara Walters) to anchor the national network news. In a candid conversation, Pak shared with us how Chung paved the way, while also becoming a model that Asian American TV newswomen were expected to mimic for generations after.

## How It Began

I was actually discovered at a Youth & Government convention, which is this YMCA program where students simulate how a state government runs. My best friend was really into it, and was going to be participating as a member of the Model State Supreme Court. So I went along, but the only role that they had left for me was to be a reporter for the Y-Witness News, a news show for the program that was broadcast on the hotel's in-house TV channel. Nobody wanted to do it because it was so embarrassing. But I took the slot just to go on the trip with her. And as it turned out, the local Bay Area ABC channel had producers at the event and saw me on TV.

Back in the Nineties, there was this federal mandate that local TV stations had to have a certain amount of educational programming for young people. So they were launching all these teen-oriented talk shows. KGO's show was called *Straight Talk 'N Teens,* and that was my first break. Then the local NBC affiliate, KRON, recruited me to host their teen talk show, *First Cut.* It was nice to make money talking to kids about issues on TV rather than working in a smoothie bar. But later I realized that a big reason these shows wanted me was because it was almost a rule that you had to have an Asian woman on the news. And the biggest reason for that was Connie Chung.

## The Connie Chung Effect

Connie Chung was so successful and so popular that everyone at the big local news stations wanted to hire their own versions of her. They were all looking for Asian female coanchors—classy Asian women who could hold it down next to an older white guy—because the decision makers, generally older white guys themselves, saw that as modern, forward-thinking, and progressive. It was a tokenism, but one I benefited from.

So that's how profound Chung's impact was. She gave a lot of young Asian women, like me, the belief that we could do this. She opened the door to real opportunities for us, which wouldn't have existed without her. But she also created this accepted version of what an Asian woman in broadcast journalism was supposed to look and act like, which we were consciously or unconsciously driven to emulate. The way she did her makeup, that's how I did my makeup—I was doing Connie Chung makeup when I was 16. And for a long time after that, I felt like I was playing a role, which was to be as close to a mini-Connie as possible, until I could figure out who I was supposed to be for myself.

## Searching for SuChin

Connie Chung made it possible for people to see a place for me in the news business. But I wanted to tell a different set of stories in a different way, to an audience of my peers. I found that opportunity at MTV.

By the time I got to MTV News, I'd figured out more of who I was. I had bright red Manic Panic hair; I was getting the chance to cover hard news, like the rescue efforts in Thailand after the tsunami. I was interviewing presidential candidates for the election, but I was also at the Video Music Awards, interviewing Kanye West. It was the best of both worlds. And in many, many ways, it was a big deal for an Asian American woman to be in that position. So yes, I was getting to make my own choices, but I was also always very aware that I had to walk the straight and narrow, because I was not going to fuck this up. There were only two dishes on the career menu I'd been offered, as a young Asian woman on MTV: there was Tila Tequila, and there was me. It was important for me to be fun and relatable, but also to be true to the values that I grew up with. I wanted to prove that I could have Manic Panic red hair and a sense of humor, but hold it down with intelligence.

Once things started to click for me, I started pitching ideas that were exciting for me and that would be relatable to my audience. I covered the premiere of *Better Luck Tomorrow,* which MTV Films was distributing, and interviewed the cast. It was the first time I saw Asian people on a movie screen that I related to, and I couldn't believe how much I'd yearned for that until I saw it. I did a documentary on plastic surgery, on "double eyelid" surgery, and went on the *Oprah Winfrey Show* to talk about it. I created, produced, and hosted the docuseries *My Life Translated,* where I let cameras follow me and other immigrant kids who were trying to figure out what it meant to be young and American and to straddle these different worlds.

## Going Out on Your Own Terms

But everything has to end. I remember when Connie Chung ended her journalism career. She'd broken every barrier and she could've decided to just say goodbye quietly, but instead she decided to go out with a bang. She'd had a pretty bad run toward the end; she was pushed out as an anchor, then she was on and off the air for three years, and finally she emerged with this talk show, *Weekends with Connie and Maury,* featuring her and her husband, Maury Povich. It was widely panned and they were headed for cancellation. So for her grand finale, she dressed up in this tight-fitting evening gown and sang this parody version of "Thanks for the Memories" for the cameras. It was meant as a joke, but when I saw it, I thought to myself, "Connie Chung just gave everyone the finger." That swan song was her saying, "I don't really need you, and I don't give a shit what you think about me."

When I left MTV, I had the opportunity to possibly go to ABC, to climb the broadcast ladder. I had a meeting with Diane Sawyer. But I chafed under the pressure I was getting to be the "next Connie Chung"—from my peers, my agent, my prospective bosses, my parents.

So I said to myself, if there's one last thing Connie has to teach me, it's that when you feel yourself being compromised—even if it's because people want you to be like Connie Chung!—don't be afraid to say no, and leave them with a swan song they'll remember. And that was it. I quit the news business.

I'm 45 now, and I'm doing a podcast called *Add to Cart,* and it's funny and wild and inappropriate, and I'm not at all embarrassed about it. Before, I'd always felt nervous that if I let myself be myself, I was going to screw things up. I no longer feel like I'm under that standard, and it's very liberating. There're so many more options on the menu when you don't have to carry the mantle of being anything but yourself. You don't have to copy anyone, or even to be a more perfect version of yourself. All you have to do is reflect the complete spectrum of humanity that we as Asian Americans represent. We're messy; own that mess. Don't be afraid to feel sadness, rage, despair, grief. And if someone tells you to be something you're not, don't be afraid to sing them a swan song.

# When Asian American Indie Features Suddenly Mattered:
# The "Class of 1997," in Retrospect

BY BRIAN HU

QUENTIN LEE    MICHAEL IDEMOTO    CHRIS CHAN LEE    REA TAJIRI    JUSTIN LIN    ERIC NAKAMURA

**THERE WAS A** time when going to an Asian American film festival was all about short films: educational, silly, raunchy, or soul-stirring works by film and video artists who'd scraped together enough equipment, financing, and crew to tell a brief, gritty story. The shorter the films, the more voices a festival could pack into a program; as a result, these early festivals weren't celebrations of auteurs, but reflections of them.

Of course short films still thrive today, and most Asian American film festivals still undertake the resource-draining task of viewing, selecting, sequencing, marketing, and awarding films under 30 minutes. But let's face it: most contemporary audiences want to see comedies, dramas, and even documentaries that play out over the course of hours, not minutes. These are the works that are most likely to spotlight high-profile subjects like Jeremy Lin or George Takei, or to be star vehicles that can print posters featuring Sandra Oh or John Cho. And fes-

tivals are compelled to court that excitement, if they want audiences and press notice.

It's easy to point to the actual moment when the Asian American indie lens suddenly refocused—shifting its gaze from shorts to features, local representation to national attention, amateur effort to professional technique. That was the year 1997, when one of the three largest Asian American film events in the nation, the San Francisco International Asian American Film Festival, screened a whopping four feature-length films in their 15th annual outing. The four films: Quentin Lee and Justin Lin's *Shopping for Fangs*; Rea Tajiri's *Strawberry Fields*; Michael Idemoto and Eric Nakamura's *Sunsets;* and Chris Chan Lee's *Yellow*.

Four features may seem paltry today, but in 1997 they spelled an arrival. They were dubbed "GenerAsian X" by some critics; the "Class of 1997" was the name that stuck. Whether or not they formed a movement, the films served as a branding opportunity to draw attention to a new wave of Asian American cinema, in the way that Black and queer cinemas rode the momentum of blistering new work by Spike Lee or Todd Haynes. And indeed, it did serve as a stepping-stone for the next decade of Asian American creators. Newcomer John Cho (who'd starred in both *Yellow* and *Shopping for Fangs*) found himself on the cusp of mainstream visibility. Cho, *Yellow* costar Jason Tobin, and *Shopping for Fangs* codirector Justin Lin would reunite for the pivotal *Better Luck Tomorrow,** with Lin emerging as one of the most successful Hollywood directors of his generation. Meanwhile, *Sunsets* codirector Michael Aki Idemoto became an Asian American indie staple, and *Strawberry Fields* lead Suzy Nakamura a perennial presence on prime-time TV (most notably in Ken Jeong's Asian American family sitcom *Dr. Ken*).

But did that amount to a sea change for Asian American cinema? Chris Chan Lee has only made one feature since. Rea Tajiri has returned to documentaries. Eric Nakamura never made another film, though he continued to coedit the standard-bearing magazine *Giant Robot*. Still, the legend of the "Class of 1997" stuck. Perhaps it's less about impact than the symbolic cool that this then-young crop of directors represented. Every reference to them today still features the iconic group photo taken of the six that year: Chris Chan Lee off dreaming in a world of his own, model eyes peering past Lin's schoolboy grin; Quentin Lee slouching into frame while a clean-shaven Idemoto and Nakamura perch behind, barely able to muster a smile. Only Tajiri looks happy to be there; there's always one sincere smile in every class photo. They look like a class of star students and misfits, ready to take on the world by tearing it down. Perhaps the class is so well remembered because Asian American cinema was craving that sort of youthful-maverick ethos that would garner wider Indiewood recognition.

You can hear that desire in the films themselves—from their whip-smart dialogue to their soundtracks laden with under-the-radar indie rock. You can see it in the faces of their young actors, in how the glittering cast of *Yellow* struts across the screen in rock-star slow motion, like reservoir dogs on the mean streets, and especially in the sunglass-sporting cool of Jeanne Chinn, who in *Shopping for Fangs* looks like she stepped out of a Wong Kar-Wai film and into a San Gabriel strip mall. Even if the "Class of 1997" didn't all make it big, they refused to be forgotten.

The festival circuit took notice. But so did those who wondered whether Asian American cinema was abandoning its mission by chasing the cool kids. As early as the following year, Lily Ng wrote in the magazine of the International Documentary Association that the 1997 festival circuit had been overly infatuated with the slick—sidelining smaller, locally oriented works, especially the documentaries and short films that had for decades been Asian American cinema's reason for existence. To their credit, the 1998 SFIAAFF opened the following year's festival with Spencer Nakasako's documentary *Kelly Loves Tony,* about as gritty and local a work as they come. But the truth is, once the Asian American festival circuit sniffed stardom, it could never really turn back.

---

* See page 226, "Tomorrow Never Dies"

# It All Began with Margaret Cho

BY JEFF YANG WITH MARGARET CHO

MARGARET CHO

**IF YOU HAD** to make a case for a moment when most of the nation saw Asian America for the first time onscreen, you could point to the movie *The Joy Luck Club,* which earned a modest $33 million back in 1993, and put its all-Asian cast and immigrant generational story in front of an audience of around 8 million, based on tickets sold. A better case could be made the following year, when a new TV show made its fall debut on ABC: *All-American Girl,* the first network primetime series to center on an Asian American family in nearly two decades—since 1976's *Mr. T and Tina,* starring Pat Morita, which lasted for just five episodes. It was the most viewed new show of the 1994 season, with almost *17 million* people tuning in to its premiere episode. The star who made this possible was **MARGARET CHO**, the era's most visible and successful Asian American stand-up comic—a fireball of raucous energy onstage, who gleefully shattered both taboos and stereotypes in her sold-out no-holds-barred performances. Little of Cho's stage show would find its way into *All-American Girl,* a restrained, paint-by-numbers culture-shock farce that locked Cho's queer, unruly persona behind awkward sitcom tropes. Although the show lasted just 19 episodes before being canceled, it still put a historic dent in the prime-time ceiling, and remains the most visible Asian American pop-culture achievement of the 1990s. Below, the comedy icon shares with us her candid thoughts on how she got to prime time, what went wrong once she did, and what she learned from the experience.

## Dragged into Comedy

When I was a kid, I had my first understanding of who I wanted to be when I saw Flip Wilson on TV in drag playing his character Geraldine. I knew someday that was going to be my job. Other kids were playing with dolls. Well, I wanted to play comedian, and to me, being a comedian meant Flip Wilson as Geraldine. So comedy for me was queer from the very beginning.

And I grew up in San Francisco, where my parents owned a gay bookstore that employed mostly people with full body tattoos who used to all go out to drag shows at night. Those workers were like my babysitters. This was back in the early Eighties, and a fad back then was something called "drag wrestling"—these outrageous wrestling events featuring drag queens—and by the time I was a teen, I was going to them with my parents' employees. It was crazy.

That's the environment I grew up in. And if you're growing up watching drag queens body-slam each other, well, the idea of getting on stage and doing stand-up comedy doesn't seem like that big of a jump.

## Failing at Passing

In my generation of Korean Americans, so many of us had parents who were coming to America with the goal in mind of getting their kids into an Ivy League school. As a result, there was this whole throughline of aspirational whiteness. You know that book *The Preppy Handbook*? It's a comedy book that spoofs aspirational whiteness, but every Korean American kid had it, and they weren't reading it for laughs. They wanted to be "preppy," to wear Ralph Lauren and play tennis, because preppy was really just code for "white." But you couldn't be blatant about wanting to be white, since Koreans are too proud about our Korean-ness. You had to protect that nationalistic pride while still figuring out how to be as close as you could possibly be to white.

Being preppy was a kind of drag. Pretending to be white without being white—except that the goal of preppy drag was to fit in at these elite universities.

And that's kind of how I related to comedy. I said that my original comedy inspiration was Flip Wilson in drag, but during the heyday of Eighties stand-up comedy, it was like everyone was doing drag. Everyone was trying to copy Jerry Seinfeld and Garry Shandling—that is, doing their style of observational comedy, which comes from a particular white male gaze—which led to all these women and nonwhite comics basically doing white male drag. You had non-Jewish stand-ups trying to be Jewish, and Jewish stand-ups trying to be WASP. You had all of these non-Black people of color trying to be Bill Cosby. Everyone was trying to escape their own identity.

For me, though, there were a lot of things that exempted me from doing that. I couldn't escape my own queerness, or the fact that I was or looked so young, the fact that I was a woman—all of that exempted me from any sort of "passing." I had no choice but to do comedy that was steeped in my identity.

## Race as Brand

Racial humor was just something that a lot of nonwhite comedians who couldn't pass had to do back then. We didn't have a choice. We didn't have the feeling that we had the right to protest stereotyping, because the stereotypes almost became a form of branding. It's hard to tell the current generation who have choices now that we didn't have choices back then—it was either that or invisibility.

I started doing comedy at age 14. I remember I was too young for them to even use photographs of me on posters. So I was doing a show, and the way they promoted me was with a flyer that featured a caricature of a coolie with a long braid and buck teeth, eating rice with chopsticks. Underneath it, it said: "Margaret Cho—Proof That the Chinese Are No Laughing Matter!" And of course, well, I'm Korean, and also, if you're a comedian, you kind of *want* to be a laughing matter, right?

So there were a lot of different things wrong with that. I wish I still had a copy of it because it really was this crazy, almost minstrel-show level of racism.

Interestingly, I took a DNA test later, and it turns out that my DNA actually is Chinese, even though my parents are from Korea. So maybe the club knew something I didn't.

## Lost in Translation

I never dreamed of the possibility that I could be on TV. But at the time, Hollywood was going out of its way to develop television shows around comedians, like *Seinfeld* and *Roseanne*. It was an industry. It was the only thing they knew what to do with comedians.

So I found myself pushed along into that industry. But the truth was that my actual comedy wouldn't be possible as a family show on network TV. You couldn't really sanitize my true experience as a queer Korean American stand-up comedian; my gayness and weirdness wouldn't translate into that type of television. But back then there were only four networks—cable was not what it is now. So we didn't have that autonomy to do a show that reflected my real self. Instead, on *All-American Girl,* they decided to infantilize my experience, to put me back home, whereas in real life, I had run away from home when I was 16. I never fought back about it. I never had a sense I could; I was in my mid-twenties and of course I'd never experienced anything like this, so I didn't know what to do.

It wasn't about "Asian authenticity." They were trying to be authentic. Back then, *Third Rock from the Sun* was successful, and to make the space references work in that show, they'd hired astronomers and people who worked at NASA as consultants. So they tried to do the same thing for *All-American Girl.* They looked for advisers for our show who had Korean language degrees! But it was such a weird approach for my show, because they were so concerned about getting the authenticity of the "Asian American experience" and not the authenticity of my experience.

## Fitting into the Box

As they were developing the show, the main issue they had with me was that I was too fat, and so I tried to get thinner to appease them. I was so focused on losing weight that they'd send out a production assistant to get diet pills and bring them to me on set. I started urinating blood because I was so sick and hungry.

At the time, I was scared of what would happen to my career if I didn't do what they wanted. I also had my management in my ear telling me not to make a fuss, saying that once the show was on air and it was a hit, I could do whatever I wanted. After all, they'd also managed Roseanne, and that's what she did.

If I'd understood what television was about back then, if I'd had any control, I wouldn't have made my show have a family setting. It's not that I wouldn't have had my family involved, because I love my family, and they're still very much involved in my life now. But I would have had my character live on her own. I would've made the show a more realistic view of what my life actually was. At the same time, I don't think it would have been possible back then.

## Everything but the Girl

When the show's ratings weren't what they wanted, they fired everybody working on the show, even the showrunner, and hired different writers. The new direction the writers were taking it was to make it like *Friends*—a twenty-something slacker story. So then you went from having a show with an all-Asian cast, to this thing where they were looking at everything through the lens of whiteness. Everybody in the new cast was white. They couldn't figure out what to do with me because the only examples they had for TV nonwhite shows were A, shows about Blackness, and B, shows about Blackness with a white savior.

For them, "Asian" wasn't considered a racial identity. And yet, Asian Americans were putting a lot of pressure on the show, and it confused them, so they ran away from it.

Most of that pressure was spearheaded by a journalist named Connie Kang. She was the first Korean American writer at the *Los Angeles*

*Times,* a real pioneer, but I didn't know who she was, and at the time, I thought, "If you're Asian, you should support me." My attitude got her mad. I was wrong, and I definitely was not being very Korean, because we're supposed to respect our elders. But I didn't see it that way, having defied my family's predisposition toward that kind of attitude. I now have a lot of regrets for not respecting Connie Kang the way I should have. You have to respect people who've paved the way for you. So I was wrong.

I realize now that for Asian American writers looking at Asian American work, you want them to be critical. You don't want people to think that just because something is Asian, Asians are going to be naturally supportive. You want other people to realize that we look at each other as individuals and not as a monolithic group, because if we can't do that, how can we expect others to do it?

At the time, there was a lot I didn't understand, even though I was living in Los Angeles. The show went on air a few years after the L.A. Riots. The last time Korean Americans had seen themselves on TV, it was in news stories of them crouching on rooftops with their rifles to defend their stores, looking like snipers. So the community was very protective of their public image, to the point of paranoia. They didn't want to be victimized, and they didn't want to be seen as victimizers. Our show couldn't possibly avoid that critical eye.

## Memories, Not Regrets

A lot of times, people say that *All-American Girl* was ahead of its time. What does being ahead of your time even mean? I look at something like *Flower Drum Song,* and I think how hard and weird it was for that movie to have come out in 1961, but there's so much truth in it. I love Jack Soo. Nancy Kwan is this fabulous showgirl. James Shigeta is a romantic lead. There's definitely a lot of problematic racial things in it, but there's also so much greatness. Some people don't look back at it fondly, but I treasure it.

So my thought on the show is that yes, I made mistakes, but I just didn't know what I was doing. There were things I should've pushed back on. But what happened happened, and what did happen was that for many people, it was the first time they saw an Asian American family on TV. I made a grand impression, and that's good enough for me.

If *All-American Girl* had been successful, I'd probably be living in Palm Springs right now, retired and tanned, and I'd have a million dogs. Success would have aged me prematurely! But are fame and success really that important? I don't know. I don't think it is anymore. The experience gave me an understanding of race, and an understanding of Hollywood—and frankly, that was more valuable.

## Girl Meets World

I love sharing my experiences with other Asian Americans coming up. We need more of our people in entertainment, to push the fact that we exist, that we're out here, that we have something to say. I want to recruit as many Asian Americans as I can into creative professions, because it's so important to have their voice. We're lost in history if we don't.

I know firsthand how hard it can be to start out and not know anything. We have to be supportive of each other. I always look to young Asian Americans who are doing different and exciting things—and there are so many now. Awkwafina inspired me, which is why I wanted to work with her. I love her. I love Bowen Yang. So many people are doing amazing stuff now, and that's really exciting. I don't have a family or kids, so seeing this next generation come up keeps me young. That, and stand-up comedy. Stand-up really is my life. It keeps me alive. And it's what I'll always do.

But I'd love to go back to television now and try again. Like, I'd love to do a reboot—that would be really fun. All of the actors from *All-American Girl* are still around. And in the reboot, I could have sons, one who's a rapper, the other who owns a food truck. It would be super meta. Very, very meta. They would basically be Dumbfoundead and Roy Choi.

# POSTCARD FROM ASIAN AMERICA

BY KRISHNA SADASIVAM

Dear RISE,

I was born in Winnipeg, Manitoba, in Canada. My childhood in a traditional Indian household felt normal, given the thriving Indian community in our small town. That all changed for me when we moved to the U.S., very much against my wishes.

Moving to Charlotte, North Carolina, made me aware of how different I was. I didn't look like anyone I knew in school. I was of an age at which I still didn't know much about my culture, and yet here I was in school representing it, like an unwilling ambassador. I had a difficult-to-pronounce name. I certainly never saw myself in any of the TV shows or movies I watched. I said "zed" for the letter "Z." I spelled "color" as "colour." Oh, and I was vegetarian.

Mom would try to pack me dosa for lunch, but I would steadfastly refuse to bring it. I didn't need yet another reason to be so obviously different. I might as well have been an alien.

Because of all this, I grew up resenting my roots. It didn't help that our family kept moving from state to state due to my father's job, meaning that I had to go through this every year.

It was only in college that I started to accept what it meant to be Indian. I made friends who understood me and showed me the beauty and value in my traditions and culture. I was no longer the only Indian on campus. And by finding a place where I fit in, I began to appreciate being different. It made me a more empathic and tolerant person. It has encouraged me to always look for ways to make people feel welcome, to try to find common ground with everyone I meet. I celebrate diversity as a strength, not a weakness. I guess I ended up as an ambassador after all.

And I'd like to imagine that the kids who made fun of my food as "weird" or "gross" back then are now the biggest fans of Indian food.

Yours,

Krishna

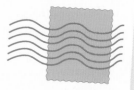

RISE
HERE AND NOW,
ASIAN AMERICA

# What's Funny?

**IN THE 1990S,** it was hard to be an Asian American comic and not talk about your race—or racism, for that matter. Part of the job of the stand-up comedian is making it clear you belong on stage; it often felt like Asian comedians first had to prove they belonged in America. Here's a selection of choice punchlines from top comics of the 1990s:

I was in Mobile, Alabama, walking down the street, and this man actually called me a chink. I got so mad. "Chink? Chinks are Chinese! I'm Korean—I'm a gook, okay? If you're going to be racist, at least learn the terminology. Get a Redneck-to-English dictionary."
**—MARGARET CHO**

I'm from the South, so I guess that makes me . . . South Korean? I'm smart because I'm Korean, I'm not so smart 'cause I'm from the South. They cancel each other out, so I guess I'm even.
**—HENRY CHO**

You're "so Pinoy" if you have the Sony sticker on your TV. You're "*hella* Pinoy" if you still have the receipt hanging from the TV in case you need to return it.
**—REX NAVARRETE**

I can't beat my dad in an argument because he grew up in Korea during the war, and I grew up in San Diego. I remember I'd come home, and be like, "Dad, my friend Billy fell off his skateboard and broke his leg!" And he'd say, "Oh yeah? My friend Han Lee, in the Korean War, his head blew up . . . now he can't comb his hair!"
**—BOBBY LEE**

Indians are cheap. We've been so dedicated to being cheap for so long, we actually invented the number zero.
**—RUSSELL PETERS**

Filipino moms sh*t on their kids' dreams. And you know I'm not lying. I told my mom I wanted to be a comedian and she cried! "Why? Why do you want to be a comedian, Josep? All your *aunties* are nurses. Your *cousins* are nurses. Do you see any clowns in this family? *Do* you, Josep? Who told you you were funny? It wasn't *me!*"
**—JO KOY**

# Asian Grocery Store

BY PHIL YU

Long before Whole Foods sold goji berries, before Netflix streamed Korean dramas, and before hipster chefs drove up the price of bone broth, we had the Asian grocery store. For many immigrant communities, the Asian grocery serves as a home base and a nostalgic cultural filling station—a place to restock and recharge with the familiar sights, sounds, and smells of somewhere not quite left behind. Whether it's a mom-and-pop shop or a supermarket chain, a weekend shopping trip and cartful of groceries were always visceral reminders of our connection to a larger extended family of peoples. Here are some of the things you might encounter at the Asian market.

# The 1990's

## The Asian American Yearbook

BY JEFF YANG, ILLUSTRATED BY LINDA CHUNG

Many of us growing up as Asian Americans never saw ourselves reflected in the coming-of-age comedies and dramas that do so much to shape adolescence in America (and no, Long Duk Dong doesn't count). We decided to reimagine what high school would've been like if we'd been classmates with some of Asian America's most memorable personalities. First up: the Nineties.

Homecoming Queen and King:
Michelle Kwan & Tiger Woods

Most Likely to Save the World:
Dr. David Ho

Golden Girl:
Kristi Yamaguchi

Varsity All American:
Eugene Chung

Most Competitive: Jeanette Lee
Scrappiest Player: Michael Chang

Best School Spirit:
Manny Malhotra

Most Likely to be President:
Gary Locke

Most Likely to Succeed:
Jerry Yang

JOIN OUR ENTREPRENEUR CLUB

Cool Guy and Cool Girl:
Keanu Reeves & Jenny Shimizu

Class Clown:
Margaret Cho

1. Video rental counter: With bootlegged VHS tapes or burned CDs of the latest in-language content from the motherland. (not pictured)

2. Baked goods section: Delicious cakes and pastries inspired by, but qualitatively different from, Western originals. That croissant has a hot dog in it and yes, it's drizzled with mayo. If you're looking for a Doraemon-themed birthday cake, you've come to the right place.

3. Asian snack haven: Shrimp chips, Pocky, Botan Rice Candy, and more—someday, your white friends will get it.

4. Old lady yelling at man behind meat counter: What are they fighting about? Wait, are they even fighting? Or is this just a really spirited conversation?

5. WAP (Weird Asian Produce): Chard, perilla, gai choy, choy sum, amaranth, burdock . . . at least, you think that's what these vegetables are called in English? What matters is that Mom really knows how to cook them.

6. "American grocery" aisle: If you must, for some reason, purchase Campbell's soup, spaghetti sauce, and white bread.

7. Latino employee: The manager speaks to him in Korean. He replies in Spanish. It works. This relationship has functionally bypassed the need for English.

8. Bags of dried stuff: You have no idea what it is, and it smells like a dusty sock, but Grandma swears it will heal whatever ails you.

9. Fancy big box of fruit: The deluxe gift set of pears or mangoes or oranges, for when you really want to show you care. And you're classy.

10. Seafood, very much alive: Sorry, kid, you're not picking out a new pet. That's tonight's dinner.

11. That auntie with all the tea: Of course, we ran into someone Mom knows. They'll be trading gossip for another twenty minutes in the middle of the fish sauce aisle.

12. Spices and condiments: Every kind of hot sauce, fermented versions of anything that can be fermented, a paradise of dried, ground-up parts of plants and sometimes animals that bring the magic to mealtime, bags of MSG proudly and defiantly on display.

13. Alcohol section: VSOP and XO darks and flammable clears. Plus yellow carbonated water in cans marked "Tsingtao" or "OB."

14. Danish/European cookie tins: Do these actually have cookies in them?

15. Rice aisle: Small (5 lbs.), Medium (10 lbs.), Large (20 lbs.), Extra Asian (50 lbs.).

16. Small child climbing on bags in rice aisle.

17. Stationery kiosk: All the gel pens and phone charms you could ever want. And of course, plenty of knock-off character plushies for your bed.

18. Car accessories: Blue LED lights for your car dash, and air fresheners that smell like Asian taxicabs. And of course, plenty of knockoff character plushies for your car back seat. (not pictured)

19. Appliance aisle: Kimchi fridges, water dispensers, and basic $10 rice cookers all the way to $500 rice cookers that have a faster processor than your laptop. (not pictured)

20. Frozen foods: Dumplings, noodles, every kind of seafood made into balls, and for some reason, Hot Pockets.

21. Bored checkout clerk: Wearing rubber gloves and elastic-banded sleeve covers, manually entering prices at lightning speed. (not pictured)

22. Someone trying to pay with Asian currency.

# FOUNDING FATHERS AND MOTHERS

## 1990s

BY JEFF YANG, ILLUSTRATED BY SOJUNG KIM-McCARTHY

**IN THE NINETIES,** a new cohort of Asian American activists and political leaders stepped forward, building on the foundations laid by the pioneers of generations before them and expanding the diversity of our representation and organizational coalitions. Here are some of the challengers and champions whose work shaped our communities in the 1990s.

**REP. BOB MATSUI:** Matsui was instrumental in passing the Civil Liberties Act of 1988, which led to an official apology for the WWII incarceration of Japanese Americans

**REP. PATSY MINK:** First Asian American woman in Congress, and first Asian American to run for president

**REP. NORMAN MINETA:** First Asian American to serve in a presidential cabinet—as secretary of commerce under Bill Clinton and transportation under George W. Bush

**SEN. DANIEL AKAKA:** Congressman and senator who fought for sovereignty for Native Hawaiians

**REP. BOBBY SCOTT:** First Filipino American congressperson

**PAUL IGASAKI:** First Asian American commissioner—and later chair—of the Equal Employment Opportunity Commission

**DALE MINAMI:** Civil rights lawyer who headed the team that successfully reopened and won *Korematsu v. United States*

**KATIE QUAN:** Labor activist and chair of the founding convention of the Asian Pacific American Labor Alliance

**HELEN ZIA:** Journalist, author, cofounder of American Citizens for Justice and lead spokesperson for Vincent Chin

**ANGELA OH:** Attorney and key spokesperson for the Korean American community during and after the 1992 L.A. riots

**MARGARET FUNG:** Attorney and founder of the Asian American Legal Defense and Education Fund

**KAREN NARASAKI:** Attorney and founder of Asian Americans Advancing Justice (AAAJ)

**STEWART KWOH:** Attorney and founder of the Asian Pacific American Legal Center (now part of AAAJ)

**IRENE NATIVIDAD:** Founder of the Global Summit on Women

**GOV. BEN CAYETANO:** First Filipino American governor

**URVASHI VAID:** Author, attorney, and former executive director of the National LGBTQ Task Force

**REP. PAT SAIKI:** Congressperson and first Asian American administrator of the Small Business Association

**ARVIND KUMAR** and **SUVIR DAS:** Cofounders of Trikone, one of the world's first advocacy groups for LGBTQ South Asians

# Anime of the People

BY JEFF YANG, ILLUSTRATED BY LINDA CHUNG

IN 1997, CARTOON Network, the biggest cable channel focused exclusively on animation, launched a new programming block that it called "Toonami." The name blended "cartoon" with the Japanese word for tidal wave, and though it was just seen as clever wordplay by the network's execs, it turned out to be wildly appropriate—because after Toonami came anime's deluge into the mainstream.

It took some months for Toonami to fully show the world what it was doing: The block's first lineup included the venerable giant-transforming-robot series *Voltron*. But while the 12-year-olds watching Toonami could sort of tell *Voltron* wasn't an American cartoon, the show's origin was mostly obscured. Audiences couldn't tell (and would likely never know) that it was an edited and adapted version of a Japanese series called *Beast King GoLion*. That was in keeping with how Japanese animation had been broadcast on U.S. TV in the past; venerable series like *Astro Boy, Speed Racer,* and *G-Force: Battle of the Planets* all had their Asian origins erased in their American airings, out of fear that the cultural differences might somehow confuse kids or offend their parents. But the Toonami block proved wildly popular, and the following year, Cartoon Network slowly began to lean into airing shows that were more difficult to disguise: *Sailor Moon, Dragon Ball Z, Gundam Wing, Ronin Warriors.* In the process, they served as a gateway for mainstream acceptance of "anime," pronounced to rhyme with Fannie Mae, not "a lime."

For Asian Americans, there was something bittersweet about the arrival of anime as a pop culture phenomenon. On the one hand, it didn't hurt for us to find ourselves experts in the stuff that everyone else was suddenly into. On the other, it felt like we were losing a secret, and the characters who used to be our private heroes were now being cosplayed by non-Asians with kanji tattoos and cat-eye makeup. Still, there's no question that the mainstreaming of anime expanded the horizons of a generation, helping them to recognize the existence of a vast and amazing world of stories beyond America's borders.

Here are some of the anime series that shaped how we grew up, and that continue to enthrall us even as adults:

WIDESCREEN WONDERS: When anime first made its way onto American screens, it was positioned as exotic esoterica, drawing an audience of college students and early true believers to midnight indie movie-house screenings. But there are more than a few works of anime that really do deserve to be seen on the largest possible screen, beginning with the canon of Hayao Miyazaki, arguably the greatest storyteller in the history of animation. Even his lesser efforts are worth viewing, but don't miss *Nausicaa of the Valley of the Wind* (1984), *My Neighbor Totoro* (1988), *Princess Mononoke* (1997), and *Spirited Away* (2001). Beyond Miyazaki, other works of must-watch big-screen anime include Katsuhiro Otomo's brilliant dystopian epic *Akira* (1990), Satoshi Kon's surreal psychological odyssey *Paprika* (2006), Mamoru Oshii's neon philosophy tome *Ghost in the Shell* (1995), and Makoto Shinkai's

blockbuster time-struck romance *Your Name* (2016).

**OLD-SCHOOL CLASSICS:** These include a bunch of TV shows that our white friends watched without even knowing they were watching anime. Your *Robotech* was my *Super Dimensional Fortress Macross* (1982). *Star Blazers*? I think you mean *Space Battleship Yamato* (1974). But works like the long-running kid-and-his-lovable-robot-cat series *Doraemon* (1979) and the boy-meets-alien rom-com *Urusei Yatsura* (1981) fall into this category, even though neither was ever broadcast on English-language American TV.

**ENDLESS EPICS:** When will these stories end? We grew up with them, our kids are still growing up with them, and maybe our grandkids will too. New versions of the ultimate fighting anime *Dragon Ball* (original, 1986; *Z,* 1989; *GT,* 1996; *Kai,* 2009; *Super,* 2015; *Super Dragon Ball Heroes,* 2018) keep on coming with no end in sight. The merry pirate adventure series *One Piece* (1999) is up to over 400 episodes now and counting. Ninja epic *Naruto* (2002) ran for five seasons before ending, but its death (as is common with ninja) was just a fake-out: a sequel series, *Naruto Shippuden* (2007) continued the series for another 500 episodes . . . after which the torch was passed to Naruto's son *Boruto* (2017), whose TV series seems destined to be just as long-lived.

**FANTASTIC VOYAGES:** When there was homework to do, we could always count on anime to sweep us off to imaginary and impossible worlds instead. The funky science fiction series *Cowboy Bebop* (1998) lasted just one season, but has enough of a huge cult following even today that Netflix is making a live-

action adaptation of it starring John Cho. *Bleach* (2004) unveiled the secrets of the afterlife. *Fullmetal Alchemist* (2006) showed us what brotherly love looks like when one brother is an empty, magically enchanted suit of armor. *Attack on Titan* (2009) is about a world where people battle to survive attacks by giant cannibalistic humanoids—like superhero sagas *My Hero Academia* (2016) and *One Punch Man* (2015) and period fantasy *Demon Slayer: Kimetsu No Yaiba* (2019). It's an incredible story where humans are revealed as the actual monsters.

**GIANT ROBOTS:** Mecha is out of fashion these days; the thrill of jumping into a giant armored battlesuit or riding the shoulder of a titanic android pal seems to have been replaced by dreams of being spirited away to be the hero of a magical RPG-style world. But those of us coming of age in the Nineties grew up dreaming we could control *Mazinger Z* (1972, released in the United States as *Tranzor Z* in the mid-Eighties), befriend *Giant Robo* (1992), roll with the robocops in *Mobile Police Patlabor* (1989), and figure out what was actually going on in *Neon Genesis Evangelion* (1996).

**STARRY-EYED SURPRISE:** For a lot of us—guys and girls—anime was the way we secretly learned about romance, which probably accounts for how bad we ended up at it. The psychic love-triangle series *Kimagure Orange Road* (1985), the goofy boy-toy comedy *Ouran High Host Club* (2006), the mixed-up magical melodrama *Fruits Basket* (2001) all taught us how to go to elaborate lengths not to admit our feelings, then repeatedly screw things up by being jealous or overconfident or tongue-tied at exactly the wrong moments.

**TWISTED IMAGINATIONS:** But there were many anime series that just couldn't be categorized, because the stories they told were too weird, disturbing, or surreal. Shows like the high-concept supernatural serial killer story sci-fi acid-trip *FLCL* (2000), *Death Note* (2006), the truthfully titled *Jojo's Bizarre Adventure* (2012), "how to kill your teacher" farce *Assassination Classroom* (2013), and laugh-out-loud psychic-powers parody *Disastrous Life of Saiki K* (2016) are all so hard to explain that it's easier to just give up and tell friends they have to watch for themselves.

**WALLET MONSTERS:** Then there were the anime programs designed to move merchandise: shows like *Yu-Gi-Oh!* (1998), *Pretty Cure* (2004), and of course, the emperor of them all, *Pokemon* (1997), which at over 1,100 episodes long has set an unbreakable record for the world's longest infomercial. Gotta buy 'em all!

# POSTCARD FROM ASIAN AMERICA

BY JENNY XU

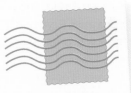

Hi RISE,

Writing in from Brooklyn, at a wild time, both for Asian America and for this book(!). I also just realized the other day that I've now lived outside of Kansas, where I grew up, for longer than I lived in it.

Living on the East Coast but being from a random state no one associates with Asian people brings out a reactionary Midwesternness in me sometimes—you mean y'all don't say "ope" when you need to squeeze right by someone?

At least it meant that when I lived in Boston—one of the most aggressively racist places I've ever been (beating out Branson, Missouri, the vaguely confederate "Orlando of the Ozarks" and my oblivious immigrant family's favorite vacation spot)—I could whip out the Kansas card when white people on the T asked me where I was from.

So what is Kansas to me, really? I was born in Shanghai, and moved to Kansas when I was in second grade. My dad is a professor, so the town in which I grew up, Lawrence, is a university town, cheerfully blue and hipster in an otherwise red state. There were Asian people there, both students and profs, and because Asian people are everywhere, we even had a local Vietnamese grocery, which we shopped at weekly, until larger Chinese and Korean grocers opened up in Kansas City, prompting us to make the 40-minute drive.

I never thought much about my Asianness there; I just felt out of place for not being homegrown, escaped via books, and spent a lot of time biking alone through the town's last few patches of tall grass. At this point, though, I've also dropped my hyper-Kansas-ness, because living through the start of the 2020s has never made me feel, for better and worse, more American than I've ever felt, and utterly Asian American.

Rock chalk,

Jenny

RISE
HERE AND NOW,
ASIAN AMERICA

# YELLOWFACE IN THE 1990S

BY NANCY WANG YUEN

The Nineties saw the practice of yellowing up by white actors finally face a reckoning—though it didn't go away completely. As yellowface faded, a new and more subtle phenomenon stepped up to take its place. "Whitewashing" was the practice of recasting roles that were originally Asian (or other nonwhite race or ethnicity) with white actors. For example, the protagonist of the Robert Heinlein novel *Starship Troopers,* Juan Rico, is Filipino. When the movie version came out in 1997, very blond, very white Casper Van Dien portrayed him as "Johnny Rico."

## "The Engineer," *Miss Saigon* on Broadway (1991), Jonathan Pryce

Jonathan Pryce originated the hit musical's Vietnamese-French lead, "The Engineer," in full yellowface when it opened in London in 1989. But when the smash hit musical transferred to Broadway, Actors Equity refused to allow Pryce to portray the role, saying that making a white actor look Asian was "an affront to the Asian community" and that "the casting of an Asian actor in the role would be an important and significant opportunity to break the usual pattern of casting Asians in minor roles." In a dramatic gesture, Cameron Mackintosh simply canceled the show. With so many jobs on the line, Equity rescinded its decision a few days later. Pryce went on to win a Tony Award for his performance. The silver lining: Filipina actor Lea Salonga, who starred as "Kim," made history as the first Asian to win a Best Actress Tony. Furthermore, because of protests from the Asian American arts community, Jonathan Pryce dropped the yellowface makeup for his Broadway run, and no white actor was ever cast as "The Engineer" in subsequent U.S. productions. Casting director Tara Rubin said in a *New York Times* interview, "We knew that the Asian American acting community had an incredibly good point, and

it was the beginning of a huge shift in the way we think about casting."

**CONVINCING OR NOT?** The yellowface was obviously unnecessary, given that Pryce won his Tony Award without it.

## "Kwai Chang Caine" in *Kung Fu: The Legend Continues* (ABC, 1993–1997), David Carradine

In this sequel to the original 1972–1975 TV series *Kung Fu,* David Carradine plays the grandson of his original character—also named Kwai Chang Caine. Apparently yellowface is hereditary!

**CONVINCING OR NOT?** David Carradine playing the older yellowface grandson of his original younger yellowface self, who just happens to share the same Asian name? No, on all levels.

## "Mrs. Noh Nang Ning" on *Tracey Takes On . . .* (HBO, 1996–1999), Tracey Ullman

Ullman remains unapologetic about doing her Chinese donut shop owner in yellowface, despite complaining about the makeup as "tough" and akin to "being buried alive." Asian American media advocates asked HBO to remove the character from the series. HBO refused, stating that "Tracey Ullman is a brilliant satirist and comedienne, and all of her work is in the spirit of fun and good humor."

**CONVINCING OR NOT?** Not at all, but that didn't put a dent in Ullman's belief as a comedian that she should be able to play anyone: "If you start questioning yourself with this PC stuff it can be really sanitizing and repress you." She also gleefully donned blackface to play "Sheneesha," a Black airport security agent. All of which may explain why *Tracey Takes On . . .* can no longer be found anywhere on streaming platforms.

### "Miss Swan" on *MADtv* (FOX, 1997–2009), Alex Borstein

Borstein claims that she based her buffoonish yellowface character "Miss Swan" on her Hungarian immigrant grandmother, but the character is easily recognizable as a crude Asian stereotype: She wore a black bowl cut wig and eye makeup that slanted her eyes, and spoke with broken speech and an indecipherable accent. Furthermore, Miss Swan worked at a nail salon (an industry in which Asians make up 76 percent of workers, according to a 2018 UCLA study). Also, it's been claimed that Miss Swan's original name was "Ms. Kwan."

**CONVINCING OR NOT?** No. And Borstein's tap-dancing to dodge complaints about the racist stereotype was even less convincing than her makeup.

## POSTCARD FROM ASIAN AMERICA

BY H'ABIGAIL MLO

Dear RISE,

Growing up in Greensboro, North Carolina, I sometimes felt torn between my Asian American and southern identities, but they intersected in the kitchen. Our pantry was a holy grail of global condiments: Carolina barbecue sauce and Tabasco; Sriracha, chile oil, and fish sauce. We celebrated every occasion with hearty meals that took hours to prepare—bún riêu, egg rolls, spring rolls, djam trong, djam wec, the works. We'd devour huge pots of sea snails seasoned with lemongrass and served with bamboo shoots—the snails hand-picked and the bamboo grown in our backyard. You'd be surprised what you can find and grow in rural North Carolina. After living here for over two decades, my family became experts in foraging food from unexpected places, a skill they brought with them from Vietnam. As Montagnards, survival was second nature. Having been repeatedly displaced from our ancestral lands in Vietnam and being displaced yet again by the war, making the most out of scarcity has become instinctive; a part of our blood. It's how my parents were raised and how they raised me.

And yet, we appreciated abundance. What I would look forward to most were summer cookouts: the peppery smell of grilled meat in the humid air, people filling their plates with curried vegetables, fatty pork, jasmine rice, and a dollop of ground Thai chile peppers. In one corner, women squatting in the shade, gossiping; in another, men standing, legs wide apart, guffawing between smokes, all exchanging stories, memories of the homeland and the refugee camps, sprinkled in between boasts about their kids and whispered questions ("Did you hear about the pastor's son?"). Kids playing and running after having their egg rolls and Chinese-takeout chicken wings. Everyone marveling at the latest addition to our community, a cooing infant. These were sacred spaces, where we built kinship and community over our shared love of food.

When I think of home, I think of this.

All my love,

H'Abigail Mlo

RISE
HERE AND NOW,
ASIAN AMERICA

# DISGRASIAN™  1990s

**IN 2007, JEN WANG** and **DIANA NGUYEN**— two friends who'd bonded over their mutual love of scotch, gossip, and pop culture— decided to launch a blog that was fueled by all three. That blog, *Disgrasian*, would keep tabs on Asian celebrities and other people of interest, sorting them into those whose behavior, attitude, or general lameness made them a "disgrace to the race," as it were, and those who were a credit to the culture. Laced with a devastatingly wicked sense of humor and a no-holds-barred approach to speaking truth to privilege, *Disgrasian* quickly became one of the most popular blogs of the early Asian American Internet. And then, Wang and Nguyen moved on, because nothing lasts forever. We asked them to get together for old times' sake, and share with us their thoughts on the Disgrasian All-Stars of the past three decades, beginning with the 1990s.

JEN WANG

DIANA NGUYEN

**JEN:** What's up, degenerates?! We're baaaaaaaa-aaaack.

**DIANA:** There's probably a whole generation of kids who don't know what a DISGRASIAN is.

**JEN:** That concept itself is DISGRASIAN.

**DIANA:** Those children are a disgrace to me! I disown them!

**JEN:** But they're not yours.

**DIANA:** EXACTLY. Nobody ghosts better than an Asian. I just *poofed* an entire generation. And that generation is saying right now, "Who are these bitches and why do they write DISGRASIAN in shouty ALL CAPS???"

**JEN:** Which brings us back to the reason we came out of retirement: to educate future generations on what it means to be DISGRASIAN! Because as a wise lady once said, "Those

who can't remember what it means to be DISGRASIAN are destined to repeat it."

**DIANA:** Disgrace and Asianness together are like soy sauce and wasabi, like Netflix and chill, like selfie cams and double chins. If someone is being DISGRASIAN, you feel shame by proxy.

**JEN:** To me, a DISGRASIAN is the person who makes you feel bad about being Asian. Like, in this culture, we've historically been invisible, right? It's actually worse to be visible and embarrassing. And since Asians never forget past offenses, let's open up these old wounds. The first decade we're going to walk our readers through is the '90s, and who and what we thought of then as DISGRASIAN.

**DIANA:** When we started the blog [in the 2000s], there were so many more Asian voices and faces in pop culture, running the gamut from astronauts to porn stars. The '90s didn't

172

have enough representation to even have an extended convo about the particular players.

**JEN:** Yup. As a teen of the era, I was desperately seeking *Asians*. For years, I was convinced Danica McKellar, Winnie on *The Wonder Years,* was Asian. My logic was: "She's got dark hair and epic bangs, she could be Filipina?" Later when I heard she was a math whiz, that just confirmed it. Only much later in adulthood did I learn she wasn't Asian. I actually felt let down! I so badly wanted to see myself and, really, to be seen.

**DIANA:** That was Margaret Cho for me. I was starting high school when *All-American Girl* (1994) aired. Along comes this Asian female comic just exploding in stand-up and onto network television with all the big boys. People knew her name and that made me feel like there was space for me there too. It was kinda like, *Is this our world to grab by the horns? Maybe!* But when I watched the show, I didn't feel good about it. I didn't have the vocabulary to articulate why. Like was her mom's accent funny to me, or was it bad for me? It didn't matter. There had been this big void for so long, then Margaret came around, and she was all I had.

**JEN:** So basically we're both saying that we can't define what it meant to be DISGRASIAN in the '90s because we couldn't even find Asians to look up to, much less look down on.

**DIANA:** I'm Vietnamese, and we were even more invisible. Like we were adjacent to the "Main Asians."

**JEN:** Except as like, nameless extras getting killed in Vietnam War movies.

**DIANA:** Or nameless hookers. Back then, the only Vietnamese guy anyone knew was Tom Vu, the infomercial guy who promised to show you how to make a million dollars so you could bone white chicks.

**JEN:** On yachts! He's the shady uncle in every Asian family that no one talks about. With unspoken "business dealings." Perpetually single. Drinks Crown Royal, is a VIP in Vegas, has stacks of *Playboy*s on the floor of his Datsun that you accidentally stumble upon when you're eight and get your first inkling of what full natural looks like.

**DIANA:** That got . . . very specific.

**JEN:** Yeah. I can't talk about that.

**DIANA:** I can't talk about my uncle's antique oak shelf of VHS porno dubs either, so I get it. Would you say shady Asians are DISGRASIAN?

**JEN:** Kind of the opposite. Because what's more American than shadiness? Anything having to do with money and vice is American AF. To me, you could argue that shady Asians are just really, really good at assimilating. And that's what America wants from us, right? Please assimilate, and don't make any noise about it.

Remember all those ballers who were funneling six figures to the Clintons and the Democratic Party in the '90s? Shady as hell. But I feel like their attitude was "Fuck it, this is what white people do to get ahead."

**DIANA:** America has one language and it isn't English, it's money. You buy your way into power, you buy your way out of trouble.

**JEN:** The '90s: an era so devoid of Asians, there weren't really even DISGRASIANs around for us to shame. Which is, itself, a shame. The next decade, however, is a whole other chapter.

**DIANA:** Just keep flipping those pages, people.

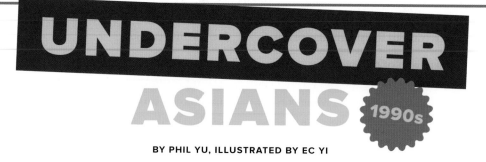

# UNDERCOVER ASIANS 1990s

BY PHIL YU, ILLUSTRATED BY EC YI

**IN OUR ONGOING** quest for representation, keen-eyed Asianspotters of the Nineties uncovered a pair of Oscar-nominated sibs, a golf champ, a Man of Steel, and more. Here are some noteworthy figures from the 1990s who you might be surprised to learn have Asian roots.

### 1. MARK-PAUL GOSSELAAR
California kid Zack Morris—the blond hair was a dye job!—on *Saved by the Bell,* Gosselaar is Indonesian and Dutch on his mother's side.

### 2. ROB SCHNEIDER
While comedian and former *Saturday Night Live* cast member Schneider's maternal grandmother is Filipina, he has somehow built a career playing gross stereotypes of brown people.

### 3. KIMORA LEE LEISSNER
Supermodel turned fashion mogul and TV-personality Leissner is the daughter of an African American father and Korean Japanese mother.

### 4&5. JENNIFER AND MEG TILLY
Before being nominated for an Oscar for *Bullets Over Broadway* as Jennifer Tilly, the squeaky-voiced bombshell was born Jennifer Ellen Chan to a Chinese American father and an Irish-Finnish-Canadian mother. So was her younger sister, Meg, nominated for an Oscar for her supporting turn in *Agnes of God.*

### 6. TYSON BECKFORD
The face (and bod) of Ralph Lauren Polo in the 1990s, Tyson Beckford is of Chinese-Jamaican descent on his father's side.

### 7. FRESH KID ICE
Christopher Won Wong, better known as Fresh Kid Ice, was a founding member of the controversial rap group 2 Live Crew. He's of Trinidadian Chinese ancestry . . . and he titled his debut solo album *The Chinaman* to make sure you knew it.

### 8. DEAN CAIN
Best known for playing Clark Kent/Superman on *Lois & Clark: The New Adventures of Superman,* Cain—born Dean George Tanaka—is of Japanese descent on his father's side.

### 9. TIGER WOODS
Golfer Woods, whose mother is Thai, Chinese, and Dutch, once famously described himself as "Cablinasian"—a self-coined abbreviation for Caucasian, Black, American Indian, and Asian.

### 10. ENRIQUE IGLESIAS
Multi-platinum pop artist Iglesias is the son of internationally celebrated Spanish singer Julio Iglesias and Filipina TV host Isabel Preysler.

### 11. FOXY BROWN
Rapper Foxy Brown (government name: Inga DeCarlo Fung Marchand) is of Chinese-Trinidadian descent, though when she was featured on a Jay-Z track, one of his verses ("Lookin' half black and Filipino") had folks speculating she was part Pinay.

GILES LI

ANIDA YOEU ALI

DENNIS KIM

MICHELLE MYERS

# RISE:
# A Poem

BY KELLY ZEN-YIE TSAI • CATZIE VILAYPHONH
GILES LI • ANIDA YOEU ALI • DENIZEN KANE
MICHELLE MYERS • BEAU SIA • MARLON ESGUERRA
EMILY C. CHANG • BAO PHI • ISHLE YI PARK
D'LO • REGIE CABICO

BEAU SIA

EMILY CHANG

BAO PHI

ISHLE YI PARK

**THROUGH THE '90S** and the 2000s, a lot of us happened to be the weird Asian that wrote performance poetry in our town. Eventually they'd call it slam poetry, or spoken word. For a lot of us, it was an outlet because we had something to say and nowhere to say it. This umbrella, Asian Pacific Islander, we negotiated, challenged, tried to grow—often uncomfortably, and often failing. We were inspired by Asian American, Pacific Islander poets and writers who came before us. Also American Indian, Indigenous, Black, Latinx, Arab, Middle Eastern, West Asian, Jewish, white, mixed, female, queer, genderqueer, trans, gender non-conforming, immigrant, refugee, adoptee. Before YouTube, before Facebook, we hustled to the open mics and the slams. We sold chapbooks because we had a connection at Kinko's, or maybe a CD, out of our bags. We hoped to make enough money to pay a bill or two, but mostly we did it because we wanted to say something and be heard. Eventually some of us met up, formed crews, formed really big crews. Some of us got into movies, organized our people, published books you could find on a bookstore shelf. We were successful because we listened to one another, we redefined success for ourselves, we made a road where none was made for us. We found each other, we built together. And we still got something to say.—Bao Phi

In celebration of Asian American spoken word's "golden age," circa late 1990s and early 2000s, we invited a dozen or so poets who were active in the era to collaborate on an original poem, exquisite corpse style. Each participant was responsible for writing a stanza, having seen only the previous poet's contribution, before passing it along to the next poet. The result: a one-of-a-kind poem about this unique moment in the scene and the rise of Asian America.

**KELLY**
Sing me, poet, the shape of my heart—
Birthed from scribbled journal pages and late-
    night street corner ciphers.
Our heads bob to the turntables' beats, weaving
    new rhythms for us.
Call us forth from these silences. Raise
    our voices. We, the unimagined, the
    undetermined—
Asian America. On every mic, amplified in every
    corner of this country, we stand.

**CATZIE**
We had practice before kindergarten, our
    parents' unofficial translators
My mother's hands worked hard, but my mother
    tongue worked harder
6th grade was a helluva drug, D.A.R.E. to call a
    fellow immigrant F.O.B.
Lucky for me, this refugee got checked by a POC
And now I recite "a planeload of bombs every 8
    minutes for 24 hours for 9 years in Laos"

**GILES**
We were made loud-mouthed and proud, and
    somehow twisted together meaning from
the scattered scripture found in the stories of
    migration. The same years that
go quiet upon every retelling, the family members
    who disappear—
From these missing pages, we drew history,
    crafted mythology,
and had no choice but to rise, even if just to keep
    from falling in on ourselves.

**ANIDA**
Yes! The poets and artists found that mythical
    nation-state called *Asian America*
with a map from ancestors of broken speak and
    paper sons.
The elders said, "*Mahal,* walk beyond Tree City,
    then follow the feedback loop,
before the reverb cross the river of yellow rage,
    there at the summit near the edge
of the 8th wonder of the world and just under the
    mango tree

**DENIZEN**
. . . we'll meet."
You'll tell me of your time in the belly.
Your tour in the war of the flea.
The bodies you lost in the water
The words you found gleaming with grief.

**MICHELLE**
Can words alone evoke an awakening?
I entreat the air but peace evades me—
Our ghosts are buried in my flesh.
My dreams circle back over time lost
    as anger sits behind my eyes and burrows in my
    chest.

**BEAU**
Learn the why of why yet to be.
How our rage got think-tanked into propaganda
    fuel.
The gold wrapper selling the white egg.
The village blindfolded in the forest together.
The maktub made trophy instead of future in the
    soil.

MARLON
*We namespeakroots into somethinggrand*
*take greatleaps that bind yellowpearls*
*singunisong wearehalftheworld ikalatmuna*
*trace YurisGraceLeesCorkys with twotongues*
*learn forallofus where wemustgo*

EMILY
We weld the golden spike where East meets
   West
no longer palimpsest pages of America
Fuck your dragon lady kung fu nerd forever
   foreigner
we rage we exist we destroy we love
we speak the exquisite language of us

BAO
Some claim being woke but are talking in their
   sleep
Asian Americans a dream no one remembers
(Unless it's a nightmare)
Our elders dying, demons roost on their chests,
Pushed down in the street, squash a walking virus

ISHLE
does it even matter? when we chronicle
our rage at disrespected elders, celebrate in joy,
& rise despite our scars (to spite da scars)? yes,
   yes, and yes.

\* gold stars scattered across da universe \*
~ your songs still echo in my heart ~ saranghe ~

D'LO
Tip Toeing Brown in the dustiest of American
   Towns, before we quietly danced backwards—
leaving to cities with boxes of lessons,
ancestors folded up in fabric, backpacks full
of reckoning, questioning the aches in our
fingers from stifled screams, picking up pens
to fight,
queer fluidity inking our poems into—a place to
   breathe, a home, a new town:
Asian America. I replace shame with the hope I
   have honored you.

REGIE
we write foot on pedal stomping the april chill
we incite a fire of poetic epiphany, spiraling
   witticisms
& hammer-winged truths, climbing a ladder of
   laughter,
our poems, a torched way out of the dark
we write to get through the unquenchable fire.

2000S

# The 2000s

BY PHIL YU

**I USED TO TRAVEL** a lot. I'd find myself on planes and other situations where strangers would attempt to make small talk, and the conversation would inevitably lead to jobs and how you make your living. I dreaded these interactions: They usually involved a mental negotiation, after sizing up the other person, of whether I wanted to disclose the fact that I run a website called "Angry Asian Man," because that always led to more questions, and I didn't feel like spending the duration of a cross-country flight elbow-to-elbow with someone who didn't like the answers to those questions. So I usually just flat-out lied and told people I'm in "web development." I'm not even sure what that actually means. It didn't matter—there were usually no follow-up questions.

*Angry Asian Man* is a blog. And I've been at it since before I knew we were calling them blogs. When I do tell people about it, I explain that it's the longest-running, most widely read independent blog devoted to Asian American news, culture, and commentary. I have no idea if this claim is actually true, but no one has called me on it yet, so it seems like a safe enough assertion. As for how long I've been doing it: I keep thinking I've done the math wrong, but I've been running *Angry Asian Man*

for over 20 years, which means I've basically been "known" as Angry Asian Man for longer than I've lived in any one place, longer than I've attended any school, longer than I've held any job. I am a professional Angry Asian Man. Do you remember what you were doing on the Internet 20 years ago? Do you remember what you were doing on the Internet last week? Twenty years in Internet time is downright ancient. And I have seen some shit.

"Why are you so angry?" I get asked this a lot. People want to know why I started *Angry Asian Man*. They want an origin story, an inciting incident—a racial slur, an act of violence—that made me so angry that I just had to run to the computer and furiously start rage typing. There is no such story. The simple truth is that I had something to say and I needed a place to say it. (The irony is that I am not even a particularly angry person, neither in the way that people usually fear, nor in the sexy, fiery Korean drama kind of way.) So I started writing and I never stopped. My first posts were short observations or just sharing links, usually accompanied by pithy commentary—much like what we do now on social media. But we were still a few years away from Facebook, Twitter, Tumblr, and the like. Those platforms didn't exist yet, so I had to create my own.

I grew up in the heart of Silicon Valley, which means, demographically, I grew up around hella Asians. The city of Cupertino,

## 2000

🎭 **Kollaboration founded** as a community-driven event to foster and showcase Asian American talent

👑 **Angela Baraquio** becomes first Asian American Miss America

🏛 **Representative Norman Mineta** becomes secretary of commerce, the first Asian American appointed to a cabinet seat. Six months later, George Bush would appoint him to his cabinet as secretary of transportation.

🎵 **Linkin Park** releases their debut album *Hybrid Theory*, establishing them as one of the most successful music acts of the decade

perhaps best known as the birthplace and headquarters of Apple Inc.—my high school's most famous alumnus is Steve Jobs—was hurtling toward an Asian-majority population as I came of age, then surging from 44 percent to 63 percent between the 2000 and 2010 Census. My childhood home was a literal stone's throw from a boba shop and a 99 Ranch Market. The Methodist church down the street holds worship services in English, Mandarin, and Korean. Growing up in a hella Asian community, I rarely felt pegged or pigeonholed with the baggage of being "the Asian guy" because lots of other guys were also the Asian guy. Or just, you know . . . guys. In the spread of high school social circles, it seemed like an Asian kid could be, yes, an overachiever or a nerd, but also a jock, a student body president, a delinquent, and/or a theater geek (like me). It was fairly easy to allow my Korean American identity to slink into the background, unacknowledged and taken for granted. It felt, at least, like something that didn't have to matter. But by the time I got to college, I was in for a culture shock.

Take this West Coast kid out of California and plunk him down in the Midwest, he's going to quickly realize two things: 1) It gets cold. Like, you-don't-own-the-right-clothes-for-this cold. 2) There are waaaay more white people here. That was me, getting dropped off my freshman year at Northwestern University in Evanston, Illinois. For perhaps the first time in my life, I experienced a subzero windchill factor, and the heightened awareness of what it felt like to be the only Asian guy in this lecture hall, in this restaurant, in this Target.

I was most acutely aware of this as one of only a handful of Asian American students studying Radio/TV/Film, a major I wore as a badge of honor. Like any red-blooded American kid, I grew up on an unhealthy diet of movies, television, and pop culture. During the Eighties and early Nineties, my parents owned a video rental store, exposing me to shelves upon shelves of VHS titles that I probably shouldn't have been exposed to. It was heaven. While Neighborhood Video & 1-Hour Photo eventually went out of business—two totally obsolete services under one roof!—my obsession as a cinephile only flourished, and college became a legit opportunity to study and pursue my passion. But somewhere along the way, as I engaged academically with film history, theory, and criticism, I was forced to reconcile the fact that so much of the media I grew up loving had never really made space for me as an Asian American. While many of my peers focused on the hands-on craft of filmmaking—directing, screenwriting, editing, etc.—I found myself writing a lot of papers and raising questions about Hollywood racism and Asian American representation. And really enjoyed it. I think I wrote no fewer than three different academic papers about *Enter the Dragon*. Yeah, I was that

## 2000

🎬 *Crouching Tiger, Hidden Dragon* released; Ang Lee's period martial arts masterpiece earns over $100 million despite having an all-Asian cast and being in Chinese with subtitles

🎬 *Romeo Must Die* is released. A breakthrough lead role for Jet Li, but best known for its aborted romantic subplot between Li and Aaliyah.

🎬 Filipino American indie film *The Debut* becomes a homegrown hit through word-of-mouth screenings

## 2001

⚾ Japanese star Ichiro Suzuki makes his MLB debut with the Seattle Mariners and ends up as both Rookie of the Year and MVP. The 10-time All Star will eventually retire with over 3,000 hits, and likely will be first Asian-born member of the Baseball Hall of Fame.

guy. And yeah, I was kind of lonely in those classes.

Not that there wasn't a significant Asian American presence on campus. And it was fighting hard to not be ignored. In the spring of 1995, the year before I arrived on campus as a freshman, student activists at Northwestern made national headlines for their efforts to establish an official program in Asian American Studies. After months of intense lobbying, only to be met with the administration's inaction and indifference, students organized a hunger strike to pressure the university to meet their demands. Seventeen students participated in the strike, which lasted 23 days, drew widespread attention and support from across the country, and ultimately resulted in the creation of the Asian American Studies Program. It would take several more years before the program was implemented. Most of the hunger strikers actually graduated before they ever got to take any of the courses they had literally starved for. But I was a direct beneficiary of their sacrifices. Four years later, I was among the students who got to enroll in some of the first classes that Northwestern officially offered under Asian American Studies. The classes that changed my life.

It all came together for me in a course called "Asian Americans in the Media," taught by Professor L. S. Kim, during a screening of Renee Tajima-Peña and Christine Choy's doc-

umentary *Who Killed Vincent Chin?* I sat there in the dark, with a growing sense of rage building in my heart as I learned, for the first time, about the brutal 1982 murder of Vincent Chin, the men who allegedly told him, "It's because of you little motherfuckers that we're out of work" before they chased him down and beat him to death with a baseball bat, and the ridiculously lenient sentence the killers received for their crime. But perhaps more important, I learned how the case galvanized a pan-Asian movement for justice, a rallying cry to be seen and heard as whole people, and a collective rebuke against the ahistorical notion that Asian Americans were victims, bystanders, or background extras in our own story.

When the film ended and the lights went up, I was angry. Angry for Vincent Chin, a life unjustly extinguished in a flash of racist violence. Angry for myself, in recognition of every slur, stereotype, and threat of violence I'd swallowed and suppressed as an Asian American, every moment I had been made to feel unwelcome and excluded in this country, the only home I'd ever known. Angry that I was only learning about this case now, nearly 20 years after the fact. Vincent Chin's murder felt like a family secret that had been purposely hidden from me. How many more of our stories were out there, withheld and untold?

Between my film classes, my Asian American Studies classes, and the burgeoning worldwide

Elaine Chao, appointed by George W. Bush as secretary of labor, becomes the first Asian American woman in a presidential cabinet

SuChin Pak joins MTV as correspondent, becoming the first regular Asian American face on MTV News

Bobby Lee joins the cast of *MADtv* as its first and only Asian American cast member; he stays with Fox's sketch comedy show for eight seasons

web, I inadvertently found a triangulation of interest and purpose . . . if not a clear career path. By the time I graduated from college, I had no idea what I wanted to do next, but knew that I had started a journey and a conversation about identity and community that I wanted to continue. However, "having strong opinions about Asian America" didn't seem like a particularly strong professional option. At least not yet. I was broke, living back home with my parents, and working a dead-end temp job. But I did have a considerable amount of free time on my hands. This Internet thing didn't seem like it was going away any time soon, so I glued together some rudimentary HTML and created a website. (I think that's "web development"?)

In February 2001, just a few minutes after midnight on Valentine's Day—a complete coincidence, by the way—I fired up the file transfer protocol, flipped the switch, and uploaded the very first version of Angry Asian Man. What I didn't know at the time was that I had just taken the first step of a journey that would define my personal and professional life for the next two decades and beyond.

I didn't expect anyone to read it. Maybe some friends and casual stumblers would find their way onto the site. The Internet was considerably smaller back then, and I just wanted to carve out my own little Asian American space on the Internet where I could sound off, throw a few stones, and run around in every room of the house. In retrospect, I was really looking for a connection, hoping my words would reach folks who had the same sense of longing for community that didn't quite always match up with the physical one around me. My website and the Internet at large were my passport to connect with something bigger than myself: a shout in the dark, a blind transmission to see if anyone out there was listening.

They were. Years later, I would hear from so many readers who shared that while growing up as the only Asian kid at their respective school or town, finding *Angry Asian Man* was a lifeline, a connection, and confirmation that a community—Asian America—was out there.

I can't believe I'm saying this like the old man that I apparently am, but I remember a time when there was no Internet, at least not in the way it is now, like a second skin in our lives. And I remember what that meant for our distributed, scattered Asian American community. Online or in person, building and cultivating community is work. It's a lot easier to retreat into old patterns, find ways of fitting in, building walls around your identity, and just growing thicker skin. I'm part of the last generation with feet firmly straddling both eras, before and after we could look at a screen and basically find out anything, at any time. And I remember when the Internet felt new, open, and undefined. Hopeful, even. When sharing a little bit of ourselves, finding fellowship in

---

**2001**

🏛 On September 11, the Twin Towers in New York and the Pentagon in Washington, D.C., are attacked by terrorists using hijacked planes. The attack permanently transforms U.S. society, changing air travel, immigration, and attitudes toward Muslims, while sparking America's longest war, in Afghanistan, as well as the Iraq War. In the wake of the attacks, South Asians and Muslims are subjected to widespread incidents of hate and violence.

**2002**

🎵 Jin the MC wins his seventh consecutive Freestyle Friday on BET's *106 & Park* and is signed to the major hip-hop label Ruff Ryders, launching his hip-hop career

🎭 David Henry Hwang's reboot of *Flower Drum Song* hits Broadway, reimagining the musical without the original's stereotypical nonsense

digital spaces and creating an online community felt like opportunities, and not liabilities.

I actually get a little wistful recalling the optimism and unguarded willingness with which we forged friendships with complete strangers on the Internet. But we did, and I'm still friends with many of them to this day. I fell comfortably into the community of Asian American bloggers, writers, and artists. Shout-outs to Disgrasians, Reappropriate, 8Asians, Sepia Mutiny, Hyphen, Giant Robot. All the LiveJournals and Xangas and message boards. We connected as fellow Asian Americans who were interested in exploring what this identity meant—not simply as a label, but as a collaborative fellowship, contributing to a project that is not yet finished; a shared struggle, a mutual celebration.

One thing I always neglect to consider when I look back on this time is how much I was still learning about who I was as an Asian American—specifically, a straight, American-born East Asian male—and my place in this community. As my blog grew in readership and influence, it might have seemed like I was operating with some level of authority, scholarship, or leadership, but there was so much I was still figuring out and learning as I went. Basic questions, like, when we say "Asian American," who exactly are we talking about? So . . . we're not

using the hyphen? Am I supposed to hate *The Joy Luck Club,* because a lot of people seem to be mad at it? (I liked it.) But also the more difficult, nuanced discussions, on hate crimes, trauma, mental health, domestic violence, misogyny, gender, sexuality, colorism. As the tools we had access to changed, we were finally able to create the spaces—via blogs, and other forms of social media—to challenge, debate, and figure these things out.

I'm still a work in progress. And all of this [gestures wildly at Asian America] is a work in progress. During the 2000s, the shape and character of our community would be forged through some of the harshest circumstances of our lifetimes.

## Your Struggle Is My Struggle

At the very start of this decade, something happened that changed the world—and specifically, our world as Asian Americans—overnight. On September 11, 2001,* 19 individuals associated with extremist group al Qaeda hijacked four airplanes and carried out coordinated attacks on targets in New York City and Washington, D.C., during which 2,977 people were killed. It was, as they say, the deadliest terrorist attack to occur on American soil. The decade, defined. The aftermath and legacy of

* See page 209, "9/11: Remembering a Tragedy and the Dark Days That Followed"

**2003**

🏀 Yao Ming enters the NBA, becomes the first Asian-born NBA all-star (eight times) and eventually, the first Asian in the Basketball Hall of Fame

🏛 Abercrombie & Fitch's release of shirts with racist graphics and slogans triggers one of the first nationwide Asian American protest movements

🎬 *Better Luck Tomorrow*, shattering both box office expectations and the model-minority stereotype, launches the directorial career of Justin Lin

🏀 Michael Chang retires from tennis; in 1989, he'd become the first Asian American and the youngest player ever to win a Grand Slam, the French Open. He is inducted into the Tennis Hall of Fame in 2008.

RISE

185

9/11 would challenge our notions of American identity and security: What does a "real" American look like? What are the true terms and conditions of citizenship? What are the sacrifices—physical and ideological—we are willing to make to feel "safe"? 9/11 would also test and retest our resolve as Asian Americans and what we stood for—if we really stood for anything—as a community.

Like most folks on the West Coast, I woke up to reports of the World Trade Center in flames. I watched the news, numb. I got ready for work. On autopilot, I somehow convinced myself that I could fulfill my job responsibilities and have a normal day. I drove halfway up the peninsula toward San Francisco before I turned around, realizing there was nothing normal I could do that day. Somewhere during that drive back, I accepted the fact that our lives were about to change. And that for entire communities, the change would be severe and devastating.

As everyone—the government, law enforcement, the media, your uncle—searched for someone to blame for the attacks, the target quickly fell on the Muslim American community, and by extension, Middle Easterners, Arabs, South Asians, and Sikhs—you know, brown folks. It became unsafe—for the brown folks. People were angry and scared, and seeking a target to focus their aggressions and fears upon. The American people have a notoriously well-documented habit of doing this.

The South Asian community was just the latest in a long history of Asian American communities, from even before the term or idea of "Asian American" existed, who have been persecuted, scapegoated, and violated. The Chinese Exclusion Act. The incarceration of Japanese Americans during World War II. The murder of Vincent Chin. Being Asian American means being invisible until you're not, and when you're not, hypervisibility comes with the blunt force of a baseball bat. Asian Americans are comfortably tolerated as model minorities, but history has clearly shown that status is tenuous and conditional.

Balbir Singh Sodhi, a gas station owner in Mesa, Arizona, was the first reported victim among dozens killed in hate crimes against Sikhs and Muslims after 9/11. Born in Punjab, India, he was Sikh, and wore a turban and unshorn beard in accordance with his faith. On September 15, 2001, four days after the attacks on the World Trade Center and the Pentagon, Sodhi was planting flowers around the front of his gas station when 42-year-old Frank Silva Roque pulled up in his truck and shot him five times in the back with a .380 handgun, killing him. Roque, who wanted revenge for the 9/11 attacks, had reportedly told a waiter at Applebee's that he was "going to go out and shoot some towel-heads." When police arrested him the next day, Roque yelled, "I am a patriot!" and "I stand for America!" Like so

## 2004

David Chang opens Momofuku Noodle Bar, launching his restaurant (and media) empire

William Hung infamously auditions for *American Idol*

Gwen Stefani introduces the "Harajuku Girls," four mute Japanese backup dancers/props who are derided by Asian Americans as a "modern minstrel show"

John Cho and Kal Penn fly high in *Harold and Kumar Go to White Castle*

*Lost* debuts on ABC, starring Daniel Dae Kim, Yunjin Kim, and Naveen Andrews

many, immediately after 9/11 and to this day, Roque erroneously associated Sodhi's appearance with those responsible for the attacks. His murder was the harbinger of a frightening new reality for brown Americans.

The murder of Balbir Singh Sodhi also inspired a generation of activists. The Sikh Coalition, an advocacy organization that defends the civil rights of Sikh Americans, was founded in response to the wave of hate violence that swept the United States in the wake of 9/11. Now the largest civil rights organization of its kind, the Sikh Coalition fights for justice, education, and equal rights on behalf of Sikh Americans. In addition to individual hate crimes and discrimination, affected communities faced rampant racial and religious profiling—particularly during air travel—targeted surveillance by law enforcement under the Patriot Act, mass deportations, and an erosion of civil rights under the pretense of national security. Many South Asian and Muslim activists, organizers, leaders, and artists cite 9/11 as the moment they found their voice, because they were forced to.

Elsewhere in the community, in the immediate days and weeks after 9/11, Japanese Americans were among the first to stand in solidarity and speak out against the suspicion and persecution of Muslim, South Asian, and Arab American communities. In Los Angeles, hundreds gathered at a Little Tokyo candle-light vigil, both to remember the victims of 9/11 and to show support for those who were being unjustly blamed for the attacks. Japanese Americans had been down this road before and they knew where it led. Speaking from authority, they were saying "hell no."

It was a contemporary model for pan-Asian unity, for standing up and speaking up on behalf of fellow Asian Americans, for Americans, for justice and fairness, a pivotal and public buying in to the idea that Asian American meant something more than a demographic box. It showed Japanese Americans putting themselves on the line, linking arms and declaring your struggle will also be my struggle.

That moment, and the aftermath of 9/11, was a lesson for me—I realized that my definition of Asian American, of community, of Asian American history and the pursuit of justice, had to be bigger, dynamic, and more inclusive. It reinforced something I'd been beginning to learn about Asian American identity: that it's an opt-in situation. Coined by activists in 1968, the term "Asian American" has been flattened over time to common usage as a general descriptor for Americans of Asian descent. But it was originally conceived as a pan-ethnic political identity to unite for social change. There's nothing inherently holding together this massive amalgamation of identities and origins. We choose to come together as a community because doing so makes us stronger in light

**2005**

Alice Wu's classic debut film *Saving Face*, a lesbian rom-com with an all-Asian cast, is released

ImaginAsian TV launches, calling itself "America's first national 24-hour Asian American network"

Hot 97's "Tsunami Song" mocks Asian tsunami tragedy, and Asian American activists launch a protest against New York City's most popular radio station in response

Steve Cheng co-founds the video streaming service YouTube, which becomes a vital launchpad for Asian American creativity

of allll the bullshit we have to face as Asian Americans. No, we are not all the same, but opting in acknowledges this shared struggle and says that we are accountable to one another. We will show up for one another, whether it's seeking justice for hate crimes to calling out bullshit in the media or fighting toward liberation for all. This realization would shape, grow, and help evolve my understanding of Asian America, through the rest of the decade and beyond.

*Angry Asian Man* gave me a voice and a unique vantage point to the highs and lows of Asian America. And contrary to the stereotype of quiet Asians, I could see that we like to fight. That we were in a fight to tell our own stories, to decide which images and narratives defined us. Decades of racist imagery, from Hollywood movies to political propaganda, informed by racism, colonialism, and conquest, have seeped their way into the consciousness of what the West views as "Asian." It dehumanizes us. It makes us smaller. It chips away at our agency and enforces the narrative of Asians as unwelcome visitors to this country. And it takes form in the most seemingly innocuous ways. But like I said, we like to scrap. And we'll use the Internet to do it. As key moments in this decade will demonstrate, if you picked a fight with us, you will be greeted with the collective fury of young, angry Asian America.

# Two Wongs Make It Wrong

In the spring of 2002, popular clothing retailer Abercrombie & Fitch decided to, as they say, fuck around and find out. The company's latest round of overpriced clothing included an assortment of Asian-themed novelty graphic T-shirts advertising fictional businesses. One of the designs, the one most people seem to remember, was for "Wong Brothers Laundry Service," evoking stereotypically cheap Chinatown labor, bachelor societies, and Ancient Chinese Secrets. The design featured an illustrated stereotypical caricature of an Asian man with slit eyes, buck teeth, and the conical (iconical?) rice paddy hat. The slogan, the kicker: "Two Wongs Can Make It White." Other shirt designs "advertised" places like Pizza Dojo ("Eat In Or Wok Out," "You Love Long Time"); Wok-N-Bowl Chinese Food & Bowling ("Let The Good Times Roll"); Rick Shaw's Hoagies and Grinders ("Good Meat, Quick Feet"); and—I'm genuinely unsure what this one was supposed to be fake-promoting—Buddha Bash ("Get Your Buddha On The Floor"). All were accompanied by racist caricatures. Man, they really loved those conical hats. These were all actual shirts, neatly folded on shelves and available for purchase at your nearest Abercrombie & Fitch store.

The college kids were the first to take notice.

## 2005

-👁- Filipina American Cristeta Comerford becomes head chef at the White House—the first woman to have the role and the first Asian American

📽 Sandra Oh debuts as Dr. Cristina Yang in *Grey's Anatomy*; her breakthrough performance eventually wins her icon status and the Golden Globe

📽 The animated *Jake Long: American Dragon* debuts, the first Disney Channel series to feature a mixed Asian American family

📽 Vietnamese American Chloe Dao wins Season 2 of *Project Runway*, becoming the first Southeast Asian reality TV winner

I first got wind of the shirts from an email forwarded from Stanford's Asian American Students' Association—there was no social media back then—which quickly spread to other campus student organizations across the country. The reaction was immediate and incendiary. Now, I'm going to be honest: I was surprised with the fury and speed of the response from these young organizers. At the time, at least in my own experience, it felt extremely difficult to get Asian American students to care about anything but grades and culture shows. Clearly, I was wrong. These shirts hit a nerve. On the other hand, it made sense. Abercrombie & Fitch's core demographic was college-age youth. One of the first unsolicited catalogs I ever received, probably when my information was sold to a mailing list after taking the PSAT, was for Abercrombie & Fitch. At my midwestern college, where Greek life was a prominent part of the social scene, Abercrombie felt like part of the starter kit. Throw on a North Face jacket and a pair of New Balance and you had the standard uniform. For some Asian American college students, the Asian-themed shirts probably felt like a betrayal and wake-up call. Abercrombie might have wanted young people to buy and wear their clothes, but they wanted the right kind of young people, if their catalogs weren't already a dead giveaway. Pretty young white people running through a field. Pretty young white people sitting on a fence. Pretty young white people kicking back in a giant tractor tire. Not you, Asians.

I'll never forget the angry student who, shortly after the controversy hit, sent me a photo of all his Abercrombie & Fitch clothes in a pile, next to a canister of lighter fluid and box of matches. The guy wasn't playing. My only thought was, dude, you own enough Abercrombie & Fitch clothing to constitute an actual pile? That could fuel a legit bonfire? Damn.

Like I said, these shirts struck a nerve.

With social media still several years away, word spread from listserv to email chain to message board to AIM chat, sans hashtags. Community members organized protests outside Abercrombie & Fitch stores across the country, from San Francisco to Chicago to Boston. Shout-out to Asian American student orgs, including but not limited to Northwestern, Stanford, Dartmouth, MIT, and Wellesley, who would not let this issue quietly fade away.

I was only about a year into running *Angry Asian Man*. It was the first time I had seen an issue among Asian Americans gain this level of traction. And it was clear that much of it was powered by the voices of Asian Americans online. The blogs were on top and in the thick

🎬 Comcast acquires and rebrands the International Channel as AZN TV, "The Network for Asian America," in an effort to create programming specifically targeted toward Asian Americans; the channel is killed in 2008

🎬 MTV launches three Asian American–targeted channels: MTV Desi and MTV Chi, featuring South Asian and Chinese-related content, followed by MTV K for Korean-related content in 2006. All three networks went off the air in 2007.

🎬 Lisa Ling, who left *The View* in 2002 to return to international reporting, brings an undercover film team into North Korea, providing a rare glimpse into the "hermit kingdom" for the National Geographic documentary *Inside North Korea*

of it, with the ability to disseminate information quickly and with ease, long before mainstream media picked up on the story. For my part, I wrote a post about the shirts, shared the images, called them racist because that's what they were, and at the end of my screed, almost as an afterthought, included Abercrombie & Fitch's corporate contact information—email, phone, mailing address, etc.—all easily found on the company's website (years before you could shout at a company's "@"). I encouraged readers to get in touch and tell Abercrombie what was up. And they did.

Abercrombie pulled the shirts from stores. "We personally thought Asians would love this T-shirt," the company's sad publicity lackey Hampton Carney later told the *San Jose Mercury News*. "It was in no way intended to offend anyone, and it hurts us that it has offended people. Everyone here at the company thought it was funny. I even polled the Asians around the office today of what they thought of the shirts, and they thought the shirts were hilarious." You see, his Asian friends said it was okay, so it must be okay. For the record, no one is allowed to cite me as their "Asian friend" to justify any kind of bullshit.

For me, the debacle was a demonstration of what was possible with the early Internet and some collective rage. It also became a turning point for my blog. It was an incredibly effective illustration of the power this website could

wield, and it changed the mission and direction of Angry Asian Man. It wasn't just a space to rant and talk shit. I could help point people at an issue, and help move people to action. That was powerful. And it gave me purpose.

If this happened today, the entire controversy would play out exclusively on Twitter and get resolved in a matter of days, if not hours. But the decade would give way to a series of such debacles, and forced into public and mainstream discourse by the Asian American community, largely by online voices. We were all learning and laying the groundwork for how to be angry online. At the core of each of the controversies that would erupt over the next eight years, from racist magazine spreads to slurs on national television, was a fight to be seen and heard as we are.

## The Devil in the Details

The April 2004 issue of *Details* magazine ran a humor piece, entitled "Gay or Asian," presented as an on-the-street field guide on how to distinguish gay men from Asian men. The piece, written by Whitney McNally, was the latest in an ongoing satirical "anthropology" feature intended to poke fun at cultural stereotypes of masculinity (previous installments included "Gay or British?" and "Gay or Jesus?") but was effectively just a laundry list of Asian stereotypes fused with bawdy double enten-

2006

🏛 The "Macaca" moment: U.S. Senator George Allen uses an obscure racial slur to refer to Indian American S. R. Sidarth, ending Allen's political career

🎬 Justin Lin takes over the *Fast & the Furious* series, steering it into one of the biggest blockbuster franchises in the world, with its third, Tokyo-set installment, *The Fast & the Furious: Tokyo Drift*

🎬 Yul Kwon wins *Survivor: Cook Islands*, a season with teams initially divided by race

🎬 *Heroes* debuts on NBC, with Masi Oka's Hiro Nakamura as arguably its central figure

dres, using tired imagery drawn from food and martial arts. It's stunning how much racism and homophobia could fit on a two-page spread, not to mention the erasure of actual gay Asian men. You have to feel sorry for the model whose photo accompanies the piece—it's likely he had no idea what he was posing for.

"One cruises for chicken; the other takes it General Tso–style," the intro read. "Whether you're into shrimp balls or shaved balls, entering the dragon requires imperial tastes. So choke up on your chopsticks, and make sure your labels are showing. Study hard, grasshopper: A sharp eye will always take home the plumpest eel." I don't even understand what most of that means, but someone sure thought they were being clever. The taxonomy points out various features of an Asian man—"Dior sunglasses," "Ryan Seacrest hair," "delicate features"—that also apparently double as telltale signs of homosexuality. A white T-shirt? Gay, apparently. "V-neck nicely showcases sashimi-smooth chest," the piece explains. "What other men visit salons to get, the Asian gene pool provides for free." I'm sorry, what?

In situations like this, you really hope that there would be at least one behind-the-scenes person—hopefully early on enough in the process—to speak up and raise the minor point that something like this might be sorta, kinda, possibly racist. It's astonishing how many

eyes and hands the "Gay or Asian" piece probably had to pass through before it saw print. Multiple people signed off on it. It speaks to how many people didn't know or didn't care, much like the Abercrombie & Fitch shirts, about this kind of casual anti-Asian racism. It's just a joke. It's just a shirt. The awareness, apologies, and accountability only emerges after the shit hits the fan, but even then, it's too often fleeting and forgotten.

The response from the Asian American community was swift, intense, and angry. Over several weeks, the magazine became the target of letter-writing and call-in campaigns, threats of boycott, numerous online petitions garnering tens of thousands of signatures, and denouncing statements from numerous civil rights and media watchdog organizations, including GLAAD, Gay Asian and Pacific Islander Men of New York, Organization of Chinese Americans, Korean American Coalition, and the Asian American Journalists Association. In New York City, a demonstration outside the offices of parent company Fairchild Publications drew hundreds of protestors (tailor-made chants reportedly included "*Details* says, 'Bonsai Ass,' we say 'In the Trash!'"—I guess you had to be there) demanding a substantial apology from *Details* and sensitivity training for editors and staff. The controversy even generated enough heat to inspire a joke on *Saturday Night Live*'s "Weekend Update" segment.

---

**2007**

**2008**

Dr. Sanjay Gupta joins CNN as medical correspondent, becoming "America's Doctor"

Gene Luen Yang's seminal graphic novel *American Born Chinese* is published

Justin Kan cofounds Justin.TV, a "lifecasting" startup that initially features Kan himself sharing his own life round the clock. When they open the service to allow others to stream, gaming emerges as a sweet spot. Kan and his team spin the game-related content off into a service called Twitch, which they later sell to Amazon for nearly a billion dollars

JabbaWockeeZ wins *America's Best Dance Crew*, launching Asian American dance crews into the mainstream spotlight

*Details* got the message. The May issue opened with editor-in-chief Daniel Peres's letter of apology, a full-throated mea culpa taking responsibility for the "Gay or Asian" piece, with the hint of an unspoken, underlying plea: we hear you, please make it stop. The white flag, waved. "Talk about fighting the good fight—and talk about having your ass handed to you," Peres wrote. Was this what the coordinated, righteous Internet fury of Asian Americans looked like? In the past, I remember feeling a little clueless when I encountered incidents like this. Angry, sure. But also clueless, and finding myself in a scramble. How are we supposed to respond? To whom do I direct my anger? Does anyone else out there feel this way? But by the time this *Details* incident hit, it was as though we had developed an effective playbook for handling these situations. Unfortunately, we would have to refer to the playbook far too often, again and again.

## Ching Chong Lessons

Danny DeVito was drunk. The veteran actor apparently showed up for his November 2006 appearance on *The View* after a night of partying, drunk off his ass, and made a fool of himself. But that's not the story. The following week, when the hosts of the ABC daytime talk show were debriefing DeVito's visit, Rosie O'Donnell joked that the incident had made international news: "You know, you can imagine in China it's like 'ching chong, ching chong chong, Danny DeVito, ching chong chong chong, drunk, *The View*, ching chong.'"

You might know what it's like to get ching chonged. If you grew up yellow in this country, at some point, you've likely been ching chonged. "Ching chong" is a lazy, racist verbal approximation of an Asian language, the result of thinking that your "foreign" tongue is an aural mess and could not possibly be deciphered as something meaningful, and is thus reduced to the falsely onomatopoetic "ching chong." One time when I was in middle school, I was waiting at a bus stop when a car of teens pulled up to the red light, music blaring. When the light turned green, the guy in the passenger seat poked his head out the window, pulled his eyes back with both hands, and ching chonged his best ching chong in my direction as they rolled past. I got drive-by ching chonged.

It's playground bullshit. It's an easy shortcut to dehumanization. Rosie O'Donnell, a grown adult, did it on national television.

The response was immediate. Five years into running *Angry Asian Man*, I had grown accustomed to being the guy people emailed and tattled to when they encountered something racist. As soon as those chings and chongs left her mouth, I started hearing from folks who had witnessed the moment on air. "Did you see what Rosie O'Donnell just did?" I hadn't—I

International Secret Agents launch live events that bring together Asian American musicians and digital celebrities

Roy Choi's Kogi Korean BBQ launches the contemporary food truck revolution and establishes him as a celebrity chef

Cung Le defeats Frank Shamrock to win Strikeforce, becoming the first Asian American to win major MMA title

Filipino American Tim Lincecum becomes the first Asian American to win the baseball Cy Young Award

was in Los Angeles; it would be another three hours before *The View* aired on the West Coast. But by then, it was like Asian America already knew what to do.

As demands for apology and threats of a boycott—directed at O'Donnell, executive producer Barbara Walters, and ABC—swiftly rolled in, Rosie went on the defensive. "She's a comedian in addition to being a talk show cohost," her spokesperson told *Page Six*. "I certainly hope that one day they will be able to grasp her humor." You see, this was actually on us, the humorless Asians who couldn't get the joke. The sophisticated comedy of "ching chong" apparently went over our heads. On her blog, O'Donnell doubled down, responding to critics:

"i am irish

i do an irish accent—make drunk jokes—stgerotypes [*sic*]

this is comedy"

This is not even close to what O'Donnell was doing with her ching chongery, but that was her story and she was sticking to it. I have to admit, more than annoyance, I felt a small swell of pride when I saw the *Gawker* headline: "Rosie O'Donnell Will Not Let a Few Angry Asians Spoil the 'Ching Chong' Fun." Yup, it's me, Rosie. Just one of these Angry Asians trying to spoil your fun. The following week, with community pressure mounting and demands for an apology from groups like UNITY: Journalists

of Color and New York City councilman John C. Liu, she addressed the issue on *The View*. "This apparently was very offensive to a lot of Asian people," O'Donnell said incredulously. "So I asked Judy, who's Asian and works here in our hair and makeup department. I said, 'Was it offensive to you?' And she said, 'Well, kinda. When I was a kid people did tease me by saying ching-chong.' So apparently 'ching-chong,' unbeknownst to me, is a very offensive way to make fun, quote-unquote, or mock, Asian accents. Some people have told me it's as bad as the N-word. I was like, really? I didn't know that." It's astounding how much casual racism can be simply written off as "oops, I didn't know." Granted, *The View* might not be the ideal place to have a nuanced discussion on racial slurs, but asking Judy in hair and makeup is . . . a start?

O'Donnell explained further that "it was never [my] intent to mock, and I'm sorry for those people who felt hurt or were teased on the playground," but added that in the future, "there's a good chance I'll do something like that again, probably in the next week—not on purpose." Not exactly reassuring. The headlines declared that O'Donnell had apologized, but this didn't seem like much more than an acknowledgment that some people might have been offended by something she said last Wednesday. Especially when she capped off the segment by admitting, "Hey, I still think it was

---

**2009**

*Slumdog Millionaire*, a British film with British Indian leads Dev Patel and Freida Pinto, is nominated for 10 Oscars, winning eight, including for A. R. Rahman's soundtrack and the movie's propulsive song "Jai Ho"

*Star Trek* icon George Takei, who had come out as gay in 2005, marries his longtime partner Brad Altman. The next year, the Takeis would be go on to become the first gay couple to compete on TV's *The Newlywed Game*.

Barack Obama is sworn in as our first Black president of the United States—and, as some noted, the closest yet to our "first Asian American" POTUS as well. since he was born in Hawaii and partially raised in Indonesia, with an Indonesian American half-sister (Maya Soetoro-Ng) and a Chinese American brother-in-law (Konrad Ng)

funny!" That's when cohost Joy Behar pointed to two Asian women in the audience, who were laughing along and nodding in agreement. Well, if these two random audience members, de facto representatives of Asian America, say it's okay, I guess it's all good. Cut to commercial.

When something like this occurs, the issue almost always evolves beyond the original offense. As painful as it is to hear a racial slur like "ching chong" laughed off and dismissed on national television, the central issue quickly became O'Donnell's defensiveness and unwillingness to take responsibility for her words, instead deflecting blame and hiding behind ignorance. God forbid anyone admits they got it wrong, while Asian Americans, once again, swallow the pain of getting mocked to our faces while everyone else chuckles and shrugs. We were resigned to accept, like so many times before, that this would probably be the end of this discussion.

But the last word actually came from a poet. Several months after it seemed the attention to this incident had more or less run out of gas, spoken word artist Beau Sia offered one last appeal to Rosie's good sense: a powerful, moving performance video entitled "An Open Letter to All the Rosie O'Donnells." Clocking in at two minutes and forty-four seconds, and shot in an elementary school classroom—because Beau is dropping knowledge—the piece draws direct lines between seemingly harmless lan-guage and the perpetuation of racial violence. The utterance of "ching chong" for laughs feels different on the receiving end of a hate crime.

"See, I don't want to be politically correct. I just want to be helpful," Sia says, addressing O'Donnell. "So there's no need to become defensive, Rosie. Ignorance is not a crime. And believe me, when it comes to accents, you are ignorant. Because 'ching chong ching chong' is not an accent. 'Ching chong ching chong' is a racist interpretation of a language often associated with being buried alive in a mine shaft or other such hate crime fun." And that's just his opening salvo. Theatrics aside, the point of all this was a helpful and noisy nudge toward doing the right thing, and not for Asian Americans to get gaslit into believing it was us, an entire community, simply suffering all along from a deficient sense of humor.

"I speak on behalf of those who don't have the opportunity to address you. For those who know what 'ching chong ching chong' feels like combined with a swinging bat. Learn from this, Rosie. Apologize, darling. Tap into the humanity I know you possess." Not an admonition, but an invitation. And like a weather balloon, Beau's poem floated out into the Internet. Far less for Rosie's sake, and much more for the culture. Even if it never reached the eyes and ears of "all the Rosie O'Donnells," the video felt like the pointed last word on what so many of us were feeling.

2009

🏛 Judy Chu elected to U.S. Congress from California's 32nd District, becoming the first Chinese American woman elected to Congress.

🏛 Dr. Stephen Chu appointed secretary of energy, becoming the first Nobel Prize winner to be appointed to a presidential cabinet. Former Washington governor Gary Locke is appointed secretary of commerce.

🎬 Ken Jeong breaks through as Chow in *The Hangover*; though controversial, the role propels Jeong into stardom

But Rosie saw it. And she apologized. The open letter somehow found its way to its intended recipient. On her blog (which also more or less resembled poetry on a regular basis) O'Donnell acknowledged receipt and offered "an open response" to Beau's poem.

> *"i apologize*
> *for any and all pain*
> *caused to any and all*
> *by my comments*
> *ignorance*
> *lack of compassion—empathy*
> *understanding*
>
> *u r right*
> *i didnt get it*
>
> *i know*
> *my intent*
> *was not to harm*
> *yet obviously i did"*

It worked. While none of the angry calls or letters or threats of boycotts really seemed to get through to O'Donnell, an eloquent word did the job. In the end, it was never really about changing one person's mind, but there is a certain satisfaction in catching that moment the light bulb flickers on.

Sometimes you need angry yells. Sometimes you need letter-writing campaigns and petitions and protests and signs. And sometimes you need a storyteller, a poet, to bear witness and make them listen.

## Telling Our Own Stories

This is the decade we would no longer wait for permission to tell our stories; we'd find new ways to tell them ourselves. We wouldn't leave our stories in the hands of Abercrombie & Fitch, *Details*, Rosie O'Donnell, Hot 97, or Gwen Stefani—at least not quietly.

This is the decade we showed up in droves to movie theaters, compelled by passionate emails forwarded five times over, to see little indie films like *The Debut, Better Luck Tomorrow, Saving Face, Robot Stories, Charlotte Sometimes,* and *Journey from the Fall.*

This is the decade we went to White Castle.

This was the decade we founded YouTube, and gave young creators who looked like us a space to share the compelling, relatable videos they were making from their backyards and bedrooms.

This was the decade we toppled political candidacies by catching their slurs on camera and making them go viral.

This was the decade we dominated dance crews, won Freestyle Friday, found the Immunity Idol and survived.

This was the decade we started winning spelling bees . . . and never stopped.

This is the decade we found our voice. It was always there. But we found a way to plug it in and amplify it. From activist groups to artist networks, we formed collectives to bring bodies to the fight, virtually and in person. We used tools to make our shouts louder. We connected. We found each other.

Glee premieres and becomes wildly popular, with Korean American Jenna Ushkowitz, Chinese American Harry Shum Jr., and Filipino American Darren Criss in major roles.

Current TV reporters Laura Ling and Euna Lee travel to the border between China and North Korea to report a story on human trafficking. They are violently apprehended by DPRK armed forces, dragged into North Korea and sentenced to 12 years hard labor. Laura's sister Lisa leads the campaign to win her freedom, which is finally obtained via the diplomatic efforts of former President Bill Clinton. Laura and Lisa Ling cowrite a bestselling book, *Somewhere Inside*, about the experience.

# SUBURBASIA:
## The Rise of the
## Asian American Suburb

BY JEFF YANG

OVER THE COURSE of the 2000s, Asian America became what demographers call a "bimodal population." This meant there were effectively two "Asian Americas," one that was increasingly affluent, professional, and educated, and one that faced cultural isolation, economic disenfranchisement, and a daily struggle to stay afloat, and the gap between the two was increasing. In the early 2000s, according to data analyzed by the Center for American Progress, 7.5 percent of Asian Americans had zero or negative wealth. By the early 2010s, that had grown to 9.9 percent. Over that time, the median net worth of the poorest 20 percent of Asian Americans fell from $11,302 to $9,319, while the median net worth of the wealthiest 10 percent grew from $1.2 million to $1.45 million.

One contributor to this phenomenon: While historically, recent immigrants from Asia were likely to arrive with little wealth and to take on low-income professions, during the 2000s, a growing number of Asian immigrants were arriving in the United States already wealthy, or came to America to take high-paying jobs via the H1-B visa program. From the mid-2000s to the mid-2010s, 300,000 Chinese immigrated to the U.S. via H1-B visas, and almost 2.2 million Indians.

Where were these wealthy Asians going? To the suburbs. Asian Americans began moving into historically white neighborhoods in Southern California and the San Francisco Bay Area, as well as parts of New York, New Jersey, Virginia, Nevada, Georgia, and even Texas: the Houston suburb of Sugar Land is 37 percent Asian American, and boasts the second-largest Hindu temple in the nation.

The suburbanization of Asian America—and the Asian Americanization of the suburbs—didn't happen without friction. Monterey Park, one of the first U.S. suburbs to have a majority Asian American population, engaged in widely publicized battles beginning in the mid-1980s over non-English signage used by Asian-owned businesses. Efforts to mandate "signs that look like America" were soon squelched, after the Asian Pacific American Legal Center (now Asian Americans Advancing Justice–LA) won a suit in federal court challenging such ordinances.

Today, the multicultural and multilingual suburbs of San Gabriel Valley are among the most economically vibrant parts of Greater Los Angeles, and the same can be said for most of the Asian "ethnoburbs" that have arisen across the nation, serving as magnets for both regional commerce and international tourism.

## OF THE 20 MOST-ASIAN CITIES IN AMERICA, ALL BUT TWO ARE SUBURBAN

| RANK | CITY | ASIAN POPULATION | ASIAN% |
|------|------|------------------|--------|
| 1 | Monterey Park, California | 60,188 | 62% |
| 2 | Waipahu, Hawaii | 63,228 | 62% |
| 3 | Cerritos, California | 51,542 | 58% |
| 4 | Honolulu, Hawaii | 387,306 | 56% |
| 5 | Aiea, Hawaii | 41,423 | 54% |
| 6 | Pearl City, Hawaii | 37,879 | 53% |
| 7 | Walnut, California | 45,106 | 52% |
| 8 | Milpitas, California | 62,840 | 52% |
| 9 | Rowland Heights, California | 46,324 | 52% |
| 10 | Ewa Beach, Hawaii | 43,874 | 50% |
| 11 | Daly City, California | 110,768 | 50% |
| 12 | Mililani, Hawaii | 45,093 | 48% |
| 13 | Rosemead, California | 61,605 | 48% |
| 14 | Alhambra, California | 85,010 | 47% |
| 15 | San Gabriel, California | 61,458 | 46% |
| 16 | Cupertino, California | 54,412 | 44% |
| 17 | Union City, California | 66,457 | 44% |
| 18 | Arcadia, California | 60,935 | 43% |
| 19 | Diamond Bar, California | 46,520 | 42% |
| 20 | Flushing, New York | 214,473 | 40% |

## LOS ANGELES'S SAN GABRIEL VALLEY: The Most Asian American Suburban Region in the Nation

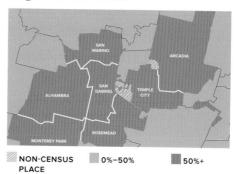

NON-CENSUS PLACE    0%–50%    50%+

## MOVING UP FAST: The Tech-Heavy South Bay Suburbs of San Francisco

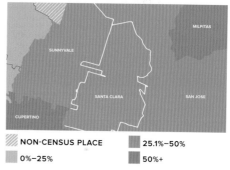

NON-CENSUS PLACE    25.1%–50%
0%–25%    50%+

## BETWEEN 1980 AND 2016, THE ASIAN AMERICAN POPULATION OF THE SAN GABRIEL VALLEY HAS SKYROCKETED

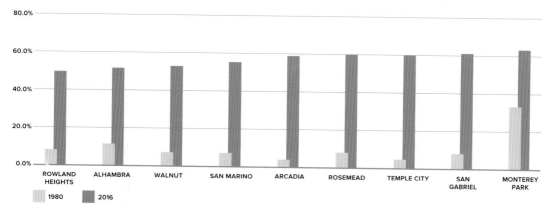

1980    2016

1. Jay Chou Chinese pop music playing on speakers—let Jay Chou's brooding mumble and soaring melodies melt your cares away.

2. TV playing K-pop music videos—perfect complexions and disturbingly precise choreography keep distracting you from your essay.

3. A mini "money tree" by the cashier, or a lucky cat, or both. Whatever brings us prosperity, right?

4. Instagram wall—more recent (post-2013), a neon sign, or fake greenery: Did you even get boba if you didn't share it on social media?

5. Posters for local community and Asian student organization events—hey, be sure to check out our culture night, and that Nineties Cantopop singer's nostalgia tour.

6. High school students playing UNO or Jenga—usually in the couch area: They've been here for three hours and bought one drink.

7. Lone grad student feverishly studying: The MCAT is 30 days away.

8. Two twentysomethings on a date.

9. The high school student: Her first and dream job. Working to earn money . . . to buy more boba.

10. Lao ban—the boss/owner. Not dressed in the uniform, usually in jeans and a polo or T-shirt, watching everything like a hawk.

11. Blenders: For mango slushies and avocado smoothies; always turning on right at an important part of your conversation.

12. Tea dispensers—let the liquid gold flow!

13. Drinks: Fruit juices; smoothies; milk tea (oolong, matcha, assam) with half 'n' half or condensed milk (Thai-style); Horlicks; coffee; "yin yang" coffee + milk tea; lemon iced tea; lemon cola.

14. Ice shaver for shaved ice, a classic dessert. In the mid-2000s, snow ice ("fluff ice") was introduced, and it changed the shaved ice game forever.

# The Boba Shop

BY PHILIP WANG

**IF CHURCHES** and supermarkets were the first baby steps for our communities in America, boba shops emerged during our teenage years, as a generation wanted to hang out in a space of their own—a place without "lunchbox moments," where they could unapologetically enjoy Asian snacks and frothy, bubbly beverages in private—or invite non-Asian friends to drop by their spot. Boba shops first popped up in Chinese enclaves in the late Nineties. By the turn of the century, they'd slid their way into the mainstream, not because America made it happen, but simply because Asians of all backgrounds took so much pride in them. Whether recent immigrant or nth-generation American-born, we made boba shops our watering holes, our community hubs, our preferred coworking spaces; a place to meet friends and play UNO for hours, a quintessential date spot, a neutral zone for family gatherings of different generations. What other place on Main Street allows all these purposes and people to converge and sit side by side? See it, smell it, hear it . . . here's your neighborhood boba shop!

# "Dis-Spelled"

BY HIBAH ANSARI, ILLUSTRATED BY KRISHNA SADASIVAM

WHEN I WAS A KID IN THE 2000S, WE WERE AT THE START OF A *PHENOMENON*...

...THE UTTER DOMINATION OF *SPELLING BEES* BY SOUTH ASIANS.

IN 1999, *NUPUR LALA* WON THE SCRIPPS NATIONAL SPELLING BEE BY CORRECTLY SPELLING *"LOGORRHEA."*

FROM THAT POINT ON, *17* OUT OF THE NEXT *20* NATIONAL BEES WOULD BE WON BY SOUTH ASIANS, INCLUDING THE LAST *12 IN A ROW.*

MY FAMILY WOULD WATCH ON TV, BECAUSE IT WAS THE ONLY TIME YOU'D SEE OUR PEOPLE ON *ESPN,* AND OUR HOME TEAM, THE *BROWNS,* WOULD ALWAYS BE IN THE WINNER CIRCLE.

GO BROWN!

BUT IT PUT A LOT OF *PRESSURE* ON THE REST OF US KIDS. ESPECIALLY THOSE OF US WHO WASHED OUT OF THE SPELLING BEE WORLD *EARLY.*

FOR ME, THAT HAPPENED IN *THIRD GRADE.* WE HAD A SPELLING BEE AT OUR SCHOOL. IT WASN'T AFFILIATED WITH THE NATIONAL COMPETITIONS, AND IT WAS ONLY BROADCAST OVER OUR *SCHOOL TV SYSTEM,* NOT ESPN. BUT EVERYONE IN MY ELEMENTARY SCHOOL WOULD WATCH IT.

AND BEING A *NERDY KID* IN GENERAL, I WAS ALWAYS REALLY *SERIOUS* ABOUT SPELLING.

SO I FIGURED I'D DO WELL. AND I *DID!* I GOT TO THE *FINAL ROUND,* WHERE IT WAS DOWN TO ME AND ONE OTHER KID.

BUT WHEN IT WAS MY TURN TO GET A WORD, THE JUDGE, *MRS. LEWIS,* STOOD UP AND SAID *"SUPERFLUSS."*

LIKE, THE WORD WAS *SUPERFLUOUS,* BUT SHE PRONOUNCED IT WITH A *"FLUSS."*

I'D NEVER HEARD THE WORD BEFORE, SO I JUST SPELLED IT LIKE IT *SOUNDED*.

SUPERFLUSS. S U P E R F L U S S. *SUPERFLUSS*.

AND OF COURSE, I WAS *WRONG*. IN FRONT OF MY WHOLE SCHOOL -- ME, THE *BROWN KID*, I GOT THE WORD *WRONG*.

AT FIRST I WAS JUST LIKE, THE SYSTEM IS *FLAWED* IF TWO OF THE *ONLY* BROWN KIDS THAT HAVE GONE THROUGH THE DISTRICT LOSE THE BEE ON THE SAME WORD.

I REALLY WAS *UPSET* ABOUT IT, SO WHEN I WENT HOME, I TOLD MY FAMILY THE STORY.

AND MY OLDEST BROTHER SAID, *REALLY?* I HAD HER AS A JUDGE TOO WHEN I WAS YOUR AGE, AND I LOST ON THE *SAME WORD* -- BECAUSE OF HOW SHE *PRONOUNCED* IT.

BUT THEN I WONDERED: DID MRS. LEWIS HAVE A *VENDETTA* AGAINST US ANSARI KIDS? OR...MAYBE IT WAS A WEIRD *TEST* OR SOMETHING?

SO WE CHECKED, AND MY BROTHER *DIDN'T* HAVE THE SAME WORD AFTER ALL -- THE WORD HE WENT OUT ON WAS *"SUPERLATIVE."* WE DIDN'T EVEN HAVE THE SAME *JUDGE!*

I MEAN, OUR PARENTS MOSTLY GREW UP LEARNING ENGLISH IN *SCHOOL*, AND THEN CAME TO AMERICA, WHERE PEOPLE MADE FUN OF THEIR *ACCENTS*.

SO MAYBE HAVING KIDS WHO ARE *SPELLING CHAMPIONS* FEELS LIKE A WAY OF PROVING SOMETHING...

EITHER WAY, THE ANSARI SIBS CLEARLY WEREN'T *DESTINED* TO BE SUPER-SPELLING-BEE CHAMPS -- UNLIKE HUNDREDS OF *OTHER* KIDS OF SOUTH ASIAN IMMIGRANT FAMILIES.

...LIKE MAYBE THAT WE *BELONG* HERE. THAT THIS IS *OUR* LANGUAGE TOO. IT'S...KIND OF A *FLEX?*

ON THE ONE HAND, STRESSING OUT OVER SPELLING CONTESTS ISN'T SOMETHING A *THIRD GRADER* SHOULD BE DOING.

ON THE OTHER, OUR PARENTS WENT THROUGH TOUGH TIMES TO GET HERE, AND WE'RE THE *PRIVILEGED* ONES.

SO IF WINNING SPELLING BEES IS A WAY TO *HONOR* THEIR HARD WORK, MAYBE WE SHOULDN'T SEE THEM AS *SUPERFLUOUS?*

JEFF YANG

PHIL YU

PHILLIP WANG

# THE ASIAN AMERICAN SYLLABUS 2000s

**HERE'S OUR LIST** of must-consume media to understand being Asian American in the 2000s, the decade in which we began to break into the mainstream, not just as individuals, but as part of broader Asian American creative, social, and political movements, in a nation that was beginning to contend with the idea of what it meant to be "multicultural."

### I'm the One That I Want

**JEFF:** This was the one-woman show, and subsequent book, that brought Margaret Cho back into all of our lives, and frankly, this was the Margaret that a lot of us wanted to have seen in *All-American Girl.*

**PHIL:** It was Cho in phoenix mode. Rising from the ashes after the crash and burn of the show, coming out again to the world as her true self, which is her best self. Acknowledging, but also defying, her critics.

**PHILIP:** Got it, I will never listen to any critics or bloggers for the rest of my life.

**PHIL:** [pregnant pause]

### The Debut

**PHIL:** A homegrown, grassroots, indie, Filipino American coming-of-age film starring Dante Basco. It was the first time he ever played an actual Filipino American kid.

**PHILIP:** By hook or by crook, they made this movie and packed people into the theaters. This was before social media, so that definitely was a community-driven effort.

### Crouching Tiger, Hidden Dragon

**JEFF:** This was the movie that disproved the big fucking lie that you couldn't fill theaters for a film with an all-Asian cast. Who were all speaking Chinese!

**PHIL:** It had fantastic performances and it was clearly something truly novel to Americans. But yeah, it shattered the idea that white people would not go and see Asians on screen and would not read subtitles.

**PHILIP:** It's just crazy to me that it was such a huge success, $100 million back in 2000—what would that be today? Maybe a $300 million movie. *Crouching Tiger* walked so *Parasite* could fly.

### Better Luck Tomorrow*

**PHILIP:** The most consequential Asian American film of this era. Justin Lin's arrival. John Cho's arrival. Sung Kang's arrival.

**PHIL:** It should've been Asian America's arrival.

**JEFF:** I love the fact that Justin made it so it's essentially the prequel to the *Fast & Furious* movies. *Better Luck Tomorrow* is part of the F&F Cinematic Universe, because Sung Kang's Han is the same character in both.

### Charlotte Sometimes; Robot Stories; The Motel; Journey from the Fall; Punching at the Sun; In Between Days; Children of Invention; Colma: The Musical

**PHIL:** Your Asian American indie movie essentials of the decade. They were all resourceful films that looked at race, belonging, and identity in a mature and unique way. They signaled that Asian American cinema was shifting into a more substantial gear.

**JEFF:** Eric Byler's *Charlotte Sometimes,* a deeply indie exploration of sex and relationships. Greg Pak's *Robot Stories,* a scrappy sci-fi anthology film about being human. Mike Kang's funny and bittersweet *The Motel*. Ham Tran's epic refugee chronicle, *Journey from the Fall,* which tells a huge story in a lean way. Tanuj Chopra's blistering urban story *Punching at the Sun*. So Yong Kim's quiet, intimate immigrant story *In Between Days*. Tze Chun's bleak but affirming *Children of Invention*. Richard Wong's deliriously fun *Colma: The Musical.*

---
\*    See page 226, "Tomorrow Never Dies"

**PHILIP:** The amazing results of maxed-out credit cards! I should say that *The Motel* was the movie that first made me want to make a feature film and not just sketches and lip-sync videos. It was so heartfelt and real.

### Monsoon Wedding

**PHIL:** Mira Nair directed this romantic comedy-drama with an all-Indian cast. It won the Golden Lion, and made $30 million on a $1.2 million budget, and it honestly deserves a lot more attention than it's gotten.

**JEFF:** I remember it was framed as this colorful, fun film with music and dance, but there's this very dark gut punch of a subplot about an elder relative grooming and molesting a young girl.

### Saving Face

**PHIL:** This is my favorite movie of this era. Undeniably one of the few that consistently holds up on rewatching, and that shows just how much talent was being overlooked in our community.

**JEFF:** My first thought after watching this was "Oh my God, that was amazing, what is Alice Wu going to do next?" And then . . . that extended hiatus! There were so many stories I'm sure she could have told. But she'd moved away from Hollywood for personal reasons. And then she came back with *The Half of It* in 2020 and showed us what we were all missing.

**PHILIP:** I think I watched it six years after it came out, after college. So it definitely held up, and I know with a lot of my queer friends, it was great to see a gay love story that was joyous.

**PHIL:** I will argue that *Saving Face* is Asian America's best and greatest romantic comedy.

### Same Difference

**PHIL:** A brilliant graphic novel by Derek Kirk Kim, with a set of stories that really sum up the alienation and awkwardness and self-doubt of being Asian American in this era.

**JEFF:** Derek has this unique ability to effortlessly mine discomfort. But this was also a book that really just showed Asian Americans being Asian American with each other, which I think was new enough to me to be just wildly refreshing.

**PHILIP:** Derek won all these awards for it, but he was also a major part of Gene Luen Yang's* crew, who basically invented Asian American indie comics.

### Shortcomings

**PHIL:** It's the only long-form work by Adrian Tomine, who's one of the preeminent graphic novelists of his generation, to really address being Asian American.

**JEFF:** Like so much of Tomine's work, it's brilliant, but it's just incredibly packed with self-loathing and misanthropy and misogyny and is very difficult to read in a lot of ways.

### The Grace Lee Project

**JEFF:** I love this movie, which is a documentary by Grace Lee about all the other people she could find who are also named Grace Lee. I think what's exceptional about this movie is how it proves you can make a documentary about anything and have it be exceptionally good.

**PHIL:** It really showed off Grace's chops as a filmmaker—this unique voice that could address a quirky topic and bring gravitas to it. I love how she managed to slip the story of Asian American activist Grace Lee Boggs into this documentary.

### Grey's Anatomy

**JEFF:** For all of us who were being pushed toward medical careers from childhood, this was the TV series we made our parents watch to show why it was a good thing we never did. The funny thing is that my sister is named Christine, and she's a doctor. And so she was called "Dr. Christina Yang" throughout her residency. It might be why she changed her name when she got married.

**PHILIP:** I think it's the first time I saw an Asian American physician on TV, portrayed amazingly by Sandra Oh**, with a full interiority around what it meant to be Asian American: pressuring yourself to be successful, getting over high-expectations parents, and all that stuff.

### American Born Chinese

**PHILIP:** Gene Luen Yang's book is not just an amazing graphic novel, it's an amazing book, period. It was the first graphic novel to be nominated for the National Book Award.

**JEFF:** Something we don't talk about is how *American Born Chinese* literally feels like a response to *F.O.B.*—the David Henry Hwang play, not the TV series. It has the same tropes of taking Chinese mythology and using it to look at diaspora, and it has a very similar lineup of characters at its core: a recent immigrant, a self-hating acculturated kid. It feels like a totally parallel work.

**PHIL:** Oh my God. Totally. Yeah. Steve in *F.O.B.* is Chin-Kee in *ABC*. I've never made that connection, but it's very obvious now.

### The Fast and the Furious: Tokyo Drift

**JEFF:** Justin Lin enters the *Fast & Furious* franchise, and brings in Sung Kang.

**PHIL:** I think this movie resurrected the franchise single-handedly. It turned a sinking ship around. *2 Fast 2 Furious,* the sequel, was almost seen as a joke. It didn't have Vin Diesel in it. People were like, why did you even make this film? But *Tokyo Drift* comes along and what Lin did with it made *2 Fast 2 Furious* relevant. He tied together a lot of disparate loose elements. And then the movies after that just were on rails. Also it introduced a lot of people in the United States to drifting.***

**PHILIP:** It was *Crazy Drift Asians.*

---

\* See page 414, "It's a Bird . . . It's a Plane . . . It's Asian Superheroes"
\*\* See page 458, "It's an Honor Just to Be Sandra"
\*\*\* See page 110, "Speed Racers"

### Finishing the Game

**JEFF:** A crazy, low-budget mockumentary about the attempt to finish Bruce Lee's unfinished final movie, *Game of Death,* which I really enjoyed. It's sad that it didn't catch fire, because it ended up being Justin Lin's last attempt at doing an indie film.

**PHILIP:** This was Justin's last indie film. But hey, dude is getting millions to make blockbusters, so I can understand why.

**PHIL:** This was a love letter to Bruce Lee. It didn't get great reviews, and it didn't make a lot of money. And Justin called in a lot of favors for it. MC Hammer is in it. James Franco. Also I'm in it for like a second, as an extra. So yeah, I wish more people saw it.

### Fortune Cookie Chronicles

**JEFF:** Fantastic book by Jenny 8. Lee, where she goes out to try to understand the origin of the fortune cookie and ends up uncovering the history of Chinese takeouts and their proliferation across America—and from there, tells this epic story about Chinese immigration to America.

### Up

**PHILIP:** Is it safe to say *Up* had Pixar's first Asian American character?

**JEFF:** Second! Edna Mode is half-Japanese. But the first lead. And the first Asian to be voiced by an Asian.

**PHIL:** There were so many Russell costumes that Halloween.

### The Hangover

**PHIL:** Say what you want about the Wolfpack, but this movie is ultimately all about Leslie Chow, Ken Jeong's* character. And it is not a warm, fuzzy character for Asian Americans, but it is a tour de force of comic acting.

**JEFF:** You read a lot that Chow is a "stereotypical" role, and the truth is, it's not. It's crazy, it's absurd, it's over the top and offensive. But Chow is not at all like any Asian character you've seen in American movies before. And if he'd been white or Black, I don't think you would've said it was stereotypical. You look at *Sixteen Candles* and Long Duk Dong, and in every scene he's in, he's the butt of the joke. Chow is the joker. He's in control because he's out of control, he's a creature of all id. My hot take: The *Hangover* trilogy is really about the Rise of Chow, like the Star Wars prequels were about the Rise of Vader. And Leslie Chow is Anakin.

### Harold and Kumar Go to White Castle

**PHILIP:** The movie that proved that Asian Americans could be hilarious stoners just like anyone else! True representation!**

**PHIL:** To this day, it still blows my mind that they were able to make this film with Kal Penn and John Cho, an Indian American and a Korean American. And then make two sequels!

**JEFF:** This movie was a turning point for Hollywood and none of us even knew it at the time.

### Planet B-Boy

**PHIL:** Benson Lee's documentary on the international b-boy circuit wasn't just brilliant filmmaking, it really introduced the world to the fact that Asians had quietly become a dominant force in breakdancing. And he made it a year before *America's Best Dance Crew* began to showcase the brilliance of Asian American b-boy crews.***

### Glee

**PHILIP:** You came for the music, but you stayed for Harry Shum Jr. and Jenna Ushkowitz as the cutest Asian American couple on TV, because they were also the only Asian American couple on TV.****

---

\*    See page 382, "Three Kings"
\*\*   See page 239, "*Harold and Kumar*"
\*\*\*  See page 270, "The Dance Crew Revolution"
\*\*\*\* See page 356, "LOVE, Asian American Style"

# 9/11: Remembering a Tragedy and the Dark Days That Followed

**THE SHADOW OF** the terror attacks of September 11, 2001, that killed nearly 3,000 people and saw the destruction of two of the most visible features of the iconic New York skyline, the Twin Towers, still looms large across our nation today. Americans of all backgrounds and walks of life continue to mourn and commemorate the event annually on its anniversary, with news networks playing back footage and interviewing survivors, and talking about the profound changes that the attacks made on American society, culture, and politics.

For many Asian Americans, however, the tragedy of the attacks was compounded in the days, months, and years that followed. Since then, South Asian Americans—particularly those of Muslim and Sikh faiths—have suffered targeted racist abuse, harassment, and attack, wrongly blamed for the horrific actions of a small group of criminal fanatics. And immigrants of all backgrounds have encountered an increasingly suspicious and hostile America, while enclaves like Manhattan's Chinatown, a low-income community in close proximity to New York's Ground Zero, experienced a drawn-out civic and economic crisis that shattered thousands of lives and shuttered hundreds of businesses . . . many of which slowly recovered, only to face repeated new impacts from SARS in 2003 and COVID in 2020. We asked three people who were immersed in the crisis—**Janice Chua**; senior staff attorney, legal services of New York City; **Simran Jeet Singh**, author, podcaster, and senior fellow for the Sikh Coalition; and **Aisha Sultan**, editor and columnist, *St. Louis Post-Dispatch*—to share with us their memories of 9/11 and the days that followed, and their thoughts on how they shaped the future of their communities.

## The Day It Happened

**JANICE:** Our teachers told us to go to the one classroom with a TV, and we all just stood there watching what was going on with shocked faces. The whole time, I was thinking about my sister who was at school downtown at the time. My family and I couldn't contact her for a few days, but she eventually was able to send us an email to say she was okay. But because transportation and streets were closed, she couldn't join us back home.

**SIMRAN:** I was a high school senior in a small town just outside of San Antonio, Texas. We began hearing rumors that there was a terrorist attack in New York right before school started, so we watched TV silently for the next couple of hours. I was born and raised in the States and felt very pained as an American, but one of the most visceral moments for me was seeing Bin Laden's photo come up on television as the primary suspect. He had a turban and a beard, and he had brown skin like mine. I knew immediately that life was about to change.

**AISHA:** My cousin, who wears a hijab, was asked to leave her university campus because they said it didn't feel like it was safe for her to stay. My brother was kicked out of his middle school classroom by his teacher for asking questions about what was going to happen next. I was nervous about my mom, who works in retail, because she wore a hijab. I knew that our place in American society had been altered in a way that might never be healed.

## The Aftermath

**SIMRAN:** In the days that followed, my family and I would take part in these huge confer-ence calls, listening to Sikhs around the country trying to organize against a backlash that had already begun. We'd hear stories of the hate incidents that they were encountering. My family and I stayed at home on lockdown, but people would drive by shouting out death threats. The big moment really came four days later, on September 15, when the first person was killed in a post-9/11 hate crime—a Sikh man in Arizona named Balbir Singh Sodhi. We knew then that we weren't overreacting. It was a reality that our lives were on the line, and that we'd need to fight for survival.

**AISHA:** I was an education reporter at the *St. Louis Post-Dispatch* at the time, and I was sent to go to schools to get kids' responses to the attacks. This was back when you could just walk into a school and talk to students. When I approached a bunch of kids, the first thing they asked was "Where are you from? Aren't you the ones attacking us right now?" The fear in their eyes told me what public reaction was going to be like for a while.

**JANICE:** Chinatown's proximity to Ground Zero meant it was hugely impacted: the economy, the infrastructure—everything was destroyed. All of Chinatown's main industries, from restaurants and food businesses to garment factories, faced revenue losses of 50 percent or more that lingered for months. There were government programs created to support people and businesses in Lower Manhattan hit hard by the attacks, but no priority was given to Chinatown and the Lower East Side, where low-income communities of color resided, and where language barriers made it hard to communicate that support was available. Four months after 9/11, the website still hadn't even been translated into Chinese. So the bulk of the grants ended up going to other downtown areas, like TriBeCa and the Financial District, that were mostly white and mostly affluent. Chinatown was virtually abandoned.

## The Long Shadow

**AISHA:** For a long time, I felt a level of anxiety I'd never felt before, almost to the point of not being able to breathe. I found myself constantly looking over my shoulder, feeling stares that seemed to question my very presence. I asked an African American veteran reporter at the paper how he dealt with that, because we all knew there were certain parts of town where if you're Black, you're made to feel that way all the time. He told me you just had to have the conviction that you deserve your place. It was good advice, but it took a long time to recover my fractured sense of belonging in America.

**SIMRAN:** Being an 18-year-old when 9/11 happened meant that in many ways, I was forged by that moment. It's not like I hadn't experienced racism before—what else could you expect if

you're a kid with a turban in South Texas? But this was the first time I began to recognize *how* racism works—the blurring that took place in order to put me into a certain category. No one actually knew where I was from, but that didn't really matter. What mattered to them was that I was part of that brown blur.

**JANICE:** 9/11 really exposed the inequalities in our system. My clients are all immigrants of color and low-income New Yorkers. The sense of fear, of anti-immigrant sentiment, that they felt after 9/11 made them afraid to pursue the rights they deserve and the benefits for which they're eligible. That didn't go away under the Obama administration—Obama deported a lot of people. But the way that entire communities were made out to be the "other," that anyone who isn't white should feel like they don't belong in this country, that's gotten so much stronger in the past four years. I continued to remind my clients that they had rights even if they didn't have documented status. It was hard to convince them of that when President Trump was trying to enact a Muslim ban, and when he put in place a public charge rule, which blocks you from becoming a permanent resident if you've ever gotten welfare benefits. These were attacks on *legal* immigration.

## Rebuilding from the Ruins

**SIMRAN:** After 9/11, Sikhs scrambled to organize. We learned we didn't have the infrastructure to deal with the challenges that we were facing. We hadn't really built institutions as a community at this point. The Sikh Coalition was an amalgamation of several different ad hoc efforts that emerged to deal with the racism we were facing, and to address the deep need for a long-term plan. Part of that was reaching out to Muslims. Post-9/11, we had been thrown into a bucket together. We realized our people were going to be treated in the same way, that our destinies and our liberation were tied up with one another. We knew that if we wanted to find a solution to these deep challenges, it would do us no good in the long run to deflect the hate that came our way over to the Muslim community.

**JANICE:** In the weeks after 9/11, Chinatown mobilized. Organizations like the Chinese Staff and Workers Association found 3,000 workers knocking at their door asking for help. They realized that their community faced a huge gap in access to government benefits. So they provided translation services, conducted surveys, and held town halls to figure out the needs of the community. They organized rallies to lobby the city and state. No one helped the community, so the community had to help itself.

**AISHA:** There was little to no positive cultural representation of Muslims in America even before 9/11; it was largely terrorists, "dirty Arabs," and so on, constantly reiterated as tropes. That stereotyping was deeply rooted in American society, but generally, you didn't feel like the government or the system was against you. After 9/11, an entire Islamophobic industry was created: to influence laws to target and vilify my community, to surveil us, to imprison us, to make our travel more difficult, and to conflate past crimes with terrorism. All of that became structural, baked into laws like the Patriot Act. But our response to all of this has been multifaceted. People recognized then that we needed to be a part of the political system, and 20 years later, we're seeing the fruit of those seeds. Muslim artists realized that we had to find ways to tell our own stories and take charge of our narratives. There's been this amazing renaissance of creative output that happened since then, and we have so many journalists and writers who are part of the conversation now, unlike two decades ago.

## Looking Ahead

**JANICE:** I'm an immigration attorney whose organization provides free legal services, and I feel like a lot of nonprofits tend to put a bandage on problems instead of listening to people to figure out what the issues really are, and what the solutions should be. With COVID-19, we're facing a crisis for immigrant communities that's even larger than 9/11. We should be at the point by now where it shouldn't be about expecting immigrants to be "strong" or ethnic enclaves to be "resilient." Immigrants and other people of color should not be expected to just bounce back on their own.

**SIMRAN:** Progress is not linear. Sometimes you overestimate what you've built. I'll say very frankly that after 9/11, the Sikh community realized that we've been in this country for a hundred years and no one had any idea who we are. So we made a concerted effort to build a presence. Eleven years later, when a white supremacist attacked a Sikh temple in Wisconsin, we had more leverage: to pull political forces, to engage other communities, to contact the media and speak for ourselves.

**AISHA:** I'm very optimistic that the Asian American community has been galvanized and activated in recent years, especially our young people. They're realizing that it's not just about defending our community, but also the African American community, LGBTQ+ persons, and every marginalized group who've faced resistance to equality and to being seen as fully human. My generation had an awakening to this, but the younger generation is fully steeped in it—and they're leading the fight.

## POSTCARD FROM ASIAN AMERICA

BY ARUNE SINGH

Dear RISE,

I didn't expect to learn anything about being Asian American outside of a bar in Utah. But I did on the night I stepped out of Vortex with three friends, to find four bros waiting outside, really mad that a guy like me had spilled a drink on them.

The hostility wasn't really a new feeling. See, I'd been born and raised in Toronto, where my peers constantly assured me that I'd never really be Canadian with a name like mine. And when I moved to Minnesota, the only thing colder than the winters was the reception given to anyone who looked like me.

You can tell me that Utah is one of the most conservative, monocultural states and I won't argue. But it's also the first place I ever found three friends who decided to stand in front of me to take the first punch.

In return for that kind of loyalty, these friends had only ever asked one thing of me—to be myself, without apology or hesitation.

I can still remember the breeze washing over my face as we walked back to our car, somehow getting out of the situation without a single punch being thrown. I looked up at the sky, exhaled with relief, and felt a firm pat on my back: "You're our brother. That's how this works."

But truly: That was the first time it felt like it had worked. These three friends had never winced at my name, felt the need to remind me how my skin color made me different, hesitated to devour my home-cooked Indian meals, or mocked the accents of my parents. And they were willing to fight so that four guys in a bar would never make me feel that being Asian made me any less American.

Guys: The next time I see you, the first round's on me.

Arune

RISE
HERE AND NOW,
ASIAN AMERICA

# How Filipino American DJs Turned the Tables on Hip-Hop

BY OLIVER WANG

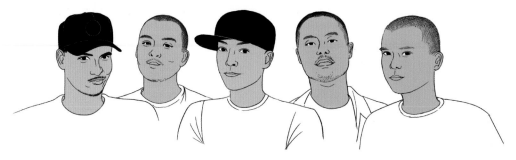

THE INVISIBLE SKRATCH PIKLZ

5TH PLATOON

**IN EARLY 1998,** the L.A.-based urban music and culture magazine *URB* released a special "DJ issue." The cover photo? Michael "Mix-Master Mike" Schwartz, Ritche "Yogafrog" Desuasido, Jon "Shortkut" Cruz, Richard "Q-Bert" Quitevis, and Dave "D-Styles" Cuasito—five members of a Bay Area DJ crew called the Invisibl Skratch Piklz, all Filipino American. Above cofounder Q-Bert's bemused face

was a tagline that read: "Are these the best DJs on the planet? The Universe?"

Asian Americans have been a part of the hip-hop scene across its four traditional pillars—rapping, b-boying/b-girling, graffiti artistry, and DJing—since at least the late '70s. But it was the last of the four in which a cohort of Asian Americans would rise to a position of prominence, or dare I say, dominance, and help develop a whole new musical subgenre.

Years before the Piklz graced that *URB* cover, their stature as the "best DJs on the planet" was already secure in their own circles. In 1991, Q-Bert, then an unknown DJ from San Francisco, had entered the prestigious Disco Mix Club World DJ competition, and shocked everyone by winning the U.S. title outright and placing a close second at the World championship stage. A year later, he returned with his Piklz cofounders MixMaster Mike and DJ Apollo Novicio. Calling themselves the Rocksteady DJs, the trio stormed their way to the world title. The following year, after Q-Bert and Mike successfully defended that title, the DMC tournament organizers asked them to voluntarily retire from competition to avoid intimidating their rivals.

The following year, after Q-Bert and Mike successfully defended that title, the DMC tournament organizers asked them to voluntarily retire from competition to avoid intimidating their rivals.

By 1995, the Piklz had established their name and lineup and were widely recognized as the world's best scratch DJs, a.k.a. turntablists. Talents like the Piklz showed that DJs could do more than just play other people's records. Through deft hand control and creative experimentation, they learned to manipulate turntable platters and DJ mixers to produce collages of sound that included rhythmic needle-scratches, beat drops, crossfades, and sped-up, slowed-down, and reversed snatches of melody, percussion, and spoken word. Turntablists don't just play records, they achieve forms of sonic wizardry that the inventors of record players would never have imagined.

The Piklz were hardly the only world-class Filipino American DJs to emerge in the 1990s.

There's Los Angeles's Beat Junkies, a multiracial crew that includes Filipino American DJs such as Nazareth "Rhettmatic" Nirza, Isaiah "Icy Ice" Dacio, Marie "Symphony" Dacio, and Chris "Babu" Oroc—the latter of whom is credited with coining the term "turntablist." In the New York Tri-State area, 5th Platoon brought together an East Coast batch of premium Pinay and Pinoy DJs, including Rhodello "Roli Rho" Roque, Candace "Kuttin Kandi" Custodio-Tan, and Vincent "Vinroc" Punsalan.

This raises an obvious question: How did the Filipino community produce so many talented DJs? There are armchair theories, some more tongue-in-cheek than others: *Spanish colonization made Filipinos adept in Western musical practices! Fil-Am youth play so many video games that they develop hand dexterity early on!* Q-Bert once even joked that it was due to the stereotypically short stature of Pinoys, which made it easier for them to stand over turntables. The most likely explanation is less colorful, but no less poignant.

One needs to travel back to the early 1970s, when a mass wave of Filipino immigration to the United States was enabled by the epochal Hart-Celler Act of 1965 and motivated by the Philippines' 1972 declaration of martial law. By decade's end, hundreds of thousands of Filipino immigrants were clustered in key suburbs on the West Coast—among them, Daly City and Fremont in the Bay Area, and Cerritos and Carson in Southern California.

The Filipino youth who came of age in those

neighborhoods grew up in a vibrant party culture. As Patrick de la Cruz of DJ crew Beyond the Limit puts it, "Being in the Filipino community, there's parties all the time. There's a party for when you're born. There's a party for when you're being christened. There's a party for when you turn 18."

> "Being in the Filipino community, there's parties all the time. There's a party for when you're born. There's a party for when you're being christened. There's a party for when you turn 18."

Naturally, with parties came music. In the beginning, guests brought vinyl singles to play on house hi-fi systems, but the disco boom introduced professional DJing to the masses, reinforcing the centrality of dance music, and within that, the DJ as the prime mover of the dance floor. By the late Seventies, intrepid Fil-Am teenagers, mostly from middle-class families, began to invest in the tools of the DJ trade: turntables, speakers, and stacks of funk, new wave, freestyle, and later, hip-hop records. They formed mobile DJ groups that brought the groove to church dances, school soirees, "debuts" (grand parties traditionally thrown for Filipina girls when they turn 18), and graduation gigs. Practically all the superstar turntablists of the Nineties got their start as mobile DJs in the Eighties—starched jeans, big hair, and all—splintering off from more traditional DJing to pursue turntablism, realizing that they loved the performative artistry of scratching more than spinning for crowds at weddings. When this younger generation of DJs began to find one another, they planted the seeds for later turntablist crews to emerge, including the Invisibl Skratch Piklz, Beat Junkies, and Fifth Platoon.

In doing so, these Fil-Am DJs paralleled the rise of pioneering Black hip-hop party DJs in the Bronx, the most important of whom were from West Indian immigrant backgrounds, including Afrika Bambaataa, Kool Herc, and Grandmaster Flash, the godfather of turntablism. That two different communities of DJs, both with roots in immigrant families, would arise on different coasts is a

> Practically all the superstar turntablists of the Nineties got their start as mobile DJs in the '80s—starched jeans, big hair, and all—splintering off from more traditional DJing to pursue turntablism.

potent reminder that immigrants have often navigated their way into American cultural relevancy via music. Though few find fame right away, most of these musical talents will spend years, even decades, perfecting their craft within their own communities before—in this case literally—scratching their way into the spotlight.

## STEPPING INTO THE CYPHER:

# Asian American Rappers

#### BY PHILIP WANG

FAR EAST MOVEMENT

**ROOTED IN AFRICAN** American culture and identity and brought to life in mostly Black enclaves like New York's South Bronx, hip-hop was embraced and further extended by other communities who connected with its message, vibe, and aesthetics in the decades after its origin—across the nation and, eventually, around the world. Led by a generation of Filipino American standouts, Asian Americans became known as innovators in the world of turntablism, and Asian American dance crews quickly became elite participants in the b-boying scene. But the road to recognition and acceptance for Asian American artists was harder when it came to hip-hop's most visible pillar, emceeing. University of California, Riverside ethnomusicology professor Deborah Wong has pointed out, "There's less of an element of race when it comes to performing on a turntable. There's more of an emphasis on what you can do with your hands, as opposed to the words coming out of an Asian mouth." It didn't help that pioneering Asian American rappers found themselves virtually alone when they started out: "Here's the scene, which is still vivid in my mind," says Jin "MC Jin" Au-Yeung, recalling the audition day that led to his legendary string of rap battle victories on BET's *106 & Park*. "Imagine 300 rappers from all across New York's boroughs. And then there's this one Chinese kid just standing there, carrying his school book bag. That was me." The rise of the Internet proved to be transformative: Asian American rap artists began discovering one another—creating and sharing their own original music, and collaborating and connecting with other Asian peers on online rap forums like AZNRaps.com, founded by a UCLA student and aspiring rapper named David "FD" Nguyen while he was still a teen in high school. In the pseudonymous chaos of these digital communities, hundreds of Asian rappers honed their craft, battled other emcees, and in a few cases, found themselves breaking out into the mainstream. Some of the most prominent were underground freestyle battle icon

**JONATHAN "DUMBFOUNDEAD" PARK** and Far East Movement (FM), the rappers who became the first Asian American musical group to hit number one on the *Billboard* charts.

Below, Park and **JAMES "PROHGRESS" ROH** of FM share with us their recollections of the Asian American rap scene's evolution and slow climb to relevance.

## First Bars

**PARK:** I started freestyling my freshman year in high school, which was around 2000. But whenever I was freestyling, someone would throw an Asian joke at me, so I had to fight back. I ended up getting into battle rapping as a defense mechanism. But it became fun, and I got a thrill out of battling. I ended up developing my style at places like Project Blowed in L.A.'s Leimert Park, which was an open mic underground workshop deeply rooted in Black history and art and music. The few other Asian MCs I knew seemed like they were always trying to sound like Asian Tupac. But at Project Blowed, I got encouraged by the Black kids there who were into different things, like anime and punk rock, to lean into my weirdness and nerdiness. The Black kids actually inspired me to be unapologetically Asian.

**ROH:** Me, Kev [Kevin "Kev Nish" Nishimura], and Jae [Jae "J-Splif" Choung] would just end up rapping and freestyling every night in parking lots. One day we decided to bring our written-out bars to the cypher and Kev shows up with, like, a bible of rhymes. Kev was born for this; Jae was the glue. And my parents were both musicians, so I had equipment, like an eight-track recorder. I'd been producing their opera concerts since I was 10. So that's how it started. But growing up in Koreatown, always being around Asians, for a long time we thought we were the only Asian American

rappers. When we saw Jin on BET, our minds were blown. And through him we discovered AZNRaps, which we had no idea existed, and when we opened it, we were like, "Holy shit! There's a lot of these guys, and they're *really* good." There were so many amazing battle rappers, lyrical miracle guys, that we knew we had to make a separate lane for ourselves, which was more positive and upbeat records.

## The Message (Board)

**PARK:** There were Asian American rappers making noise back in the Nineties, like Mountain Brothers. But I couldn't say I was a part of it back then. I didn't really connect with other Asian rappers until the Internet made it possible, sites like AZNRaps. Some people made fun of AZNRaps, but honestly, it was one of the first national networks of Asian rappers online. Those message boards had everybody from Jin,* to Far East Movement, to Flowsik, to Snacky Chan—really, like all the big Asian American rappers who were doing their thing. Some were already selling mixtapes and had street teams putting up posters for upcoming albums.

**ROH:** Being on AZNRaps was a rite of passage for all Asian American rappers at the time, when the forums were popping. There were different rooms, like the main forum was where people dropped records and people would comment. And then you'd also have "battle

---

* See page 221, "MC Jin's Greatest Spits".

rooms": some were "key styles" where you'd type out your rhymes, others were "audio battles" where you'd be paired up against someone and have a week to write, record, and post, and people would vote. There were actually big-ass tournaments.

**PARK:** The East Coast guys were doing it heavy. They really embodied that New Yorker vibe—like Decipher [Danny Chung] and Lyricks [Rick Lee, now one half of the rap duo Year of the Ox]. Lyricks was one of the first guys to go viral, and he was sort of my archnemesis for a while. We were both coming up on different coasts, and he beat me in a battle.

**ROH:** Lyricks, when it comes to just raw bars, like backpacker rap, yeah he's unbeatable.

**PARK:** But there was also a West Coast movement of Asian American rappers. We had organized events like Kublai Kwon's Asian Hip Hop Summit in 2002 with Jupitersciples, Denizen Kane, Magnetic North, Blue Scholars, SoleSides, and Lyrics Born. You saw these names pop up again and again from event to event.

**ROH:** Let's talk about Lyrics Born [Tom Shimura], who's part of Latyrx [with Lateef the Truthspeaker]. For a guy to be that lyrical and have that gravelly powerful voice along with melodies—it was shocking when we first heard it. You still don't have other emcees who rap like him.

**PARK:** I need to shout out so many great artists: Bambu [Jonah Deocampo], Key Kool [Kikuo Nishi] and the rest of the Visionaries, and Organic Thoughts. The scene was bigger than anyone knew back then, or knows now.

## Making a Name

**ROH:** We started off calling ourselves "Emcees Anonymous" because we wanted to be judged based on our music. But people asked us why we weren't representing for our people, whatever that meant. So we changed our name to Far East Movement to prove we weren't scared of who we are. We said, "Let's rep our people front and center, get it out of the way, and get back to making music about drinking and partying."

**PARK:** I was on the Internet since I was young, so I was making a name for myself online. I don't remember how I came up with "Dumbfoundead." I think I just heard the word "dumbfounded" and thought it was an old word people don't say anymore, and I switched it up to add "dead." I thought I was being so clever! I actually tried changing it to "Parker" a few years ago. My fans weren't having it, though.

## The Next Era

**ROH:** We got our first real break on *The Fast and the Furious: Tokyo Drift* soundtrack. Justin Lin gave us a shot on the soundtrack; our song was in a very nominal part of the movie, and we were ready for our scene to get cut, but Justin fought to keep it in for us. We got a fat check because of it, and it was the first time we could go full-time with our music. After that, we started getting show offers, and the funny part is that a lot of people would book us thinking we were the Teriyaki Boyz, this rap supergroup from Japan who did the movie's title track. We never corrected them! But what we were doing was still so far out from the mainstream, especially as Asian artists, that the momentum didn't last as long as if we weren't Asian, but with the same opportunities. So we had to keep reinventing ourselves; we were still trying to find ourselves. We went from being backpack rappers to doing, like, Latin hip-hop. For one show in Long Beach, we mixed our old raps with some Daft Punk, and people really fucked with it. That totally changed our shows. It eventually opened us up to exploring electronic music, and creating songs like "Girls on the Dancefloor" and "Like a G6."

**PARK:** They're my big brothers now, but at the time FM was popping off, I couldn't stand them! I was so cocky and competitive. They were doing all this club music, and as an underground artist, I felt like I had to hate it. But looking back, what they did was so incredible. Getting to the *top spot on the charts* is incredible. I mean, let's be honest, I only said "fuck the labels" because no one would sign me! And at the time, the AZNRaps era was changing. The forums were fading out and artists were moving to YouTube. You had new artists breaking on YouTube who were significant. Kids like Timothy DeLaGhetto [Tim Chantarangsu], J-Reyez [Justin Cho], and D-Pryde [Russell Llantino] were making covers, rapping on other people's beats and garnering so many views. No one talks about it as much anymore, but that era was big. It was when we were basically our own small businesses, booking shows at colleges, selling merch, and seeing each other on the road. All these Asian student organizations at different universities across the country, like, fed us for a decade.

## Passing the Mic

**PARK:** For a while, YouTube was a scene; now it's a platform. Soundcloud was a scene for a minute. Now it's just part of everything. Now it's the Internet.

**ROH:** Even TikTok is coming on, and creating this equal playing field for new artists coming up. And music is just so global now. Who could've predicted Rich Brian [Indonesian rapper Brian Imanuel, who blew up in 2016 with a YouTube rap called "Dat $tick"]?

**PARK:** 88 Rising [which represents both Rich Brian and Park] is now a huge part of elevating Asians in the hip-hop scene. But even outside of 88, we're seeing artists building their own independent movements. People like this young Vietnamese dude, Kid Trunks [Minh Nguyen]. Audrey Nuna [Audrey Chu] is a Korean girl from New Jersey who's breaking out. Ruby Ibarra is leading this new generation of Filipino women; they're out there, doing their own thing. What's key is that being Asian in the industry is still important to these artists. Asian kids need role models, and in hip-hop, there aren't many. More than just having a scene for Asian rap, we just need to encourage Asian American artists to go out there and do their thing, so they can show others that it's possible to make a living out of music, to build a brand, to have a future.

**ROH:** I love when kids coming up tell me that we've dropped some of their favorite records and that seeing us do it gave them the courage to keep going. I never wanted to think of myself as a stepping-stone, but everybody kinda is. So if we can be part of someone else's process, that's great for me.

# MC Jin's Greatest Spits:
## "Don't Make Me Start Rapping in Chinese on the Microphone"

*AN INTERVIEW WITH MC JIN*

MC JIN

**HE WAS LIKE** a kung fu fighter, taking on all challengers, soundly defeating each with cunning and quickness, until there were none. For seven straight weeks in 2002, a Chinese American kid was the biggest name in battle rap, and he did it all off the top, on national television.

Jin Au-Yeung would be the first to admit that he was an outsider. A transplant from Miami, he had been in New York less than a year when he answered an open casting call for rappers and rode the train to Harlem, where he found himself the only Asian emcee in a sea of hungry hopefuls representing the five boroughs. But that was nothing new: Jin and his brash flow were already a fixture in NYC's battle-rap scene, where rhymes are wielded like weapons and aggressive wit, bravado, and antagonism are rewarded. He was accustomed to being the only Asian in the room—and accustomed to putting up proof that he belonged there. Jin, then 19, knew a strong showing on BET's freestyle showcase could be his calling card. The rules were simple: when the beat drops, each emcee gets 30 seconds to lay lyrical waste to their opponent. No cursing allowed. The combatant with the nicest rhymes, as ruled by a panel of judges, wins and returns as the reigning champ the following week, to face off against another challenger. Seven consecutive wins gets you inducted into the Freestyle Friday Hall of Fame. And one by one, Jin did that.

MC Jin's legendary seven-win streak on the BET show *106 & Park*'s "Freestyle Friday" is a cultural milestone: it earned him a record deal with the Ruff Ryders label—a first for an Asian American solo rapper—and a guarantee that he'd get name-checked in all discussions of Asian emcees, in perpetuity.

In the two decades since his big break, Jin has forged an international career in music, acting, and comedy. Here, he looks back at those epic seven weeks, breaking down the battles and rhymes that landed him an undisputed place in the rap pantheon.

**WEEK 1**

## Hason vs. Jin

*"If you make one joke about rice or karate NYPD be in Chinatown searching for your body"*
In case six-time champ Hason was planning on spitting stereotypical cracks at the Asian guy, as experience would suggest, Jin decided to beat him to the punch. "It was a calculated risk because I was going first. I don't really know what angle he's going to take, but if I were to look at the statistics, there was a 99.8999 percent chance that he was going to reference

something about me being Asian. Is it fortune cookies? Is it Mr. Miyagi? I don't know, but there's a chance that he's going to say that. So for me, the calculated risk was beating him to the punch and in some way, hopefully defuse that."

For the record, Hason took the bait and went in for a "fried wonton" joke. Then, to everyone's surprise, the champ choked and gave up with time to spare. And we had a new champion.

### WEEK 2

## Jin vs. Sterling

*"You wanna say I'm Chinese, son, here's a reminder*
*Check your Timbs, they probably say 'Made*
*    in China'"*

Having unseated the champ, Jin was out to prove his debut wasn't a fluke. Perhaps predictably, this week's challenger hurled a barrage of basic Asian jokes he'd likely been preparing all week. Unfazed, Jin fired off an opening shot that basically ended the battle: "I was like, yo, this dude literally just did a whole round of back-to-back-to-back Chinese jokes. So when I looked at him, I was like, this is it. *'Check your Timbs.'* That line was pretty much composed during his round, at that moment when I'm looking at this guy and he's just going off about fried rice. After I got that line out, I knew it connected with the audience and the judges and the DJ. I just had to run out the clock."

### WEEK 3

## Jin vs. Skitzo

*"Four more weeks and I'm in the Hall of Fame*
*    with Poster Boy*
*Then you can join my street team and put up*
*    posters, boy"*

Week three saw Jin at his angriest. The gentleman's agreement of a freestyle battle is improvisation, or at least the pretense that your rhymes are made up on the spot. Not only did the challenger, Skitzo, come prepared with actual props for his punchlines, one of his jabs joked that he had naked pictures . . . of Jin's sister. On a previous week's broadcast, Jin had shouted out his kid sister, who was struggling with an illness at the time. So this was personal: "I'd battled enough prior to Freestyle Friday to be able to condition myself, at least within battling, that everything in the battle is in the battle. And I guess that was probably the only time in my battle career where something in real life was put into my opponent's material. It stung for a bit, but it wore off really quick. But if you watch the clip, when it was my turn, there was an added sense of ferocity."

### WEEK 4

## Jin vs. Logan

*"By the way, my little sister has something to say*
*'There's no way you'll beat my brother on*
*    Freestyle Friday'"*

By the fourth week, Jin had hit a groove. For fans following his Freestyle Friday journey, he sent the challenger on his way with a farewell message—from his sister: "I had a strong showing, and this was the week following the naked pictures guy. So that's why I came with that one line, just as a closer, *'By the way, my sister has something to say . . .'* which, in my opinion, isn't like the most complex or mind-shattering lyric, but I think the way I said it definitely won a lot of people over."

## WEEK 5

# Jin vs. Lucky Luciano

*"Ask your girl, I was doing something at her house*
*Matter fact, she had my eggroll and my*
*    dumplings in her mouth"*

It's a crude line, Jin admits, though arguably tame by most rap battle standards. But he also says "eggroll and my dumplings" basically saved the battle: "If you remove that line from my verse, I definitely think it could have gone either way. If anything, it actually could have gone in favor of Lucky Luciano. There are parts where I'm stumbling a little and it's evident I'm kind of irritated, because about five or six seconds into my round, the beat skips. And then a few beats later it skips again. Within a 30-second verse, if the beat skips twice, you're fighting an uphill battle. In the first half, I'm spending a good amount of time just trying to catch the beat back. If it wasn't for the *'ask your girl...'* line, we might not be doing this interview."

## WEEK 6

# Jin vs. Skyzoo

*"I got fans across the country, Jin is who*
*    they feeling*
*Last time he had a fan, it was spinning on*
*    the ceiling"*

Pound for pound, emcee to emcee, this was Jin's favorite week—and it was another battle that could have gone either way. Jin admits he probably only had the edge because he went second: "If I was a judge, I would have asked for one more round. One of the judges, I think Timbaland, was like, 'I wanna see a round two!' When he said that, I tried not to show it in my face, but inside I was like, 'Nah man, let's just end this.' The emcee in me was ready to go another round, but the regular Jin was like, just pick me. But this battle, out of all seven, probably aged the best to me 20 years later. Me and him, we was both on our A game that day."

## WEEK 7

# Jin vs. Sean Nicholas

*"You ain't a reggae artist and I ain't hating on you*
*Stop lying, Miss Cleo is more Jamaican than you"*

On the cusp of his final battle, the hype around Jin was through the roof. Unbeknownst to everyone, he had signed with Ruff Ryders, and planned on announcing the deal on *106 & Park* after his seventh win. But first he had to actually win, and there was backstage buzz that this week's challenger, Sean Nicholas, wasn't going to make that easy for Jin. The buzz turned out to be . . . overstated. After a strong opening shot—a Bruce Lee joke, no less—Nicholas stumbled, and his round quickly deteriorated into a verse best described as a reggae-inspired mess. In that moment, Jin knew it was over; he just had to hammer the nail in the coffin: "When he finished, I knew right away. I was going to hit him with a 'Ms. Cleo' line [referring to a famous infomercial psychic who sported a Jamaican accent]. It's crazy how these things process in a battle rapper's head. That line, I knew if I could get it out clean and connect it, it was going to be a walk in the park."

And the rest is history. "Experience has shown me so far that when these things are actually unfolding and you're in it and living it and experiencing it, you don't really think too much about what it means for your legacy," says Jin. "You don't even really know. But in hindsight now, man, it's something that I'm very proud of. I'm humbled."

# The Trials of Dr. Wen Ho Lee

STORY: HELEN ZIA AS TOLD TO JEFF YANG
ART: GLENN URIETA

JOHN CHO

KARIN ANNA CHEUNG

PARRY SHEN

# The Long Legacy of Asian America's First Killer Movie

BY PHIL YU

**THE LEGEND OF** Justin Lin's indie feature *Better Luck Tomorrow* begins with a made-for-Hollywood moment. The way some people told it, a fight broke out at the 2002 Sundance Film Festival after its screening. There was yelling! Someone apparently threatened to kill someone? And then: Roger Ebert, the late dean of American movie critics, stepped up, delivered a stunning monologue to the crowd, and saved the day.

SUNG KANG

ROGER FAN

JASON TOBIN

The truth behind the myth is a little less cinematic. It wasn't a fight—not a physical one, anyway—but an uncharacteristically heated Q&A session afterwards, in which a critic attacked the movie for its "amoral" portrayal of Asian Americans, prompting America's most revered film writer to stand up to defend it, asking his fellow critic if he'd have told white people how to represent their community. The moment became a baptism by fire, announcing the arrival of a pivotal work in the Asian American pop culture canon, and it inarguably gave an indie cinema Cinderella story the potential for a fairy-tale ending.

Made on a string of maxed-out credit cards, barrels of sweat equity, and a generous leap-of-faith investment from an unlikely celebrity benefactor, the film made a raucous splash at Sundance that earned it a distribution deal with MTV Films and a place in history. Two decades later, the story of *Better Luck Tomorrow*—getting it made and getting it seen—remains a remarkable lesson in resilience, community, and shooting your shot. We reunited the film's principal cast—**PARRY SHEN** ("Ben"), **ROGER FAN** ("Daric"), **JASON TOBIN** ("Virgil"), **SUNG KANG** ("Han"), **KARIN ANNA CHEUNG** ("Stephanie"), and **JOHN CHO** ("Steve")—to discuss the movie's creative and professional impact on their careers, that wild Ebert moment, and the film's game-changing legacy for Asian American cinema and the community at large.

## Pounding the Pavement

*Most of the performers who'd eventually become the stars of* Better Luck Tomorrow *had been at the business of acting for years, pounding the pavement with little opportunity or progression in their careers. Their biggest roles until then might've been guest starring on a "Chinatown episode" or two—a TV police procedural's occasional foray into an Asian enclave to solve a case involving human trafficking, gang violence, or tainted tofu. By the time the auditions for* Better Luck Tomorrow *came along, some were actually on the verge of quitting the business.*

**PARRY:** I was about six years into my career doing a lot of guest-star stuff—the standard fare, "Hi, I'm the delivery boy." I knew who Jason and Roger were because we would always be up against each other for roles. But we could never work together, because they'd only be willing to cast one Asian guy on any given show. One of us would get it. The others would go home.

**SUNG:** At that time, I would say I was pretty hopeless. I was wondering if this was the right career choice—I was on my way out, man. There were a few people working—it was the era of Russell Wong, Jason Scott Lee, and Dustin Nguyen—and they were kind of like the light that gave me hope when I started. I mean, hey, they had careers, so maybe I can too. Then reality set in. When you don't have a course of action to achieve your dreams and passion, you feel like you're in some kind of purgatory.

**ROGER:** It was frustrating, because you felt like you could do so much more, but pretty much anything available out there didn't even let you flex five percent of your muscles. Right before *Better Luck Tomorrow* started casting, I went to Australia for like a month. I was ready to call it quits. But two hours after I got off the plane back home, I went to this barbecue and some guy came up to me and said, "Hey, you should audition for this," and gave me a phone number. I called it and I think it was [writer/producer] Ernesto Foronda. I was like, "Hey, I heard you guys are doing a movie." And he's like, "Who's this?"

**JASON:** I arrived from Hong Kong in 1993. By the time I got the audition for *Better Luck Tomorrow,* I was already pretty jaded. I got the call for the audition, it was on a Sunday at UCLA, and at the time I was like, "Goddamn it, a Sunday?" I hadn't seen the script yet. But I read through the sides and did some improv, worked on it with another actor. I remember getting the feeling that I was going to fucking tear it apart, grab it by the horns and really go for it. Afterwards, I knew I'd given a pretty good audition.

**KARIN:** I'd never auditioned for a feature film. I actually saw the casting notice after auditions were already over! But I was standing outside a concert for John [Cho]'s band, Left of Zed, because somebody was supposed to get me into the show. Just then, Justin Lin walks by with a friend, who says, "Hey, this is the girl I was telling you about." I was like, "Oh, isn't it too late?" And he was like, "No, just send in your headshot." I found out later that Justin thought I was underage because I couldn't get into the concert, but I was in my twenties. And that's how I got the audition for Stephanie.

**JOHN:** I had worked with Justin once before. He and Quentin Lee had directed a film called *Shopping for Fangs,* which was the first thing I did on film after I graduated from college. I remember meeting with Justin at a coffee shop and discussing the script. It was around right after I had done *American Pie,* when I was just getting "MILF" screamed at me every day of my life. It felt so silly to get recognized for that.

# Beyond the Chinatown Episode

*Loosely inspired by the notorious real-life "Honor Roll Murder" that rocked Southern California in 1992,* Better Luck Tomorrow *follows a group of high school overachievers whose cheat-sheet ring leads to an escalating series of criminal schemes. The film centers on a darkly complicated portrayal of Asian American youth unfettered by authority—there isn't a single parent in the movie. (Were Asian American films allowed to do that?) It felt dangerous, almost illicit, and most certainly made without Mom and Dad's permission.*

**PARRY:** When the script for *Better Luck Tomorrow* came along, they wanted me to play the role of Ben. I'm used to flipping through a script to the middle, to page 40—"That's where *you* come in." Here, I was on page one. I'd never been given the opportunity to even read something like that. But the shoot was going to conflict with pilot season. I asked the other guys what they were planning on doing and everybody, unanimously, was like, "Fuck pilot season. Who cares?" Even if we got a show, it would be some ridiculous, tiny part. With *Better Luck Tomorrow,* we had the potential to do things we normally never got a chance to do.

**ROGER:** When we finally ended up on set, we actually got to see all these people that you were always forced to compete against, and we saw that they were actually pretty darn good. It was a lot of fun. It was like the first time all of us really got to flap our wings and do what we felt like we were capable of doing.

**JASON:** I remember thinking if this wasn't an Asian cast, it was the kind of movie that would've been Oscar-nominated. It was that good of a script. I really felt like we had gold in our hands, and that feeling just continued throughout the rehearsal and the shoot. There was always this sense that we were making something special.

**JOHN:** I just thought it was a good piece of writing. And there was also the excitement of seeing a bunch of Asian characters on a page. At that point, if I had a career to speak of, it was being the one Asian guy in a scene or something. I would say that's one of the takeaways I had from shooting, what it was like working with so many Asian Americans. That was and still is unusual.

**KARIN:** I'm so glad that I didn't know until after we were done with the film that every freaking Asian American actress out there had auditioned for it. Because I was nervous. But these guys . . . I have to say, if you think my performance is any good, it's because I had these amazing, seasoned actors to work with. It was the best school I could have ever gone through, watching these guys. I felt very fortunate to start my career working with professionals who were so skilled and amazing at their craft. They really pushed me to be better.

## Hammer Time

*Making an independent film costs money. Making an independent film without compromising your vision is damn near impossible. Better Luck Tomorrow was made on a lot of debt and a lot of faith. On the strength of the script, the actors all deferred their salaries to put funds back into the film. Even so, the production eventually ran out of money. Faced with imminent shutdown, Justin Lin pulled out his Hail Mary: he made a call to MC Hammer. Yes, that MC Hammer.*

**PARRY:** Justin had met Hammer at some sort of event, got a chance to talk to him, and he really listened to Justin. Because Justin was so passionate, and you could tell that from his words.

**SUNG:** It was at a consumer electronics convention downtown, when the Canon XL-1 was coming out. One of the first three-chip consumer video cameras. Justin was down there looking for options to shoot the film. Hammer was there too for some reason, I guess he was a techie or something. So they were both looking at the camera, and Hammer asked, "Hey kid, do you know anything about this camera?" Justin shared whatever he knew. And then Hammer asked, "So what do you do?" And Justin responded, "One day, I want to be a filmmaker." So Hammer gave him his phone number. Justin hung on to it, and kept that number pinned on his corkboard.

Well, two years later, we're getting ready to shoot *Better Luck Tomorrow,* and the investors ask Justin to recast the film with all Caucasians. They said they would give him more money, like a million bucks for it. And Justin just pulled out. That night he called Hammer out of the blue and said, "Hey, you remember me?" And Hammer was like, "No." But he listened to Justin anyway. And he said, "All right, well, I don't have Hammer Time money anymore, but I'm going to send you ten grand." So he just wired ten grand to Justin! That's why in *The Fast and the Furious: Tokyo Drift,* Justin put Hammer on all the billboards in Tokyo. Because Hammer saved the movie.

## The Right to Be Whoever the Hell They Want to Be

*It was at the third screening of* Better Luck Tomorrow's *Sundance premiere when all hell broke loose. During the Q&A, film critic Jim Fouratt berated Lin, demanding to know "Why would you, with the talent up there, and yourself, make a film that is so empty, amoral for Asian Americans and for Americans?" His remarks set off a fiery debate among audience members who jumped to the film's defense, most notably Roger Ebert, who admonished Fouratt, saying, "Asian American characters have the right to be whoever the hell they want to be. They do not have to 'represent' their people." The much-publicized moment made* Better Luck Tomorrow *the talk of the festival.*

**KARIN:** That guy basically said, "How can you do this to your people?"

**SUNG:** It was basically a loaded compliment. "Hey, obviously, you guys know how to make a film, the actors know how to act, and there's competence up there, but . . . *how dare you? Shame on you for portraying your people this way!*" And I remember I looked over at Jason, because he looked like he was going to punch someone.

**JASON:** It sucked out all the air in the whole room. And I just got so angry—the audacity to tell me what I can or can't do! My responsibility to my community is to be the best goddamn actor that I can be, not to put some perfect human being on screen for you. I could feel this rage coming up inside of me. So I just went straight into character: I think I said something like "I'm gonna fuckin' kill you!" pretending to lift my shirt up to show Virgil's fake gun, or

whatever it was. Then the room just erupted with laughter. It shattered the silence. People started getting up and talking.

**SUNG:** God bless Roger Ebert for being there and standing up. He said that our only responsibility to our communities was to make a good film. And that's what we did, but then people were uncomfortable with us going outside of our model-minority box. Ebert was like Moses parting the seas.

**JOHN:** I wasn't there for this screening. But it sounds like a movie scene in and of itself, you know? It was preposterous that Ebert—the foremost film critic in the world—stood up to defend our film. It's also complicated, and indicative of the time, that we needed a white man to defend us. And it speaks to the shift in how people were viewing Asian Americans, that somebody would object to our characters having secret dark motives. It definitely wasn't what white audiences were used to seeing, which were good Asians or bad Asians, and never anything in between.

**KARIN:** I remember after the screening, the afterparty had this huge block of ice with a huge ahi tuna on it—an entire fish—and they're cutting sashimi for us. And I'm like, what the fuck? "Pour Some Sugar on Me" by Def Leppard came on, and we were all standing there half crying, half laughing about what we just went through. Every time I hear that song now, I see you guys in a circle, dancing, saying to each other, "What the fuck just happened?"

**SUNG:** Do you guys remember our film rep, Jeff Dowd? He was the dude *The Big Lebowski* was based on. He was at that screening. He told me, in his career, he'd never seen something like that. And he said, "Enjoy it, because you might never have this experience again." And he was right. I never did.

## Out of the Box

*On the strength of Ebert's unusual endorsement and its status as a certified Sundance hit,* Better Luck Tomorrow *was acquired by MTV Films. But it became evident that the studio did not know what to do with the movie. The film would have to rely on Asian American community buzz, a grassroots screening tour, and word of mouth, largely powered by the pre–social media Internet. When it opened in limited theatrical release in 2003, it played to sold-out houses and took in the year's highest per-screen average at the box office.*

**PARRY:** *Better Luck Tomorrow* was MTV Films' first purchase. They were kind of like the rogue production studio underneath the Paramount Classics banner. But Paramount apparently didn't really want this movie. [Paramount Classics' co-president Ruth Vitale publicly stated that she hated it.] I think finally someone from the *Los Angeles Times* who had seen it basically confronted Sherry Lansing, the president of Paramount at the time, and said, "You have one of the best movies of the year under your banner and you guys haven't done anything with it. What's going on?" And of course, Sherry had no idea what was going on either. So she scheduled a screening and watched it while Justin was waiting outside. When she came out, she gave him a big hug and said, "We are going to release this." But it took the head of the studio to push Paramount Classics to make it happen.

**JOHN:** I remember touring to support the movie and just understanding how hard it was.

Because it was so boots-on-the-ground, you know? You think, well, people buy TV commercials and buy an ad in the Calendar, and that's how it works, right? It's like, no, you gotta go around and do screenings and go to colleges. We did it retail.

**SUNG:** We were able to mobilize a lot of people through email. We hit all these universities and Asian American organizations across America—we kind of got a taste of what it feels like to be a Backstreet Boy. It wasn't one person that had to be an ambassador for the movie—all of us did. We're so different, but the thing that unified us was that we were all there for the right reasons.

**KARIN:** We made the old-school Gold Open happen, basically. The guerrilla version of a Gold Open.

**JOHN:** It seems like a foregone conclusion now, but when we were making it, there was actually some question as to whether or not the Asian American community would receive the movie well. And I remember now being pleasantly surprised at how intense and opposite that reaction was, that people were actually not only ignoring what could've been seen as a "negative" portrayal, but they were actually really into the active repudiation of the goody-goody stereotype. They were like, go ahead. Chop this tree down.

**SUNG:** All of a sudden you saw all these other people that looked like you at these venues. And among them there was this—and I use this word in the kindest way—desperation for their voices to be heard. I would meet young men and women who were thanking us for representing them. It was shocking. It's like they had been waiting for this their whole lives.

## The Day After No Tomorrow

Better Luck Tomorrow *was a bona fide break-through, but it never quite jump-started a movement—or opened up careers—in the way many involved with the film had hoped. Professionally, the film became a badge of honor for the actors . . . but badges, even honorable ones, don't pay the bills.*

**ROGER:** When we were at Sundance, it seemed like everyone's careers were going to be catapulted to the moon. But when you look back in retrospect, the way the game is played, Sundance is really more of a director's medium. So it was very interesting. Justin was more than generous with all of us, trying to help every actor, every writer, every producer get a foot in the door. But the whole system of Hollywood was trying to just find the next big director.

**SUNG:** There was kind of a grandiose hope that it would lead to jobs right away. At least for me there was. All the fervor at Sundance, where suddenly you're in the trades and people around you are talking to real agents. You get a taste of what real Hollywood is, right?

**JASON:** Let's not forget, at that point, we had still not been paid a penny for *Better Luck Tomorrow*. We had all done the film on copy and credit. I think the hope for all of us was that a hit film at Sundance meant that we would have a career, and money in our pockets to be able to survive and actually live off acting.

**ROGER:** For the whole year before the release, we were taking a lot of meetings. But right when the movie came out, all of a sudden it just ended. My phone completely stopped ringing. It was really a wake-up call. It's like, if you're not hot on the iron right now, the business won't find any incentive to sell you. That was tough to go through.

**SUNG:** I went back to waiting tables, dude. I remember after that film came out, I was waiting tables and meeting people who had seen the film. They were like, "Hey, you look like that guy in that movie. Why are you back to zero?" It took like six years again before I booked *Tokyo Drift,* because Justin directed a film that could actually pay me and I could finally say I was living off acting money. But that was years later. The whole representation game evaporated for us after Sundance.

**ROGER:** John was already on a certain trajectory. He was already ahead of us, from a career perspective. But still, I expected at least one or two or three of us to be on a TV series or something by that time. The fact that it didn't happen was a big surprise to me.

## The Better Luck Club

*Defying expectations on every step of its journey,* Better Luck Tomorrow *offered an exciting vision of what Asian American cinema could be. It was also a calling card for Justin Lin, who went on to become the director and chief architect of* Fast & Furious, *one of the biggest movie franchises of all time. In 2020, the* Los Angeles Times *polled critics and film influencers to name "The 20 Best Asian American Films of the Last 20 Years."* Better Luck Tomorrow *topped the list.*

**JOHN:** It was the arrival of a really legitimate pop director like Justin Lin. That was the real discovery of the movie, that there was an Asian American filmmaker who had the potential to be a world-class filmmaker. To me, that was

> "The burden of 'breaking through' is a lot for one film to carry. I realized things weren't just going to change overnight, because you need a whole slew of work out there. You need the *Fresh Off the Boats*. You need the *Saving Faces*. You need the comedy, you need the horror, you need the action. You've got to have the whole rainbow."

a distinguishing moment in our history, and it was clear how quickly the community got behind him. If there's anything that informed what our potential future was, it was having this new, exciting creator.

**ROGER:** It was the first time in my life I felt the shared energy of a lot of people with unrealized dreams, who all got together with a little bit of coaxing from Justin, who pointed all of us in the exact same direction. We were underdogs. This film really should not have gotten made, but there was something about layering all these people together and pushing forward. Doors opened up left and right, saving us when we really needed it. To this day, I don't think I've ever seen anything like that from a professional standpoint, where a group of people come together and all of a sudden, small miracles happen.

**KARIN:** It was a gift to work with these guys, true passionate artists who are so skilled in their craft—and none of them was selfish. I believe that when you take the steps to express yourself, and you're doing what's right for you, you will change the world. Stick to your thing and do it. If your gut tells you who you are, why try to play to the expectations of some white dude?

**PARRY:** I'm still amazed at the experience of going to colleges and hearing Asian American kids say that they changed their science-based majors to acting, because they saw someone actually doing it. Or opening weekend, when we were only screening in four cities, and kids were taking buses from, like, Pennsylvania all the way to New York City because that was the closest theater, just to support the film.

**SUNG:** The burden of "breaking through" is a lot for one film to carry. I realized things weren't just going to change overnight, because you need a whole slew of work out there. You need the *Fresh Off the Boats*. You need the *Saving Faces*. You need the comedy, you need the horror, you need the action. You've got to have the whole rainbow. What we had was this one edgy indie film.

**JASON:** I often call *Better Luck Tomorrow* the gift that keeps on giving. It's been 20 years, which is incredible, and every actor goes through ups and downs, but this film still gets me work. It still gives me a lot of credibility. The fact that it's had such a profound effect, and we're all sitting here talking about it, is a testament to what I'm saying. We were part of a wave, and it's still going. It wasn't a light switch; it took two decades. But it's the kind of film that we might be talking about again in another ten years. Let's go ahead and set up that Zoom meeting for ten years from now.

# The Cartoon Characters That Shaped Our Kidhood

**BY JES VU, ILLUSTRATED BY LINDA CHUNG**

**FOR SOME OF** us who grew up as latchkey kids, watching over ourselves while our immigrant parents were hard at work, cartoons were our companions while we were alone. For others, they were held out as an incentive to make us study, or watched stealthily as a secret distraction from studying. For still others, they offered a way to better understand a culture—or a language—that didn't quite feel like our own. And while Asians may have been mostly absent from live-action TV, if we looked closely, we could usually find our faces, names, and sometimes even voices represented in the colorful world of cartoons. Here's a timeline of some of the most memorable animated Asians of American TV, and a handful of favorites shared by some of our favorite Asian American animation veterans.

## The Golden Age

*There were just a handful of pioneering Asian characters in the earliest days of animation, and the best you could say about them was they didn't know any better at the time.*

**HASHIMOTO-SAN FROM *HASHIMOTO-SAN* (1959):** Amazingly, the first Asian character to star in their own American toon was a mouse named Hashimoto-san, created by Asian American animation pioneer Bob Kuwahara. Fourteen shorts featuring the Japanese mouse and his family were created between 1959 and 1963, with imagery we'd find stereotypical today (acutely slanted eyes, broken English, and chopstick lettering)—but for the era, even this representation was a breakthrough.

**CHARLIE CHAN FROM *THE AMAZING CHAN AND THE CHAN CLAN* (1972):** It would be 13 years before another animated Asian family showed up in cartoons—and of course, the family in question was that of Charlie Chan, the racist stereotype created by Earl Derr Biggers and portrayed on film by a series of white men in yellowface. Incredibly, the animated Chan was voiced by veteran Chinese American actor Keye Luke, who'd played Chan's "Number One Son" in many of the films—making this the only time the character was ever acted by an actual Asian. The series focused on Chan and his 10 kids (who had a band!) traveling around to solve mysteries in the transforming Chan Van.

**PENROD POOCH FROM *HONG KONG PHOOEY* (1974):** Not quite an "Asian" character, Penrod Pooch, an anthropomorphic dog working as a janitor in a human world, reads as Black (he's voiced by the iconic Scatman Crothers). When crime strikes, however, he leaps into action as a masked kung-fu superhero named Hong Kong Phooey. The theme song was wildly offensive—"Hong Kong Phooey, number-one super guy…chicky chong chicky chong"—but something about the show

made it feel less like mockery and more like a clumsy showcase of Black and Asian solidarity. Maybe because literally all of the other characters were human … and white?

## The Silver Age

*By the 1980s and '90s, cartoons actively tried to incorporate diversity in their lineups—but frequently ended up leaning into stereotypes, even as they earnestly included Asian characters.*

**GI FROM *CAPTAIN PLANET AND THE PLANETEERS* (1990):** Gi, voiced by Janice Kawaye, hailed from "Asia" (not a *country* in Asia—just Asia) and was bearer of the Water Ring, which, when grouped with rings held by a diverse group of four other kids, summoned the eco-superhero Captain Planet.

**KIMI WATANABE-FINSTER FROM *RUGRATS* (1991):** Kimiko, voiced by Dionne Quan, is a perky, ponytailed Japanese American toddler whose mother, Kira Watanabe, marries Chuckie Finster's father, Chas, making her Chuckie's stepsister.

**WANDA FROM *THE MAGIC SCHOOL BUS* (1994):** Voiced by Lisa Yamanaka, Wanda is a tomboy and the smallest but feistiest member of Ms. Frizzle's highly diverse class.

**PHOEBE HEYERDAHL FROM *HEY ARNOLD!* (1996):** Phoebe, voiced by Anndi McAfee, is Helga's best friend and the smartest girl in football-head Arnold's class. One of the earliest biracial Asian cartoon characters, her father is depicted as Japanese, though it's not clear why his last name is Heyerdahl.

**CONNIE SOUPHANOUSINPHONE IN *KING OF THE HILL* (1997):** Connie, voiced by Lauren Tom, is the smart and kind daughter of the Hill family's neighbor and nemesis, loudmouthed Kahn Souphanousinphone. Her actual name, as we learn during the series, is "Kahn Jr."

**AMY WONG FROM *FUTURAMA* (1999):** Amy, voiced by Lauren Tom (who brought to life so many amazing Asian animated characters!), is Planet Express's rich, spoiled, airheaded intern.

## The Millennium

*A full three decades after* The Amazing Chan, *the arrival of the 2000s saw a number of cartoons centered on Asian protagonists and their families. And even in shows where Asian characters weren't the leads, a conscious attempt was made to avoid cliché depictions.*

DAN SANTAT, CREATOR, *THE REPLACEMENTS*

### Quick Kick, *GI Joe: A Real American Hero* (1982)

"I loved Quick Kick because he didn't have a stereotypical accent, and basically cracked jokes in the form of puns and sarcastic remarks, much like myself, while being the GI Joe martial arts expert. In the cartoon, he's introduced as a karate movie actor who was abandoned in the Arctic by his director and survived solely on granola bars that were left over on the frozen set. In the comic, he's described as a basketball player who was turned down by leagues because of his height, leading him to decide to become proficient in various martial art forms instead. He literally is an animated version of a bunch of Asian friends who I grew up with, so when I see him on the screen it's like seeing an old friend."

**JADE CHAN (AND JACKIE) FROM *JACKIE CHAN ADVENTURES* (2001):** This series depicted Jackie Chan as a kung-fu archaeologist (voiced not by Jackie but by James Sie), using mystical talismans in a war between good and evil. Jackie's 12-year-old Chinese American niece Jade, voiced by Stacie Chan, is his constant sidekick and smarter half.

**JAKE LONG FROM *AMERICAN DRAGON: JAKE LONG* (2005):** Jacob Luke "Jake" Long, voiced by Dante Basco, is a laid-back biracial Chinese American skate kid with the magical powers of a Chinese dragon, inherited through his Chinese mother's side of the family.

**JUNE FROM *LITTLE EINSTEINS* (2005):** June is a six-year-old Asian American ballerina, voiced by Erica Huang, who goes on extremely educational adventures with her three multiracial friends and their magical rocketship.

**BALJEET TJINDER FROM *PHINEAS AND FERB* (2007):** Baljeet, voiced by Maulik Pancholy, is the friend and neighbor of the two protagonists, who's constantly swept up into their crazy ideas. He frequently bemoans his girl problems, but by series finale ends up in a couple with **GINGER HIRANO** (voiced by Michaela Zee, Ming-Na Wen's daughter!) in one of the first animated depictions of a multiethnic Asian American relationship. Ginger's elder sister **STACY**, voiced by Kelly Hu, frequently appears as the best friend of Candace, Phineas and Ferb's elder sister and nemesis.

**KAI LAN FROM *NI HAO, KAI LAN* (2008):** Kai Lan, voiced by Jade Lianna Peters, is a bilingual Chinese American girl who teaches manners and Mandarin to her friends, all of whom are talking animals.

---

VYVY NGUYEN, ACTRESS/CONSULTANT, *BOJACK HORSEMAN*, *THE HARPER HOUSE*

## Mr. Hyunh, *Hey Arnold!*

"As a Vietnamese American, it was so nice to see someone like Mr. Hyunh from *Hey Arnold!* who looked and sounded like my relatives, and who, despite having a strong accent, was never mocked for it. The heartbreaking Christmas special in particular helped me better understand what my own parents had experienced as refugees fleeing Vietnam, which I'd previously been too young to properly grasp. Most importantly, Mr. Hyunh's identity wasn't completely shaped around war. He was a beloved and integral part of the boardinghouse—and turned out to also be an incredibly talented country music singer!"

DANIEL CHONG, CREATOR, *WE BARE BEARS*

## Russell, *Up* (2009)

"Russell from Pixar's *Up* struck me as a really positive reflection of Asian American representation largely because, well, nobody ever pointed out he was Asian—Russell was just a fun, optimistic, and earnest kid trying to get a wilderness badge, not defined by his ethnicity, which is totally how I operated growing up. The inspiration for Russell was a Korean American director at Pixar, Peter Sohn—his personality and features are all reflected in Russell, highlighting how just the presence of diversity in the workplace can naturally lead to thoughtful representation in a huge and successful animated movie."

1. Executive director of festival doing 10 things at once

2. Other staff of festival doing 20 things at once

3. Corporate sponsor representatives—you can tell because they're the only ones in suits

4. The guy who put all his friends' tickets on his card and is anxiously waiting for them to show up five minutes before showtime

5. Asian American celebrity

6. Group of fans surrounding Asian American celebrity

7. Other Asian American celebrity trying to be conspicuously inconspicuous

8. Group of Asian American YouTubers who've produced their first feature

9. Sheepish latecomer asking staff to let him sneak in quietly

10. Asian American Film Studies major explaining the elaborate details of this one scene to his friends

11. Fans in cosplay there for that one anime film

12. First-time indie director surrounded by all of her huge extended family who are there to root her on

13. White film critic from major newspaper, did not quite understand the movie so will praise the art direction and cinematography

14. Pop-up boba tea stand (not pictured)

15. Bone marrow donation registry booth (not pictured)

16. Long lines at the bar spilling out of the VIP party (not pictured)

17. Photo booth/shoot

18. Red carpet step-and-repeat

19. People in IT'S AN HONOR JUST TO BE ASIAN shirts

20. People in STAY ANGRY shirts

# The Asian American Film Festival

BY JEFF YANG

There are many spaces that allow our diverse community to converge, but Asian American film festivals are in many ways unique: They're both local—hosted by cities from Boston to Honolulu—and national, in that they represent a cross-country distribution circuit through which Asian American narrative visions can be seen by hundreds of thousands of people who might not ever have had the chance to be exposed to them. And international, for that matter: long before *Parasite* won the Oscar for Best Picture, Asian American film fests were often a gateway to the United States for notable works from Asia and the Asian diaspora. But for those of us who've attended them for decades, they're something more: they're a locus for an extended family of people who gather every year around their shared love for our stories and our people. Here's what attending an Asian American film festival is like, from those of us who've seen them as our second home.

KAREN CHAU, CREATOR, *NI HAO, KAI LAN*

## Edna Mode, *The Incredibles* (2004)

"Edna is brilliant, loyal, powerful, armed with crystalline clarity and purpose and a huge heart. She's brutally honest, and has no filter—and nor did she need one to succeed. Her philosophy and pearls of wisdom are memorable rules I strive to live by. 'I never look back, *dahling*. It distracts from the now.' 'Yes, words are useless, gobble gobble.' I love her work-life principles, her no-bullshit attitude, and the way that she makes every decision with thought and consideration in her costumes. That approach in life and work is awesome. On top of that, she's hilarious, and her comedic timing is perfection. Unfortunately, despite being depicted as half Japanese and half German, she was voiced by *Incredibles* director Brad Bird. That was a shortsighted decision—and a wasted opportunity."

VIDHYA IYER (STAFF WRITER, DISNEY JUNIOR'S *MIRA, ROYAL DETECTIVE*)

## Juniper Lee, *The Life and Times of Juniper Lee* (2005)

"Juniper was one of my favorite characters. It was fun to see an Asian lead just having adventures and going on missions—I wanted to be a spy as a kid and loved mission-driven shows. The badass action sequences and the supernatural bent of the show mixed some of my favorite aspects of cartoons, and I watched it without fail after school!"

## The Modern Era

*Cartoons have never been more innovative or diverse; with Asian Americans a dominant force behind the scenes as animators and showrunners, depiction of Asians in animation is often more rounded and complex than in live-action shows.*

**SANJAY PATEL FROM *SANJAY AND CRAIG* (2013):** Sanjay, voiced by Maulik Pancholy, is a 12-year-old Indian American boy who goes on adventures with his best friend, Craig, who happens to be a snake.

**CONNIE MAHESWARAN FROM *STEVEN UNIVERSE* (2013):** Connie, voiced by Grace Rolek, is protagonist Steven Universe's best friend-turned-girlfriend, who matures from timid nerd to sword queen.

**HIRO AND TADASHI HAMADA FROM *BIG HERO 6* (2014):** In the Disney animated feature, Ryan Potter voices robotics prodigy Hiro, who inherits the wellness robot Baymax from his elder brother Tadashi (Daniel Henney) and converts him into a crimefighting hero.

**CHLOE PARK FROM *WE BARE BEARS* (2015):** Chloe, voiced by Charlyne Yi, is the best friend of the series' three titular bears.

**ANNE BOONCHUY FROM *AMPHIBIA* (2019):** Anne (Brenda Song), is the first Thai American protagonist of an American animated series, which follows her adventures as she tries to reunite with lost friends Sasha (a white character, voiced by Asian American Anna Akana!) and Marcy (Haley Tju) in a world ruled by frogs.

**MIRA FROM *MIRA, ROYAL DETECTIVE* (2020):** Mira (Leela Ladnier) is a young girl named as Jaipur's royal detective, solving crimes with her pet mongooses—mongeese?—Mikku and Chikku.

KAL PENN

JOHN CHO

# *Harold and Kumar*

## How a Pair of Potheads Stormed Hollywood's White Castle

BY ANNA JOHN

**IN 2004, A UNIQUE** stoner comedy blazed its way into America's hearts. *Harold and Kumar Go to White Castle* was an audaciously bizarre film featuring two best friends who go on an epic quest to sate their munchies. For Asian Americans, however, it was groundbreaking—the first Hollywood buddy film to feature two Asian American leads. The fact that it went on to become a three-movie franchise, while turning Kal Penn and John Cho into first-tier Hollywood stars, was almost icing on the cake. Co-creators **HAYDEN SCHLOSSBERG** and **JON HURWITZ** sat down with actor/director **SUJATA DAY** (HBO's *Insecure*), actor **LEE SHORTEN** (Amazon's *The Man in the High Castle*), and writer **GAUTHAM NAGESH** for a conversation on *Harold and Kumar*'s impact and continuing legacy.

### Representation Matters

**JON HURWITZ:** In high school, Hayden and I hung with a pretty multicultural group. We all looked different from one another, but at the end of the day, we were all just American teenagers going to high school in New Jersey. And you know, one of our best friends was the real Harold Lee, and we had very good pals from debate team named Shanker and Saiket. Once we started writing scripts together, the very first script we sold had two characters at the center that were basically versions of us, but their best friends were Harold and Kumar. We ended up putting Harold and Kumar somewhere in every screenplay we wrote after that. None of those movies ended up getting made, but we built this lasting affection for those characters.

**HAYDEN SCHLOSSBERG:** We gradually realized *they* were the interesting ones. Sometimes characters stay with you and they won't let you go! We were also aware of the lack of representation of Asians onscreen. We'd seen enough teen comedies with "Long Duk Dong"–type characters; that obviously didn't reflect reality as we knew it.

**JON:** And then, to be honest, John Cho was in *American Pie,* and every time we went out with Harold, people would shout out, "Hey, it's the MILF guy!" It's not even like they look that much alike, but John was one of the few Korean American faces out there at the time. So in a weird way, when we started writing *Harold and Kumar,* it was in part because we were confident that there was someone who could star in it.

**HAYDEN:** We met Kal during the process of casting. And we'd seen his work, and it turned out Kal's from New Jersey like we are, and he was in speech and debate too, so it sort of like all came together. But what really sealed the deal for us was John and Kal talking about how they felt a sense of responsibility—that it wasn't just a role. We all understood there might be a college class watching this someday.

## An Accent on Authenticity

**HAYDEN:** We were protective of the characters. One thing we did put in was "no accents," because we needed the reader to have that in mind. So many execs over a certain age would just assume, "Well, they've got to have accents, otherwise what's funny about it?"

**JON:** Yeah, that was the big thing that I remember in the character descriptions. It said "no accent," in all caps. That was us trying to portray the characters authentically. And you have to have the right partners. I remember our very first meeting with Nathan Kahane, who's a producer on the movie and is now running the motion picture group at Lionsgate, he picked up on what we were doing, and he said, "If you make this, you gotta make this movie with me, because I guarantee it will continue to be *Harold and Kumar Go to White Castle* through to the end."

## What *Harold and Kumar* Meant to Us

**GAUTHAM NAGESH:** When I saw it, I was 21. I'd dropped out of Cornell and was living at home, working as a substitute teacher and smoking a lot of weed. I distinctly remember watching it with my high school friends and thinking that I'd never seen anything remotely resembling us in Hollywood before. I think *Gandhi* was the only English-language movie with Indians in it that had really penetrated American consciousness. So we had that, we had Apu on *The Simpsons,* we had immigrant stories, and that was it. There was nothing depicting the lives of kids who were born here, who didn't have an accent, who were American. So it felt revolutionary.

**LEE SHORTEN:** I'm adopted. I grew up in a small Australian town raised by white parents. I wasn't just the only Asian in my friend group, I was the only person of color. I was the "Twinkie," as Harold jokingly calls himself in the movie. When I saw *Harold and Kumar* it was a huge deal, because I'd never seen myself represented that way.

**SUJATA DAY:** It was really nice to see Asian and Indian faces on screen that reflected the people around me. But also, there's a scene in which Kumar is interviewing for med school, and it's clear he completely doesn't give a shit. Well, I had that same interview, for a six-year med program that I did not want to attend, and *Harold and Kumar* definitely inspired me to throw away my engineering degree and pursue acting and writing. I can honestly say that it was a movie that changed my life.

## Smoking Out Stereotypes

**LEE:** While Asians have a lot more representation now in Hollywood, the stories are very specific. They're important, don't get me wrong. I love that we had *Crazy Rich Asians*. But I also long for us to just be people on the screen, where our ethnicity is not a central defining characteristic or a main narrative drive. And I feel like *Harold and Kumar* nailed that in a way that was unique then, and in many ways still is.

> We were protective of the characters. One thing we did put in was "no accents," because we needed the reader to have that in mind.

**HAYDEN:** Hollywood always lags behind reality; I think the aftereffects of *Harold and Kumar* are still being seen now, and there'll only be more opportunities over time. My hope was that we'd inspire Asians to say, "Hey, you know what, maybe *I'll* write or direct a movie." Sometimes we talk about how we've made a lot of Asian American parents frustrated.

**LEE:** Well, one thing I'll say about *Harold and Kumar* is it's held up really well. People these days talk about how it's so hard to do com-

edy now, but you guys gave a good example of "punching up," making it so the stereotypes are almost always inverted or the butt of the joke.

**HAYDEN:** Stereotypes exist. We know some people think a certain way, but they shouldn't, so how do we explore that in an entertaining way? We had this attitude of "Hey, let's play with that. If we poke all the bears, then they won't feel like we're harping on one."

**SUJATA:** Part of it is the diversity of the cast. Beyond Kal and John as the leads, the film included so many races. I mean, Gary Anthony Williams as Tarik Johnson, his scene in prison, where Harold says, "What are you in for?" And he responds, "For being Black." That's painfully relevant today, when Black people are being shot for no reason.

**JON:** It's upsetting that people could have made that same point about injustice 20 years before us. When we wrote that scene, our hope was we wouldn't still need to make that point today.

## So What Does the *Real* Harold Think?

**JON:** He loves the movies. He and John became very good friends through this process. There was a brief period when Harold was between jobs that coincided with when John was going on a multi-country tour for *Star Trek*; John had a plus one for his junket, but his wife couldn't go. So Harold ended up going with him, and it was like *Harold and Harold Travel the World*. It was their adventure, and it was amazing.

**HAYDEN:** I would've watched a documentary on that trip so hard.

# Elevated or Appropriated?

# "Asian Night": The Asian Party Scene

BY PHILIP WANG

**IN THE 1990S** and 2000s, a new phenomenon began to spread across major cities like New York, San Francisco, and especially Los Angeles: the Asian party scene, consisting of dedicated "Asian Nights" promoted by enterprising operators who saw a rising demand among Asian Americans for the chance to mix, mingle, and make bad decisions in their own (semi)private venues. Serving this market was lucrative: "The promoters who were crushing it were probably making $10,000 in cash per party, and they were doing two or three parties a week," says stand-up comedian Paul Kim, a veteran of L.A.'s Asian Nights. "And on special nights, like New Year's Eve, they were probably clearing $40,000 or more." Kim remembers how crazy the scene was at its peak: "I don't remember ever seeing clubs that packed—they were breaking the fire code every week, 2,000 people cramming into clubs that maxed out at

a thousand," he says. "You'd be running into people you hadn't seen since high school, from afterschool programs, from church."

The main reason for this boom: a surge in Asian American post-grad professionals, who saw Asian Nights as rare opportunities to meet other single Asians, or simply to reunite with the old college crews and let off steam. "You know, all the way through college, many of us were pushed to focus on that 'aspirational model-minority' stuff," says Kim. "So we didn't have a chance to really cut loose or meet people— a lot of us grew up in environments where we weren't off the leash ever, with parents who wouldn't let us go hang out. So these events were where we came together."

We asked some of the pioneering promoters and party people of the Asian American nightlife scene to share with us their memories of the club circuit's heyday.

---

I was going crazy every weekend. Like, I literally was working just to party on the weekend. You'd head out to the club and everybody was always wearing dark clothes, black leather jackets. You'd see a lot of guys just kind of looking around, and a lot of girls in crowds kind of dancing with one another, and maybe it would take all night for someone to try to cut in. Still, it was an opportunity for us to meet and mingle with people in an adult environment that just didn't exist anywhere else after college.

—PAUL KIM

It all started in K-Town. In the Nineties, K-Town was a special place for a lot of us—sort of this exclusive hiding place just for Koreans, where you could let your hair down and seriously party it up. There was underage drinking. There was indoor smoking. There was underage clubbing.

—PAUL KIM

One of the things we did with our crowds that stood out was bottle service. Asians actually were the ones who introduced bottle service—VIP tables with full bottles—to America!

—CARL CHOI, cofounder, Climax Global

We brought go-go dancing back into the American scene. Our approach was to do these Vegas-style mega club events with thousands of people each night at huge venues, strobe lights everywhere—it was like a theme park. Our crowd loved to flash with their cars at the valet, and with the money they spent at the bar, but ultimately they just really wanted to hang out with other Asians at the time, and we created a haven for that.

—BILLY CHEN, cofounder, Visionshock

At the time it was very rare to see other ethnicities hanging out, quote unquote, on our turf, you know? I feel like 1995 to 1999 were the heydays of K-Town, where every weekend, every Koreatown club was popping. It didn't matter where you went, because it was literally popping everywhere, totally packed. And not just the clubs: the bars were all at capacity. And that's when I launched KTown213, because we wanted to just capture the essence of that scene, the true K-Town spirit. And that was 2000. But we had a lot of issues with taking photos in K-Town—people didn't want to be put on camera. And then Asian promoters—Visionshock, Climax, and many more—started to become big players in the party game in Hollywood.

—JONATHAN LEE, founder of KTown213, an early website that offered news, event listings, and photo galleries of the Asian party scene

A lot of Asian promoters began by putting together club events as fundraisers for college organizations. But pretty soon, different brands and types of events catering to different niches began to form. At Climax, we ended up creating a network that went from San Diego to San Francisco, and eventually expanded to New York, Atlanta, Houston, and Philadelphia. We had different nights, from the "18 and over" student crowd to glammed-up events that attracted big spenders. Asian nightlife was a category, but there were a lot of subcategories.

—CARL CHOI

Whatever city we spread to, there was always a lot of support. Ultimately, we were trying to create a circuit that we could take Asian American artists through, like MC Jin and Far East Movement. In their early days, I took them on tour through these parties.

—CARL CHOI

In the early days, Asians never got credit for the amount of money and people we were bringing into major Hollywood clubs. I recall in 2001, my friend, a club owner, was filling out a census, reporting how many white and Black people came to his events. But there was no box to report Asian Americans, so he just grouped us as "white."

—CARL CHOI

If you go back to Asia, you'll see that we're nocturnal creatures—among Asians, all our business is done at night, so nightlife is part of our DNA. You have people who wanna go out and have fun, and in the early 2000s, before dating apps, to meet other guys and girls. Our parties gave Asian men and women a platform to stand out and connect.

Yeah, it was common in Koreatown booking clubs, but we brought the service to high-end Hollywood venues, and soon our "Asian Nights" were generating more money than any white event. Club owners couldn't believe it, so they replicated our model. Now bottle service has been adopted across all ethnicities, and is a staple of nightlife around the world. But it started with Asians.

—BILLY CHEN

It ended up as a pan-Asian scene, but that didn't happen all at once. At least in L.A., where we were operating the strongest, it started with Chinese and Korean Americans—students who came from the college scene. Then we had Vietnamese crowds coming up from Orange County. The next wave to join in were the rich parachute kids: first Indonesians, then Taiwanese, then Mainland Chinese. Toward the later years of our companies, it was just a mix of everyone.

—CARL CHOI

In San Francisco we obviously saw a big tech crowd; all the conversations were always about how much they hated L.A. Out in New York, we were limited to bars essentially, so people would just come by for like 10 minutes, then bounce. We didn't make money out there—it was more for branding. Atlanta was very Korean and had more of an older graduate-school scene. But some cities like Houston and San Diego stayed collegiate. We had a good run in D.C., where the crowd was a mix of Vietnamese and Korean. But the parties never got too large out there because the venues just weren't that big.

—CARL CHOI

But we knew what we did. We knew the force that we were. Our companies brought eyes to the power that Asians possessed in an industry that didn't even have a checkbox for us. And on a personal level, we created a place for Asians to network, to meet future husbands and wives, and just be unapologetically Asian.

—BILLY CHEN

# THE STYLE LIST 2000s

BY FAWNIA SOO HOO

**BY THE 2000S,** clothes designed by Asian Americans were dressing down and up—becoming must-wear apparel in which to be seen on the block, and on the red carpet. Here are five Asian Americans who shaped the decade's streetwise and upmarket looks.

## OPENING CEREMONY

**BEST KNOWN FOR:** Being *the* destination for hard-to-find, buzzy brands and exclusive collaborations

**SIGNATURE LOOK:** Downtown cool kid goes global

**ASIAN INSPIRATION:** Carol Lim and Humberto Leon developed Opening Ceremony inspired by a two-week trip they took together to Hong Kong

Korean American Lim and Peruvian Chinese American Leon revolutionized the millennial fashion landscape in 2002 by debuting Opening Ceremony in New York with their own savings and a small business loan. The concept store quickly became a tastemaker with its curated mix of emerging American labels, like Rodarte and Proenza Schouler, and its savvy introduction of high-low international favorites, like Topshop, Havaianas, and Acne, to the U.S. market. In 2015, O.C. introduced its own in-house line, but in 2020, due to the COVID-19 pandemic, they closed all of their brick-and-mortar stores.

## KIMORA LEE LEISSNER

**BEST KNOWN FOR:** That louche cat logo

**SIGNATURE LOOK:** Baby tees, bedazzled jackets, low-rider denim

**ASIAN INSPIRATION:** Metallic obi belts, kanji characters on distressed T-shirts, Japanese floral embroidery, Devon Aoki walking the runway and in their Fall 2002 ad campaign

Former model and Karl Lagerfeld muse Lee Leissner, who is of African and Japanese descent, was the first designer to carve out a place for women in the male-dominated streetwear category. She grew her brand Baby Phat by Kimora Lee Simmons, originally founded in 1999 under then-husband Russell Simmons's Phat Farm umbrella, into a billion-dollar company at its peak. The line (which Leissner reacquired in 2019) has been a favorite of celebrities, including Aaliyah, Lil' Kim, and Paris Hilton.

## NAEEM KHAN

**BEST KNOWN FOR:** The strapless, silver sequined gown Michelle Obama wore to her first state dinner in 2009, which honored the prime minister of India

**SIGNATURE LOOK:** Luxurious red-carpet glamour

**ASIAN INSPIRATION:** He incorporated artistry learned from his father and grandfather, who had designed clothing for Indian royalty, into his collections.

After honing his design skills under Halston, in 2003 the Indian American designer launched his own evening-wear label, which quickly became a red-carpet mainstay among celebs like Jennifer Lopez and Beyoncé. He's also become known internationally for dressing royalty, including Queen Noor of Jordan and Catherine, Duchess of Cambridge—notably for her 2016 visit to the Taj Mahal.

## JASON WU

**BEST KNOWN FOR:** Michelle Obama's floral-embellished, white one-shoulder inauguration gown, which now is displayed at the Smithsonian's National Museum of American History

**SIGNATURE LOOK:** Modern Americana with international flair

**ASIAN INSPIRATION:** Mao-era military greens, Qing Dynasty embroideries, and mandarin collars in his irreverent Fall 2012 collection that explored "What is Chinese?"

Just a year after launching his label in 2007, the New York City–based Taiwanese Canadian designer received industry accolades as a finalist for the CFDA/*Vogue* Fashion Fund award. But it was First Lady Michelle Obama who made him a household name by wearing his gowns to both of President Barack Obama's

inaugural balls—as well as on her March 2009 *Vogue* cover.

## PHILLIP LIM

**BEST KNOWN FOR:** The architectural and zippered top-handle Pashli bag, which was also reimagined for the popular 2013 Target collaboration

**SIGNATURE LOOK:** Effortless, yet experimental city chic

**ASIAN INSPIRATION:** Qipao influences—and all-Asian models—for his brand's fifth-anniversary show, held in 2010 at the Forbidden City in Beijing

The Thailand-born Chinese American designer began his fashion career working at Barneys New York. After his Los Angeles–based first line, Development, shut down, Lim connected with longtime partner Wen Zhou in 2005 to establish a new brand, 3.1 Phillip Lim. (Both were 31 at the time.) Lim's new brand skyrocketed to success, receiving the CDFA Award for Emerging Talent in Womenswear in 2007, followed by the ongoing support of First Lady Michelle Obama, who wore 3.1 Phillip Lim multiple times—including a Lim dress and coat set for the state arrival ceremony of Chinese president Xi Jinping and First Lady Peng Liyuan in 2015. But Lim's relationship with the White House paused after the Obamas departed: he issued a statement to *Women's Wear Daily* politely declining to dress Melania Trump, stating that he and the Trumps do not "share a similar set of values."

## Boys of the Millennium:

You've got a first-generation iPod that fits in the sizable pockets of your cargo pants. Are you an athlete? Well, you're wearing a LIVE STRONG bracelet, that should be sporty enough. And while you probably don't play rugby, you at least wear a shirt with stripes on it. If you're a preppy boi, make that "shirts": you're wearing multiple tops at the same time—you've layered that rugby shirt over a Lacoste polo, and maybe that polo over a T-shirt. Either way, the collar's popped and the sleeves are rolled. If it's a hot day and you're feeling casual, it's time for just the tee—which has the Sriracha label printed on it, and that's now your whole personality.

Or maybe you're a bad boy: If so, you're so Hoobastanky that you've got a pair of ear gauges. Your hair is medium-long with curtain bangs. It's as if your forehead spread those hairs open to greet the day while the beats of the Neptunes danced in your head.

Whichever style you cop, you've both definitely got at least a dozen pairs of Nike Dunks in multiple colorways.

## Girls of the Millennium:

You're a Bratz Doll come to life, with a closet of candy-colored separates and a few metallic pieces that shine like they're from outer space. You like tiny shirts, maybe tube tops, softened up with something fuzzy: either your own big hair, or a fluffy cropped cardigan to keep your arms warm. Make sure to wear high heels with your toes crammed into an absurdly pointed toe because, again, you're a kewpie doll sweetie pie who doesn't need her feet to function!

It's the 2000s, and Y2K clearly did something to clothing proportions: tanks go down to your thighs, jeans stop below your hips. You're wearing micro-layered miniskirts with big thick belts that don't hold up anything, but just function to communicate "Hi! This is where my waist is!" Also, you seem to believe leggings are pants. Most of your shirts are longer than a top but shorter than a dress. What can one do with these . . . these . . . what should we call them? Tunics? You might try putting them over Seven Jeans or True Religion (like "My Humps," thank you, Black Eyed Peas). Or throw them over leggings, which are still not pants, and accessorize with pointed ballet flats and a skinny scarf.

# The Asian American Reality TV Hall of Fame

BY CYNTHIA WANG, ILLUSTRATED BY TAK TOYOSHIMA

**YOU COULD SAY** that reality TV put Asians in the spotlight before "reality" did. From the beginning of the reality explosion in the early 2000s, unscripted series gave undiscovered dancers, singers, chefs, designers, and, well, ordinary people a chance to shine—and sometimes not shine—in front of millions. Among these hundreds of aspiring contestants were dozens of Asian Americans. For many of us, they represented our first chance to see and root for someone who looked like us on prime-time TV.

Daniel Lue, *Survivor*'s first Asian male castaway, underscores how rare it was for us to be represented in those days. When he saw that Shii Ann Huang had been cast in Season 5's competition, set in Thailand, he was sure he'd have no chance to get on the show: "It made me nervous because I was thinking CBS might not cast two Asian Americans in a row."

Fortunately for us he was wrong, and we got to see him in 2003 on Season 6, living off meager rations in the Amazon and speaking Mandarin with ally Matthew von Ertfelda. Although he got voted out after three episodes, his adventures were seen by an average of 22 million viewers a week. "A lot of guys sent me emails asking for advice on working out," he says. "I especially received a lot from guys from Asian countries—and this was before YouTube and Instagram. They saw me, and it inspired them."

Being on *Survivor* changed Lue's life, too. The former Houston-based corporate tax accountant moved to Los Angeles to fulfill his childhood dream of becoming an actor, and has since built a résumé that includes prestige shows like *Bosch* and *Lucifer*.

By dashing through obstacles, facing off in wild competitions, and bearing with all kinds of grueling and embarrassing circumstances, the Asian Americans of reality TV gave us a "home team" to root for, while expanding the context of what society thought Asians could do, achieve, or behave like. Here are the reality stars who paved the way.

## The Champions:

**2003**

JUN SONG, *Big Brother,* Season 4: Song, *Big Brother*'s first nonwhite winner (a status she'd hold till Season 19!) and the first to never receive a single eviction vote, used her cooking skills and secret alliances with her ex-boyfriend Jee Choe (also in the house, due to an *X-Factor* twist, but evicted on Day 61!) to become one of the earliest Asian American reality TV champs.

**2005**

CHLOE DAO, *Project Runway,* Season 2: Vietnamese American designer Dao was among the leaders throughout most of her season. She triumphed over both the competition and her own self-doubts to be the first Asian American to take the $100,000 prize.

**2006**

YUL KWON, *Survivor,* Season 13: Korean American lawyer and management consultant Kwon won the uniquely structured Cook Islands contest—which had its castaway teams initially divided up into racially segregated groups—with devastating strategy, strong social skills, and of course, those impeccable pecs. He returned after a 14-year hiatus in 2019 for *Survivor: Winners at War,* placing 14th.

**2007**

APOLO ANTON OHNO, *Dancing with the Stars,* Season 4: Already an Olympic gold medalist for short-track speed skating, Ohno partnered with Julianne Hough to take the win. (He would also place 5th in 2012 on Season 15's All-Star reunion competition, partnered with Karina Smirnoff.)

TESSA HORST, *The Bachelor,* Season 10: Horst got the final rose from Andy Baldwin; they broke up four months after the May 2007 finale.

HUNG HUYNH, *Top Chef,* Season 3: Vietnamese American Huynh won Season 3, set in Miami, after a run in which he was seen as cocky and arrogant—a persona he chose to cultivate. Hung is currently chef de cuisine at Morimoto Asia, at the Disney Springs resort.

**2009**

TAMMY AND VICTOR JIH, *The Amazing Race,* Season 14: The pair of siblings, both attorneys, took a whatever-it-takes attitude all the way to the winner's circle of Season 14, taking advantage of several legs that were set in China, given that they were the only contestants fluent in Chinese.

**2008**

KRISTI YAMAGUCHI, *Dancing with the Stars,* Season 6: Skaters clearly have an edge—pun intended. Partnered with Mark Ballas, Yamaguchi became the second gold-medal-winning Asian American ice star to take the win on *DWTS.*

**2010**

NICOLE SCHERZINGER, *Dancing with the Stars,* Season 10: Filipino-Hawaiian Scherzinger, who first came to fame as one of the winners of the music-group reality show *Popstars,* showed she can dance as well as she can sing by winning her season, partnered with Derek Hough. She's now a judge on Fox's idols-in-disguise reality contest *The Masked Singer.*

**2011**

HINES WARD, *Dancing with the Stars,* Season 12: The Black and Korean American former Pittsburgh Steelers star partnered with Kym Johnson to show off triumphant footwork in Season 12.

RAJA GEMINI (A.K.A. SUTAN AMRULL), *RuPaul's Drag Race,* Season 3: The first and only Asian American winner of *Drag Race* to date, Amrull beat out another Asian American—Filipino American Manila Luzon (a.k.a. Karl Philip Michael Westerberg)—in a finale lip-sync-off to take the crown. He subsequently worked as head makeup artist for *America's Next Top Model* for eight seasons.

PAUL QUI, *Top Chef,* Season 9: Filipino American Qui won eight of 16 elimination challenges en route to his victory. Unfortunately, all the talent in the world can't make up for domestic violence. In 2018, he was arrested for allegedly assaulting his then-girlfriend while intoxicated. Though the chef denied punching her, he admitted he knocked her and her son out of the way in the process of drunkenly trashing their apartment. In April 2018, charges were dropped when the alleged victim refused to cooperate with prosecutors.

## 2012

**CHRISTINE HA**, *MasterChef,* Season 3: Vietnamese American self-taught chef Ha—the first and only legally blind contestant in the show's history—beat out dozens of rivals to win the third season of *MasterChef*, stunning the judges with her extraordinary palate, her disciplined execution, and her thorough command of culinary techniques.

**ANYA AYOUNG-CHEE**, *Project Runway*, Season 9: The Trinidadian American, whose heritage includes a mix of ancestries, including Chinese, Indian, and Caucasian, represented Trinidad and Tobago as its 2008 Miss Universe candidate—designing her own wardrobe for the pageant—before winning the ninth season of *Runway* as a runaway fan favorite.

**KRISTEN KISH**, *Top Chef*, Season 10: Korean American Kish, an adoptee, almost found herself eliminated during the Seattle season, but beat her way back into the main competition from the show's "Last Chance Kitchen" to become just the second female winner in *Top Chef* history. In 2014, Kish made headlines when she publicly came out as gay.

## 2014

**NATALIE ANDERSON**, *Survivor*, Season 29: Sri Lankan American Anderson and her twin sister, Nadiya, competed in the San Juan del Sur season, with Nadiya being the first contestant voted out and Natalie winning the whole shebang. Anderson also competed in *Survivor: Winners at War,* and finished as runner-up. The sisters also competed in two seasons of *The Amazing Race,* Seasons 21 and 24.

**MEI LIN**, *Top Chef,* Season 12: Chinese American Lin won the Boston season, and was promptly hired by Oprah Winfrey as her personal chef. She opened her first restaurant, Nightshade, in 2019 in Los Angeles.

## 2013

**TESSANNE CHIN**, *The Voice,* Season 5: Chin, a Jamaican Chinese crooner from a musical family, won her season as part of Team Adam, while garnering the highest number of votes in *Voice* history. (As an aside: While she didn't win, Korean American Dia Frampton was runner-up on the inaugural season of *The Voice* in 2011!)

**CATHERINE GIUDICI**, *The Bachelor*, Season 17: Filipina American Giudici won the final rose from Sean Lowe, and married him the following year. They have three children—Samuel Thomas, Isaiah Hendrix, and Mia Meija.

## 2017

**KENTARO KAMEYAMA**, *Project Runway*, Season 16: Japanese-born Angeleno Kameyama blew away the judges with his idiosyncratic sensibility and classically inspired designs. A music scholar and composer, Kameyama also showed off his musical chops during the show, playing host Tim Gunn an original piece, "Kentaro and the Dead Cat," that he wrote after finding and burying a deceased feline.

**LEX ISHIMOTO**, *So You Think You Can Dance,* Season 14: Hip-hop/contemporary dancer Ishimoto didn't just win his season—he also found love, in the form of the season's third-place finisher, Taylor Sieve. (He wasn't the only one: his fellow Japanese American contestant, Koine Iwasaki, who came in second, is dating fourth-place finisher Kiki Nyemchek.)

## 2018

SHIN LIM, *America's Got Talent,* Season 13: Lim isn't your garden-variety illusionist. in 2015, the Chinese Canadian American won the world championship in Close-Up Card Magic, and parlayed that into two mind-blowing appearances on *Penn & Teller's Fool Us*—he fooled them both times!—and then a Season 13 triumph on *America's Got Talent,* dazzling the judges and even making Simon Cowell speechless with awe, a magic trick all of its own.

KAYCEE CLARK, *Big Brother,* Season 20: Filipino American Clark, a receiver for the San Diego Surge of the Women's Football Alliance, dominated physical competitions while forging an ironclad alliance with fellow houseguests who dubbed themselves "Level Six." Her athletic prowess and strategic skill led to her winning the season in a close 5–4 vote.

HANNAHLEI CABANILLA, *So You Think You Can Dance,* Season 15: Filipino American contemporary dancer Cabanilla was a fan favorite through most of her season, while bonding with celebrity judge and fellow Filipina Vanessa Hudgens.

## 2019

KODI LEE, *America's Got Talent,* Season 14: Lee, who is blind and autistic, first performed in public at age six, when he spontaneously began accompanying an a cappella group that was singing nearby. They thought he was so amazing that they asked him to stay with them all day. His "perfect pitch, perfect memory, and perfect timing," in his mother Tina Lee's words, are combined with a magical, soulful voice that transported the judges, especially Gabrielle Union, who handed him a Golden Buzzer that sent him directly to the finals—where he won with a breathtaking cover of Leona Lewis's "You Are the Reason."

BAILEY MUÑOZ, *So You Think You Can Dance,* Season 16: Muñoz became the second Filipino American in a row to win the competition, and the first b-boy.

## 2020

MELISSA KING, *Top Chef,* Season 17: King placed as a finalist—behind eventual winner and fellow Chinese American Mei Lin—in Season 12, but returned for this All-Stars season in Los Angeles, winning the title and the designation of fan favorite. She has won more single-season challenges than any other competitor on the show.

# WILLIAM HUNG DOES NOT NEED YOUR SYMPATHY

BY CYNTHIA WANG

**IN 2003, A** 20-year-old UC Berkeley civil engineering student in an aloha shirt took the stage at *American Idol*'s Season 3 auditions and told host Ryan Seacrest, "I want to make music my living."

With number 32716 taped across his chest, William Hung proceeded to deliver a rendition of Ricky Martin's "She Bangs," complete with staccato dance moves, that could most charitably be described as earnest. Notoriously cranky lead judge Simon Cowell cut him off: "You can't sing, you can't dance. What do you want me to say?" Hung replied simply, "I already gave my best, and I have no regrets at all."

Hung may have been fine with how things went, but the public had many, *many* opinions. In a pre-Facebook, pre-YouTube, and pre-anything-social age, more than 29 million viewers saw Hung's audition as soon as it aired and reacted as you might expect: with cringes, laughter, condescension, and in some cases, horror.

Not everyone hated Hung; in fact, he had a sizable contingent of supporters who found him to be an inspirational example of someone following his dreams against all odds, with confidence, passion, and optimism. But some of his harshest critics could be found among the Asian American community—not because they hated him personally, but because the frankly

WILLIAM HUNG

racist mockery he faced spilled over to them as well. The logic went: Why would Hollywood producers set up an obvious non-talent to bomb on a national scale except to heap derision on other Asians? It couldn't have been easy for Hung either, to be laughed at by non-Asians and given the cold shoulder by those in his own community.

But with typical cheer, Hung, now 37, simply says, "I would say that you cannot please everybody. You have to focus on your own mission, and my mission is to bring happiness to the world—to help people try something new, without being judged or ridiculed."

And there were upsides to his instant fame, too. "I was living my dream life," he says. "My first album, *Inspiration,* was the number one independent album on *Billboard* and sold over 250,000 copies. I was getting opportunities to perform all over the world. I got commercial deals with big companies like AT&T and Jack in the Box. But I knew it couldn't last forever."

After the cameo movie and TV appearances began to fade out, Hung—who had dropped out of Berkeley to pursue his music career—got serious and finished school, graduating from California State University, Northridge with a degree in mathematics. He worked as a crime analyst for the L.A. County Sheriff's Department, before transitioning to the L.A. County Department of Health. He got married and divorced—and appeared on *Idol* to perform a reprise of "She Bangs" in 2016. Now, he's harnessing all of his experiences into a career as a motivational speaker, and toward helping clients work themselves up to a place where they're confident enough to deliver TED Talks.

But the shadow of his *Idol* days still follows him. Comedian Jimmy O. Yang told podcast host Joe Rogan during an interview on his show that Hung "set us [Asian Americans] back, like, 10 years."

Hung, who's heard it all, shrugged it off. "I'm OK with that because he's just saying his opin-

ion and at least he was civil about it," he says. "Everybody has a right to their own opinion."

But Hung hasn't given up on his fans. He still livestreams on the Livit app and offers up paid shout-outs on Cameo. And those fans aren't there for his music; they're there for his legacy as someone who defiantly crashed the gates when they were still mostly shut for Asian Americans. "I would say there were more Asians willing to put themselves out there to try to get on various talent shows after my audition," he says. "It's been a long, long process to get to where we are today."

And along the way Hung got to meet Ricky Martin, the original singer of his signature song: "It was so surreal," he says. "I never thought it would be possible!"

# POSTCARD FROM ASIAN AMERICA

BY CHRISTINA MAJASKI

Dear RISE,

I'm a fortysomething liberal Korean adoptee single mom in conservative central Minnesota, and I only really like five people and a few animals. I grew up mostly in Germany because my dad was in the military. And while I was raised "white"—like many other transracial adoptees back then—being a part of the military community gave me some exposure to other cultures.

But that said, I did not grow up feeling at all Asian and was ashamed of the little Asianness I had. I mean, I didn't learn how to use a rice cooker until a friend freaked out on me about it. As a result, I led the most inauthentic twenties a person can live, trying to co-opt identities that were not mine—I have a picture of myself with cornrows that, now that I think of it, should be burned.

I guess I didn't really feel "Asian" until I had my daughter, at 30. I've always wanted her to understand the privilege that comes with being half white, and to be proud of being half Asian . . . while living in central Minnesota. We've embraced our Asianness together through travel, watching TV (*Bling Empire!*) and reading books; so while she might pass for white with people who don't look closely, she now loudly celebrates being Asian and being part of this community—so loudly that I don't know if I should be more proud or afraid. But it's given me faith that in new generations to come, there will be fewer Asian kids growing up lost, even in areas where they're the only Asian people anyone might ever know.

And yes, because I know you want to ask: As I write, it's April and there's still snow up here. A blizzard might break out any minute.

Always Asian,
Christina

RISE
HERE AND NOW,
ASIAN AMERICA

# THE ASIAN AMERICAN PLAYLIST:

# The 2000s

BY RICHIE "TRAKTIVIST" MENCHAVEZ

| Song Name | Time | Artist | Notes |
|---|---|---|---|
| "Pursuit of Happiness" | 6:36 | Steve Aoki remix feat. Kid Cudi, MGMT, Ratatat | They call him the "Asian Jesus"—for his long-haired, bearded looks and for his ability to resurrect songs in new and transcendent forms. As a Grammy-nominated DJ, producer, entrepreneur, and philanthropist, Aoki has become one of the most recognizable Japanese American faces in the world. This 2009 remix, which has generated almost half a billion combined streams and views, continues to be a staple in his DJ sets, which famously include throwing cakes at fans, crowdsurfing on inflatable rafts, and popping bottles and spraying champagne on listeners. Perhaps it's his status as son of wrestler turned Benihana founder Rocky Aoki that gave Aoki his work ethic and instinct for performance, both of which have contributed to his status as one of the highest-paid DJs in the world—and the holder of a Guinness World Record for "most traveled musician." |
| "In the End" | 3:36 | Linkin Park | When this rap-rock hybrid track was first released as the fourth single from Linkin Park's debut album *Hybrid Theory*, it received just average reviews. In fact, it originally almost didn't make the album. To everyone's surprise, however, the song, with its signature piano riff, has managed to stand the test of time, becoming one of the band's most recognizable songs and accumulating over one billion views for its video on YouTube. Two of the band's founding members are Asian American: vocalist, rhythm guitarist, producer, and primary songwriter of the band Mike Shinoda is Japanese American, while DJ, turntablist, and video director Joe Hahn is Korean American. Both have inspired a generation of rock/hip-hop fusion fans around the world. |

SCAN THE
QR CODE TO
DOWNLOAD
THE PLAYLIST

| Song Name | Time | Artist | Notes |
|---|---|---|---|
| "Learn Chinese" | 4:33 | MC Jin | One might dismiss this song as a gimmick on first listen. You might even find it offensive, given its usage of the controversial, orientalist "Arabian riff" and demeaning lyrics from Yellowman's "Mr. Chin." But context is everything: this was the first single off of Jin's 2004 album *The Rest Is History*, released after his unprecedented signing with Ruff Ryders/Universal, which made him the first ever Asian American solo rapper signed by a major record label. With production from hip-hop's elite—Kanye West, Swizz Beatz, Just Blaze, Wyclef Jean—it debuted at #54 on the Billboard 200 and spent seven weeks on *Billboard*'s Top R&B/Hip-Hop Albums, debuting at #12, eventually selling over 100,000 units in the United States and over 250,000 worldwide. |
| "That Girl" | 3:49 | David Choi | Korean American singer, songwriter, and producer Choi is one of the primary artists responsible for the wave of Asian American visibility and success during YouTube's formative years. "That Girl" is an essential listen, not only because it's his most popular studio-produced track, but because it perfectly showcases the signature, heartfelt folk-infused pop style that helped him capture the hearts of over a million YouTube subscribers worldwide. As one of the platform's earliest adopters, it was his experimental video "YouTube: A Love Song" in 2006 that unexpectedly went viral, changed his life, and revealed the medium's possibilities for our underrepresented community. |
| "Umbrella" | 3:48 | Marié Digby | Singing to the camera with bad lighting, accompanying herself with guitar in front of her living room couch, Digby's simple but brilliant acoustic cover of Rihanna's "Umbrella" skyrocketed her into YouTube fame in 2007; it has since amassed over 22 million views. Biracial Japanese American Digby had already been signed to Disney's Hollywood Records since 2005, and strongly believed that the posting of simple videos like this one would give her visibility in the leadup to her debut. She was absolutely right. *Unfold* debuted at number 29 on the Billboard 200 in April 2008, and has since sold over 400,000 albums worldwide, in both English and Japanese. |

| Song Name | Time | Artist | Notes |
|---|---|---|---|
| "We Could Happen" | 3:36 | AJ Rafael | Rafael, a Filipino American singer, songwriter, actor, and director from Riverside, California, was one of YouTube's earliest adopters. He relied on his talent, consistency, and authentic connection to fans for his success in gaining a million subscribers—something that took over a decade. However, his significance goes beyond numbers: with his hundreds of collaborations, AJ made it popular for YouTubers to work with other artists, building a community that helped to unleash a tidal wave of Asian American representation on the platform. "Starlit Nights" was the first original Rafael posted to YouTube, a joyous keyboard-driven power ballad that he wrote for and dedicated to his then-girlfriend. |
| "Valentine" | 2:30 | Kina Grannis | It's appropriate that "Valentine" is Grannis's most popular song. It's a chill, sweet track about falling in love every day. And that's it. The millions of "Kinerds"—the name her fans have given themselves—around the world haven't just fallen in love with her music, they've fallen in love with her. A biracial Japanese American, Grannis was YouTube's first Asian American breakout star, after she won a 2008 contest that led to her music video being played during Super Bowl XLII and landed her a contract with major label Interscope Records. Amazingly, she chose to decline the label deal due to a mismatch of creative visions. It proved to be the right decision for her: Grannis's independently released album *Stairwells* debuted at number 139 on the Billboard 200, demonstrating that a major label record deal wasn't required for success as an Asian American artist. |
| "Lemonade" | 3:01 | Jeremy Passion | In the mid-2000s, "Lemonade" became a prime pick for amateur balladeers hoping to catch the attention of the object of their affection. Filipino American Passion is a singer, songwriter, producer, and one of the first Asian/Filipino Americans to go viral online; he's also considered a pioneer of the acoustic R&B/soul movement. In fact, "Lemonade" reached such a wide audience that it was part of a 2018 plagiarism controversy involving Daniel Caesar and H.E.R.'s Grammy Award–winning song "Best Part." Make sure to check out his latest version of the song done with his supergroup MPG, a collaboration with fellow YouTubers Melissa Polinar and Gabe Bondoc. |

| Song Name | Time | Artist | Notes |
|---|---|---|---|
| "Callin' Out" | 3:34 | Lyrics Born | Who's the funkiest rapper alive? My pick is Lyrics Born, and if yours isn't, I don't want to hear it. Born Tsutomu "Tom" Shimura, the rapper, singer, producer, and actor has had a career spanning a quarter century. In the process, he's obliterated stereotypes by becoming the first Asian American rapper to release 10 studio albums, and the first to release a greatest hits compilation. "Callin' Out," from his debut solo album *Later That Day*, was a breakout hit that led to his becoming the first Asian American to play major music festivals like Coachella and Lollapalooza. |
| "You Oughta Know" | 2:55 | Das Racist | In the early to mid-2000s, South Asians began to blow up in hip-hop. M.I.A.'s "Paper Planes" and Punjabi MC's "Beware of the Boys ft. Jay-Z" became major hits. So when a pair of Indian Americans—Himanshu "Heems" Suri and Ashok "Dapwell" Kondabolu (brother of comedian Hari)—and Afro-Cuban/Italian American Victor "Kool A.D." Vazquez, collectively known as Das Racist, went viral for their novelty song "Combination Pizza Hut and Taco Bell," hip-hop heads were not sure how seriously to take them, or if they should take them at all. They followed up with two mixtape gems that made their critics shut up and sit down. From the *Shut Up, Dude* mixtape, "You Oughta Know" is a classic track built around a sped-up Billy Joel sample that showcases their unconventional style—lyrically playful, provocative, and sometimes profound. |
| "Cough Syrup" | 4:09 | Young the Giant | Within the first 30 seconds of hearing "Cough Syrup," I knew I had to add it to my collection. It was the compelling and somewhat haunting vocals that completely drew me in. Upon researching the band, I discovered that the lead singer Sameer Gadhia is Indian American—making him one of the first South Asian rock frontmen. Young the Giant's continued success demonstrates that Asian Americans can run with rock's best. |
| "Gee" | 3:22 | Girls' Generation | With the rise of social media and YouTube in the 2000s, K-pop began to spread its appeal beyond Korea, in a phenomenon referred to as Hallyu or the "Korean wave." One of the groups most responsible for the leading edge of this wave is Girls' Generation, a nine-girl pop army, two of whom were Korean American—Tiffany Young and Jessica Jung. Pop decorated with smatterings of techno, "Gee" is the electro-bubblegum hit that skyrocketed the group to fame, eventually becoming one of Korea's most popular songs of the decade. |

# Bhangra Is the Beat

BY PHILIP WANG

FOR MANY ASIAN American students, dance teams were a major part of college life. If you weren't on a team, you knew someone who was, or you at least saw them around campus. But while Filipinos, Southeast Asians, and East Asians leaned into b-boying and hip-hop—with stand-out college dance teams like UC Irvine's Kaba Modern laying the groundwork for Asian American domination in competitions like *America's Best Dance Crew*—South Asian Americans built community and created a hotly contested national competition circuit based on contemporary and classical dance forms like garba, kathak, Bollywood-style dance, and especially bhangra, a traditional Punjabi dance that has emerged as a unique art form of the South Asian diaspora, often infused with modern choreography and the swagger of hip-hop. In the process, it's brought disparate young people together, instilling in them a unique sense of shared community and cultural pride. We asked some veterans of the bhangra world to share their experiences with us: **RITESH RAJAN** (Netflix's *Russian Doll*), an actor and former bhangra instructor who was his dance team's captain at New York University; **SALEENA KHAMAMKAR**, a bhangra choreographer and previous coordinator at UC San Diego; and **SHIVANI BHAGWAN** and **CHAYA KUMAR**, dancers and founders of the bhangra YouTube channel "BFunk," which has 1.7 million subscribers.

PHOTO COURTESY OF DA REAL PUNJABIEZ

## Planting Seeds

**RITESH:** Bhangra dance evolved out of the motions of Punjabi farmers as they planted and harvested, and it's still most associated with Punjabi Sikh culture, though it has evolved to be a part of mainstream dance and music culture in India. My parents listened to bhangra music—there's a rich history of bhangra being a form of escape for Indian youth in the U.K. But for me growing up, it was a sonic backbone of parties, weddings, and family gatherings. And it got a huge boost during the early 2000s when people in the Indian community in the United States and Canada started forming dance teams to replicate the Bollywood experience at their school's cultural shows.

**SHIVANI:** Bollywood movies have been around since the Forties, so cinema, dance, music—we all grew up with them around our homes. That's why you have so many South Asian kids drawn to join dance teams once they get to college.

**SALEENA:** To be clear, most schools will have a separate Bollywood dance team and bhangra team. Bollywood teams tend to incorporate more Western dance styles into their performances; bhangra teams tend to be more traditional and focus on the different styles within bhangra. Most people who join bhangra teams grew up with it.

**CHAYA:** I grew up in Dallas, Texas, and Shivani in Michigan. We both danced as kids; a lot of Indian parents encourage dance because they say they want their children to be well-rounded, which is funny because only one thing still matters at the end: academics. But once I tapped into Indian dance, it just consumed me.

**RITESH:** I grew up in a very white town. At home I was very Indian, but at school I was more "American." So joining a team was the first time I got to experience Indian culture *with* my peers. My team being fusion with hip-hop and bhangra was kind of symbolic of my own sort of journey trying to balance two cultures, and it really sort of shaped my identity moving forward.

**SALEENA:** I grew up in Las Vegas, so I was also a little bit more detached from other Indians—I was one of five of us in my high school. I wanted to join a dance team in college to find that sense of Indian community.

## Cultivating Bonds

**RITESH:** The social incentive is a big reason for joining bhangra teams. It helps that the learning curve isn't that steep. The point of entry is friendly enough that a lot of people can join even if they haven't danced before.

**SALEENA:** It's so cliché, but you really become family when you're on these teams and at these shows with people who have the same background and goals as you, loving the same music. It's a family away from home.

**CHAYA:** There's a sense of mutual accountability and responsibility. You're representing your school, you're representing yourself, you're representing your culture. All that together gives you this high that's so addictive.

**SHIVANI:** In a way it felt like we were living double lives: going to class in the morning, then going straight to choreographing and dance practice, and repeat. And our parents had no idea that this is what we were doing.

## Growing Together

**RITESH:** Bhangra dance has been around for a long time, but what really catapulted it into something new was the organized Indian dance competitions. The shows connected South Asians across the country. I was making friends in Texas, Philadelphia, Los Angeles—they made the community really grow.

**SALEENA:** When you go to these competitions, everyone is like you and likes the same kind of music. You play a bhangra song and everyone busts out their moves. We were all living and breathing this dance and culture together.

**SHIVANI:** And it got pretty serious. You could fail all your exams, but still feel accomplished if your team got first place.

## Gathering the Harvest

**CHAYA:** Social media has made everything more accessible—it's made learning and sharing so much easier.

**SALEENA:** Now we're seeing people from all backgrounds and cultures wanting to learn bhangra, and it's awesome. It's very exciting because you feel seen: They understand me! We're becoming normalized!

**SHIVANI:** There was a trend on TikTok where everyone was dancing to a bhangra/hip-hop fusion song and a lot of people were actually learning bhangra moves—respectfully, not making fun of it. So we're seeing way more awareness now. There's a growing appreciation for bhangra as a real dance form, instead of some foreign, exotic thing.

**SALEENA:** When we first started pitching major dance studios about teaching bhangra classes, they would tell us, "No, we can't have a class like that, it's not a real style, it's a cultural dance." This was just a few years ago; now we get messages from the same studios that rejected us to come in and teach. This style of dance has become legitimized, and this means we can prove that Indian dance can be a career. We're showing people it can be something that can be forever in your life.

**RITESH:** That's really great, because for a lot of students, dancing on a team was their last hurrah before they were sent off to medical school, having to work 20 hours a day as an investment banker: "Well, it's been fun, now I'm going to go live in the middle of an oil field in Texas where everyone's racist."

**SHIVANI:** Now dance teams are seen as stepping-stones to a future instead of just a club, because new kids who are starting out can see that previous members have become professional actors or dancers.

**RITESH:** A bhangra team, the Desi Hoppers, won *World of Dance* a few years ago! My mom was texting me the whole time: "Did you see them? Did you see that?"

**SHIVANI:** My grandparents were the ones who immigrated here, so in some ways I feel more American than Indian. What happens when I'm a grandparent? So my goal is to keep my culture from being diluted for the future. I know younger generations and even people in my generation who think it's uncool to be Indian. I want to show them that you can have both and be proud.

# The Dance Crew Revolution

ILLUSTRATED BY JEF CASTRO

**WHAT WE CALL** hip-hop dance today is a fusion of styles first performed at New York block parties and L.A. freestyle jams to music ranging from up-tempo funk to the staccato break beats that fueled the rise of rap. Inspired by African dance but incorporating moves from modern, jazz, swing, tap, and even martial arts and gymnastics, hip-hop's electric, expressive, and continuously evolving forms have made it the heart of contemporary dance, and have spread it far beyond the urban Black American communities from which it began.

In 1984, Crazy-A—a leader of Japan's offshoot of the Bronx-based Rock Steady Crew—brought breakdancing to Tokyo's Yoyogi Park, where b-boys still gather to battle on weekends. In 1992, a Korean American music promoter named John Jay Chon took a b-boy VHS tape to Seoul and shared it with dancer friends; it ended up sparking a breakdance scene that's one of the most innovative and competitive in the world today.

Chon was far from the only Asian American drawn to hip-hop dance in the early Nineties. The same year as Chon's fateful trip, a Filipino American freshman at the University of California, Irvine named Arnel Calvario pitched the idea for a new dance troupe to the president of Kababayan, the college's Filipino cultural club. Instead of traditional dances, the group—Kaba Modern—would focus on hip-hop dance. Soon, dance crews were popping up throughout the West Coast, producing some of the most talented hip-hop dancers in the nation.

The popularity of *American Idol* guaranteed that dance competitions would soon follow, and in 2005, one of the most visible Asian hip-hop-inspired dancers on TV, former *In Living Color* "Fly Girl" Carrie Ann Inaba, would become a judge on *Dancing with the Stars* and a choreographer on *So You Think You Can Dance.* But it was *ABDC*—better known as *America's Best Dance Crew,* produced by former *Idol* judge Randy Jackson—that brought dance crews to the mainstream in 2008. (An elite squad from Kaba Modern even competed in the show's first season, finishing third.)

It must have shocked MTV's young, 13–34 demo to see Asian American–led crews dominating the show with humor, athleticism, and awe-inspiring tricks. In the first six seasons of the show, crews led by Asian dancers hoisted the contest's trophy high, year after year.

"People take it for granted that all crews are from the [Black] 'hood," Jackson told *People* magazine in 2009. "No, they are in every 'hood, not just the Black 'hood! JabbaWockeeZ has one of everything in there, Latin kids, Asian kids, and Black kids. I just love how through dance and through this music and this culture, everybody just comes together."

Added *ABDC*'s Filipino American creative director and supervising choreographer Napoleon D'umo, who with wife Tabitha formed the lyrical hip-hop choreography duo Nappytabs, "If you're Filipino, you know that you either sing or dance, [so naturally] our Asian population on the show is really big."

*ABDC* is gone, but Asian American crews continue to shine in shows like *So You Think You Can Dance* and *World of Dance*; first-season winners JabbaWockeeZ even have their own Las Vegas casino residency!

**Winners of *America's Best Dance Crew*:**

**JabbaWockeeZ,** Season 1, 2008
**Super Cr3w,** Season 2, 2008
**Quest Crew,** Season 3, 2009 (also won Season 8 All-Stars, 2015)
**We Are Heroes,** Season 4, 2009
**Poreotix,** Season 5, 2010
**I.aM.mE,** Season 6, 2011 (founding member Di "Moon" Zhang).

# Pioneers of Asian American YouTube

BY PHILIP WANG

**I UPLOADED MY** first YouTube video in March of 2006. We were drawn to it because Wong Fu Productions' own website had maxed out on download capacity due to a little student film we'd released called *Yellow Fever,* and YouTube offered free bandwidth and an online video player—two factors we take for granted in this age of endless livestreaming. But back in 2006, YouTube was laying a path to an unknown, unclaimed frontier—one where anyone could easily share and consume videos made by anyone. And while "anyone" really does mean "anyone," the fact is that many of the earliest adopters and pioneers of this revolutionary platform were Asian American.

When people tell me that, as one of the early channels to get millions of views, we were "pioneers," it makes me feel weird; when we were starting, we didn't know we were becoming part of a golden era for Asian American content creators—a term that didn't even exist at the time. No one really even understood what we were doing, why we were doing it, or where it was headed.

But now that we're seeing infants learning how to navigate YouTube, and teens making millions off of it, I can see why we're seen this way. (Partially because, we old!) If the true meaning of being a pioneer is facing the unknown, pushing through obstacles, and helping to carve a path through a new and risky landscape for others to follow, Wong Fu Productions and other incredibly talented Asians did just that—pointing our cameras at ourselves from our bedrooms, garages, and backyards to create videos, first for our own enjoyment and then for millions of others. Little did we know these unassuming videos would ultimately raise a generation of Asian kids who'd find representation not through TV and movies, but through tiny boxes on a computer screen.

### KevJumba

**WHO:** Kevin Wu, joined July 27, 2006

**STYLE:** Personal stories and low-fi comedy sketches

**BREAKOUT VIDEO:** "Ask KevJumba," 15 million views

**CURRENT SUBSCRIBERS:** 3 million

**SIGNATURE QUOTE:** "Team Jumba! I like it!"—Papa Jumba

**DESCRIPTION:** Wu's relatable storytelling (with frequent cameo appearances by his hilarious real-life dad, "Papa Jumba") made him a wholesome heartthrob.

### HappySlip

**WHO:** Christine Gambito, joined August 31, 2006

**STYLE:** Character-based comedy

**BREAKOUT VIDEO:** "Mixed Nuts," 4.7 million views

**CURRENT SUBSCRIBERS:** 600,000

**SIGNATURE QUOTE:** "Put it in purse!"

**DESCRIPTION:** Gambito, who took the name HappySlip from her mother's pronunciation of "half a slip," was the Filipino family for us all, playing multiple members of her extended clan and sharing Filipino inside jokes with the world.

### NigaHiga

**WHO:** Ryan Higa, joined July 20, 2006

**STYLE:** Sketch comedy, stories, parodies, music videos

**BREAKOUT VIDEO:** "How to Be a Ninja," 55 million views

**CURRENT SUBSCRIBERS:** 21 million

**SIGNATURE QUOTE:** "TEE HEE!"

**DESCRIPTION:** Higa went from being an obscure high school student living in Hilo, Hawaii, to becoming YouTube's number-one most subscribed creator. As NigaHiga, his hilarious skits and rants became a standard for the platform's content creators. Higa was likely the most-beloved Asian American personality of a generation, and may still be.

### Communitychannel

**WHO:** Natalie Tran, joined September 12, 2006

**STYLE:** Character-based comedy, sometimes with stick-figure animation

**BREAKOUT VIDEO:** "ERROR," 1.8 million views

**CURRENT SUBSCRIBERS:** 1.8 million

**SIGNATURE QUOTE:** "It's porno music-slash-comment time!"

**DESCRIPTION:** Not all the Asian faces breaking barriers in the early days of YouTube were from the United States. Tran's offbeat (and profanity-laced) humor came to us from Sydney, Australia, and focused on situational humor and her own self-induced awkwardness.

**Timothy DeLaGhetto**

**WHO:** Timothy Chantarangsu, joined September 28, 2006

**STYLE:** Personal stories, sketches, rap (formerly as Traphik)

**BREAKOUT VIDEO:** "No Racial!," 3.1 million views

**CURRENT SUBSCRIBERS:** 4.8 million

**SIGNATURE QUOTE:** "Love, peace, skeet, cheese"

**DESCRIPTION:** A triple threat of acting, singing, and rapping, Tim had humor rooted in hip-hop, and his raunchy talent allowed him to cross over into TV shows like MTV's *Wild 'N Out*. His YouTube handle—which he no longer uses—was inspired by a fake name used by Will Smith in *Fresh Prince of Bel-Air*: "Rafael De La Ghetto."

---

**Just Kidding Films**

**WHO:** Joe "Jo" Jitsukawa and Bart Kwan, joined August 18, 2007

**STYLE:** Character-based comedy, music videos, talk

**BREAKOUT VIDEO:** "Korean History Channel," 1.5 million views

**CURRENT SUBSCRIBERS:** 1.6 million

**SIGNATURE QUOTE:** "Do da Unco Sam"

**DESCRIPTION:** The wild duo of Kwan and Jitsukawa became known for off-the-wall sketches and music videos based on a variety of caricatures. After adding Geo Antoinette (who later married Kwan) they transitioned into a talk and commentary format, Just Kidding News, with a full team of rotating panelists.

**Michelle Phan**

**WHO:** Michelle Phan, joined July 18, 2006

**STYLE:** Makeup demos and beauty advice

**BREAKOUT VIDEO:** "Lady Gaga makeup tutorials" (34 million to 54 million views)

**CURRENT SUBSCRIBERS:** 8.9 million

**SIGNATURE QUOTE:** "Have fun and good luck!"

**DESCRIPTION:** The queen of YouTube beauty. Makeup and beauty is a massive genre now, but it all started with Phan's tutorials, which shed a light on Asian beauty techniques and paved the way for all the beauty gurus who've come along since. Phan went on to partner with Lancôme, cofound Ipsy, and launch her own cosmetics line: EM Cosmetics.

---

**Blogilates**

**WHO:** Cassey Ho, California, joined June 13, 2009

**STYLE:** Health and fitness

**BREAKOUT VIDEO:** "Pop Pilates for beginners," 13 million views

**CURRENT SUBSCRIBERS:** 5.3 million

**SIGNATURE QUOTE:** "Omg I'm dying are you dying?"

**DESCRIPTION:** Ho changed the face of fitness. In an industry dominated by blonde, white women, Ho's optimistic vibe and energetic personality showed that Asian women could be strong and outspoken, while leading millions to change their bodies and lives with her unique upbeat brand of at-home exercise.

## THE MUSICIANS

# A YouTube Playlist

**BY PHILIP WANG**

YouTube allowed hundreds of Asian American talents to break through and be seen (and heard) on an infinite stage by singing their own cover versions of pop favorites—putting new spins (and new faces) to hit music. And once they had your attention, their own original singles solidified you as a fan.

**Display:**

## ▼ Related Videos

"That Girl," David Choi
(January 10, 2007, 9.7 million views)
The singer-songwriter-producer whose signature was never smiling. Choi's ability to write and produce his own songs allowed him to create acoustic ballads that became soundtracks in Korean dramas and first-dance songs at hundreds of weddings.

"When We Say," "We Could Happen," AJ Rafael
(July 28, 2009, 7.4 million views; September 15, 2010, 8.3 million views)
Rafael created the unofficial Filipino anthems with these songs. Gifted on both guitar and piano, he turned his talents along with his personality into a cornerstone of the YouTube music community. Along with Jeremy Passion, Gabe Bondoc, Jesse Barrera, and JR Aquino, Rafael made Filipino male vocalists a YouTube subgenre in itself.

"Valentine," "In Your Arms," Kina Grannis
(February 13, 2009, 23 million views; February 28, 2011, 14 million views)
Grannis's sweet songbird voice and memorable stop-motion music videos turned her into a worldwide sensation. After being featured on a Super Bowl ad, Grannis utilized YouTube to take control of her own career and she has flourished ever since—most notably being featured in the film *Crazy Rich Asians,* singing a cover of "Can't Help Falling in Love" for its famous wedding scene.

Jayesslee, Cathy Nguyen, Jason Chen, and Joseph Vincent
The boys- and girls-next-door of YouTube covers. Their amazing renditions of major songs made fans look for their versions over the originals. And yeah, we all had crushes on them, too.

# FOUNDING FATHERS AND MOTHERS

2000s

BY JEFF YANG, ILLUSTRATED BY SOJUNG KIM-McCARTHY

**BY THE 2000S,** Asian American leaders were on the front lines of the fight for equity and inclusion and rising into the mainstream of the political establishment. Here are some of the advocates and power brokers whose work shaped our communities in the 2000s.

**BRUCE YAMASHITA:** Yamashita enlisted in the Marines, only to be subjected to racial taunts and abuse throughout his boot camp experience. When he was disenrolled, allegedly due to "poor performance and leadership failure," he filed a civil rights suit against the service that ultimately led to the Marines issuing an apology to him and commissioning him as a captain.

**AI-JEN POO:** Poo is the executive director of the National Domestic Workers Alliance; codirector of Caring Across Generations, an advocacy coalition focused on improving long-term care for the elderly; and cofounder of Supermajority, which trains women to be leaders, organizers, and activists.

**GEORGE TAKEI:** Best known as *Star Trek*'s Sulu, Takei has been an impassioned advocate for inclusion and Asian American representation. In 2005, he came out as gay, and since then has been one of the most visible activists for LGBTQ rights, and played a key role in winning marriage equality.

**KAMALA HARRIS:** Harris served as San Francisco district attorney and California attorney general for decades, before successfully running for senator in 2017, and then being elected as the first woman, first African American, and first Asian American vice president of the United States in 2020's historic election.

**RINKU SEN:** Former executive director of the racial justice organization Race Forward, Sen is now executive director of the Narrative Initiative and a member of the board of directors of the Women's March.

**CHANNAPHA KHAMVONGSA:** Founder and former executive director of Legacies of War, a nonprofit dedicated to raising awareness of the history and residual impact of the Vietnam War–era bombings of Laos.

**DORIS MATSUI:** Founder and former executive director of Legacies of War, a nonprofit dedicated to raising awareness of the history and residual impact of the Vietnam War–era bombings of Laos.

**MIKE HONDA:** Honda served as U.S. representative from 2001 to 2017, and was a vice chair of the Democratic National Committee and the chair of the Congressional Asian Pacific American Caucus.

**ELAINE CHAO:** Chao was secretary of labor under President George W. Bush and secretary of transportation under President Donald Trump.

**GARY LOCKE:** The first Chinese American to serve as governor (for the state of Washington), Locke went on to serve as secretary of commerce in the Obama administration, and then to be the first Chinese American to serve as U.S. ambassador to China.

**STEPHEN CHU:** Chu is a Nobel Prize–winning physicist who served as secretary of energy under President Barack Obama. He has been an active advocate for aggressive response to the climate change crisis.

**BOBBY JINDAL:** Jindal was the first Indian American in history to be elected to Congress as a Republican, and the first to serve as governor (for the state of Louisiana).

**MEE MOUA:** The first Hmong American woman to be elected to a state legislature, Moua went on to become president and executive director of Asian Americans Advancing Justice.

**CHRISTINE CHEN:** Chen is the founder and executive director of the Asian American voting rights organization APIAVote and the former national executive director of the Organization of Chinese Americans.

1. Shoes outside of temple, people confused as to whose is whose

2. Priest leading prayers in Sanskrit, which no one understands

3. People with leg cramps and kids fidgeting while kneeling on the floor during prayers (no extended legs and you can't sit cross-legged either)

4. Kid feeling envious of the kids playing outside in the parking lot, because their parents didn't make them sit inside during service

5. Gifts for the temple, like fruits and flowers

6. People greeting the deities, starting with Ganesha, pressing hands together in namaskara and making offerings

7. Pujari delivering the puja, chanting in Sanskrit, and blessing sacred objects: rice, oil lights, incense, etc.

8. Worshippers prostrating themselves, men flat on the floor, arms outstretched, women kneeling and touching their heads to the floor, hands in front of head

9. Worshippers sitting in quiet meditation

10. Worshipper snoring in quiet meditation

11. Sacred lamp being passed from devotee to devotee—whoops, someone burned himself

12. Applying tilak

13. Group of children sitting in half-circle listening to Indian mythology stories and coloring pictures of gods

14. Adolescent boys reading Indian god comics

15. Gossiping aunties on food prep duty

16. Asian Scout troop meeting

17. Teens playing basketball, all of them wearing Jeremy Lin jerseys from different teams

18. Teens playing volleyball—maybe a bit too seriously, someone's gonna get hurt

19. Communal after-service potluck lunch for congregations:
    - big vat of brown liquid with chunks of meat in it
    - big vat of curry
    - dumplings
    - gigantic pot of rice
    - various other kinds of entrées, side dishes, and desserts
    - condescending person setting out elaborately made Asian dish
    - embarrassed person setting out Costco cheese plate
    - a Chinatown bakery cake (you know the kind) celebrating someone's 68th birthday
    - orangeade

20. Too-cool teens hanging out back sneaking a smoke

21. Tetris-like parking lot with at least six or seven pairs of cars that are absolutely identical (minivans, Honda Civics, Toyota Celicas), to cause confusion when people are looking for their cars after service

22. Shuttle vans, always white with the denomination logo painted on the side and name both in English and translated

# Finding Our Religion

BY JEFF YANG

**FOR MANY ASIAN AMERICANS**, the church, temple, or mosque isn't just a house of worship—it's a cultural hub and the regular gathering place of communities that may be distributed across hours of distance. Places of faith provide a space where traditions and language can be cultivated and passed on to the next generation (though the next generation doesn't always appreciate it), and where those youth can make friends, and maybe more, with people who share their heritage. One thing that most Asian places of faith have: in addition to feeding the soul, they usually also feed the body, with communal meals that offer a time for the dispersed members of a diaspora to feel like members of an extended family, if only for a few hours. Here's a tongue-in-cheek look at some of our houses of worship, as we and our friends remember them.

54

# The Do-Over
## Hollywood Remakes Asian Films
BY PHIL YU, ILLUSTRATED BY CHI-YUN LAU

**IT'S ONE THING** to be inspired by stories from another culture. Kurosawa was inspired by Shakespeare! George Lucas was inspired by Kurosawa! But it's another when you strip away all of the cultural specificity and nuance that made a story's original premise interesting down to the high-concept bone, then sprinkle on some Scarlett Johansson and call it a day. From the early 2000s on, that seemed to be Hollywood's recipe for the Asian Remake—Asian stories, hold the Asians—resulting in works with varying degrees of failure, fidelity, and Richard Gere. For Asian Americans, the process ended up choking off opportunity, because a.) Asian Americans weren't getting the shot to play the lead even in English-language versions of Asian stories and b.) the less-than-stellar results of many of these facelifts led studios to associate anything Asian with the smell of death . . . including Asian American stories. Here's a roundup of remakes—the Asian original, the Hollywood do-over, and what may have gotten lost in translation.

| THE JAPANESE ORIGINAL | THE HOLLYWOOD REMAKE |
| --- | --- |
| **ANTARCTICA (1983)** Based on the true story of an ill-fated 1958 Japanese expedition to the South Pole, this is a survival drama about a team of abandoned sled dogs who must survive on their own for months until rescue comes. | **EIGHT BELOW (2006)** The Disney remake of this story spun a decidedly sunnier version of the facts—and whitewashed the cast, including the poor dogs, transforming them from Japanese Karafuto-ken to standard huskies. |
| **HACHIKO MONOGATARI (1987)** A drama telling the true story of Hachiko, a loyal Akita who waited every day at the train station for his owner to return home from work, continuing to do so nine years after his master's death. | **HACHI: A DOG'S TALE (2009)** The tear-jerking remake moved the iconic train station to Rhode Island and starred Joan Allen and Jason Alexander, with Richard Gere as Hachi's beloved owner. |
| **EAT DRINK MAN WOMAN (1994)** Ang Lee's mouth-watering family dramedy, centering on a Taiwanese master chef and his three grown daughters, should not be viewed on an empty stomach. | **TORTILLA SOUP (2001)** Moving the family drama and food porn to Los Angeles, this remake serves up a fresh Mexican American take on the tale, while preserving much of the charm of the original. |
| **GHOST IN THE SHELL (1995)** Mamoru Oshii's anime cyberpunk thriller, following a cyborg security agent on the trail of a mysterious hacker, is widely considered a landmark achievement in animation. | **GHOST IN THE SHELL (2017)** Notoriously starring Scarlett Johansson as a Japanese woman in a white woman's body, this soulless endeavor feels like it was made by someone whose main takeaway from the source material was "Ooh, cool Asian shit." |

46. Men entering mosque separately, some dressed in Western garb and others in traditional kurta; some wear head coverings and some don't

47. Skateboarding girls and boys running, being scolded by aunties

48. Some Black Muslim neighbors visiting the congregation

49. Guy with impressive beard stroking his enviously as he looks at someone with an even more impressive beard

50. People seated listening to imam, some stretching out legs that have gone to sleep

51. People removing their shoes before entering temple

52. Shoes outside of temple, people confused as to whose is whose

53. Aunties wearing beautiful salwar kameez

54. Uncles in kurtas

55. Younger men wearing business casual outfits (jackets and open-necked shirts, khakis)

56. Younger women wearing outfits with long skirts

57. At least one younger woman getting disapproving stares for wearing an outfit with a not-long-enough skirt

58. Grandmas not-so-secretly trying to make matches for their grandkids

23. Pastor, senior and Asian "from the old country"

24. Translator, who's doubling the length of the sermon by repeating every line in English

25. Kid who's really inappropriately dressed in shorts and a T-shirt with a rude slogan on it

26. Kid making paper airplanes or origami out of the service program

27. People singing hymns in an Asian language and English at the same time, creating cacophony

28. Prim and proper auntie singing louder than everyone, in operatic voice that's a little off-key

29. Musicians who are wannabe rockers or classical prodigies or both

30. Thug uncle, actually very devout

31. Napping person leaning forward

32. Napping person leaning backward

33. Family who's a guest of a member, asked to stand up and introduce themselves and feeling really awkward

34. Young adults still wearing the same black club clothes they wore the night before because they came straight from having hangover soup after partying all night

35. That one girl everyone knows is going to Harvard

36. That one girl everyone knows is going to get pregnant

37. "Good boy" who's secretly a delinquent and only the kids know it

38. Someone brought a hamster

39. Youth service in English being delivered by earnest second-gen leader; one kid who looks angry because his question about whether God ever has to pee was ignored

40. Teenager group with leader who is suspiciously hot and is the crush of all the girl teens, to the annoyance of the boy teens

41. Baby room for loud toddlers, with one kid obviously too old to be there

42. Shoes outside of mosque, people confused as to whose is whose

43. In tower, muezzin leaning out of window and preparing to call the faithful to prayer

44. People washing their hands and faces, preparing to enter the mosque

45. Women with different kinds of head coverings or none—plus some younger women who don't wear head coverings (head covering is a choice, not a requirement; what's required is thoughtfulness and modesty) entering mosque

| THE JAPANESE ORIGINAL | THE HOLLYWOOD REMAKE |
|---|---|
| **SHALL WE DANCE? (1996)** <br> In Masayuki Suo's sweet comedy, a successful but unhappy salaryman finds the missing passion in his life when he secretly signs up for ballroom dance lessons. | **SHALL WE DANCE? (2004)** <br> The remake boasted some big talent—Jennifer Lopez and, yes, Richard Gere—but removed from the context of rigid Japanese society, it never quite lived up to the charm and nuance of the original. |
| **RINGU (1998)** <br> In Hideo Nakata's J-horror classic, a cursed videotape (VHS!) kills the viewer seven days after watching it. Nobody who saw *Ringu* ever looked at waist-length black hair the same way again. | **THE RING (2002)** <br> Heard the one about the cursed videotape? Hollywood did. By ringing up $250 million at the box office, *The Ring* broke open the dam for western remakes of Asian horror films starring scared white people. |
| **IL MARE (2000)** <br> In this Korean romantic fantasy, two occupants of the same seaside house begin a back-and-forth correspondence separated in time by two years, by way of a magical mailbox. | **THE LAKE HOUSE (2006)** <br> The Chicago-set re-do reunited *Speed* stars Keanu Reeves and Sandra Bullock—though they're rarely on screen together given the film's conceit—and the time travel shenanigans still made no sense. |
| **BANGKOK DANGEROUS (2000)** <br> Directed by twin brothers Danny and Oxide Pang, this stylish Thai shoot-'em-up follows a deaf-mute assassin for hire living and killing in the Bangkok underworld. | **BANGKOK DANGEROUS (2008)** <br> Same title. Same directors. Same setting. Same story. But this one had Nicolas Cage! |
| **KAIRO (2001)** <br> Kiyoshi Kurosawa's unnerving cult hit techno-horror thriller features two parallel stories about spirits trying to invade the world of the living via the Internet. | **PULSE (2006)** <br> This dull Hollywood remake traded the unique, creepy atmosphere of the original for juiced-up visual effects, reducing it to another boilerplate teen horror flick. |
| **MY SASSY GIRL (2001)** <br> This offbeat Korean romantic comedy, about an average joe whose life is turned upside down after he meets the titular sassy girl, was a massive blockbuster across Asia. | **MY SASSY GIRL (2008)** <br> This regrettable direct-to-DVD remake swapped It-girl Jeon Ji-hyun for Aught-girl Elisha Cuthbert and the simple, sad truth: it wasn't the original and never could be. |
| **INFERNAL AFFAIRS (2002)** <br> Tony Leung and Andy Lau lead a stacked cast in the acclaimed cat-and-mouse crime saga about undercover crooks and cops on opposite sides of the law. | **THE DEPARTED (2006)** <br> This was, arguably, the whitest remake on this list, in that it traded Hong Kong cool for aggro-Irish gruff. But maybe that's what it took to be The Movie That Finally Earned Martin Scorsese His Oscar. |
| **JU-ON: THE GRUDGE (2002)** <br> The crowning achievement of this J-horror mega-franchise, which spawned over a dozen movies, is that it cursed the world with the scary pale cat boy. | **THE GRUDGE (2004)** <br> Director Takashi Shimizu remade his own movie for Hollywood, keeping the story in Japan, with scary pale cat boy returning to terrorize attractive white Americans. |
| **A TALE OF TWO SISTERS (2003)** <br> In Kim Jee-woon's exquisite psychological horror drama, a former psychiatric patient returns home, only to clash with her stepmother and ghosts of their family's past. | **THE UNINVITED (2009)** <br> Let's be real: Asian ghosts are just scarier. But this creepy Maine-washed remake still wove a halfway decent horror yarn, all the way up to the movie's cunning reveal. |

# What's Funny? 2000s

**BY THE 2000S,** it was less of a rarity to see Asians on stage and on screen. As a result, while Asian American comedians still frequently explored issues of race and identity in their acts, there was more room for complexity and nuance in their jokes—which often played off of the expectations of non-Asians as much as the traits and foibles of Asians.

My people, what do we have going for us? Nail salons. Vietnamese nail salon owners are the best at sales. They'll compliment you and insult you at the same time. "Oh, your hair looks good, just not on you. Come inside, I'll fix it for you."
**—DAT PHAN**

You know how Asians communicate by talking about their kids. My uncle is like, "My Danny is discovering a cure for cancer!" So my dad responds, "Well, my daughter has a full scholarship at Duke!" "What about Kenny? What's Kenny doing?" Silence. "My daughter has a full scholarship at Duke!"
**—KEN JEONG**

Buddhism's cool; it's a very laid-back religion. It's the only religion I know where the god you prayed to is more out of shape than you. That rocks.
**—KEVIN KATAOKA**

I'm actually adopted by white people. You know, the devils. I don't say this because they didn't love me, I say this because they raised me in Bethlehem, Pennsylvania, where there isn't a lot of me. I don't expect the kids in my elementary school to know the difference between Korean, Chinese, or Japanese, but one time, a little girl came up to me and called me a freaking *Eskimo*.
**—KEVIN SHEA**

I grew up in a small town. But somehow I never understood racism. One day I walked home from school, and this kid yelled at me, "Why don't you go home and eat your rice?" And I was like, "Yep, that's what I'm about to do, how'd you know I was hungry?" And then he shouted, "I bet you have a small penis!" I said, "You got me there!" I'm thinking to myself, "Well, what do you expect? I'm seven years old."
**—KEVIN CAMIA**

# The Wonderful World of White Saviors

BY PHIL YU, ILLUSTRATED BY JEF CASTRO

**HOLLYWOOD RULE #44:** You can set a movie anywhere in the world, in any era of history, and still somehow find a way to put a white hero smack-dab in the center. Meet the tried-and-true trope commonly referred to as the White Savior. Whether it's war-torn China or modern gangland Japan, white dudes somehow manage to creep into settings and narratives where they can demonstrate that they're more skilled at being "Asian" (e.g., doing martial arts, samurai stuff, or some kind of mystical shit) than actual Asians, putting them in prime position to romance the local ladies, and of course, Save the Asians. The bleak truth? White Saviors are primarily there to save the box office, because it's quite likely that none of these films or TV series would have gotten produced without their respective white star front and center on the poster. Here are our picks for the top 10 whitest White Savior movies, from the Nineties to now.

### Come See the Paradise (1990)
**WHITE SAVIOR:** Dennis Quaid
**WHO GETS SAVED:** Japanese Americans in Manzanar, California
What's Dennis Quaid doing at the center of this romantic drama, one of the few mainstream feature films to depict the incarceration of Japanese Americans during World War II? Falling in love with the boss's daughter, Tamlyn Tomita, of course.

### Snow Falling on Cedars (1999)
**WHITE SAVIOR:** Ethan Hawke
**WHO GETS SAVED:** Japanese Americans on San Piedro Island, Washington
In this legal drama, based on the bestselling novel, Hawke's postwar small-town newspaper editor investigates a murder case against a Japanese American man (Rick Yune) . . . who happens to be married to the Nisei gal who broke his heart (Yuki Kudoh). Awkward.

### The Last Samurai (2003)
**WHITE SAVIOR:** Tom Cruise
**WHO GETS SAVED:** The Way of the Samurai in Japan, 1870s
Tom Cruise goes to Japan. Tom Cruise gets captured by rebel samurai. Tom Cruise learns about honor and stuff. Tom Cruise learns Japanese. Tom Cruise learns samurai swords. Tom Cruise falls in love with the widow (Koyuki Kato) of a Japanese guy he killed. Tom Cruise. Is. The. Last. Samurai.

### The Forbidden Kingdom (2008)
**WHITE SAVIOR:** Michael Angarano
**WHO GETS SAVED:** China, unspecified ancient times
We were promised something epic: action legends Jackie Chan and Jet Li on screen together for the

first time, costarring in a wuxia tale based on the classic novel *Journey to the West*. What we got: a not-so-epic story centering on a white kid (Angarano) magically transported to ancient China, to save it.

## Gran Torino (2008)

**WHITE SAVIOR:** Clint Eastwood

**WHO GETS SAVED:** Hmong Americans in Detroit, Michigan, the present

A disgruntled, get-off-my-lawn Korean War veteran overcomes his own racism, befriends a Hmong American teen (Bee Vang) and his family (e.g., the Good Asians), and—spoiler alert—literally dies, Jesus-style, to save them from the neighborhood gang (e.g., the Bad Asians).

## The Flowers of War (2012)

**WHITE SAVIOR:** Christian Bale

**WHO GETS SAVED:** Virginal Chinese schoolgirls in Nanking, China, 1937

This historical drama is technically a Chinese film, directed by iconic Chinese filmmaker Zhang Yimou, no less. But somehow, the story of the 1937 Nanking Massacre still ends up getting told through the eyes of—who else?—a white American (Bale) who learns the meaning of sacrifice and honor amidst the atrocities of war.

## No Escape (2015)

**WHITE SAVIOR:** Owen Wilson

**WHO GETS SAVED:** Owen Wilson's family in an Extremely Dangerous Asian Country

A white American family moves overseas to an unnamed Southeast Asian country, only to find themselves running for their lives from lots of scary armed Asians when they find themselves in the middle of a violent uprising. Technically, the White Saviors here just save themselves, but we'll count it.

## The Great Wall (2016)

**WHITE SAVIOR:** Matt Damon

**WHO GETS SAVED:** China, unspecified ancient times

The real "ancient Chinese secret" is that the Great Wall of China was actually erected to defend against a deadly horde of marauding monsters. So it's a good thing Matt Damon and his ponytail were there, to shoot them with arrows and save China.

## Iron Fist (2017)

**WHITE SAVIOR:** Finn Jones

**WHO GETS SAVED:** All of us, when Netflix killed this joke

Raised by monks, Danny Rand is the Living Weapon—a master martial artist who wields the mystical force known as the "Iron Fist" to protect the secret land of K'un L'un. Rand also quotes Buddhist texts, meditates, and is an expert in using chopsticks. Sadly, no amount of movie magic could convince viewers that Finn Jones is even the tiniest bit proficient in martial arts. (Typical fight cinematography: Rand grimaces, says something about K'un L'un, ducks into the shadows to throw a punch.)

## The Outsider (2018)

**WHITE SAVIOR:** Jared Leto

**WHO GETS SAVED:** The Shiromatsu clan

In postwar Japan, a former American serviceman (Leto) ascends the ranks of the Japanese underground, eventually working his way up to becoming the head of his yakuza clan. Along the way, he gets a tattoo, falls in love with his sworn brother's sister (Shiori Katsuna), and kills a lot of Japanese dudes. Okay, *gaijin*.

# YELLOWFACE IN THE 2000S

BY NANCY WANG YUEN

**BY THE 2000S,** Hollywood was beginning to see that yellowface was an abhorrent practice—but not well enough to understand that the frequent alternative, simply casting white actors in Asian roles, should also be seen as abhorrent. Hollywood's whitewashing era began in earnest this decade. Meanwhile, when yellowface portrayals did occur, it was always with the excuse of satire, as if playing a character for laughs was enough to excuse the way the practice invariably leaned into racist caricature and ugly xenophobic tropes.

### "Asian minister," *I Now Pronounce You Chuck and Larry* (2007), Rob Schneider

Yes, Schneider is a quarter Filipino. But as he proved here, it's quite possible to have ancestry and still offer up a deeply offensive yellowface performance. Schneider's unnamed "Asian minister" was as cringeworthy as Mickey Rooney's in *Breakfast at Tiffany's,* with taped-back eyes, a bad bowl-cut wig, buck teeth, and a stereotypical nonsense accent. **CONVINCING OR NOT? NOT CONVINCING.** But it convinced many Asians to vote Schneider off of Team Asian.

### "Feng," *Balls of Fury* (2007), Christopher Walken

Walken gives a typically weirdo performance here as a criminal mastermind who looks like a cross between Fu Manchu and Dracula, wearing long robes and a puffy black wig with a thick braid. Though he speaks more like Christopher Walken (or someone pretending to be Christopher Walken) than an Asian caricature, the inexplicably orientalist look pushes the role into yellowface cosplay—accentuated by the design of the set from which he delivered most of his lines, a Chinese chaise elevated on a platform with an Asian paper screen in the background. **CONVINCING OR NOT? NOT CONVINCING.** No one would think this look was anyone other than Christopher Walken cosplaying as Faux Manchu.

### "Mr. Wong" in *Norbit* (2007), Eddie Murphy

Mr. Wong is one of the most elaborate transformations ever undergone by Murphy, who prides himself on his ability to create and embody characters of many different races and backgrounds in his movies. But the outcome was an all-too-typical yellowface performance, featuring a stereotypical accent (e.g., pronouncing "L"s as "R"s) and copious amounts of racially loaded humor ("Norbit, when he was just little boy, had a pee-pee the size of an egg roll").

**CONVINCING OR NOT? NOT CONVINCING.** Mr. Wong does not look particularly Asian—he's simply coded as Asian by his jaundiced skin, ching-chong accent, and random Chinese food jokes.

### "Fu Manchu" in *Grindhouse* (2007), Nicolas Cage

This is a bit of a special case, in that Cage's performance as old-school villain Fu Manchu in a faux parody trailer that appears between the movie's "double feature" installments is intended to be a fully aware depiction of a white man in yellowface; his catfish mustache, gold finger claws, elaborate velvet Orientalist robe, and maniacal laughter are intended to reproduce the traditional yellowface Fu Manchu performances of yore. But by engaging in this resurrection, director Rob Zombie is essentially celebrating one of the most grotesque legacies of pulp cinema as something worthy of nostalgia.

**CONVINCING OR NOT? CONVINCING—**in the sense that Cage looks like the yellowface villain he's mimicking. There's no question what we see on screen. But while the trailer is meant to invoke absurdist kitsch, the very brief scene reads more like dated racism.

### "Guru Pitka," in *The Love Guru* (2008), Mike Myers

Even though Mike Myers isn't *technically* playing an Indian person (he's a white orphan adopted by "Guru Tugginmypudha," who's played by . . . Ben Kingsley!), his performance still embraces the central elements of brownface caricature:

- Fake Indian accent (check)
- Fake Indian name (check)
- Tunic, flower garland, bead necklaces, and exaggerated beard (check)
- Fake sitar-playing (check)
- Caricature spirituality, including putting hands in namaste pose as a greeting (check)
- Elephant ride (check)
- Bad Bollywood dance scenes (check)

**CONVINCING OR NOT? NOT CONVINCING— OR FUNNY.** Myers threw every Indian cultural and religious stereotype he could find into this film, which is widely seen as having permanently tarnished Myers's stardom. Louder for white actors in the back: doing raceface can kill careers!

### "Ben Campbell" and "Jimmy Fisher" in *21* (2008), Jim Sturgess and Jacob Pitts

The film *21* was adapted from Ben Mezrich's bestselling book *Bringing Down the House,* which told the true story of the MIT blackjack team—most of whom were Asian American in real life. The movie version chose to whitewash the team's Asian American mainstays, Jeff Ma and Mike Aponte, by renaming them and recasting them with white actors. (Even the team's elder statesman, "Mickey Rosa," played by Kevin Spacey, was based partly on Asian American professor John Chang.) In response to the whitewashing critique, producer Dana Brunetti admitted he simply didn't believe people wanted to watch Asians on screen: "Believe me, I would have loved to cast Asians in the lead roles, but the truth is, we didn't have access to any bankable Asian American actors that we wanted."

**CONVINCING OR NOT? NOT REMOTELY CONVINCING.** As Mezrich makes clear in his book, the Asian faces of the MIT team were actually a critical facet of their success: Casino operators have long gotten used to seeing young Asian men bet large amounts of cash and were thus less suspicious of the team members' high-stakes play. If they'd been mostly white, it would've put casino observers on alert much earlier.

### "Speed Racer" in *Speed Racer* (2008), Emile Hirsch

The Wachowski siblings whitewashed the entire cast of *Speed Racer,* based on the 1967 anime series of the same name, though to be fair, they followed the cue of its U.S. translators—who took a show titled *Mach GoGoGo,* following the high-test adventures of Go Mifune, his girlfriend Michi Shimura, and the rest of the Mifune clan, and reframed everyone as Caucasian. Still, they couldn't fully disguise the series' Japanese cultural cues; not so with the live-action remake, which fully removed all traces of Asianness from the Racer family, making them white, Midwestern, and frankly boring.

**CONVINCING OR NOT? EH, SURE, CONVINCING**—if your goal was to drain all remaining flavor from a set of already bleached characters. The filmmakers tried to make up for it by casting K-pop idol Rain in a minor, semi-villainous side role.

### "Goku" in *Dragonball Evolution* (2009), Justin Chatwin

This terrible live-action adaptation of one of the most popular Japanese anime franchises of all time decided to cast Chatwin (everyone

In response to the whitewashing critique, producer Dana Brunetti admitted he simply didn't believe people wanted to watch Asians on screen.

reading this: *Who???*) as Goku, the legendary Saiyan warrior. Except that *Dragonball Evolution* dispensed with Saiyans and most of the rest of Akira Toriyama's lore and story, in favor of simply making "Son Goku" an ordinary martial artist who gets special training from Master Roshi (Chow Yun-Fat). One could argue that Goku in the original source is an alien, and thus not "Asian" per se, but then again, the character of Son Goku is actually an interpretation of Sun Wukong, the Monkey King of Chinese legend.

**CONVINCING OR NOT? NOT REMOTELY CONVINCING.** The film ended up getting trashed by fans, critics, creator Toriyama, and even, ultimately, the movie's screenwriter, Ben Ramsey, who publicly apologized for "dropping the dragon ball."

## POSTCARD FROM ASIAN AMERICA

BY JEN WANA

Dear RISE,

Growing up in the suburbs of Chicago, my Thai immigrant parents tried their best to fit in. They spoke to us only in English, enrolled me in gymnastics and Girl Scouts, and—even though we were Buddhist—my mom placed a Christmas tree by our front window with empty gift-wrapped boxes underneath it every December.

High school was the first time I was ever around other Asians, and we found confidence in numbers. The rest of our school was consumed with football and Guns N' Roses; my friends and I went to Depeche Mode concerts and wore tapered Z. Cavaricci pants. When ballots were handed out for homecoming queen, a tradition that had never involved minorities at our school, I gathered votes for one of our Asian friends, who surprisingly went on to win. Some kids booed her as she went up to receive her crown, but she held her head high. It gave me a sense of pride to see her defiance. I realized then that it only takes a simple action to make an impact.

Still, as a Thai American, I always felt like a minority even among other minorities. I ingratiated myself to the chic Filipino girls in high school. In college, I joined the Chinese students club because I didn't have another option. But by junior year, I'd founded a new group at my school—the Asian Student Union, all ethnicities welcome.

We all deserve spaces where we can come together as a community, and still be our whole selves. Only then can you truly feel like you belong.

Your friend,
Jen

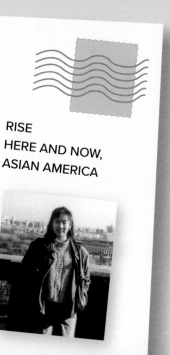

RISE
HERE AND NOW,
ASIAN AMERICA

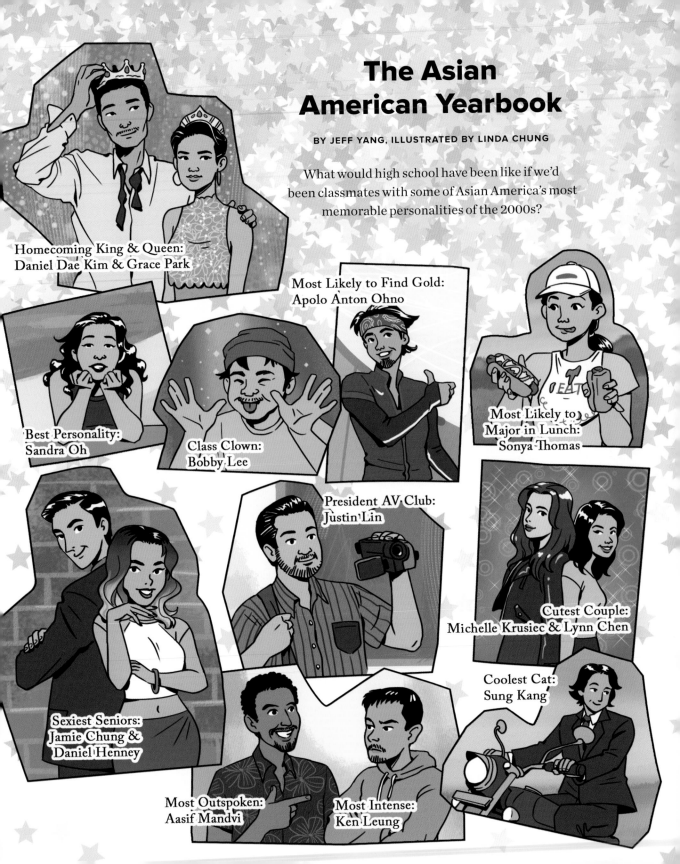

# The Asian American Yearbook

BY JEFF YANG, ILLUSTRATED BY LINDA CHUNG

What would high school have been like if we'd been classmates with some of Asian America's most memorable personalities of the 2000s?

Homecoming King & Queen:
Daniel Dae Kim & Grace Park

Most Likely to Find Gold:
Apolo Anton Ohno

Best Personality:
Sandra Oh

Class Clown:
Bobby Lee

Most Likely to
Major in Lunch:
Sonya Thomas

President AV Club:
Justin Lin

Cutest Couple:
Michelle Krusiec & Lynn Chen

Sexiest Seniors:
Jamie Chung &
Daniel Henney

Coolest Cat:
Sung Kang

Most Outspoken:
Aasif Mandvi

Most Intense:
Ken Leung

# THE 2000s

Most Likely to Take Over the World: Kelly Hu

Choir Queen: Vanessa Hudgens

Best Bromance: John Cho & Kal Penn

Superhero in Training: Masi Oka

Lady Boss: Mindy Kaling

Shop Class Heroes: Vern Yip & Grant Imahara

Best Person to be Stranded with on a Desert Island: Yul Kwon

Debate Club VIP: Lisa Ling

Most Likely to Become a Doctor: Sanjay Gupta

Biggest Badass: Cung Le

Most Likely to Be a Disney Princess: Brenda Song

Most Likely to Become a Former Doctor: Ken Jeong

# DISGRASIAN™ 2000s

**WE'RE BACK WITH JEN WANG** and **DIANA NGUYEN**, the blogatrices of Disgrasian, as they give their takes on the Disgrasian All-Stars of 2000s, an era that you could call "peak Disgrasian."

**DIANA:** Wasssuuuuuuuuup??

**JEN:** WASSSUUUUPPP?? Oh man, I hated the "wasssuuuup" thing.

**DIANA:** Me too. Add it to the infinite list of things I loved to hate in the Aughts. So much material that we had to start a blog!

**JEN:** It seemed like the 2000s saw a sudden jump in our visibility. The Internet became an opportunity to represent yourself without having to go through these traditional gatekeepers. It felt like Asians had "arrived," and we needed to talk about that.

**DIANA:** And by talk about that, we mean "talk shit about that." Shitty representation offenses seemed criminal back then. It was like, y'all, we're finally getting airtime and you're making it smell like fart.

**JEN:** It was the stuff that brought up the scars of the '80s and '90s, that sense of shame— if it was highly visible but stereotypical, nerdy, or one-dimensional, it was probably DISGRASIAN.

**DIANA:** While new media was exploding with a whole spectrum of Asian American portrayals, old media was still holding on to this tiny bucket of hackneyed ideas: buck teeth, ching-chong accents, Coke bottle glasses, small dicks, bad driving.

JEN WANG    DIANA NGUYEN

I mean, being a nerd is obviously really dope if it's your jam! But it's a different story if it's just this one caricature you're confined to, and the portrayal isn't your choice. That lack of agency, that powerlessness, it's a trigger. It makes us all feel at risk.

**JEN:** Because being Asian in America had finally started to feel cool. There was this sense that we were beginning to transcend that specter of embarrassment and foreignness and otherness, that perceived inability to ever really be American.

We were starting to see Asian faces all over fashion. Behind the scenes and on the runway. In the '90s, there was only Jenny Shimizu. She was my inspo for shaving my head in college. I got mistaken for a boy all the time!

**DIANA:** You were definitely as hot as Jenny, just without the Calvin Klein contract.

**JEN:** Too bad, since achieving her "just emerged from the hood of a muscle car" mechanic look cost a lot of Calvins! We also had the rebirth of Margaret Cho. She did her one-woman show *I'm the One That I Want* in '99, and the film came out in 2000. I was so scarred from *All-*

*American Girl* that I didn't even want to watch it at first. I think I was resigned to the idea that audiences didn't want authentic Asian voices; they just wanted our voices shoved through a white mainstream meat grinder. I assumed that even her own stand-up would get turned into processed meat, a cringe bologna, if you will. But when I finally forced myself to watch, I was blown away. She didn't need anyone's permission to speak anymore, and she damn sure didn't need anyone's approval. Fuck network TV! Fuck the Nielsens! No more gatekeepers for this bitch! Remember how when we started the blog, we considered Margaret Cho our patron saint?

**DIANA:** Mutha Margaret. Don't forget we also started the blog to Free the Harajuku Girls. Our first foray into social justice.

**JEN:** I will never forgive or forget Gwen Stefani for that.

**DIANA:** Hashtag never forget. What about Lucy Liu? Arguably the biggest Asian American star of the Aughts. I was still in high school and at the height of my teen awkweirdness when *Ally McBeal* became a TV juggernaut. I wasn't into the show, but I was very into her Ling Woo character. She was powerful, gainfully employed, went toe-to-toe with the dudes, *and* super sexy. I was a too-nice virgin with forehead acne and those qualities were all things I wanted, so I saw it as aspirational rather than problematic. Then she was in *Charlie's Angels* alongside Cameron Diaz and freakin' Drew Barrymore. They were hay-haired Hollywood It girls, and she was giving them a run for their money. Like, One of Us is an Angel!!!

**JEN:** Speaking of Hollywood, do you remember Rachel Lee, leader of the "Bling Ring," who went around with all of her friends stealing shit from celebrity homes? Sofia Coppola made a whitewashed version of her story.

**DIANA:** Sofia Coppola makes a whitewashed version of *every* story. A movie set in Japan without any meaningful Japanese characters, a movie set during the Civil War without any meaningful African American characters . . .

**JEN:** I guess we should be grateful she actually hired an Asian actor to play Rachel? LOL. People always assumed Rachel Lee was DISGRASIAN, but I thought she was fucking amazing. She stole diamonds and Dior from celebs too dumb to lock their doors. She used a beta version of Google Maps to find Paris Hilton's house! Hats off to you, Rachel!

**DIANA:** I think she's a good example of someone who gave the appropriate number of fucks for her situation, which is to say zero, which is cool even though technically she is a legit criminal. Maybe her parents are mad at her, but we ain't.

**JEN:** Yeah, not DISGRASIAN.

**DIANA:** You know who is, was, and perhaps may always be the essence of DISGRASIAN? Tila Tequila. I'd like to thank her for being an incipient member of our hit list. She may have actually been the very first person that I wrote about.

**JEN:** It brought you extra shame that she was also a Nguyen.

**DIANA:** [bows head in shame]

**JEN:** Tila was a walking disaster. She called herself a singer, but her songs were garbage. She got to star in her own reality show, and it was boring and fake AF. The only thing she really excelled at was MySpace. When MySpace died it seemed like the beginning of her career, but you could argue it was actually the beginning of the end.

There's something heartbreaking about an Asian person who's busted for being an imposter. People of color in general have Imposter Syndrome. And the particular strain of Imposter Syndrome that Asians suffer from is not feeling like we belong here. We're constantly interrogated about where we're *really* from or told to go back to where we're *really* from. But we're never supposed to be HERE.

**DIANA:** She was an object in her own story, not the subject. It was as if she was impersonating a no-fux person, but she actually gave all the fucks. Any person who's an "influencer" of any generation gives all the fucks. She was always trying too hard. And didn't she also do a lap as an alt-right Nazi?

**JEN:** Yup, before converting to being an alt-Christ religious zealot. I will say that she shot her shot, though. Godspeed, girl. Make every career opportunity you can out of your talents, even if you don't got any.

**DIANA:** DISGRASIAN Hall-of-Famer for sure. At least that's something!

**JEN:** We talked a lot about Bai Ling then, too, and kind of put her and Tila in the same bucket. She was always doing crazy stuff, like showing up naked at the grocery store, *Chinglish* spilling out of her mouth. "Oop, my tit fall out again! Ruh-roh!"

**DIANA:** Time has softened my heart for Bai Ling. In retrospect, she was fairly harmless.

**JEN:** Exactly. I wouldn't lump her together with Tila at all now. Bai Ling had a lane, she stayed in that lane, and that lane was white-hot-mess entertainment. I'm sure she speaks

English a lot better than she let on and she's not drunk all the time. It seems a lot like performance art, looking back on it.

**DIANA:** Good for Bai Ling! I love a good redemption narrative. You know who still sucks, though? John Yoo.

**JEN:** 100 percent DISGRASIAN. He's this great, brilliant legal mind, teaches at Berkeley law school, and then he goes to work for George W. Bush and uses that talent to twist legal language to accommodate torture. You don't have any fucking moral compass at that point.

When you're in that position, you have so much power. Your job is about life and death. Do better.

**DIANA:** Is that so much to ask? And speaking of irredeemable trash bags, there's also Michelle Malkin.

**JEN:** We made Michelle Malkin "DISGRASIAN OF THE WEAK" once and then she wrote a one-word post on us: "Disgrasian" and linked it to our piece. Immediately, a tsunami of hate mail from her crazy-ass fans. That was fun, actually. So much bad spelling.

**DIANA:** We were asked to rape and kill ourselves many, many times, but they did not succeed in convincing us. Take that, bitches!

**JEN:** "We hope you get swine flu and die!" Guess what, asswipes? We didn't.

**DIANA:** She was a real treat. I think what makes Michelle Malkin super DISGRASIAN is—to roll with this highway theme—that she totally had a lane and just fucking off-roaded it. She went the "racist sellout" path and she didn't even do it well. Nobody even cares who Michelle Malkin is now.

**JEN:** She wanted to be Ann Coulter or Laura Ingraham and she fucking failed. I mean, sell your soul and it gets you nowhere? That must suck.

I didn't even want to bring Malkin up and memorialize her mediocrity because she's so irrelevant—but she recently went to a banquet with Kyle Rittenhouse's mother and those two were just cheesing at the camera like it was prom, after sonny boy Kyle had murdered two unarmed people in the street during a protest for Black lives. That's when I knew we had to memorialize her as the POS she really is.

**DIANA:** Yeah. Fuck you and your shitty shooty-play for relevance.

**JEN:** Do you remember Azia Kim?

**DIANA:** That girl who pretended to be a Stanford student because she couldn't tell her parents she didn't get in, right? I have so much empathy for my fellow Asian American under-achievers.

**JEN:** And I clearly have a soft spot for Asian female "victimless crime" perps. It seems really hard to impersonate a Stanford student. There are key cards! Meal plan cards! Your fake ID card for your fake identity! So many cards. This is elaborate and exhausting to me. As some-body who can't lie, I appreciate when people do it well.

**DIANA:** As someone who would rather com-mit 100 crimes than disappoint my parents, I really appreciate people who can figure out a high-level workaround.

**JEN:** She wasn't hurting anybody. She wanted to be a Stanford student like millions of other Asians and went for it in the way that she knew how. I'm not mad about that. There's some-thing heartbreaking, too, about an Asian per-son who's busted for being an imposter. People of color in general have Imposter Syndrome more than white people. And the particular strain of Imposter Syndrome that Asians suf-fer from is not feeling like we belong here. Like here, in this country. We're constantly interro-gated about where we're *really* from or told to go back to where we're *really* from. But we're never supposed to be HERE. This has been going on for generations.

**DIANA:** I feel for Azia Kim too. Being so bro-ken by your family and fearful of bringing them shame that you would pull a con this big, that isn't even really on you. This girl isn't DISGRASIAN, she's someone I want to offer a hug.

**JEN:** On that note, let's hug it out for the 2000s. It was a golden age for DISGRASIAN. We spent, like, 90 percent of our time drunk on scotch while writing about people's boobs falling out of their dresses. There was a lot of fun and froth. Things got a lot darker as we entered the second decade of the millennium, which we'll get to in our next and last chapter.

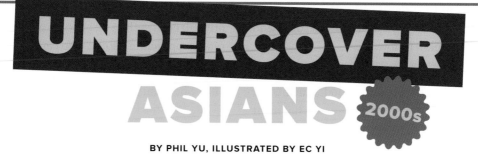

# UNDERCOVER ASIANS 2000s

BY PHIL YU, ILLUSTRATED BY EC YI

**FELLOW ASIANSPOTTERS,** in the new millennium our search for representation leads us to a former *Saturday Night Live* cast member, multiple Grammy-winning artists, a Super Bowl MVP, and more secretly Asian discoveries. Here are some noteworthy personalities of the 2000s who you might be surprised to learn are multiracial members of Team Asian America.

### 1. NORAH JONES
Born Geethali Norah Jones Shankar, the multi-Grammy-winning singer-songwriter is the daughter of legendary Indian sitar virtuoso Ravi Shankar.

### 2. KELIS
R&B artist Kelis Rogers, whose milkshake brings all the boys to the yard (damn right, it's better than yours), is Chinese Puerto Rican on her mother's side.

### 3. VANESSA HUDGENS
Actress and singer Hudgens, who rose to fame starring in the *High School Musical* film series, is the daughter of an Irish French Native American father and Filipino mother.

### 4. TYGA
Controversial rapper Tyga, born Michael Ray Nguyen-Stevenson to a Black and Vietnamese American mother, apparently got his nickname because of his childhood resemblance to golfer Tiger Woods.

### 5. MICHELLE BRANCH
Double platinum-selling singer Branch is of Dutch Indonesian ancestry on her maternal grandmother's side.

### 6. AMERIE
The singer behind "1 Thing" and other bangers, Amerie Mi Marie Rogers—or simply Amerie, as she is known—is the daughter of an African American father and Korean mother.

### 7. FRED ARMISEN
For much of his life, *Saturday Night Live* and *Portlandia* star Armisen believed his paternal grandfather was Japanese, only to learn in 2017 that he was actually Korean.

### 8. NICOLE SCHERZINGER
Pussycat Dolls frontwoman, *Dancing with the Stars* winner, and TV talent judge Scherzinger was born Nicole Prescovia Elikolani Valiente to a Filipino American father and Native Hawaiian Russian mother.

### 9. KAREN O
The badass vocalist for Yeah Yeah Yeahs was born Karen Lee Orzolek in Busan, South Korea, the daughter of a Korean mother and Polish father.

### 10. HINES WARD
Born in Seoul to an African American father and Korean mother, former Pittsburgh Steelers wide receiver Ward is now an advocate for social acceptance of mixed-race youth in South Korea.

**2010S**

# The 2010s

BY PHILIP WANG

**THREE MONTHS BEFORE** the 2010s officially began, I already knew there was going to be something really special about the decade to come. It was September 6, 2009, and I was standing at the side of the stage at the San Gabriel Mission Playhouse, watching David Choi perform his debut single "I Won't Even Start" to an audience of about 1,500 young Asian American fans. It was his final song of the night at the International Secret Agents Concert, ISA for short—a grassroots event that Wong Fu Productions organized in partnership with our friends, the band Far East Movement, and it was the first to bring together rising Asian American YouTube artists for live shows.

Now, I'd been to many Asian American concerts prior to this particular night, and I'd seen many Asian American singers before this particular performance. But what made this one different—what made this moment stand out—was when David *stopped* singing.

Because that's when all 1,500 people continued to sing the song, reciting his lyrics by heart. Typically, I'm not the type to recognize defining moments while they're happening, but as I stood there in the dark, listening to the auditorium fill with the collective voice of fans who knew every word of a song that had never been on the radio, by an Asian American artist who'd never been promoted by a mainstream label, I knew we were seeing something remarkable. It was something that couldn't have happened before. And to me, it was an indication that we were embarking on a new chapter of Asian American culture.

Before this, there had been moments that galvanized Asians and brought us together. The 2000s saw us utilizing the maturing Internet and still-primitive social media to begin to organize music concerts like the Asian Hip Hop Summit, annual talent shows like Kollaboration, and Asian American film festivals in cities around the country. All of these were crucial for creating places for our aspiring artists to be seen—to be given a stage, a screen, a space to perform where once there'd been nowhere else to go. We used online forums and email listservs to get the word out, and although some artists had fanbases, most events were more like showcases, presenting the Asian American offerings that mainstream film and radio weren't giving us, and we attended them with almost a sense of responsibility. That's how I felt in 2005 when I attended my first Asian film fest, the San Diego Asian Film Festival. I had no idea what I was going to watch, and chose to see *The Motel* solely because I'd heard one of the guys from *Better Luck Tomorrow*, Sung Kang, was in it and I wanted to back him up. I'd gone

---

## 2010

♪ Far East Movement hits #1 with "Like a G6," becoming the first Asian American music group to hit the top of the *Billboard* charts. (The artist they knocked down to number 2? Honolulu-born and half-Filipino Bruno Mars—an FM friend and collaborator.)

🔆 Adopting a graphical language created in Japan, Unicode introduces the modern emoji set; the iconic set of icons transforms digital communications

🎬 Ryan "Nigahiga" Higa becomes the first Asian American to have the #1 most subscribed channel on YouTube

🎬 *Outsourced* airs on NBC as the first network TV series with a nearly all-Indian cast

to my first Kollaboration, a reality-style competition that brought together Asian American artists from regional contests all across the country, for a similar reason: to show my support for the idea that Asian Americans had talent that deserved an audience.

But this moment with David Choi was different. Despite the fact that I'd already been in the YouTube world for three years by then, this was the first time I had a real feeling that a big change was about to come. Because here we were, at this massive concert organized by indie artists, with a lineup of performers who all had followings that they'd created and nurtured on their own via YouTube, outside of any mainstream system. Here was a concert hall filled with fans who didn't have to be *convinced* to be there, but actually lined up in droves to buy tickets to see these artists, whom they viewed the same as anyone on the radio. It was an underground scene, but the most wholesome one you could imagine, fueled by young Asian Americans who were taking representation into their own hands as both creators and as consumers. For the first time, it felt like Asian America was ready to emerge from local community center events to step onto the main stage, not as a backup singer, not as a supporting character, but front and center, with thousands of people singing with them and cheering them along.

---
*  See page 100, "How to 'AZN'"

To be honest, I'd never expected us to get here—hell, I never expected to even be part of the movement myself. But because of Wong Fu Productions, I got a front-row seat to all the major shifts that would happen in the 2010s, not just in media, but in our collective culture and identity.

## Growing Up AZN

I grew up in the Nineties, the product of immigrant parents in the East Bay of the San Francisco Bay Area. While the town I grew up in was predominantly white, I feel lucky that my parents always kept Asian families, kids, and culture around me. As a result, there was never a time when I tried to push away my Asian identity—and I definitely never wished I was white. (Maybe the only thing I envied were the "American snacks" the other kids had at lunchtime, but that was it.) I had no "lunchbox moment," I had no demeaning memory of a non-Asian girl rejecting me. If the other kids didn't like me, I figured it was because of *me*, not because of my race. Frankly, I'm not sure which is worse on a kid's self-esteem—but either way, when the late '90s came along, I was in eighth grade and searching for any way to be accepted and cool.

And that's when I very naturally fell into AZN PrYdE.

"AP," as "AZN Pryde"* was sometimes fur-

2010

🎬 *The Walking Dead* premieres with Steven Yeun as Glenn Rhee; Yeun becomes a fan favorite and a firestorm is unleashed when his character is killed off

🏛 Jean Quan elected mayor of Oakland, becoming the first Asian American woman mayor of a major U.S. city

2011

💡 Canadian Godfrey Gao becomes the first Asian male model for Louis Vuitton; he would sadly pass away of cardiac arrest in 2019, at just 35

🎬 Indonesian American Raja wins Season 3 of *RuPaul's Drag Race*, becoming the first Asian queen to win

ther abbreviated for extra coolness, looked different to different people. Some embraced AP as part of the gang scene. Others just saw it as an opportunity to change our image, to bring Asian influence to the Y2K. Leaning into my AZN Pryde was intentional and aspirational, because I associated the image and lifestyle with being cool and confident in being uniquely Asian. But another reason was natural selection, essentially: all through middle school I'd had friends from a wide range of backgrounds, but once I hit high school, I noticed that at lunchtime when I wanted to discuss class notes and tests, most of the non-Asians in my friends' group were only interested in talking about football tryouts or parties. There was nothing wrong with that, but I needed to know what was on the exam! In my high school, the majority of the Asians ate in the cafeteria. I began eating there with them because we could relate to each other's struggles, interests, and yes, academic anxieties. The cafeteria was so clearly Asian that it was nicknamed "Chinatown"—which is pretty problematic, looking back, but at the time, we owned it.

So as a suburban teen in the early 2000s, I found myself surrounded by Asians, absorbing everything AZN I could: driving Honda Preludes and Mitsubishi Eclipses, burning mix CDs of K-pop and Mando-pop, and having endless talks about strategy to win in *Star Craft II* and *Gunbound*. Living in the East Bay, we would have to drive over 30 minutes just to get boba in Berkeley, or Korean BBQ in Milpitas. But we did it: It was what we had to do to consume our culture. To immerse ourselves in it.

For me, the AZN Pryde phenomenon had three lasting effects on my future.

It started very innocently, with AOL. When I was in seventh grade and our family first got AOL, I decided to go with "wongfuphil" for my screen name: clean, simple, and with a bit of alliteration. It was an in-joke to my friends: "Wong Fu" was what I called a faux martial arts style that I'd made up. And yes, my legal last name is not Wong, but Wang, but at that age, I didn't know the complicated reasons why my name wasn't spelled like it sounded—immigration history, the limitations of English phonetics—so I went with Wong to be more "accurate" in the one place I had control: the Internet. The rest is history . . . I wish I had a better story as to how I came up with the name of the company I've been a part of for two decades ( like, it was inscribed in a scroll and delivered to my parents by a monk on the eve of my birth, "He shall be known as Wong Fu"), but it was ultimately the result of AZN Pryde–based screen name selection when I was 12.

The AZN era also saw the arrival of boba in America. I can still recall my friends driving 30 minutes for our first ever boba shop experience in 1999. I instantly associated going to get boba with being a "cool Asian," which led to

2012

🏛 Jose Antonio Vargas "comes out" as undocumented; the Pulitzer Prize–winning Filipino American journalist becomes a major figure in the national dialogue on immigration

💡 UCLA student Alexandra Wallace's mockery of Asians in the library ("Ching Chong Ling Long") goes viral

🏛 Gary Locke becomes the first Chinese American to serve as U.S. ambassador to China

 *The Mindy Project* debuts on Fox, the first network show to topline a South Asian American woman

me working for a boba shop for half my college life. Even after graduation, I stayed close to the boba life by frequently working *at* tea shops: Instead of being the typical "screenwriter at a coffee shop working on his screenplay," I was the "YouTuber at a boba shop working on his latest video." This close relationship I had to boba tea and the culture surrounding it ultimately led me to wanting to add to it—in 2019 I opened up Bopomofo Cafe with my friend and cofounder Eric Wang.

Finally, the AZN era was also when my heart came of age. I was experiencing relationships for the first time, Asian R&B groups were giving me a soundtrack for my teenage angst, and the ubiquitous cartoon artwork of "Jonny Angel" was providing the "Asian love" representation I couldn't see on TV or in movies. It sounds weird to say today, but I saw myself in—or aspired to be like—those drawings, like many other Asians of that era, who also vibed along with the emotions of their creator, Jonny Ngo. Because of what I saw and latched onto as a teen, because of what I experienced myself, I had no shame or doubt in the idea that Asians could be romantic with each other, both in person and on screen, which would all eventually shape my own work at Wong Fu Productions.

Given that AZN Pryde was such a large part of my formative adolescent years, it's no wonder that I ended up entering the UC system for college, and found myself living in a dorm pop-ulated mostly by other Asian Americans. It was in this densely-Asian-concentrated environment that Wong Fu Productions would sprout and gradually begin extending its influence in the community. But like I said, that was never part of the plan. In fact, there *was* no plan.

## Accidental Creators

Yes, we may roll our eyes at "chopsocky" kung fu stereotypes, but as a kid I *loved* those movies. I watched every Jackie Chan movie—even the deep cuts like *Thunderbolt* and *Twin Dragons*—thanks to the probably pirated VCDs my dad would rent for us. As a teen, *Dragon: The Bruce Lee Story* was one of the first films I recall making me cry. I cheered when Jet Li crossed over to Hollywood in *Lethal Weapon 4* and stepped into the lead with Aaliyah as his almost-romantic partner in *Romeo Must Die*.

But that had been the extent of my expectations for Asians in Hollywood. All I saw was Asians getting little chances here and there; I thought that was all we could ever get, and that we should just be happy with it. I most certainly never saw myself as having a future as a director. Did I enjoy making videos with the home camcorder? Absolutely. Did I try to turn all of my English writing projects into video projects? Yup. But unlike most aspiring filmmakers, Asian American or not, I never felt like directing was my calling. It was just too out

2012

🎬 A remake of the cult thriller *Red Dawn*—which was about a Soviet invasion of the U.S.—alters the invading force to China. However, after China complains, the attacking force is digitally altered to North Korea.

🎬 *Cloud Atlas* is released; in one segment of the cryptic film, Jim Sturgess, who starred in the whitewashed film *21*, plays a Korean guy in horrific yellowface

🎵 PSY's "Gangnam Style" goes viral and becomes inescapable

🏀 Jeremy Lin ushers in Linsanity with an improbable NBA debut

of reach—too foreign to my experience. Even when I made Visual Arts my major at UC San Diego, it was only because I'd convinced my parents and myself that "entertainment" was a *business*, and I was essentially going into business. I dreamed of eventually finding a good desk job at best. That's what happens when there are so few examples of success, and no sense from the few who'd found their way into the industry that you, too, could follow them.

There was no front door for me. But I found a side door that was just barely cracked open. With my college friends—and eventual business partners (I guess it became a business after all)—Wesley Chan and Ted Fu, I founded Wong Fu Productions.

In the beginning, it wasn't anything formal. There was no mission statement, no expectations, there was barely intention. We were making skits and lip-syncs for fun and we just wanted our friends to see. A suitemate at the time was Internet savvy and got us a domain and server. To share a video we'd send a link to our friends on AIM, one by one down the buddy list, and they would have to download the file from that link to our server, and play the video from their desktop media player. (THAT SENTENCE SOUNDS SO ARCHAIC AT THIS POINT!)

And a lot of people did just that. Soon our videos became events people would anticipate. Every finals season, Wong Fu Productions would have something to share, know-

Credit: Melly Lee

ing everyone was on their computers at the time. Through this consistency (and I'd like to believe, genuinely quality 240p content), we gained more and more viewers. First around campus at UCSD. And then we heard friends at other UCs were watching. Over the quarters we'd see our web stats with downloads from all around the U.S., Canada, and even Australia. We were freaked out, never having imagined it'd be possible for our homemade videos to be shared around the world.

Every step forward was a surprise, like when our servers maxed out after we released our short film *Yellow Fever*. We were forced to find free bandwidth options, and that's the main reason we started using YouTube! We just kept cracking that side door open a little more each time to see where it led. By the late 2000s, Wong Fu, along with several other Asian American creators, had found a way to explore our

**2013**

Steven Universe premieres with a predominantly Asian American voice-acting cast behind the scenes—mostly playing non-Asian roles

Nina Davuluri becomes the second Asian American and first Indian American to be crowned Miss America

**2014**

Mark Takano elected to California's 41st congressional district, becoming the first openly gay person of Asian descent in Congress

Chinese SF novel *Three Body Problem*, translated into English by Ken Liu, is published, and becomes the first Asian novel to win a Hugo Award

creativity without having to expose ourselves to the traditional challenges of breaking into Hollywood.

At its start, YouTube wasn't seen as a destination for aspiring performers or creators. If you were truly serious about your career, you pounded the pavement and went the traditional route. But when the traditional route wasn't an option because of family expectations or a lack of resources, relationships, or precedent, young Asian Americans would create and upload videos for fun on YouTube. And some of them were blessed by the viral video gods, and fame landed in their laps almost by accident, while they sang to webcams in their bedrooms, or in our case, filmed little skits around our neighborhood.

None of us were trying to find "audiences" as Hollywood defined them, but the fans found us anyway—helped by the community that early Asian YouTubers formed with one another, collaborating, cross-promoting, and building an ecosystem of shares, likes, and follows. It was organic; we had no expectations of what a following on YouTube might turn into, and what a huge bubble of Asian creators we would become during the early days of YouTube.

For the three of us, Wong Fu Productions was the only way we had to tell our stories. The only reason any of us actually started taking it seriously as careers was because the demand for us was there. I'll never forget the first time Wes, Ted, and myself went on tour, having been invited to speak at universities across North America. As we met our fans face-to-face, I was blown away to hear that people had driven from Virginia to see us in Pennsylvania (both states that were foreign to this California boy)—a journey of six hours round-trip. When we visited Calgary, in the middle of Canada, hundreds of people waited in the snow for the chance to watch our homemade videos.

So yes, seeing this type of support made it clear that we'd stumbled upon something that we couldn't take for granted. Whatever this was, we had to see it through and take it as far as we could. And that's how I somehow ended up as a writer-director. Not because I'd been a young cinephile with a dream, but because a generation of Asian American kids pushed me into it. But as social media transformed the cultural landscape, our community of Asian creators expanded, and so did our horizons.

## Asians Finding/Creating Representation Online

I often say that I got lucky with Wong Fu Productions because we started making content at the perfect intersection of the disruption of distribution, through the arrival of consumer high-speed Internet—and production, via major advancements in digital video. (I also consider myself lucky that I avoided the

2014

2015

🏛 In New York, Officer Peter Liang accidentally shoots and kills unarmed Black man Akai Gurley

🏛 Dr. Vivek Murthy is confirmed as 19th surgeon general of the United States, the first Asian American to fill that role

🎙 Ruthie Ann Miles becomes the first Asian American to win a Tony Award for Best Featured Actress in a Musical, for her turn as Lady Thiang in *The King and I*

🎙 88Rising founded by Sean Miyashiro, as a record label and management company seeking to "bridge the gap between Asian and American music"

shadow of Long Duk Dong in the 1980s, unlike some of my older peers.) With these technologies available to me (and with*out* the chip on my shoulder from *Sixteen Candles*), I joined many other Asians in participating and contributing in spaces we had little chance to be a part of before.

What had been stopping us?

"Opportunity" is one limitation our community often laments about when discussing our lack of representation. But "permission" and "visibility" are also part of the problem: What good is an opportunity if those in charge don't let you express yourself authentically within it? And what good is even authentic creative expression if no one ever gets to see your work?

All three of these barriers began crumbling with the rising power of social media platforms on smarter mobile devices in the 2010s. *Opportunity:* All you needed was a phone and the world was at your fingertips—just pick an app and find your calling. *Permission:* On social media, no one was your boss. You decided what you wanted your content to be and how you wanted to create it. *Visibility:* Your hard work would no longer be hidden behind anyone else's brand—your brand was yourself, and fans who saw you might be inspired to emulate you, thus repeating the cycle all over.

Of course not every person was going to take advantage of this leveled playing field, but you could imagine that for Asians who faced a huge barrier of entry to the world of entertainment in decades past, this was a relatively easy way to explore our passions and turn them into a profession.

To be honest, if it hadn't happened so serendipitously, I might not have been one of those bold risk takers myself. I still clearly remember that when I graduated in 2006, all my friends and family had no understanding of what I was going to do with an "online following." There was no legitimized path toward legitimacy. There was no way to "monetize" the audience. Which reminds me . . .

There's one more major barrier for Asians to pursue any type of passion: *cash.* Very few of us are raised in situations where we're encouraged to move to a new city with just a dollar and a dream. Our parents did that so that *we* wouldn't have to—even if we wanted to. Who cares about finally having a platform to express ourselves? If Asian Americans were going to venture out en masse away from the traditional, financially secure jobs that our parents had dreamed of for us, there had to be a system in place for us to earn a living.

The first platform to establish that in a meaningful way was YouTube, with Google AdSense and its Partner Program. Bing Chen, YouTube's global head of creator development and management, spearheaded this initiative in the late 2000s, and by the early 2010s, the

---

*Allegiance* comes to Broadway; inspired by George Takei's experiences as an incarcerated youth during WWII, *Allegiance* is the first wholly original Broadway musical with a mostly Asian cast in decades

Viet Thanh Nguyen publishes his debut novel *The Sympathizer*; it goes on to win the Pulitzer Prize

WIth her lawsuit, *Pao v. Kleiner Perkins*, Ellen Pao takes on sexism in Silicon Valley and starts a nationwide conversation about gender inequality

Groundbreaking TV series *Fresh Off the Boat* airs on ABC, becoming the first Asian American family sitcom to air for a complete season on network TV and goes on for six seasons

Partner Program had become a key source of revenue for creators on the platform. In the early days of the Internet, monetization of digital content was initially frowned upon as "selling out"; soon, however, it became normalized. This transformed the digital landscape: ad dollars increased, sponsorships and branded content became widely accepted, and people started to get used to paying for memberships and subscriptions. All these societal behaviors opened the door even further for hobbies to turn into professions.

Having overcome the shame of asking for money, and with making content becoming a realistic way to earn a living, a wave of Asian Americans embraced the chance to become creators-entrepreneurs. Before the 2010s, only the boldest and most fortunate broke through, and for years before that, you were doomed to life as a starving dreamer. But the popularization and normalization of platforms like Instagram, Patreon, Kickstarter, and even Tik-Tok didn't just create stars: it opened the way for a thriving middle class of artists and businesspeople. The existence of this less risky midzone attracted many Asians to finally explore the multitude of talents and interests that they'd sidelined for years. We picked up our cameras and started documenting our dining adventures like FoodWithSoy to become professional foodies. We picked up pens and showcased our doodles like AmandaRachLee to turn journaling into a job. We picked up microphones and shared our unique voices like #GoodMuslimBadMuslim and AsianBossGirl (and "They Call Us Bruce," of course) to create culturally impactful podcasts.

With a burgeoning sense of autonomy, Asian "influencers" began popping up and dominating on every platform, across a wide range of verticals from chefs, to fashion stylists, to tech reviewers, and even motivational speakers! So many industries and professions that previously would've never allowed us in had no choice but to accommodate us once they saw we were in demand. Who could say no to a million followers?

How difficult was it for a typical Asian American to get a food review show on television, or multipage spreads in a fashion magazine, or their own national talk radio show? If your answer is "impossible," you're not far off. But social media made attaining those coveted positions a hell of a lot easier than in the Nineties or even the 2000s. Asian influencers began to fill in the gaps of our representation on their own terms. Leveraging our massive homegrown audiences, we parlayed our successes to break into mainstream outlets as well—those food shows and fashion magazines that had turned their noses up at prior generations of our talent. And in many cases, we weren't going to them—they were coming to us. By this point, the shows and magazines

**2015**

🎬 *Master of None* premieres on Netflix; the groundbreaking series created by Aziz Ansari and Alan Yang becomes a huge hit for the streamer

🎬 Cameron Crowe's *Aloha* is released, featuring Emma Stone as "Allison Ng"—a casting choice that generates "whitewashing" backlash

🎵 Model and John Legend spouse Chrissy Teigen becomes a social media superstar

🏛 Bobby Jindal runs for president, becoming the first Indian American to do so

needed our audiences more than we needed theirs. And that's how we got to see David So judge dishes on Netflix, Lauren Riihimaki host a craft show on HBO, Cassey Ho on the cover of *Health* magazine, and Roi "Guava Juice" Fabito with a line of kids' toys at Target.

With more and more Asians becoming visible in these verticals, it was inevitable that certain categories of creativity would have a significantly higher Asian presence than others. Which meant that ironically, the 2010s saw the birth of a new set of Asian stereotypes, even as we reclaimed some old ones.

## The New Stereotypes

For generations, Asian Americans have pushed back against stereotypes that have dogged us through the decades—weird foreigner, exotic temptress, screaming thug, silent coolie. These were the only lenses through which Hollywood let the world see us—but that was in an era where Hollywood controlled 100 percent of what America was exposed to in the media.

What emerged as that control began fading away in the 2010s, and Asians could redefine our own narrative? A lot of boba. Okay, that's not all, but that's a *lot* of it. (Hell, we have two pieces about boba in this book.) Now, I'm the last person to roll my eyes at boba becoming deeply tied to Asian American identity—to be fully honest, I love the odd sense of unity and

empowerment that boba symbolized for us beginning in the 2010s—and the other "new stereotypes" that started being associated with Asians in that decade were equally positive in their own way.

Did you know being a "food blogger" is the number-one Instagram aspiration among Asian Americans? Fine, I have no data to prove that, but something's gotta explain all the photos we take of our meals. With so much variety, our innate adventurous appetites, and such a vast array of cross-cultural influence, it was perhaps just a matter of time before Asians became trendsetters and opinion leaders when it came to food. Whereas once we were just being asked to calculate how to split the check, now we were being asked about the best places to dine, and what to order once you got there. And if K-pop was South Korea's biggest export to America, a close second was *mukbang*—eating huge meals on camera. Again, I have no data to support that statement . . . but if you've seen anyone chowing down on massive slabs of salmon and two dozen crab legs on YouTube, just remember that that was our thing first.

The "Asian dancer" was also a stereotype that became cemented in the 2010s. Yes, there's now an assumption that "all Asians are good at dancing," and with good reason. The most visible and highest scoring dance teams on shows like *America's Best Dance Crew* and *World of Dance* were predominantly and visibly Asian

**2016**

🏛 Japan officially apologizes for World War II "comfort women," after over half a century of refusal to do so

🐒 Comedian Ali Wong breaks into the big time with *Baby Cobra*; the Netflix stand-up special turns Wong (and her outfit) into a cult phenomenon

💡 TikTok comes to America from China and becomes the social platform of choice for Gen Z

🎬 Korean Canadian family sitcom *Kim's Convenience* debuts on CBC and becomes a huge hit—and an even bigger one when it debuts on Netflix

American.* After winning titles, many of those teams and dancers went on to start studios and build massive brands online like the Kinjaz and Movement Lifestyle, garnering hundreds of millions of views, and inspiring even more young Asians to pursue dance as a hobby or career.

Meanwhile, as Asian cultural imports like anime, K-pop, and e-sports rose in popularity in North America, so did their association with Asian Americans. To be fair, 95 percent of us are fans of at least two of those three. (I don't know why I keep citing totally unsupported statistics.) But jokes aside, all of these new associations served as proof that there was more to our community and identity than had ever previously been seen.

As a result, a generation of Asians coming of age in the new millennia felt less need to assimilate into the communities around them, whether white, Black, or Latinx. The more our own culture became established, and the cooler the rest of the world thought it was, the less reason we had to feel hangups about the old stereotypes that shadowed us as well. Martial arts may have been cringy for some before the 1990s, when it was all that anyone thought we could do. Now, YouTube videos of people blowing out birthday candles with nunchucks get two million views overnight. In the past, being a doctor might have been seen as a boring,

parentally approved career. But what about an Asian doctor who does TikTok dances and raps parodies of *Hamilton* as a way to give helpful public health advice?

Asian Americans live in a whole new world of representation. We're finally making the point more clearly that it wasn't being depicted as kung fu fighters or math whizzes that was the problem; the problem was when those were the only way we were ever depicted. All marginalized groups want is to be seen as complex, multifaceted, and human, and for Asians, the 2010s is when we finally stopped waiting around for others to give us the chance to do so and did it for ourselves.

Remember, this was the decade when Jeremy Lin took over the world for a month in 2012. As Linsanity** unfolded, I specifically remember wondering if I was living in an alternate reality. As a diehard Yao Ming fan, when he retired in 2011, I firmly believed that it would be at least a decade before another Asian star would emerge, and decades before we ever saw an Asian *American* excel in the league. But just one year later, Lin had become a household name and ESPN was writing feature stories about bias against Asian Americans in sports. It was truly unbelievable: America finally got to see a version of the "Asian baller" archetype we were all familiar with within our community, but

---

\*   See page 270, "The Dance Crew Revolution"
\*\*  See page 322, "Remembering Linsanity"

**2016**

**2017**

🎬 *The Great Wall* released, featuring Matt Damon as a warrior in . . . China?

🏛 Kamala Harris is elected to U.S. Senate, becoming the first Indian American to serve as a U.S. senator

🏛 Former South Carolina governor Nikki Haley becomes U.S. ambassador to the UN, the first Asian American to fill that role

🎭 *KPOP* debuts off-Broadway and becomes a commercial and critical hit, headed to Broadway

📖 *Little Fires Everywhere* by Celeste Ng tops the bestseller lists and is later adapted into a TV series on Hulu

on the grandest stage, in the most epic of performances. And we didn't stop there: we kept challenging the conventional image of an "All-American athlete" throughout the decade, with Korean American Chloe Kim winning gold at the Winter Olympics, Chinese American Taylor Rapp getting drafted in the second round by the Los Angeles Rams, Naomi Osaka on her way to being a perennial Grand Slam winner in tennis, and Kim Ng getting hired by the Miami Marlins as the first woman and first Asian American GM of a Major League Baseball team.

This was also the decade that Andrew Yang*** went beyond everyone's expectations—especially those of his fellow Asian Americans—in his long-shot run for president. Watching his rise, I once again had the knee-jerk reaction I did with Jeremy Lin: "Can this really be happening already?" Yang actually became the first presidential candidate I ever donated to—but not for any political reason. I was returning a favor: My first encounter with him was via email in 2009 when he was still the CEO of the test preparation company Manhattan Prep, long before he had any presidential aspirations. He'd messaged Wong Fu Productions out of the blue, saying he was a fan of what we were doing at the time, and wanted to help support us by buying some ad space on our website. He admitted it wasn't much, but that it'd give us some "pizza money" at the very

least. This was one of the first "brand deals" we'd ever struck, long before anyone was really paying us for sponsorships, and it was support we really appreciated. He was such a fan of our growing channel that he also offered us a ton of business advice—which was all way over our heads at the time. Long story short, I was grateful for his early enthusiasm for us, and overwhelmed by how far he, and we, had come in just a little over a decade.

Rising representation in places where we'd never been seen gave Asian Americans more confidence in embracing our collective identity, but also more comfort in celebrating our differences. The 2010s saw a huge increase in content and creators specific to South and Southeast Asian communities, along with increased awareness and intersectional inclusion of the queer Asian community, the multiracial community, and the adoptee community. If the 2000s was about Asian Americans realizing that there were a lot more of us than we had once felt or believed, the 2010s was when we began activating our true potential by both uniting in, and diverging from, our monolithic labeling.

## Connected Like Never Before

Mobile devices meant that the greater Asian diaspora finally had a tool to unify virtually

***　See page 458, "The Math of Andrew Yang"

---

-ϙ- Simon Tam wins his Supreme Court case to register "The Slants" as a trademark, setting a new precedent regarding "objectionable" marks

📖 *Andi Mack* debuts on Disney Channel, the first live action show on the channel to focus on an Asian American family

📖 Scarlett Johansson takes on the role of Japanese American Motoko Kusanagi in *Ghost in the Shell*, prompting . . . many questions

📖 *The Big Sick* is released; lead actor Kumail Nanjiani is nominated for a Best Original Screenplay Oscar, along with his wife, Emily V. Gordon

instantly around causes that needed ground-swells of support. Although the Asian American community still struggles with fragmentation in many regards, when it counts we also know how to connect like Voltron to call out whitewashed casting or cultural appropriation, or on the positive side, to amplify our heroes or buy out movie theaters to support our creators.

I felt the direct benefits of social-media-driven support when Wong Fu Productions made our first feature film, *Everything Before Us*, in 2014. I'd actually tried making a movie in 2008 the "traditional" way, writing a script with Asian leads and shopping around town to different production companies, only to have the amazing experience of having white executives tell me that casting Asians was bad business. "There are no bankable Asian American stars," they said. When we told them we already had an online audience and didn't need a "bankable star," it meant nothing to them. At the same time, I also learned that entertainment marketers grouped us together with white audiences when looking at demographics, meaning our spending power and attendance was literally erased, and actually absorbed, by white people. The ignorance and arrogance that that demonstrated drove me to double down on Wong Fu's YouTube endeavors.

Fast-forward to 2013 and Visual Communications, a nonprofit cultivating and advocating for Asian American filmmakers, chose to sup-port this first film of ours with a small grant (thanks, Phil Yu!). At this time, crowdfunding was just taking off, and it seemed like the perfect time to activate our audience toward supporting one of our projects with money instead of just eyeballs. Our campaign on IndieGoGo raised over $350,000 thanks to our grassroots marketing and the loyal backing of our fans, and Wesley and I got to make a movie with an *all* Asian American cast—completely ignoring the advice of those producers six years prior.

And what terrible advice that truly was, as the rest of the decade would prove.

In 2014, *Fresh Off the Boat* premiered. The Asian American community was so unprepared to have anything like it—the first primetime network sitcom featuring an Asian American cast in two decades—that we were half ready to reject it even before it premiered. With concerns over Asian accents, casting choices, and even the title, it was impossible for the entirety of the Asian American community to purely appreciate this major step in representation, because we were debating what type of representation we even wanted. Thankfully, Asian Americans changed their minds, and it went on to become a hit show, Asian America's first hit show, lasting six seasons and 116 episodes, and cementing Randall Park and Constance Wu as stars, while introducing us to Hudson Yang! Then in 2016, Alan Yang and Aziz Ansari won Emmys for their writing on *Master of None*,

2018

🐾 Filipino American Robert Lopez, composer of *Avenue Q* and *Frozen*, becomes the first double EGOT (Emmy, Grammy, Oscar, and Tony winner)

🎬 *Crazy Rich Asians* makes $240 million at the global box office—the first blockbuster film directed by and primarily starring Asian Americans

🎬 Hasan Minhaj's breakthrough news/comedy show *Patriot Act* debuts on Netflix

🎬 The adaptation of Jenny Han's YA bestseller *To All the Boys I've Loved Before* becomes a huge hit on Netflix

for an episode focused on the Asian immigrant experience—demonstrating that we had voices worth listening to. That same year, Ali Wong's *Baby Cobra* took the country by storm, showing a raunchy and hilarious side of Asian women few had seen since Margaret Cho.

But the true test of our community's collective power came in 2018, when *Crazy Rich Asians* was set to be released. I remember how much weight was put on this film to succeed—unfairly, perhaps—but we literally Had. No. Other. Choices. As much discourse and debate as there was about the story, cast, and once again, the title, it was undeniable that this film had to do well in order to prove to the system that we deserved a place at the table and more swings at bat. So while I didn't relate to the story from a personal basis—I am far from a Crazy Rich Asian—I found what I could relate to within it and the aspects I wanted to support. And unlike decades past, the vast majority of the community now understood what was on the line. API leaders also recognized how the film's success would have lasting effects beyond the movie itself, and organized across groups and industries to purchase entire screenings of the film and distribute tickets to those in need, to ensure a strong opening weekend. For the first time, Asian Americans stood up to prove that we were a demographic that couldn't be ignored.

And yes, I'll never forget the first time I saw the *Crazy Rich Asians* movie poster hanging at a bus stop. A bus stop! The image of two Asian romantic leads in a major motion picture was so foreign to even me. It made me feel exposed, but also proud, and it hit me that I'd never had this feeling in my life before. I pulled over and took a picture . . . of a bus stop. Was this how white people felt every week when they saw their movie posters plastered around town?

That initial feeling of surprise and awkwardness began to fade, as more posters and billboards followed *Crazy Rich Asians* in the final years of the decade. Randall Park and Ali Wong in *Always Be My Maybe*, Awkwafina in *The Farewell*, Hasan Minaj's *Patriot Act*, Henry Golding in *Last Christmas*. Seeing billboards featuring Asians around town almost became . . . normal. (Though admittedly none of them could top seeing the one billboard we had featuring Harry Shum Jr. and Kina Grannis in our own series, *Single by 30*, back in 2016!)

With all these films and shows—but really, all the money they generated—we finally saw Hollywood accept the idea that Asian Americans could be "bankable stars."

To illustrate how quickly things changed, I need to tell you about the "Unforgettable" Gala, an annual event created to celebrate Asian American achievements in entertainment. Think of it as the Asian Golden Globes, only not as much of a hot mess? At the beginning of the 2010s, the awards for Best Actor were

---

🎵 BTS hits number one on Billboard 200 album charts, becoming the first K-pop group to achieve mainstream American (and global) embrace

🏛 Subtle Asian Traits founded; the invite-only Facebook group quickly grows to millions in size, repping young diasporic Asians from around the globe

📈 Gold House founded, gathering prominent Asian American creators and entrepreneurs together with a focus on lifting up other Asian Americans

🏂 At the Pyeongchang Olympics, 17-year-old Chloe Kim wins the women's snowboarding halfpipe, becoming the youngest woman ever to win Olympic gold in the event

regularly given to actors who had scored a *supporting* spot in some (or any) major Hollywood film. And it wasn't even a competition between different actors—in many cases, there would only be one nominee. This isn't a knock on our actors. This was an indication of the scraps we were given, and how we *still* celebrated them, because they were all we had.

Fast-forward to the 2019 gala, and some of the actors who were winning awards weren't even showing up—because now they were at the *actual* Golden Globes.

## The Difference a Decade Can Make

Things continue to change quickly. *Parasite* won Best Picture and Best Director, as a Korean movie with subtitles! Sandra Oh got a Best Lead Actress Golden Globe, the very first for an Asian American! Steven Yeun and Riz Ahmed, both nominated for Best Actor Oscars . . . against one another! Seeing all this, I found myself having similar feelings as when I saw Jeremy Lin and Andrew Yang in newspaper headlines, and when I encountered that *Crazy Rich Asians* poster at the bus stop. Were we really supposed to overcome our challenges so quickly?

And then I have to remind myself, this didn't happen quickly at all. As we've shown, it took a slow grind over the course of decades to *finally* get to this first checkpoint.

Because that's really where we are still. And the worst thing we can do right now is be content, because there is actually so much further we need to go. That being said, we deserve a hearty pat on the back for the immense progress we made in the 2010s. I recall, as recently as 2014, going to an Asian American movie premiere and not loving it—yet, agreeing with peers that we had to publicly support the film still, because "we weren't there yet" where we could be selective. But imagine having so much Asian content that we didn't have to feel obligated to back everything! Now that would be progress.

Well, it's the 2020s, and you know what? It feels like we're there. The Asian American community has reached new levels of confidence in critiquing our own. And I'm not talking about broad protests rooted in fear that a single misstep will set us back. We're seeing honest discussions over what's progress, and what can be improved on.

On one hand, that makes our individual jobs harder; on the other, it pushes us to do better work. The best result of this newfound energy?

Asian Americans now have choices.

Some will sing along with Olivia Rodrigo, while others vibe to NIKI. Some will cry watching *Minari*, while others get drunk to *Bling Empire*. Some will buy Fareed Zakaria's [or Dr. Sanjay Gupta's] new book, while others buy LilyPichu's latest merch. In 10 short years we went from "take what we can get" to "picky eaters." But either way, it's clear that we're still hungry.

2019

🎬 Asian Canadian Lilly Singh becomes the first person of South Asian descent to host an American major broadcast network late-night talk show

🎬 *Always Be My Maybe* debuts on Netflix; Randall Park and Ali Wong's exquisitely Asian American rom-com becomes a huge hit

🎬 Bong Joon-Ho's *Parasite* wins the Cannes Palme d'Or and then four major awards at the Oscars, including Best Picture

🎬 Bowen Yang joins the cast of *Saturday Night Live*, *SNL*'s first obviously Asian American cast member (although past cast members Fred Armisen and Rob Schneider are of multiracial Asian descent)

🎬 Awkwafina wins Golden Globe for Best Actress for her turn in Lulu Wang's *The Farewell*

# THE ASIAN AMERICAN PLAYLIST:

# The 2010s

BY RICHIE "TRAKTIVIST" MENCHAVEZ

| # | TITLE | |
|---|---|---|
| 1 | **"Like a G6"** <br> Far East Movement | Released in 2009, this became the first number one hit on the *Billboard* charts for an all-Asian band, with over half a billion combined views and streams across various platforms, so it goes without saying that this song was monumental. Based in Koreatown, Los Angeles, Far East Movement is a hip-hop and electronic group whose members are a pan-Asian mix: Chinese/Japanese (Kevin "Kev Nish" Nishimura), Korean (James "Prohgress" Roh and Jae "J-Splif" Choung, who later left the group), and Filipino American (DJ Virman). With catchy lyrics heavy on bottle-popping and club hopping, laid down over a bass-heavy, electro-dance backtrack, "Like a G6" made music history when it hit number one (and incredibly, was 1 and 2 with Filipino/Puerto Rican Bruno Mars's "Just the Way You Are," whom they'd bumped from his position at the top spot a week earlier). Also worth noting: The song was created with the help of The Cataracs, a production duo that includes Indian American Niles Hollowell-Dhar—now one of the world's top EDM DJs under the stage name KSHMR. |
| 2 | **"That's What I Like"** <br> Bruno Mars | Hawaiian-born Bruno Mars, whose mother is Filipina American, is one of the best-selling artists of all time and a living icon of our generation. "That's What I Like" is the infectiously bouncy R&B track that won him Song of the Year, Best R&B Song, and Best R&B Performance at the 2018 Grammy Awards. Asian American magic runs deep in the song: it was produced by The Stereotypes, a production team that includes Chinese American Jonathan Yip. The working relationship between Mars and The Stereotypes goes back to 2007; in fact, The Stereotypes produced a 2009 song by Far East Movement called "3D" that marks Mars's first recorded appearance as a singer. What an incredibly full-circle milestone in our musical history! |

SCAN THE
QR CODE TO
DOWNLOAD
THE PLAYLIST

**3** **"Crush"**
Yuna, featuring Usher

Don't be fooled by Yuna's butterfly-soft voice—the Malaysian-born, devout Muslim singer-songwriter and fashion icon is a powerhouse. This is her first *Billboard* chart-topping hit, a duet with R&B icon Usher from her third studio album, *Chapters*. Honest, personal, sweet, and sultry, the song helped Yuna make history as the first Malaysian singer to be nominated for a BET Award.

**4** **"The Worst"**
Jhene Aiko

Aiko's distinctly sensual and feathery voice, and emotive and vulnerable yet unapologetic lyrical stylings, have made her one of music's most prominent R&B divas. She's the child of a Japanese, Spanish, and Dominican mother and African American, Native American, German, and Jewish father, and her visibility and success have challenged the longstanding Black-white dichotomy in R&B and hip-hop. "The Worst" is the breakout hit from her debut EP *Sail Out,* and garnered her her first nomination for Best R&B Song at the 2015 Grammys.

**5** **"Best Part"**
H.E.R., featuring
Daniel Caesar

At just 23 years old, with only two albums released, H.E.R.—a backronym for Having Everything Revealed—has received 15 Grammy nominations, and won three: Best R&B Album of the Year in 2018, and Song of the Year and R&B Song of the Year for "I Can't Breathe" and "Better Than I Imagined" in 2021. Born to a Filipina mother and Black father, the singer, songwriter, and multi-instrumentalist initially kept a purposefully low and mysterious profile, in order to put her music center stage. "Best Part," an acoustic duet with Daniel Caesar that won them a Grammy for Best R&B Performance, shot her into the limelight. In an age in which too much attention is placed on image, numbers, and virality, H.E.R. proves that selflessness, vulnerability, and excellent music can still be a formula for success.

**6** **"Safe"**
Dumbfoundead

At the start of 2016, the #OscarsSoWhite hashtag triggered a conversation on the lack of diversity in American entertainment, while the #StarringJohnCho campaign visually highlighted Asian America's absence in Hollywood's star-power conversation. "Safe," a hip-hop track from Korean American rapper and actor Jonathan "Dumbfoundead" Park, provided the perfect call to arms, every line packed with his signature scintillating wit, stinging social commentary, and razor-sharp delivery. To drive his point home, Dumbfoundead accompanied the song with a brilliant music video that superimposed his face over the faces of white actors in popular movie scenes, #StarringJonathanPark style.

| # | TITLE |
|---|-------|

**7**    **"Midsummer Madness"** 88rising featuring Rich Brian, Joji, Higher Brothers, August 08

88rising, the hybrid record label, marketing firm, and creative agency founded by Sean Miyashiro, a Korean Japanese American media and marketing savant, and Jaeson Ma, a Chinese American serial entrepreneur, has been doing its best to shift the needle on Asian visibility in the American and global music industries. "Midsummer Madness," a supergroup song from the collective, features their flagship artists Rich Brian (Indonesian), Joji (Japanese/Australian), Higher Brothers (Chinese), and August 08 (African American). It's a quality feel-good song that isn't overtly "Asian" in lyrical content despite being delivered in both Chinese and English. It expresses the spirit of a brand that aims to capture the loyalty of the Asian diaspora around the world.

**8**    **"Don't Call Me"** TOKiMONSTA, featuring Yuna

TOKiMONSTA is a Korean American DJ, the founder of Young Art Records, and a record producer widely recognized for defining the sound of modern electronic music. Featuring Malaysian songstress Yuna, "Don't Call Me" was the lead single off of TOKiMONSTA's third studio album, *Lune Rouge*. The track showcases her compositional prowess, combining futuristic melodies with beats filled with a colorful mixture of hip-hop, soul, and dance. In 2019, the album received a Grammy Award nomination for Best Dance/Electronic Album, making her the first woman and first Asian American to be so honored. Even more stunning: prior to completing the album, she battled to recover from two brain surgeries for moyamoya disease, which left her unable to speak or to comprehend music for months afterward.

**9**    **"Run or Hide"** Run River North

Run River North is a kick-ass indie rock band whose members happen to be Korean American. Originally formed in 2011 as a sextet named Monsters Calling Home, the band was propelled into national headlines after a DIY music video they recorded in their Honda cars unexpectedly garnered them an offer to perform on *Jimmy Kimmel Live!* "Run or Hide," the lead single from their second album, *Drink from a Salt Pond,* undoubtedly showed that the band had come into its own. The record was aggressive, edgy, cohesive, and a clear step away from the acoustic folk sound for which they'd become known, while authentically capturing the collision of emotions within the band that eventually led to three members quitting.

**10** **"Your Best American Girl"**
Mitski

According to biracial Japanese American singer-songwriter Mitsuki Laycock—better known as Mitski—this song is simply about love. But artists don't always get to determine what their music means to the masses. With lyrics that are both elusive and candid, subtle and turbulent, "Your Best American Girl" was an anthem for many Asian Americans, especially those who are mixed race and women—a relatable account of the pain experienced in assimilating into whiteness, and the power that comes from self-acceptance. "Your Best American Girl" was named the 13th best song of the 2010s by *Rolling Stone*.

**11** **"Goddess"**
Krewella w/Raja Kumari & NERVO

The half–Pakistani American sister duo known as Krewella survived a long, public onslaught of sexist online abuse by the EDM community, led by renowned producer Deadmau5. They've achieved success as female artists of color in a predominantly white boys' club, launched their own label, Mixed Kid Records, and are thriving as fully independent artists. Leaning on their motto of "East Meets West," the South Asian–inspired electro-pop track "Goddess" is an irrefutable roar of empowerment and a clear reflection of their evolved sound, created in collaboration with electronic duo NERVO and Indian American rapper Raja Kumari.

**12** **"Us"**
Ruby Ibarra featuring Rocky Rivera, Klassy, and Faith Santilla

There are songs, and then there are anthems. There are music videos and then there are visual masterpieces. In "Us," a woman who wears many hats—rapper, poet, music producer, film director, and research scientist—Ruby Ibarra created both. The compelling track, off of her debut album, *CIRCA91,* isn't just a triumphant celebration of the Filipina diaspora, but also a defiant exploration of social injustice, colorism, and the struggles of immigration and assimilation for people of color. In featuring fellow Pinay rappers Rocky Rivera and Klassy and spoken-word artist Faith Santilla, this song also provides a direct challenge to gender inequality, in hip-hop and in society at large. The album was released under Beatrock Music, the longest-running independent hip-hop record label founded and operated by Asian Americans, whose artist roster includes groundbreaking artists like Bambu, Prometheus Brown, and Fatgums, just to name a few.

| # | TITLE |
|---|-------|

**13**    **"Big Fax"**
Anika Khan

Khan is a Bengali rapper, singer, and entrepreneur, the child of a freedom fighter in the Bangladesh Liberation War. Khan is a standout in a recent surge of rappers of South Asian descent, given his unique balancing act in managing his success as an artist and the adversity he's experienced from the U.S. immigration system. In fact, he almost quit music completely while fighting to become a citizen: as he raps in "Big Fax," "They think I'm a threat, but I'm an addict to the belief." Produced by MEMBA, a production duo featuring Indian American Ishaan Chaudhary, "Fax" is a hefty track showing Anika's life out loud, while rallying brown and Black folks to join in celebration of the beautiful aspects of being an immigrant.

**14**    **"Yellow"**
Katherine Ho

Ho's cover of "Yellow"—originally performed by the iconic band Coldplay—was the most memorable song from the global blockbuster hit movie *Crazy Rich Asians,* and significant not just for Ho's lovely Mandarin-language rendition, but for its significance in reclaiming the word "yellow." The story of how the cover came about is fascinating: The track was originally intended for Li Wenqi, who had popularized a version of the song retitled "Liu Xing" during the popular Chinese TV singing competition *The Voice of China.* After Li declined the offer, the film's music supervisors were able to get Katherine Ho to take on the track in her stead. Then they ran into trouble clearing the rights to recontextualize the song—but a now-famous heartfelt appeal from director Jon Chu directly to the members of Coldplay finally convinced the band to let it happen. The rest is soundtrack history.

**15**    **"We Could Happen"**
AJ Rafael

Rafael, a Filipino American singer, songwriter, actor, and director from Riverside, California, was one of YouTube's earliest adopters. He didn't experience a meteoric rise to fame like many other artists, but relied on his talent, consistency, and authentic connection to fans for his success in gaining a million subscribers—something that took over a decade. However, his significance goes beyond numbers: with his hundreds of collaborations, AJ made it popular for YouTubers to work with other artists, building a community that helped to unleash a tidal wave of Asian American representation on the platform. "Starlit Nights" was the first original Rafael posted to YouTube, a joyous keyboard-driven power ballad that he wrote for and dedicated to his then-girlfriend.

# Hashtag
# #ASIANAMERICA

## BY JEFF YANG

**THE 2010S SAW** Asian America emerge as a political and creative force that demanded to be seen and heard, and a big reason for our surge into greater visibility was our overwhelming presence on social media—a place where our fragmented and distributed communities could link together, and our collective voice amplified.

By the mid-2010s, based on data from Pew Research, 95 percent of English-speaking Asian Americans were on the Internet. And we weren't just "on" the Internet—we were *always* on, fueled by superfast connectivity (84 percent of English-speaking Asian Americans already had broadband, versus two-thirds of other Americans) and mobile wireless (91 percent of English-speaking Asian Americans were smartphone owners, versus two-thirds of other Americans). On average, Asian Americans spent 4 hours and 42 minutes per day online on some kind of Internet-connected device, versus 4 hours and 14 minutes for Americans as a whole. For a population largely frozen out by traditional media, mobile technology and fast Internet provided us with both the tools to express ourselves and a potential audience the size of the world.

By the end of the 2010s, a wave of younger Asian Americans, digitally immersed virtually from birth, had come online. Today, the Asian American Internet population is the most youthful on the Web: almost two-thirds of Asian American Internet users are between the ages of 18 and 34, versus 41 percent of Asian Americans as a whole. And they're not just consumers—they're creators, many with enormous followings, on YouTube, Instagram, Twitter, and especially the fastest growing and most influential new social platform, TikTok. Three of the top 10 most followed TikTokers in the world are Asian American: The fourth most popular TikTok creator, digital illusionist Zach King, with 58 million followers, is of Chinese, Austrian, and Nicaraguan descent. Number 6, musician SpencerX (Spencer Polanco Knight), at 52 million, is Chinese and Ecuadorian, and number 10, dancer JustMaiko (Michael Le), at 47 million, is Vietnamese American.

The TikTok generation isn't just having fun online. They're educating and elevating one another, busting myths and spotlighting under-the-radar truths. They're speaking out for social justice. And they're mobilizing to make real-world impact—raising money for worthy causes, boosting voter registration and civic participation, and making politics both readily accessible and deeply personal.

## ONLINE ASIAN AMERICANS TEND TO BE YOUNGER ON AVERAGE—WITH A MEDIAN AGE OF 33.5, VERSUS 39 FOR AMERICANS OVERALL

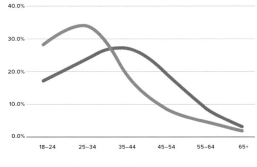

Pew Internet Tracking Project, 2000

**They're hardcore Internet users—far more likely to use the Internet daily than other Americans, and staying on longer when they do**

### % OF EACH GROUP WHO GOES ON THE INTERNET DAILY

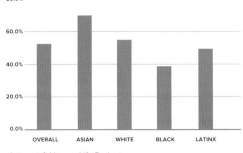

Pew Internet & Human Life Project

**40%**
of Asians spend two or more hours online when they're using the Internet (versus 29% of Americans overall)

**15%**
spend four or more hours online

### THEY'RE MORE LIKELY THAN ANY OTHER GROUP TO USE THE INTERNET TO GET AND SHARE INFORMATION

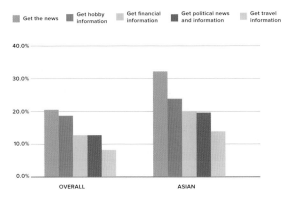

### AND THEY'RE MORE LIKELY TO HAVE A WIDE RANGE OF DIGITAL DEVICES IN THEIR HOUSEHOLDS

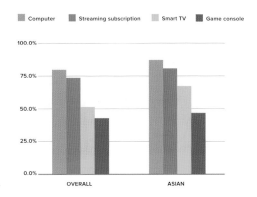

# Remembering Linsanity

BY JEREMY LIN, AS TOLD TO PHILIP WANG
ILLUSTRATED BY MOLLY MURAKAMI

THEY STARTED CALLING IT "*LINSANITY*." AND IT WAS ***CRAZY***.
LINSANE! #17 GO KNICKS
KNICKS
I KEPT SCORING. WE KEPT WINNING. EVERY NIGHT, I THOUGHT IT WAS GOING TO END, AND EVERY NIGHT I KEPT PRAYING IT WOULDN'T.
BUT EVERYTHING REALLY CHANGED THE NIGHT WE PLAYED THE ***LAKERS***. THE MEDIA ASKED ***KOBE BRYANT*** ABOUT ME. AND HE SAID WHAT HE SAID.
I don't even know what he's done... What the $*#$% is going on? Who is this kid?
...if he's playing well, I'll just have to deal with him.
I GUESS YOU COULD SAY THAT WAS THE ULTIMATE UNDERDOG GAME. BUT YOU KNOW WHAT? I'M USED TO IT.
So... you think Kobe knows who Jeremy Lin is now?
BRYANT 24
17
The Knicks ***WIN!***
Jeremy Lin scores a game-high, ***career-high 38 points*** against the Lakers!
AFTER THAT GAME, MY LIFE BEGAN CHANGING SO FAST. PEOPLE BEGAN STALKING MY FAMILY, TRYING TO TAKE ADVANTAGE OF ME. AND AS EVERYONE ELSE'S EXPECTATIONS OF ME CHANGED, I STARTED CHANGING MY EXPECTATIONS OF MYSELF.
NEW
LIN 17
MY WHOLE LIFE, I WAS ALWAYS UNDER THE RADAR AND NO ONE CARED ABOUT ME. NOW, HALF THE WORLD NEEDED ME TO SUCCEED, AND THE OTHER HALF WAS WAITING FOR ME TO FAIL.
DREAMS AND EXPECTATIONS OF EVERY
(EVER)
WHEN WE FINALLY LOST A GAME, ESPN RAN AN ARTICLE ON US. AND WHEN I SAW THE HEADLINE, I THOUGHT, "THERE'S NO WAY THAT WAS AN ACCIDENT."
Orchestra's on the other side of campus!
ESPN
Chink in the Armor
BUT TO BE HONEST, IT DIDN'T EVEN FAZE ME. IT WAS ONLY A HEADLINE. I'D HEARD WORSE BACK IN MY COLLEGE DAYS.
Open your eyes! Go back to China!
MY TIME IN THE NBA REMINDED ME OF HOW SYSTEMIC RACISM IS IN AMERICAN SOCIETY, AND HOW IT SOMETIMES PITS PEOPLE OF COLOR AGAINST EACH OTHER.
IT ALSO SHOWED ME HOW MUCH ASIAN AMERICANS NEED HEROES... AND HOW HARD IT IS TO BE THE ONLY ONE, STANDING IN FOR THE DREAMS OF A WHOLE COMMUNITY.

TRUTH IS, I COULDN'T EVEN PROCESS THE IMPACT I WAS HAVING ON ASIANS, I WAS SO YOUNG AND NAIVE. LET ME EXPLAIN THE ONLY WAY I CAN: THROUGH NARUTO.

I RELATE TO NARUTO'S STORY SO MUCH, BECAUSE HE'S JUST TRYING TO BE A GREAT NINJA. AND AS HIS SKILLS GROW, ALL OF A SUDDEN EVERYONE ELSE AROUND HIM CHANGES THEIR VIEWS OF HIM, AND HE DOESN'T KNOW WHY IT'S HAPPENING. *THAT WAS ME.*

THE GAMES WERE COMING SO FAST, I WAS STILL JUST TRYING TO MAKE IT TO THE END OF THE SEASON. I KNEW MY FUTURE WASN'T GUARANTEED.

BUT I CAN'T SAY IT WASN'T A *BLAST.* WHEN I MENTIONED THAT I LIKED PINEAPPLE SHORTCAKES, FANS STARTED SENDING THEM TO ME. ALSO, I GOT ONE OF THOSE ALL-YOU-CAN-EAT CARDS FROM CHIPOTLE!

BUT SERIOUSLY, I JUST WISH I HAD THE CHANCE TO SLOW DOWN AND *EMBRACE* WHAT WAS HAPPENING,

INSTEAD OF LETTING EVERYONE ELSE AND THEIR THOUGHTS AND OPINIONS OF ME SHAPE HOW I WAS SUPPOSED TO INTERPRET THAT EXPERIENCE.

AND THEN, *26 DAYS* LATER, IT WAS OVER.

OVER THAT TIME AND OVER THE YEARS, I WENT FROM

"OH, THAT WAS SO COOL!" TO

"I'M SCARED" TO "I'M JADED" TO "I'M BITTER" TO "I'M ANGRY AND RESENTFUL."

BUT NOW I'VE COME FULL CIRCLE.

I'VE BEEN HUMBLED. I LEARNED TO CHERISH THOSE MEMORIES. I LOVE THAT I HAD THAT. I LOVE WHO I AM. I LOVE WHAT I'VE BEEN ABLE TO DO, AS THAT GUY IN THE MIDDLE OF *LINSANITY.*

AND NOW, LOOKING BACK, *"LINSANITY"* WAS A MOMENT IN TIME,

BUT IT WAS ALSO A MENTALITY...

A COMBINATION OF FAITH AND PERSEVERANCE THAT PROVED DREAMS AND MIRACLES CAN HAPPEN WHEN YOU GIVE YOURSELF A SHOT TO SUCCEED.

YOU GOT TO PUT YOURSELF IN A POSITION WHERE YOU CAN DO SOMETHING, VERSUS SITTING BACK AND LETTING THINGS HAPPEN.

OUR STORY IS JUST BEGINNING.

AND SO IS MINE.

JEFF YANG

PHIL YU

PHILLIP WANG

# THE ASIAN AMERICAN
# SYLLABUS 2010s

**HERE'S OUR LIST** of must-consume media to understand being Asian American in the 2010s, the decade of Asian America's pop jubilee.

### Hawaii Five-0 (2010)

**PHIL:** A remake of the Sixties cop show that promised to be a whole new way of telling a story set in the only state in the union that's majority Asian American.

**JEFF:** Daniel Dae Kim and Grace Park were literally front and center on all the billboards! And then the show turned out to really be all about the two white guys.

**PHILIP:** Disappointed but not surprised. The most important thing about the show was Daniel and Grace quitting because they were sick of being disrespected. Shots fired.

### Nikita (2010); Elementary (2012); Killing Eve (2018)

**PHIL:** The first TV drama to have an Asian American woman as its title lead—Maggie Q, who's biracial Vietnamese American, born in Hawaii.

**PHILIP:** So we're probably overdue for another remake? Maggie wasn't the only Asian American woman to star in a TV thriller series, though: Lucy Liu starred as Dr. Joan Watson, a gender-flipped version of Sherlock Holmes's mystery-solving partner, in CBS's *Elementary*.

**JEFF:** And then there was *Killing Eve*! This was the show that finally put Sandra Oh where she belonged: at the center of the spotlight, brilliantly playing Eve Polastri in a role that wasn't Asian—or American—in the British books on which the show was based.

### The Walking Dead (2010)

**PHIL:** The most beloved character in this series was Glenn Rhee. Then they killed Glenn Rhee.

**PHILIP:** But the relationship between Glenn and Maggie was like the spine of the show. How often do you see an Asian guy like Steven Yeun play a romantic lead on TV? It took the zombie apocalypse to make it happen.

**JEFF:** Glenn died so Steve Yeun could live.

**Outsourced (2010); The Mindy Project (2012); Master of None (2015); Quantico (2015)**

**JEFF:** *Outsourced,* set in a call center in Mumbai, only lasted one season and it had lots of problematic things going on, but it was also the first time you could turn on U.S. network TV and see a screen full of brown faces.

**PHIL:** Who were standing behind the white leads. But yes. It did open up an era in which we started to see real South Asian representation on TV, though. Mindy Kaling, best known for *The Office,* created and starred in *The Mindy Project* for six seasons. Aziz Ansari created *Master of None* for Netflix. And Priyanka Chopra played an FBI agent in ABC's *Quantico.*

**Agents of Secret Stuff (2010); Hang Loose (2012); Everything Before Us (2015)**

**PHILIP:** These features were early attempts by YouTubers to cross over into more traditional media formats. *Hang Loose* was Kevin "KevJumba" Wu's first stab at a movie, costarring Dante Basco and Justin Chon. *Agents,* starring Ryan Higa and Arden Cho, got 35 million views!

**JEFF:** You directed it! And you also made *Everything Before Us,* a sci-fi romance featuring Aaron Yoo and Brittany Ishibashi.

**PHILIP:** Good times.

**In the Family (2011); Seoul Searching (2015); Gook (2017)**

**PHIL:** I loved *In the Family*, about a gay Asian American man trying to keep his son after his partner dies. Patrick Wang wrote it, directed it, starred in it, and distributed it himself. You will never see more indie grit than that.

**JEFF:** Unless you want to talk about Benson Lee's *Seoul Searching,* a nostalgic teen comedy about kids at a "summer cultural tour" in Korea, or *Gook,* Justin Chon's breakthrough black-and-white drama, set during the L.A. Riots. All movies made on passion that capture unique slices of Asian American life during the decade.

**Agents of S.H.I.E.L.D. (2013); Big Hero 6 (2014)**

**JEFF:** This was Disney giving us superheroes—on TV, with Ming-Na Wen and Chloe Bennet playing members of an elite squad of Marvel Universe operatives, and on the big screen, with *Big Hero 6,* an anime-inspired crime-fighting team set in an alternate reality where America is Asian, and the Bay Area has been replaced with a city called "San Fransokyo."

**PHILIP:** Girls swooned over Tadashi Hamada!

**Seeking Asian Female; Linsanity; 9 Man; Twinsters; Abacus: Small Enough to Jail (2016); Minding the Gap (2018); Origin Story (2018)**

**PHIL:** Here's your essential Asian American docs-of-the-decade pack. *Seeking Asian Female* explores the phenomenon of mail-order brides, and it's a train wreck that you can't look away from. *Linsanity* brings us back to Jeremy Lin's special moment.

**JEFF:** Both of us are briefly in it! I'm just a voice, though. *9 Man* is an incredible look at this unique sport, a kind of volleyball played by Asian Americans in amazingly competitive tournaments, and *Twinsters* is about Korean adoptee Samantha Futerman—who starred in *The Motel*—accidentally discovering over social media that she has a long-lost identical twin who was adopted in France!

**PHILIP:** *Abacus* is about the only bank that was ever penalized after the financial crisis, a small family-run bank in New York's Chinatown. *Minding the Gap* made Bing Liu one of the hottest rising directors in Hollywood.

**PHIL**: *Origin Story* is Kulap Vilaysack's brilliant journey to find her biological father, which she documented on film. It's a must-watch.

**Vietnamerica: A Family's Journey (2011); Ms. Marvel: No Normal (2014); Pashmina (2017); The Best We Could Do (2018); New Agents of Atlas: War of the Realms (2019)**

**JEFF:** Essential graphic novels. *Vietnamerica* and *The Best We Could Do* are lovely takes on family histories by Vietnamese American artist-writers. *Ms. Marvel: No Normal* is what introduced Kamala Khan, the first Muslim superhero, to the Marvel Universe.

PHIL: *Pashmina,* about a girl coming to terms with her family's secret history, tells a different kind of Indian American story. And *New Agents of Atlas* showcases Greg Pak's all–Asian American superhero team, who come together for dim sum and also to save the world!

### The Interview (2014)

JEFF: In *The Interview,* Randall Park plays Kim Jong-Un and he is fantastic in it, but this film came out as we were shooting the first season of *Fresh Off the Boat.* Everyone was super freaked out, including Randall, that North Korean spies were going to kill us all. It was wild how much of an outsized impact this relatively small film had on geopolitical matters.

PHIL: The movie led North Korea to hack Sony, so all this dirt came out and we could see what Hollywood says about us behind our back—including the fact that Aaron Sorkin, who was supposed to write the script of this movie about high-frequency traders called Flash Boys, emailed Sony to say, "There are no Asian movie stars. You can't make this with Asians."

PHILIP: Right. He was like, "If we're going to do this, everybody's white, right?" Again: disappointed but not surprised.

### Allegiance (2015); Vietgone (2015); Cambodian Rock Band (2018); Soft Power (2018)

PHIL: This was an incredible decade for Asian American musical theater. *Allegiance* was George Takei's dream project, inspired by his childhood incarceration with his family during World War II.

JEFF: *Vietgone* and *Cambodian Rock Band* brought different Southeast Asian family stories to life, through rap and rock. And *Soft Power* is David Henry Hwang's masterpiece.

PHIL: It's basically a riff on *The King and I,* with the genders swapped and Hillary Clinton as the king. Not joking, it's amazing.

### Selfie (2014); Fresh Off the Boat (2014); Dr. Ken (2015); Kim's Convenience (2016)

PHILIP: *Selfie* only aired for like seven episodes before it was moved to streaming and then canceled, but it has a huge cult following: John Cho and Karen Gillan in a rom-com!

JEFF: But if *Selfie* hadn't been canceled, we might not have gotten *Fresh Off the Boat*! *FOTB* took over *Selfie*'s slot.

PHIL: I forgot that! *Dr. Ken* is based on Ken Jeong's real life as a medical doctor before turning to comedy. And *Kim's Convenience,* based on a play by Ins Choi, was on Canadian TV but it became a big global hit on Netflix. And then Simu Liu got cast as a Marvel superhero!

JEFF: Remember when these three Asian family sitcoms were on at once? Now they're all gone.

### Into the Badlands (2015); Warrior (2019)

PHIL: With these two shows, we finally had legit martial arts on TV for the first time in decades.

JEFF: *Into the Badlands* put Daniel Wu into a dystopian future. *Warrior* was Bruce Lee's posthumous idea about a fighter looking for his sister in Gold Rush San Francisco. No one saw it because it was on Cinemax!

PHILIP: So everyone's going to discover it four years from now and be like, yo, that was great, what happened, where is it now? Whoops, too late. (Wait: a miracle—HBO Max saved it!)

### Make It Pop (2015); Andi Mack (2017); Hala (2019); PEN15 (2019)

PHIL: This was a decade for Asian American coming-of-age stories. *Make It Pop* was a Nickelodeon dram-com about three Asian American girls trying to . . . start a K-pop band? Over on Disney, you had *Andi Mack,* which was about an Asian American girl who finds out her elder sister is actually her mom.

JEFF: *Hala* is about a skateboarding Pakistani American teen girl. And *PEN15* stars and was cocreated by thirtysomething comedian Maya Erskine, who plays a tween version of herself. It's brilliant and super-awkward.

**The Sympathizer (2015); The Leavers (2017); Little Fires Everywhere (2017); Dear America: Notes of an Undocumented Citizen (2018); On Earth We're Briefly Gorgeous (2019)**

**JEFF:** The 2010s' necessary lit library. *The Sympathizer* won Viet T. Nguyen the Pulitzer Prize. Lisa Ko's *The Leavers* was a finalist for the National Book Award. *Dear America* is Jose Antonio Vargas's memoir of growing up undocumented in America. *On Earth We're Briefly Gorgeous* is Ocean Vuong's breakthrough, a fragmentary semi-memoir. And *Little Fires Everywhere,* Celeste Ng's second novel, about mothers fighting for custody over an adopted Chinese girl, was a huge bestseller and a Hulu miniseries.

**Crazy Ex-Girlfriend (2015); The Good Place (2016); Single Parents (2018)**

**PHIL:** Three different series, all giving TV a new take on Asian guys—the Asian dudebro. *Crazy Ex-Girlfriend* featured Vincent Rodriguez III, playing a Filipino American—we actually get to see his huge extended family. Manny Jacinto in *The Good Place* plays Jason Mendoza as almost too dumb to function. Jake Choi is a sweet out-of-his-depth single dad in *Single Parents*.

**Ali Wong: Baby Cobra (2016)**

**PHIL:** This special launched Ali Wong into superstardom, and inspired dozens of people to costume themselves or their kids in Ali's signature striped maternity dress for Halloween!

**The Big Sick (2017); Searching (2018)**

**PHILIP:** Two low-budget movies that blew up expectations at the box office! Kumail Nanjiani and his wife, Emily V. Gordon, wrote a fictional version of their actual relationship—which was interrupted when Gordon had to be put into an induced coma!—and were nominated for an Academy Award for Best Screenplay. And in *Searching,* John Cho stars as a dad looking for his daughter the modern way: by Googling her.

---

* See page 448, "She, Rose"

**Rogue One (2016); Star Wars: The Last Jedi (2017)**

**JEFF:** Asians finally arrive in the Star Wars Universe. Where were we before? It took us a while to dig out of that Sarlacc pit.

**PHIL:** *The Last Jedi* gave us Kelly Marie Tran!*

**Ghost in the Shell (2017)**

**PHILIP:** The nail in the coffin for whitewashing. Scarlett Johansson ran out of arguments to explain why she was playing a Japanese woman, and the movie was a huge flop.

**To All the Boys I've Loved Before (2018); Always Be My Maybe (2019)**

**JEFF:** Two Netflix rom-coms, two giant hits. *To All the Boys,* based on Jenny Han's bestseller, was one of the most watched films in Netflix history.

**PHIL:** *Always Be My Maybe* was wished into existence by fans after Ali Wong said she wanted to do a rom-com with Randall Park! It's so good. And it made us fall in love with Keanu again.

**The Farewell (2019); Hustlers (2019); Parasite (2019)**

**JEFF:** These three films made it clear that Asians were in Hollywood to stay. *The Farewell* was Lulu Wang's autobiographical story of her family's refusal to tell her grandma that she had terminal cancer. It confirmed director Wang and Awkwafina as superstars. *Hustlers* was Constance Wu's team-up with Jennifer Lopez, playing strippers who scam clients—it was a huge success and showed Constance can do anything.

**PHIL:** *Parasite* changed the game. An Asian movie winning Best Picture. An Asian winning Best Director. That does not happen. Until now.

**The Terror: Infamy (2019)**

**PHIL:** For its second season, AMC's horror anthology was set in a Japanese American internment camp during World War II. Made you wonder why no one ever thought of the idea before.

# Asian American YouTube Crosses Over

BY PHILIP WANG

**BY THE END** of the 2000s, YouTube had begun to completely shift the terrain of media. There was no way to easily categorize what was happening, but in the decade that followed, what was once a chaotic Wild West of content began to take shape as a legitimate and lucrative platform. The term "new media" was coined. Networks were formed. Advertising dollars began pouring in, and Asian content creators began to learn how to succeed in a brand-new system. A growing number began to cross over into the mainstream, because digital content *was* the new mainstream. At the beginning of YouTube's rise, Hollywood didn't know what to do with it, but by the 2010s, they knew: YouTube was where they'd discover some of their most innovative and interesting new talent. There was no more accidental fame, no more inexplicable novelty. Creators were joining the platform with intent, following models they'd seen before, and taking their achievements to another level by forging new and innovative paths.

## RocketJump

**WHO:** Freddie Wong

**STYLE:** Action comedy, special FX

**BREAKOUT VIDEO:** *Real Life Portal Gun*, 2010

**CURRENT SUBSCRIBERS:** 9 million

**SIGNATURE QUOTE:** "So Man Created RocketJump, and It Was Leet"

As one of the first YouTube creators to consistently go viral with his special-effects-laden videos, one-time *Guitar Hero* champion Wong built an empire with comedy videos satirizing games, gamers, and gaming tropes. In 2013, he launched a production company, RocketJump, and created the popular web series *Video Game High School*. Along the way, mainstream media discovered him: He made a video with Key and Peele, and he's been a guest on *Conan O'Brien* and *Jimmy Kimmel*. His brother Jimmy Wong is also a YouTuber (and was a star of Disney's live-action version of *Mulan*).

## JusReign

**WHO:** Jasmeet Singh Raina

**STYLE:** Sketch and musical comedy

**BREAKOUT VIDEO:** *Shit White Guys Say to Brown Guys*, 2012

**CURRENT SUBSCRIBERS:** 1 million

**SIGNATURE QUOTE:** "I'm brown, I wear a turban, old white ladies are scared of me"

Indian Canadian JusReign's offbeat and observational humor has made his videos extremely unique and shareable, both within the Desi community and beyond. He is currently writing, producing, and starring in a new series, *Late Bloomer,* executive produced by comedian Russell Peters for the CBC.

## Ryan's World

**WHO:** Ryan Guan

**STYLE:** Unboxing

**CURRENT SUBSCRIBERS:** 28 million

**SIGNATURE QUOTE:** "WHOAAAAAAA!"

The most subscribed-to Asian American YouTube channel, produced by the highest-paid YouTube creator, stars a nine-year-old boy from Texas. With over 45 BILLION views since he launched his channel in 2015, Ryan built a monster video empire before even hitting double digits in age. His simple but wildly popular unboxing videos led to toy lines at Walmart and Target and Ryan-branded video games. He currently stars in a TV show on Nick Jr., already in its third season!

## Superwoman

**WHO:** Lilly Singh

**STYLE:** Character sketch comedy

**BREAKOUT VIDEO:** *How Girls Get Ready*, 2013

**CURRENT SUBSCRIBERS:** 15 million

**SIGNATURE QUOTE:** "What up, everyone, it's ya gurl Superwoman!"

Toronto native Singh went from making videos about her Indian parents and culture to becoming the first woman of color late-night host on network TV! In 2019, she was tapped to host *A Little Late with Lilly Singh* on NBC, and can now be frequently seen making videos with celebrity pals like Will Smith, Zendaya, and The Rock.

## Liza Koshy

**WHO:** Elizabeth Shaila Koshy
**STYLE:** Comedy sketches
**CURRENT SUBSCRIBERS:** 18 million
**SIGNATURE QUOTE:** "Little Brown girl, OUT!"

Koshy's ascent actually began on Vine, Twitter's short-lived short-video platform. After amassing 7 million followers there, she transitioned to YouTube, where she became the fastest person ever to reach 10 million subscribers. With this powerful fan base behind her, she went on to create content with Will Smith, Alicia Keys, and Barack and Michelle Obama. As an actor and producer, she's hosted the revivals of MTV's *TRL* and Nickelodeon's *Double Dare,* and starred in series and movies on Hulu, YouTube Originals, and Netflix, and was part of the Emmy Award—winning documentary *Creators for Change*.

## Bretman Rock

**WHO:** Bretman Rock Sacayanan
**STYLE:** Beauty, comedy, vlogs
**BREAKOUT VIDEO:** *How to Contour,* 2015
**CURRENT SUBSCRIBERS:** 8.3 million
**SIGNATURE QUOTE:** "Gooooood motherfuckin morning, bitch!"

Philippines-born, Hawaii-raised Bretman Rock was a star just waiting to be noticed. Once he began vlogging, his humor and wild personality drew millions of followers, fast-tracking him onto *Time*'s "30 Most Influential Teens" list, and winning him the Beauty Influencer Award at the 45th People's Choice Awards. He now has a show on MTV, *MTV Following: Bretman Rock.*

## BuzzFeed Creators

**WHO:** Steven Lim, Eugene Lee Yang, Ashly Perez
**STYLE:** Food, hosting, comedy

BuzzFeed ruled the video world in the mid-2010s, and among their strongest creators were three Asian Americans. Creating content on BuzzFeed's highly demanding schedule, the trio ended up producing the platform's most successful shows and videos. Series like Lim's *Worth It,* Yang's *Try Guys,* and Perez's *Unfortunatly Ashly* set the tone for a new wave of YouTube content.

### AsianGirlSquad

**WHO:** LaurDIY (Lauren Riihimaki), MissRemiAshten (Remi Ashten), MissTiffanyMa (Tiffany Ma), Mia Soyoko

**STYLE:** Lifestyle creators/girl gang

**CURRENT SUBSCRIBERS:** LaurDIY (8.8 million), MissRemiAshten (2.5 million), MissTiffanyMa (1.85 million), Mia Sayoko (4.4 million)

The 2010s saw the birth of a new tribe on YouTube: the lifestyle influencer. These YouTubers didn't just do makeup reviews, or provide fashion tips, or show off their travel experiences—they did all of that and everything in between, with millions looking to them as big sisters and celebrities, sharing the intimate details of their lives, from meal prep to relationship breakups, while also teaching crafts and life hacks. At the forefront of this movement were members of the AsianGirlSquad, a quartet of these personalities who frequently also united to support one another and spend Girl Time together.

### Fung Bros

**WHO:** David and Andrew Fung

**STYLE:** Culture and food commentary, music

**BREAKOUT VIDEO:** *Things Asian Parents Do*, 2013

**CURRENT SUBSCRIBERS:** 2.2 million

**SIGNATURE QUOTE:** "Let's go!"

Originally from Seattle, the Fungs relocated to L.A. in 2010, and subsequently immersed themselves in the culture of the San Gabriel Valley. Leveraging their love of hip-hop, hoops, and food, the Fungs established themselves as culinary tastemakers. In 2015, they landed a show on A&E's FYI channel, *Broke Bites: What the Fung*.

### ClothesEncounters

**WHO:** Jenn Im

**STYLE:** Fashion, beauty, vlogs

**BREAKOUT VIDEO:** *Room Tour*, 2012

**CURRENT SUBSCRIBERS:** 3 million

**SIGNATURE QUOTE:** "Hey everyone, it's Jenn!" Im's path to success has served as a model for a generation of fashion and beauty vloggers. Rising to popularity while still in college with "fashion haul" and Outfit of the Day videos, she went on to start her own makeup and clothing lines, setting the bar for self-made social media influencers.

### Joji

**WHO:** George Kusunoki Miller

**STYLE:** Comedy (retired), music

**CURRENT SUBSCRIBERS:** 7.6 million (Filthy Frank); 1.3 million (Joji)

**SIGNATURE QUOTE:** "You want some tap water?"

Did you know the Harlem Shake challenge that took over the world in 2013 was started by a Japanese Australian YouTube creator then going by the name of Filthy Frank? While Miller's content could be controversial, there's no doubt that he left his mark on Internet culture. Focusing on his music persona, Joji, beginning in 2017, Miller performed on *The Tonight Show with Jimmy Fallon* and went on to become a platinum-selling artist after signing with 88rising.

# The Seven Stages of PSY

**BY EUNY HONG, ILLUSTRATED BY JAMIE NOGUCHI**

**PARK JAE-SANG**, better known as **PSY**, is what you'd get if you took the template for a Korean pop star and reversed it. The loose-cannon goofball rapper is more **POTATO-SHAPED** than willowy, and at the time of his global breakout was the ripe age of **35**—by K-pop standards, practically dead. He also had the temerity to write his own songs, eschewing the neatly packaged bubblegum confections of the country's expert pop producers, and was what Koreans call a ddan-dda-ra—a phrase mimicking the sound of a pompous trumpet. When

record execs and culture ministers were considering what musical exports might best serve the nation's soft-power needs, PSY wasn't even on the radar. Which is why no one was more shocked than Koreans when he burst out of YouTube and into the record books with his video for "**GANGNAM STYLE**," the first in history ever to reach **ONE BILLION VIEWS**. For better or for worse, over several months in 2012, PSY was everywhere. Here's how the "Gangnam style" phenomenon evolved, in **SEVEN EVOLUTIONARY STAGES**:

**STAGE 1: "CHUBBY LITTLE NEWCOMER"**

*JANUARY 7, 2012: PSY* MAKES HIS *INTERNATIONAL DEBUT* IN JAPAN, WHERE HE HOLDS UP A SIGN SAYING "IN KOREA, I'M A FAMOUS SINGER KNOWN FOR DRIVING AUDIENCES WILD, BUT HERE TODAY, I'M JUST A CHUBBY LITTLE NEWCOMER."

**STAGE 2: "TUBE NOOB"**

*JULY 15, 2012: "GANGNAM STYLE"* DEBUTS ON YOUTUBE. PSY'S SATIRE OF THE *KOREAN ELITE*—TO WHICH HE BELONGED AS SON OF A *TECH TYCOON*—POKES FUN AT BOTH OLD AND NEW SEOUL.

**STAGE 3: "WTF?"**

*JULY 29, 2012:* RAPPER *T-PAIN* TWEETS ABOUT "GANGNAM STYLE"; ENDLESS RETWEETS FOLLOW. NON-KOREANS HAD NO IDEA WHAT TO MAKE OF PSY. TO BE FAIR, KOREANS DIDN'T EITHER.

**STAGE 4: "THE CIRCUS"**

PSY IS PARADED AROUND AS A KIND OF *EXOTIC CURIOSITY*, TEACHING HIS SIGNATURE *HORSE DANCE* TO EVERY MAJOR TALK SHOW HOST IN AMERICA, AND A LOT OF THE MINOR ONES.

**STAGE 5: "PHENOMENON"**

PSY BECOMES THE "*IT BOY*" OF GLOBAL ENTERTAINMENT—AND ON *DECEMBER 21, 2012,* "GANGNAM STYLE" BECOMES THE FIRST VIDEO TO GET *1 BILLION VIEWS* ON YOUTUBE.

**STAGE 6: "BACKLASH BEGINS"**

"GANGNAM STYLE" HITS *MAX SATURATION*. PSY'S WONDERFUL PISTACHIOS *SUPER BOWL AD* IS THE STRAW THAT BREAKS THE INVISIBLE HORSE'S BACK. HIS 2013 FOLLOW-UP, "*GENTLEMAN*," GETS "ONLY" 900 MILLION VIEWS. "*HANGOVER*"—HIS 2014 SNOOP DOGG COLLAB—GETS 200 MILLION.

**STAGE 7: "THE LEGACY"**

PSY DOESN'T *DISAPPEAR*, HE JUST *RETURNS TO KOREA*. MEANWHILE, "GANGNAM STYLE" PRIMES THE WEST FOR K-IDOLS LIKE *BTS* AND *BLACKPINK*.

AND JUST BY BEING AN *ASIAN GUY IN THE LIMELIGHT*, PSY ARGUABLY HELPED PAVE THE WAY FOR THE POP CULTURE EMERGENCE OF *ASIAN AMERICANS*. BECAUSE IF WHITE AUDIENCES CAN EMBRACE A WEIRDO LIKE PSY, MAYBE *ASIAN FACES* AREN'T BOX OFFICE POISON AFTER ALL?

## CLAWING BACK AT TIGER MOM:

# How Amy Chua's Parenting Memoir Triggered Vitriol and Self-Reckoning

**BY EUNY HONG**

*The Battle Hymn of the Tiger Mother,* the 2011 parenting memoir written by Yale Law professor Amy Chua, forever changed the global discourse not only on child rearing, but also on cultural differences and multiple identities. Chua's book was a sassy, tongue-in-cheek reflection of how she reconciled her Chinese upbringing with her American values, as well as those of her Jewish American husband, while bringing up a pair of strong-willed daughters who upended everything Chua thought she knew. The book addressed a question that's at the core of the American experience: How do you decide which lessons inherited from your immigrant parents are worth passing along to the next generation?

At least, that's the book Chua *thought* she'd written. The public disagreed—and came after her with pitchforks. Chua's central parenting premise was what she called the Virtuous Circle: "What Chinese parents understand is that nothing is fun until you're good at it. To get good at anything you have to work, and children on their own never want to work, which is why it is crucial to override their preferences." Western parents, she argued, placed too much value on boosting a child's self-esteem—rather than giving the child the tools to *earn* a reason to feel good about themselves.

At the same time, critics felt that Chua's approach to instilling the Virtuous Circle was harsh: rejecting the birthday card her then-four-year-old younger daughter Lulu made for her as showing insufficient effort, threatening to burn Lulu's stuffed animals after an imperfect piano rendition, and of course, "no play dates, no sleepovers, no school plays; and no complaining about not being in school plays."

Some saw Chua's book as throwing down a gauntlet—or a grenade. According to Chua, she received almost "immediate death threats," with flames erupting on all sides: Western parents who felt their parenting style was being attacked, white people who accused her of anti-white bigotry, survivors of child abuse, and of course, legions of second-generation Asian Americans who recounted the scars of their own tiger upbringing. Some defenders of Chua, however, did point out that humming beneath the rage at Chua was a xenophobic fear of Chinese hegemony, as could be seen in some of the more patently racist reactions to the *Wall Street Journal*'s "extract" of the book, headlined "Why Chinese Mothers Are Superior."

Despite the controversy—or because of it—the book sold like New Year's rice cakes. Here's a look at how the Tiger Mom discourse played out in public.

1. The world first learned of Tiger Mom through a *Wall Street Journal* "extract" from her memoir titled "Why Chinese Mothers Are Superior" (January 8, 2011). As a result of that article, a war cry ensued before the book was even released (January 11, 2011), though Chua revealed to *Rise* coauthor Jeff Yang in the *San Francisco Chronicle* that the article and its headline were edited differently than she expected: "I was very surprised. They didn't even hint . . . that I get my comeuppance, and retreat from this very strict Chinese parenting model." She goes on the talk-show circuit to explain to people that she didn't intend for it to be a parenting "how-to."

2. "It was the 'Little White Donkey' incident that pushed many readers over the edge," wrote *Time* magazine's Annie Murphy Paul (January 20, 2011)—the one in which Chua shares how she forced her daughter Lulu to practice a piano piece under threat of burning all her stuffed animals. On the other hand, there were those who rallied around the importance Chua placed on practice, practice, practice, including Husna Haq, who wrote in the *Christian Science Monitor,* "Having been raised by Indian parents, I'm not so outraged. How many families have graduated all four kids as valedictorian . . . followed, four years later, with four more *summa cum laude* college grads? Clearly, my parents did something right."

3. In an op-ed entitled "Amy Chua Is a Wimp" (January 17, 2011), *New York Times* columnist David Brooks wrote: "Practicing a piece of music for four hours requires focused attention, but it is nowhere near as cognitively demanding as a sleepover with 14-year-old girls" (January 17, 2011). Also in the *Times,* Janet Maslin's book review called *Tiger Mother* a "diabolically well-packaged, highly readable screed ostensibly about the art of parenting. In truth, Ms. Chua's memoir is about one little narcissist's book-length search for happiness" (January 17, 2011).

THE COLBERT REPORT

AMY CHUA

SEASON 7 E 14 · 01/25/2011

Amy Chua explains how she tried to raise her two daughters the same way her strict Chinese immigrant

## Betty Ming Liu ⑥

### Parents like Amy Chua are the reason why Asian-Americans like me are in therapy

**≡ ▐HUFFPOST▐**

⑦ **Tiger Mother Haunts Obama's SOTU**

**≡ NEW YORK POST ⑤**

## Why I love my strict Chinese mom

**4.** Chua appeared on *The Colbert Report* (January 25, 2011) for a fairly friendly interview, in which Stephen Colbert posited that Chua was tapping into American xenophobia and fear of losing its superpower status. "There's a political component here," he said. "We're terrified of the Chinese, ever since the opening of the Olympic Games. We think they've got more discipline than we do!" His take on the American response: "Mothers across America, they think you're wrong but privately think maybe you're right, and doubt how they're raising their own children."

**5.** Chua's elder daughter, Sophia Chua-Rubenfeld, 18 years old at the time, penned an op-ed, "Why I love my strict Chinese mom" for the *New York Post,* framed as a letter to her Tiger Mom. She wrote, "One problem is that some people don't get your humor," but she acknowledged, "I admit it: Having you as a mother was no tea party." The piece helped to soften the public's view of Chua . . . for about five seconds.

**6.** Asian Americans who hated their Tiger Mom upbringings began to speak out, including former *New York Daily News* columnist Betty Ming Liu, who wrote, "Parents like Amy Chua are the reason why Asian Americans like me are in therapy."

**7.** President Barack Obama, while not naming Chua, was widely thought to have alluded to the book in his January 25, 2011, "State of the Union" address. Appealing to Republicans who wanted to cut back on investment in research and education, he warned that in doing so, they would be letting China get ahead: "This is our generation's Sputnik moment," he said. "At stake is whether new jobs and industries take root in this country or somewhere else . . . Just recently, China became home to the world's largest private solar research facility, and the world's fastest computer." But was tiger mothering the solution or the threat?

R
I
S
E

# The Evolution of Asian Memes

### BY PHILIP WANG

**A MEME IS** an idea that has a life of its own—replicating itself across a population or social platform by encouraging people to share it. On the Internet they can take many forms: widely replicated stunts (the "ice bucket challenge"), frequently recycled phrases ("I'm not crying, you're crying"), or viral hashtags (#Oscars-SoWhite). But the most common is the image meme—quirky pics of famous or anonymous individuals that are shared again and again with new captions by the extremely online. Many early image memes treated Asians as the butt of racist jokes, but as Asian American influence over the Internet grew, image memes evolved into a way of reclaiming stereotypes and making inside jokes that only other Asians might appreciate, and finally as a means to fight back. Sharing image memes was actually the original purpose of the Facebook megagroup Subtle Asian Traits, which has evolved into one of the largest Asian diasporic communities on the Internet. Image memes also served as a viral outreach tool for Andrew Yang's insurgent 2020 campaign for president. So don't sleep on memes: sure, they generate laughs, but they've also united millions around the world, powered political campaigns, and spread awareness of important issues. Not bad for a bunch of clip art!

## PHASE ONE
## That's Racist!

The dark side of image memes is that—especially in the early years of social media—they were often at our expense, featuring wildly racist depictions of Asians, with captions that reinforced ugly attacks on our names, our food, and our looks. When anyone can slap a new slogan on an image and throw it anonymously onto the Internet, it probably shouldn't come as a surprise that the worst in people will float to the surface.

## Leaning into Stereotypes

As Asian Americans became a larger part of the cultural conversation, the focus of Asian memes evolved to incorporate perceptions of Asians as geeky grinds with overbearing parents—in short, the model minority. What's interesting is that many of these memes were shared not just by non-Asians but by Asians as well, who tended to treat them more as rueful, self-deprecating critique. The most popular of these image memes: **"High Expectations Asian Father,"** the disembodied, disappointed face of South Korean actor Jeon Mu-Song on a geometric green background, who, beginning in 2010, served as the Internet's favorite avatar for Asian parental angst. Joining HEAF in the Asian meme nuclear family the following year, after the publication of Amy Chua's controversial book *Battle Hymn of the Tiger Mother*: **"Tiger Mom,"** a stock photo of a forbidding Asian mother against a tiger-stripe background, whose quips tended to be more about control and emotional unavailability, in contrast to HEAF's focus on academic achievement. Stock photos of **nerdy-looking Asians** were frequently used to portray Asians as embracing the values of HEAF/Tiger Mom and prizing grades and studying above

all things—although a countermeme, **"Asian Baller,"** also became popular, using a picture of Korean American design school student Tim Kim in the midst of a pickup basketball game to illustrate the idea of Asian kids who wistfully aspire to a different, less academic destiny.

## Disrupting and Reclaiming Stereotypes

By the late 2010s, social media platforms like Instagram's **AsiansNeverDie** and Facebook's **Subtle Asian Traits** had risen to prominence on the backs of a never-ending feed of humorous, heartfelt, and in some cases, painfully honest memes. The content shared to their members tended to be inside jokes uniting Asians within a common cultural struggle—often incorporating stereotypical ideas, but presenting them as social commentary rather than just for laughs. As Kerry Kang, a cofounder of Subtle Asian Traits, says, "The rise of Asian memes in our culture is happening because our generation has learned to actually embrace some of these stereotypes as a symbol of our shared heritage and upbringing experiences. And that's powerful."

Some common meme formats shared on these platforms include **"starter packs"**—assemblies of pictures that define an Asian subculture. Commentaries on **cultural duality**—for example, memes about being a "traditional" Asian by day and a hard-partying ABG (Asian Baby Girl) by night. And, of course, memes about the **uncanny youthfulness of Asians** ("Asian don't raisin"/"gold don't fold").

## Weaponized Memes

Somewhere along the way, Asians also began using our meme-generating skills to switch targets from making fun of ourselves toward calling out microaggressions, social double standards, and white privilege. Memes became a means not just to generate a quick laugh, but to strike out at people and institutions who were guilty of misrepresenting Asians, and to seize back agency over our cultural narrative.

# Other Memes

### ANIMEMES

As anime rose in mainstream popularity, **anime-based memes** became increasingly popular, with the Internet-savvy anime community drawing from an endless well of characters and content to create iconic reactions.

### "Confused Anime Guy," 2011

From 1991 anime TV series, *The Brave Fighter of Sun Fightbird*

### "Man of Culture," 2016

From a 2010 episode of *Arakawa Under the Bridge*

### "Surprised Pikachu," 2018

From 1997 *Pokemon,* Season 1, Episode 10, "Bulbasaur and the Hidden Village"

## CELEBRITY EXPRESSION MEMES

Other popular Asian memes include just barely recognizable "rage-comic"-style contour drawings, derived from photos, of Asian celebrities, some of which have become part of the Internet's fundamental meme vocabulary.

"Bitch please," 2010: NBA Hall of Famer Yao Ming

"My brain is full of fucks," 2009: global action star Jackie Chan

## K-POP FANCAMS

More recently, K-pop fans have joined the fun, creating their own homage memes of favorite K-pop "biases" and editing together "fancams"—edited videos of their favorite K-pop artists in iconic performances—that were initially used to boost trending K-pop hashtags, but more recently have become a social media weapon to troll racists and hijack alt-right tweet threads.

K-Pop Fancams vs. The Man

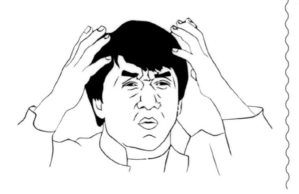

# APPRECIATION OR APPROPRIATION?

BY JEFF YANG

**IT'S A PERENNIAL** debate that pops up every time someone non-Asian (and usually, famous) lectures us all on "the right way" to do something traditionally Asian or shares a "reinvented" expression of Asian heritage; incorporates "Asian-inspired" symbols, patterns, or shapes into designs; or engages in general dumbassery related to ethnic-specific customs, costumes, or communication styles: Is this a flattering homage, or an arrogant act of cultural piracy?

The categories that most commonly trigger controversy are basically the "four Fs":

- **FASHION:** qipaos, kimonos, or saris; nonsense character tattoos
- **FOOD:** ridiculous fusion fare; "upscale" versions of food that was eaten for survival
- **FAITH:** mimicry or mockery of religious iconography or practices
- **FOLKWAYS:** clumsy "Westernizations" of Asian legends, heroes, heritage art forms, and traditional pastimes

But it's not actually that difficult to avoid stumbling into cultural appropriation—it just takes some humility, sincerity, and willingness to put in work; we've even created the following flowchart to guide your way.

## Flowchart

**START HERE** →

**Are you the original creator of the thing you're putting out into the world?**

— YES → **It's your thing. Do what you wanna do.** *"Proper credit should be assigned for this quote to the Isley Brothers, the classic Black R&B group who were an iconic part of Motown's success*

— NO → **Have you reached out to partner with the original creator(s)?**

— NO → **Do it. Come on. It's not that hard. And it's important.** — GOT IT, WILL DO → **Copying of work of marginalized creators happens all the time, because the perception is that if you're nonwhite, poor, immigrant, indigenous, untrained, "amateur," or otherwise not yet validated by the establishment, your work isn't seen as real.**

**THE WORK IS NOT TIED TO A SINGLE INDIVIDUAL THAT I CAN PLAUSIBLY CONTACT**

— YES, BUT THEY'RE NOT INTERESTED OR AVAILABLE → **Sometimes reaching out is impossible, because of the passage of time or the unavailability of access to original creators. If you choose to proceed, remember that "disinterested/unavailable" people may still react to what you do after the fact.**

→ **Are the original creator(s) being harmed by what you're doing?**

— NO → **Do you meaningfully share an identity, culture or heritage with the creator(s) of the work?**

— YES →

**THEY'RE WORKING ON IT!**

342

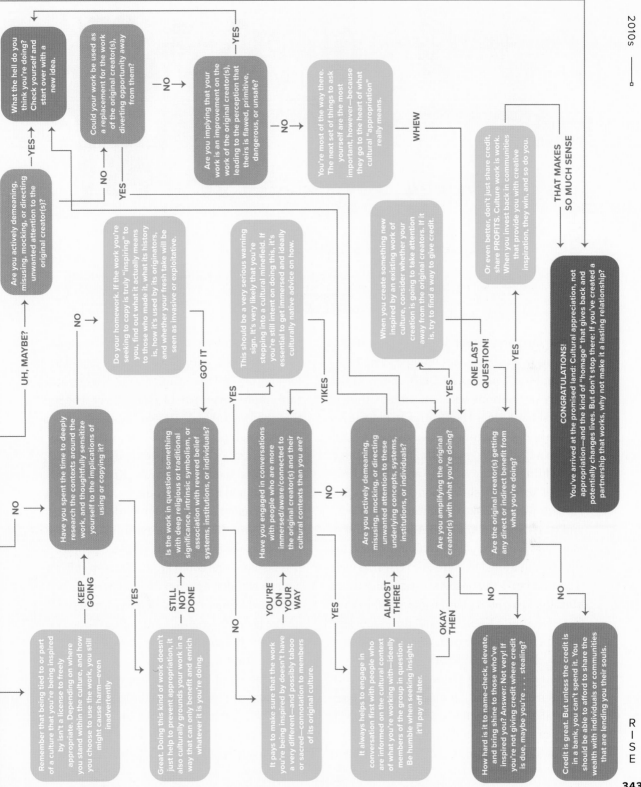

# Hallyu Like Me Now

The Rise of Korean Pop Culture in America (and Everywhere Else around the World)

BY EUNY HONG

ILLUSTRATED BY JEF CASTRO

**LOOK AROUND, AND** you'll see that BTS is the world's most popular boy band, despite the fact that they sing in a language that is native to only two nations on earth. In fact, they're the first band since the Beatles to have three albums land together on the Billboard 200 within a 12-month span. Streaming channels are fighting over the rights to air *subtitled* versions of Korean TV shows. Bong-Joon Ho's film *Parasite* won the 2020 Oscar for Best Picture—and Best Director, and Best Adapted Screenplay, and also, as almost an offhanded flex, the Best International Feature Film Oscar as well. Korean food is the hottest thing (sometimes literally) to hit both high cuisine and the street food scene, and Korean beauty products now have their own shelves at CVS and Sephora.

It's safe to say that South Korea now has a reputation for being a place where cool stuff comes from. And yet, just 70 years ago—after the end of the Korean War—Korea was one of the poorest nations in the world.

How did we get from there to here? Well, it wasn't an accident. South Korea's government and private industry have spent the last quarter-century collaborating to build this pop culture empire, in pursuit of a soft-power strategy that they've dubbed "Hallyu," or the "Korean Wave." Their plan was to raise the nation's geopolitical and economic profile by encouraging a global feeding frenzy for Korean entertainment and lifestyle products, and the plan has succeeded beyond their wildest expectations. It's not the first time nation-states have tried to make friends and influence people in this fashion; one could argue that pop culture has always been America's secret weapon. But never has a blueprint for global cultural pollination been so programmatically and bureaucratically designed (which makes it even more stunning that it's worked).

The seeds of Hallyu were planted in 1994, when a South Korean economic commission published a white paper pointing out that the export revenue of the film *Jurassic Park* was the equivalent of 1.5 million Hyundai cars. The paper's conclusion, which then-president Kim Young-sam vociferously endorsed, was: *Why can't we become pop culture exporters, too? Why are we focusing on getting our hands dirty with assembly line crap like* 멍청이*\**?

So the South Korean government began to set things in motion, initially on a small scale, doing things like giving the Korean Consulate in Hong Kong the budget to translate a hit Korean drama, *What's Love All About,* into Cantonese. And the Korean pop culture export plan would likely have remained a half-assed effort had it not been for an epic regional emergency: the Asian Financial Crisis of 1997–1998.

Beginning in Thailand, the crisis felled most of the rest of emerging Asia like dominoes. When it hit Korea, the nation was sent into a tailspin of debt, forcing the nation in 1997 to take out an IMF loan under extremely harsh stipulations. President Kim declared the day of the loan signing a "Day of National Mourning."

Two things came out of the crisis. The first was that the South Korean government decided it needed to rip up its existing heavy-metal economic blueprints and reorient around pop and electronica—that is to say, culture export and technology. The government made huge investments in creating a high-speed Internet network that gave residents of Greater Seoul, e.g., about half of the country's population, the fastest average Internet speeds in the world.

The second was that a new generation of young upstarts was handed the reins over major parts of the culture economy, partly because the seniority system that dominates the Korean business world had been disrupted by the crisis, and partly because the government's injection of money into culture and tech sectors led to projects being greenlit even for

*	schmucks

the more eccentric talents in Korean entertainment. With money and relatively little supervision, a wave of creators went nuts—unleashing a wild variety of unexpectedly cool works on an unsuspecting nation.

With this creative renaissance running at full tilt, Korea decided it had what it took to build an entire ecosystem of cool, pushing on a wide array of fronts: music, television, film, even cuisine. In the late 1990s, the Korean Ministry of Culture created a special division just for the promotion of these four areas, while the government set aside a sizable slush fund to use for "emergency" pop culture measures (like bailing out the music industry when its survival was threatened by piracy, or building a giant government-subsidized K-pop arena). By the 2000s, the Korean Cool industry had become a self-feeding beast: it no longer required government support to sustain itself, though the government is always ready to jump in if a pop culture emergency erupts.

By the 2010s, this had led to a strange new reality for Asian Americans, in which Asians—including and maybe especially Asian men!—had become aspirational standards of beauty, and people of all backgrounds were learning to speak Korean, not because their parents were forcing them to, but because they wanted to be able to sing along to their favorite songs or even become K-pop stars themselves. And why not pursue that dream? Some of the most popular K-pop idols in the business aren't native Korean, including half of the blockbuster girl band Blackpink (Rosé is a Korean New Zealander, and Lisa is Thai). If Hong Kong action films started the process of making Asians cool and anime brought it to the next level, Hallyu could be what finally seals the deal.

# GENERASIAN GAP

2010s

BY TESS PARAS

NATHAN RAMOS PARK, SONAL SHAH, TESS PARAS,
AND PHILIP WANG; PHOTOGRAPHED BY MOLLY PAN

The 2010s are a Tale of Two Lewks—crispy or ripped, tailored or draped.

## Dapper Dudes

You're the very picture of a gent, sporting slim, tucked shirts, even slimmer pants, hems cuffed to show some ankle, and those Sperry Top-Siders. Maybe even a smart little fedora (hey, Bruno Mars can pull it off)!

## Boho Beaus

You're always ready for yoga, with your long hair in a man-bun or a short pony. Drop the crotch of those pants, and put that knit beanie on—doesn't matter how hot it is outside. Make sure you have a flannel around your waist. Get the V-neck with a deep V-neck; if you think it's deep enough, make it deeper until your crotch hairs say hi. Basically, wear everything Eugene Lee Yang from BuzzFeed ever wore when he walked around Hollywood.

## Dapper Dames

Everything's soft and satiny, and your shoulders are cold. You've got a full face of makeup. Brows are back. Lipstick is happening. American Apparel has yet to be canceled, and you and your gals look like you're ready to go to the club at all hours. It's always 1:00 a.m. somewhere!

On the opposite side of this look? . . . Uh, oh, we went Boho.

## Boho Belles

Dress for Coachella, or at least like you're Coach-jealous because you didn't go. Hold a T-shirt cutting party with your friends! If you're too anxious with scissors to make your own rips, buy shirts at Forever 21 with holes in them already! Wear bracelets. Not just one— you need a stack. Prayer beads, leather, mix 'em up. Extra-long belts, floral patterns, wild hair, flowy and impractical gauze robes over short-shorts that barely cover up your gender. Now we're talking!

# THE STYLE LIST 2010s

### BY FAWNIA SOO HOO

**BY THE 2010S,** Asian American fashionistas were branching out beyond retail and the runway, and into prominent (or dominant) roles in styling, digital influence, and activism. Here are five Asian Americans who helped fashion converge with media, entertainment, and social justice.

## PRABAL GURUNG

**BEST KNOWN FOR:** The custom-designed red dress that Michelle Obama wore to the White House Correspondents Dinner in 2010

**SIGNATURE LOOK:** Modern femininity with edgy shapes, bold color, and arty prints

**ASIAN INSPIRATION:** His signature cut-out dress silhouette, based on a Nepalese saree Before his 2009 debut at New York Fashion Week, the Nepalese American designer honed his skills apprenticing under Manish Arora. He earned a degree from Parsons School of Design before working at Cynthia Rowley and then as design director at Bill Blass. Upon the launch of his line, international style icons, including Oprah Winfrey, quickly embraced his designs. First Lady Michelle Obama wore a watercolor dress from Gurung's spring 2010 collection while presenting her 2009 inauguration gown to the Smithsonian Institution. In 2021, newly sworn-in Vice President Kamala Harris wore a custom purple dress and jacket to the presidential inaugural prayer service. Gurung is also a philanthropist and activist, regularly speaking out for LGBTQ+ rights, body positivity, and inclusivity.

## JEANNE YANG

**BEST KNOWN FOR:** Jason Momoa's pink velvet Fendi tuxedo (and matching scrunchie) at the 2019 Oscars

**SIGNATURE LOOK:** Expertly tailored suiting, experimental textures, exuberant color play

**ASIAN INSPIRATION:** "A little bit old Korean grandpa with a little bit of badass Japanese" for John Cho's tapered joggers suit by Zegna, which he wore to the 2019 Independent Spirit Awards After considering a career in politics, Los Angeles–raised Korean American Yang pivoted to fashion, first as associate publisher and managing editor of *Detour* magazine, and then as one of the premier men's stylists to the stars, falling into the profession after dressing music videos for Blink-182 and Weezer. She began her working relationship with Keanu Reeves during *The Matrix* promo rounds in 1999, and has continued to reinvigorate the red carpet ever since, while amplifying the personal styles of A-list clients like Jason Momoa, Kumail Nanjiani, Robert Downey Jr., and sweet Alan Kim from the Oscar-nominated *Minari*. Style runs in the family: Yang's brother Ben, a.k.a. "Ben Baller," is a jeweler to the stars, and collaborates with artists like A$AP Rocky for his own personal clothing line, Superism.

## AIMEE SONG

**BEST KNOWN FOR:** Being an influencer before the term "influencer" went mainstream

**SIGNATURE LOOK:** Elevated and eclectic SoCal cool

**ASIAN INSPIRATION:** International Asian bloggers like Bryanboy and Susie Bubble

While still a college freshman studying interior architecture, in 2008, Korean American Song pioneered the digital content creation space with her fashion, travel, and lifestyle blog, "Song of Style." Song became a Fashion Week front-row fixture and street-style star in the early 2010s, and has since built out her influencer empire with numerous brand collaborations, personal jewelry and apparel lines, and two books, *New York Times* bestsellers *Capture Your Style* and *Aimee Song: World of Style*.

## EVA CHEN

**BEST KNOWN FOR:** Her signature #EvaChen-Pose, featuring a designer outfit, bag, and shoes, and fresh fruit

**SIGNATURE LOOK:** Insta-happy street style

**ASIAN INSPIRATION:** Her chic Taiwanese mother, who lent Chen her first Chanel bag

The first head of fashion partnerships at Instagram, Chen is a trailblazer in the convergence of digital, social, and traditional media. As a beauty editor at *Teen Vogue,* Chen gained a substantial Instagram following during the early years of the platform; in 2013, Anna Wintour handpicked the native New Yorker to oversee an e-commerce joint venture for *Lucky* magazine. In 2015, Chen joined Instagram in a role newly created for her—a harbinger of the future of fashion media.

## BOBBY KIM, A.K.A. BOBBY HUNDREDS

**BEST KNOWN FOR:** Creating a community of streetwear devotees. Jonah Hill, and rappers Kid Cudi, Tyler, the Creator, and the members of Odd Future would chill at the shop on Fairfax Avenue in Los Angeles in the early days of The Hundreds (fashion model Luka Sabbat was a Hundreds intern).

**SIGNATURE LOOK:** Irreverent graphic T-shirts in '80s-inspired black or '90s-referential multicolors

**ASIAN INSPIRATION:** Paying homage to the slide favored by the Asian American teens in Kim's '90s SoCal community, with The Hundreds' x Fila collaboration. (He cast all–Asian American models in the 2017 campaign, which was shot by Filipino American photographer Alexander Spit.)

In 2003, along with law school classmate Ben Shenassafar, Kim confounded The Hundreds, an L.A.-based streetwear brand. Their business model bridged the burgeoning skate-style trend and the booming world of online pop culture, as The Hundreds grew into a multimedia platform. The Hundreds is particularly known for its inspired collaborations with nostalgic pop culture entities, from Garfield to Amoeba Records. In 2019, Kim released his first book, *This Is Not a T-Shirt: A Brand, a Culture, a Community—a Life in Streetwear,* about his unique personal and professional journey.

# Asians All the Rave

BY PHILIP WANG

**HI, I'M YULTRON.** I went to my first rave in the late-2000s, and I've pursued DJing and producing as a career ever since.

The stereotype is that Asians are nerdy and don't party, but the truth is, Asians love partying more than anyone else. And the rave and festival scene is where Asian Americans proved it, by carving out our own spaces—literally, you could always see the massive groups of Asians in the crowd. Maybe you can attribute it to the culture of strict rules and guidelines a lot of us grew up with, or the stereotypical tendency that's been placed on us to not show emotions or express ourselves publicly. But at raves and festivals, usually at the trance stage, we found excuses to break free from both, leaving our comfort zones for the first time. Maybe it was the drugs? Okay, it was *definitely* the drugs. But it was also the amazing music that went with them, and the chance to share the experience with thousands of other people.

Electronic music first became popular in Europe, and let's be honest, it's still a very white thing. But Asians really helped build up that scene, funding it with all the VIP tickets and merchandise we buy. We're a big part of the community, and we rarely get acknowledgment for that. Even as a professional in the industry, I still feel like I face barriers. I know why they don't put me on the covers, or why I'm not featured. But I do what I do for my love of the music and of the people who enjoy it. I do it for the Asian teen who messages me after a show telling me his parents won't let him pursue music—but that I've inspired him to go for it anyway. I do it for all the music listeners who are surprised when they find out their favorite DJ is Asian. To them I say: Fuck yeah, I'm Asian!   **—YULTRON**

**AO BEATS · ARIUS · ARMNHMR · DABIN · ELEPHANTE**

**FAR EAST MOVEMENT · GRYFFIN · GENT & JAWNS · GINGEE**

**GIRAFFAGE · THE GLITCH MOB · HOTEL GARUDA · JOSH PAN**

**KEN LOI · KREWELLA · KSHMR · LAIDBACK LUKE · MANILA KILLA**

**MARK REDITO · QRION · ROBOTAKI · SHAWN WASABI · SHOGUN**

**SOFTEST HARD · STARRO · STEVE AOKI · SWEATER BEATS**

**TOKIMONSTA · YAEJI · YULTRON · ZHU**

**JAMES "PROHGRESS" ROH:** Asians love Ecstasy, man. I remember from 1998 to 2002, when all the raves were still underground, they'd be filled with Asians and they'd be rolling, raved out of their minds.

**TOKIMONSTA:** As an Asian woman starting in the industry, I had so many people doubting my skills. They thought I had a boyfriend making my music. At this point, my career speaks for itself and I've thrived, along with many Asians, in the electronic space. And there's a reason for that. As Asian American children, we bear the burden of our parents' struggles. Every time your parents tell you about what it took them to provide you with a good life, that's another ten-pound weight you carry! And of course, love is never spoken out loud; maybe it's shown through gestures like cooking instead. Well, you know where there's no pressure, and instead just love, affection, and full acceptance? Raves. Rave culture has always provided that sense of radical acceptance, but Asian Americans thirst for it the most.

**SOFTEST HARD:** My first rave ever was a Skrillex concert. From then on out, I fell in love with the music and feeling. How could you not fall in love with something that fills your body up with joy and takes you on a roller-coaster ride of happy emotions? It's more than just music. It's bringing people together, strengthening bonds, and empowering not only my fellow Asians, but everyone all over the world.

**SHAWN WASABI:** As an artist, a lot of my stuff is very Filipino inspired—I really like using Southeast Asian sounds in my work. But I also draw a lot of inspiration from anime and video games like *Super Mario* and *Dance Dance Revolution*. I feel like, being Asian American and getting exposed to these melodies and rhythms so much as kids, there was a predisposition in place

for a lot of us toward electronic music. There are lots of talented Asian Americans making art and music who can't pursue it full-time. More of us need to work to mentor others. This industry is all about "Who do you know?" We already make up so much of the audience at these music festivals. I wish the performance lineups were more inclusive, and accurately reflected how much our communities show up and contribute.

**KEN LOI:** Music has always been a part of my life. I was a stereotypical piano child. I was never a rave kid. When I did attend, it was because I wanted to see how people responded, how the DJ mixed each song, and to take in the culture. ETD POP '06 in San Francisco was the first massive event I attended. After that I was hooked, and spent the next six years learning to produce. This was at a time when there were no YouTube tutorials! But there's been progress in some ways; we see a lot more Asian representation in every aspect of electronica now.

**MANILA KILLA:** Growing up, a lot of my Asian peers were extremely talented. But as we grew up, despite all that real talent, most of them worked toward the traditional route, so I felt I had to do the same. Being an Asian DJ was pretty rare even just 10 years ago, so in the beginning my identity actually held me back from pursuing my passion. It wasn't until after high school, when I discovered Asian artists who were making dance music, that I changed my perspective. Asians have continually been excluded from many cultural movements. But a small portion of electronic music now has a hardcore, dedicated Asian fan base. Now, even more than ever, I'm getting messages about how what I've done has inspired others. That keeps me wanting to push further. That makes me proud of being Asian.

stage and multiple monitors so you'll never miss a lyric. Both options include:

- Saran-wrapped controller: Because *soju* spilling is not a matter of whether, but when.
- A button to call for service, either more drinks, more food, or why is this thing repeating "Bohemian Rhapsody" over and over?
- A karaoke system with pitch control (not that the veterans are going to need it; they know what tracks are exactly in their range) and a scoring system that will always give you 100 if everyone sings at once but tell you "Nice try! 54!" when it's your solo.
- Tambourines for the backup dancers.
- Expensive fruit platters: Somehow, watermelon is *always* in season.
- Snacks and even full entrée menus: Kimchi *chigae* from a *noraebang* is the equivalent of wings at a strip bar. Oh yeah, the wings are also amazing.

6. ***Soondobu* spot:** When you think "drunk food," it's gotta be tofu soup, right?

7. ***Seolleongtang* spot:** Unless it's ox-bone broth—boiled for hours until it's milky white and seasoned at the table with salt, pepper, and other chopped and minced condiments if you really need them. A life-giving elixir.

8. **That slightly shady 24/7/365 Korean diner:** After-after-hours fare served by *ajumma* waitresses who've seen it all and will carefully put hot bowls in places at the table where there aren't snoring heads.

9. **The 21st birthday party:** Not that people necessarily waited till they were 21 to party in K-Town, but hey, have a blast with your legal ID!

10. **The parking lot fight:** Someone looked at someone the wrong way or flicked a cigarette at a fender. Stay clear because it's about to get serious.

11. **Booking club:** The heyday of clubs where servers pull women over to drink with random groups of men at their request is gone, but yes, back in the day, this was a thing.

12. **The neighborhood bar:** A spot for Koreatown natives who want to chill away from white hipsters and San Gabriel parachute kids driving Lamborghinis with Supreme stickers on them. Only in K-Town can you get bottle service at a dive bar.

13. **The Korean cab:** Long before Lyft and Uber, there was the *ajusshi* passing out business cards that he knew you'd need later in the night. Cheaper than taxis, and in some cases, they'll even organize to drive your car home for you when you're in no condition. *That's* service.

14. **The hipsters:** Sometime in the mid-2010s, K-Town started to gentrify. Perhaps because of its proximity to Hollywood and downtown, or maybe because of Roy Choi's bulgogi tacos, but K-Town suddenly began to swarm with non-Asians—mostly sticking to the Bermuda Triangle around Chapman Plaza.

15. **Second-floor lounge:** There's a door guy downstairs who's not going to let you in if you're not Korean. Sorry.

16. **Mexican markets:** They call it Koreatown, but the neighborhood is actually 53 percent Hispanic. Latinx businesses are nestled in between the Korean bars, restaurants, and cafés on most blocks, reflecting the area's unique blend of cultures.

17. ***Jimjilbang*:** The 24-hour Korean spa, where you can roast in a sauna, soak in a near-boiling tub (and then a freezing one), get a power massage or scrubdown, or just sleep—yes, overnight stays are an option, if you don't mind crashing on a folding lounge chair next to dozens of other zonked-out patrons. This is where all those Korean cab *ajusshi*s go after their shifts, before rolling out to pick up the morning hangover crowd.

# A Night in Koreatown

BY JON PARK AND JEFF YANG

**LOS ANGELES'S KOREATOWN** isn't the only K-Town in America—there are thriving Korean commercial enclaves in New York City; in Annandale, Virginia; in Dallas, Texas; and outside of Atlanta, Georgia—but it's essentially the motherland outside the motherland, home to several thousand Korean businesses and around 25,000 Korean Americans, a population that, on weekends, doubles . . . or triples. K-Town has long been a dining, drinking, and partying home base for Korean Americans, but since the Nineties, they've been joined by other Asians and non-Asians as well, seeking an all-night neighborhood where the evening begins after work and doesn't end till morning. "I think it was food culture that first made K-Town popular to non-Koreans," says Jon Park, better known by his rap name Dumbfoundead. "As Korean food became popular, you had folks like Anthony Bourdain coming in, the media coming in, and evervyone else followed. And of course, after you eat, you have to drink, right? And then after you drink, well, it just goes from there." Where does it go? Check out this look at L.A.'s K-Town when the lights go down.

**Il-Cha (Round 1):** Dinner and drinks—this is where you lay down a foundation for the evening.

**Ee-Cha (Round 2):** The first bar—you might go somewhere with bottle service or cocktails, you probably play drinking games.

**Sam-Cha (Round 3):** The second bar, for *soju* or beer, everyone's already drunk so it doesn't really matter, and you'll probably have bar snacks to keep the night going.

**Sa-Cha (Round 4):** The main party—that's where the dancing, mingling, and meeting up with other crowds comes in.

**O-Cha (Round 5):** Karaoke, because a night out should end on a high note.

**Late-night snack (optional)**—If people are still hungry or just want to go head-down on a table.

**Hangover breakfast (probably not optional)**—If people are still out when the sun starts to rise.

1. **AYCE KBBQ:** L.A. pioneered all-you-can-eat Korean barbecue, which admittedly offers less *banchan* and probably lower-quality meat, but the *soju*'s still the same. If you trust $19.99 unlimited beef, this is where you start your night.

2. **Upscale KBBQ:** A spot that hangs up photos with actors who've eaten there, both Korean and Hollywood. You'll have the option of private rooms, and the servers might cook the meat for you. The brisket is *wagyu* and the intestines are small.

3. **Valet parking:** Like you have a choice? Parking spots in K-Town on a weekend only exist in fairy tales. The good thing is that while Beverly Hills just a few miles away charges $25 a car, the valets in K-Town will take your $5 and put your car somewhere you probably don't want to ask about, driving like a stuntman all the way. Warning: Those lots close at 1:00 a.m. on the dot even though you're now five blocks away and belting Nineties R&B at a *noraebang*.

4. **Noraebang (small room):** *Noraebang* literally means "sound room," and that's what these are: karaoke in a private room for you and your friends. You might choose a small room for just a few friends if you want to work on your standards with low stakes.

5. **Noraebang (big room):** Do you have 15 or 20 pals and a desire to stage your own personal arena concert? The big room is yours, complete with

# LOVE,
# Asian American Style

BY LINDA GE, ILLUSTRATED BY SISI YU

**MOST ASIAN AMERICANS** who came to adulthood in the last three decades grew up watching very few people who looked like us in popular culture. The real unicorn, however, was seeing two Asian American characters flirt, romance, and *fall in love*. That's why, for many of us, the 1961 movie musical *Flower Drum Song* occupies such a unique place in pop culture, despite its cringey stereotypes and convoluted plot. It takes dashing James Shigeta, hilarious Jack Soo, sensational Nancy Kwan, and lovely Miyoshi Umeki and puts them in a love quadrangle that resolves over the course of two hours and a dozen song and dance numbers. They're romantic. They're sexy. And most of all, they're abundantly, defiantly Asian American, sorting out their soulmate issues on the streets of San Francisco. Since then, we've seen Hollywood serve up romances between Asian and Asian-ish characters in real and fairy-tale versions of the exotic East—Aladdin and Jasmine (Asian-ish)! Mulan and Li Shang . . . kinda!—but it wasn't until the 2000s that we finally began seeing Asian Americans coupling up on screen again. Here's our roster of the hottest Asian American matches we remember from film and TV:

## 2002: Ben and Stephanie, *Better Luck Tomorrow*

This seminal piece of Asian American cinema from future superstar director Justin Lin was a darkly comic thriller with no real promise for a happy ending. Ben (Parry Shen) might have been the stereotypical Asian sidekick in any other movie, longing for the bad boy's girl but quietly accepting being her friend. Instead, *Better Luck Tomorrow* gave him and Stephanie (Karin Anna Cheung) a kiss, a shot at love, and, well, an ambiguous finale.

## 2004: Jin and Sun, *Lost*

This one's a bit of a cheat, since Jin (Daniel Dae Kim) and Sun (Yunjin Kim) were two South Koreans cast away among a group of mostly American plane crash survivors, and the setting was a weird island in the middle of nowhere. But their story, which went from embodying terrible stereotypes of patriarchy and loveless marriage to becoming one of the most tender, nuanced, and ultimately heart-wrenching depictions of love between Asians in Hollywood history, still felt very familiar to any of us who heard the right stories from our parents (or their friends).

## 2004: Wil and Vivian, *Saving Face*

Alice Wu's iconic 2004 hit indie film is still one of the only Asian American lesbian romances ever to be put on screen. It was notable for subverting both Chinese and LGBTQ stereotypes—in part by simply allowing Wil (Michelle Krusiec) and Viv (Lynn Chen) to actually end

JIN & SUN

BEN & STEPHANIE

MIKE & TINA

WIL & VIVIAN

MARCUS & SASHA

LOUIS & JESSICA

PAX & DEVI

up together, happy (and parentally approved), as one might expect in any good rom-com.

## 2009: Mike and Tina, *Glee*

Yes, there were some cringey jokes about the fact that they were both Asian (what exactly is an "Asian kiss"?), but in Mike (Harry Shum Jr.) and Tina (Jenna Ushkowitz), for the first time we saw two Asian characters on TV mostly treated as just a couple of American teenagers who fall in love, have drama, fight, get back together, have more drama, have sex, break up, and almost get married.

## 2015: Louis and Jessica, *Fresh Off the Boat*

In a subversion of one-note, stereotypical immigrant Asian parents, the ABC sitcom allowed its central Taiwanese couple to grow and evolve, both together and as individuals, as they raised their three sons and reckoned with living in their new country. And even though no Asian wants to think about our parents kissing, Louis and Jessica even got to do that, now and again—as well as regularly allude to having sex (they did have three sons!). It helped that the series gave them six full seasons to become more actualized, fully human characters—still the longest running of any Asian-led show in Hollywood history.

## 2018: Nick and Rachel, *Crazy Rich Asians*

Can you believe that it took until 2018—more than half a century after *Flower Drum Song*!—for us to get another full-blown romantic comedy featuring two Asians from a Hollywood studio? It was worth the wait: the swoonwor-thy love journey of Rachel (*Fresh Off the Boat*'s Constance Wu) and Nick (Malaysian British newcomer Henry Golding) made for a true blockbuster, despite (or because of!) its all-Asian cast.

## 2019: Marcus and Sasha, *Always Be My Maybe*

While *Crazy Rich Asians* depicted an opulent and exotic Singapore, the love connection of Marcus (*Fresh Off the Boat*'s Randall Park) and Sasha (comedian and former *FOTB* staff writer Ali Wong) was a decidedly middle-class American affair. But the rom-com was its own noteworthy hit for Netflix, while also serving as a testament to just how long it can take two charismatic, A-list-worthy Asian American stars to get to a point where they can play the leads in a mainstream American romantic comedy. The answer: 15 years, which is how long Wong and Park had been friends, watching each other toil in stand-up comedy and in supporting roles, before Hollywood was ready for their response to *When Harry Met Sally*.

## 2020: Pax and Devi, *Never Have I Ever*

Adolescent girls aren't usually allowed to express their sexual desires on screen; Asian ones, even less so. So this Mindy Kaling–created teen sex comedy, featuring Indian American Devi (Maitreyi Ramakrishnan) and her droolworthy crush Paxton Hall-Yoshida (hapa Japanese American Darren Barnet), would've already been a rare bird even if it didn't feature a super-cute on-again, off-again romance between two Asian American teens. And, according to Netflix, 40 million viewers to date approve!

# What's Funny? 2010s

**BY THE 2010S,** Asian Americans were entrenched at every tier of comedy—from top headliners to edgy up-and-comers—and the proliferation of talent really allowed Asian stand-ups to stake out their own distinctive approaches to talking about race . . . if they chose to at all. Some inverted and disrupted stereotypes; others knowingly embraced them. Some consciously occupied intersectional personas, making it clear how standing at the nexus of identities made them different from Asian peers. But perhaps the biggest shift was that Asian comics felt less of a need to explain where they came from, minting jokes that assumed audiences knew something about Asian culture—or were Asian American themselves.

I got into comedy to pursue my real dream, which is to do temporary administrative support. Temp jobs are weird. One time I was in a job for a year and then when I was leaving they had me train my permanent replacement. I was like, why would you have your least invested employee train your hopes and dreams for the future?
**—APARNA NANCHERLA**

If you're a bad driver with this face, it's a nightmare. I feel like I've seen every version of "of course!" expression in L.A., and when I see it I want to roll down my window and say, "Excuse me, sir, I'm not a bad driver because I'm Asian, I'm a bad driver because I won't wear my glasses and I text, okay? It's a personal choice."
**—JOEL KIM BOOSTER**

I'm from Jilin, China, but I came to the United States when I was 24 to study at Rice University in Texas. That wasn't a joke . . . until now.
**—JOE WONG**

My real name isn't Jimmy. That's my English name. My Chinese name is Man Shing. It stands for "10,000 Success." I had very ambitious parents. And now I'm telling dick jokes and doing tai chi on stage. But Jimmy was just an arbitrary name, which I picked because it was easy. My dad, he picked the name Richard. I asked him, "Dad, why'd you choose the name Richard?" And he said, "Because I want to be rich." It makes so much sense!
**—JIMMY O. YANG**

My husband is Asian, which shocks a lot of people. Because usually Asian American women who wear these kind of glasses and have a lot of opinions like to date white dudes. Go to any hipster neighborhood in any major city and that shit is a Yoko Ono factory. But it can be nice to be with somebody of your own race. Because you get to go home and be racist together. You get to say whatever you like. Don't gotta explain shit. My husband is half Filipino and half Japanese. I'm half Chinese and half Vietnamese. And we spend a hundred percent of our time shitting on Korean people. It's amazing. It's what love is built on.
**—ALI WONG**

There's a restaurant in my neighborhood called Sheng Wang. Spelled exactly like my name. All my friends insist I have to go eat there. Secretly I agree, but I don't know why. I don't know what kind of fantasy we expect to pan out! Like I walk in there, everyone freaks out, oh my God, it's him. We've been waiting for you. The prophecy has begun. I look around, and there's baby pictures of me everywhere.
**—SHENG WANG**

So I was at a party last week and this guy came up to me and asked, "Hey, where are you from?" So I told him. "I'm from Queens, New York." "No, I mean, where are you really from?" For those of you who don't know, that's code for "Why are you not white? I noticed your skin is a different color than mine. Why this pigment?" I was offended, clearly. Because this man had judged me by the color of my skin, and not its more important qualities, like its softness and smoothness.
**—HARI KONDABOLU**

Growing up was kind of tough. I had a unibrow . . . on my lip. I would comb my face, like Chewbacca. And kids in middle school can be mean. This kid shouted at me, "Hey, you have a mustache." So I ran home. I didn't want to tell my mom about it, because I didn't want to offend her about her beard. And I go into my dad's drawer and I shave it off. The next day I get to school, and the same kid is like, "You have a mustache!" And my best friend was like, don't worry. I'll handle it. "Hey yo, no she doesn't. She used to. But she shaved it off!" And he turns to me like, yeah! Dude, that was not a victory.
**—KIRAN DEOL**

It's been a big year for me. I got married. And I had an Indian wedding, the most expensive way to tell the world I was going to try to be monogamous. I did it for my wife, and I did it for my white friends. All of my white friends were like, Hasan, oh, look at all the colors, oh my God, what is this, cumin? You're eating rice, Chris, relax.

**—HASAN MINHAJ**

I love video games, and a new *Call of Duty* came out and it looks so good. Then I found out that one of the levels is called "Karachi." Yep, the city I grew up in! They're basically like, "Your hometown is now a battlefield, how many points can you get, Kumail?" I was able to convince myself that I'd have an advantage over everybody, because I'd know all the locations already. I'd be like, "Hey, we can hide in here, guys! I used to rent movies in this place! Mr. Sadiki will give me shelter. He once fixed my VCR for free!"

**—KUMAIL NANJIANI**

My nephew's about to start kindergarten. Kindergarten in America is all about macaroni pictures and finger painting. When I went to kindergarten in the Philippines, we were making handbags.

**—NICO SANTOS**

It's such a weird stereotype to have associated with your ethnicity: that Asian parents want their kids to be doctors. But it's true. And when Asian parents want their kids to be doctors, helping people is at the bottom of the list. If it even makes the list! For them, helping people is like the unfortunate byproduct of becoming a healthcare professional. Don't let it get in the way of what it's really about—the money and the prestige.

**—RONNIE CHIENG**

I was at a Chinese restaurant the other night, and it was a chic modern one. Like, the hostess was white, that's what we're dealing with. But they had this really cute cocktail program there, and one of the drinks was called a "Shanghai mule," which is cute, right? It's like a Moscow mule, but just slightly less homophobic. And then I realized that I am also a Shanghai mule, because I'm Chinese and I will not reproduce. I'm also a mule in that I stick drugs in my ass. Wow. I mean, I saw myself on that menu. Like, representation matters, you guys!

**—BOWEN YANG**

# The FAQ About Apu

BY JEFF YANG

HARI KONDABOLU

**IN 2012, STAND-UP** comedian **HARI KONDABOLU** was working as a writer on W. Kamau Bell's TV show on FX, *Totally Biased*. Kondabolu pitched a segment where Bell would discuss Mindy Kaling's new show *The Mindy Project* and how big it was for Indian American representation—considering Apu, the Indian character on Fox's *The Simpsons*, was the only thing representing the community for years. Bell said it was great, but that the bit would only work if Kondabolu did it. At first he was reluctant, responding that he was focused on writing for the show, not performing. Bell then said he'd fire him if he didn't do it. So Kondabolu did, basing it on observations he included in a hilarious 2008 mini-mockumentary, *Manoj*. That turned into the seed for Kondabolu's 2017 documentary called *The Problem with Apu*, featuring Kal Penn, Maulik Pancholy, Aasif Mandvi, and Hasan Minhaj, among other South Asian performers, talking about their experiences being called "Apu," or being mocked with his catchphrases or accent. The documentary generated backlash from people who professed love for the character, but had a real impact: it got Hank Azaria, the white voice actor behind Apu, to decide to no longer do the character. We asked Hari to give us some answers to questions he gets about Apu even today . . . half a decade after his documentary.

## So who's Apu?

Apu Nahasapeemapetilon is an Indian immigrant character who first appeared on *The Simpsons* in the early Nineties, when I was in fourth grade. At the time, I thought the idea of an Indian character on a show I enjoyed was great, because when you're not invited to the table, you gladly accept the scraps. It wasn't so complicated then because I was a kid, but essentially I was happy they even acknowledged we existed. I didn't question more than that. But there's this made-up dichotomy that says something isn't racist just because it's funny. The fact is, things can be both racist and funny—and that's the problem. When racism is made funny, when it makes people laugh and it can dig under the skin that way, that's when people are willing to allow for it to exist.

## What's the issue with Apu?

To me, it's obvious: Apu is a white guy, Hank Azaria, doing an imitation of a stereotypical Indian character. His name is ridiculous. He owns a convenience store—and owning a Kwik-E-Mart isn't itself racist, but the way Apu is depicted certainly is. There's nothing wrong with small business owners! A lot of people in our community work hard to survive in that realm. But how he's depicted doesn't reflect their reality. If you're Indian, you watch the show and you instantly know that our community didn't have anything to do with creating the show or the character. And part of it is that the way he's voiced is over-the-top ridiculous.

## What makes Apu racist?

The way Azaria does the voice isn't based on an Indian person's accent. It's based on how [British comedian] Peter Sellers did Indian accents. So it's not even a white guy doing an Indian accent, it's a white guy doing a white guy doing an Indian accent. Maybe somewhere down the road it's based in some shred of reality, but by the time it comes out of Apu's mouth, it's overdone to a degree that makes it clearly a non-Indian's view of how an Indian talks. The fact is, there's no such thing as an "Indian" accent any more than there's an "American" accent. We have so many different regions—shit, we have dozens of different languages. So the purpose of Apu's accent isn't accuracy, it's laughter. And it's not to get me to laugh, it's to get non-Indians to laugh. And by non-Indians, by and large, I mean "white people."

## If he's a racist caricature, why has he stuck around?

I don't think they ever expected the show to go on for 30 years! People loved the character of Apu when he was added to the cast. They thought he was hilarious, so the writers kept writing to him. Over time, that's made him more three-dimensional. But the fundamental issue that he's an Indian character voiced, conceived of, and written by non-Indians is still there.

## Why did you feel like it was important to call this out?

Look, I didn't make my documentary to talk to South Asians. There are no Indians watching my doc and feeling shocked, like, "Oh my God! We were made fun of because of *Apu*? How did I miss this entire phenomenon during the Eighties, Nineties, and early 2000s?" This wasn't me *mak-

ing* it a thing—it was *already* a thing. We grew up watching this shit, and it's not like it ever stopped being racist. And white people were not talking about it, so I realized that the racism conversation would have to start with us.

## What's the documentary about?

In exploring Apu, I wanted to talk about the experience of growing up in this country with only one mainstream representation of us—this cartoon character—and how it's part of a larger American history of racist caricature, and how if you don't nip something like this in the bud, it survives and people move on. In doing so, I wanted to share as many of our stories as we could. It was like a love letter to my community, in a lot of ways.

## How was it received?

Most people who hated *The Problem with Apu* haven't seen it. I'm saying that honestly, because I think it's hard to hate. I think you can dislike it, you can disagree with it, but to straight-up hate it? You've either made up your mind about it and you're going in trying to figure out how to destroy it, or you didn't watch it in the first place. I got a lot of hate mail from outside the U.S., particularly from South America. The doc wasn't even available outside the U.S., so a lot of backlash was from people just reading about it online.

## Are you happy at the outcome?

Maybe part of the joy of that has been sucked out by the death threats? I'm happy that Hank Azaria stopped doing the voice, and that he's apparently really invested in anti-racist education now and has done a lot of reading, and that's great. I'm glad that at least one white person got something out of it. But whenever he talks about how he rethought his decision to do Apu, he never gives the documentary any credit, which is part of the erasure. Like white people come to the conclusion to be less racist without us having to yell about it. Yay, white people! Come on—I got death threats so that you could figure it out.

## What about the future?

Apu is going to live on, with someone else doing the voice. And that's fine. I'm not saying we should delete scenes from the past. I'd rather they exist to remind people of where the character came from. But the real victory for me came when Disney made its cartoon *Mira, Royal Detective.* They did everything right: They cast all brown people, they got voice coaches and cul-

tural consultants. And the creator, Sascha Paladino, is a white guy, but he reached out and told me he got every single writer and producer to watch *The Problem with Apu* before they even started working. The idea that this cartoon featuring South Asians was done with so much love and respect for another generation of young people—not just South Asian kids, but kids in general—that's amazing. I realize that I impacted *that,* and that's the closure I want. That's the next wave of South Asians in animation. Who gives a *fuck* about *The Simpsons*? We're the main characters in this. That still blows my mind.

Apu reflected the era in which he was created. But people always want to move past racism. We know what you thought of us. You recorded it. Own that, then we can talk about moving on.

## POSTCARD FROM ASIAN AMERICA

BY MIA IVES-RUBLEE

Dear RISE,

Growing up as a disabled, Korean transracial adoptee in the South was extremely isolating. There were few Asians and even fewer Koreans. Still, it wasn't until my elementary school years that it became evident to me that I wasn't the same race as my family. My parents tried to connect me with my birth culture. They gave me books on South Korea and sent me to language school. I left after getting teased for being in "beginner" classes. Meanwhile, kids at my regular school would comment about my eyes or hair. I'd be told I spoke "good English" and how "lucky" I was to be "saved" by my parents. I couldn't explain why the things they said were hurtful.

In middle school, I got involved in adapted athletics. It was a chance for me to test my physical bounds past what all the doctors said I could do. It gave me validation and even pride in having a physical disability—and it was the first time I became friends with another Asian American. Everyone confused us for one another, as we were the only two Asians in wheelchair track and field. But I looked up to and was inspired by her.

But it wasn't until college that I became close friends with another Asian. She helped me gain comfort in my Asian identity. I began exploring my culture (and yes, its food), and it felt liberating. Having her guide me toward reconnecting to my identity—and give me the words to explain my experiences with anti-Asian sentiment—helped me come into my own.

Now I work as a civil rights organizer in AAPI spaces, connecting and empowering Asian American communities. I've had the opportunity to visit the land of my birth. When I come back home to the South, I'm much more cognizant of my background—in fact, these days, I often feel more comfortable in Asian American spaces than I do in others. I've found a sense of peace in who I am, and I hope others are able to find it as well.

In solidarity,
Mia, a.k.a. 미혜

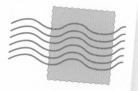

RISE
HERE AND NOW,
ASIAN AMERICA

# #StarringJohnCho

## BY WILLIAM YU

In 2016, Hollywood Didn't Care about Asian American Stories. #StarringJohnCho Proved That the World Demanded Them.

Back then, film news included Scarlett Johansson getting cast as Motoko Kusanagi in *Ghost in the Shell* and Tilda Swinton filling the role of The Ancient One, a Tibetan, in *Doctor Strange*. Even Oscar-winning screenwriter Aaron Sorkin had recently said the quiet part out loud: "There aren't any Asian movie stars." It was clear that, even if they weren't outright racist, Hollywood's creatives had shockingly little imagination.

I decided that if you couldn't envision what an Asian movie star looked like, I'd literally show you. Without anyone's permission, I Photoshopped actor John Cho onto hit movie posters and launched a Twitter account to anonymously share my #StarringJohnCho creations. The Internet ran with it. And then, NBC, the BBC, and CNN came calling.

I expected pushback: "People don't know who he is!" Tell that to the hundreds of thousands of John Cho stans. "He has no leading-man experience!" John Cho anchored *Selfie,* a whole broadcast sitcom—which, though short-lived, proved he could be a romantic lead. "Does he get good reviews?" Yes. Next question. "Asians don't sell tickets!" Maybe you've heard of a little franchise called *Harold and Kumar*?

But this campaign wasn't just about John, and it wasn't just about money. Yes, diverse films do better financially and are better returns on investment. But it's also the case that great films are built around great characters—from courageous superheroes or to swoonworthy romantics—that also showcase our humanity. Our passions. Our pains. Our dreams. All of us deserve to see our flaws and joys depicted onscreen.

And now, Hollywood is changing. But things can move faster. *Crazy Rich Asians* director Jon M. Chu said, "One of the first things that made me want to make a movie like [*Crazy Rich Asians*] was the #StarringJohnCho movement. It was as if a light turned on."

We need to turn on more lights.

#StarringJohnCho snowballed from an Internet meme into a global movement because people made it their own, and amplified that Asian representation matters to them. The demand and the dollars are there. Now it's up to Hollywood to deliver. Because we're ready to pull the culture forward—with or without their permission.

## John Cho on #StarringJohnCho

"The timing of this campaign was so perfect, in the sense that Asian Americans were ready to assert themselves and the public at large was probably primed to accept the idea in a way they hadn't before. And you were really taking advantage of a new medium—the Internet—to discuss these ideas. And I would argue that I worked for the campaign because I have a reputation for being chronically underused. It was

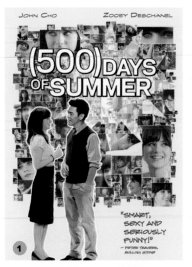

1

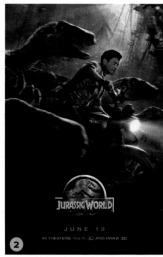

2

3

6

"When you see the
group poster you go,
'What is keeping some-
thing like this from hap-
pening? It seems com-
pletely natural, now that
I'm looking at it.'"

4

5

8

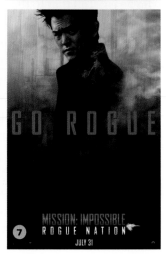

7

CREDIT: CREATED BY WILLIAM YU; USED WITH PERMISSION

an interesting way to talk about [representation]—a socially acceptable way of bringing up the issue. And now, I feel more optimistic. There are more writers. There's a different consciousness. It's like the four-minute mile: It's universally agreed that a human being cannot go under four minutes, and then somebody does. And then for some reason, there's a whole bunch of people who run a sub-four-minute mile."

## POSTER REACTIONS

**1** *500 Days of Summer*

"For almost every poster, I'm like, 'What is that haircut?' That's my primary thought. Great movie—that would have been fun to do. As someone who grew up in the '90s, there's an emotional link to it. It's faded, but [there was a time when] I did want to do a very straight-ahead rom-com."

**2** *Jurassic World*

"Being on a motorcycle—dope. I've only done it once, very briefly, on one of my first movies, *Better Luck Tomorrow*. But I would like to get back on a motorcycle on-screen again."

**3** *21*

"This one was the most provocative. If I understand the history of this story, they were all MIT kids, right? And they were Asian. This is one where I went, 'That's the poster that it should've been.' With me or anybody else. That was taken from us."

**4** *Spectre*

"This seemed to be the biggest stretch. But yeah, good suit . . . that kind of thing would be fun."

**5** *The Martian*

"I don't know why, but I found this one the most effective. I always find faces the most effective on posters. I always think it's a mistake when one doesn't have a human being in it. I especially was tickled because I thought the movie was so good. We all know there are Asian American astronauts, this is easily plausible. An Asian American in this story is completely plausible."

**6** *Me Before You*

"For whatever reason, I had the most mixed feelings about this one. I didn't want this to fall into the anachronistic, Asian male political stance where it's awesome to be on-screen with white girls. That that's the pinnacle of success . . . This poster made me think of that political angle. [But] the other thought I had was that it was probably the best Photoshop job."

**7** *Mission: Impossible*

"That's a cool picture. I just thought that worked . . . it seems like to me you could've made it. It seemed the least Photoshop-y. I just, 'Whoa. Cool. Let's go sell that somewhere.'"

**8** *Avengers: Age of Ultron*

"It's interesting that this works. Because it's a bunch of characters, and you go, 'Oh, there's an Asian face in there.' So it simultaneously pops, but is also completely plausible. When you see the group poster you go, 'What is keeping something like this from happening? It seems completely natural, now that I'm looking at it.' I thought, 'He's really challenging you. Because a studio head or a casting director, if they were charged with making a character in that universe Asian, it wouldn't be Captain America. That's the one where they'd go, 'That guy's gotta literally look like corn.' So I thought that was the ballsiest one."

# Fresh Off the Boat: A Retrospective

BY JEFF YANG AND PHIL YU

**IN 2013, A CALL** went out seeking actors for a TV show that—if it made it to broadcast—would be the first prime-time network sitcom to focus on an Asian American family in 20 years. That show was *Fresh Off the Boat,* and it starred Randall Park and Constance Wu as Louis and Jessica Huang, Forrest Wheeler and Ian Chen as their middle and youngest kids Emery and Evan, and finally, Hudson Yang—my eldest son—as irrepressible Eddie, the younger avatar of real-life chef Eddie Huang, whose brash, hip-hop-inflected bestselling memoir served as the series' very loose inspiration. Six seasons and 116 episodes of groundbreaking TV later, Hudson had made the role fully his own, as had Randall, Constance, Forrest, and Ian, etching themselves into pop culture as Asian America's favorite family. In the process, they didn't just make history—they made the future. I sat down with Phil, who was deeply involved with the show throughout its six-year life, to unpack and reminisce our feelings about its epic run.

**PHIL:** So this is a little different from the rest of our pieces, because you're really in this story directly. *Fresh Off the Boat* clearly impacted your life more than the 95 other things we talk about in the book.

**JEFF:** Yeah. True. You were there too, for a lot of it—for the first season, you and Jenny Yang did an unofficial after-show program called *Fresh Off the Show.* But your POV is still more outside in than inside out, so I was hoping you could talk from the standpoint of having been immersed in the modern history of Asian American TV. Like you kept that running annual list of all the Asians on TV, right? What was it called?

**PHIL:** It was called "All the Asians on TV."

**JEFF:** Right! So I can talk about this from a first-person perspective, and you can bring in that bigger context. So let's just begin by talking about when you first heard about the show.

**PHIL:** I think I heard about it like everybody else. I read in the trades that they were adapting Eddie Huang's book, and that it was going to be done by Nahnatchka Khan, who I already knew from *Don't Trust the B---- in Apartment 23.*

**JEFF:** What was it that popped for you about the show when you saw the news?

**PHIL:** My first reaction was, oh my God, this is about a family. So immediately this isn't just one Asian as part of an ensemble, or even a show with one Asian star. Because this is a fam-

ily, it's built in that there's going to be four, five, maybe six major roles for Asians. And because I'd invested so much of my time and energy doing this Asian census of prime-time scripted network television, it hit me that this one show would, in one fell swoop, account for probably half the Asians on TV.

**JEFF:** The funny thing is that the show was pretty off the radar for me. I wasn't living in L.A., I was in New York. And I was a cultural critic, but I was no longer a TV reviewer. So I didn't really have a reason to specifically be focused on pilot season. Especially because every season there's a new Asian American pilot, but nothing ever gets made. It gets announced, and then it doesn't get picked up.

**PHIL:** Right. I mean, Randall Park was in half a dozen pilots that never got picked up. So why should we believe in anything?

**JEFF:** Exactly. But, the other thing is, it was based on Eddie Huang's life. And I had known Eddie, I'd interviewed him before. Which later was part of the origin story of Hudson Yang. But by the time the show was on my radar, I didn't connect it to Eddie's book, because for some reason they'd changed the show's name from *Fresh Off the Boat* to *Far East Orlando.*

And they'd changed the names of most of the characters. The original treatment bore very little resemblance to the book. So I had no reason to associate the two. I just thought that it was wild how a pilot looking for a bunch of Asian Americans was coincidentally coming along as my son had gotten all hot on potentially being on TV.

**PHIL:** What was that like? You and I were friends and we communicated pretty regularly, but it was definitely a weird convergence of my interests. One minute I'm counting Asians on TV and then the next, you're telling me, "Hey, my kid's auditioning for this show." You, of all people, Jeff Yang, your kid is being thrown into the middle of this. And I do remember you sharing with me the news about Eddie reaching out to you after Hudson's audition.

**JEFF:** Yeah, he messaged me saying, "Yo, is this your kid on this tape?" Because he saw the

name, and Hudson had mentioned that his dad was a writer for the *Wall Street Journal.* And that was the first time it clicked that this was *Fresh Off the Boat.* But Eddie went on to say: "You know, he totally shouldn't be auditioning for this role." Hudson was auditioning for the middle kid, who's supposed to be the smooth, goody-goody teacher's pet. And my reaction was "Ouch." But Eddie's explanation was to say, "No no no, I'm not saying he sucks, he's great, kid's got swag. He's just not right for that role. He should be auditioning for my role. Me, as a kid." And I said, "Are you kidding? Isn't that the star role? You do know he's never been on TV before." But Eddie was adamant that he wanted to set up an audition for Hudson to read for his role. And he did. I brought Hudson back in to read again at this separate audition, and a few days later, I get a call. "This is Melvin Mar. I'm the executive producer of this show, and it may sound crazy, but can you get on a plane next week?"

**PHIL:** Oh man. That's when you flew out for the chemistry read? We had dinner on that trip. I remember Hudson falling asleep in the booth next to you.

**JEFF:** The kid was nine, time zones are rough. Which actually is a part of the story too. Anyway, this chemistry read, they had a bunch of kids they were testing for each of the three Huang brothers. And the other kids were all models, athletes, martial arts experts, actors with all this experience. And then Hudson, who was two or three years younger and the size of a walnut.

**PHIL:** I cannot believe how small he was back then and how tall he is now. It's a good thing he started younger because he had more room to go before he turned humongous, which is the dead end for cute little sitcom kids.

**JEFF:** Yeah, the show would've ended three seasons earlier. Or they would've written him out and Jessica would've magically given birth to a daughter, or they'd adopt a white kid or something. Sitcom rules. Anyway, they had a bunch of options for each kid and every hour they'd let one of them from each set go. It was very reality show. Fresh off the island. Every hour I was thinking, at some point this ride is going to be over for Hudson, I hope he's cool with it. But it kept going. And in the end, it was Hudson and Forrest Wheeler and Ian Chen, and they brought in Randall and Constance and read for the first time as a family.

**PHIL:** Speaking of Constance, she was a real discovery. Constance had done theater and some commercials and guest-starring stuff. I

remember that nobody knew who she was and then she was cast, and then she became the breakout star of the series. There was some drama about Randall being cast too, because he's Korean American and the family was Taiwanese. But this was really about getting an Asian American family on prime-time TV for the first time in 20 years, and Randall was the linchpin to making that happen.

**JEFF:** Melvin had already determined that Randall was both a known quantity and an unknown one, in the sense that everybody who had ever seen what he did loved him, but he hadn't really gotten his big break. Most of America still knew him from one episode of *The Office,* where he played "Asian Jim." Which makes me really think, how many other over-looked Asian stars are out there just waiting for a break? Constance, who'd never really done comedy, she rolls into this show and she has the timing and the beats and builds this totally unique persona that generations from now people will be rediscovering and point-ing back to as a classic TV character. For me, Jessica Huang is Archie Bunker. She's Fonzie. Constance made Jessica into *Fresh Off the Boat*'s Fonzie.

**PHIL:** *Fresh Off the Boat* forced people to relearn how to watch Asians on TV. We came in with all this dread, ready to flee. And there's this term that me, Jenny Yang, and my wife, Joanna Lee, came up with on the night of the premiere. We were hosting this live viewing of the show in Little Tokyo at the Japanese American National Museum. It had sold out pretty much instantly, but we had no idea how people were going to react. So the three of us were feeling giddy but also nervous. And we realized that's the feeling we got whenever we saw ourselves on-screen, this feeling of excite-ment-slash-dread, like, "Oh God, please don't embarrass us." And we said, "We need a name for this." So we came up with the term "rep sweats." We knew instantly that's what it was: rep sweats. The feeling of being conditioned to want to see yourself but bracing yourself for it to suck.

**JEFF:** So that's where we were. Our standard

had been set at "please don't suck." We're Asian. We should be aiming higher than that. That's absolutely a B-minus ambition, but we'd been beaten down so far for so long by Holly-wood that just not sucking was going to be good enough for us.

**PHIL:** But then we're watching along with the audience. And we're like, "Oh, the perfor-mances are pretty good. And the script is pretty good." And then the scene happens in the prin-cipal's office where Louis and Jessica come to Eddie's defense, and I got teary-eyed. I still do when I rewatch it today. I thought to myself, "That didn't go the way I thought it was going to go." It was so different from what I'd expected or feared. I said to myself then, "Okay, we can get there with this. This might just work."

**JEFF:** Well, you were way ahead of us. Because we were a midseason replacement, so we actually shot 13 episodes before airing even one. The cast had to crank out a baker's dozen shows, without knowing if they were ever going to air, or what the reaction would be once they did. And here's the crazy thing: The show that was in the slot that we ended up getting was *Selfie,* a romantic comedy starring John Cho and Karen Gillan. And the first few episodes of that were pretty bad, but by episode four or five, it was starting to be amazing. If the show had managed to figure out the charming chemistry they ended up having a little bit faster, or if the network was a little more patient with it, who knows if we'd even have gotten on the air. Certainly not in that slot. And even then, it was a little gut-wrenching, because it felt like they were giving us the Asian Death Slot. Like retail locations where every store shuts down in a few months, here we were, replacing a canceled show starring an Asian American with a new show starring Asian Americans. A show that had 13 episodes in the can, which they couldn't change even if they wanted to. We just had to cross our fingers that people would like it.

**PHIL:** And while you were shooting that first half-season was when *The Interview* came out. With Randall as Kim Jong-un.

**JEFF:** Yeah, that was bizarre. We were shooting, and at first people were like, "it's going to be great, this is going to turn him into a huge star. It's gonna be great for the show." And the next thing you know we're all afraid the Fox Studios lot was going to be hit with a nuclear weapon. I think that's just one sign of how snakebit *Fresh Off the Boat* was from the beginning, and how much it had to overcome just to make it on air.

**PHIL:** It was the last show picked up to series that year, right?

**JEFF:** Yeah. At the stroke of midnight on the deadline day, they picked up *Fresh Off the Boat* and *Cristela*. It was the season they made good on the idea that ABC was going to bring a different look to TV, because ABC also picked up *Black-ish*. A game-changing year for TV and for Hollywood. But if you look back, ABC has

really been behind virtually every attempt to crack Asian families into prime time. Not just *All-American Girl,* which was on ABC, but two decades before it, *Mr. T and Tina*, which starred Pat Morita. But you know, after all that, Hudson almost didn't make it onto the show.

**PHIL:** The dumplings.

**JEFF:** His greatest love and greatest nemesis. I wasn't able to bring him to L.A. for the pilot table read because I was in Austin, Texas, for work, so his mom took him, and they basically got off a plane and headed to the studio for this evening read. Hudson hadn't eaten, but they told her that there'd be food there. And the studio had catered Din Tai Fung, and his mom told him he could go to town. The next thing you know, I'm getting a phone call and Melvin Mar is saying, "Can you get on a plane to L.A. tonight?" And I say, what happened? And it comes out that Hudson ate 30 dumplings, got hit with the time zone shift—remember the time zone shift—and during the table read, in between his scenes, he put his head down on the table, and at one point even put the script over his face to block out the light. The ABC folks were like, "The kid's performance is fine, but does he really want the role? How can we build a show around a kid who's sleeping between his scenes?" Then Eddie calls me, right while I'm talking to Melvin, and he's laughing his ass off saying, "Dude, your kid ate 30 dumplings and went into a food coma. I would've done exactly the same thing." But ABC was not amused, and Melvin had come up with a plan to save him—shooting a test scene in costume the next morning. And they wanted me to be there for it. It was the first time I'd ever taken a flight with three connections, but I made it. He was professional, he hit his lines

on the dot, and the ABC folks were mollified enough to let things go forward.

**PHIL:** The groundbreaking Asian American sitcom, almost derailed by dumplings.

**JEFF:** I should've told Melvin that Din Tai Fung is basically his Achilles' heel. But that was just the beginning. Remember the Television Critics Association kickoff?

**PHIL:** Oh yeah, dude, I was there. This journalist at the TCA raised her hand during the cast Q&A and asked, "Hey, I wanted to know, I love the Asian culture and I was just thinking, am I going to see chopsticks on the show or is it more Americanized?"

**JEFF:** I remember the whole cast was just frozen for a second. And then, rapid-fire, Constance is like, "Yeah, we've got some chopsticks. We'll have a lot of chopsticks." And Randall says, "The original name for the show was going to be *Chopsticks*." It brought down the house. But instead of being about how groundbreaking the show was, all the stories coming out of TCA were talking about the "Chopstick Moment."

**PHIL:** It was a harbinger of things to come. This idea that if you're going to put an Asian family on TV and they're not "Americanized," then it would be all about the "chopsticks." People started picking it apart just based on the trailer—months before the show was broadcast.

**JEFF:** The very week it premiered, Eddie Huang wrote a piece for *New York* magazine saying that he thought the show had taken his book and turned it into sitcom chop suey, instead of the go-hard black comedy he wanted. And he was right! But there's also a sense that you make a deal with Disney, you know what you're getting into. What would the show have been if it were on a different network, and been the show Eddie wanted?

**PHIL:** I don't think it had that detrimental of an effect on the show. It definitely made people nervous. It added to the rep sweats epidemic.

**JEFF:** It was trial by fire, but with flamethrowers, from all sides, from the industry, from the audience, even from the community. We had to build things up from the "It's about chopsticks" level. And in some ways I wonder if the show was made possible because you just couldn't kill it. It got stronger because it survived all these pitfalls.

**PHIL:** But it had to be carried over those pitfalls. You did all these public viewings across the country, just four-walling the series.

**JEFF:** Yeah, I still remember the premiere episode, we had a viewing event and over 1,500 Asian Americans showed up to this nightclub my friend Bobby Kwak owned, just to literally watch TV together on a big screen. There were lines around the block, and the police made us turn away hundreds of people.

**PHIL:** We had a parallel experience over on the West Coast. Jenny Yang and I organized that screening at the museum, and it was packed and there was a line down the block. It's not like we didn't have TVs at home. But even after all the craziness, especially after all the craziness, everybody wanted to see it together. People still post pictures from that night: "Remember when…?" And I know they did the same for the New York event, and the ones you organized in D.C., in San Francisco, in L.A.

**JEFF:** It was amazing because we've seen so many gritty indie films do this. But this was a network TV show, and it felt like we still had to carry it over the goal line on a grassroots level. You were doing the live *Fresh Off the Show* series the whole first season.

**PHIL:** We did it in front of a live studio audience! We had an Asian snacks sponsor, we rented the VC office, and we had a crowd in there every week. And great guests from the show: We had Hudson and the other boys on. We had Ali Wong, who was a writer on the show at the time; we had Camilla Blackett, also a writer; we had Melvin and Natch. It was a part of the whole effort around the community to just get this thing going. But to me, the funniest thing is still that it was you, in the middle of this, dealing with the fact that it was your son on TV.

**JEFF:** Yeah. I already had on my conscience the feeling that I was a part of *All-American Girl*'s demise. Because I had written a negative review back then, and it haunted me for decades. I actually quit being a TV reviewer after that, because I realized how much power there was in being someone who would give thumbs up or down. Before the Internet, before everyone now being a pundit, you could actu-

ally kill a show or movie. And Hudson getting this gig basically meant I had to quit writing for the *Wall Street Journal*—they were very kind, saying, "It's fine if you don't write about entertainment," but that was 90 percent of what I was writing about. So yeah, I was all in on making this work, because too many people had sacrificed to make it happen. And 20 years off the air was long enough, you know?

**PHIL:** I remember being on set a lot that first season. I had courtside seats because the show was being shot around the corner from my house. I remember being on set for the episode with the big block party scene, which was supposed to be episode two but ended up airing as episode three. And I remember Hudson was super uncomfortable with this sequence where he had to grab the butt of Honey, played by Chelsey Crisp.

**JEFF:** That scene showed how much the show eventually evolved, because Eddie's character changed so much from there, and so did Honey. Both moved away from those sitcom archetypes of the pervy loudmouthed kid and the "hot neighbor." Because they became more like who they are in real life. Hudson was 10 years old, and doing this thing even as a gag just felt so disrespectful—he's this little nugget of a kid and she's a grown woman. He ended up on the verge of tears, and Jake Kasdan, who was directing the episode, called for a break, told everyone to go away, and sat down with Hudson on this pile of mats. He talked to him about how hard it was to grow up as a kid in this business. Because Jake's dad is Lawrence Kasdan, a Hollywood legend, he knows what it was like, growing up second-generation Hollywood. He told Hudson, if you don't want to do it, we'll kill it. It's a throwaway sight gag. We'll rewrite this scene right here and now. But if you do do it, I promise we will not let it make you or Chelsey look bad. And he said, "There are a lot of kids who get eaten up in this business, and I will tell you now, we will not let that happen to you." And he and Melvin and Natch made good on that promise. They were always there to back him and the other boys up, and to spend the time to talk them through things and give them the support they needed.

**PHIL:** It took a village to raise that kid, and it took a nation to make this show survive. We should talk a little about how it ended.

**JEFF:** The tweets.

**PHIL:** The tweets. When the show was renewed for a sixth season, Constance reacted by basically showing how angry and disappointed she was. And people were shocked, because usually actors celebrate when their shows survive.

**JEFF:** But to put things into context, Constance had become one of the biggest stars in Hollywood, she'd been in *Crazy Rich Asians,* she'd gotten award nominations and had her pick of big film projects to do. And what people forget is that when she was first cast, some shady manager had put out that she was four years younger than her real age. But she was turning 32 when the show started, and she was turning 35 when *Crazy Rich Asians* changed everything. And by the time she was in *Hustlers,* which confirmed she was a huge movie star talent, she was past that—past an age when Hollywood starts treating actresses differently, in terms of what roles you get to play. Her reaction was based on that: the show was probably on its last legs, everyone was signed up to do seven seasons, and renewal meant she'd have to turn down a movie role she'd fought hard to

get. It was an indelicate situation. But I understood where it came from.

**PHIL:** I think there was no question she was going to keep going on to bigger things. So many people from the show did. Ali Wong became a superstar. Randall has blown up. Melvin and Jake and Natch are running Hollywood.

**JEFF:** The show broke all the conventions, overcame all the snakebites, and it showed how you could be universal while being specific—telling the story of Asian Americans through the lens of an explicitly Taiwanese Chinese family. The show shot an episode in Taiwan! Growing up, I never ever thought I'd see that happen. Flying to Taiwan was such a flex. And then it was over—and I remember Hudson crying nonstop after the series wrap, because this had been half his life. Those tears were about how much he was going to miss his second family. But also he was afraid of what would come next for him, a kid who'd spent six years being on camera in one role. Was there even going to be another chance for him?

**PHIL**: People take for granted how much *Fresh Off the Boat* changed things. Hollywood is different now. There are more chances, for him and for Asians across the board. Because the big legacy of *Fresh Off the Boat* is that now shows like this can exist, and it's a normal thing. It made it safe for Asian American shows to not have to be special.

But it still blows my mind that a month after the final episode aired, COVID hit. And all of this latent racism burst out into the culture.

**JEFF:** I think that part of the reason we've been able to weather all of this is that we had personalities and leaders who were able to come forward and defy the violence and bigotry. And that we as a community felt like we could hold our heads up. And that people outside of our community were able to empathize with us, to see us as human, to stand up as allies. If *Fresh Off the Boat* and *Crazy Rich Asians* and everything that came after helped to make that possible, it was all worthwhile.

# THE *FRESH OFF THE BOAT* STARTER KIT

One of the most fun aspects of the Huang family's television journey was the opportunity to explore themes and storylines that were unique to Asian American identity and community—things you hadn't seen on any other show in television history. Here are 10 episodes that showcase some of the uniquely familiar Asian American themes and "firsts" that *Fresh Off the Boat* brought to primetime network TV.

## ADOPTEES

### Season 1, Episode 8: "Phillip Goldstein"

Albert Tsai, who'd later go on to star in *Dr. Ken*, ABC's Asian American family sitcom vehicle for Ken Jeong, plays an adopted Chinese Jewish kid who becomes Eddie's friend, and then nemesis—humorously bringing to light some of the issues related to transracial Asian adoption.

## LUNAR NEW YEAR AS A REAL HOLIDAY

### Season 2, Episode 11: "Year of the Rat"

From Halloween to Hanukkah, holiday-themed episodes are an American sitcom tradition. But in 2016, *Fresh Off the Boat* became the first network show to ever devote a special "holiday episode" to Lunar New Year—a tradition they would revisit over several seasons.

## THE "OTHER NAME"

### Season 2, Episode 20: "Hi, My Name Is . . ."

While opening his first bank account, Evan grapples with whether to use his American or his Chinese name. Jessica and Louis explain how they adopted their own "easier to pronounce" American names, in a hilarious and poignant reflection on names, assimilation, and bicultural identity.

## SHOES OFF, ORANGES OUT

### Season 2, Episode 23: "The Manchurian Dinner Date"

When Eddie's fake Asian girlfriend (it's complicated) shows up at his doorstep, she presents his parents with a traditional box of oranges and takes off her shoes before entering the house. (That's something even the Huangs notoriously didn't do, explained away as the result of the intersection of Louis's "wide-ass feet" with cowboy boots.) Seeing this display of authentic Chineseness causes Jessica to cry literal tears of happiness.

## THE HOMELAND

### Season 3, Episode 1: "Coming from America"

In the Season 3 premiere, family drama sends the Huangs to Taiwan. Filmed on location in Taipei, the episode is an ambitious reverse fish-out-of-water take on what happens when an Asian American immigrant family returns to the motherland.

## THE BIG BOX

### Season 3, Episode 6: "What Would Jessica Do?"

Jessica's obsessive love of bargains—often garnered through negotiations that feel more like mafia coercion—is a running joke in the series, but this episode demonstrates the unique love Asians have for a certain Big Box Discount Warehouse store. Okay, we'll name it by name, because the episode does too: this episode is about Costco.

## TURNING AMERICAN

### Season 3, Episode 9: "How to Be an American"

Over the course of several episodes, the show thoughtfully explored the meaning of citizenship, culminating in this episode, featuring Jessica's unexpectedly moving naturalization ceremony.

## THE ASIAN FLUSH

### Season 3, Episode 17: "The Flush"

Eddie learns about the "Flush" (an allergic reaction many alcohol-consuming Asians know) the hard way when he takes a sip of beer—and turns bright red, in what has to be the first PSA for Asian Flush on U.S. TV.

## THE "MOTHER TONGUE"

### Season 4, Episode 16: "Ride the Tiger"

In the show's third observance of Lunar New Year, the Huangs engage in a friendly contest to see who can go the longest speaking only in Mandarin. It comes down to a challenge of wills between Evan and Jessica, and 50 percent of the episode's dialogue ends up being performed in Mandarin.

## STUDY TOURS

### Season 5, Episode 21: "Under the Taipei Sun"

In Season 5, in the series's 100th episode (guest-starring Simu Liu of *Kim's Convenience* and Marvel's *Shang-Chi!*), Eddie goes back to Taiwan, this time as part of a cultural exchange program that for all intents and purposes is the show's analog of the "Love Boat."*

---

\* See page 118, "Setting Sail on the Love Boat"

# OUR FAVORITE FAMILY

The Huangs filled our screens for six seasons, bringing Nineties nostalgia and a defiantly Asian American POV to primetime that didn't stop to explain cultural nuances or inside jokes—if you knew, you knew. If you haven't yet binged the show, here's a quick intro to the members of Asian America's first family, who over the course of 116 half-hour slices of life made us laugh, made us cry, and along the way, made history.

## RANDALL PARK
### AS LOUIS HUANG

**CHARACTER QUOTE:** *"Sometimes you have to spend money you don't have to make it seem like you have money that you don't spend."*

**DESCRIPTION:** As Taiwanese immigrant restaurateur Louis, Park was the Asian sitcom dad of America's dreams—funny, kind, pop-culture savvy, and always willing to lend a hand, even an unwanted hand, to those in need. He was best known for hair that won't quit (he even installed a sit-down salon blow-dryer to keep it perfectly coiffed) and his love of Halloween, the holiday that let him be anyone he'd ever aspired to be: Mr. T, KISS lead singer Gene Simmons, Jerry Seinfeld, Super Mario, the Godfather . . . or Mad Cow Disease?

**RANDALL ON *FRESH*:** "Every step of the way was a surprise to me. When I first heard that the project was in development, I was like, that's great, good luck with that. When I found out It was getting picked up for a pilot, I was like, that's amazing. We got a pilot! That's already a victory. And then I got cast in the pilot, and it was just mind-blowing. And then the pilot got picked up to series. And again, I could not believe it. I was like, let's celebrate this and really cherish the first three episodes, because we're going to get canceled after the first. I really feel lucky to have been a part of it. When I was on the set, every day I'd look at the props and the people and how high the ceilings of the sound stages were, and think, gosh, I'm so lucky to be here."

## CONSTANCE WU AS JESSICA HUANG

**CHARACTER QUOTE:** *"No one seems to appreciate how I'm good at everything I do."*

**DESCRIPTION:** Jessica was the brains, beauty, *and* brawn of the Huang family (regularly demonstrating almost superhuman physical abilities, like braining a runaway thug with a thrown onion from two blocks away). But Wu brought vulnerability, eccentricity, and endless charm to a role that could've been an easy stereotype—turning her into a character never before seen on U.S. television, and the show's breakout star. As much as Louis loved

Halloween, Jessica loved Christmas—when she would arrange her collection of holiday porcelain mice and dress up as the only real Santa, Lao Ban Santa, the boss of all Santas, to exhort her kids to do better in the year to come.

**CONSTANCE ON *FRESH*:** "What being Jessica really taught me is that we need to be more conscious about what we mean by breaking stereotypes. Because traditionally that means doing the opposite of what is expected. So instead of being good at math, they're really bad at math and doing a bunch of drugs. But the truth is, stereotypes are harmful not because they're inherently wrong, but because they reduce and flatten people. Jessica cracked open stereotypes because while she had 'tiger mom' qualities, she wasn't reduced to only those qualities. She was so much more."

**HUDSON YANG AS EDDIE HUANG**

**CHARACTER QUOTE:** *"Hey, this is what you signed up for, remember? You knew my way could get messy, but it works."*

**DESCRIPTION:** Brash, boisterous, lazy, lovable, Eddie was the heart and soul of the show, even after it became an increasingly ensemble story after the first season, when focus shifted from Eddie's trials as a square peg in a round hole in school and in his family and toward a wider-angle look at the intersections between the Huangs and the (mostly white) world around them. But his love of hip-hop still defined much of the show's unique vibe, and led to memorable cameos from the likes of Busta Rhymes, Wu-Tang's RZA, and DMX.

**HUDSON ON *FRESH*:** "When I first started out on the show, I was such a little kid, I was running around, eating everything, making noise. It took me a while to realize that it was a job—it felt too fun to be a job—but I started to take it seriously when I realized how much it impacted people. I'd get messages from people about how Eddie was exactly like they were, growing up, and how important it was to see someone like them on TV. I love that we gave people that: a chance to see themselves."

**FORREST WHEELER AS EMERY HUANG**

**CHARACTER QUOTE:** *"The number-one dating rule is to listen to a woman. Especially when she's talking about horses."*

**DESCRIPTION:** The middle kid of the Huang family, Emery had in many ways the hardest role to play: a mediator, a peacemaker, a calm

> "It felt too fun to be a job, but I started to take it seriously when I realized how much it impacted people. I'd get messages from people about . . . how important it was to see someone like them on TV. I love that we gave people that: a chance to see themselves."

oasis in the center of the chaotic Huang-icane. As seasons went by, Emery's perfection as the popular kid that everyone loved—especially the girls—got dented by both puberty and reality, as the world became too complicated for him to get by as the Huangs' resident nice guy.

**FORREST ON** *FRESH*: "Emery was the well-adjusted middle brother. Things came easily to him, letting him be the happy-go-lucky, no worries, 'just being me' sibling who brought an air of balance to the family. I related to him; he had the same sensibilities as I do. But I'm an only child, so one of the best things about the show for me was that it gave me a chance to have brothers."

### IAN CHEN
### AS EVAN
### HUANG

**CHARACTER QUOTE:**

*"God forgives unconditionally. But I don't."*

**DESCRIPTION:** The youngest kid in a family sitcom is usually the smartest one in the family, but Evan—a meticulous, mother-loving prodigy, too adult for his short pants but not grown-up enough to give up his Beanie Babies—was a television original, whether ruling the local homeowners' association with a tiny iron fist or putting big bro Eddie in his place.

**IAN ON** *FRESH*: "Being on *Fresh Off the Boat* was a dream come true. It was definitely really important as the first show featuring an all–Asian American cast in 20 years, and it was kind of like a stepping-stone to having more diverse shows on television. When I was first cast I was so young I didn't really think about what we were doing—I just thought that it would be really cool to see myself on television. And now the whole world has seen us."

### LUCILLE
### SOONG
### AS JENNY
### "GRANDMA"
### HUANG

**CHARACTER QUOTE:** *"Oh, is the princess lonely? My feet were bound when I was seven."*

**DESCRIPTION:** The only member of the Huang household who regularly stood up to—and more often than not, came out on top against—the elemental force that was Jessica Huang, Grandma Jenny was a ride-or-die partner in crime for her eldest grandson, Eddie, and an unpredictable variable in every episode. And she spoke mostly Mandarin for the better part of six seasons—making her likely the first, and certainly the longest-running, Chinese-speaking main cast member in network prime-time TV.

**LUCILLE ON** *FRESH*: "When I was filming *55 Days at Peking* in 1962, the studio cast a white English actress to play the Chinese empress. Now we have Asian actors to play Asians. It has been a long journey. It was so much fun playing Jenny. She had so many faces, she was kind, smart, and crafty. A lot of fans still stop me in stores to tell me 'You were my favorite.' I really enjoyed being a grandma. But only on TV, ha ha!"

DANIEL DAE KIM    KEN JEONG    RANDALL PARK

# THREE KINGS

*The slow rise and late bloom of three of Hollywood's*
*most visible and beloved Asian American actors*

### BY PHILIP WANG

**IF YOU ASK** anybody to name an Asian American actor off the top of their head, there's a pretty good chance they'll respond with one of the following three names, and maybe all of them: **DANIEL DAE KIM**, **KEN JEONG**, and **RANDALL PARK**. Kim first became a household name on NBC's iconic science fiction series *Lost*. Jeong sprang into visibility—literally—in the anarchic comedy *The Hangover*. And while Park is still remembered for a tiny cameo he had in the long-running sitcom *The Office* as "Asian Jim," it was his role as Asian America's dad in *Fresh Off the Boat* that brought him the attention that he'd long deserved.

And that (and the fact that all three happen to be Korean American men) is something Kim, Jeong, and Park have in common: They've been doing amazing work in Hollywood for a very long time, but only really began to receive appreciation as A-list actors decades after they'd already proven their worth, because that's how long it took for this industry to give them credit for it. Not that they were "given" anything—because if there's one thing their careers show, it's that for Asian Americans to receive the respect they're due, it has to be demanded.

We talked to them about their long journeys to the top, the frustrations they felt along the way, the defiant choices they made to take control of their careers and destinies—and the commitment they've each shown to reaching back to others who are farther behind on the path.

## The First Step Is the Hardest

*Even just beginning down the path of being a performer was a challenge. All three had to overcome skepticism from their loved ones and their own self-doubt, before even making the vital choice to embrace a creative career.*

**KEN:** I grew up in North Carolina, and had no aspirations at all to go into entertainment as a kid. I always had a sense of humor, but even through high school, I never did any theater. It wasn't until right before graduation that there was this mock male beauty pageant, and

I decided to participate. I sang "Three Times a Lady" by Lionel Richie and got a standing ovation—I was 16, and it was like a *Napoleon Dynamite* moment. I should mention, I graduated from high school when I was 16. But I went to Duke University with every intention to be a pre-med student, and then on a whim I took an "Intro to Acting" class my sophomore year. That's when I was really bitten by the acting bug. I applied to Duke's theater school and actually got accepted, and was contemplating switching over because I was failing organic chemistry. My dad got real with me, though: he knew I was talented, but he said to me, "Do you think a guy who looks like you could succeed in L.A.? Can you deal with the rejection?"

Knowing how much my parents sacrificed so I could go to Duke, I made the very difficult decision to quit drama and stay pre-med. My last semester in college, I did as much theater as I could, thinking it would be my last hurrah.

**RANDALL:** Growing up in L.A., I loved comic books—I even made my own, and bound them together myself with a stapler. They were generally pretty dirty. And because I was a shy kid, it was through these comic books that I started finding an inkling of a voice. It wasn't until I went to UCLA, though, that that voice would turn toward the Asian American community. The funny thing is, I didn't even want to go to UCLA, because I knew there were so many Asians there—I had a very diverse friend group as a kid and I'd never been really surrounded by Asians. But as soon as I stepped into the dorms, I met so many Asian Americans and it was kind of magical, like it was what I'd been missing my whole life. My English TA encouraged me to explore writing, and that's when I started writing plays. And because two other friends

of mine, Dave Lee and Derek Mateo, were also writing plays, we decided to form a little theater group, which was just the three of us at first, three Asian dudes. I was learning about so many Asian American issues, opening my eyes to all the ways in which I'd been marginalized even within my own group of friends as a kid, all the frustrations I'd had that I didn't link to my Asianness back then. Those were the kinds of issues we wrote about, and this makeshift theater company of ours, which we called Lapu the Coyote That Cares, really started taking off on campus.

**DANIEL:** Looking back, when I was starting out, I really didn't realize how bad it was going to be, even while I lived through it. I thought we had a long way to go, but I felt like things were changing—that it wasn't that bad—because in the 1990s, I remember working with older actors telling me stories about how lucky I was, and how many more opportunities there were for me than they had. For example, at the time there was this first push toward what was then called "color-blind" casting in the theater. There were some prominent companies championing the multicultural casting in their productions of the classics—that's how I got to be in *Romeo and Juliet* back in 1991. But had I known then how difficult the next 30 years were going to be, I don't know if I would've even begun to walk down this road. I'm very grateful to be where I am today, but it was really difficult getting here. Because the only way you get better at any skill is by practice. By repetition. And if you're an Asian actor, and you rarely get the chance to act, how are you going to get any better? And of course, then you've just fulfilled the perception that there are no "experienced" Asian actors.

## Grinding Upward

*The only option they had was to stay committed and keep honing their craft, hoping for that first big break.*

**DANIEL:** I started with small parts in theater, and then bigger parts in theater, and then really tiny parts in TV, like a medical examiner on *Law & Order*—basically, I hit every Asian trope. And then I decided to go back to grad school for acting. This business was hard enough as an Asian, so I wanted to concentrate on the things that I could change and control, which for me was getting better at the craft of acting.

**RANDALL:** I started taking as many acting classes as I could after graduating, since I had never taken one in college. I had no road map to get started in Hollywood, but I knew I had to get good at the craft; whenever I made any sort of money, I put it toward a class or a workshop. That was my life, just scrounging for opportunities to act.

**KEN:** Once I got into med school, I leveraged that to convince my parents to let me do what I wanted for my "last summer." And what I wanted was to take an acting class at UCLA. But it was also around this time that I discovered stand-up comedy and started to do open mics. Even when I started med school, I just kept doing it—maybe only once every three months, because med school was so intense I had no bandwidth. But in my mind, stand-up could only be a hobby. I was going to be a doctor, and stand-up would be my golf.

## Cracking the Ceiling

*There was no "big break" for a long time. Even when opportunity knocked, it knocked softly, and there was always the fear that it would be a fickle guest, ready to bolt at any moment.*

**RANDALL:** Our college theater group became something of a phenomenon around campus, just by word of mouth. We'd be turning people away at the door, lines would wrap around buildings to buy tickets, and more and more talented people were joining—like Ali Wong! But eventually I graduated, and I didn't want to stop. So I built a stage in my parents' backyard out of scrap wood I'd found around the neighborhood. It even had a full bar. And a lot of the energy and hunger for the stories we were doing in college followed us to this new theater group. At this point, I was working a day job as a graphic designer, spending all my nights and weekends on acting, and I was also doing stand-up comedy. It was clear that I had the passion to pursue performing as a full-time gig. But I had no idea how to do that. Like, I knew some people who were succeeding, but I thought I couldn't follow their specific paths. I came to learn later that there *is* no single path. So I got little breaks here and there, but nothing ever felt like it was going to change my life. My first regular role was on MTV's *Wild 'n Out,* but I was still working at a Starbucks while on that show. I was still paying off my student loans.

**DANIEL:** For a long time, every Asian actor I know would have to wait for the "Chinatown episode." On the one hand we were encouraged that there even were "Chinatown episodes," but the reality is it's not just about the number of roles out there, but the quality of them. My generation all ended up having early reels filled with triad members or unscrupulous businessmen. But I made my way up to eventually being a series regular on a sci-fi show on cable called *Crusade*, because back then, if you were Asian the only place you could ever be regular cast was on a sci-fi show, and that was thanks to Gene Roddenberry and George Takei. So it was a slow progression until I got *Lost.* But even then, I never felt like my life had changed. To celebrate the second-season renewal, I bought myself a plasma TV, because I'd never had enough money for a big TV before—it was a congratulatory gift to myself. But I was so concerned that I was going to get killed off the show that I never threw away the box! And the box would just sit in my place as a constant reminder that whatever I had could get taken away from me at any time. I still have that philosophy. I don't take my career for granted.

**KEN:** I always thought that I'd just end up as a full-time physician just doing comedy on the side. And maybe I'd get to rub elbows with Daniel or John Cho at special events, and that was fine. Even when I quit my doctor job at 37, I wasn't looking to be rich or famous; I was just looking to be a good actor, because I thought it was too late for me to be anything but a character actor. And I'd resigned myself that if that well dried up, I would've just gone back to being a doctor, and I wouldn't even have regretted it. It was like Michael Jordan playing baseball and then going back to hoops. But one of the character roles I got was for *Knocked Up.* It was the most difficult audition of my life, because I was called in directly to do a table read with ALL the actors and Judd Apatow, and casting told me, hey, just to be clear, you still don't have the gig. I was scared shitless. But after the table read, Judd came up to me and said, "Fantastic job." Fast-forward to after the filming, he said to me, "You're my discovery, and I'll take care

of you." My relationship with him led to me getting a lot of other roles—one of them being *The Hangover,* which essentially changed everything for me.

## Hitting the Wall

*When a chance to really be seen did finally come along, it came with heartaches—and backlash from forces beyond the industry, including ones close to home.*

**KEN:** I actually initially turned down the role in *The Hangover,* because Mr. Chow was originally written as a 60-year-old man. And my wife, Tran, was going through breast cancer treatment at the time, and I was afraid I would be distracted. But after talking to her, I took the role, because I wanted to make her laugh. So my goal from the beginning with Mr. Chow was to play a stereotypical character so hard that the stereotype would be shattered. It was my intention to trust the audience—that they'd know I was doing this as a meta joke. The character wasn't written in that way, so I ended up having to make up a lot on the fly. Even the naked scene I did was in imitation of Will Ferrell in *Old School,* another Todd Phillips movie. If I'd just done the role as it was given, people would say, "Yeah, we've seen this before." But if I took it farther, if I took it so far it came out the other side, they couldn't say that. It was the only way I could let myself do the role and live my absolute truth. And ever since, I've never played another live-action role with an accent. I broke that role, and I'm not doing it again.

**DANIEL:** When *Lost* first came out, the reaction to my character, Jin, was not a positive one, especially from the Korean community. I got a lot of backlash for playing a domineering Asian man, and I also got a lot of backlash for my language skills. It was heartbreaking that the very people that I cared about most were the ones I got criticized by the most. I will say that things changed once the character turned a little bit and the show became a bigger hit. But it definitely wasn't a love story from the Asian American community at the start.

**RANDALL:** I finally landed this great role in *The Interview,* and sure, it was playing a murderous dictator, but I thought it was going to be a turning point in my career. That's what everyone was telling me, and I started believing it. But then the actual North Korean government threatened the United States over the film, it became a huge security risk, and I saw my big moment crumble before me. The movie was being pulled from big theaters. I was being told I needed security at my house. I remember being a little depressed because I had been fed the idea by so many people that this was going to be my big break. And also because of the death threats.

## Breaking Through

*But decades into their careers, each finally landed in roles that showed them for who they are: talented, appealing, capable of connecting with audiences and playing roles that put them at the center of the screen. They didn't get there without help—and that helped them recognize the importance of setting an example for the future, and giving back to the community.*

**RANDALL:** At the same time as I was doing *The Interview,* I was also attached to *Fresh Off the Boat.* I still remember executive producer

Melvin Mar approaching me with the book and saying he wanted me to play the dad. A part of me was like, "Really? You want me to play this? Did you know I'm not that famous?" But another part of me was like, "Well, it's okay, because this show is never going to get made." But then it made its way through the system, and even so, I think it just barely got through. And then we ran for six seasons.

**KEN:** Thank God there was *Fresh Off the Boat,* because without *Fresh Off the Boat* there is no *Crazy Rich Asians.* There certainly would be no *Dr. Ken,* which is ironic, because at the time I was thinking it wouldn't be possible to get *Dr. Ken* made, because *Fresh Off the Boat* was already out there. I still get choked up thinking about it because it was actually Melvin Mar who went to bat for us, showing up on set at our pilot taping and then telling the ABC execs that they had to put us on the air. So it's literally *Fresh Off the Boat* that made my dream to have my own show come true, and it's still my favorite thing I've ever done, because I created, wrote, and acted in it. And it broke the "rule of one." It's amazing to me that there were two Asian American shows on the same network, and none on any other network except ours. So shout-out to Melvin and to Samie Falvey, who's Korean American and was head of comedy at ABC at the time, for championing both shows. We proved we can all get there together. And I've taken that to heart. I've supported and invested in Asian American independent films. I've made it a point to try to give back, because I've learned it's less about being famous than it is what you do with your fame.

**DANIEL:** After *Lost* I had a pretty high profile, and I was pitched to join the cast of the reboot of *Hawaii Five-0.* I'll just say that it was a role that changed my life, but also came with a lot of lessons. When they refused to put me and Grace Park on the same level as the white leads, I decided to leave the show. And when I did, the studio initially prepared a statement for me to use, so my exit wouldn't be seen as a big deal. But I refused to sign off on it, because it was untrue. I felt that by agreeing, I'd be perpetuating a problem. Because of that, my departure became a big story. And I'm glad that it meant something in particular to Asian Americans, because so often we're underemployed—not unemployed, but underemployed. Once we get to the higher levels, not just in entertainment but everywhere, we somehow stop moving up the ladder. We're recruited just to be the grunts. When you look in the C-suites, we're not there. The perception is that we're very qualified for entry-level work, but once we get to leadership positions, we're not qualified. I firmly believe we need to stand up to demand the respect we've earned.

## Are We There Yet?

*Now they've gotten to a place where they can make a difference—each of them not just starring in, but producing work for others. There wasn't a path laid out for them, but they're making sure they're laying a path out behind.*

**KEN:** When I first started, there were so few of us that everyone was under a microscope. Today, I look around, and I'm one of many. Well, I look forward to being one of a million someday. I tell my kids all the time that they have the freedom now to do whatever they want—art, acting, whatever they want, so of course they'll probably rebel and become doctors. But it all boils down to that freedom of choice. And I want that freedom of choice too. I think I've earned it. I want the ability to work on projects not just with *an* Asian writer, but with *only* Asian writers. That way if we disagree, whatever happens, it's still an Asian who's going to win.

**RANDALL:** I have a production company now. I feel it's like starting all over again. There are so many new things to learn and it's a new kind of battleground. I don't like getting caught up in celebrating too much, because there's still so much more work to be done. Yes, the dam has broken! But it wasn't like we saw one accomplishment happen after the other. It's more like there was this big constipated mass of talent that finally burst through from all the hard effort that came before. And I know that that's a disgusting metaphor. But my point is, I'm finally optimistic.

**DANIEL:** Everything happens as a direct result of the sequence of events before. It's slow. It's not always steady. It took a perfect storm for us to finally even get the chance we have now. But as I get older now, I think about legacy a lot more. Over the decades I've seen with my own eyes many Asians in our business who have *not* helped other Asian Americans. We need to strive to inspire and lead in our community. You get these awards saying you're a "pioneer," and yes, it's a compliment, but pioneers are the ones getting stuck with thorns and hit in the face with branches. Well, you'd better be clearing the forest for people behind you. You'd better be reaching back and taking hands and leading the way, because why should others suffer the same way you did? You need to do it, or otherwise, it won't get done.

# The Road to *Crazy Rich Asians*

BY JON M. CHU, AS TOLD TO JEFF YANG; PENCILS: CHRISTINE NORRIE; INKS & COLORS: TAK TOYOSHIMA

AFTER THAT, I REFUSED TO SHOW IT TO ANYONE. WHICH IS BAD, SINCE A WHOLE CREW OF FOLKS *WORKED* ON IT.

AND I NO LONGER MADE FILMS FOCUSED ON PEOPLE WHO LOOKED LIKE *ME*. I WAS AFRAID OF TOUCHING THAT NERVE AGAIN.

JUSTIN BIEBER

@GWAILO

BUT BY MY SIXTH MOVIE, I REALIZED: I KNOW HOW TO MAKE MOVIES. AND I KNOW HOW TO GET A MOVIE *MADE*, WHICH IS NOT THE SAME.

AND THEN I STARTED GETTING ALL THESE *EMAILS* ABOUT THIS BOOK, *CRAZY RICH ASIANS*.

...THINGS STARTED TO *HAPPEN*.

*#STARRINGJOHNCHO* WENT VIRAL. ASIAN AMERICANS WERE GOING *WILD* OVER THE IDEA THAT SEEING OURSELVES AT THE CENTER OF THE SCREEN COULD MAKE A *DIFFERENCE*.

@JOHNTHECHO

CRAZY RICH ASIANS
KEVIN KWAN

**CUPERTINO CUZ:** OMG IT'S SO GOOD

**SIS:** HAVE YOU READ IT?

**MOM:** YOU NEED TO MAKE THIS!

CRAZY RICH ASIANS KEVIN KWAN

I DIDN'T THINK IT'D *WORK*. AND IF SO, I DIDN'T THINK *I* WAS THE ONE TO DO IT. BUT THEN...

OH GOO, IT'S *RANDALL!*

*CAPE*, THE COALITION OF ASIAN PACIFICS IN ENTERTAINMENT, HAD ITS 25TH ANNIVERSARY *GALA*.

*HUDSON*, OVER HERE!

LOVE YA, *CONSTANCE!*

AND IT FELT *DIFFERENT*. THE CAST OF *FRESH OFF THE BOAT* WAS THERE, BEING TREATED LIKE MOVIE STARS!

EVERYONE WAS GORGEOUSLY DRESSED, TALKING, DANCING...IT WAS FUN! *SOMETHING* HAD CHANGED.

OK!

SO I FINALLY CRACKED OPEN THE *BOOK*.

THE PROTAGONIST IS NAMED RACHEL *CHU*? AND THE CHU SIDE OF HER FAMILY LIVES IN *CUPERTINO*?

WHERE *I* GREW UP?

...AND RACHEL HAS A *COUSIN* WHO MAKES *MOVIES*?

TURNS OUT MY COUSIN IS PALS WITH THE AUTHOR, *KEVIN KWAN*, WHO INCLUDED STORIES SHE TOLD HIM ABOUT *OUR* FAMILY. THAT DIRECTOR WAS *ME!*

# University Culture Fest

BY ESTHER TSENG AND JEFF YANG

**FOR A LOT OF US,** college is where we "became Asian American." It was the first time we encountered other people who came from ethnic backgrounds different from our own, but shared experiences we found ironically familiar. Across crowded rooms, and usually over some kind of dumplings, we exchanged stories, celebrated, commiserated, and forged the first tentative bonds of something that felt like community. More often than not, this process took place in the leadup to, or on the night of, that one big event in most Asian American student organization calendars: the annual "Culture Festival," which brought together people from across the spectrum of Asian American campus groups to, well, put on a show, designed to show off talent, demonstrate solidarity, and pay homage to old traditions and contemporary pop obsessions. The Culture Festival usually combined elements of drama, comedy, ethnic music and dance, martial arts, hip-hop, and maybe even a runway featuring fashion or "traditional dress," all anchored by earnest emceeing by student leaders or local broadcast personalities. However the festival might be organized—some had ambitious overarching themes and strict quality-control screening for inclusion, others were variety shows featuring a hodgepodge of volunteer performances—they provided a yearly showcase for the diverse backgrounds and unexpected gifts of Asian American students, while giving the participants an excuse to engage in collaboration and foster camaraderie over many weeks spent together as directors, curators, choreographers, dance partners, sparring opponents, and cast and crew. The planning and preparation were as important in building bonds as the final festival performances themselves. Welcome to University Culture Festival night!

1. Nervous backstage manager urgently muttering through headset mic. The show's about to start, where the heck is the guy who operates the head part of the "lion dance" lion?

2. In bathroom behind the stage: Guy who operates the head part of the "lion dance" lion, at urinal (wearing the lion head)

3. Back half of lion, freaking out

4. Racks of ethnic clothing donated by local parents

5. Wooden sets painstakingly built and painted, which will be used for one five-minute performance and then immediately recycled

6. Culture Fest Best in Show trophy: it's not much but it comes with a $100 gift certificate for the local Korean BBQ

7. Big Greek letters for the Asian frat's lip-sync performance

8. Asian student coalition co-presidents (popular guy + woman who does all the actual work) delivering a welcome full of awkward puns on the word "Asian" ("You all look am-Asian!" "What a celebr-Asian!")

9. Impeccably coiffed local broadcast anchor who cannot wait to move up to a bigger market

10. Dean of multicultural affairs impatiently standing by, holding a proclamation stating how much the school appreciates their multicultural-ness

11. Rows of folding chairs

IT WAS A STORY OF AN ASIAN AMERICAN GOING TO *ASIA* AND BEING TREATED LIKE A *FOREIGNER*, THEN HAVING TO PROVE SHE *DESERVED* TO BE THERE.

IT WAS *XIAO GWAILO!* BUT THIS TIME, I WAS GOING TO MAKE SURE THE *WHOLE WORLD* WOULD SEE IT.

I *WANT* THIS MOVIE. *I'M* THE GUY.

I KNEW EXACTLY HOW IT HAD TO BE DONE. WE HAD TO ASSEMBLE THE *ASIAN AVENGERS.*

I WANTED TO WORK WITH *CONSTANCE WU* AND *JIMMY O. YANG.*

I WAS TOTALLY BLOWN AWAY BY *AWKWAFINA'S* YOUTUBE STUFF.

I LOVED *RONNY CHIENG* ON *THE DAILY SHOW* AND *GEMMA CHAN* ON *HUMANS.*

BUT WE HAD TO DECIDE *WHERE* WE WERE GOING TO MAKE THIS. *NETFLIX* WANTED IN! NO WORRIES ABOUT *BOX OFFICE.* FORGET *CRITICS.* 200 MILLION SUBSCRIBERS AROUND THE *WORLD!*

AT THE SAME TIME, WE HAD SOMETHING TO *PROVE* TO *HOLLYWOOD.* TO THE *WORLD.* TO *OURSELVES.* IT HAD TO BE IN THEATERS. AND *WARNER BROTHERS* WANTED TO MAKE THAT *HAPPEN.*

NETFLIX OFFERED US A *LOT* OF MONEY. MORE THAN I'D MADE IN MY *LIFE.* GUARANTEED *CREATIVE CONTROL.* MASSIVE *MARKETING* DOLLARS, PLUS THE SECOND AND THIRD MOVIES *LOCKED IN* UP FRONT.

WARNER BROTHERS CAME IN AND, WELL, LET'S JUST SAY THEY WERE *LOWER.* *WITHOUT* THE SAME GUARANTEES.

WE RECOMMEND YOU GO WITH NETFLIX. IT'S LIKE WINNING THE *LOTTERY.*

YOU GET *EVERYTHING* YOU WANT!

EVERYTHING *EXCEPT* THE PROOF WE'D BEEN LOOKING FOR: THAT AN ALL-ASIAN CAST COULD CRASH THE *GATES.*

NETFLIX

WB

NETFLIX

12. Enthusiastic parents of one of the performers with flower bouquet and sign "WE LOVE YOU RAJ"

13. Skeptical parents of another performer thinking, "This is where we see if 20 years of violin lessons pay off"

14. Non-Asian students who are attending as part of an "experience other cultures" assignment, taking notes

15. Student photographers each trying to get a better shot than the others

16. Precision hip-hop dance crew whose leader is making them go through their routine one more time

17. Totally casual hip-hop dance crew that's formed a cypher and is just fooling around doing head spins and flares

18. Bhangra dance team, in full effect

19. Ribbon and fan dancers

20. A disgruntled former classical prodigy who now performs electric violin in a neon tuxedo

21. Improv troupe in T-shirts and jeans, mugging at each other and breaking up in hysterics, "Just get it all out now before we go onstage"

22. Fashion show models getting last-minute hem pins

23. Martial artists stretching; one guy has his shirt off because he's ripped and wants to flaunt it

24. Distracted nunchuck guy accidentally hitting someone in the crotch

25. Rock band tuning guitars and air-drumming; at least two non-Asians are in the band, but just focus on the Asian lead singer

26. "Parade of Nations" performers lining up and adjusting their ethnic dress

27. Traditional instrument performers getting ready (erhu, pipa, dizi, tabla, etc.)

28. A cappella group, overdressed in black tie and tails

29. Beatboxer wearing sunglasses and holding a drum pad

30. Potluck cuisine being laid out, the most generic dishes from across the Asian diaspora: dumplings, bulgogi, boba, lumpia, samosas, but also, there's pizza

31. Stray floor dumpling

32. Cases of off-brand bottled water donated by local businesses

33. Guy surreptitiously loading up a plate of food

34. Organizer about to drop the hammer on guy surreptitiously loading up a plate of food

35. Sponsorship banners from insurance agents, local bank, travel agency

36. Folding registration table with volunteers trying to check in a line of latecomers arriving on Asian time

37. "Are you sure my name isn't on there? Did you look under 'Wang' instead of 'Wong'?"

38. Guy trying to pay with a credit card

39. Volunteer trying to explain that they can't take credit cards

40. Merch table for Asian rock band, being staffed by a band member's significant other

# FOUNDING FATHERS AND MOTHERS

## 2010s

BY JEFF YANG, ILLUSTRATED BY SOJUNG KIM-McCARTHY

**BY THE 2010S,** a new generation of Asian American leaders had arrived, representing an array of divergent ideologies and policy priorities. For the first time, there were enough Asian Americans in key areas in government that they could afford to disagree, and they often did. Here are some of the reformers and rebuilders who, in the 2010s, led a major political maturation in the Asian American community.

**PRAMILA JAYAPAL:** Jayapal is the first South Asian American woman to serve in the U.S. House of Representatives. A cochair of the Congressional Progressive Caucus, she has been a leader on immigration issues, the fight for Medicare for All, and a $15 minimum wage.

**GRACE MENG:** Meng, the first Asian American to be elected to represent New York in the U.S. House, has been a prominent voice in the pushback against anti-Asian bias and hate crime in the wake of COVID-19.

**JUDY CHU:** The first Chinese American woman elected to the U.S. House, Chu has been a leader on immigrant rights, and in 2012 sponsored a bill that led to an official apology for the Chinese Exclusion Act. She is the chair of the Congressional Asian Pacific American Caucus.

**TED LIEU:** Lieu, an Air Force veteran and reservist, was one of the most vocal leaders against the policies and behavior of President Donald Trump, both in the House and online. He was one of the managers for Trump's second impeachment.

**MAZIE HIRONO:** The first Asian American woman and the first Buddhist to be elected to the Senate, Hirono, a cancer survivor, has been a vocal advocate for expanded healthcare and women's reproductive rights.

**TAMMY DUCKWORTH:** Duckworth is the first Thai American to serve in the U.S. Senate. A decorated veteran who lost both legs in the Iraq War, she is the first disabled woman to be elected to the Senate, and in 2018 became the first senator to give birth while in office. She has been credited with saving the Americans with Disabilities Act.

**NIKKI HALEY:** Haley was the first Asian American woman to serve as governor, and when appointed UN ambassador by President Donald Trump, the first Indian American appointed to a cabinet-level position.

**MARK TAKANO:** Takano was the first openly gay Asian American in the House. A former public school teacher, he has been a leader in education.

**RO KHANNA:** Elected to the U.S. House with the backing of many of the most prominent entrepreneurs in Silicon Valley, Khanna has been an active leader on technology issues, as well as on the environment and electoral reform. He was cochair of Senator Bernie Sanders's presidential campaign in 2020.

**RAJA KRISHNAMOORTHI:** Krishnamoorthi was the first Indian American to preside over the U.S. House as speaker pro tempore. He has been a key voice on worker training, climate change, and the opioid epidemic during his time in office.

**STEPHANIE MURPHY:** The first Vietnamese American woman to serve in the U.S. House, Murphy has been a major force for immigration rights, gun control, and police reform.

**TULSI GABBARD:** An Iraq War veteran, Gabbard was elected to the U.S. House in 2012, and chose not to run for reelection after her campaign for president in 2020. She was known for her close relationships "across the aisle" while serving.

**AMI BERA:** Bera is a prominent centrist voice in the U.S. House who has been a key leader in climate change and—as a medical researcher—in healthcare-related issues.

# Asian Celebrity Chefs

BY ESTHER TSENG
ILLUSTRATED BY KITKAT PECSON

**AS THE FIRST** queen of culinary multimedia, Julia Child is usually considered America's first "celebrity chef," writing out the recipe for what it took to cultivate megabrands and devoted followings ever since. There were a few notable early exceptions to the notably white (and also male) realm of celebrity chefs: beginning in the 1960s, Boston-based restaurateur Joyce Chen launched what would become a cookbook, restaurant, and kitchenware empire, mostly out of sheer hustle. She introduced Northern Chinese–style dumplings (under the guise of "Peking ravioli") to the American palate, and was instrumental in bringing the wok into the U.S. mainstream; her PBS cooking show *Joyce Chen Cooks* was filmed on the same set as Julia Child's *The French Chef* (in part because Child was a fan). Sadly, Chen's series only ran for 26 episodes; it would fall to an immigrant from Hong Kong, Martin Yan, to establish the first real foothold in the culinary media mainstream: since he debuted in 1978, he's made over 1,500 episodes and counting of his beloved cooking show *Yan Can Cook*.

But it wasn't until the 2000s that Asian Americans really began to come into their own as true stars in the culinary firmament, propelled by the foodie phenomenon and the boom in reality TV cooking contests. Guides like Zagat and Michelin sent aspiring gourmets out to search star-blessed restaurants by the likes of San Francisco's Corey Lee, New York's Anita Lo, and Los Angeles's Nobu Matsuhisa. And Asian Americans like Mei Lin, Kristen Kish, and Sheldon Simeon became household names after their appearances on shows like *Top Chef*. Here's a selection of some of the most influential of this bumper crop of foodie favorites.

## ROY CHOI

**BEST KNOWN FOR:** Igniting the haute food-truck movement

Roy Choi's contributions to the culinary world are many, but his legacy began with the humble Kogi taco truck, where he applied his formal culinary training to his personal mission of feeding the people, putting gourmet fusion food on wheels. Bright, Korean-influenced flavors inform his cooking, while his populist sensibilities shape how he approaches his business, which is first and foremost focused on making really good food really accessible to the masses. He's expanded his restaurant empire from Los Angeles to Las Vegas and now has an illustrious TV presence. From his Netflix collaboration with director Jon Favreau, *The Chef Show*, to his public TV social-justice documentary series, *Broken Bread*, it's clear Choi is just getting started.

**SIGNATURE DISH:** The Kogi short rib taco

## PIM TECHAMUANVIVIT

**BEST KNOWN FOR:** Going from food blogger to Michelin-starred chef In 2001, then working in Silicon Valley, Pim Techamuanvivit launched her blog Chez Pim; it quickly became beloved, and not only for its sharp insights on food and restaurants. It allowed her to go from following engineers around with clipboards to commanding an army of loyal foodies—who, beginning in 2004, helped her raise hundreds of thousands of dollars a year for charity via her annual event, Menu for Hope. In 2014, she decided to go from keyboard to kitchen, opening her restaurant Kin Khao in San Francisco, and won a Michelin star the following year. In 2018, she was asked to take over a second Michelin-starred restaurant, Nahm, in Bangkok. She now shuttles between the Bay Area and Bangkok, while promoting her unique everything-from-scratch approach to Thai cuisine to both hemispheres.

**SIGNATURE DISH:** Rabbit green curry

## DAVID CHANG

**BEST KNOWN FOR:** The Momofuku restaurant and media empire Noodle Bar. Ssäm Bar. Milk Bar. Ko. These are just a sampling of the restaurants in Chang's empire—and that's just counting New York City. Chang's restaurants have pushed a truly Asian American food experience into mainstream consciousness, featuring menu items that draw from his Korean ancestry, his Japanese training, and his American childhood. Chang's all-inclusive approach to food is why he's responsible for helping popularize cereal milk as a food ingredient and for mainstreaming the concept of "umami." Along the way, Chang launched a short-lived but wildly influential magazine called *Lucky Peach,* and hosts a regular podcast, *The Dave Chang Show*, where you can hear him holding forth about topics such as the racism and the bad science entrenched in the demonization of MSG, and his hit Netflix show *Ugly Delicious.*

**SIGNATURE DISH:** The Momofuku pork bun

## NIKI NAKAYAMA

**BEST KNOWN FOR:** Reinventing *kaiseki* The inaugural season of David Gelb's addictive culinary Netflix documentary series, *Chef's Table,* turned Niki Nakayama into an international sensation after its episode sharing the story of her life, how she met the love of her life (wife Carole Iida, who is also her business partner and sous-chef), and how she challenged the patriarchal world of *kaiseki,* the multicourse seasonal, regional, chef's choice cuisine of Japan that at its highest levels is almost exclusively made by male chefs. Her version of the traditional Japanese multicourse progression, as served at her 18-seat Los Angeles restaurant n/naka, showcases not just deft technique but the best and freshest ingredients California has to offer. No wonder it's one of the most difficult reservations to obtain in L.A.

**SIGNATURE DISH:** Abalone pasta

## PREETI MISTRY

**BEST KNOWN FOR:** Her outspoken views on being immigrant, brown, and queer

Born in London but now based in the Bay Area, Mistry launched a catering company, Saffron Hill, then joined Bon Appetit Management Company as executive chef, where she oversaw food service at Google, before coming to fame as a contestant on Season 6 of *Top Chef*. Her fun, vibrant take on Indian fare made her restaurants Juhu Beach Club and Navi Kitchen a celebrated part of the eclectic Northern California dining scene and garnered her two coveted James Beard nominations as Best Chef of the West. But what has made Mistry stand out isn't just her cuisine—it's her candid commentary on race, gender, colonialism, and white supremacy and how they impact the culinary world and hospitality industry, which she has shared in essays, speeches, and directly in the faces of some of the grand old men of cooking. Now she's got her own line of spice blends called Spicewalla so home cooks can create their own Indian dishes.

**SIGNATURE DISH:** Manchurian cauliflower

## PADMA LAKSHMI

**BEST KNOWN FOR:** Hosting *Top Chef*

The former model, actress, and cookbook author cemented her status as food TV royalty through her longtime role as host and judge of the show that has virtually defined modern-day culinary celebrity: *Top Chef*. But she's also been an avid advocate for women's health, equity in the restaurant industry, and immigrant rights. She combines her activism with her passion for food on her travel and food series for Hulu, *Taste the Nation*, where she visits towns and cities all over America to learn about the signature cuisines of ethnic enclaves, and the cultures and peoples behind them.

**SIGNATURE DISH:** Her grandmother's Madras lemon rice

## EDWARD LEE

**BEST KNOWN FOR:** The LEE (Let's Empower Employment) Initiative

Edward Lee is a Brooklyn-born, NYU-educated Korean American chef, who became an adopted son of the American South after visiting Kentucky for the Derby in 2001. He moved there the following year, and began cooking modern Southern fare as chef at Louisville's celebrated 610 Magnolia, which he now owns, along with multiple other restaurants in Louisville and Washington, D.C. He's been nominated for a James Beard Award four times, competed on Season 9 of *Top Chef*, and even hosted a season of PBS's *The Mind of a Chef*. But he really captured the attention of the food world when he launched his nonprofit, The LEE Initiative, in 2018, which is focusing on making social change in and through the restaurant industry. Its Women Chefs Program has trained and mentored dozens of female stars in the making, helping to redress the culinary world's gender imbalance. And after COVID shut down restaurants across the nation, LEE raised funds to reopen them as community kitchens, feeding people in need over 300 meals a day.

**SIGNATURE DISH:** Collards and kimchi

## COREY LEE

**BEST KNOWN FOR:** Those three Michelin stars Regularly named as one of the most talented chefs in the nation, Lee is one of just 14 American chefs with a restaurant that has been awarded the Michelin Guide's highest possible honor—three stars. Benu's contemporary tasting dishes incorporate flavors and ingredients from his ancestral Korean culture, but also an array of others, both Asian and Western. But his restaurant/culinary art project In Situ, located at the San Francisco Museum of Modern Art, is perhaps even more fascinating: In Situ features a menu that replicates and showcases the greatest dishes of the most celebrated chefs in the world.

**SIGNATURE DISH:** Barbecued quail

## DANNY BOWIEN AND ANTHONY MYINT

**BEST KNOWN FOR:** A punk-populist approach to fine food

The pair—Bowien, a Korean adoptee who grew up in Oklahoma, and Myint, a Burmese Chinese American from Virginia who forged his eclectic palate after a 31-country tour of the globe's culinary traditions—met in San Francisco and immediately began partnering on a series of dining experiences: Mission Street Food, Mission Burger, and finally Mission Chinese Food, a pop-up restaurant within an existing Chinese restaurant, which was named Best New Restaurant in America by *Bon Appétit*. Standalone locations in Manhattan and Bushwick, Brooklyn, followed, as Myint began focusing his time on culinary sustainability issues and climate change, cofounding the nonprofit Zero Foodprint. Beginning in 2017, Mission Chinese's Manhattan location was beset with allegations of abuse, exploitation, and mismanagement—for which Bowien ultimately apologized.

**SIGNATURE DISH:** Kung pao pastrami

## J. KENJI LÓPEZ-ALT

**BEST KNOWN FOR:** Unifying art and science in haute cuisine

López-Alt, the son of geneticist and immunologist Frederick Alt and, on his mother's side, grandson of legendary chemist Koji Nakanishi, literally has science in his blood—which explains the methodical, empirical approach he brought to his work as test cook and editor at *Cook's Illustrated* magazine and *America's Test Kitchen,* and to the food blog Serious Eats, where he is currently chief culinary consultant. His long-running *Serious Eats* column, The Food Lab, became the source for his *New York Times* best-selling and James Beard Award–winning book *The Food Lab: Better Home Cooking Through Science,* which has become holy writ for food nerds everywhere.

**SIGNATURE DISH:** His painstaking, brilliant home re-creation of an In-N-Out Animal Style Double Double burger

Best Dressed:
Tan France

Most Popular Junior:
Kelly Marie Tran

Most Popular Senior:
Randall Park

Most Likely to Take
Over the World:
Ali Wong

Varsity All-American:
Jeremy Lin

Freshman Honors Society:
Maitreyi Ramakrishnan & Hudson Yang

Six Seasons
and a
MOVIE

Dream Duet: Harry Shum Jr. &
Jenna Ushkowitz

Community Service Award:
Danny Pudi

Sweetest Siblings:
Alex & Maia Shibutani

Best-Decorated Locker:
Joanna Gaines

Girlboss:
Kim Ng

Drama Club Queen:
Constance Wu

Cool Girls:
Lilly Singh, Liza Koshy, Olivia Munn, Chloe Bennet

# The Asian American Yearbook: the 2010s

BY JEFF YANG,
ILLUSTRATED BY LINDA CHUNG

What would high school have been like if we'd been classmates with some of Asian America's most memorable personalities of the 2010s?

Homecoming King & Queen:
Steven Yeun & Awkwafina

Class President:
Kamala Harris

Debate Club President:
Ted Lieu

Most Likely to Succeed:
Naomi Osaka

Mathlete of the Year:
Andrew Yang

s Sweetheart:
a Condor

The Bros:
Vincent Rodriguez III, Jake Choi,
Ross Butler, Manny Jacinto

Fight Club President:
Daniel Wu

Likely to Be Shredded:
il Nanjiani

Most Likely to Be Shredding:
Chloe Kim

Most Likely to Be Shirtless:
Simu Liu

Dancing Queen:
Carrie Ann Inaba

# Gaming While Asian

**ASIANS AND VIDEO GAMES** have a long and almost symbiotic history: Many of the most influential platforms and gaming brands—Nintendo, PlayStation, Sega, Capcom, SNK, Konami, Bandai Namco, Nexon, NCSoft, Tencent—come from Asia. And today, many of the top pro players in the surging world of e-sports are Asian and Asian American, as are some of the most popular game streamers.

We asked Twitch cofounder **KEVIN "KLIN" LIN**, Streamer **LESLIE "FUSLIE" FU**, Pro League of Legends player **HAI "SIMPLYHAI" LAM**, and e-sports commentator **SUE "SMIX" LEE** to take us through the evolution of the modern Asian gamer.

**KLIN:** Where's everyone from? I grew up in New Orleans.

**SMIX:** Queens, New York.

**FUSLIE:** Cupertino, California.

**SIMPLYHAI:** Grandville, Michigan. I was one of 25 Asian kids in my school. But I always spent a lot of time with my Asian club in high school.

**KLIN:** Same, I had one Asian friend as a kid. But I mostly played video games with non-Asian kids.

**SMIX:** I grew up around lots of Asians in New York and had the privilege of not even realizing I was a "minority" until college. I had an older brother who was into games. He didn't let me play with him, but he let me watch. By osmosis I started to love gaming as well.

**FUSLIE:** Same! I remember sneaking in to play *Starfox* on N64 when my brother wasn't around. But other than that, the stuff I was playing was Neopets, *Roller Coaster Tycoon*, Pokémon.

**SMIX:** Did anyone go to PC bangs as a kid? In middle school I remember going with my brother to play *Counter-Strike 1.6*.

**KLIN:** We didn't have LAN centers where I grew up. There was one place that had a bunch of Sega Genesis and Super Nintendos, but TBH I mostly went to arcades at the mall. Those were the best times.

**SMIX:** Sounds better than PC bangs. I just remember everything was dirty and dark. But maybe I was going to shitty PC bangs!

**SIMPLYHAI:** I've only ever been to one, and I couldn't afford to go often. It was more comfortable to be at my desk in my room anyway than to be surrounded by a bunch of other people eating at the keyboard and getting food all over the computers.

**SMIX:** Yeah, the mouse was always sticky from spilled drinks. At least I hope it was spilled drinks.

**FUSLIE:** I didn't even start playing PC games until college. It was one summer when I was switching directions in my career, I was basically lost and had some time. My roommates, all Asian guys, were playing *League of Legends*, and I was curious. So I downloaded it and after about 10 games, I was hooked. I was like, "Oh, this is so fun." And then I found

**SIMPLYHAI:** Which I was already a part of!

**SMIX:** What was your rank on the leaderboard?

**SIMPLYHAI:** At one point I was number one. But I went back down to 50. This was back in 2013 and e-sports wasn't really a thing yet. *League of Legends* really popularized it in North America. *LoL* were the first to offer huge cash prizes, and that's honestly what drew me in to compete.

**SMIX:** As an O.G. *Star Craft* fan, I have to say those seeds were planted by avid *Star Craft II* fans and the e-sports industry in South Korea. Tournaments had been happening there for years, with big prize money and a robust culture around *Star Craft*. People around the world would download illegal stream links on forums like TeamLiquid.net to watch the events. I'd help translate the videos in real time!

**KLIN:** This was around the time when we were noticing that the community was using Twitch to broadcast games. Before that, it was a service to stream anything live. But we ended up leaning into gaming culture, because we looked at the data and saw it was going to be huge.

**FUSLIE:** That made a home for people like me! My first stream was in 2015 and even then, it was still just a little corner of the Internet.

**SMIX:** Now streaming and e-sports are so much more normalized. There are so many events now. Asians are always at the top.

**SIMPLYHAI:** That affected us in North America because younger Asian American

have a place here." When I was growing up i was hard to feel comfortable in your own skin

**FUSLIE:** Definitely. My friends encouraged me to stream because they thought that as an Asian female playing *LoL* I'd stand out While it helped me get my first 50 followers there's a ceiling for female streamers. All the top Twitch channels are male, because a lot of people still refuse to look at women as serious gamers. They can't process that we can be as good or better. Which is why I feel what I do is so important! I get letters from teenage girls telling me, "I'm Asian and I really look up to you. You made me realize that I can play games and make it a job."

**SMIX:** That said, when you look at the elites, the top 50 to 100 content creators on Twitch, there actually aren't that many Asians On the other hand, we're definitely not a minority—we have quite a few Asian Americans who are making a name for themselves And the creators on OfflineTV, like Scarra LilyPichu, Pokimane, Disguised Toast, Yvonnie, and you, Fuslie—the exponential growth of your followings has done a lot! To see a very solid group of mostly Asians become such a presence inspires more Asian Americans to follow, and they'll get to that level even faster

**FUSLIE:** I watched Asian YouTubers like Ryan Higa, KevJumba, and Wong Fu, and felt super represented by them. It's pretty cool knowing that my friend group on Twitch is creating that same wave for the next generation. We're entertainers at the end of the day and we're showing that there are other avenues outside of being an actor or filmmaker to express yourself and stand in the spotlight

# Coming Out in Public

## BY EUGENE LEE YANG

**I WAS 18** when I first came out to my parents. They were totally blindsided. My mom cried a little. My dad actually pulled out a medical textbook and he said, "I don't understand this, but too much of the gay sex, you lose"—*checks textbook*—"anal elasticity."

EUGENE LEE YANG

We left things up in the air and barely discussed it again until I publicly came out over 15 years later.

Let's back up a little bit.

I was born Korean. But being from a small town in Texas, I didn't have much access to other Asian Americans. I wish I had. Instead, I was just "the Asian kid" in my class, with no one to compare myself to. In some ways, that put me in a mental bubble where I had no idea of the buttload of issues already awaiting me when it came to pursuing art as an Asian.

I was born to be an artist. Ever since I was a baby, I'd gravitated toward the arts. At my *dol,* the traditional Korean one-year birthday ceremony where a child determines his future based on what object he randomly grabs from things put in front of him, I grabbed the paintbrush. Despite some hesitation, my parents supported me as I joined dance, theater, and choir. But Hollywood, of course, never felt tangible. Outside of Margaret Cho's *All-American Girl,* the only Asians I saw on screen were in martial arts movies, or the K-dramas my dad got from the Korean rental store.

Finally, I was born gay. It was sixth grade when I really knew it—but no one else did. I was already acting, not only as a "straight-pass-ing" kid, but also as a "good Asian boy." Those were two cultural roles that forced me to conceal myself until I finally came out, resulting in the aforementioned lecture on anal elasticity.

But even once I was out of the closet, their mentality was: "I don't understand the closet, so I'm gonna ignore the closet. We don't have any closets in this house!" Asians sometimes coexist without engaging. Communicating through invisible walls was a family pastime, and even though I knew my parents loved me, they kept up those walls for a long time.

Being Asian, queer, from the South, and pursuing art—that was a set of intersections that were unique in my family and my community. Going to Los Angeles, which I thought was a liberal artistic mecca, fulfilled my dreams of leaving my small town. But I found out that L.A. was weirdly another kind of small town. In Texas, I got bullied for being Asian. At USC, my professors would tell me to make a script more—or less—"Asian" for effect. It was a weird experience to conceal parts of my otherness in Texas, only to have my otherness leveraged and manipulated once I came to L.A. Both versions of this sense of being different were damaging, and the constant head-to-head tension I faced, as an artist, as an Asian American, and as a gay man, explains a lot of how my public coming-out journey ended up being delayed.

Add to that the guilt I harbored thinking about my parents grappling with having everyone know that they had a gay son, and having to explain that to their rural Christian Korean friends. I felt so indebted to my parents for even allowing me to go to film school; my goal became to stay *behind* the camera and someday, way down the line maybe, getting so successful in my career while making an unabashedly queer film, that no one back home could even question my life choices. If I was taking care of myself and doing well based on my identity, my identity wouldn't be a burden on them.

That plan changed when I realized I didn't have to wait for that award-winning film. The early 2010s were beautiful and messy when it came to digital media: diverse voices were rising, and every company run by *non*-diverse voices was trying to figure out how to negotiate, control, and exploit those voices. BuzzFeed was one of them. After years of participating in diversity showcases and Asian American film labs, I took a job as one of their first video producers, thinking I'd only be there for a year.

I never intended on being a YouTube performer, mainly because I wanted the control over my narrative to be so specific—especially as a gay person—and the idea of becoming a digital star, whose entire career and work would likely be steeped in my identity, didn't coalesce peacefully in my mind. At first, I didn't even want to be in any videos. But with limited resources and a mandate to create video after video, I found myself becoming a recurring personality on camera, and to my surprise, people really gravitated toward me. With each video hitting millions of views, and my social media numbers skyrocketing, I started to question why people were following me, becoming hyper-aware of how I presented myself, especially as a gay Asian man on *The Try Guys,* a comedy show costarring three cisgender white men. Digital media expected me to lay my iden-

tity bare. I had to grapple with my parasocial relationship with viewers: "How much of my real self do I give to them?" In some ways, as I became more established in the digital space, I ended up building myself a new closet.

I'd been out to my professional circles and friends, and my first video was even based on my gay identity. But it wasn't until 2018 that I began openly talking and posting about being gay. I realized that my dream of making world-changing work to change the lives of young people's lives was already happening. Publicly coming out no longer had to be a far-off thing. It was important to me to have the chance to really start positively impacting the LGBTQ community as I was starting to do with the Asian community—which is why my official 2019 coming-out video was the most important work I've produced thus far.

It wasn't about the "what"—for all intents and purposes, I was already out—it was about the "why." Just like being Asian American, being queer isn't simply a label or a single moment. Coming out is a continuous journey, a constant evolution, an ongoing conversation that some of us are lucky to be able to express through art, and share through social media.

Now you have big stars like Lilly Singh and Anna Akana, all normalizing the queer experience, thanks to YouTube. Out and proud, young, queer, Asian American YouTubers are showing up with fierceness and veracity, and they're part of the engine of LGBTQ Asian grassroots movements. They're loud. Loud is something we've stereotypically not been. And as a naturally loud, unabashedly flamboyant dude, I've come to own my beautiful, queer Asianness. It's taken most of my life, but my parents are starting to embrace it, too.

# DISGRASIAN™

JEN WANG            DIANA NGUYEN

**ONE LAST ROUND** with **JEN WANG** and **DIANA NGUYEN**, the namers of names and flamers of flames, offering up their takes on the All-Stars of the 2010s—the end of the *Disgrasian* era, because social media had become a cancel culture clusterfuck, and no one's wanted to read anything longer than a #hashtag since.

**JEN:** We're done after this, right? I forgot how tiring it is to talk shit about people.

**DIANA:** I'm exhausted and need a nap before I become a zombie. Thankfully, the 2010s literally just ended.

**JEN:** Lit-rally.

**DIANA:** Speaking of dead-eyes, allow me to remind you of golf's greatest robot of excellence, Tiger Woods. We blogged quite a bit about Tiger when he fell from grace.

**JEN:** When he cheated on his wife and then wrapped his car around a tree?

**DIANA:** Like so many superior athletes, he was bred to be excellent at only one thing from birth—all he knew to care about was golf at the expense of everything else. But then he went through this personal and very public shame, and in a way, it humanized him. I think we'd be gentler about him today, because the scope of what DISGRASIAN means to us has changed.

**JEN:** I attribute it to us being older and looking at these people in hindsight. Let's face it, being Asian is rough. The demands on you—to be excellent, to represent your family or, more

preposterously, your entire race—they're so unforgiving. When you're Asian and you fuck up, you don't get forgiveness. We basically pioneered cancel culture! There are two cultural forces at play—Asian cancel culture and the American culture of anti-Asian racism, with its stereotypes and the perpetual "othering." One of those forces alone is enough to crush somebody. I have so much more empathy for our people now—canceled within our own culture, and erased by the culture we're supposed to adopt.

**DIANA:** So the people we think are DISGRASIAN in the 2010s are not the sort of people we would call out in the Aughts.

**JEN:** Right. These DISGRASIANs are the Big Bad. Over the last 10 years, we, as a country, have started to acknowledge on a real level that racism is a systemic problem. Calling someone or something racist before this time centered much more around individuals or the behavior of individuals. But we're understanding now how racism is a product of a larger system, one that creates incentives for racist behavior.

**DIANA:** So DISGRASIANs in this era are truly irredeemable, because they're complicit in maintaining an oppressive system.

**JEN:** Translation: They're canceled.

**DIANA:** *Translasian:* They are dead to us and we are no longer family. On that note, let's talk about Amy Chua, a.k.a. Tiger Mom!

**JEN:** Oh, Tiger Mom. I don't know if I was being contrarian when her first book came out, but I gave her a wider berth than I think she deserves now. When I read her book, I didn't understand why somebody like her, who's second generation and "Tiger-parented" herself, would choose to impose this style of parenting on her own children. Any person with a modicum of self-awareness would know that is incredibly fucked up. But I also recognized her argument that the book was a memoir, not a how-to guide, so maybe she wasn't just defending a broken, traumatizing system.

Then she came out with *The Triple Package,* which reinforced the model-minority stereotype, and then defended Brett Kavanaugh. It became clear that self-promoting and victim-blaming were her "brand," and that brand has real-life harmful consequences. And that's what I'd define as DISGRASIAN, in a post-*Disgrasian*-the-blog world.

**DIANA:** You want to talk about brands, you know how there's always that fucking kid who's trying not to be bullied by aligning themselves with the bullies? That to me is Dinesh D'Souza.

**JEN:** He's the Asian the system trots out and tokenizes to justify everything they do. Like when racists say, "I have a Black best friend and he isn't offended."

**DIANA:** If you don't look at things holistically, if you're just playing these little strategy games to advance your own ass, that behavior is DISGRASIAN, because all you give a shit about is your own ass and not the beautiful Asian asses of the community around you.

**JEN:** Anything else is ass-backwards.

**DIANA:** That is an ass-tute point.

**JEN:** The two of us are kinder, gentler, and wiser than we were two decades ago. We realize now that for a lot of you out there, it's not your fault. We wouldn't make fun of you today.

**DIANA:** We began our contribution to this book talking about how minuscule Asian representation used to be. That's grown to the point where there are now myriad representations of Asian identity. The way we're represented matters a little less now because that spectrum has broadened. We have more breathing room. But it's clear who the real toxic people are.

We've been careening around the information age for over 30 years and come out wiser *and* dumber; we have more access to the truth and more ways to escape it. Pop culture was once contained in a silo and now, pop culture *is* culture. Our democracy was nearly burnt to the ground by a failed reality star who tweeted racist policy and made "Kung Flu" viral, all while letting over half a million people—especially people of color—die from the most catastrophic virus we've seen in 100 years. So what disgraces us is anything that maintains cycles of harm and doesn't lift everyone up.

**JEN:** More Asians now have agency to control the narrative. And if you're taking that narrative in the wrong direction, that's on you. You chose this path, and that's why you're DISGRASIAN. Translation: Fuck you very much. Your Asian card has been officially revoked. But to everybody else . . . have a nice day!

# UNDERCOVER
## ASIANS 2010s

BY PHIL YU, ILLUSTRATED BY EC YI

**BACK ON IT,** Asianspotters—our quest for representation of the Asian kind continues! This decade uncovers several chart-topping hitmakers, a couple of Marvelous heroes, an NBA champion basketball coach, and more. Here are some familiar faces from the 2010s who you might be surprised to learn are part of the Asian American nation.

### 1. BRUNO MARS
Mega-platinum-selling, multi-Grammy-winning singer Mars was born Peter Gene Hernandez to a Filipina mother and Puerto RicanAshkenazi Jewish father.

### 2. DAVE BAUTISTA
The former six-time world champion professional wrestler turned actor is the son of a Filipino father and Greek mother, which is why he rocks arm tattoos of the flags of Greece and the Philippines.

### 3. CHLOE BENNET
Best known for *Marvel's Agents of S.H.I.E.L.D.,* actress Bennet was born Chloe Wang (her father, Bennet Wang, is Chinese American) and she had a pop music career under that name in China; she took her stage name when she had trouble booking American gigs under her Asian legal surname.

### 4. HAILEE STEINFELD
One of the youngest Oscar nominees ever, for her performance in *True Grit,* actress and singer Steinfeld is of Filipino and African American ancestry on her maternal grandfather's side.

### 5. DARREN CRISS
Actor/singer Criss, whose mother is Filipina, starred on *Glee* and won an Emmy for his starring role as spree killer Andrew Cunanan in *The Assassination of Gianni Versace: American Crime Story.*

### 6. OLIVIA RODRIGO
Disney star Rodrigo, who is Filipina on her father's side, broke streaming records and topped charts around the world with her smash hit debut single "Drivers License."

### 7. ANDERSON .PAAK
Born Brandon Paak Anderson, rapper, singer, songwriter, and multi-instrumentalist Anderson .Paak is of mixed Korean heritage—his mother is an adoptee of Black and Korean descent.

### 8. ERIK SPOELSTRA
Miami Heat head coach Spoelstra, whose mother is Filipina, is the first Asian American head coach in the history of the four major North American sports leagues—and also the first to win a championship.

### 9. H.E.R.
The acclaimed R&B singer-songwriter behind "Hard Place," known professionally as H.E.R., was born Gabriella Sarmiento Wilson to a Filipina mother and African American father.

# YELLOWFACE IN THE 2010S

BY NANCY WANG YUEN

**BY THE 2010S,** yellowface was thankfully almost gone. But whitewashing, the practice of reframing of nonwhite roles to allow the casting of white actors, more than picked up the slack. Fortunately, most if not all of the prominent movies that embraced this path ended up being box-office disasters—a far more convincing reason for Hollywood to stop engaging in whitewashing than complaints from nonwhite communities.

### "Raj" in a TV ad for Popchips (2012), played by Ashton Kutcher

Kutcher, best known for starring in *That '70s Show,* slathered on the brownface to portray an Indian Bollywood producer named Raj in an ad for the corn snack Popchips. In addition to the makeup, fake mustache, and an embroidered tunic, Kutcher spoke in fake Indian accent and danced around like a clown. Popchips initially responded to critiques of the commercial's by saying it was meant for laughs, and that they "embrace all types of shapes, flavors and colors, and appreciate all snackers, no matter their race or ethnicity." They eventually pulled the ad. **CONVINCING OR NOT? ONLY AS A MODERN BENCHMARK FOR BROWNFACE.** In a 2015 episode of the Netflix series *Master of None,* Ravi Patel's character asks Aziz Ansari's character, "Is it like the Popchips commercial?" as a way to gauge whether a performance was offensive.

### "Hae-Joo Chang" in *Cloud Atlas* (2012), played by Jim Sturgess

The film's intention was to capture a humanity that transcends "tribal differences," according to Lana Wachowski, one of the film's directors; as a result, the filmmakers decided to have multiple actors play

different characters of different racial backgrounds. But the use of makeup to change the eye shape of Jim Sturgess—plus having him speak English in a faux-Korean accent—made this attempt at social commentary into an offensive yellow-face performance. Why would Jim Sturgess's Korean character even speak accented English rather than Korean (with subtitles) in a future "Neo-Seoul"? And while Doona Bae and Halle Berry appear in "white-face" makeup to play white characters, there's no equivalency between the history of white actors playing nonwhite roles in problematic ways, and the rare actor of color who plays a white role. **CONVINCING OR NOT? MADE STURGESS THE GO-TO WHITE DUDE TO PLAY ASIANS.** In addition to this role, he also performed as the whitewashed Asian American lead in *21* (2008).

### "Aang," "Katara," and "Sokka" in *The Last Airbender* (2010), played by Noah Ringer, Nicola Peltz, and Jackson Rathbone

The case of *The Last Airbender,* the movie

adaptation of the popular animated TV series *Avatar: The Last Airbender,* is a complicated one. Although the original series takes place in a fantasy world, the creators acknowledged that the world's cultures were inspired by Asian and Indigenous peoples. M. Night Shyamalan's choice to cast white actors in all but one of the major roles in his live-action adaptation led an advocacy group to coin the term "race-bending" to protest the casting decisions, "playfully borrowing the concept of manipulating elements (bending) from the *Avatar* universe."

**CONVINCING OR NOT? THAT MISSES THE POINT.** The issue isn't really authenticity, it's opportunity. With the chance to give Asian actors a major opportunity to star in a huge franchise, Shyamalan—himself Indian American—chose to pass the buck. Worse yet, he cast his only Asian lead and other dark-skinned actors as the villainous Fire Nation, causing some to suggest that the film fueled stereotypes of darker people as evil.

**"Allison Ng" in *Aloha* (2015), played by Emma Stone**
In Cameron Crowe's film, Stone is supposed to be a quarter Chinese, a quarter Hawaiian—and half Swedish, which apparently canceled out the other two quarters. The casting of Stone led to outrage among Asian and Native Hawaiian communities, to which director Crowe responded that the point of the character was that she was super proud of her non-white heritage even though she seemed, to all appearances, to be white. He did not respond to the response to his response, which was that he could've easily just cast a biracial actor.

**CONVINCING OR NOT? NO, BUT AT LEAST EMMA STONE IS SORRY.** When host Sandra Oh joked at the 2019 Golden Globe Awards that *Crazy Rich Asians* was "the first studio film with an Asian American lead since *Ghost in the Shell* and *Aloha,*" Stone shouted "I'm sorry!" from her seat.

## "The Ancient One," in *Doctor Strange* (2016), played by Tilda Swinton

In the comic books, "The Ancient One" is a mystical Tibetan man who hails from the fictional Himalayan kingdom of Kamar-Taj. Director Scott Derrickson decided to whitewash (and gender-bend) the character, because he couldn't imagine any version of the role that "wouldn't be offensive to Asians." He chose to cast Swinton and describe her as a Celtic sorcerer who apparently booked a Himalayan timeshare.

**CONVINCING OR NOT? WHITEWASHING IS ALWAYS A ONE-WAY STREET.** If you're going to cast a British actor as The Ancient One, why not cast an Asian as Dr. Strange? (We know why.)

**"Major" in *Ghost in the Shell* (2017), played by Scarlett Johansson**
In perhaps the most infamous case of Hollywood whitewashing, Johansson played "Major," a cybernetically enhanced human, in the live-action adaptation of a manga series set in a futuristic Japan. Johansson has insisted that she "would never attempt to play a person of a different race." But the movie ends up revealing that the Major is in fact a Japanese woman, whose soul has been decanted into a white woman's body. After Johansson was cast, news leaked that Paramount and DreamWorks had tested out post-production visual effects that would have made Johansson appear "more Asian."

**CONVINCING OR NOT? IT MADE SCARLETT JOHANSSON THE POSTER CHILD FOR WHITEWASHING.** It didn't help that she has consistently argued against casting critiques, insisting that she "should be able to play any person, or any tree, or any animal."

# It's a Bird . . . It's a Plane . . . It's Asian Superheroes

BY JEFF YANG, ILLUSTRATED BY KOLBE YANG

**MANY ASIAN AMERICANS** turned to superheroes for inspiration because there were so few places we could see ourselves as heroes of the un-super variety. While it's not like there were many Asian American comic book icons either, if we squinted a little, we could reimagine Superman as Clark Kang, Batman as Bruce Wei, Spider-Man as Peter Park—we could project our own faces and identities into the capes and cowls of these extraordinary beings, and lift ourselves up, up and away from our decidedly ordinary lives. Over the past few years, we've finally gotten to a point where we don't have to pretend that Asian American superheroes exist—and two writers have been disproportionately responsible for this shift: **GENE LUEN YANG**, who broke out as an indie graphic novelist and went on to create DC's Chinese "New Super-Man," and **GREG PAK**, who reinvented the Incredible Hulk with his introduction of Korean American super-genius Amadeus Cho. We got them together to talk about what inspired them about superheroes as kids, and why Asian American superheroes are important.

## Secret Origins

**GREG:** My mom was the kind of mom who bought markers and crayons and paper instead of coloring books. So I've been drawing since I was a little kid. And I've been writing comics, professionally anyway, for 16 years. I've written over 550 individual books over the years.

**GENE:** I started collecting comic books in the fifth grade. I was not good at sports, but I really liked drawing. And as an immigrant's kid, comics felt like a refuge to me. Me and my best friend, who was half Japanese, half Jewish, would hang out and we'd make comics together and get his mom to Xerox them, and then we'd sell them to our friends for 50 cents apiece. I remember when a girl in my class bought one, and I was like, wow, because of comics, a girl talked to me. Pretty soon after that, I just became a comic book nerd.

## In from the Outside

**GENE:** When we were growing up, nobody would go to school wearing a Spider-Man shirt. Unless you wanted to get a wedgie.

**GREG:** Comics are where weirdos have congregated forever. It's a little hard to wrap your head around it now, because superhero comics have become the driving force of American pop culture, but comics traditionally have been an outsider art form. So as Asian Americans, facing a wall that made it harder for us historically to become pop culture creators, gravitating to comics just made sense.

## Getting Personal

**GREG:** In college, I started getting into manga. What drew me in was that it's an Asian medium with Asian protagonists, but unencumbered by issues with that identity. They're just culturally Asian, doing their thing. And then dealing

414

with giant robots and demons and whatever. They have millions of issues, but being Asian isn't one. That made me conscious of the power of combining genre stories and underrepresented protagonists. It felt like a way of pulling in everybody.

**GENE:** For me, it was that back then in the Nineties, comics were just not doing well as an industry. Marvel Comics had declared bankruptcy! We'd go to conventions and there were more exhibitors than attendees. Everything was kind of falling apart. So when I fell in with this group of indie Bay Area cartoonists, we decided we were just going to make our comics as personal as possible. And because most of us were Asian American, that's what was personal to us.

## You Are What You Draw

**GREG:** I remember when *American Born Chinese* came out, reading it and just being blown away. I told people that it was the best depiction of a certain Asian American male experience I'd ever seen, in any format. It was incredibly moving and uncompromisingly intimate—you could tell there was no one breathing down Gene's neck saying, "Try to make this more universal." So when I moved into comics, I happened to have the chance to create a new superhero. I pitched this Asian American character and literally, nobody said boo. Nobody ever said, "Does he have to be Asian?" That ended up becoming Amadeus Cho.

**GENE:** I'm a huge fan of Amadeus Cho. He feels like somebody I would've hung out with! There's a scene in *Totally Awesome Hulk* where basically all the Asian American superheroes in the Marvel Universe get together and eat

Korean barbecue, and then they have a super-powered fight over the check. And then they go and sing karaoke. That blew me away. I thought, "I have waited all my life to read this."

**GREG:** It was a chance to show that there's a huge multiplicity of Asian American experiences, even in a superhero reality. I try to avoid the term "authenticity," because what is authentic? There's 18 million authentic Asian American experiences, you know what I mean?

## Moving to the Core

**GENE:** At the same time, when you think about characters like Shang-Chi, the appeal of him historically has been that he is the other—you weren't supposed to read the comic and think *you're* Shang-Chi, you were supposed to read the comic and look at Shang-Chi and be like, *wow, that dude is awesome and crazy and a little bit alien.*

**GREG:** Which is why I appreciated characters like Jubilee for being Asian American at a time when almost all of the comics characters were exoticized, orientalist versions of some kind of Asian. She's Asian, but she's never quoted as Asian. I've talked to people who are like, wait, Jubilee is supposed to be *Asian*?

**GENE:** It's how these things evolve. I have a student who did this whole survey of Asian American representation in middle-grade fiction, and her thesis was that at the beginning you have stories where there are no Asian American characters. And then you move on to a phase where there are Asian American characters, but their being Asian is not a part of the story—they're just Asian in name. And then you get to a point where Asian American-ness is the main focus of the story. And then you move on where you have Asian Americans dealing with problems that are not specifically Asian American, but who live in a very Asian American way and deal with those problems in a very Asian American way. So it could be zombies, but they deal with them from an Asian American core.

**GREG:** That's when you get Amadeus Cho. And Kamala Khan, Ms. Marvel, who's Pakistani American and Muslim and has to deal with those aspects of her life, even as she's being a superhero.

## Super Normal

**GENE:** Didn't you have a scene in *Agents of Atlas* where everyone has to take their shoes off before they go inside? It was amazing. All these superhero boots lined up outside the headquarters.

**GREG:** These kinds of things in stories matter not just because they make us see ourselves, but because when you see these superheroic beings that look like us, that do the things we do as Asian Americans, it normalizes us to everybody else. Like maybe you never would have hung out with Shang-Chi before, but you would now, because the dude sings karaoke. You'd be all over it.

**GENE:** Yeah. It's totally different now. We live in a time when Asian American superheroes fight for the check, go to bone marrow drives, and eat Spam. This may be the most Asian American moment for superhero comics ever.

# POSTCARD FROM ASIAN AMERICA

BY SUYIN SO

Hey RISE,

Greetings from 1989. And greetings from Marion, Indiana, population 30,000, four of whom at this moment are me, my parents, and my older brother, all transplants from New York. Growing up in a sports-obsessed small factory town, my life is equal parts John Mellencamp and The Smiths. I go to pep rallies and basketball games and then head home to listen to "The Boy with a Thorn in His Side" on repeat.

Like all the other Asians in Marion—maybe 20 other families?—my family is here for work. There are enough of us here to be more than a novelty, but too few to form a real community. To be Asian—to engage in Asianness—we have to travel. We drive three hours to shop and eat in Chicago's Chinatown. Once in a very long while, we fly for days to visit my family in Indonesia.

And until high school, I'm consistently the only Asian kid in my class, occupying a negative space labeled "Other" in an all Black and white community. My 8th grade perm is white-girl-aspirational perfection, but I know and feel that I'm different—despite my friends (mostly white) constantly telling me, "I don't see you as any different." I understand I'm meant to appreciate this, but it feels like a weak excuse for the casual, everyday racism I regularly encounter. It's all a part of the confusing, continuous push-pull of identity in America: "You're one of us, if you let us erase you."

Learning to embrace my difference is a journey I'm still on today.
Love,
Suyin

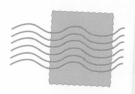

RISE
HERE AND NOW,
ASIAN AMERICA

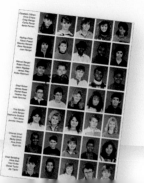

# BEYOND

# Beyond

BY JEFF YANG, PHIL YU, AND PHILIP WANG

**THIS FINAL ESSAY** was supposed to start off . . . differently. Back when we first began writing, we imagined this essay as framing a "Beyond" for Asian America that focused on the continued rise in our narrative profile—highlighting prominent Asian creators, athletes, politicians, and entrepreneurs from an emerging generation of influencers and tastemakers.

We were going to interview budding leaders who were building on the progress we'd covered over the past three decades and ask them questions about what they hoped to see in the future. And we had good reason to be optimistic: We anticipated the releases of *Raya and the Last Dragon*, Disney's first animated "Princess" feature inspired by Southeast Asian mythology, and of *Shang-Chi and the Legend of the Ten Rings*, Marvel's first movie centering around an Asian superhero with a nearly all-Asian cast. Redress for the egregious yellowface of David Carradine's *Kung Fu* was coming in the form of a reboot, starring Olivia Liang as a martial arts expert (and Harvard Law dropout, because of course). There was early buzz about Lee Isaac Chung's gorgeous rural Korean American story *Minari*—which would go on to be nominated for six Academy Awards, including Best Picture, Best Director, Best Original Score, Best Original Screenplay, Best Actor (for Steven Yeun), and Best Supporting Actress (for Yuh-Jung Youn, who would go on to become just the second Asian actress to win an Oscar in Hollywood history).

Things seemed to truly be looking up.

But as we complete this now in spring 2021, one year into a pandemic that has utterly changed the world and drastically impacted our community, our view of what's "Beyond" has shifted. The racialization of COVID-19 as a "Chinese" disease by political leaders, including and especially the former president of the United States, brought back recurring nightmares of prior eras when Asians have been scapegoated and subjected to social exclusion and random attack: Muslims, Sikhs, and South Asians targeted in the wake of 9/11. The false spy allegations against Wen Ho Lee in 2001. The scaremongering campaign finance investigations of the late 1990s. The murder of Vincent Chin in 1982. The hatred spawned by propaganda campaigns in repeated wars against Asian countries dating back to World War II, when Japanese Americans were unjustly incarcerated by their own government; the anti-immigration laws that targeted Asians throughout the early 20th century, and the massacres and lynchings of Chinese workers in the late 19th.

"I remember seeing Trump on TV calling COVID-19 the China virus; my partner and I just looked at each other and said, 'Well, there goes our safety,'" says Filipino American hip-hop artist Ruby Ibarra. "Him saying this right now is going to cause a ripple effect of hatred toward Asian Americans. And right before this, we'd been on such an upward trajectory."

The virus that put our society into deep freeze seemed to paralyze our progress. The raw, bitter bigotry that it laid bare in many around us—political leaders, online acquaintances, total strangers even, sometimes former friends—underscored the fact that the narratives we've sought to change are deeply rooted in stubborn soil. And the violence that has been waged against our communities since then has shaken all of us to our core.

While hate crimes in general decreased by 7 percent in 2020, targeted attacks on Asians increased by over 150 percent over the same period. Stop AAPI Hate, a nonprofit coalition that formed to collect reports of anti-Asian incidents across the nation, revealed that they'd collected nearly 3,800 incidents in roughly a year, since the beginning of the pandemic, with 68 percent taking place against women. And the most visible and violent incidents happened to our most vulnerable: elders living in ethnic enclaves, who were culturally unprepared for attack and physically unable to fight back (with some exceptions, notably Xiao Zhen Xie, the 75-year-old San Francisco shero who beat her assailant unconscious with a nearby wooden board, then donated the hundreds of thousands raised for her injury recovery to organizations fighting anti-Asian hate).

Asian Americans will tell you that this hate and hostility directed toward our community are not new sentiments—they've just been given the green light to be out in the open, unchecked. Growing up and simply existing in this country requires a too-often unspoken level of tolerance for pain and silent suffering, a resigned acceptance of every unwelcome joke, slur, or act of violence. It accumulates and suffocates us under the weight of each generation. But the notion that Asians are suddenly waking up, finally, to fight back is ahistorical (and frankly, harmful). At each step in our story, our community has struggled, raised our voices, and stood up to lift up activists, organizers, fighters, and leaders. This is just the latest threshold, the point at which someone, too many of us, could not take it anymore.

The past 12 months have forced us to watch and endure what seemed like daily, heartbreaking attacks against our most vulnerable. A community doesn't endure this type of pain and tragedy without coming out transformed. A little sadder. A little harder. But also, a little stronger and more determined. Now, the rising generation is more resolved than ever to come together to demand meaningful and lasting change from institutions that have revealed themselves as unable or unwilling to protect us, much less sustain and elevate us.

"We're at a breaking point right now. We're in a position where we need to be vocal—because lives are literally on the line," says Dan Matthews, a rapper, activist, and documentary filmmaker better known as Dan AKA Dan. "As a Korean adoptee, this is something that I've internalized: the need to get other non-Asian communities—which, for us, includes our own families—to care about and understand the issues we face here in the United States as Asian Americans."

Over the course of the past year, existing leaders have stepped up and new activists have found their voices, amplifying our urgent concerns, rallying support for our essential workers, highlighting the social and economic and physical impact of the disease on our communities, and especially, pushing back on the groundswell of bigotry that has erupted in its wake. They've built coalitions with one another and with allies, underscoring that—as was the case in the very first days of the Asian American movement—no division can exist between our needs and those of Black, Latinx, and Indigenous peoples, that none of us are good until all of us are good, a refrain we frequently heard as we spoke to some of the young leaders and creative talents who are poised to take us forward into the Beyond.

"None of us are good until all of us are good" means ensuring that we're not just "diverse," but inclusive, pushing for our spaces, movements, and organizations to reflect the full breadth of our ethnic representation:

"I grew up in the Nineties, and most places I went back then, Southeast Asians basically didn't even exist—it was just like, 'Aren't you all Chinese?'" says Sahra Nguyen, founder and CEO of Nguyen Coffee Supply, a craft roaster of single-source Vietnamese coffee. "There was just no room for any level of nuance. We're seeing a major difference now."

And it means we aren't just including, but focusing on intersections, by elevating women and women's issues in the conversation:

"The stigmatization and intense scrutiny that follows publicly discussing sexual violence is relentless, and ignorance of these issues runs rampant in our communities," says Lacy Lew Nguyen Wright, associate director of BLD PWR, which unites diverse actors and athletes to advance social change and racial justice. "At times I feel like Asian American women are blamed for our own silence. We need to be able to openly discuss our traumas and demand what we need to heal and reclaim the voices so many didn't think we had."

And by putting queer identities at the center rather than pushing them to the margins:

"From the beginning of my career, I was just very openly talking about being Indian and being gay," says actor and organizer Nik Dodani, in discussing his own activist journey. "I was just very straight about it. I mean—I was very direct about it. I was never an actor that was in the closet, either about my race or about my sexuality."

It also means recognizing that we will not always see eye to eye, and acknowledging that the road Beyond won't be smooth or easy. As Asian Americans, we're constantly forced to negotiate the lines between what makes us different from one another and what we have in common. Every iteration of our identity has demanded that we consider who's being drawn into the picture, and who's being left out.

Yet that's equally true of our nation as a whole, never more than today, an era when the phrase "Make America Great Again"—whose America? Great for whom?—still echoes.

If America is the "grand experiment," as it is often called, in many ways, Asian America is a great experiment within that grand experiment—a test case to see if an identity that was originally adopted out of political purpose can foster a resilient sense of cultural passion, and frame a shared narrative that is both firm enough to last across centuries and elastic enough to weather the inevitable ways in which it will be stretched by changing demographics and increasingly complex self-definitions.

"Historically, Asians Americans have dealt with being seen as the perpetual foreigner—being systematically erased, from our history to our stories to our present-day news. Things are different today. The world is going through a reckoning and our generation is starting to speak up," says Amanda Nguyen, advocate for victims of sexual assault and the engine behind the drafting and passage of the Sexual Assault Survivors' Rights Act, which passed unanimously through Congress in 2016 and was signed into law by President Barack Obama.

So while Asian America is an experiment, it's now one that we're running for ourselves, not being subjected to by others. We of previous generations had to learn for ourselves how to defy and to demand, overcoming both internalized inferiority complexes and family-imposed impulses to keep our heads down and our mouths closed. But the rising generation is comfortable raising its voice, filling the room.

"Growing up as a first-generation kid of immigrants, we were just always in a state of survival—we were like, 'just give us anything and we'll be happy with it,'" says Linh Nguyen, executive director of RUN AAPI, a group seeking to harness the emerging political voice of Asian Americans. "But this next generation, they're so fucking good at demanding better. The way they're self-organizing in such beautiful and organic ways—I never grew up like that. I'm a believer in the next generation."

There's plenty of reason to believe. As anti-Asian harassment rooted in COVID devolved into brutal, random violence, a bold and outspoken cohort of political leaders stepped forward on behalf of our stricken community. And in particular, after the tipping-point horror of the murder of eight people—six of them Asian American women—outside of Atlanta by a white man who claimed that he simply wanted to "eliminate sexual temptation," it was Asian American women elected officials like Bee Nguyen, first Vietnamese American elected to Georgia's House of Representatives; Yuh-Line Niou, the first and still only Asian American woman to represent New York in its State Assembly; Michelle Wu, the first Asian American to serve on Boston's city council; State Senator Stephanie Chang, the first Asian American woman to represent Michigan in its state legislature; and Representative Grace Meng, the first Asian American to represent the state of New York in the House, who provided comfort, direction, and purpose in a time of heartrending despair.

And now, as the world begins to wake from its slumber, we find ourselves reviewing hard truths the ugly events of these pandemic months have taught us: When we are not included, we are invisible. When we put ourselves at the mercy of the fears and fantasies of others, we lose agency over our work, our creations, our very bodies. When we don't demand to be seen in all our multiplicities, when we don't take up space, we become vulnerable. We become victims.

"I want to see us normalize arm hair and Thursday night leftovers, unapologetically enjoying ourselves just as we are," says Maitreyi Ramakrishnan, the young Tamil Canadian lead of the Netflix television series *Never Have I Ever*. "Right now, simply existing as a brown girl, without saying anything, shows the world that people who look like me are valid. But that's not enough. We aren't just one character. And we shouldn't have to compromise to be relatable, or to be forced into the shadows of white narratives."

For generations, Asians have been lucky to be the last box checked off in statehouses and boardrooms, in marketing meetings and casting calls. Those leading us Beyond are reinforcing the message that we aren't an afterthought, but an asset, a pool of untold tales and undiscovered talents and full, rich voices that are only just beginning to speak.

"We're going to see a rise in representation across many areas, to move from a sense of narrative scarcity to narrative plenitude," says Nimarta Narang, literary editor of *Brown Girl Magazine*. "Our definition of success, of perfection, of what it means to be Asian American must be ever-evolving as we move forward into the future, while reconciling with the past. We have been taught to accept each crumb we were given, because for us, speaking up was taboo for so long. Now is the time for our voice to grow and expand."

A big part of that growth and expansion will mean exploring and understanding what it means for us to be a part of a global Asian diaspora. Because this moment should have taught us how much our fate as Asian Americans is tethered to how America sees our mirrored reflections in Asia, and elsewhere in the world. Throughout history, our ties to a worldwide web of other Asians has been used against us: to question our loyalty and patriotism, to attack and condemn us for the perceived sins of overseas doppelgangers, to exclude and isolate us in our own home. We need to turn those from a liability to a strength. Because they mean a future in which we're not a minority of America, but a majority of the world.

Our elders fled wars and revolutions, seeing America as a land of peace, of hope—of opportunity. Now, as America seeks to revitalize its economy and to rebuild relations with international partners, we're the ones who represent opportunity for our nation—and for the globe.

Perhaps we can see an example in the stories of Filipino American entrepreneurs Roland Ros and Rexy Dorado. Raised and educated in the U.S., Ros and Dorado were both drawn back to the Philippines after college, joining forces to do nonprofit work on behalf of their motherland. There, a chance encounter with a Filipino ambassador pushed them in a new direction.

"He said, you invest in startups in the U.S., but when you come to the Philippines, you do the typical Filipino American thing—that messianic 'Oh, I'm going to do a clean water project, I'm going to alleviate poverty' attitude," remembers Ros. "Why don't you invest in a technology startup here? That's what would make a real impact."

As they put their minds on ways to answer the ambassador's challenge, Ros and Dorado realized that their desire to reclaim their culture was a feeling shared by a globally distributed Filipino population. "We are dispersed all over the world, and yet we're looking for connection with other Filipinos," says Ros.

They built an app called Kumu, short for "Kumusta," slang for "how are you?" in Tagalog. Initially designed as a messaging platform, it quickly became obvious that people were much more interested in a secondary feature of the app, which allowed anyone to open up a video room and start livestreaming to viewers from anywhere. This led to a stroke of revelation: Why not leverage the distributed talent of Filipinos and turn the app into a way for creators to connect with a global audience? Since then, Kumu has allowed thousands of artists to earn full-time income performing for audiences around the world.

Today, Kumu is currently the number one social app in the Philippines. It's number six in Canada, number 18 in the U.S., and number five in Australia.

"The Filipino diaspora is the key. But there are other people out there launching startups like this for their own diasporas," says Ros. "So many of my Vietnamese, Thai, Chinese, and Korean American counterparts have all at the same time gone back to build businesses in their 'home' countries. That link between Asian Americans and Asia that used to be seen as something to struggle against is now beginning to be seen as empowering. It's very fascinating."

And that may well be the next chapter of our progress. To move not just beyond the past and this present moment, but beyond our self-imposed barriers and borders.

"Something has changed," says Nik Dodani. "A sense of common identity around being

Asian has begun to solidify, and there's a growing understanding of how we're all connected, even if we have different cultural backgrounds and maybe are in different parts of the world. We know what we share. We feel more solidarity. I don't want to call it a renaissance, because that means rebirth. I think this might just be the birth of a brand-new thing."

Spotted on set during our "Generation Gap" photo shoot: AJ Rafael's arm tattoo

W KAMAU BELL

JEFF CHANG

RYAN ALEXANDER HOLMES

MONICA MACER

SHAWN TAYLOR

# BLACK AND ASIAN:

## A Conversation

As we look to the future of America, it's clear that a long-over-due conversation must take place between Black and Asian communities: one that acknowledges the complicated, some-times ugly, sometimes beautiful history that the two groups have shared, and that addresses our very real areas of conflict, and equally real opportunities for coalition and collaboration. As we look to the 2020s and beyond, we asked some astute cultural observers—Black, Asian, and both—to dip a toe into the waters of a discussion that will define the decades to come.

W. KAMAU BELL IS A WRITER, COMEDIAN, AND HOST OF THE CNN SERIES *UNITED SHADES OF AMERICA*

JEFF CHANG IS A HISTORIAN AND MUSIC CRITIC, AND AUTHOR OF THE SEMINAL HIP-HOP HISTORY *CAN'T STOP WON'T STOP*

RYAN ALEXANDER HOLMES IS AN ACTOR, BEST KNOWN FOR *DEAR WHITE PEOPLE*

MONICA MACER IS SHOWRUNNER AND EXECUTIVE PRODUCER OF NETFLIX'S *GENTEFIED* AND CBS'S *MACGYVER*

SHAWN TAYLOR IS A COFOUNDER OF THE NERDS OF COLOR AND THE BLACK COMIX ARTS FESTIVAL

## An Interwoven History

*Asians and Black Americans have an ample shared past, albeit one that has been submerged deep beneath the waters of our culture.*

**JEFF CHANG:** As Asians we have to understand that the Black freedom struggle is the reason that we're here. We tend to think the story of what we owe the Black community starts in the 1960s, during the Civil Rights Movement, but we have to take it further back. The 1960s is really the second or third revolution that led to our rights being expanded. The reason Asians even first came here in large numbers was because, when slavery ended, there was a demand for labor from Asia to build the West Coast—coolie and plantation labor from China, Japan, the Philippines, and everybody else down the line. And the reason we were able to *stay* here is because of the Black struggle that won the rights of the 14th Amendment, which created birthright citizenship.

**SHAWN TAYLOR:** Of course in the late '60s and '70s, there were a lot of Black folks who were liberatory agents for the rights of recent immigrants, including Asians. But I think what you see is that the very fact of that fight becomes a power imbalance that creates backlash. It's similar to when you give someone a gift, and they resent you for it. That's how it sometimes feels when you see anti-Blackness expressed by Asian Americans. There's obviously this love of the fruits of Black labor—the rights we've won, the culture we created—but not of Black people. Like much of America, you love what we do, but not who we are.

**W. KAMAU BELL:** But we have to also acknowledge that it goes both ways. Like, for years, I didn't know anything about Yuri Kochiyama, who was a close comrade and sister in the struggle with Malcolm X and held his head in her lap when he was shot and dying—where was that scene in the movie? Why hasn't that story been told? So I think that those of us in Hollywood and the media especially need to work harder and louder to build out our history in intersectional ways.

**RYAN ALEXANDER HOLMES:** I'll put my own education out as an example. The neighborhood that I grew up in was about 60 percent Asian. But we didn't learn anything about Asian American history in school—literally, nothing. If we had, maybe we would have understood America in its real context. And if they'd also actually taught African American history, we'd realize how connected we actually are. As someone who's Black and Asian, I've always felt that wedge there between both my communities. And if we just understood our histories, the things we have in common, the wedge might be replaced with connection and celebration of who we are.

## Living in the Intersections

*The lines between our communities are not as easy to draw as one might think—but standing with a foot in each can be difficult.*

**RYAN:** I'm Black and Chinese. I grew up in San Marino, which has been called the Chinese Beverly Hills. It's mostly white and Asian, and the only Black person in my school was my brother and me, combined. I didn't grow up with Black people other than my father—but I was taught how to be "Black" by those Asian and white kids. Because I didn't act Black to them, they encouraged me to be stereotypically Black. My dad came home one day to see me sitting there with a do-rag on my head, blasting Tupac and shouting obscenities—and he grabbed that right out of my head. He said, "I don't know what the fuck you're doing right now, but let me teach you what Black is, because this ain't it."

On the other hand, I never felt Asian enough, even though I was raised by the Asian side of my family. It wasn't until George Floyd's murder, when I wrote a piece about how I felt being Blasian, that things really changed for me. To my surprise, most Asians who read it were supportive. It made me want to focus on moving forward and celebrating my Asian heritage, not being afraid to be out loud with it—to say the things that I want to say as an Asian American. To no longer feel like a Chinese man trapped in a Black person's body.

The reason Asians even first came here in large numbers was because, when slavery ended, there was a demand for labor from Asia to build the West Coast—coolie and plantation labor from China, Japan, the Philippines, and everybody else down the line.

**KAMAU:** Man, I remember I was a little kid, looking at Bruce Lee, going, "Mom, are you sure that's not my dad? I mean, look at our noses." But for real, when I discovered Bruce I was hooked—I felt this deep connection with him, as a cultural figure and as a personal inspiration. In the last year, after watching Bao Nguyen's documentary *Be Water* and reading a lot of his writings, I've also been able to see what his role was as an anti-racist. Living in San Francisco, I feel very connected to the Chinese American community, but I am very clear that I'm not Chinese American and I'm totally fine

with that—it's all love.

During the pandemic, it was frustrating to see hate crimes being committed against Asians because of who was president at the time. I was also frustrated because the Chinese government had directed blame toward African nationals in China, and rumors were spreading there that they were the reason for the virus. I spoke up about it on social media, and got people angry at me from all sides. I ended up turning that experience into an essay I posted about how we're all in this together, and how I learned that from Bruce Lee.

## A Nation of Separation

*Events like the L.A. Riots, in which Black and Asian communities were pitted against one another while law enforcement stood back to defend majority-white neighborhoods, are painful evidence of the way that racial power structures are preserved and reinforced. Communities of color are encouraged to make each other scapegoats for inequities that are part of America's basic operating system.*

**MONICA:** I'm Black and Korean, and it was really painful in the Nineties in New York and in California. It felt like a constant clash between the African American community and the Asian American—specifically the Korean American—community.

**RYAN:** During the L.A. Riots, my mom, who's Chinese, was in the wrong area at the wrong time and rocks were thrown at her car. At the time, my parents had been together for three or four years, and even though they lived 20 minutes away, my Chinese family did not interact with us at all. But when they saw how my mother was treated, and how involved my dad was as a lawyer in the wake of the Riots—that made my Chinese family question why they weren't involved in their grandsons' lives.

**MONICA:** There's just a divide-and-conquer mentality in our society. I think that's where the tension comes from. We're constantly encouraged to fight each other, as opposed to banding together. The breakthrough moments of the Civil Rights Movement came because there was so much camaraderie and unity between Black and Jewish advocacy groups. We need to realize, like they did, that if we join together, we can outnumber everyone else.

**SHAWN:** When the Riots happened, I felt like a cultural switch got turned off. My circle of friends had been a very multicultural group, but they started siloing off. I remember when the Mountain Brothers, this very influential Asian American hip-hop group, dropped their album in the late '90s. Black people in my circle wanted to bury the album. It may seem inconsequential, but it hurt me so bad, because it made me realize how bad the fracture was. Seeing anti-Asian behavior among African Americans, among Caribbeans and West Indians and Spanish-speaking Black folks . . . to me, that was a really horrific thing. And I do believe that the Rodney King incident led to that—it caused a hyper-metastasis of this cancer into the bones of our culture that led to a fracture that we're still trying to heal.

**JEFF CHANG:** White supremacy is a motherfucker. It puts us into competition with each other, it creates this hierarchy, and it expects us all to beg to be white. And people immigrating here already have that in their minds. They get anti-Blackness injected into them, and say to themselves, well, at least we're never going

to be at the bottom. And that's how you get a Soon Ja Du, and the dehumanization of Black people that led her to shoot a young Black girl. It comes out of white supremacy.

Asian Americans have to break out of this. We have to be able to make a choice. We have to get off our asses and choose whether we're down for white supremacy or whether we can be down for Black freedom, which means freedom for all.

## Freedom to Speak

*Conversation between our communities is essential. But how can it begin when many of us are trained to think we shouldn't even have a voice—especially those who exist within both cultures, and often feel accepted by neither?*

**RYAN:** When I was attending drama school, I played a white man in every play that I was in. The whole time I was saying, Can I just be myself? Can I do that? When do I get to do that? Because representation is powerful. I cried during both *Black Panther* and *Crazy Rich Asians*. Look, Black people in a dope-ass spaceship flying into their secret futuristic world and saying, "We're home." I started sobbing at *Crazy Rich Asians* just because they were playing mahjong! I'd never seen any of that shit on a big screen before, you know?

My dream is to write my own show about being Blasian, because when you're Blasian in Hollywood, you just don't really have a place to go.

**MONICA:** Even in my own brain, I didn't think my story was worth watching. But a Korean American executive encouraged me to write a pitch based on my life story growing up as a Black Korean person in Chicago, and I sold it.

So, I hear what you're saying, "Can I do that?" But representation for us is growing. Even just looking at Naomi Osaka, seeing her just doing what she's doing, that's big. Like Naomi, I grew up playing tennis, and seeing someone who is half black and half Asian crushing it in tennis, taking the baton from Serena Williams, being politically vocal—that representation matters.

> We didn't learn anything about Asian American history in school—literally, nothing. If we had, maybe we would have understood America in its real context. And if they'd also actually taugh African American history, we'd realize how connected we actually are. As someone who's Black and Asian, I've always felt that wedge there between both my communities.

## Into the Future

*Nothing is going to change on its own, and the choices we make today will become the difference we see tomorrow.*

**KAMAU:** What we need in 10 years is the power to change things ourselves. If we're talking about Hollywood, we need the representation in the room to help greenlight projects. And yes, we need studio diversity programs, but ultimately all of that is sort of nibbling around the edges. That's why a lot of Black folks like me have sort of backed off on Tyler Perry. That guy's worth a billion dollars. He owns a studio, and he can set the stakes of what the game is going to look like next. And then you have peo-ple like Ava DuVernay, Shonda Rhimes, Kenya Barris, Ryan Coogler. If they position themselves, they can be studio owners too. That's what we really need to get Hollywood interested in making our interesting stories

**JEFF:** On a social level, it's a fantasy that everything will just get better as older racist folks die off. Folks choose to act, or they choose to let things go. Well, we can't let anti-Black racism and white supremacy go. We're living in a historic moment right now. It's on us to make the choices in our daily lives and in the way that we raise our families and in our communities to not let that happen.

**SHAWN:** I think there's also a self-esteem issue that we need to address. I think that a lot of us need to believe we can make those choices. That if we stand together, Black and Asian, we can rise above this moment.

Bruce Lee has been dead for 40 years, and we're still talking about him—that's impact. Hip-hop has changed since I first fell in love with it, but we're still talking about its impact. We're still talking about Richard Pryor. We're still talking about Yuri Kochiyama and Grace Lee Boggs. These are people who have made gigantic footprints.

So yes, white supremacy is a motherfucker, but fuck white supremacy. There's a level of power when you don't even have to worry about the enemy. And I think that when more of us act from that place of agency, we'll get there. Buckminster Fuller said something along the lines of: You don't fight the existing system. You create a new one to make the old one obsolete.

PARVESH CHEENA    DUSTIN NGUYEN    DANTE BASCO    TIYA SIRCAR

# After "Asian August": A Conversation

**ON AUGUST 15, 2018,** *Crazy Rich Asians* opened. It felt to a lot of us like the beginning of a new era for Asian Americans on-screen. That was amplified two days later on August 17, when Netflix's *To All the Boys I've Loved Before*, a teen rom-com starring Vietnamese American Lana Condor, became one of its most-watched movies ever. The unexpectedly big August 31 opening of *Searching*, a lean, brilliant thriller starring John Cho and directed by Aneesh Chaganty, served as an exclamation mark—Asian August? Yes, this was #AsianAugust! Not just a month, but a movement. But would this magical moment really lead to an overnight transformation of an industry that had spent a century excluding, erasing, and distorting Asian stories and voices? Three years after Asian August, we gathered a group of veteran Asian American performers, **PARVESH CHEENA**, **DUSTIN NGUYEN**, **DANTE BASCO**, and **TIYA SIRCAR**, to talk about their journeys through the lean times of Hollywood, and their hopes for and anxieties about what's coming next.

## How It Started

*For a lot of Asian American performers, discovering that you're Asian—and that being Asian is an obstacle to doing what you love—was a rude awakening.*

**PARVESH:** I was a theater student, a kid from the Chicago suburbs, and I was gay. But you know how you can be Asian *or* gay, and you can't be both sometimes? Well, I felt like I was like a white guy—I did musicals throughout high school without any issue. And then 9/11 happened. I got followed around at an Old Navy by a suspicious clerk. I complained about it to my friend—who's Black—and she said to me: "Welcome to being Black." Honestly, that was the first time I realized, "Oh, I guess I'm Indian." Getting cast in *Barbershop* brought me out to Los Angeles, but *Outsourced* in 2010 was my big TV break.

**DUSTIN:** I was born in Vietnam, but came to the United States in 1975 when I was 10 years old. I knew I always wanted to make movies from my first moment sitting in the cinema—when the lights went down, it created such a magical feeling. I didn't set out to be an actor! But I started acting in the Eighties, and got very lucky to be cast on a show called *21 Jump Street.*

**DANTE:** I'm Filipino American and was born in the Bay Area in Pittsburg, California. I actually came to Los Angeles as a break dancer when I was 10. Being Filipino and American in the Bay Area—well, being Filipino in the Bay is its own thing. I wasn't as conscious of being Asian as I was of being a child of hip-hop. But that changed when I came into the world of Hollywood. My big break was playing Rufio in Steven Spielberg's *Hook* in 1991.

**TIYA:** I'm Indian American, Bengali American, born and raised in Dallas, Texas. I started dancing when I was two, before discovering musical theater. And I immediately knew I wanted to act: I'd beg my parents to let me at least try to get a commercial agent in Dallas. They said, "Absolutely not." But they let me perform, just not professionally, so I took classes and was a part of as many productions as possible in high school. In college, I got two different degrees: one in theater and dance, and a business degree in marketing. My parents are both professors with Ph.D.s and they're Indians— so there was this double whammy of pressure and expectation. In my mind, my first break was being in a movie called *17 Again,* which starred Matthew Perry and Zac Efron. But I guess *The Internship,* with Owen Wilson, was a much more major milestone.

## On the Shoulders of Giants

*Some had mentors or role models to look toward for inspiration and support. Others, not so much.*

**DUSTIN:** I looked up to people like Pat Morita, James Shigeta, Clyde Kusatsu, and Mako. But as you moved along the industry, opportunities for Asians were few and far between. I'm sure the climate is different now. But then? One out of every 20 auditions I took would be a "non-Asian" role. You'd go in, you knew you never were going to book.

**DANTE:** Dustin was one of my inspirations in the community! People like Dustin and Ernie Reyes Jr. looked out for me like big brothers. It was cool to come to Hollywood having Asian cats before me who had succeeded, set up a lane, and who were willing to help.

- Outer clothing left by front door in a pile
- Basket full of cloth masks
- Plastic "visor" masks and N95s
- Box of latex gloves
- Hand sanitizer
- By the door, many pairs of shoes and slippers
- Woman washing hands in scalding hot water with antiseptic soap
- Hand sanitizer
- Bleach wipes
- Dining table with laptop, papers, files, cat lounging on keyboard
- Hand sanitizer
- Children's books, toys on floor
- Younger son watching Chinese TV with Grandma while also playing Nintendo Switch
- Grandma is sewing a mask
- Children's books, toys on floor
- Hand sanitizer
- Older son on Zoom "listening" to a lecture but clearly paying more attention to a second window containing a Minecraft game
- More books and toys, different floor
- Too many toothbrushes and too many bottles of different products due to grandparents moving in
- Hand sanitizer
- Man in home office on Zoom with relative who's obviously sick, feverish, and sneezing. Another window on separate screen shows a spiking chart with COVID-19 contagions
- Too many mobile devices plugged into power strip with USB adapter

- Books and toys, basically everywhere
- Hand sanitizer
- Daughter recording a selfie TikTok dance
- Grandpa looking through a refrigerator that's been completely packed; freezer has pork, chicken, and beef for a month
- Teacups and mugs everywhere, most with varying levels of (old) liquid
- Big pots on the stove steaming
- Piles of snacks in pantry for stress eating: instant noodles, shrimp crackers, cans of milk tea, potato chips, seaweed, cookies
- Produce on the counter (garlic, onions, squashes, cabbage, etc.)
- A ton of flour, pasta, beans, canned fish, Spam, pickles
- Giant package of toilet paper in pantry
- Hand sanitizer
- Backyard garden thriving under the care of Grandma
- Mostly empty streets
- A few businesses with signs indicating they've shuttered
- Discarded masks on the ground
- A sign pointing to a local testing station
- An Asian medical worker in scrubs walking by in a mask
- Unmasked white people castigating Asian medical worker for . . . something
- Bus parked by the road; someone inside is sanitizing it
- Joggers staying carefully six feet apart from one another

# Life During COVID

BY JEFF YANG AND FRANKIE HUANG

**NORMALLY, OUR HOMES** have been a place of comfort, but for much of 2020, home has been . . . everything. Sealed in by the COVID-19 pandemic, many of us have had to spend day and night within our four walls, trying to be productive, entertaining ourselves, doing our best to stay connected but not overwhelmed by news, getting used to a degree of extreme closeness with some of our loved ones and extreme distance with others.

Outside, the world beyond our front door has transformed into a hostile place that resembles America, but feels more like the Twilight Zone. Streets are almost deserted; restaurants, laundromats, cafés, gyms, schools, office buildings are all empty, doors shut, lights out. Your N95 is secure on your face as you walk down the street, the few people you see trigger loneliness, but also fear. Are they wearing a mask? Are they coughing? Are they looking at you with contempt? You just want to go buy some groceries for the week, and you can see that the line outside the Asian supermarket winds around the block, and one of the store walls still has the faint signs of a hastily scrubbed away GO BACK HOME from a vandal attack several nights before. You pick up the pace, as a white person with her mask pulled down under her chin whispers "CHINA VIRUS" in your direction.

This was living la vida COVID while Asian. And we won't forget it anytime soon.

**DUSTIN:** I should hire you as my publicist.

**TIYA:** My first year was challenging. I don't know if there was so much camaraderie, because it didn't feel like there were many South Asian women doing comedy back then that I could look at and say, that is a blueprint for what I want to do. Now, there's Mindy Kaling. But her rise has sort of been contemporaneous with my career.

## "All Ethnicities"

*The biggest challenge in the days before "Asian August" was also one of the biggest opportunities: roles that were written as ethnically ambiguous. Pro: Being able to play a part that isn't anchored in stereotypes. Con: Playing a part that isn't anchored in anything at all.*

**PARVESH:** Over the past decade, I realized that a lot of my humor as a brown, Asian, gay man has been in service to white supremacy. It's really weird. As I've brought these characters to life, I've found myself thinking, "I'm not like those other gays! I'm straight-acting!" Or, "*Their* house smells like curry. *We* eat pizza." So there was always this deflection of my identity, and it was usually in the service of frat boys in *Dude, Where's My Car?*–type comedy.

**DANTE:** What choice did we have back then? "All Ethnicities" roles. We always joked about it being a casting breakdown when it said that, because we all knew what it meant: in the end it would go to that ethnically ambiguous white guy. That's "All Ethnicities."

**TIYA:** Well, "All Ethnicities" was the name of the game for much of my career. You go to these auditions, you'd always see the same set of girls—one Japanese American, one Chinese American, a few Black girls, a few white girls, and maybe one other Indian girl. They were the ones doing comedy. So I ended up getting cast almost exclusively for these ethnically ambiguous characters named "Amy" or "Ashley," where the character just happens to be South Asian, but nothing about the character is specific. The first pilot that I booked, my character's name was "Harper Holly."

**DUSTIN:** Maybe it's because I'm a guy, but I was resigned early on to the fact that all the parts I was ever going to get were Asian. Now of course, I had personal aspirations to go beyond that, but it was just reality for me. I took this acting class, and we had a guest—a famous photographer who'd come in to do our headshots. He did an exercise with us to help us figure out what "type" we were in this industry. To others, he said, "the ingenue," "the girl next door," or "the jock." Then he looked at me and he said, "You know, you'd work a lot if you were in Hong Kong." That was my type: Asian.

**DANTE:** But what kind of Asian? When I go to auditions for an Asian role, they always subtly try to find out what brand of Asian I am—because it's never the one they were thinking about. So at auditions, when they basically ask me, "What are you?" I respond, "What's the role?" They say, "It's Chinese." I respond with "My grandmother on my dad's side is part Chinese." One time, they said the role was Mexican. I told them: "The Spaniards did to us what they did to them." Because of our history, Filipinos are such a mixed race, so I've ended up playing so many different ethnicities.

One of the first TV shows I recurred in was *The Wonder Years*—I played Fred Savage's best friend. It wasn't written as an Asian role, but one of the things I tell young actors of color is, you gotta be better than the white kids. You have to beat white kids out for white kid parts, period. And you have to build relationships with other actors of color. Not just Asians. When I came into Hollywood, it was just white and Black. So my career, from *Moesha* to *Hanging with Mr. Cooper,* I ended up being just as much anchored in Black Hollywood.

## Boxed In

*While ethnic-specific roles offered the opportunity to bring texture, truth, and authenticity to a character, they also could be restrictive— in part because there were so few with many talented actors seeking to fill them, and in part because they created new hurdles that non-Asians rarely had to face.*

**TIYA:** It wasn't until 2010 that there were roles I was called in for that were specifically South Asian. But then they told me I wasn't "authentically" Indian enough! I'm from Texas. What do you want from me? I'm as Indian as I am, and I'm bicultural. During pilot season, I auditioned for a show where the lead's name was "Rebecca." What are the odds they were going to actually cast me? I can do the role, but the moment there's a family involved, are they going to cast me and a brown dad and a brown brother? Forget it. That was the story of my life for a long time. It's only recently that things started to change. In *The Internship,* my character's name was Neha Patel—the first specifically Indian American character I'd ever played.

**DANTE:** I always say this about *ER,* which was one of the longest-running medical shows on television: Where's the Filipino nurses? On *ER*?! In the last season or two, we finally got an Indian doctor—but where were those nurses?!

**PARVESH:** We want accuracy. We want representation. We don't want to be swirled into "All Ethnicities." But at the same time, we also don't want to always be boxed into the restrictions of hyper-accurate ethnic distinction, which is something white actors don't have to face. I say Brown a lot now instead of Indian because technically, if my grandparents who were born in Lahore were born today, they'd be Pakistani.

**DANTE:** Well, if I got to wait to be Filipino in a movie, I don't have a career.

## When the Earth Moved

*The big shift began before Asian August. But Asian August hopefully sealed the deal.*

**DUSTIN:** I spent a lot of the last decade working in Vietnam. And while I was there, I started to see Korean cinema starting to cross international borders. I started to see more and more interest in Asian pop culture. And then *Crazy Rich Asians* came out, and I was like, wow, okay, it took quite a while since *The Joy Luck Club* for something like this to come out. And this isn't an art house film. This is commercial. This is from a major studio, and it made a lot of money.

**DANTE:** But even before *Crazy Rich Asians,* there was the digital media scene, a whole Asian American community on YouTube with folks like KevJumba and Ryan Higa, showing young Asian Americans just being people. So many of them were among the most subscribed channels on YouTube during its early eras. We weren't in network TV or mainstream films, but these kids were garnering these huge audiences, and some of them were making $100,000 a month—that was incredible to me. These kids were doing something far beyond what Hollywood was doing, and ultimately that had a huge impact.

**PARVESH:** True, though if I had to put the date on when things really felt like they were starting to shift, I'd say 2016—the beginning of the Trump era. It was such a political pivot to a conservative white nationalist agenda that, well, say what you want about Hollywood, but it had to react to that. During Obama, I still played a lot of stereotypical brown roles. Since 2016, I've gotten roles for gay characters, for complex Indian characters, and I'm not grateful for Trump. I'm really grateful for Gen Z. Because they will not stand for it—this generation is vocal when things aren't right.

## How It's Going

*After Asian August, more doors are open for Asian American creators. But just because doors are open doesn't mean everyone can walk through—or that they can't be closed again. The only solution: cutting more doors in the wall.*

**DUSTIN:** I moved to Vietnam because around 2000, I hit a glass ceiling as an actor, and I knew it would also be difficult for me to direct and produce the stories that I wanted to tell in America. I'd done a film called *Little Fish* as Cate Blanchett's love interest. After that film, I thought it would change how people saw Asian people—how they saw me—but it didn't. So I went back to tell stories in my native tongue.

The interesting thing is that the first few films I produced, directed, and acted in there were then picked up for distribution here in the United States. It made me realize the industry was becoming more global, and that from an artist's point of view, you don't have to be in Hollywood to create content.

**DANTE:** I feel you. I produced a film in the Philippines. The building of bridges to Asians globally, and hooking into the star systems and financial resources out there—the world has changed. It's so much more fluid than it was even 10 years ago. The game in this town up till now has been to go to the studios and beg for money, and yes, that's always going to be part of the game, but that's no longer the only game.

**TIYA:** But things are even changing there. In 2018, I was cast as the lead of an ABC series called *Alex Inc.,* opposite Zach Braff. And the character is based on a real woman who's Persian American, but when they offered me the role, they changed her background to be Indian American. Then they asked if they could make my character Hindu, because they really wanted to do a Holi episode. And then they made her from Texas, like me. The role became much easier to draw because these were my own experiences. My parents even came into the writers' room so the producers could pick their brains. My dad was writing out explanations on a whiteboard.

It was mind-boggling to not only play an Indian American, but specifically a Bengali American. And they cast a Bengali American actress to be the mom, Anjali Bhimani, who spoke Bengali on the show! It never happened before, and I hope it happens again.

**DANTE:** Our future has to go beyond representation. We need to create a self-sustaining system of our own, where we're the arbiters of the art we're making. We can't depend on Hollywood to spend $30 million on a *Crazy*

*Rich Asians*. We have to be putting out our own $300,000 films every month. Until then, we're at the whims of other people writing things for us.

**DUSTIN:** As actors, we're just a color in a painting. We need painters: writers and directors. We need storytellers who are telling stories through our filters. You're seeing more of that now. There's a lot of Asian directors making amazing work. That's where the changes are gonna take place.

**TIYA:** My hope is that in 10 years, we don't have to have this conversation. Because it'll be so much less noteworthy when an Asian is the lead in a film. We'll just be: "Oh, another one?"

# POSTCARD FROM ASIAN AMERICA

BY DINO RAY RAMOS

Dear RISE,

Picture it: 1979. Lackland Air Force Base, San Antonio, Texas. It's almost midnight, raining and Rovena Ramos is about to give birth to the most handsome Filipino American boy that the world will ever see. Also . . . he is going to grow up to be a bad bitch. And that bad bitch . . . is me.

Yes, my father, Froilan Ramos, was in the military—the Air Force, to be specific. So of all places, Texas was where my cultural identity as an Asian American took shape. I was surrounded by whiteness; that's not an attempt to throw shade, just a fact. I had Black and LatinX friends, but white was still the majority—and as far as Asian people were concerned, they were limited to family and family friends. I admit I fell into the trap of "white proximity equals white acceptance." And even though my dad was a leader and staunch advocate for the Filipino community, in my youthful rebellion, I distanced myself from both my culture and my dad's example.

Fast forward a decade later, and I'd embraced my father as a role model. I went to Texas A&M University, where I became the president of the Philippine Student Association, connecting me with my heritage, and putting me in a position to advocate for the entire Asian community, for my fellow LGBTQ+ peers, and for marginalized people in general. That in turn fed into my work as a journalist at the university paper, and when I graduated, at the *Oakland Tribune*, *San Francisco Chronicle*, *Deadline*, and numerous other publications. My latest venture, a website called Diaspora, has been called by some the "*Village Voice* of Hollywood trades." And by some, I mean me.

So when people ask: Are there Filipinos in Texas? My answer would be: "Yes, there are Filipinos in Texas. In fact, there are Filipinos everywhere around the world. There are Asians all around the world." If you didn't know, now you know.

LYLAS,
Dino

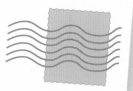

RISE
HERE AND NOW,
ASIAN AMERICA

# The Essential
# Awkwafina 12-Pack

BY JEFF YANG AND PHILIP WANG,
ILLUSTRATED BY JIA SUNG

**AWKWAFINA—BORN NORA LUM** in Queens, New York—now seems to be everywhere. She's leveraged her considerable talents as a musician, actress, comedian, author, and larger-than-life personality to go from novelty rapper/bodega worker to A-list celebrity in half a decade, and now can count some of the biggest movies in recent Hollywood history to her credit, as well as her own comic memoir series, *Nora from Queens*. We took a refreshing look at her rise to almost-overnight success, popping the bottles on a dozen projects that have defined her surging career so far.

1. "My Vag": Awkwafina first burst into public prominence with her comedy rap song and video "My Vag," a hilarious celebration of her girl parts. When the video went viral, she got fired from her job as a publicity assistant at Rodale Books.

2. *Girl Code*: In 2014, Awkwafina joined the cast of MTV's unscripted comedy show *Girl Code* for its third and fourth seasons. In 2015, she became cohost for the series's talk show spinoff, *Girl Code Live,* which only lasted one season.

3. *Tawk*: Awkwafina launched a talk show called *Tawk,* which first ran on YouTube and then was picked up by Verizon Media's Go90 network. It was honored at the Webby Awards and nominated for a Streamy in 2016.

4. *Ocean's 8*: In 2018, Awkwafina appeared in the all-woman Ocean Trilogy spinoff *Ocean's 8* as a street hustler and pickpocket who helps heist a $150 million Cartier necklace from the Met Gala. Her character's name is Constance.

5. *Crazy Rich Asians*: Which is a coincidence (or is it?), because in 2018, Awkwafina would also star opposite Constance Wu in Jon M. Chu's blockbuster romantic comedy hit, *Crazy Rich Asians,* as Peik-Lin Goh, the college best friend of Wu's character Rachel Chu.

6. *Saturday Night Live*: Hosting *Saturday Night Live* is one of the most sought-after gigs in Hollywood—and Awkwafina became the first Asian American woman asked to take it on in almost two decades (with Lucy Liu being the first—and until then, only—in 2000).

7. *The Farewell*: Interestingly, director Lulu Wang says she'd actually cast Awkwafina in *The Farewell* before her breakout appearance in *Crazy Rich Asians,* but—the reality of indie filmmaking being what it is—her movie made it to theaters afterward. Just as well: the success of *Crazy Rich Asians* pulled people into theaters to see Awkwafina play her first lead, as a girl at odds with her family over their unwillingness to tell her grandmother that she has terminal cancer . . . a performance that garnered her a Golden Globe and copious critical praise.

8. *Jumanji: The Next Level*: Awkwafina next found herself cast in the sequel to the 2017 hit *Jumanji: Welcome to the Jungle,* as thief and pickpocket Ming Fleetfoot. Though the role wasn't huge, the movie was—earning $800 million globally, and confirming Awkwafina as an A-list star.

9. Promo voice for the Queens, New York, 7 Train: In 2020, as a promo for her semi-autobiographical

Comedy Central series *Nora from Queens,* Awkwafina took over the prerecorded conductor announcements on her native New York borough's 7 train, using her raspy voice to tell people key facts like "The poles are for hands only, people!"

10.  *Nora from Queens*: Awkwafina gets to tell her life story, or at least a hilariously over-the-top version of it. People find out that her real name is "Nora Lum," that she's half Chinese and half Korean, and that she's from Queens! With B. D. Wong as her father, Jonathan "Dumbfoundead" Park as her brother, and Bowen Yang (of *SNL*) as her cousin, and guest appearances from the likes of Ming-Na Wen, Harry Shum Jr., and Simu Liu! The show was enough of a success that it was renewed for a second season even before it premiered.

11.  *Raya and the Last Dragon*: Awkwafina costars in her first Disney Princess movie, as Sisu, a water dragon who might just be the last hope for the people of Kumandra, a land inspired by Southeast Asian culture and legend. Not her last Disney Princess movie, though: She's slated to appear in the live-action version of Disney's *The Little Mermaid* as the seagull Scuttle.

12.  *Shang-Chi and the Legend of the Ten Rings*: On top of everything else, Awkwafina was tapped to star in Marvel's first Asian American superhero movie, opposite Simu Liu (cast as Shang-Chi). And it's clear that as big a splash as she's made already, the best for Awkwafina is still ahead.

# Talking with the Founders of Subtle Asian Traits

### BY PHILIP WANG

## From Procrastination to Global Phenomenon

The first ever post on Subtle Asian Traits

**IT WAS SEPTEMBER 2018,** on the other side of the world in Melbourne, Australia, and nine friends who'd met at Chinese language school were facing their final exams. To distract themselves from the grind, they decided to turn their group chat into a private Facebook group—membership by invite only—where they would post funny memes that would highlight small experiences growing up Asian. The name of the group: Subtle Asian Traits. Over the next few months, SAT, as insiders call it, began to spread like wildfire—jumping out of their immediate friend group and extending to other cities in Australia, before finally crossing oceans to connect Asian Australians with their overseas counterparts. The group is now approaching two million members, and features tens of thousands of posts of user-submitted content weekly. Cofounder **KERRY KANG**, admin **EUGENE SOO,** and moderator **ZOE IMANSJAH** shared with us their experiences of founding and running a viral phenomenon that somehow managed to unite the global Asian diaspora—while also shedding light on both how relatably similar and wildly diverse that diaspora actually is.

## Humble Beginnings

**EUGENE:** The original concept was just to try to encapsulate the Asian experience in one sentence. A lot of early posts were jokes about hoarding plastic bags and napkins.

**KERRY:** The whole idea was linking us as minorities in our countries, while showing we have these shared niche experiences that aren't limited to the culture in which we grew up and maybe really aren't that niche. We also didn't want to be dragging other cultures; we wanted it to be positive. And that led us toward this mission to be a platform that's as inclusive as possible of stories and experiences across the diaspora.

**EUGENE:** We chose to use a Facebook group because that gave us the sense of community. Everyone is able to post and contribute content by themselves, so it's much more of a collaborative field rather than a one-sided content machine. But then again, Facebook Groups were designed to be for 50 to 60 people.

## Unexpected Growth

*In just three months, the group grew to over a million members around the world.*

**EUGENE:** We just told people to invite all their Asian friends on Facebook. There was no marketing—our growth was totally organic.

**KERRY:** To be honest, 10K was always our goal, but since we founders are Chinese, we saw eight as a lucky number. So we tracked our growth with the number eight. When we hit 88,888, we took a screenshot and shared it with the group, thinking, wow, amazing. Then it hit 888,888.

But in a way, the real feeling that we were getting big was when we expanded from Melbourne to Sydney, because we didn't expect it to go farther than Melbourne. And then it reached the U.K. in three months, and we hit a million. If you ask us when it truly started feeling like it was getting out of control, though, it was when the U.S. nation attacked.

## America versus Australia

*Once the group reached the United States, the tone of the group began to change.*

**EUGENE:** Australians—how do I say this nicely?—we're a society that doesn't give a lot of shits in general. So it was a really, really big learning experience over the past two years for us to understand American culture, because there is quite a massive difference.

**KERRY:** Funny enough, one of the first examples where we felt this division was in the whole boba versus bubble tea debate. I genuinely did not realize that the Americans had an agenda where it had to be one or the other.

**EUGENE:** Aussies were feeling prideful about being the origin of SAT. And when all these Americans started joining, there was definitely a sentiment of "Why are the Americans bringing in all these expectations of what SAT should be?" And the Americans were just like "Too bad."

## With Growth Comes Responsibility

*More members meant more opinions. A group meant for memes had to start grappling with politics and controversial current events.*

**EUGENE:** There were so many things coming at us so quickly all at once that we had to learn how to handle and cope with.

**ZOE:** As a moderator, I just wanted to share memes that made me laugh, or cute stories. But I would start getting messages in my inbox saying I was a racist, or threatening me because I didn't post about something. It definitely made me step back and ask myself, "Why am I doing this? Is this something that I want to endure, just because I want to create a community that I care about?" When SAT first started, it was a small group of 16- to 18-year-olds. Then, almost overnight, we were like, "We have to run this global group now!" At one point, our pending queue was at like 60,000 posts, and we spent all-nighters scrolling through to approve them.

**EUGENE:** The responsibility we feel for the group has never been greater. If anything, the longer we've had to manage the group, the more responsibility and attachment we feel for it. To be honest, though, it does get very draining on our entire team. We're still students with daily lives, not making any money doing this. But we'll still get dozens of people messaging us at 3:00 a.m. like, "Hi, can you approve my posts, you terrible person?"

**ZOE:** We have group rules, and they're very simple to follow. Be kind, be courteous, don't use hate speech, don't discriminate. People forget that we're a private group, and that we can ban or mute them if they break those rules. But it's what we have to do to ensure the group survives.

## Subtle Asian EVERYTHING!

*As it grew, SAT became a meme in itself, with imitation pages popping up all over: Subtle Asian Dating, Subtle Asian Cooking, Subtle Curry Traits.*

**EUGENE:** I view it less as them trying to copy us or make fake versions of us than just trying to make a spin-off version for whatever their niche is.

**ZOE:** In SAT, there just happens to be more East Asian content, because there are more people of East Asian descent in the group submitting. I'm Indonesian, and there's a Subtle Indonesians group that I'm a member of—and over there, I'm like, "Oh my gosh, this is really funny. I relate to this too!"

**KERRY:** The fact is, it's very hard for us to cater to all needs. So we actually appreciate some of these niche groups, because then they allow all those other conversations to happen.

## What's Next?

*Come for the memes; stay for the humanity.*

**KERRY:** Our mission is to connect Asian individuals globally and to create a community that celebrates the similarities and differences within our cultures and subcultures. That's what we continue to strive for.

**ZOE:** The content in SAT has definitely changed a lot from what it was in the beginning. It grew from being a meme page to now, people sharing their own interests and personal experiences. It's not just "oh, funny relatable jokes"; we have people acknowledging their Asian parents' sacrifices, we have stories of people coming to terms with their sexuality. That's what keeps us going, when people are taking their own personal lives and putting them out there for this community to see as an example, breaking down barriers.

**KERRY:** We do acknowledge that we're young. However, we have a lot of experience, enthusiasm, and motivation to grow this as a cultural phenomenon. We came along around the same time as *Crazy Rich Asians, To All the Boys I've Loved Before,* all these different things that launched empowering Asian movements. And now, we kind of sit in the forefront of it.

**EUGENE:** However long this goes, I just hope that people remember us in a positive light and that we were a force for good, and that we had a positive impact when we were around.

# BTS: Inside the American ARMY

BY REBECCA SUN

**THE PARADOX OF** Bangtan Sonyeondan is that it is at once the most quantifiably popular, famous, and successful pop artist of the moment, yet also, to anyone outside of its considerable ARMY fanbase, the most opaque and impenetrable. This dual quality—and the fact that BTS's reign coincides with the social media age—lends itself extremely well to memery, the ultimate dialect of the insider. And although, unlike many other K-pop groups, nobody in BTS is Asian American, the phenomenon of being seen as simultaneously ubiquitous and frustratingly foreign (even, dare one say, inscrutable) parallels the experience of being one. No wonder, then, that even as ARMY remains a resolutely diverse battalion, for Westerners of Asian descent BTS's ascension to pop culture sovereignty simply hits different. Witnessing "locals"— K-pop slang for Muggles, essentially—throw themselves at the feet of such an unabashedly Asian, thoroughly modern entity is aspiration porn at its finest, a hope that as BTS goes, so goes Asian America.

In honor of BTS's most sacred number, here are seven memes—one for each member—that have resonated the most with the Asian American experience.

### President Namjoon

ARMY have conferred this title upon BTS's leader, RM (né Kim Namjoon), as a reference not just to his position within the seven-member group but also to the respect and authority he has come to command in unlikely spaces, such as the UN General Assembly.

if you dont think jin is handsome just remember that he trended on twitter in korea for stepping out of a car

## Car Door Guy

Even casual fans know Jin as "Worldwide Handsome," the half-tongue-in-cheek moniker the oldest member has given himself. But before BTS became worldwide famous, Jin was first known as "Car Door Guy" to netizens desperately searching for the identity of the handsome fella exiting his SUV to hit the red carpet at the 2015 Melon Music Awards. With each media appearance, new SEO-friendly nicknames for various members trend on Twitter like scales falling from locals' eyes.

## Minstradamus

What Suga wants, Suga gets. Rapper-producer Min Yoongi isn't shy about boldly publicizing his goals for the group, which have included performing at awards shows (check), filling stadiums (check), and reaching No. 1 on the Billboard Hot 100 chart (check). His goals turned prophecies are proof that frank ambition can be rewarding. Next up: The Grammys . . .

@ELMXRIACHI

winter dior          summer dior

6:54 PM · 06 Jul 19 · Twitter for iPhone

## J-Hope's Dior fit

J-Hope's talk show persona is as sunny as his stage name, but his duality was on full display during the rapline's performances of "Outro: Tear" on the Speak Yourself tour. Spitting and looking fire in an all-black commando-inspired getup from Dior Homme's Kim Jones, who designed custom outfits for the tour, J-Hope's instantly iconic look signified both an imprimatur from haute couture and a reminder that these boys are actually men.

**A Male Stage Designer Considered Leaving His Girlfriend for BTS's Jimin**

"I'm now confused about my sexual orientation."

여친이랑 헤어지겠습니다. 오늘부로 전 게이 입니다

ㅋㅋㅋㅋㅁ진 지민이 너 안 만나 져 씻고 자라ㅋㅋㅋ

고백도 하기전에 차이다니ㅜ 얼굴이랑 춤이 랑 목소리 너무 섹시도발...부채라도 되고싶 다

## Once you Jimin, you can't Jimout

Also known as "The Jimin Effect," Urban Dictionary defines this phenomenon as Jimin's ability to "effortlessly snatch locals," in other words, make stans of an unsuspecting public, particularly men. His sinuous dancing, airy tenor, and ineffable charisma are not about attaining or subverting Western standards of machismo, but rather redefining masculinity on his own terms.

## Taehyung's vibe check

As more and more Western celebrities, locals, and media members attempt to hop onto the BTS bandwagon for clout, V's expressions and mannerisms don't lie. Whether sitting through interviews or posing for selfie requests, Kim Taehyung can sniff out the trend-chasers and the fakes.

cherry⁷
@chucklesbts
Follow

i don't trust anyone who doesn't pass taehyung's vibe check

1:24 AM - 21 Sep 2020

28,697 Retweets 101,148 Likes

**TOP DEFINITION**

## golden maknae

a beautiful hot <u>Korean</u> man <u>named</u> <u>Jungkook</u>.

*The golden maknae was <u>so hot</u> in <u>Spring day</u>.*

via giphy

**by namjooniscute February 20, 2018**

👍 57   👎 0

## Golden Maknae

BTS's youngest member is not only its most well-rounded in terms of vocals, dance, and rap ability; if Jungkook was a high school archetype he'd be the homecoming king. (Just a sampling of his documented skills to date: archery, track and field, wrestling, taekwondo, filmmaking, painting, sketching, bowling, e-sports, and innumerable random variety show games.) JK recently addressed his nickname in the 2020 documentary *Break the Silence,* confessing that he feels pressure to live up to his reputation. Sounds about relatable.

# She, Rose

## An Interview with Kelly Marie Tran

### BY JEFF YANG

KELLY MARIE TRAN

**IN 2015, LIFE** changed forever for **KELLY MARIE TRAN**, a young actress and comedian who was plucked from obscurity to become a lead in one of the biggest multimedia franchises in the world—*Star Wars.* As Rose Tico, a determined and feisty member of the Rebel resistance, she embodied the hopes, dreams, and fantasies of millions of Asian Americans who'd never seen ourselves reflected at the franchise's supergalactic scale. But like the Force, becoming Rose had its dark side: legions of toxic fans keyed in on Tran as an unwelcome outsider in a set of stories that had up to then centered on white heroes, harassing her on social media, committing gross acts of racist and misogynist digital vandalism on public platforms showcasing her new character, and ultimately causing her to retreat from the public landscape entirely after the widespread release of *The Last Jedi.* But Tran would not be silenced forever. She returned in 2018 with an op-ed essay in the *New York Times,* in which she talked about her experience of going "down a spiral of self-hate, into the darkest recesses of my mind, places where I tore myself apart." She concluded the essay with a defiant statement, proudly owning her identity as a woman and as a Vietnamese American: "My real name is Loan. And I am just getting started." She joined us to talk about her rise to Rose, and the next step in her voyage—voicing the first Southeast Asian American Disney Princess, Raya, in the animated feature film *Raya and the Last Dragon.*

*At first, the very idea of getting cast as Rose Tico seemed impossible—so Tran decided to embrace that it would never happen, and make choices for herself, not for a role that might never come*

When the opportunity to audition for *Star Wars* came along, I was still working a full-time day job. I was going out for things all the time and I was getting really close, but I was not able to support myself financially on the little bits that I was doing acting-wise. I was doing sketches for *College Humor.* I was doing tiny parts on sitcoms. And then I got an email about

reading for "Untitled Rian Johnson Project," which after a little Googling, you could pretty much immediately figure out what that was. Just getting that audition was a huge success for me. "Wow! They want to see me!"

So I went through what turned out to be a six-month audition process because they were seeing people in London and New York and L.A.—everywhere. And the whole time I thought I was not going to get it. That saved me, because I didn't have the desire to manipulate the experience. I was just, how cool is it that I get to be here?

I remember getting the call about the

London test from my agent—I was actually in Chicago at the time, because there was an air flight deal, a hundred dollars, L.A. to Chicago. I'd gotten this diversity scholarship to study with Second City, so I went to Chicago to meet the woman who had chosen me for this scholarship. I remember thinking that I wanted to remind myself there was stuff for me outside of *Star Wars*. And I got this call from my agents while I was on the train there: "Do you have your passport with you?" And I said "No." "Well, you have to come back now, because you need to go to London."

I don't know how I got the courage to do it but I said to myself, "I need to give myself the privilege to just be here, to be in Chicago for this moment." I'd set this meeting for myself, and I was not going to change it. I mean, the *audacity*. But this is the only way I know how to explain it: There was something telling me that I needed to listen to that voice inside. And it worked out. I had my meeting at Second City. And I think it gave me some confidence to have spoken up for myself in that way. But then, yeah, I flew back to L.A., grabbed my stuff, jumped on a plane to London, put on this costume, and did this camera test for this incredible thing that I knew I absolutely was never going to be a part of, but I still was going to be able to tell my kids about someday.

I think that gave me the ability to not come from a place of fear. To not come from a place of "What do these people want?" I just trusted that if I was really present, something good would happen. Or not! I was well aware that so many people didn't even get the chance to audition.

And after that, it's weird. I just went back to my day job, answering phones and picking up dry cleaning and getting coffee. I found out I got the gig when I was on my lunch break at this office job. I went to the casting office and Rian was there and producer Ram Bergman was there and they offered me the part. And then, God, my first reaction was "Wait, you actually want to give me this opportunity?" I'd been so busy treading water that I'd never thought about how I would actually do the job.

But then, boom, I got out of my apartment and moved to London without anyone knowing. For "the secret project." I think the press release that announced that I was actually involved at all came out the day that we started shooting. So I had already been in London for three or four months training and, yeah, that was my first day on set. Crazy. And I guess I don't really have a formula to explain how I handled that transition. I just credit my family and my friends for all of the incredible support they've given me.

*Getting the role meant fighting fear, overcoming doubt, and staying grounded—all of which took honest self-assessment and a village of friends and family*

If you want to know what fear sounds like, it sounds like this: "Kelly, you're crazy. You should go to grad school. This is never gonna work out." It took me some time to decipher how to run my life from a point of love, from a point of confidence, and from a point of honoring myself, and I feel like I'm finally at the point where I know what I want and I'm fighting for myself. But it wasn't an easy or a quick journey at all.

I think that an actor's part-time job is just staying sane. It's not really something growing up that I was aware of at all, how strange it is to work in this world and the ways in which it can change. My entire realm of normalcy changed. I remember my first test for *Star Wars* was the first time I'd ever been in business class on a plane, and I was confused by so much about it. I didn't know that "sleep suits" were a thing. And then they put me in this hotel, I remember looking at this lemon that came with the food and it had a see-through white thing around it. I said, "What is this?" And I spent 10 minutes taking it off. And then afterwards they explained, "Kelly, that's so the seeds don't fall into food." I grew up with parents who are both refugees from the Vietnam War. My dad worked at Burger King for the last 40 years. My mom worked managing funerals. I was not exposed to any of this.

So to stay grounded was all about staying close to the people that I came up with, this ragtag group of people who were just trying to make it in this crazy world. And a lot of them are thriving now too! That's the best part of it for me. My success is one thing, but to be able to see friends who came from the same place I did really coming into their own power—that's the shit I live for!

*But as challenging (and sometimes heartbreaking) as it was to become Rose, it opened doors, both for the Asian American community, who'd never seen ourselves represented in that fashion before, and for Tran herself—who went on to be cast as Disney's first-ever Southeast Asian American "Princess," in* Raya and the Last Dragon

I think that I had a very similar experience about Raya as I did about Rose. When I found out I was going to get the opportunity to play this part, my first reaction was "I fought for this, can I actually *do* this?"

*Star Wars*, Disney Princesses, these are so much bigger than you and me. So I take that position with a lot of responsibility, wanting to make sure I never emphasized some sort of stereotype, or reinforced some sort of negative idea.

And the truth of the matter is that when you are a person of color in spaces that have not historically been made for people of color, your existence is automatically political whether you like it or not. That's just the way it is.

Playing Raya was not only a dream come true, because I was a huge Disney kid growing up, it also comes with that sense of responsibility. I was so proud of the ways that I advocated for certain things. What are the ways that I could uplift voices that have not been uplifted before? What are the ways in which I could honor this culture?

This was a big, blockbuster movie honoring Southeast Asia. When's the last time we got something like that? It's rare that I've been a part of something that felt intrinsically part of my being. The history embedded within Raya is very much part of the cultures that I grew up in. I could step into her shoes and know exactly what it felt like to have lost someone because of conflict, or to have had to leave home because of war.

And it's important that we had Qui Nguyen and Adele Lim as writers and that our head of story was also from Southeast Asia. They also had this in their blood and their bones. With Raya, for the first time I used all the parts of me. That, as an actor, is the best thing that you can hope for.

That said, being a Disney Princess is a huge

WTF for me. Knowing how much those movies cost and how much they sculpted my childhood, to be part of that legacy now, how do I process that?

When the movie promo started, I had a day off, and I spent it driving all over L.A. and just finding every billboard for it and taking pictures with them. And I'm going to quote Daniel Dae Kim here, he said this to me the other day: "We know how important this is and how rare it is. The goal is for our kids to not even blink when a movie like this happens. Because it'll be so normal for them." I think about that a lot.

## POSTCARD FROM ASIAN AMERICA

BY BRIAN, ALLISON, AND ELI CHI

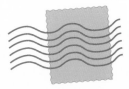

Dear RISE,

Hi from Minnesota and New York! The three of us are second-generation Chinese American kids. Our parents were both born in Cuba and immigrated to America before meeting in New York City.

We grew up in the white suburbs of Massachusetts and Connecticut, but took many trips to Boston and New York Chinatowns to eat with our grandparents, aunts, uncles, and cousins, and stock up on groceries and food to bring back home. If we weren't eating Chinese food, we were eating Cuban food—*lechon asado*, *fricase de pollo*, *platanos*, *flan*, and more. We grew up always being asked, "Have you eaten yet? Are you hungry? Do you want some more?"—all questions that were signs of love.

When we were teenagers, we moved halfway across the country to Minnesota. Suddenly we couldn't find Chinese or Cuban food that could compare to the food we ate on the East Coast. Slowly, however, we discovered some local gems like Hmong Village, United Noodle, and El Burrito Mercado where we could find familiar ingredients like bok choy, fermented bean paste, and sazón.

We always felt that our strongest connection to Chinese and Cuban culture was through food. It's become our main way of learning about our family heritage as we've gotten older and become prouder of our cultures. And food comforted us through the pandemic—after being apart for over a year, we can't wait to gather around the table together for a delicious feast.

Xo

Brian, Allison, and Eli

RISE
HERE AND NOW,
ASIAN AMERICA

ANDREW YANG

# The Math of Andrew Yang

## BY PHILIP WANG,
## ILLUSTRATED BY JAMES YANG

**ON NOVEMBER 6, 2017,** Andrew Yang—a Taiwanese American entrepreneur who'd run a test preparation service and sold it to Stanley Kaplan, then founded a nonprofit called Venture for America—launched his unlikely candidacy for president of the United States. He'd never held public office, nor even run for anything—yet, building on innovative and maybe wild-sounding ideas, he got attention, and then began gaining momentum. The most popular of the "wild-sounding ideas" he evangelized: Universal Basic Income, the notion of giving people "free money" to provide them with economic security and job mobility. Yang built his campaign by leveraging the Internet, amassing an army of extremely online supporters who called themselves the "Yang Gang." They created tens of thousands of memes celebrating him and bashing his critics (and the media, for failing to give him coverage in proportion to his polls or fundraising— and for mislabeling him with the wrong names or wrong photos) and filled social media with pictures of blue caps, the color his campaigns chose for their headgear, as a contrast to the red hats of Trump supporters. Emblazoned on that headgear: Yang's campaign slogan MATH, which was both an acronym for "Make America Think Harder" and a stereotype-tugging joke— Yang would frequently, to laughs from some circles and groans from others, refer to himself as an "Asian guy who likes MATH."

By February 11, 2020, after the Iowa and New Hampshire primaries, Yang decided to drop out of the race and endorse former VP Joe Biden. But along the way, he managed to shock the world with the most successful presidential campaign by an Asian American candidate ever, given that the other Asian American in the race, Senator Kamala Harris, had dropped out of the primaries three months before, on December 3, 2019. Senator Harris would eventually become Biden's running mate and is now vice president; Yang ran for mayor of New York, and began as an unlikely frontrunner (though he ultimately conceded, after a campaign beset by media controversies).

Still, it's clear that the 2020 primaries marked the beginning of a new era for Asian Americans in politics. In keeping with his love of math, here's a look back at Yang's historic race—by the numbers.

# $1000
THE AMOUNT YANG WANTED TO GIVE TO EVERY AMERICAN AS A MONTHLY "FREEDOM DIVIDEND"

# 42%
THE PERCENTAGE OF YANG'S SUPPORTERS WHO SAID THEY WOULD NOT SUPPORT ANY OTHER CANDIDATE AFTER HE DROPPED OUT ON FEBRUARY 11, 2020

Though Yang endorsed Joe Biden, who eventually became the Democratic nominee, and then president, four in 10 of his supporters said they would support only Yang—the highest "unique loyalty rate" among the candidates in the primary.

# 44
ANDREW YANG'S AGE WHEN THE 2020 PRIMARIES BEGAN

making him the fifth-youngest candidate in the race, after Representatives Seth Moultin (40), Tulsi Gabbard and Eric Swalwell (both 39), and Mayor Pete Buttigieg (37). If elected, he would have entered office at age 45, making him the second-youngest president in history, after President John F. Kennedy (43).

# 44:36
THE TOTAL AMOUNT OF TIME YANG SPOKE, ACROSS THE EIGHT DEMOCRATIC DEBATES THAT TOOK PLACE BEFORE HE DROPPED OUT

His highest talk time, 10:44, came in the sixth debate; he did not qualify for the seventh debate, and dropped out after the eighth one.

# 17,226
THE NUMBER OF VOTES YANG EARNED IN THE TWO STATE CONTESTS IN WHICH HE COMPETED BEFORE WITHDRAWING

8,914 votes in Iowa's caucus, about 5.1% of the total first alignment vote, and 8,312 votes in New Hampshire's primary, about 2.8% of the total vote.

# $41.6 MILLION
THE AMOUNT YANG RAISED DURING HIS CAMPAIGN

# $2.8 TRILLION
THE AMOUNT THE "FREEDOM DIVIDEND" WOULD HAVE COST

which Yang would have raised through a 10% value-added tax on business transactions, a 0.1% tax on financial transactions, taxing capital gains and carried interest at normal income rates, a $40 per ton carbon tax, and a removal of the wage cap on the Social Security payroll tax.

# 400,000
THE NUMBER OF PEOPLE WHO CONTRIBUTED TO YANG'S CAMPAIGN

half of it in amounts of $200 or less.

# 70%
THE PERCENTAGE OF YANG'S SUPPORTERS WHO WERE 44 OR YOUNGER

the highest percentage of any candidate—compared to 42% of Democratic voters as a whole.

# 8%
YANG'S HIGHEST POLL NUMBER

in a poll conducted by Emerson Polling on January 23, 2020. The poll put him in fourth place, behind former VP Joe Biden (30%) and Senators Bernie Sanders (27%) and Elizabeth Warren (13%)—leading to the trending hashtag #YANGSURGE.

# 19%
HOW YANG POLLED AT PEAK AMONG ASIAN AMERICANS

in a poll conducted by Morning Consult on December 19, 2020. The poll put him in third place among Asian Americans, behind former VP Joe Biden (24%) and Senator Bernie Sanders (20%).

# A Sign of Things to Come

BY MAYA L. HARRIS, ILLUSTRATED BY SUHUN SHIN

## "You may be the first to do many things in life, but make sure you're *not* the last."

**MOMMY HAD A LOT OF SAYINGS.** This particular one was repeated whenever my sister Kamala or I achieved some significant milestone, often having been the first woman or person of color—or both—to have accomplished whatever it was we'd done. It was one of many ways Mommy conveyed not only her high expectations for us, but what she expected *from* us.

It was also a description of her own story: a mission-driven journey powered by strong egalitarian beliefs and a deep faith in her ability to improve the world around her. Mommy had a curiosity that stretched well beyond the continent of her upbringing. Raised with a confidence that gave her the courage to chart her own course, she left her parents' home (then in Calcutta) as a teenager to pursue graduate studies in America in 1958. She became a scientist, and as she poured herself into her primary life goals—raising her two daughters and curing breast cancer—this petite, brown woman with an accent was undeterred by the fact that hers was an academy dominated by white men. By the sheer force of her intelligence, determination, and wit, Mommy elicited respect and admiration in the classroom, in her laboratory, and among her peers. And it was her example of hard work, unflinching determination, and commitment to excellence that shaped how Kamala and I grew up.

Both of our parents came to the United States to pursue their studies: our father from Jamaica and our mother from India. They met at UC Berkeley during the height of the Civil Rights Movement, and quickly became entrenched in the activism of the moment. Their marches, debates, sit-ins, and student meetings would all be frequent topics of family dinner conversations. Our earliest lessons in life were about equality, fairness, justice, and human dignity, learned not by rote or in the pages of a history book, but by our parents' example—and in living color.

Perhaps it's not surprising, then, that Kamala and I grew up aspiring to lead lives dedicated to pursuing justice in the public interest. We both saw law school as the bridge that could take us there, but in charting our paths, we pursued different (if complementary) routes.

Being the eldest, Kamala went to law school first, and upon graduating she sought out a position as an assistant district attorney—a decision not obvious to our family and friends and one, she'd later recount, she had to defend like an academic thesis. Of course, Kamala understood from our own life experience that equal justice under law was an aspiration that fell short of the reality, especially in communities of color. But what she also knew was that the same system too often deployed to repress

could also protect, and that prosecutors could be a force for institutional change.

The year Kamala graduated from UC Hastings College of the Law, I began my first year at Stanford Law School. But I chose to scale the mountain of justice from a different side. I went to law school not just wanting to be a lawyer; I wanted to be a *civil rights* lawyer. As a direct beneficiary of *Brown* and busing, voting rights and affirmative action, I'd experienced firsthand how law could shape the social justice landscape with lawyers as agents of social change. So that's what I wanted to do.

In 2003, after having spent a decade practicing and teaching law (as well as serving as reportedly the country's youngest law school dean at age 29, a story for another day!), I joined the nation's largest affiliate of the American Civil Liberties Union as Racial Justice Project director. Immediately, I plunged into a hotly contested election battle, helping to lead the statewide fight against a controversial California ballot initiative, Proposition 54, which sought to ban state and local governments from collecting any data on race and ethnicity, with devastating consequences for communities of color.

That same year, Kamala launched her first campaign for San Francisco district attorney—a political battle that was no less intense. It wasn't just that she was running against a well-known incumbent; no one who looked like us had ever been elected DA, despite the city's progressive reputation. Getting there would be hard and hard-fought.

Throughout that election year, Kamala and I were in constant communication, strategizing and sharing the high and low moments characteristic of every campaign. As a public servant, she had valuable insights into Prop 54's negative consequences for government. I'd share my advice and volunteer on her campaign when I wasn't on the trail myself.

Even out campaigning independently, we were never far apart: repeatedly, as I traveled Northern California attending "No on Prop 54" campaign events, I'd finish speaking at some rally when someone would come up to me afterwards and say a version of: "You remind me of that sharp sister who's running for district attorney in San Francisco. Do you know her?"

I'd proudly reply: "Well, yes, I do know that 'sharp sister.' She's *my* sharp sister. And in case you had any doubt, she's the older one."

On a special election ballot, my campaign ended first: we defeated Prop 54, the first victory for progressives in recent memory against a draconian ballot initiative, and I could now dedicate more time to Kamala's campaign. Beating all odds, Kamala made it into a runoff election against the incumbent and, four weeks later, prevailed at the ballot box—becoming the first non–white male district attorney of San Francisco since the office's founding in 1856.

As anyone who has worked in politics knows, the crucible of a campaign forges unique bonds among those who share the experience. Compounding that for Kamala and me was our sisterhood, both as actual sisters and as young women of color lawyers who felt an obligation to change our world for the better—from different, equally essential, vantage points. That sense of duty, opportunity, and shared responsibility only grew as we took on larger platforms.

By the time Kamala was running for U.S. Senate—after having been twice elected state attorney general—I was serving as senior policy advisor on Hillary Clinton's presidential campaign. Hillary had hired me to help lead development of her domestic policy agenda; in addition to our mutual love of policy, we bonded over being the only expectant grandmas in the campaign's leadership. Not often enough in American politics have we seen someone of Hillary's intelligence, commitment, and fortitude break down so many barriers. Hillary manifested Mommy's "first but not the last," and one of my sorrows is that Mommy passed before I could introduce them.

I'll always remember Election Night 2016 as a cauldron of conflicting emotions, the very definition of bittersweet. After nearly two years of pouring my heart and soul into Hillary's race, I was devastated watching the returns roll in with other campaign staff members at the Javits Center in New York. And yet, at the same time, my shock and sadness mixed with pride and hope watching Kamala's election to the U.S. Senate by a landslide.

Still, in that moment, I could not have foreseen what the future held in store. Two years later, on the path paved by Shirley Chisholm, Hillary Clinton, and so many others, my one and only sister would launch her campaign for the presidency and ask me to join her as campaign chair. It was the culmination of lives led in parallel, in different circles but with the same purpose of advancing equity. And it was the natural result of growing up to be what we've *always* been: our mother's daughters.

In due time, yet another of Mommy's sayings ("everything happens for a reason") would prove prescient. While there was no denying the disappointment that we did not succeed in the historically large primary election field, there's no doubt that experience prepared Kamala to take up the mantle as Joe Biden's running mate in the general election.

On Election Night 2020, a flood of emotions again swept over me. Familial pride, to be sure. My "Akka" (the Tamil word for "older sister" I was taught as a child) had soared to this greatest of heights. Along the way, she had become a symbol of hope for so many, a personification of what they could achieve, and what all of us, working together, could aspire to.

And compounding my personal joy was an immense sense of pride in the collective sisterhood. Having grounded my career in the fight for racial and gender equity, Kamala's ascent marked the manifestation of a democratic evolution I'd advocated for years: that women of color, particularly Black women, were the beating heart of our democracy. That our voices—as voters and as political candidates—were becoming increasingly potent, influencing political outcomes. That our leadership would lift and advance all Americans. That November night, I couldn't help but take a step back and say, "We did that, y'all!"

I dearly wish Mommy could have been with us that evening to witness Kamala step into history. This first-generation daughter of immigrants, as the first woman, the first Black woman, the first woman of South Asian descent to be elected vice president of the United States. To see Kamala beaming, dressed in suffragist white, declaring to the world that charge we knew so well: "While I may be the first woman in this office, I will not be the last."

Yet as much as I have missed Mommy's physical presence at these milestones she made possible, I know she would've been quick to remind both Kamala and me that this was the beginning—not the end—of the journey.

"I'm proud of you girls," she'd say, with a smile bursting from deep within. Then, not a split second later, she'd playfully chide us: "Okay, enough—now, *get back to work!*"

SANDRA OH

# It's an Honor Just to Be Sandra

*AN INTERVIEW WITH SANDRA OH*

**HOLLYWOOD HAS NEVER** truly known what it has in Sandra Oh, who has quietly built a career as one of the most talented, adaptable, and appealing actors in the business, without ever receiving the industry recognition she truly deserves; without ever being talked about as an "A-list" performer; without ever getting offers to play above-the-title roles. That is, until 2018, when BBC America offered her the role of Eve Polastri in their adaptation of crime novelist Luke Jennings's "Villanelle" novels—a white character in the original novels. Oh's performance was universally acclaimed, garnering her a Lead Actress Emmy nomination. But for many of us, the line she uttered in the show's opening musical number was the most memorable part of the night: when told by the hosts that it was the first nod in the category ever given to an Asian actress, she responded, "It's an honor just to be Asian." Oh shared with us the long road she walked to get to that point, and why the line sums up how she feels today, and how she hopes future generations will feel as well.

## Oh, Canada

I grew up outside Ottawa, Canada. I began dancing when I was four. My parents made me do it because I was pigeon-toed and they heard it was a way to fix that, but I loved it—I loved the sensation of being onstage and moving my body and expressing myself, and just being as big and as truthful as possible. Then, at age 10, I did my first play in school, *The Canada Goose*, and that opened everything for me. There was nothing like the feeling of connecting with and reaching an audience for me. I was hooked. At age 15, I started working in front of the camera. At the time, I was in a student improv group called Skit Row High, like "Skid Row"; it was a bad pun but a very good improv troupe. Alanis Morissette, who's from Ottawa, was a part of our troupe for a hot second—I actually sang backup for her in one sketch!

One of the girls in the troupe had an agent, and her agent asked if she knew any young Asian actresses. Well, she did—me—so I got signed, and I started doing things like PSAs and industrial videos. My first on-camera job was an anti–drinking-and-driving short film. I learned a lot from that, no kidding.

I always had a basic understanding that I was an Asian person in a white society. I grew up in Canada, with a lot of safety and privilege in a close-knit Korean Canadian community. But it was a small community and church, in a very white community. So yes, there was always the sting of knowing I couldn't go out for the lead parts.

But I was extremely driven, and I wanted to do everything. I was in this high school show called *Denim Blues*, which was sort of inspired by *Degrassi High*. And then I was on another show where I was, like, the best friend of the best friend—basically two girls away from the blond girl. These were small roles, and I was clearly not a priority, the makeup artists never understood how to do my face, but I didn't give a shit why I got a job or how small my role was. I just wanted to be in front of that camera, so I took it all.

And then after I left school, I got the lead in a film called *The Diary of Evelyn Lau* for the Canadian Broadcasting Channel, based on Evelyn's book about her life on the streets. And then I met Mina Shum and was able to star in her film *Double Happiness*. I was 21, and these experiences made me realize how much I had to give, and how eager I was to give the world all my work, all my soul, and all my talent. So I moved to Hollywood.

## Go Back Where You Came From

I think it's good to land in Hollywood when you're young and driven—you have a little bit more energy to push through things. But there was this very specific moment I experienced when the systemic racism that we experience as Asian artists just hit me. It was when I was first taking meetings with agents. And one in particular, she was a big agent, and very intimidating, and she made me wait a long time. When she finally saw me, she said: "Listen. I'm going to tell you the truth, because no one else will. Go home. Go back home and get famous. Because I can tell you, I have an Asian actress in my roster and she hasn't gone out for anything in six months. There's really no place for you here."

And at this point, I'd starred in A-level theater. I'd been nominated for the equivalent of the Best Actress Emmy in Canada—and I'd won the equivalent of Canada's Best Actress Oscar. So I thought to myself, where else could I go to get famous, if not here? I remember going back to the place where I was staying and calling my mentor and just shaking and crying. I could have quit then and gone home.

But I was *extremely* driven.

## Know When to Walk Away

I stuck it out. I got some guest-starring roles and did short films. And then the following year, I landed a regular role in HBO's *Arli$$,* and I did that for six years. And even then, after that show ended, it didn't open any real doors for me. I did a couple of indie films, including *Sideways,* which got great reviews, but that didn't open any doors either. I was still just getting offers for supporting parts. So I finally set myself a growth goal: I wanted to get to the point where I felt I had the ability to walk away.

Then I got a call for *Grey's Anatomy.* They brought me in for the role Chandra Wilson eventually got: the hospital chief of staff, Dr. Bailey. But as I read the script, I realized that the show was really the interns. It was a show about students and teachers, and the students were the meat of it. So I asked my agent what other roles were open, and it turned out they hadn't cast Cristina at that point. I looked at the part, and said to myself, "This is a better fucking role." She's the antagonist in the pilot. Cristina and Meredith Grey meet, and they're instant rivals.

So they brought me in to test for Dr. Bailey, but I was adamant I wanted to get the shot to play Cristina instead. And because I'd gotten there early, I ran Cristina's lines with them, just so Shonda Rhimes and the other executive producers could see what I could do as

Cristina. After that, as I was waiting to do my test, my manager called and said, "Walk out." You have to sign your contract before you test, and they weren't willing to sign the deal my team thought I deserved. Well, that was my growth goal: to be able to say no. So I said, "I have to leave. Bye!" And I walked out of the audition. And they gave me the role! They cast me, and I never even tested.

I played Cristina—they gave her the last name "Yang" after they cast me—for 10 seasons. And I'm so thankful for the opportunity. But I got the role because I was willing to walk away, and I always said to myself that I would hold on to that willingness to say no, to leave a situation if it was no longer feeding me or challenging me. And after a decade doing a role, you get to that point. So I did let Cristina go, and it was a painful but necessary decision.

## Finding Eve

I was nominated for an Emmy every year for five years for playing Cristina Yang. I won a Golden Globe and a Screen Actors Guild award for Best Supporting Actress. Even then, when I left in 2014, no job offers. So I just did what I did early in my career: concentrated on growing as an actor. I did a lot of theater. I did another film with Mina Shum. I worked with John Ridley. And it dawned on me that for all of my success, I was just never going to have the same career trajectory as Charlize Theron or any of the Emmas or any of the Jennifers.

Here's a sign of how beaten down I felt. When my agent called me to say they were offering me *Killing Eve,* I didn't know what part I was being offered. I looked through the script and I couldn't see myself in any of the characters. And that's when my agent told me that they wanted me for the lead. For Eve. The character in the title.

And that's the moment that I realized how deep the internalized racism had been for me by that point in my career. I couldn't even see the part I was supposed to be playing. I'd gone from a place of tremendous possibility and confidence when I was very young to not even being able to see myself on the page.

> That's the moment that I realized how deep the internalized racism had been for me by that point in my career. I couldn't even see the part I was supposed to be playing. I'd gone from a place of tremendous possibility and confidence when I was very young to not even being able to see myself on the page.

## Wearing Your Pride

So things have obviously been different in the past few years. But a lot of it is timing: the timing of *Killing Eve,* the timing of *Crazy Rich Asians,* the timing of society, ultimately, being ready for me to be where I wanted to be. To let me represent who I really am.

That was summed up by the line they gave to me in the opener of the 2018 Emmys. I was up for a Lead Actress Emmy for *Killing Eve,* and I had tough competition, and they asked me to say this line about being nominated: "It's an honor just to be Asian." And I jumped on it. I knew I could do the line, make it funny and make it true, because it *was* true. I wasn't worried that it would be taken the wrong way. But you just don't know when something's going to go viral. Everyone was talking about it the next day, and even then I thought it would bubble up and fade away. Until the shirt. Jeff Yang made

the shirt, and the shirt became a thing. I wore it on Instagram with my family before the Golden Globes. I wore it when I hosted *Saturday Night Live*! I'm so glad it happened, because I see people wearing it all over as just a celebration of pride in being ourselves.

That's something I've tried to bring to my choices as an actor. In the third season of *Killing Eve,* I got them to set it in New Malden, which is a Koreatown in the UK—and I could do that because I was also an executive producer. By that point in the story, Eve needs to retreat and to find a sense of home. Seeing her make mandu spiritually grounds the character. Hearing Korean spoken gives flavor to her background. And for the first time, I'm finally getting film roles where my character's name is Korean. That's significant for me—people are calling me by a Korean name on-screen. I'm doing *Umma,* a psychological horror film written and directed by Iris Shim, and it's very significant for me, in part because I do not speak Korean and I had to learn Korean for it. Just deeply confronting my ancestral language was very, very challenging. And then there's *Raya and the Last Dragon,* which is so amazing, because Awkwafina is so fucking busy, and there are two kids in it who are going to be fucking busy, and Kelly Marie Tran's dance card is full—that is what we need to see, our next generation out there working. If the industry is going to change, that's how it's going to change.

We have a new generation of storytellers coming up. We have a little bit more freedom to write and talk about what we want to write and talk about. We aren't as afraid it's all going to go away if we wake up. It's been thrilling for me just to have been able to be a part of that. You could say, it's an honor.

SIMU LIU

KUMAIL NANJIANI

# The First Action Hero

BY PHILIP WANG

**OVER THE PAST** decade, Marvel has been minting the biggest characters, biggest stories, biggest movies, and biggest stars in cinematic history. So the announcement that they were making not one, but *two* movies featuring Asian superheroes was a blockbuster for those of us who hadn't grown up seeing ourselves depicted as heroes at all by Hollywood, much less those of the "super" variety. **SIMU LIU** went from starring in the beloved Korean-Canadian sitcom *Kim's Convenience* to being cast as Shang-Chi, Master of Kung Fu, in Marvel's *Shang-Chi and the Legend of the Ten Rings.* **KUMAIL NANJIANI**, star of HBO's *Silicon Valley* and, with his wife, Emily V. Gordon, an Oscar-nominated screenwriter for their semi-autobiographical indie movie hit *The Big Sick,* was unveiled as Kingo in Marvel's *The Eternals.* We brought them together for a discussion on the great responsibility that comes with great power.

## Fighting for Representation

**KUMAIL:** I'm from Pakistan, and I only moved to America in 1997. So for most of my life, I watched a lot of Hollywood stuff, but I also watched a lot of Bollywood. That meant I got to see action movie stars who looked like me—and these guys were awesome. I feel very lucky that I grew up seeing myself reflected on-screen in these kinds of roles, which are still very rare for people who look like me in the United States. I don't know, if I'd grown up here in America, if I'd have had the confidence to even go for this

role. I really feel for kids who've grown up never seeing themselves as heroes.

**SIMU:** I was born in China, and grew up in Canada since I was five. The first time I saw Jackie Chan's poster in a movie multiplex, I felt so much pride that he'd finally broken into Hollywood. Since then, I've made sure to watch all of his American movies. Not all of them were great. I even watched *The Tuxedo*! So I'll always be a fan of his. Asians who grew up in the West went through different things and developed in different ways because of the things we were subjected to here. We have unique stories to tell. And this idea that Asian people have to do martial arts in order to have value, in order to deserve an American audience, is something we're struggling against as well.

**KUMAIL:** You're literally Master of Kung Fu!

**SIMU:** Ha! But the fact that there are aspects to my character that are quintessentially Asian American is very important to me. I'm not just about fighting.

**KUMAIL:** Superheroes are always fighting. If they're not fighting villains, they're fighting each other.

**SIMU:** Well, I'm glad Shang-Chi isn't fighting Kingo. Kingo would win. You're the descendant of literal gods, or something. And these days you're three times my size.

**KUMAIL:** I don't know, man, I've seen your recent pictures. And the way you can move is amazing. Anyway, we're not going to fight! We'll team up and crush everybody else.

## Humor as a Superpower

**KUMAIL:** I was on a sitcom that I loved for many years, *Silicon Valley*. I remember when I first started comedy, all I wanted to do was just someday be host at the Des Moines Funny Bone. That was my goal! And then as you progress in your journey, your goals change. Right before I started talking to Marvel, I remember thinking I really love action movies, but I do not have access to being cast in them because I don't look a certain way. So I made a conscious decision to change the way I look, because these roles have a very artificial, physical barrier to them, and I wanted to take that barrier out of the picture. That way if I failed, I was going to be failing on my own terms.

**SIMU:** I've always wanted to be an action hero! In 2015, I even wrote, shot, and acted in a short superhero film with money I cobbled together by myself. But the truth is that my experience with comedy in *Kim's Convenience* helped me immensely in taking on this superhero role. Because Marvel understands that the heroic archetype has shifted away from the overly macho standards of the Seventies and Eighties, like the Schwarzeneggers and Stallones. Comedic timing, charisma, a little self-deprecation, that's what people want and appreciate now.

## The Human in Superhuman

**KUMAIL:** For the longest time, if you were a brown guy in Hollywood, you were only gonna audition for two kinds of parts: you're going to be a cabdriver or you're going to be a terrorist. And in both sets of parts, you're going to have that thick Hollywood Brown Guy accent. I remember how stunned I was when I first started auditioning in America that people would ask me to "make it a little bit more funny." Now I knew exactly what that meant. They wanted the accent. And I decided early on that I wasn't going to play up my accent for comedy. So that led to some awkward moments in the audition room: "When you say 'funny,' what do you mean?" "Well . . . you know." "No, I don't." When I saw guys like Kal Penn playing roles that weren't doing that, it was groundbreaking.

**SIMU:** This is going to sound cliché, but with great power comes great responsibility. We're taking on these massive roles, and that means we have this extra layer of thought we have to put into this. We can't just focus on creating great characters, we have to think about the stereotypes that will be associated with us, like it or not. For Shang-Chi, there were many ways that it could have gone wrong. So we weren't going to have Shang-Chi speak in weird Asian parables. We were never going to have him say "honor." Thankfully we had Asian Americans on board as director and writer—Destin Daniel Cretton and David Callaham—to find the humanity in this story, you know?

**KUMAIL:** Oh, I know! I was so nervous I was actually shitting myself about this role. But the first time I met Chloe Zhao, our director, I was like, "Oh, she's going to take care of me. She's going to make sure I don't suck in this thing." Because she's such a badass, she's such a force of nature, such a smart person, such a truly, truly wonderful filmmaker, I knew she would make sure I wasn't going to embarrass anyone in this.

**SIMU:** Same. I nearly crapped my pants when I got the screen test offer for Shang-Chi, because I'm not the tallest, not the best-looking, not the best at martial arts or anything else, and here I had to be the representative hero of an entire population of billions of people.

**KUMAIL:** It's a very easy trap to fall into. If you're part of a group that hasn't been represented for so long, you only want to play pure, perfect beings. But that's just as reductive in some ways as playing negative stereotypes.

**SIMU:** I auditioned as a human being. But now I'm supposed to be the perfect specimen of all East Asian men? That wasn't going to happen. I didn't want that to happen. This is the first Asian Marvel superhero, and I just wanted him to be this guy that you might see walking out of a boba shop onto the streets in L.A.

> There are over a billion South Asians in India alone. Just do the math. There are more talented people than me, funnier people, people that act better. I had to get over this constant feeling that it should not be me doing this.

**KUMAIL:** I'm sure my own community would like me to portray this role as this idealized picture of goodness, knowledge, and wisdom. But I don't think that's my job. My job is to portray this one specific person, flaws and all. And we're only put in this position because there aren't enough of us getting these chances. Because the more people that do, the more we have the freedom to play complex characters without feeling like we're letting everyone down each time.

To be the first South Asian superhero in a big Hollywood movie is a lot to carry. But all I can do is represent myself the best I can while being aware of that responsibility. I mean, there are over a billion South Asians in India alone. Just do the math. There are more-talented people than me, funnier people, people that act better. I had to get over this constant feeling that it should not be me doing this. And at the end of the day, it is me. But hey, at least now I'm jacked.

## Aiming for Higher Ground

**KUMAIL:** I wanted to approach my character as an inversion of the stereotypes I saw while auditioning as an actor. We're always depicted as nerds, so I wanted him to be cool. We're depicted as weak, so I wanted him to be seen as strong. And we're depicted as angry terrorists, so I wanted him to be full of joy. Basically, just the exact opposite of all the ways I'd seen myself represented in American pop culture.

**SIMU:** And it's not just about the roles, but their context and status within the story. How many times have I played the "Asian Guy Getting Yelled At," or the "Asian Guy Getting Scared about Stuff"? I'm supposed to be playing a CIA agent, but when they cut to me, my mouth is open, I'm confused and worried, and have no idea what to do and nothing to contribute. How fucking low status is that? We have to push for higher status in our own stories.

**KUMAIL:** We have to not be afraid to take up space in predominantly white spaces without apologizing for it.

**SIMU:** And in your case, that means literally taking up physical space.

**KUMAIL:** Look, my character's secret identity is a Bollywood movie star. Those guys are fucking huge—Google them, they're specimens. For this character, I had to credibly look like those guys.

Besides, Asian men are desexualized, while Asian women are hypersexualized. That's where some of that responsibility kicked in. If I was gonna be the first brown superhero, I wanted to make sure he looked like he'd fit in next to Thor or Captain America—the physical types white guys get to be all the time. And that got some people upset for some reason, because it was challenging things in their head about what brown guys can do.

## A Time for Heroes

**SIMU:** Given the current climate of anti-Asian violence we're living in, the timing of our films is insane. At the same time, we've always been facing degrees of this kind of hatred. So it's incredibly important for the world to see us as heroes—and more important, as humans.

**KUMAIL:** I started doing stand-up comedy in America right after 9/11, so I'm very aware of how South Asian and Arab Muslims were the default bad guys in Hollywood for a very, very long time. When that's all people see, it trickles down into how we act in the real world—we don't want to play into that.

> It's a double-edged sword, being the first to challenge these default images, but also shouldering all the expectations that come along with that.

**SIMU:** It's a double-edged sword, being the first to challenge these default images, but also shouldering all the expectations that come along with that. You and I are going to be the people who have to plant that flag. You won't always remember the sixth or the seventh guy, but the first you know they'll remember.

**KUMAIL:** But let me just acknowledge that we're living our dreams, right? We get to be superheroes! And while we're the first, we're already starting to see more: I want to shout out the *Ms. Marvel* TV series they're making starring Iman Vellani. There are so many little girls who are going to watch her, and it's going to change the way they see themselves.

**SIMU:** I hope our films make Asians, especially young Asians, feel like they belong. I want them to feel okay taking up all the space they want, not just in our own circles, but in white ones as well. Don't be afraid to stand up tall. When you walk down that street, walk like you fucking own it.

# Afterword

STORY: JEFF YANG, PHIL YU, & PHILIP WANG   ART: KRISTAN LAI

# CONTRIBUTORS

**ANIDA YOEU ALI** continues to be an artist, educator, and global agitator whose search for that mythical place called Asian America led her to cocreate numerous non-hyphenated spaces and collectives for hybrid Asians to exist before confusing acronyms and social media became a thing.

**HIBAH ANSARI** is a journalist at *Sahan Journal*, where she covers immigrants in Minnesota. She specializes in telling the stories of marginalized communities in unique and collaborative ways.

**JEREMY ARAMBULO** is a Los Angeles–based cartoonist and musician, creator of the graphic novel *A Challenge*, and writes/performs songs with Fluorescent Beige and Born That Guy.

**REGIE CABICO** is the first Asian American and queer poet to win the Nuyorican Poets Cafe Grand Slam in 1993, later taking top honors in three National Poetry Slams.

**JEF CASTRO** is a former Asian Avenue "member of the week," an artist, psychic medium, and one half of SooJ and Jef, whose mission is to promote sustainability and spirituality while living tiny in the PNW.

**EMILY C. CHANG** is an actor, producer, and television writer who was one-fourth of the performance poetry group I Was Born with Two Tongues.

**ALLISON CHI** is a designer, art director, and pie enthusiast living in New York.

**LOUIE CHIN** is an illustrator living in New York.

**JON M. CHU** is the director of such blockbuster films as *G.I. Joe: Retaliation*, *Now You See Me 2*, the iconic *Crazy Rich Asians*, and the joyous movie musical *In the Heights*.

**LINDA CHUNG** is a visual development artist for animation and has worked on shows such as Hulu's *Solar Opposites* and DreamWorks' *Kipo*.

**D'LO** is a Tamil Sri Lankan American queer/trans solo theater artist/actor/writer/comic, but he is (and was also once known mostly as) a poet!

**MARLON UNAS ESGUERRA** is a public high school teacher, a writer, and a runner, transplanted from Chicago to Queens, New York.

**JENN FANG** is the founder and editor of Reappropriate, the longest-running Asian American race, identity, and feminism blog.

**JAMIE FORD** is the *New York Times* bestselling author of *Hotel on the Corner of Bitter and Sweet*, *Songs of Willow Frost*, and *Love and Other Consolation Prizes*.

**LINDA GE** is a screenwriter and journalist who was most recently a writer on The CW's *Kung Fu* and Peacock's *Vampire Academy*.

**ROBIN HA** is a South Korean–born cartoonist based in Washington, D.C. She's the author of the *New York Times* bestseller *Cook Korean!: A Comic Book with Recipes*, and her graphic novel memoir, *Almost American Girl*.

**DR. THAO HA** is a Vietnam-born, Texas-raised California sociology professor with expertise on Vietnamese in the South, and an advisor and associate producer of the award-winning documentary *Seadrift* (2019).

A lawyer, policy advocate, and writer, **MAYA HARRIS** has been an influential voice at the intersection of politics, public policy, and civil rights for over two decades.

**EUNY HONG** is the author of *The Birth of Korean Cool: How One Nation Is Conquering the World Through Pop Culture*; *The Power of Nunchi: The Korean Secret to Happiness and Success*; and *Kept: A Comedy of Sex and Manners*.

**BRIAN HU** is the artistic director of Pacific Arts Movement and associate professor of television, film, and new media at San Diego State University.

**FRANKIE HUANG** is a Beijinger American writer and illustrator who loves to paint cats and pull noodles from scratch.

**TODD INOUE** writes about music, soccer, and culture from his San Jose home.

**MIA IVES-RUBLEE** is a disabled Korean American transracial adoptee who works as a community organizer, advocate, and writer.

**ANNA JOHN** is an activist, journalist, and emerging screenwriter in Hollywood, California. Previously, she was a senior reporter covering race and class at NPR, and a cofounder of the seminal South Asian American blog, Sepia Mutiny.

**SHING YIN KHOR** is a Malaysian American Ignatz-winning cartoonist and immersive experience designer exploring personal memoir, new human rituals, and collaborative worldbuilding through graphic novels and installation art.

**DENNIS SANGMIN KIM** used to be called Denizen Kane and doesn't get around much anymore.

**TAYEN KIM** is an artist who calls herself a draw-er (which she is trying to make a word), working in visual narrative doing storyboarding, directing, writing, and facilitating creative communities.

**SOJUNG KIM-McCARTHY** is a Korean-born illustrator based in the U.K. She writes and illustrates stories about being different, finding new home, and belonging.

**KRISTAN LAI** is an illustrator and visual storyteller whose work focuses on reimagining environments, memories, and dreamscapes.

**CHI-YUN LAU** is a Boston-based illustrator and designer who enjoys making cool art.

**JESSICA HJ LEE** is a Korean-born illustrator/art director based in San Francisco. She loves visual storytelling and draws a lot of inspiration from her childhood growing up in different places.

**GILES LI** is a father of three who has worked in the nonprofit and philanthropic sector for more than 20 years.

**JEREMY LIN** spent nine years in the NBA, enthralling the world in 2011 when his outstanding play sparked what the media called "Linsanity." He went on to win a championship with the Toronto Raptors in 2019.

**STEPHANIE LIN** is an illustrator, designer, and 3D artist who loves visual storytelling and dabbling in hobbies.

**CHRISTINA MAJASKI** is a Korean adoptee writer, editor, and mom based in Minnesota.

**RICHIE "TRAKTIVIST" MENCHAVEZ** is a Filipino American DJ, music archivist, and the founder of TRAKTIVIST, whose mission is to bring more visibility and sustainability to artists that are Asian American.

**H'ABIGAIL MLO** is a Montagnard writer, organizer, and founder of Voices of the Highlands from Greensboro, North Carolina, and based in Philadelphia.

**MOLLY MURAKAMI** is a cartoonist and illustrator from Minneapolis, Minnesota. She likes making work about family, shared histories, identity, and of course, sports.

A founding member of the spoken word group Yellow Rage, **MICHELLE MYERS** is an award-winning poet/educator who draws from her experiences as a biracial Korean American woman to write poetry challenging misconceptions of Asianness.

**DIANA NGUYEN** is an L.A.-based writer, producer, mom, and cofounder of the culture blog Disgrasian (2007–2013). She would love to pet your dog.

**THUC DOAN NGUYEN** founded #StartWith8Hollywood. She's a contributor to *The Daily Beast*, *Esquire Magazine*, *VICE*, *Refinery29*, *Southern Living*, and others. Thuc's a translator for the Academy Award–nominated *Last Days in Vietnam*.

**JAMIE NOGUCHI** is a Washington, D.C.–area cartoonist/illustrator and cocreator/illustrator of the young adult graphic novel series *School for Extraterrestrial Girls*.

Best known for her graphic novel *Cheat*, **CHRISTINE NORRIE** is a comic artist who has been nominated twice for the coveted Eisner Award.

**MOLLY PAN** is a Los Angeles headshot and portrait photographer who obsesses over cats, plants, and Dungeons & Dragons.

**TESS PARAS** is an actress, writer, and director whose satirical comedy videos on YouTube went viral and is now most recognized for her roles on *Just Add Magic* and *Crazy Ex-Girlfriend*.

**ISHLE YI PARK** is the first woman poet laureate of Queens, New York, 2021; Na Hoku Hanohano Award–nominated island musician; and author of *The Temperature of This Water* and *Angel & Hannah: A Novel in Verse*.

**KITKAT PECSON** designs apps and websites, makes colorful illustrations and the occasional wedding invite. She lives in New York.

**BAO PHI** is a Viet Nam–born, Minneapolis-raised spoken word artist, published poet, children's book author, arts administrator, and father.

**ERIN QUILL** has a BFA from CMU and is most known for having been an original Broadway cast member of *Avenue Q* and for her blog, Fairy Princess Diaries.

**DINO-RAY RAMOS** is a Los Angeles–based Filipino American journalist who is the founder of Diaspora and has written for the *Oakland Tribune*, *San Francisco Chronicle*, and *Deadline Hollywood*.

**KRISHNA M. SADASIVAM** is a former electrical engineer turned professional illustrator/cartoonist with clients including the LORE Podcast, Microsoft, White Hat Security, *CARtoons Magazine*, and more.

**SUHUN SHIN** is a South Korean artist practicing both traditional and digital painting in her hometown—Nairobi, Kenya. She likes long walks on the beach and spends most of her time painting in the sun.

**BEAU SIA** expands metaphor, develops culture, and bridges understanding through his relationship with poetry.

**ARUNE SINGH** is director of brand, editorial for Skybound Entertainment. Previously he was VP of marketing for BOOM! Studios and had key exec roles at Syfy and Marvel Entertainment

**SUYIN SO** is the daughter of two ethnically Chinese Indonesian immigrants based in Brooklyn, where she lives with her husband and three children. She cofounded Central Queens Academy Charter School.

Filmmaker and writer (beyondasiaphilia.com) **VALERIE SOE**'s latest documentary, *Love Boat: Taiwan*, was released in 2019 and has played to sold-out festival audiences across North America and in Taiwan.

**FAWNIA SOO HOO** is a Brooklyn-based fashion, beauty, and entertainment writer, with bylines including *Hollywood Reporter*, *Elle*, *Nylon*, and *Fashionista*.

**CHELSEA ST. CLAIR** is a creative strategist and consultant living in Hollywood.

**REBECCA SUN** is senior editor of diversity and inclusion at *Hollywood Reporter*.

**JIA SUNG** is an artist and educator born in Minnesota, bred in Singapore, now based in Brooklyn. She was a 2018–2019 Smack Mellon Studio Artist and Van Lier Fellow, and is currently an adjunct professor at RISD.

**AGNES CHUNG TALDE** is an award-winning journalist and actress. She owns and operates the food and beverage group Food Crush Hospitality with her celebrity chef husband, Dale Talde.

**TAK TOYOSHIMA** is the creator/illustrator of Secret Asian Man comics, the first nationally syndicated comic strip featuring an Asian American main character.

**KELLY ZEN-YIE TSAI** is an award-winning interdisciplinary artist, performer, and musician based in Brooklyn, New York.

**ESTHER TSENG** is a Los Angeles–based freelance food and culture writer. Her work has appeared in the *Los Angeles Times*, *Bon Appétit*, *Food & Wine*, and more.

Illustrator and comics artist **GLENN URIETA** is best known for Papercut Kids and his work in the superhero anthologies *Secret Identities* and *Shattered*.

**CATZIE VILAYPHONH** is a multimedia artist and award-winning writer, half of the spoken word poetry group Yellow Rage, and founder of Laos in the House, which promotes storytelling in the Lao American refugee community.

**JES VU** is a Los Angeles–based Vietnamese American creative organizer, cultural consultant, and producer.

**JEN WANA** is a Thai American writer whose work has appeared in the *New York Times* and the *Washington Post*'s "The Lily." He is also the author of *How to Choose the Best Preschool for Your Child*.

**CYNTHIA WANG,** former features editor at *TV Week*, is a Sydney-based pop-culture writer and editor. She covered five Olympics, six *Survivor* locations, and every major award show during an 18-year career at *People*.

**FRANCES KAI-HWA WANG** is a journalist, essayist, and poet focused on issues of Asian America, race, justice, and the arts.

**JEN WANG** is one-half of the Artist Formerly Known as Disgrasian, a culture blog (2007–2013) written from an unapologetically Asian American women's perspective. She lives and works in Los Angeles.

**OLIVER WANG** is a professor of sociology at CSU–Long Beach, pop culture writer, and cohost of the Heat Rocks podcast.

**CLARISSA WEI** is a freelance journalist based in Taipei. Her work is centered on the food and culture of the greater China area.

**JENNY XU** is a book editor based in Brooklyn.

**EUGENE LEE YANG** is a filmmaker, actor, producer, author, director, activist, and Internet celebrity best known for being one-fourth of the YouTube group The Try Guys.

**JAMES YANG** is a Brooklyn-based award-winning illustrator and the 2020 Dr. Seuss Geisel Award winner for *Stop! Bot!* for the most distinguished American book for young readers.

**KOLBE YANG** is an illustrator and creator of the card game Red Bean: Dragon Slayer.

**EC YI** is a Seattle-based illustrator and comics artist from Boston, who probably should be drawing more right now.

**PAULA YOO** is a book author, TV/feature screenwriter, and freelance musician who lives in Los Angeles.

**SISI YU (JINGYI YU)** is a freelance illustrator from China, based in Brooklyn, New York. She's interested in the juxtaposition of street culture and her Chinese heritage, and journaling unique stories in visual forms.

**WILLIAM YU** is a Korean American screenwriter and the creator of the viral social media project #StarringJohnCho, which sparked a global conversation about Asian American representation in media. He is based in Los Angeles.

**NANCY WANG YUEN** is a sociologist and author of *Reel Inequality: Hollywood Actors and Racism*.

**HELEN ZIA** is an Asian American journalist, author, and activist. Her books include *Asian American Dreams*, *My Country vs. Me* (with Dr. Wen Ho Lee), and most recently, *Last Boat Out of Shanghai*.

# ACKNOWLEDGMENTS

**THE AUTHORS WOULD** like to thank the team that made *Rise* possible, especially:

Project manager Jes Vu, whose tireless coordination and hustle were the glue that held this book together; our agent, Rachel Vogel, who believed in us from the beginning; illustrator Julia Kuo and our fab designer Allison Chi for breathing life into every page; art director Mark Robinson, the entire crew at HarperCollins Mariner, and especially, our brilliant, inspirational, painstaking, patient—and yet, when necessary, persistent—editor Jenny Xu;

Our incredible squad of writers and artists, and the dozens of interviewees who generously offered their time and insight, including: Tamlyn Tomita, Ming-Na Wen, Lauren Tom, Rosalind Chao, Rita Hsiao, Peilin Chou, Parry Shen, Roger Fan, Sung Kang, Jason Tobin, Karin Anna Cheung, Jon Hurwitz, Hayden Schlossberg, Gautham Nagesh, Lee Shorten, Sujata Day, John Cho, Daniel Dae Kim, Ken Jeong, Randall Park, Hari Kondabolu, Sandra Oh, Kelly Marie Tran, SuChin Pak, Saagar Shaikh, Shaan Baig, Jin Au-Yeung, Jonathan Park, Paul "PK" Kim, John Lee, Billy Chen, Carl Choi, Ritesh Rajan, Saleena Khamamkar, Shivani Bhagwan, Chaya Kumar, W. Kamau Bell, Jeff Chang, Ryan Alexander Holmes, Monica Macer, Shawn Taylor, Yultron, James "Prohgress" Roh, Tokimonsta, Softest Hard, Shawn Wasabi, Ken Loi, Manila Killa, Eugene Lee Yang, Gene Luen Yang, Greg Pak, Kerry Kang, Eugene Soo, Zoe Imansjah, Simu Liu, Kumail Nanjiani, Ruby Ibarra, Alessandro Roco, Sahra Nguyen, Lacy Lew Nguyen Wright, Nik Dodani, Amanda Nguyen, Linh Nguyen, Maitreyi Ramakrishnan, Nimarta Narang, Roland Ros, Rexy Dorado, Carter Jung, Mike Munar, Michael Chang, Kaila Yu, Jonny Ngo, Kevin Lin, Sue Lee, Hai Lam, and Leslie Fu;

Our families and loved ones, who helped raise us so we could rise: YeWon Min, Hudson Yang, Skyler Yang, Bailing and David Yang, and Dr. Christine Yang Kauh; Joanna Lee, Adeline Lee-Yu, Jang Ok and Boo Sung Yu, Hannah Yu, and Sarah Yu; and Nancy C. Wang, Li-Ho Wang, Phyllis Wang, and Helen Wu;

Additional thanks to Anirvan Chatterjee, Keone Young, Kristina Schake, Melvin Mar, Alex Contraviwat, Traci Kato-Kiriyama, Valarie Kaur, and Tanzila "Taz" Ahmed;

And to those who were lights in the darkness urging us on through this weird and often horrific year: our friend, colleague, and sometime mentor Corky Lee, the undisputed unofficial Asian American photographer laureate, who passed away at 73 of COVID-19 on January 27, 2021; Vice President Kamala Harris, the first Black person, first Asian American, and first woman to ever hold the office in our nation's history; and Xiao Zhen Xie, the 75-year-old Chinese American grandmother in San Francisco who, after getting punched brutally in the face, grabbed a board and beat her white male attacker until he had to be carried off crying in a stretcher. Xie then announced that she was donating the nearly $1 million that had been crowdfunded for her medical expenses to fight anti-Asian hate, because, in her words, "People must not submit to racism."

Thank you, Grandma, we honor and respect you.

# INDEX

# CREDITS